Lecture Notes in Computer Science   8972

Commenced Publication in 1973
Founding and Former Series Editors:
Gerhard Goos, Juris Hartmanis, and Jan van Leeuwen

FoLLI Publications on Logic, Language and Information

Subline of Lectures Notes in Computer Science

Johan van Benthem · Sujata Ghosh
Rineke Verbrugge (Eds.)

Models of Strategic Reasoning

Logics, Games, and Communities

 Springer

Editors
Johan van Benthem
Institute for Logic, Language
    and Computation
University of Amsterdam
Amsterdam, Noord-Holland
The Netherlands

Rineke Verbrugge
Institute of Artificial Intelligence, Faculty
    of Mathematics and Natural Sciences
University of Groningen
Groningen
The Netherlands

Sujata Ghosh
Computer Science Unit
Indian Statistical Institute
Chennai, Tamil Nadu
India

Cover illustration: "Geisha playing Go" by Kikukawa Eizan (1790–1848),
from the collection of Erwin Gerstorfer, with permission.

ISSN 0302-9743   ISSN 1611-3349   (electronic)
Lecture Notes in Computer Science
ISBN 978-3-662-48539-2   ISBN 978-3-662-48540-8   (eBook)
DOI 10.1007/978-3-662-48540-8

Library of Congress Control Number: 2015951803

LNCS Sublibrary: SL1 – Theoretical Computer Science and General Issues

Springer Heidelberg New York Dordrecht London

Printed on acid-free paper

Springer-Verlag GmbH Berlin Heidelberg is part of Springer Science+Business Media
(www.springer.com)

Preface

Strategic behavior is the key to social interaction, from the ever-evolving world of living beings to the modern theater of designed computational agents. Several crucial dimensions come together in acting strategically. One dimension is that of agents having individual goals and intentions that they try to realize by taking decisions based on their current information and preferences, which may involve influencing others as well. A second dimension of strategies is the longer temporal horizon of agents having plans for dealing with complex scenarios of events unfolding over time, where, in particular, it is essential to respond in an optimal manner to what others do, or sometimes also to lead the way. Merging all these individual strategies results in forms of group behavior in which stable patterns of behavior may emerge representing some sort of equilibrium that is optimal for all. More generally, what we see at work here is a third, social dimension of group structure and collective goals and actions.

Strategies are often associated with recreational games such as chess and bridge. Strategies can also be associated with games in the sense of economic game theory, covering many social interactions such as selling one's house or playing the stock market. Finally, strategies play a role in using or even designing social software such as proper protocols for holding meetings or working toward a treaty that limits global warming. In the course of such scenarios, optimal strategies may involve the most delicate phenomena, for example, a balance between public and private information or between public and private goals.

Given this variety of games and strategic behavior across so many different spheres of life, studies of strategies can be found in many disciplines. Game theory is one major source of insights, but there are others. Strategies occur as generalized algorithms in computer science, where games have become an influential model for multi-agent systems for interactive computation by large networks of processors. In logic, strategies have supplied new models for valid reasoning or successful model checking. In philosophy, strategies for planned intentional behavior have entered the realm of ethics, philosophy of action, and social philosophy. In mathematics, intuitions about strategies in infinite games fuel the search for new axioms in the foundations of set theory. And the list keeps growing. Strategies in evolutionary games are a powerful model in biology, and combinations of ideas from both classic and evolutionary games are making their way into the study of meaning in linguistics as a communicative equilibrium, and into cognitive science, where strategies provide the link between *knowing that* and *knowing how*, and, more generally, learnability of cognitive skills.

This book aims at understanding the phenomenon of strategic behavior in its proper width and depth. It is based on a workshop held at the Lorentz Center in Leiden in 2012, emanating from the NWO project "Strategies in Multi-agent Systems: From Implicit to Implementable" on strategies as a unifying interdisciplinary theme. The aim of the workshop was, by bringing together congenial experts, to create a comparative view of the different frameworks for strategic reasoning in social interactions occurring in game theory, computer science, logic, linguistics, philosophy, and the cognitive and social sciences. The workshop participants were (and are) active researchers in these areas, and they engaged in wide-ranging outreach discussions. The authors of this book represent a fair sample of the people involved and the themes that emerged. We have grouped their contributions as follows.

Reasoning About Games

Part 1 of this book is concerned with reasoning about information and rational inter-action in the paradigmatic arena of games, with ideas coming mainly from the con-temporary interface of game theory and logic. Eric Pacuit, in his chapter "Dynamic Models of Rational Deliberation in Games" develops an interesting perspective on strategic reasoning in dynamic games, in which players take turns. Pacuit shifts the focus from the usual solution concepts and players' beliefs about other players' choices, to the processes of deliberation that underlie the participants' strategic choices in such dynamic games.

Next we have two chapters presenting distinct perspectives on strategies in dynamic games. In his chapter "Reasoning About Strategies and Rational Play in Dynamic Games," Giacomo Bonanno focuses on the counterfactual considerations implicit in the definition of a strategy of a player: What would the player do at information sets that are actually never reached? Bonanno highlights the implications of such counterfactual beliefs on the belief revision of players in dynamic games. In the process, he provides a fresh look at what is meant by the rationality of a player in terms of her choices and beliefs.

Andrés Perea, on the other hand, considers strategies as plans of actions, concen-trating on the choice part only, rather than the belief part. Assuming such a notion of strategy in his chapter "Finite Reasoning Procedures for Dynamic Games," he shows that for finite dynamic games, the infinitely many conditions associated with the concept of common belief in future rationality can be tackled using a finitary proce-dure. In all, Part I provides the reader with the flavors of the various notions of strategies discussed in the literature on game theory.

Formal Frameworks for Strategies

Next, Part 2 of this book is concerned with formal frameworks for representing strategies, geared toward an analysis of their laws and their behavioral complexity, with an emphasis on combining techniques from logic, philosophy, computation, and automata theory. Nils Bulling, Valentin Goranko, and Wojciech Jamroga, in their chapter "Logics for Reasoning About Strategic Abilities in Multi-player Games," provide a rich description of an approach to strategies from an external observer's perspective, which has proved to be very useful in programming and verifying multi-agent systems. This approach, based on alternating-time temporal logic (ATL) and its variants, does not focus on players who reason based on the presumed rationality of other players. Instead, the objects of analysis are the players' and groups' objective abilities to apply strategies guaranteeing that their goals are achieved, regardless of whether their opponents are rational and independently of the strategies applied by their opponents.

In their chapter "Using STIT Theory to Talk About Strategies," Jan Broersen and Andreas Herzig provide a detailed account of seeing-to-it-that (STIT) frameworks used in the analysis of strategies. They also investigate the connections between the STIT frameworks and the ATL frameworks described in the previous chapter, focusing on various properties of strategic reasoning.

The reader will encounter automata-theoretic approaches to strategies in the context of large dynamic games in the chapter "Automata and Compositional Strategies in Extensive Form Games," authored by Soumya Paul, R. Ramanujam, and Sunil Simon. They consider on-the-fly strategizing in games where the players only have a limited view of the game structures and hence need to resort to partial strategies for the relevant subgames.

This second part of the book ends with the chapter "Languages for Imperfect Information" by Gabriel Sandu, in which he looks into the game-theoretical semantics for different logics. The chapter mainly focuses on independence-friendly (IF) logics. Distinctive features of semantical games are considered, in accordance with different game-theoretical concepts, aiding in a logical analysis of games of imperfect information.

Strategies in Social Situations

Finally, Part 3 of this book explores current uses of strategies in social situations with a range of examples coming from natural language use and scenarios in cognitive psychology and in the social sciences. Michael Franke and Robert van Rooij explore strategic aspects of communication in their chapter "Strategies of Persuasion, Manipulation, and Propaganda: Psychological and Social Aspects." Using decision theory and game theory, they first shine a light on the psychological question of what a communicator should undertake in order to manipulate someone else to adopt a certain opinion: Which information should she convey, and in which manner? Subsequently, the authors adapt DeGroot's model of opinion dynamics to tackle a more sociological question: Which individual agents should the manipulator address in order to effectively influence certain groups in society?

Jan van Eijck, in his chapter "Strategies in Social Software," shows how knowledge of design and analysis of algorithms in computer science may be fruitfully applied to mechanism design in social situations, taking into account that the participants in society may be aware of the mechanisms and may attempt to strategically turn these mechanisms to their own advantage. He illustrates his points by presenting various examples of strategic situations, such as a prisoner's dilemma with punishment for cheaters, the tragedy of the commons, and voting procedures.

Wrapping Up

The book rounds off with Johan van Benthem's chapter "Logic of Strategies: What and How?," which presents some perspectives on the future of logical studies of strategies in the width suggested by this book.

Many common themes and working habits tie together the various chapters in this book, with logic often serving as the lingua franca that facilitates communication between fields. Moreover, many of the themes addressed by our authors cross between disciplines, where they often raise fundamental issues, such as the delicate interfaces of deliberate versus automated behavior, or of short-term versus long-term behavior, and more broadly, the interplay of theory and empirical reality, including the mixed world of today, where theory-driven design of social software and ICT hardware can lead to new forms of behavior.

We hope that this book will show the reader that strategies are a worthy subject of study in their own right, that they provide a common thread that connects many academic fields, from the humanities to the sciences, and that an improved understanding of strategies can also impact directly on how we behave and how we shape the social world around us.

Acknowledgments

The unique facilities at the Lorentz Centre in Leiden fostered lively discussions about Models of Strategic Reasoning: Logics, Games, and Communities, during the workshop "Modeling Strategic Reasoning," February 20–24, 2012. We would like to thank Sietske Kroon, Mieke Schutte, and Henriette Jensenius for their great suggestions and their professional and friendly support around the workshop. The workshop participants played a large role in the contents of the chapters and the coherence of the book as a whole. In addition to the authors, we therefore thank Alexandru Baltag, Anton Benz, Dietmar Berwanger, Robin Clark, Harmen de Weerd, Francien Dechesne, Ulle Endriss, Amanda Friedenberg, Pietro Galliani, Amélie Gheerbrant, Nina Gierasimczuk, Rainer Kessler, Barteld Kooi, Maartje Raijmakers, Bryan Renne, Ben Rodenhäuser, Olivier Roy, Cristián Santibáñez, Floor Sietsma, Sonja Smets, Jakub Szymanik, Nicolas Troquard, Paolo Turrini, Dirk Walther, and Andreas Witzel.

Most crucially, we are grateful to the authors of the chapters in this book. They were willing to distribute first drafts of their chapters and have them critiqued in special sessions by the workshop participants and in several rounds of reviews at later stages. Special thanks are due to the anonymous reviewers for their dedication to provide the chapter authors with useful, constructive feedback during the in-depth reviewing process involving several versions of each chapter. In addition to the reviewers who have already been mentioned as authors, workshop attendees, or editors, we thank Oliver Board, Thomas Bolander, Edith Elkind, Davide Grossi, Pelle Guldborg Hansen, John Horty, Tomohiro Hoshi, Christof Loeding, and Burkhard Schipper.

The picture on the front cover of this book is the woodblock print "Geisha Playing Go" by Kikukawa Eizan (1787–1867), from the collection of Erwin Gerstorfer, whom we would like to thank for his generous permission to use this beautiful print that conjures up the themes of this book.

July 2015

Johan van Benthem
Sujata Ghosh
Rineke Verbrugge

Contents

Reasoning About Games

Dynamic Models of Rational Deliberation in Games

Eric Pacuit[✉]

Department of Philosophy, University of Maryland, College Park, USA
epacuit@umd.edu

Abstract. There is a growing body of literature that analyzes games in terms of the "process of deliberation" that leads the players to select their component of a rational outcome. Although the details of the various models of deliberation in games are different, they share a common line of thought: The rational outcomes of a game are arrived at through a process in which each player settles on an optimal choice given her evolving beliefs about her own choices and the choices of her opponents. The goal is to describe deliberation in terms of a sequence of belief changes about what the players are doing or what their opponents may be thinking. The central question is: What are the update mechanisms that match different game-theoretic analyses? The general conclusion is that the rational outcomes of a game depend not only on the structure of the game, but also on the players' initial beliefs, which dynamical rule is being used by the players to update their inclinations (in general, different players may be using different rules), and what exactly is commonly known about the process of deliberation.

Keywords: Epistemic game theory · Dynamic epistemic logic · Belief revision

1 Introduction and Motivation

Strategies are the basic objects of study in a game-theoretic model. The standard interpretation is that a strategy represents a player's *general plan of action*. That is, player i's strategy describes the action that player i will choose whenever she is required to make a decision according to the rules of the game.

Traditionally, game theorists have focused on identifying profiles of strategies that constitute an "equilibrium" (e.g., the Nash equilibrium and its refinements). A typical game-theoretic analysis runs as follows: Given a game G, there is an associated *solution space* S_G describing all the possible *outcomes* of G. In a one-shot game (called a **strategic game**; see Sect. 2.1 for details), this is the set of all tuples of strategies (a tuple of strategies, one for each player, is called a **strategy profile**)[1]. Abstractly, a **solution** for a game G is a subset of the

---

[1] The assumption is that once each player settles on a strategy, this identifies a unique outcome of the game. This is a simplifying assumption that can be dropped if necessary. However, for this chapter, it is simpler to follow standard practice and identify the set of "outcomes" of a game with the set of all tuples of actions.

© Springer-Verlag Berlin Heidelberg 2015
J. van Benthem et al. (Eds.): Models of Strategic Reasoning, LNCS 8972, pp. 3–33, 2015.
DOI: 10.1007/978-3-662-48540-8_1

solution space S_G. The subset of S_G identified by a solution concept is intended to represent the "rational outcomes" of the game G.

Suppose that $S \subseteq S_G$ is a solution for the game G. The elements of S are privileged outcomes of G, but what, exactly, distinguishes them from the other outcomes in S_G? The standard approach is to require that for each profile in S, players should not have an incentive to deviate from their prescribed strategy, given that the other players follow their own prescribed strategies. This is an *internal* constraint on the elements of a solution set since it requires that the strategies in a profile are related to each other in a particular way. This chapter takes a different perspective on the above question by imposing a different constraint on the profiles in S: Each player's prescribed strategy should be "optimal" given her *beliefs* about what the other players are going to do. This constraint is *external* since it refers to the players' "beliefs", which are typically not part of the mathematical representation of the game.

It is not hard to think of situations in which the internal and external constraints on solution concepts discussed above are not jointly satisfied. The point is that players may have very good reasons to believe that the other players are choosing certain strategies, and so, they choose an optimal strategy based on these beliefs. There is no reason to expect that the resulting choices will satisfy the above internal constraint unless one makes strong assumptions about how the players' beliefs are related[2]. The external constraint on solution concepts can be made more precise by taking a "Bayesian" perspective on game theory [46]: In a game-theoretic situation, as in any situation of choice, the *rational choice* for a player is the one that maximizes expected utility with respect to a (subjective) probability measure over the other players' strategy choices. A sophisticated literature has developed around this simple idea: it focuses on characterizing solution concepts in terms of what the players know and believe about the other players' strategy choices and beliefs (see, for example, [7,22,26,60] and [63] for a textbook presentation).

In this chapter, I shift the focus from beliefs about the other players' choices to the underlying *processes* that lead (rational) players to adopt certain strategies. An early formulation of this idea can found in John C. Harsanyi's seminal paper [42], in which he introduced the *tracing procedure* to select an equilibrium in any finite game:

> The n players will find the solution s of a giving game G through an intellectual process of *convergent expectations*, to be called the *solution process*....During this process, they will continually and systematically modify [their] expectations—until, at the end of this process, their expectations will come to converge on one particular equilibrium point s in the game G.   (original italics) [42, pg. 71]

The goal of the tracing procedure is to identify a unique Nash equilibrium in any finite strategic game. The idea is to define a continuum of games in

---

[2] For example, one can assume that each player *knows* which strategies the other players are going to choose. Robert Aumann and Adam Brandenburger use this assumption to provide an epistemic characterization of the Nash equilibrium [10].

such a way that each of the games has a unique Nash equilibrium. The tracing procedure identifies a path through this space of games ending at a unique Nash equilibrium in the original game. Harsanyi thought of this procedure as "being a mathematical formalization of the process by which rational players coordinate their choices of strategies."

Harsanyi, in collaboration with Reinhard Selten [43], turned these basic ideas into a beautiful theory of equilibrium selection. This theory is now part of the standard education for any game theorist. Nonetheless, it is not at all clear that this theory of equilibrium selection is best interpreted as a formalization of the players' processes of "rational deliberation" in game situations (see [72, pgs. 154–158] for a discussion of this point). In this chapter, I will critically discuss three recent frameworks in which the players' process of "rational deliberation" takes center stage:

1. Brian Skyrms' model of "dynamic deliberation," in which players deliberate by calculating their expected utility and then use this new information to recalculate their probabilities about the states of the world and their expected utilities [72].
2. Robin Cubitt and Robert Sugden's recent contribution that develops a "reasoning-based expected utility" procedure for solving games (building on David Lewis' "common modes of reasoning") [31, 33].
3. Johan van Benthem *et col.*'s analysis of solution concepts as fixed-points of iterated "(virtual) rationality announcements" [3, 15, 18, 20, 21].

Although the details of these frameworks are quite different, they share a common line of thought: In contrast to classical game theory, solution concepts are no longer the basic object of study. Instead, the "rational solutions" of a game are arrived at through a process of "rational deliberation". My goal in this chapter is to provide a (biased) overview of some key technical and conceptual issues that arise when developing mathematical models of players deliberating about what to do in a game situation.

2 Background

I assume that the reader is familiar with the basics of game theory (see [52] and [2] for concise discussions of the key concepts, definitions and theorems) and formal models of knowledge and belief (see [19, 57] for details). In this section, I introduce some key definitions in order to fix notation.

2.1 Strategic Games

A **strategic game** is a tuple $\langle N, \{S_i\}_{i \in N}, \{u_i\}_{i \in N} \rangle$ where N is a (finite) set of players; for each $i \in N$, S_i is a finite set (elements of which are called actions or strategies); and for each $i \in N$, $u_i : \Pi_{i \in N} S_i \to \mathbb{R}$ is a utility function assigning real numbers to each outcome of the game (i.e., tuples consisting of the choices for each player). Strategic games represent situations in which each player makes a single decision, and all the players make their decisions simultaneously. If $s \in \Pi_{i \in N} S_i$ is a strategy profile, then write s_i for the ith component of s and s_{-i} for the sequence consisting of all components of s except for s_i (let S_{-i} denote all such sequences of strategies).

Recall from the introduction that the *solution space* S_G for a game G is the set of all outcomes of G. Since we identify the outcomes of a game with the set of strategy profiles, we have $S_G = \Pi_{i \in N} S_i$. This means that a "solution" to a strategic game is a distinguished set of strategy profiles. In the remainder of this section, I will define some standard game- and decision-theoretic notions that will be used throughout this chapter.

Mixed Strategies. Let $\Delta(X)$ denote the set of probability measures over the finite[3] set X. A **mixed strategy** for player i, is an element $m_i \in \Delta(S_i)$. If $m_i \in \Delta(S_i)$ assigns probability 1 to an element $s_i \in S_i$, then m_i is called a **pure strategy** (in such a case, I write s_i for m_i). Mixed strategies are incorporated into a game-theoretic analysis as follows. Suppose that $G = \langle N, \{S_i\}_{i \in N}, \{u_i\}_{i \in N} \rangle$ is a finite strategic game. The **mixed extension** of G is the strategic game in which the strategies for player i are the mixed strategies in G (i.e., $\Delta(S_i)$), and the utility for player i (denoted U_i) of the joint mixed strategy $m \in \Pi_{i \in N} \Delta(S_i)$ is calculated in the obvious way (let $m(s) = m_1(s_1) \cdot m_2(s_2) \cdots m_n(s_n)$ for $s \in \Pi_{i \in N} S_i$):

$$U_i(m) = \sum_{s \in \Pi_{i \in N} S_i} m(s) \cdot u_i(s).$$

Thus, the solution space of a mixed extension of the game G is the set $\Pi_{i \in N} \Delta(S_i)$.

Mixed strategies play an important role in many game-theoretic analyses. However, the interpretation of mixed strategies is controversial, as Ariel Rubinstein notes: "We are reluctant to believe that our decisions are made at random. We prefer to be able to point to a reason for each action we take. Outside of Las Vegas we do not spin roulettes" [69, pg. 913]. For the purposes of this chapter, I will assume that players choose only pure strategies. Mixed strategies do play a role in Sect. 3, where they describe each players' beliefs about what they will do (at the end of deliberation).

Nash Equilibrium. The most well-known and extensively studied solution concept is the **Nash equilibrium**. Let $G = \langle N, \{S_i\}_{i \in N}, \{u_i\}_{i \in N} \rangle$ be a finite strategic game. A mixed strategy profile $m = (m_1, \ldots, m_n) \in \Pi_{i \in N} \Delta(S_i)$ is a Nash equilibrium provided for all $i \in N$,

$$U_i(m_1, \ldots, m_i, \ldots, m_n) \geq U_i(m_1, \ldots, m_i', \ldots, m_n), \qquad \text{for all } m_i' \in \Delta(S_i).$$

This definition is an example of the *internal* constraint on solutions discussed in the introduction. Despite its prominence in the game theory literature, the

---

[3] Recall that I am restricting attention to finite strategic games.

Nash equilibrium faces many foundational problems [68]. For example, there are theoretical concerns about what the players need to *know* in order to play their component of a Nash equilibrium [10, 62]; questions about how players choose among multiple Nash equilibria; and many experiments purporting to demonstrate game-theoretic situations in which the player's choices do not form a Nash equilibrium. Nash equilibrium does not play an important role in this chapter. I focus, instead, on the outcomes of a game that can be reached through a process of "rational deliberation".

Iteratively Removing Strategies. A strategy $s \in S_i$ **strictly dominates** strategy $s' \in S_i$ provided that

$$\forall s_{-i} \in S_{-i} \ \ u_i(s, s_{-i}) > u_i(s', s_{-i}).$$

A strategy $s \in S_i$ **weakly dominates** strategy $s' \in S_i$ provided that

$$\forall s_{-i} \in S_{-i} \ \ u_i(s, s_{-i}) \geq u_i(s', s_{-i}) \quad \text{and} \quad \exists s_{-i} \in S_{-i} \ \ u_i(s, s_{-i}) > u_i(s', s_{-i}).$$

More generally, the strategy s strictly/weakly dominates s' **with respect to a set** $X \subseteq S_{-i}$ if S_{-i} is replaced with X in the above definitions[4]. Suppose that $G = \langle N, \{S_i\}_{i \in N}, \{u_i\}_{i \in N} \rangle$ and $G' = \langle N, \{S'_i\}_{i \in N}, \{u'_i\}_{i \in N} \rangle$ are strategic games. The game G' is a **restriction** of G provided that for each $i \in N$, $S'_i \subseteq S_i$ and u'_i is the restriction of u_i to $\Pi_{i \in N} S'_i$. To simplify notation, write G_i for the set of strategies for player i in game G. Strict and weak dominance can be used to *reduce* a strategic game. Write $H \longrightarrow_{SD} H'$ whenever $H \neq H'$, H' is a restriction of H and

$$\forall i \in N, \forall s_i \in H_i \setminus H'_i \ \exists s'_i \in H_i s_i \text{ is strictly dominated in } H \text{ by } s'_i$$

So, if $H \longrightarrow_{SD} H'$, then H' is the result of removing some of the strictly dominated strategies from H. We can iterate this process of removing strictly dominated strategies. Formally, H is the result of iteratively removing strictly dominated strategies (IESDS) provided that $G \longrightarrow^*_{SD} H$, where $\longrightarrow^*$ is the reflexive transitive closure[5] of a relation $\longrightarrow$.

The above definition can be easily adapted to other choice rules, such as weak dominance. Let $\longrightarrow_{WD}$ denote the relation between games defined as above using weak dominance instead of strict dominance[6]. Furthermore, the above

---

[4] Furthermore, the definitions of strict and weak dominance can be extended so that strategies may be strictly/weakly dominated by *mixed strategies*. This is important for the epistemic analysis of iterative removal of strictly/weakly dominated strategies. However, for my purposes in this chapter, I can stick with the simpler definition in terms of pure strategies.

[5] The reflexive transitive closure of a relation R is the smallest relation R^* containing R that is reflexive and transitive.

[6] Some interesting issues arise here: It is well-known that, unlike with strict dominance, different orders in which weakly dominated strategies are removed can lead to different outcomes. Let us set aside these issues in this chapter.

definition of iterated removal of strictly/weakly dominated strategies can be readily adapted to the mixed extensions of a strategic game.

There are a number of ways to interpret the iterative process of removing strategies, defined above. The first is that it is an algorithm that a game theorist can use to find an equilibrium in a game. The second interpretation views the successive steps of the removal process as corresponding to the players' *higher-order beliefs* (i.e., player i believes that player j believes that player i believes that...that player i will not play such-and-such strategy). Finally, the third interpretation is that the iterative process of removing strategies tracks the "back-and-forth reasoning" players engage in as they decide what to do in a game situation (i.e., if player i does not play such-and-such a strategy, then player j will not play such-and-such a strategy, and so on).

Bayesian Rationality. In this chapter, I am interested not only in solutions to a game, but also what the players *believe* about the outcomes of a game. Let $G = \langle N, \{S_i\}_{i \in N}, \{u_i\}_{i \in N} \rangle$ be a strategic game. A probability measure $\pi \in \Delta(S_{-i})$ is called a **conjecture** for player i. The **expected utility** of $s \in S_i$ for player i with respect to $\pi \in \Delta(S_{-i})$ is:

$$EU_\pi(s) = \sum_{\sigma_{-i} \in S_{-i}} \pi(\sigma_{-i}) \cdot u_i(s, \sigma_{-i}).$$

We say that $s \in S_i$ maximizes expected utility with respect to $\pi \in \Delta(S_{-i})$, denoted $MEU(s, \pi)$, if for all $s' \in S_i$, $EU_\pi(s) \geq EU_\pi(s')$.

* * * * * * *

One conclusion to draw from the discussion in this section is that much can be said about the issues raised in this chapter using standard game-theoretic notions. Indeed, it is standard for a game theorist to distinguish between the *ex ante* and *ex interim* stages of decision making[7]. In the former, the players have not yet decided what strategy they will choose, while, in the latter, the players know their own choices but not their opponents'. However, the *process* by which the players form their beliefs in the *ex interim* stage is typically not discussed. The frameworks discussed in the remainder of this chapter are focused on making this process explicit.

2.2   Game Models

A **game model** describes a particular play of the game *and* what the players think about the other players. That is, a game model represents an "informational context" of a given play of the game. This includes the "knowledge" the players have about the game situation *and* what they think about the other

---

[7] There is also an *ex post* analysis when all choices are "out in the open," and the only remaining uncertainties are about what the other players are thinking.

players' choices and beliefs. Researchers interested in the foundations of decision theory, epistemic and doxastic logic and formal epistemology have developed many different formal models to describe the variety of informational attitudes important for assessing decision maker's choices in a decision- or game-theoretic situation. See [19] for an overview and pointers to the relevant literature. In this section, I present the details of a logical framework that can be used to reason about the informational context of a game.

Syntactic issues do not play an important role in this chapter. Nonetheless, I will give the definition of truth for a relevant formal language, as it makes for a smoother transition from the game theory literature to the literature on dynamic epistemic logic and iterated belief change discussed in Sect. 5.1. Consult [19,57,58] for a discussion of the standard logical questions about axiomatics, definability, decidability of the satisfiability problem, and so on.

Epistemic-Plausibility Models. Variants of the models presented in this section have been studied extensively by logicians [13,17,19], game theorists [23], philosophers [51,74] and computer scientists [25,48]. The models are intended to describe what the players know and believe about an outcome of the game.

The first component of an epistemic-plausibility model is a nonempty set W of **states** (also called **worlds**). Each state in a game model will be associated with an outcome of a game G via a function σ, called the **outcome map**. So, for a state w, $\sigma(w)$ is the element of S_G realized at state w. Let $\sigma_i(w)$ denote the ith component of $\sigma(w)$ (so, $\sigma_i(w)$ is the strategy played by i at state w). The atomic propositions are intended to describe different aspects of the the outcomes of a game. For example, they could describe the specific action chosen by a player or the utility assigned to the outcome by a given player. There are a number of ways to make this precise. Perhaps the simplest is to introduce, for each player i and strategy $a \in S_i$, an atomic proposition $play_i(a)$ intended to mean "player i is playing strategy a." For a game $G = \langle N, \{S_i\}_{i \in N}, \{u_i\}_{i \in N}\rangle$, let $\mathsf{At}(G) = \{play_i(a) \mid i \in N \text{ and } a \in S_i\}$ be the set of atomic propositions for the game G.

There are two additional components to an epistemic-plausibility model. The first is a set of equivalence relations $\sim_i$, one for each player. The intended reading of $w \sim_i v$ is that "everything that i knows at w is true at v". Alternatively, I will say that "player i does not have enough information to distinguish state w from state v."

The second component is a *plausibility ordering* for each player: a pre-order (reflexive and transitive) $w \preceq_i v$ that says "agent i considers world w at least as plausible as v." As a convenient notation, for $X \subseteq W$, set $Min_{\preceq_i}(X) = \{v \in X \mid v \preceq_i w \text{ for all } w \in X\}$, the set of minimal elements of X according to $\preceq_i$. This is the subset of X that agent i considers the "most plausible". Thus, while the $\sim_i$ partitions the set of possible worlds according to i's "hard information", the plausibility ordering $\preceq_i$ represents which of the possible worlds agent i considers more likely (i.e., it represents i's "soft information").

Putting everything together, the definition of an epistemic-plausibility model is as follows:

Definition 1. *Suppose that $G = \langle N, \{S_i\}_{i \in N}, \{u_i\}_{i \in N} \rangle$ is a strategic game. An* **epistemic-plausibility model** *for G is a tuple $\mathcal{M} = \langle W, \{\sim_i\}_{i \in \mathcal{A}}, \{\preceq_i\}_{i \in \mathcal{A}}, \sigma \rangle$ where $W \neq \emptyset$; for each $i \in \mathcal{A}$, $\sim_i \subseteq W \times W$ is an equivalence relation (each $\sim_i$ is reflexive: for each $w \in W$, $w \sim_i w$; transitive: for each $w, v, u \in W$, if $w \sim_i v$ and $v \sim_i u$ then $w \sim_i u$; and Euclidean: for each $w, v, u \in W$, if $w \sim_i v$ and $w \sim_i u$, then $v \sim_i u$); for each $i \in \mathcal{A}$, $\preceq_i$ is a well-founded (every non-empty set of states has a minimal element)[8] reflexive and transitive relation on W; and σ is an outcome map. In addition, the following two conditions are imposed for all $w, v \in W$:*

1. *if $w \preceq_i v$ then $w \sim_i v$ (plausibility implies possibility), and*
2. *if $w \sim_i v$ then either $w \preceq_i v$ or $v \preceq_i w$ (locally-connected).*   ◁

Models without plausibility relations are called **epistemic models**.

Remark 1. Note that if $w \not\sim_i v$, then, since $\sim_i$ is symmetric, I also have $v \not\sim_i w$, and so by property 1, $w \not\preceq_i v$ and $v \not\preceq_i w$. Thus, I have the following equivalence: $w \sim_i v$ iff $w \preceq_i v$ or $v \preceq_i w$. In what follows, unless otherwise stated, I will assume that $\sim_i$ is defined as follows: $w \sim_i v$ iff $w \preceq_i v$ or $v \preceq_i w$.

For each strategic game G, let $\mathcal{L}_{KB}(G)$ be the set of sentences generated by the following grammar[9]:

$$\varphi := play_i(a) \mid \neg \varphi \mid \varphi \wedge \psi \mid B_i^{\varphi} \psi \mid K_i \varphi$$

where $i \in N$ and $play_i(a) \in \mathsf{At}(G)$. The additional propositional connectives $(\rightarrow, \leftrightarrow, \vee)$ are defined as usual and the dual of K_i, denoted L_i, is defined as follows: $L_i \varphi := \neg K_i \neg \varphi$. The intended interpretation of $K_i \varphi$ is "agent i knows that φ"[10]. The intended interpretation of $B_i^{\varphi} \psi$ is "agent i believes ψ under the supposition that φ is true".

Truth for formulas in $\mathcal{L}_{KB}(G)$ is defined as usual. Let $[w]_i$ be the equivalence class of w under $\sim_i$. Then, local connectedness implies that $\preceq_i$ totally orders $[w]_i$, and well-foundedness implies that $Min_{\preceq_i}([w]_i \cap X)$ is nonempty if $[w]_i \cap X \neq \emptyset$.

---

[8] Well-foundedness is only needed to ensure that for any set X, $Min_{\preceq_i}(X)$ is nonempty. This is important only when W is infinite – and there are ways around this in current logics. Moreover, the condition of connectedness can also be lifted, but I use it here for convenience.

[9] There are other natural modal operators that can. See [57] for an overview and pointers to the relevant literature.

[10] This is the standard interpretation of $K_i \varphi$ in the game theory literature. Whether this captures any of the many different definitions of knowledge found in the epistemology literature is debatable. A better reading of $K_i \varphi$ is "given all of the available evidence and everything i has observed, agent i is informed that φ is true".

Definition 2 (Truth for $\mathcal{L}_{KB}(G)$). *Given an epistemic-plausibility model* $\mathcal{M} = \langle W, \{\sim_i\}_{i \in \mathcal{A}}, \{\preceq_i\}_{i \in \mathcal{A}}, \sigma \rangle$. *Truth for formulas from* $\mathcal{L}_{KB}(G)$ *is defined recursively:*

- $\mathcal{M}, w \models play_i(a)$ *iff* $\sigma_i(w) = a$
- $\mathcal{M}, w \models \neg\varphi$ *iff* $\mathcal{M}, w \not\models \varphi$
- $\mathcal{M}, w \models \varphi \wedge \psi$ *iff* $\mathcal{M}, w \models \varphi$ *and* $\mathcal{M}, w \models \psi$
- $\mathcal{M}, w \models K_i\varphi$ *iff for all* $v \in W$, *if* $w \sim_i v$ *then* $\mathcal{M}, v \models \varphi$
- $\mathcal{M}, w \models B_i^\varphi\psi$ *iff for all* $v \in Min_{\preceq_i}([w]_i \cap [\![\varphi]\!]_\mathcal{M})$, $\mathcal{M}, v \models \varphi$

Thus, i believes ψ conditional on φ, $B_i^\varphi\psi$, if i's most plausible φ-worlds (i.e., the states satisfying φ that i has not ruled out and considers most plausible) all satisfy ψ. Full belief is defined as follows: $B_i\varphi := B^\top\varphi$. Then, the definition of plain belief is:

$$\mathcal{M}, w \models B_i\varphi \text{ iff for each } v \in Min_{\preceq_i}([w]_i), \mathcal{M}, v \models \varphi.$$

I illustrate the above definition with the following coordination game:

Bob

	l	r
u	3,3	0,0
d	0,0	1,1

Ann

The epistemic-plausibility model below describes a possible configuration of *ex ante* beliefs of the players (i.e., before the players have settled on a strategy): I draw an i-labeled arrow from v to w if $w \preceq_i v$ (to keep minimize the clutter, I do not include all arrows; the remaining arrows can be inferred by reflexivity and transitivity).

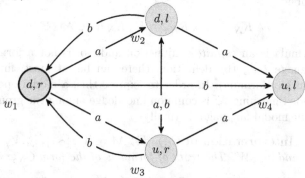

Following the convention discussed in Remark 1, we have $[w_1]_a = [w_1]_b = \{w_1, w_2, w_3, w_4\}$, and so, neither Ann nor Bob knows how the game will end. Furthermore, both Ann and Bob believe that they will coordinate with Ann choosing u and Bob choosing l:

$$B_a(play_a(u) \wedge play_b(l)) \wedge B_b(play_a(u) \wedge play_b(l))$$

is true at all states. However, Ann and Bob do have different *conditional* beliefs. On the one hand, Ann believes that their choices are independent; thus, she believes that $play_b(l)$ is true even under the supposition that $play_a(d)$ is true (i.e., she continues to believe that Bob will play l even if she decides to play d). On the other hand, Bob believes that their choices are somehow correlated; thus, under the supposition that $play_b(r)$ is true, Bob believes that Ann will choose d. Conditional beliefs describe an agent's *disposition* to change her beliefs in the presence of (perhaps surprising) evidence (cf. [49]).

Common Knowledge and Belief. States in an epistemic-plausibility model not only represent the players' beliefs about what their opponents will do, but also their *higher-order* beliefs about what their opponents are thinking. Both game theorists and logicians have extensively discussed different notions of knowledge and belief for a group, such as common knowledge and belief. These notions have played a fundamental role in the analysis of distributed algorithms [40] and social interactions [28]. In this section, I briefly recount the standard definition of common knowledge[11].

Consider the statement "Everyone in group X knows that φ." With finitely many agents, this can be easily defined in the epistemic language $\mathcal{L}_{KB}$:

$$K_X\varphi \; := \; \bigwedge_{i\in X} K_i\varphi,$$

where $X \subseteq N$ is a finite set. The first nontrivial informational attitude for a group that I study is *common knowledge*. If φ is common knowledge for the group G, then not only does everyone in the group know that φ is true, but this fact is completely transparent to all members of the group. Following [6], the idea is to define common knowledge of φ as the following iteration of everyone knows operators:

$$\varphi \wedge K_N\varphi \wedge K_N K_N\varphi \wedge K_N K_N K_N\varphi \wedge \cdots$$

The above formula is an *infinite* conjunction and, so, is not a formula in our epistemic language $\mathcal{L}_{KB}$ (by definition, there can be, at most, finitely many conjunctions in any formula). In order to express this, a modal operator $C_G\varphi$ with the intended meaning "φ is common knowledge among the group G" must be added to our modal language. Formally:

Definition 3 (Interpretation of C_G). *Let $\mathcal{M} = \langle W, \{\sim_i\}_{i\in\mathcal{A}}, V\rangle$ be an epistemic model[12] and $w \in W$. The truth of formulas of the form $C_X\varphi$ is:*

$$\mathcal{M}, w \models C_X\varphi \quad \textit{iff} \quad \textit{for all } v \in W, \textit{ if } wR_X^C v \textit{ then } \mathcal{M}, v \models \varphi$$

where $R_X^C := (\bigcup_{i\in X} \sim_i)^*$ is the reflexive transitive closure of $\bigcup_{i\in X} \sim_i$.

---

[11] I assume that the formal definition of common knowledge is well-known to the reader. For more information and pointers to the relevant literature, see [34,36,57,76].

[12] The same definition will, of course, hold for epistemic-plausibility and epistemic-probability models.

It is well-known that for any relation R on W, if wR^*v then there is a finite R-path starting at w ending in v. Thus, $\mathcal{M}, w \models C_X\varphi$ iff every finite path for X from w ends with a state satisfying φ.

This approach to defining common knowledge can be viewed as a recipe for defining common (robust) belief. For example, suppose that $wR_i^B v$ iff $v \in Min_{\preceq_i}([w]_i)$, and define R_G^B to be the transitive closure[13] of $\cup_{i \in G} R_i^B$. Then, **common belief of** φ, denoted $C_G^B\varphi$, is defined in the usual way:

$$\mathcal{M}, w \models C_G^B\varphi \text{ iff for each } v \in W, \text{ if } wR_G^B v \text{ then } \mathcal{M}, v \models \varphi.$$

A probabilistic variant of common belief was introduced in [55].

3   Reasoning to an Equilibrium

Brian Skyrms presents a model of the players' process of deliberation in a game in his important book *The Dynamics of Rational Deliberation* [72]. In this section, I introduce and discuss this model of deliberation, though the reader is referred to [72] for a full discussion (see, also, [1,45] for analyses of this model).

To simplify the exposition, I restrict attention to a two-person finite strategic game. Everything discussed below can be extended to situations with more than two players[14] and to extensive games[15]. Suppose that $G = \langle \{a, b\}, \{S_a, S_b\}, \{u_a, u_b\} \rangle$ is a strategic game in which $S_a = \{s_1, \ldots, s_n\}$ and $S_b = \{t_1, \ldots, t_m\}$ are the players' strategies, and u_a and u_b are utility functions. In the simplest case, deliberation is trivial: Each player calculates the expected utility given her belief about what her opponent is going to do and then chooses the action that maximizes these expected utilities. One of Skyrms' key insights is that this calculation may be informative to the players, and if a player believes that there is any possibility that the process of deliberation may ultimately lead her to a different decision, then she will not act until her deliberation process has reached a stable state[16].

Deliberation is understood as an iterative process that modifies the players' opinions about the strategies that they will choose (at the end of the deliberation). For each player, a **state of indecision** is a probability measure on that player's set of strategies—i.e., an element of $\Delta(S_i)$ for $i = a, b$. Note that each state of indecision is a *mixed strategy*. However, the interpretation of the mixed strategies differs from the one discussed in Sect. 2.1. In this model, the interpretation is that the state of indecision for a player i at any given stage of the deliberation process is the mixed strategy that player i would choose if the player stopped deliberating. It is the players' states of indecision that evolve during the deliberation process.

---

[13] Since beliefs need not be factive, I do not force R_G^B to be reflexive.

[14] However, see [1] for interesting new issues that arise with more than two players.

[15] See [72], pgs. 44 – 52 and Chap. 5.

[16] See [72], Chap. 4.

Let $p_a \in \Delta(S_a)$ and $p_b \in \Delta(S_b)$ be states of indecision for a and b, respectively, and assume that the states of indecision are *common knowledge*. One consequence of this assumption is that the players can calculate the expected utilities of their strategies (using their opponent's state of indecision). For example, for $s_j \in S_a$, we have

$$EU_a(s_j) = \sum_{t_k \in S_b} p_b(t_k) u_i(s_j, t_k),$$

and similarly for b. The **status quo** is the expected utility of the current state of indecision:

$$SQ_a = \sum_{s_j \in S_a} p_a(s_j) \cdot EU_a(s_j) \qquad SQ_b = \sum_{t_k \in S_b} p_b(t_k) \cdot EU_b(t_k).$$

Once the expected utilities are calculated, the players modify their states of indecision so that they believe more strongly that they will choose strategies with higher expected utility than the status quo. Players can use various rules to update their states of indecision accordingly. In general, any dynamical rule can be used so long as the rule *seeks the good* in the following sense:

1. The rule raises the probability of a strategy only if that strategy has expected utility greater than the status quo.
2. The rule raises the sum of the probabilities of all strategies with expected utility greater than the status quo (if any).

Deliberation reaches a **fixed-point** when the dynamical rule no longer changes the state of indecision. It is not hard to see that all dynamical rules that seek the good have, as fixed-points, states of indecision in which the expected utility of the status quo is maximal. To illustrate Skyrms' model of deliberation with an example, I give the details of one of the rules discussed in [72]:

Nash dynamics. The **covetability** of a strategy s for player i is calculated as follows: $cov_i(s) = \max(EU_i(s) - SQ_i, 0)$. Then, **Nash dynamics** transform a probability $p \in \Delta(S_i)$ into a new probability $p' \in \Delta(S_i)$ as follows. For each $s \in S_i$:

$$p'(s) = \frac{k \cdot p(s) + cov_i(s)}{k + \sum_{s \in S_i} cov(s)},$$

where $k > 0$ is the "index of caution" (the higher the k, the more slowly the decision maker raises the probability of strategies that have higher expected utility than the status quo).

In addition to assuming that the initial states of indecision are common knowledge, it is assumed that each player can *emulate* the other's calculations, and that each player is, in fact, using the same dynamical rule to modify her state of indecision. Given that all of this is common knowledge, the states of indecision resulting from one round of the deliberation process will, again, be common knowledge and the process can continue until a fixed-point is reached.

A simple example will make this more concrete. Consider the following game between two players, Ann (a) and Bob (b)[17].

Bob

	l	r
u	2,1	0,0
d	0,0	1,2

Ann

There are two pure Nash equilibria $((u, l)$ and $(d, r))$ and one mixed-strategy Nash equilibrium where Ann plays u with probability $2/3$ and Bob plays l with probability $1/3$. Suppose that the initial state of indecision is:

$$p_a(u) = 0.2, \; p_a(d) = 0.8 \quad \text{and} \quad p_b(l) = 0.9, \; p_b(r) = 0.1.$$

Since both players have access to each other's state of indecision, they can calculate the expected utilities of each of their strategies:

$$EU_a(u) = 2 \cdot 0.9 + 0 \cdot 0.1 = 1.8$$
$$EU_a(d) = 0 \cdot 0.9 + 1 \cdot 0.1 = 0.1$$
$$EU_b(l) = 1 \cdot 0.2 + 0 \cdot 0.8 = 0.2$$
$$EU_b(r) = 0 \cdot 0.2 + 2 \cdot 0.8 = 1.6$$

If the players simply choose the strategy that maximizes their expected utilities, then the outcome of the interaction will be the off-equilibrium profile (u, r). However, the process of deliberation will pull the players towards an equilibrium. The status quo for each player is:

$$SQ_a = 0.2 \cdot EU_a(u) + 0.8 \cdot EU_a(d) = 0.2 \cdot 1.8 + 0.8 \cdot 0.1 = 0.44$$
$$SQ_b = 0.4 \cdot EU_b(l) + 0.6 \cdot EU_b(r) = 0.9 \cdot 0.2 + 0.1 \cdot 1.6 = 0.34$$

The covetabilities for each of the strategies are:

$$cov_a(u) = \max(1.8 - 0.44, 0) = 1.36$$
$$cov_a(d) = \max(0.34 - 0.44, 0) = 0$$
$$cov_b(l) = \max(0.2 - 0.34, 0) = 0$$
$$cov_b(r) = \max(1.6 - 0.34, 0) = 1.26$$

Now, the new states of indecision p'_a and p'_b are calculated using Nash dynamics (for simplicity, I assume that the index of caution is $k = 1$):

---

[17] This game is called the "Battle of the Sexes". The underlying story is that Ann and Bob are married and are deciding where to go for dinner. Ann would rather eat Indian food than French food, whereas Bob prefers French food to Indian food. They both prefer to eat together rather than separately. The outcome (u, l) is that they go to an Indian restaurant together; (d, r) is the outcome that they go to a French restaurant together; and (u, r) and (d, l) are outcomes where they go to different restaurants.

$$p'_a(u) = \frac{p_A(u)+cov_a(u)}{1+(cov_a(u)+cov_a(d))} = \frac{0.2+1.36}{1+1.36} = 0.221183800623$$

$$p'_a(d) = \frac{p_a(d)+cov_a(d)}{1+(cov_a(u)+cov_a(d))} = \frac{0.8+0}{1+1.36} = 0.778816199377$$

$$p'_b(l) = \frac{p_b(l)+cov_b(l)}{1+(cov_b(l)+cov_b(r))} = \frac{0.9+0}{1+1.26} = 0.87787748732$$

$$p'_b(r) = \frac{p_b(r)+cov_b(r)}{1+(cov_b(l)+cov_b(r))} = \frac{0.1+1.26}{1+1.26} = 0.12212251268$$

The new states of indecision are now p'_a and p'_b, and we can continue this process. On can visualize this process by the following graph, in which the x-axis is the probability that Bob will choose r and the y-axis is the probability that Ann will choose u[18].

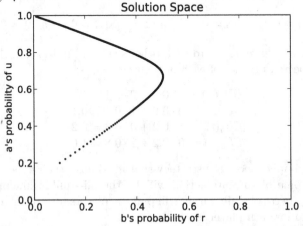

The deliberation reaches a fixed-point with Ann and Bob deciding to play their part of the Nash equilibrium (u, l). In fact, Skyrms shows that under the strong assumptions of common knowledge noted above and assuming that all players use dynamical rules that seek the good, when the process of deliberation reaches a fixed-point, the states of indecision will form a Nash equilibrium[19].

4   Strategic Reasoning as a Solution Concept

A key aspect of the iterative removal of dominated strategies is that at each stage of the process, strategies are identified as either "good" or "bad". The "good" strategies are those that are not strictly/weakly dominated, while the "bad" ones are weakly/strictly dominated. If the intended interpretation of the iterative procedure that removes weakly/strictly dominated strategies is to represent the players "deliberation" about what they are going to do, then this is a significant assumption. The point is that while a player is deliberating about what to do in a

---

[18] This graph was produced by a python program with an index of caution $k = 25$ and a satisficing value of 0.01. A satisficing value of 0.01 means that the process stops when the covetabilities fall below 0.01. Contact the author for the code for this simulation.

[19] The outcome may end in a mixed-strategy Nash equilibrium.

game situation, there may be strategies that cannot yet be classified as "good" or "bad". These are the strategies that the player needs to think about more before deciding how to classify them. Building on this intuition, the *reasoning-based expected utility procedure* of [32] is intended to model the reasoning procedure that a *Bayesian* rational player would follow as she decides what to do in a game.

At each stage of the procedure, strategies are **categorized**. A categorization is a *ternary* partition of the players' strategies S_i, rather than the usual binary partition in terms of which strategies are strictly/weakly dominated and which are not. The key idea is that during the reasoning process, strategies are accumulated, deleted or neither. Formally, for each player i, let $S_i^+ \subseteq S_i$ denote the set of strategies that have been accumulated and $S_i^- \subseteq S_i$ the set of strategies that have been deleted. The innovative aspect of this procedure is that $S_i^+ \cup S_i^-$ need not equal S_i. So, strategies in S_i but not in $S_i^+ \cup S_i^-$ are classified as "neither accumulated nor deleted". The reasoning-based expected utility procedure proceeds as follows: The procedure is defined by induction. Initially, let $D_{i,0} = \Delta(S_{-i})$, the set of all probability measures over the strategies of i's opponents, and let $S_{i,0}^+ = S_{i,0}^- = \emptyset$. Then, for $n \geq 0$, we have:

- Accumulate all strategies for player i that maximize expected utility for *every* probability in D_i. Formally,

$$S_{i,n+1}^+ = \{s_i \in S_{i,n} \mid MEU(s_i, \pi) \text{ for all } \pi \in D_{i,n}\}.$$

- Delete all strategies for player i that do not maximize probability against *any* *probability distribution*

$$S_{i,n+1}^-\{s_i \in S_{i,n} \mid \text{ there is no } \pi \in D_{i,n} \text{ such that } MEU(s_i, \pi)\}.$$

- Keep all probability measures that assign positive probability to opponents playing accumulated strategies and zero probability to deleted strategies. Formally, let $D_{i,n+1}$ be all the probability measures from $D_{i,n}$ that assign positive probability to any strategy profile from $\Pi_{j \neq i} S_{i,n+1}^+$ and 0 probability to any strategy profile from $\Pi_{j \neq i} S_{i,n+1}^-$.

The following example from [32] illustrates this procedure:

Bob

		l	r
u		1,1	1,1
m_1		0,0	1,0
m_2		2,0	0,0
d		0,2	0,0

Ann

For Bob, strategy l is accumulated since it maximizes expected utility with respect to every probability on Ann's strategies (note that l weakly dominates r). For Ann, d is deleted, as it does not maximize probability with respect to any probability measure on Bob's strategies (note that d is *strictly* dominated by u). Thus, we have

$$S_{a,1}^+ = \emptyset$$
$$S_{a,1}^- = \{d\}$$
$$S_{b,1}^+ = \{l\}$$
$$S_{b,1}^- = \emptyset$$

In the next round, Ann must consider only probability measures that assign positive probability to Bob playing l, and Bob must consider only probability measures assigning probability 0 to Ann playing d. This means that r is accumulated for Bob[20] and m_1 is deleted[21] for Ann:

$$S_{a,2}^+ = \emptyset$$
$$S_{a,2}^- = \{b, m_1\}$$
$$S_{b,2}^+ = \{l, r\}$$
$$S_{b,2}^- = \emptyset$$

At this point, the procedure reaches a fixed-point with Bob accumulating l and r and Ann deleting d and m_1. The interpretation is that Bob has good reason to play either l or r and, thus, must *pick* one of them. All that Ann was able to conclude is that d and m_1 are not good choices.

The general message is that players may not be able to identify a *unique* rational strategy by strategic reasoning alone (as represented by the iterative procedure given above). There are two reasons why this may happen. First, a player may accumulate more than one strategy, and so the player must "pick"[22] one of them. This is what happened with Bob. Given the observation that Ann will not choose b, both of the choices l and r give the same payoff, and so Bob must *pick* one of them[23]. Second, players may not have enough information to identify the "rational" choices. Without any information about which of l or r Bob will pick, Ann cannot come to a conclusion about which of u or m_2 she should choose. Thus, neither of these strategies can be accumulated. Ann and Bob face very different decision problems. No matter which choice Bob ends up picking, his choice will be rational (given his belief that Ann will not choose irrationally). However, since Ann lacks a probability over how Bob will pick, she cannot identify a rational choice.

5   Reasoning to a Game Model

The game models introduced in Sect. 2.2 can be used to describe the informational context of a game. A natural question from the perspective of this

---

[20] If Bob assigns probability 0 to Ann playing d, then the strategies l and r give exactly the same payoffs.

[21] The only probability measures such that m_1 maximizes expected utility are the ones that assign probability 1 to Bob playing r.

[22] See [56] for an interesting discussion of "picking" and "choosing" in decision theory.

[23] Of course, Bob may think it is possible that Ann is irrational, and so she could choose the strictly dominated strategy d. Then, depending on how likely Bob thinks it is that Ann will choose irrationally, l may be the only rational choice for him. In this chapter, we set aside such considerations.

chapter is: How do the players arrive at a particular informational context? In this section, I introduce different operations that transform epistemic-plausibility models. These operations are intended to represent different ways a rational agent's knowledge and beliefs can change over time. Then, I show how to use these operations to describe how the players' knowledge and beliefs change as they each deliberate about what they are going to do in a game situation.

5.1   Modeling Information Changes

The simplest type of informational change treats the source of the information as *infallible*. The effect of finding out from an infallible source that φ is true should be clear: *Remove* all states that do not satisfy φ. In the epistemic logic literature, this operation is called a *public announcement* [37,65]. However, calling this an "announcement" is misleading since, in this chapter, I am not modeling any form of "pre-play" communication. The "announcements" are formulas that the players incorporate into the current epistemic state.

Definition 4 (Public Announcement). *Suppose that $\mathcal{M} = \langle W, \{\sim_i\}_{i \in \mathcal{A}}, V \rangle$ is an epistemic model and φ is a formula (in the language $\mathcal{L}_K$). After all the agents find out that φ is true (i.e., φ is* **publicly announced***), the resulting model is $\mathcal{M}^{!\varphi} = \langle W^{!\varphi}, \{\sim_i^{!\varphi}\}, V^{!\varphi} \rangle$, where $W^{!\varphi} = \{w \in W \mid \mathcal{M}, w \models \varphi\}$; $\sim_i^{!\varphi} = \sim_i \cap W^{!\varphi} \times W^{!\varphi}$ for all $i \in \mathcal{A}$; and $\sigma^{!\varphi}$ is the restriction of σ to $W^{!\varphi}$.*

The models $\mathcal{M}$ and $\mathcal{M}^\varphi$ describe two different moments in time, with $\mathcal{M}$ describing the current or initial information state of the agents and $\mathcal{M}^{!\varphi}$ the information state *after* all the agents find out that φ is true. This temporal dimension can also be represented in the logical language with modalities of the form $[!\varphi]\psi$. The intended interpretation of $[!\varphi]\psi$ is "ψ is true after all the agents find out that φ is true", and truth is defined as

- $\mathcal{M}, w \models [!\varphi]\psi$ iff [if $\mathcal{M}, w \models \varphi$ then $\mathcal{M}^{!\varphi}, w \models \psi$].

A public announcement is only one type of informative action. For the other transformations discussed in this chapter, while the agents do *trust* the source of φ, they do not treat it as infallible. Perhaps the most ubiquitous policy is *conservative upgrade* ($\uparrow\varphi$), which lets the agent only tentatively accept the incoming information φ by making the best φ-worlds the new minimal set and keeping the old plausibility ordering the same on all other worlds. A second operation is *radical upgrade* ($\Uparrow\varphi$), which moves *all* the φ worlds before all the $\neg\varphi$ worlds and otherwise keeps the plausibility ordering the same. Before giving the formal definition, we need some notation: Given an epistemic-plausibility model $\mathcal{M}$, let $\llbracket\varphi\rrbracket_i^w = \{x \mid \mathcal{M}, x \models \varphi\} \cap [w]_i$ denote the set of all φ-worlds that i considers possible at state w and $best_i(\varphi, w) = Min_{\preceq_i}(\llbracket\varphi\rrbracket_i^w)$ be the best φ-worlds at state w, according to agent i.

Definition 5 (Conservative and Radical Upgrade). *Given an epistemic-plausibility model $\mathcal{M} = \langle W, \{\sim_i\}_{i \in \mathcal{A}}, \{\preceq_i\}_{i \in \mathcal{A}}, \sigma \rangle$ and a formula $\varphi \in \mathcal{L}_{KB}$, the* *conservative/radical upgrade* of $\mathcal{M}$ with φ is the model $\mathcal{M}^{*\varphi} = \langle W^{*\varphi}, \{\sim_i^{*\varphi}\}_{i \in N}, \{\preceq_i^{*\varphi}\}_{i \in N}, V^{*\varphi}\rangle$ *10:44 AM 9/11/2015 with* $W^{*\varphi} = W$, *for each* i, $\sim_i^{*\varphi} = \sim_i$, $V^{*\varphi} = V$ *where* $* = \uparrow, \Uparrow$. *The relations* $\preceq_i^{\uparrow\varphi}$ *and* $\preceq_i^{\Uparrow\varphi}$ *are the smallest relations satisfying:*

Conservative Upgrade

1. *If* $v \in best_i(\varphi, w)$ *then* $v \prec_i^{\uparrow\varphi} x$ *for all* $x \in [w]_i$; *and*
2. *for all* $x, y \in [w]_i - best_i(\varphi, w)$, $x \preceq_i^{\uparrow\varphi} y$ *iff* $x \preceq_i y$.

Radical Upgrade

1. *for all* $x \in [\![\varphi]\!]_i^w$ *and* $y \in [\![\neg\varphi]\!]_i^w$, *set* $x \prec_i^{\Uparrow\varphi} y$;
2. *for all* $x, y \in [\![\varphi]\!]_i^w$, *set* $x \preceq_i^{\Uparrow\varphi} y$ *iff* $x \preceq_i y$; *and*
3. *for all* $x, y \in [\![\neg\varphi]\!]_i^w$, *set* $x \preceq_i^{\Uparrow\varphi} y$ *iff* $x \preceq_i y$. ◁

As the reader is invited to check, a conservative upgrade is a special case of a radical upgrade: the conservative upgrade of φ at w is the radical upgrade of $best_i(\varphi, w)$. A logical analysis of these operations includes formulas of the form $[\uparrow\varphi]\psi$ intended to mean "after everyone conservatively upgrades with φ, ψ is true" and $[\Uparrow\varphi]\psi$ intended to mean "after everyone radically upgrades with φ, ψ is true". The definition of truth for these formula is as expected:

- $\mathcal{M}, w \models [\uparrow\varphi]\psi$ iff $\mathcal{M}^{\uparrow\varphi}, w \models \psi$
- $\mathcal{M}, w \models [\Uparrow\varphi]\psi$ iff $\mathcal{M}^{\Uparrow\varphi}, w \models \psi$

The main issue of interest in this chapter is the limit behavior of iterated sequences of announcements. That is, what happens to the epistemic-plausibility models *in the limit*? Do the players' knowledge and beliefs stabilize or keep changing in response to the new information?

An initial observation is that iterated public announcement of any formula φ in an epistemic-plausibility model must stop at a limit model where either φ or its negation is true at all states (see [14] for a discussion and proof). In addition to the limit dynamics of knowledge under public announcements, there is the limit behavior of beliefs under soft announcements (radical/conservative upgrades). See [14] and [21, Sect. 4] for general discussions. I conclude this brief introduction to dynamic logics of knowledge and beliefs with an example of the type of dynamics that can arise.

Let $\mathcal{M}_1$ be an initial epistemic-plausibility model (for a single agent) with three states w_1, w_2 and w_3 satisfying r, q and p, respectively. Suppose that the agent's plausibility ordering is $w_1 \prec w_2 \prec w_3$. Then, the agent believes that r. Consider the formula

$$\varphi := (r \vee (B^{\neg r}q \wedge p) \vee (B^{\neg r}p \wedge q)).$$

This is true at w_1 in the initial model. Since $[\![\varphi]\!]_{\mathcal{M}_1} = \{w_3, w_1\}$, we have $\mathcal{M}_1^{\Uparrow\varphi} = \mathcal{M}_2$. Furthermore, $[\![\varphi]\!]_{\mathcal{M}_2} = \{w_2, w_1\}$, so $\mathcal{M}_2^{\Uparrow\varphi} = \mathcal{M}_3$. Since $\mathcal{M}_3$ is the same model as $\mathcal{M}_1$, we have a cycle:

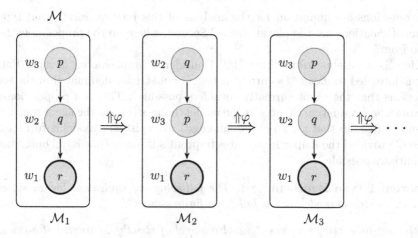

In the above example, the player's conditional beliefs keep changing during the update process. However, the player's non-conditional beliefs remain fixed throughout the process. In fact, Baltag and Smets have shown that every iterated sequence of truthful radical upgrades stabilizes all non-conditional beliefs in the limit [14]. See [12,38,58] for generalizations and broader discussions about the issues raised in this section.

5.2   Rational Belief Change During Deliberation

This section looks at the operations that transform the informational context of a game *as the players deliberate about what they should do in a game situation*. The main idea is that in each informational context (viewed as describing one stage of the deliberation process), the players determine which options are *"optimal"* and which options the players ought to avoid (guided by some choice rule). This leads to a transformation of the informational context as the players adopt the relevant beliefs about the outcome of their *practical reasoning*. The different types of transformation mentioned above then represent how confident the player(s) (or modeler) is (are) in their assessment of which outcomes are rational. In this new informational context, the players again think about what they should do, leading to another transformation. The main question is: Does this process *stabilize*?

The answer to this question will depend on a number of factors. The general picture is

$$\mathcal{M}_0 \overset{\tau(D_0)}{\Longrightarrow} \mathcal{M}_1 \overset{\tau(D_1)}{\Longrightarrow} \mathcal{M}_2 \overset{\tau(D_2)}{\Longrightarrow} \cdots \overset{\tau(D_n)}{\Longrightarrow} \mathcal{M}_{n+1} \Longrightarrow \cdots,$$

where each D_i is some proposition describing the "rational" options and τ is a model transformer (e.g., public announcement, radical or conservative upgrade).

Two questions are important for the analysis of this process. First, what type of transformations are the players using? Second, where do the propositions D_i come from?

Here is a baseline result from [18]. Consider a propositional formula Rat_i that is intended to mean "i's current action is not strictly dominated in the set of actions that the agent currently considers possible". This is a propositional formula whose valuation changes as the model changes (i.e., as the agent removes possible outcomes that are strictly dominated). An epistemic model is **full** for a game G provided the map σ from states to profiles is onto. That is, all outcomes are initially possible.

Theorem 1 (van Benthem [18]). *The following are equivalent for all states w in an epistemic model that is full for a finite game G:*

1. *The outcome $\sigma(w)$ survives iterated removal of strictly dominated strategies.*
2. *Repeated successive* **public announcements** *of $\bigwedge_i \mathsf{Rat}_i$ for the players stabilize at a submodel whose domain contains w.*

This theorem gives a precise sense of how the process of iteratively removing strictly dominated strategies can be viewed as a process of deliberation (cf. the discussion in Sect. 2.1). See [4] for a generalization of this theorem focusing on arbitrary "optimality" propositions satisfying a monotonicity property and arbitrary games. A related analysis can be found in [59], which provides an in-depth study of the upgrade mechanisms that match game-theoretic analyses.

5.3   Rational Belief Change During Game Play

The importance of explicitly modeling belief change over time becomes even more evident when considering *extensive games*. An extensive game makes explicit the sequential structure of the choices in a game. Formally, an extensive game is a tuple $\langle N, T, \tau, \{u_i\}_{i \in N} \rangle$, where

- N is a finite set of players;
- T is a tree describing the temporal structure of the game situation: Formally, T consists of a set of nodes and an immediate successor relation $\rightarrowtail$. Let O denote the set of leaves (nodes without any successors) and V the remaining nodes. The edges at a decision node $v \in V$ are each labeled with an action. Let $A(v)$ denote the set of actions available at v. Let $\rightsquigarrow$ be the transitive closure of $\rightarrowtail$.
- τ is a turn function assigning a player to each node $v \in V$ (let $V_i = \{v \in V \mid \tau(v) = i\}$.
- $u_i : O \rightarrow \mathbb{R}$ is the utility function for player i assigning real numbers to outcome nodes.

The following is an example of an extensive game:

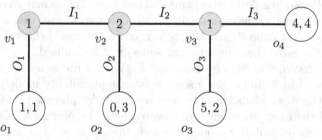

This is an extensive game with $V = \{v_1, v_2, v_3\}$, $O = \{o_1, o_2, o_3, o_4\}$, $\tau(v_1) = \tau(v_3) = 1$ and $\tau(v_2) = 2$, and, for example, $u_1(o_2) = 0$ and $u_2(o_2) = 3$. Furthermore, we have, for example, $v_1 \longmapsto o_1$, $v_1 \rightsquigarrow o_4$, and $A(v_1) = \{I_1, O_1\}$.

A **strategy** for player i in an extensive game is a function σ from V_i to nodes such that $v \mapsto \sigma(v)$. Thus, a strategy prescribes a move for player i at *every possible node where i moves*. For example, the function σ with $\sigma(v_1) = O_1$ and $\sigma(v_3) = I_3$ is a strategy for player i, even though, by following the strategy, i knows that v_3 will not be reached. The main solution concept for extensive games is the *subgame perfect equilibrium* [71], which is calculated using the "backward induction (BI) algorithm":

BI Algorithm: *At terminal nodes, players already have the nodes marked with their utilities. At a non-terminal node n, once all daughters are marked, the node is marked as follows: determine whose turn it is to move at n and find the daughter d that has the highest utility for that player. Copy the utilities from d onto n.*

In the extensive game given above, the BI algorithm leads to the following markings:

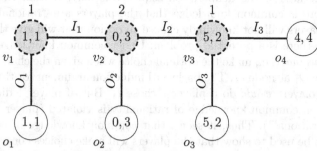

The BI strategy for player 1 is $\sigma(v_1) = O_1$, $\sigma(v_3) = O_3$ and for player 2 it is $\sigma(v_2) = O_2$. If both players follow their BI strategy, then the resulting outcome is o_1 ($v_1 \mapsto o_1$ is called the *BI path*).

Much has been written about backward induction and whether it follows from the assumption that there is common knowledge (or common belief) that all players are *rational*[24]. In the remainder of this section, I explain how epistemic-plausibility models and the model transformations defined above can make this

---

[24] The key papers include [8,9,16,39,75]. See [61] for a complete survey of the literature.

more precise. The first step is to describe what the players believe about the strategies followed in an extensive game and how these beliefs may change during the play of the game. I sidestep a number of delicate issues in the discussion below (see [24] for a clear exposition). My focus is on the players' beliefs about which outcome of the game (i.e., the terminal nodes) will be realized.

Suppose that $a, a' \in A(v)$ for some $v \in V_i$. We say **move a strictly dominates move a' in beliefs** (given some epistemic-plausibility model), provided that all of the most plausible outcomes reachable by playing a at v are preferred to all the most plausible outcomes reachable by playing a'. Consider an initial epistemic-plausibility model in which the states are the four outcomes $\{o_1, o_2, o_3, o_4\}$, and both players consider all outcomes equally plausible (I write $w \approx v$ if w and v are equally plausible—i.e., $w \succeq v$ and $v \succeq w$). Then, at v_2, O_2 is not strictly dominated over I_2 in beliefs since the nodes reachable by I_2 are $\{o_3, o_4\}$, both are equally plausible, and player 2 prefers o_4 over o_2, but o_2 over o_3. However, since player 1 prefers o_3 to o_4, O_3 strictly dominates I_3 in beliefs. Suppose that R is interpreted as "no player chooses an action that is strictly dominated in beliefs". Thus, in the initial model, in which all four outcomes are equally plausible, the interpretation of R is $\{o_1, o_2, o_3\}$. We can now ask what happens to the initial model if this formula R is iteratively updated (for example, using radical upgrade).

$$o_1 \approx o_2 \approx o_3 \approx o_4 \quad \overset{\Uparrow R}{\Longrightarrow} \quad o_1 \approx o_2 \approx o_3 \prec o_4 \quad \overset{\Uparrow R}{\Longrightarrow} \quad o_1 \approx o_2 \prec o_3 \prec o_4$$

$$o_1 \prec o_2 \prec o_3 \prec o_4 \quad \overset{\Uparrow R}{\nwarrow}$$

This sequence of radical upgrades is intended to represent the "pre-play" deliberation leading to a model in which there is common belief that the outcome of the game will be o_1. But, what justifies both players deliberating in this way to a common epistemic-plausibility model?

The correctness of the deliberation sequence is derived from the assumption that there is common knowledge that the players are "rational" (in the sense, that players will not knowingly choose an option that will give them lower payoffs). But there is a potential problem: Under common knowledge that the players are *rational* (i.e., make the optimal choice when given the chance), player 1 *must* choose O_1 at node v_1. The backward induction argument for this is based on what the players *would* do if player 1 chose I_1. But, if player 1 did, in fact, choose I_1, then common knowledge of rationality is violated (player 1's choice would be "irrational"). Thus, it seems that common knowledge of rationality, alone, cannot be used to show that the players will make choices consistent with the backward induction path. An additional assumption about how the players' beliefs may change during the course of the game is needed. The underlying assumption is that the players are assumed to be unwaveringly optimistic: No matter what is observed, players maintain the belief that everyone is *rational* at future nodes.

There are many ways to formalize the above intuition that players are "unwaveringly optimistic". I briefly discuss the approach from [15] since it touches on a number of issues raised in this chapter. The key idea is to encode the players' strategies as conditional beliefs in an epistemic-plausibility model. For example, consider the following epistemic-plausibility model on the four outcomes of the above extensive game:

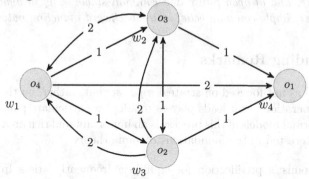

It is assumed that there are atomic propositions for each possible outcome. Formally, suppose that there is an atomic proposition o_i for each outcome o_i (assume that o_i is true only at state o_i). The non-terminal nodes $v \in V$ are then identified with the set of outcomes reachable from that node:

$$v := \bigvee_{v \rightsquigarrow o} o.$$

In the above model, both players 1 and 2 believe that o_1 is the outcome that will be realized, and the players initially rule out none of the possible outcomes. That is, the model satisfies the "open future" assumption of [15] (none of the players have "hard" information that an outcome is ruled out). The fact that player 1 is committed to the BI strategy is encoded in the conditional beliefs of the player: both $B_1^{v_1} o_1$ and $B_1^{v_3} o_3$ are true in the above model. For player 2, $B_2^{v_2}(o_3 \vee o_4)$ is true in the above model, which implies that player 2 plans to choose action I_2 at node v_2.

The dynamics of actual play is then modeled as a sequence of public announcements (cf. Definition 4). The players' beliefs change as they learn (irrevocably) which of the nodes in the game are reached. This process produces a sequence of epistemic-plausibility models. For example, a possible sequence of the above game starting with the initial model $\mathcal{M}$ given above is:

$$\mathcal{M} = \mathcal{M}^{!v_1}; \mathcal{M}^{!v_2}; \mathcal{M}^{!v_3}; \mathcal{M}^{!o_4}$$

The assumption that the players are "incurably optimistic" is represented as follows: No matter what true formula is publicly announced (i.e., no matter how the game proceeds), there is common belief that the players will make a rational choice (when it is their turn to move). Formally, this requires introducing an *arbitrary public announcement operator* [11]: $\mathcal{M}, w \models [\,!\,]\varphi$ provided that, for all formulas[25] ψ, if $\mathcal{M}, w \models \psi$ then $\mathcal{M}, w \models [!\psi]\varphi$. Then, there is *common stable*

---

[25] Strictly speaking, it is all *epistemic* formulas. The important point is to not include formulas with the [!] operator in them.

belief in φ provided that $[\,!\,]C^B\varphi$ is true, where $C^B\varphi$ is intended to mean that there is common belief in φ (cf. Sect. 2.2). The key result is:

Theorem 2 (Baltag, Smets and Zvesper [15]). *Common knowledge of the game structure, and of open future and common stable belief in dynamic rationality, together, imply common belief in the backward induction outcome.*

6 Concluding Remarks

This chapter has not focused on strategies *per se*, but, rather, on the process of "rational deliberation" that leads players to adopt a particular "plan of action". Developing formal models of this process is an important and rich area of research for anyone interested in the foundations of game theory.

> The economist's predilection for equilibria frequently arises from the belief that some underlying dynamic process (often suppressed in formal models) moves a system to a point from which it moves no further.
>
> [22, pg. 1008]

Many readers may have been expecting a formal account of the players' *practical reasoning* in game-theoretic situations. Instead, this chapter presented three different frameworks in which the "underlying dynamic process" mentioned in the above quote is made explicit. None of the frameworks discussed in this chapter are intended to model the players' practical reasoning. Rather, they describe deliberation in terms of a sequence of belief changes about what the players are doing or what their opponents may be thinking. This raises an important question: In what sense do the frameworks introduced in this chapter describe the players' *strategic reasoning*? I will not attempt a complete answer to this question here. Instead, I conclude with brief discussions of two related questions.

6.1 What Are the Differences and Similarities Between the Different Models of Strategic Reasoning?

The three frameworks presented in this paper offer different perspectives on the standard game-theoretic analysis of strategic situations. To compare and contrast these different formal frameworks, I will illustrate the different perspectives on the following game from [70, Example 8, pg. 305]:

Bob

		l	r
Ann	u	1, 1	1, 0
	d	1, 0	0, 1

In the above game, d is weakly dominated by u for Ann. If Bob knows that Ann is rational (in the sense that she will not choose a weakly dominated strategy), then he can rule out option d. In the smaller game, action r is now strictly dominated by l for Bob. If Ann knows that Bob is rational and that Bob knows that she is rational (and so, rules out option d), then she can rule out option r. Assuming that the above reasoning is transparent to both Ann and Bob, it is common knowledge that Ann will play u and Bob will play l. But now, what is the reason for Bob to rule out the possibility that Ann will play d? He knows that Ann knows that he is going to play l, and both u and d maximize Ann's expected utility with respect to the belief that Bob will play l.

Many authors have pointed out puzzles surrounding an epistemic analysis of iterated removal of weakly dominated strategies [5, 27, 70]. The central issue is that the assumption of common knowledge of rationality seems to conflict with the logic of iteratively removing weakly dominated strategies. The models introduced in this paper each provide a unique perspective on this issue. Note that the idea is not to provide a new "epistemic foundation" for iterated removal of weakly dominated strategies. Both [27] and [41] have convincing results here. Rather, the goal is to offer a different perspective on the existing epistemic analyses.

I start with Skyrms' model of rational deliberation from Sect. 3. There are two Nash equilibria: the pure strategy Nash equilibrium (u, l) and the mixed Nash equilibrium, where Ann plays u and d each with probability 0.5 and Bob plays strategy l. Rational deliberation with any dynamical rule that "seeks the good" (such as the Nash dynamics) is guaranteed to lead the players to one of the two equilibria. However, there is an important difference between the two Nash equilibria from the point of view of rational deliberators. Through deliberation, the players will *almost always* end up at the pure-strategy equilibrium. That is, unless the players start deliberating at the mixed-strategy Nash equilibrium, deliberation will lead the players to the pure-strategy equilibrium. This makes sense since playing u will always give a greater expected utility for Ann than any mixed strategy, as long as there is a chance (no matter how small) that Bob will play r. I can illustrate this point by showing the deliberational path that is generated if the players start from the following states of indecision: (1) Ann is playing d with probability 1 and Bob is playing l with probability 1; (2) Ann is playing u and l with probability 0.5 and Bob is playing l with probability 0.95; and (3) Ann is playing u with probability 0.5 and Bob is playing r with probability 0.5.[26]

---

[26] These graphs were generated by a python program using a satisficing value of 0.001 and an index of caution of 50. The reason that the simulations stopped before reaching the pure Nash equilibrium is because the simulation is designed so that deliberation ends when the covetabilities fall below the satisficing value.

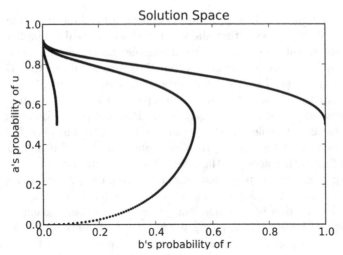

The second perspective comes from the reasoning-based expected utility procedure discussed in Sect. 4. For Ann, u is accumulated in the first round since it maximizes expected utility with respect to all probability measures on Bob's strategies. No other strategies are deleted or accumulated. Thus, the procedure stabilizes in the second round without categorizing any of Bob's strategies or Ann's strategy d. So, u is identified as a "good" strategy, but d is not classified as a "bad" strategy. Furthermore, neither of Bob's strategies can be classified as "good" or "bad".

Finally, I turn to the approach outlined in Sect. 5. An analysis of this game is discussed in [59]. In that paper, it is shown that certain deliberational sequences for the above game do not stabilize. Of course, whether a deliberational sequence stabilizes depends crucially on which model transformations are used. Indeed, a new model transformation, "suspend judgement", is used in [59] to construct a deliberational sequence that does not stabilize. The general conclusion is that the players may not be able to deliberate their way to an informational context in which there is common knowledge of rationality (where rationality includes the assumption that players do not play weakly dominated strategies).

Each of the different frameworks offers a different perspective on strategic reasoning in games. The perspectives are not *competing*; rather, they highlight different aspects of what it means to reason strategically. However, more work is needed to precisely characterize the similarities and differences between these different models of rational deliberation in games. Such a comprehensive comparison will be left for another paper.

6.2   What Role Do Higher-Order Beliefs Play in a General Theory of Rational Decision Making in Game Situations?

Each model of deliberation discussed in this chapter either implicitly or explicitly made assumptions about the players' *higher-order* beliefs (see Sect. 2.2). In the end, I am interested only in what (rational) players are going to do. This, in turn, depends only on what the players believe the other players are going to do. A player's belief about what her opponents are thinking is relevant only because they shape the players first-order beliefs about what her opponents are going to do. Kadane and Larkey explain the issue nicely:

> "It is true that a subjective Bayesian will have an opinion not only on his opponent's behavior, but also on his opponent's belief about his own behavior, his opponent's belief about his belief about his opponent's behavior, etc. (He also has opinions about the phase of the moon, tomorrow's weather and the winner of the next Superbowl). *However, in a single-play game, all aspects of his opinion except his opinion about his opponent's behavior are irrelevant, and can be ignored in the analysis by integrating them out of the joint opinion.*"
>
> [46, pg. 239, my emphasis]

A theory of rational decision making in game situations need not *require* that a player considers *all* of her higher-order beliefs in her decision-making process. The assumption is only that the players recognize that their opponents are "actively reasoning" agents. Precisely "how much" higher-order information *should* be taken into account in such a situation is a very interesting, open question (cf. [47,64]).

There is quite a lot of experimental work about whether or not humans take into account even second-order beliefs (e.g., a belief about their opponents' beliefs) in game situations (see, for example, [30,44,73]). It is beyond the scope of this chapter to survey this literature here (see [29] for an excellent overview). Of course, this is a *descriptive* question, and it is very much open how such observations should be incorporated into a general theory of rational deliberation in games (cf. [53,54,77]).

****

A general theory of rational deliberation for game and decision theory is a broad topic. It is beyond the scope of this chapter to discuss the many different aspects and competing perspectives on such a theory[27]. A completely developed theory will have both a normative component (What are the normative principles that guide the players' thinking about what they should do?) and a descriptive component (Which psychological phenomena best explain discrepancies between predicted and observed behavior in game situations?). The main challenge is to find the right balance between descriptive accuracy and normative relevance. While this is true for all theories of individual decision making and reasoning, focusing on game situations raises a number of compelling issues. Robert Aumann and Jacques Dreze [2, pg. 81] adeptly summarize one of the most pressing issues when they write: "[T]he fundamental insight of game theory [is] that a rational player must take into account that the players reason

---

[27] Interested readers are referred to [72] (especially Chap. 7), and [35,50,67] for broader discussions.

about each other in deciding how to play". Exactly how the players (should) incorporate the fact that they are interacting with other (actively reasoning) agents into their own decision-making process is the subject of much debate.

References

1. Alexander, J.M.: Local interactions and the dynamics of rational deliberation. Philos. Stud. **147**(1), 103–121 (2010)
2. Apt, K.R.: A primer on strategic games. In: Apt, K.R., Grädel, E. (eds.) Lectures in Game Theory for Computer Scientists, pp. 1–33. Cambridge University Press, Cambridge (2011)
3. Apt, K.R., Zvesper, J.A.: Public announcements in strategic games with arbitrary strategy sets. In: Proceedings of LOFT 2010 (2010)
4. Apt, K.R., Zvesper, J.A.: Public announcements in strategic games with arbitrary strategy sets. CoRR (2010). http://arxiv.org/abs/1012.5173
5. Asheim, G., Dufwenberg, M.: Admissibility and common belief. Games Econ. Behav. **42**, 208–234 (2003)
6. Aumann, R.: Agreeing to disagree. Ann. Stat. **4**, 1236–1239 (1976)
7. Aumann, R.: Correlated equilibrium as an expression of Bayesian rationality. Econometrica **55**(1), 1–18 (1987)
8. Aumann, R.: Backward induction and common knowledge of rationality. Game Econ. Behav. **8**, 6–19 (1995)
9. Aumann, R.: On the centipede game. Game Econ. Behav. **23**, 97–105 (1998)
10. Aumann, R., Brandenburger, A.: Epistemic conditions for Nash equilibrium. Econometrica **63**, 1161–1180 (1995)
11. Balbiani, P., Baltag, A., van Ditmarsch, H., Herzig, A., Hoshi, T., De Lima, T.: 'Knowable' as 'known after an announcement'. Rev. Symb. Log. **1**(3), 305–334 (2008)
12. Baltag, A., Gierasimczuk, N., Smets, S.: Belief revision as a truth-tracking process. In: Proceedings of the 13th Conference on Theoretical Aspects of Rationality and Knowledge, TARK XIII, pp. 187–190, ACM (2011)
13. Baltag, A., Smets, S.: ESSLLI 2009 course: dynamic logics for interactive belief revision (2009). Slides available online at http://alexandru.tiddlyspot.com/#%5B%5BESSLLI09%20COURSE%5D%5D
14. Baltag, A., Smets, S.: Group belief dynamics under iterated revision: Fixed points and cycles of joint upgrades. In: Proceedings of Theoretical Aspects of Rationality and Knowledge (2009)
15. Baltag, A., Smets, S., Zvesper, J.A.: Keep 'hoping' for rationality: A solution to the backwards induction paradox. Synthese **169**, 301–333 (2009)
16. Battigalli, P., Siniscalchi, M.: Strong belief and forward induction reasoning. J. Econ. Theor. **105**, 356–391 (2002)
17. van Benthem, J.: Dynamic logic for belief revision. J. Appl. Non-Class. Log. **14**(2), 129–155 (2004)
18. van Benthem, J.: Rational dynamics and epistemic logic in games. Int. Game Theor. Rev. **9**(1), 13–45 (2007)
19. van Benthem, J.: Logical Dynamics of Information and Interaction. Cambridge University Press, Cambridge (2011)
20. van Benthem, J., Gheerbrant, A.: Game solution, epistemic dynamics and fixed-point logics. Fundam. Inform. **100**, 1–23 (2010)

21. van Benthem, J., Pacuit, E., Roy, O.: Towards a theory of play: A logical perspective on games and interaction. Games **2**(1), 52–86 (2011)
22. Bernheim, B.D.: Rationalizable strategic behavior. Econometrica **52**(4), 1007–1028 (1984)
23. Board, O.: Dynamic interactive epistemology. Games Econ. Behav. **49**, 49–80 (2004)
24. Bonanno, G.: Reasoning about strategies and rational play in dynamic games. In: van Benthem, J., Ghosh, S., Verbrugge, R. (eds.) Models of Strategic Reasoning. LNCS, vol. 8972, pp. 34–62. Springer, Heidelberg (2015)
25. Boutilier, C.: Conditional logics for default reasoning and belief revision. Ph.D. thesis, University of Toronto (1992)
26. Brandenburger, A.: The power of paradox: some recent developments in interactive epistemology. Int. J. Game Theor. **35**, 465–492 (2007)
27. Brandenburger, A., Friedenberg, A., Keisler, H.J.: Admissibility in games. Econometrica **76**(2), 307–352 (2008)
28. Chwe, M.S.-Y.: Rational Ritual. Princeton University Press, Princeton (2001)
29. Colman, A.: Cooperation, psychological game theory, and limitations of rationality in social interactions. Behav. Brain Sci. **26**, 139–198 (2003)
30. Colman, A.: Depth of strategic reasoning in games. TRENDS Cogn. Sci. **7**(1), 2–4 (2003)
31. Cubitt, R.P., Sugden, R.: Common knowledge, salience and convention: A reconstruction of David Lewis' game theory. Econ. Philos. **19**(2), 175–210 (2003)
32. Cubitt, R.P., Sugden, R.: The reasoning-based expected utility procedure. Games Econ. Behav. **71**(2), 328–338 (2011)
33. Cubitt, R.P., Sugden, R.: Common reasoning in games: A Lewisian analysis of common knowledge of rationality. Econ. Philos. **30**(03), 285–329 (2014)
34. van Ditmarsch, H., van Eijck, J., Verbrugge, R.: Common knowledge and common belief. In: van Eijck, J., Verbrugge, R. (eds.) Discourses on Social Software, pp. 99–122. Amsterdam University Press, Amsterdam (2009)
35. Douven, I.: Decision theory and the rationality of further deliberation. Econ. Philos. **18**(2), 303–328 (2002)
36. Fagin, R., Halpern, J., Moses, Y., Vardi, M.: Reasoning about Knowledge. The MIT Press, Cambridge (1995)
37. Gerbrandy, J.: Bisimulations on planet Kripke. Ph.D. thesis, University of Amsterdam (1999)
38. Gierasimczuk, N.: Knowing one's limits: Logical analysis of inductive inference. Ph.D. thesis, Institute for Logic, Language and Information, University of Amsterdam (2011)
39. Halpern, J.: Substantive rationality and backward induction. Games Econ. Behav. **37**(2), 425–435 (2001)
40. Halpern, J., Moses, Y.: Knowledge and common knowledge in a distributed environment. J. ACM **37**(3), 549–587 (1990)
41. Halpern, J., Pass, R.: A logical characterization of iterated admissibility. In: Heifetz, A. (ed.) Proceedings of the Twelfth Conference on Theoretical Aspects of Rationality and Knoweldge, pp. 146–155 (2009)
42. Harsanyi, J.: The tracing procedure: a Bayesian approach to defining a solution for n-person noncooperative games. Int. J. Game Theor. **4**, 61–94 (1975)
43. Harsanyi, J., Selten, R.: A General Theory of Equilibrium Selection in Games. The MIT Press, Cambridge (1988)
44. Hedden, T., Zhang, J.: What do you think I think you think? strategic reasoning in matrix games. Cognition **85**, 1–36 (2002)

45. Jeffrey, R.: Review of the dynamics of rational deliberation by Brian Skyrms. Philos. Phenomenol. Res. **52**(3), 734–737 (1992)
46. Kadane, J.B., Larkey, P.D.: Subjective probability and the theory of games. Manag. Sci. **28**(2), 113–120 (1982)
47. Kets, W.: Bounded reasoning and higher-order uncertainty. Working paper (2010)
48. Lamarre, P., Shoham, Y.: Knowledge, certainty, belief and conditionalisation. In: Proceedings of the International Conference on Knowledge Representation and Reasoning, pp. 415–424 (1994)
49. Leitgeb, H.: Beliefs in conditionals vs. conditional beliefs. Topoi **26**(1), 115–132 (2007)
50. Levi, I.: Feasibility. In: Bicchieri, C., Chiara, L.D. (eds.) Knowledge, Belief and Strategic Interaction, pp. 1–20. Cambridge University Press, Cambridge (1992)
51. Lewis, D.K.: Counterfactuals. Harvard University Press, Cambridge (1973)
52. Leyton-Brown, K., Shoham, Y.: Essentials of Game Theory: A Concise Multidisciplinary Introduction. Morgan & Claypool Publishers, San Rafael (2008)
53. Meijering, B., van Rijn, H., Taatgen, N., Verbrugge, R.: I do know what you think I think: Second-order social reasoning is not that difficult. In: Proceedings of the 33rd Annual Meeting of the Cognitive Science Society, pp. 1423–1428 (2010)
54. Meijering, B., van Rijn, H., Taatgen, N., Verbrugge, R.: What eye movements can tell about theory of mind in a strategic game. PLoS ONE **7**(9), e45961 (2012)
55. Monderer, D., Samet, D.: Approximating common knowledge with common beliefs. Games Econ. Behav. **1**, 170–190 (1989)
56. Morgenbesser, S., Ullmann-Margalit, E.: Picking and choosing. Soc. Res. **44**(4), 757–785 (1977)
57. Pacuit, E.: Dynamic epistemic logic I: Modeling knowledge and beliefs. Philos. Compass **8**(9), 798–814 (2013)
58. Pacuit, E.: Dynamic epistemic logic II: Logics of information change. Philos. Compass **8**(9), 815–833 (2013)
59. Pacuit, E., Roy, O.: A dynamic analysis of interactive rationality. In: Ju, S., Lang, J., van Ditmarsch, H. (eds.) LORI 2011. LNCS, vol. 6953, pp. 244–257. Springer, Heidelberg (2011)
60. Pearce, D.G.: Rationalizable strategic behavior and the problem of perfection. Econometrica **52**(4), 1029–1050 (1984)
61. Perea, A.: Epistemic foundations for backward induction: An overview. In: van Benthem, J., Gabbay, D., Löwe, B. (eds.) Proceedings of the 7th Augustus de Morgan Workshop, pp. 159–193. Texts in Logic and Games, Amsterdam University Press (2007)
62. Perea, A.: A one-person doxastic characterization of Nash strategies. Synthese **158**, 251–271 (2007)
63. Perea, A.: Epistemic Game Theory: Reasoning and Choice. Cambridge University Press, Cambridge (2012)
64. Perea, A.: Finite reasoning procedures for dynamic games. In: van Benthem, J., Ghosh, S., Verbrugge, R. (eds.) Models of Strategic Reasoning. LNCS, vol. 8972, pp. 63–90. Springer, Heidelberg (2015)
65. Plaza, J.: Logics of public communications. In: Emrich, M.L., Pfeifer, M.S., Hadzikadic, M., Ras, Z.W. (eds.) Proceedings, 4th International Symposium on Methodologies for Intelligent Systems, pp. 201–216 (republished as [66]) (1989)
66. Plaza, J.: Logics of public communications. Synthese **158**(2), 165–179 (2007)
67. Rabinowicz, W.: Does practical deliberation crowd out self-prediction? Erkenntnis **57**, 91–122 (2002)

68. Risse, M.: What is rational about Nash equilibrium? Synthese **124**(3), 361–384 (2000)
69. Rubinstein, A.: Comments on the interpretation of game theory. Econometrica **59**(4), 909–924 (1991)
70. Samuelson, L.: Dominated strategies and common knowledge. Games Econ. Behav. **4**, 284–313 (1992)
71. Selten, R.: Reexamination of the perfectness concept for equilibrium points in extensive games. Int. J. Game Theor. **4**(1), 25–55 (1975)
72. Skyrms, B.: The Dynamics of Rational Deliberation. Harvard University Press, Cambridge (1990)
73. Stahl, D.O., Wilson, P.W.: On players' models of other players: theory and experimental evidence. Games Econ. Behav. **10**, 218–254 (1995)
74. Stalnaker, R.: Knowledge, belief, and counterfactual reasoning in games. Econ. Philos. **12**, 133–163 (1996)
75. Stalnaker, R.: Belief revision in games: Forward and backward induction. Math. Soc. Sci. **36**, 31–56 (1998)
76. Vanderschraaf, P., Sillari, G.: Common knowledge. In: Zalta, E.N. (ed.) The Stanford Encyclopedia of Philosophy. Spring 2009 edition (2009)
77. Verbrugge, R.: Logic and social cognition: the facts matter, and so do computational models. J. Philos. Log. **38**(6), 649–680 (2009)

Reasoning About Strategies and Rational Play in Dynamic Games

Giacomo Bonanno[(✉)]

Department of Economics, University of California, Davis, USA
gfbonanno@ucdavis.edu

Abstract. We discuss the issues that arise in modeling the notion of common belief of rationality in epistemic models of dynamic games, in particular at the level of interpretation of strategies. A strategy in a dynamic game is defined as a function that associates with every information set a choice at that information set. Implicit in this definition is a set of counterfactual statements concerning what a player would do at information sets that are not reached, or a belief revision policy concerning behavior at information sets that are ruled out by the initial beliefs. We discuss the role of both objective and subjective counterfactuals in attempting to flesh out the interpretation of strategies in epistemic models of dynamic games.

Keywords: Rationality · Dynamic games · Common belief · Belief revision · Counterfactual reasoning

1 Introduction

Game theory provides a formal language for the representation of interactive situations, that is, situations where several "entities" - called players - take actions that affect each other. The nature of the players varies depending on the context in which the game theoretic language is invoked: in evolutionary biology (see, for example, [47]) players are non-thinking living organisms;[1] in computer science (see, for example, [46]) players are artificial agents; in behavioral game theory (see, for example, [26]) players are "ordinary" human beings, etc. Traditionally, however, game theory has focused on interaction among intelligent, sophisticated and rational individuals. For example, Aumann describes game theory as follows:

> "Briefly put, game and economic theory are concerned with the interactive behavior of *Homo rationalis* - rational man. *Homo rationalis* is the species that always acts both purposefully and logically, has well-defined goals, is motivated solely by the desire to approach these goals as closely as possible, and has the calculating ability required to do so." ([3], p. 35)

---

[1] Evolutionary game theory has been applied not only to the analysis of animal and insect behavior but also to studying the "most successful strategies" for tumor and cancer cells (see, for example, [32]).

© Springer-Verlag Berlin Heidelberg 2015
J. van Benthem et al. (Eds.): Models of Strategic Reasoning, LNCS 8972, pp. 34–62, 2015.
DOI: 10.1007/978-3-662-48540-8_2

This chapter is concerned with the traditional interpretation of game theory, in particular, with what is known as the *epistemic foundation program*, whose aim is to characterize, for any game, the behavior of rational and intelligent players who know the structure of the game and the preferences of their opponents and who recognize each other's rationality and reasoning abilities. The fundamental problem in this literature is to answer the following two questions: (1) under what circumstances can a player be said to be rational? and (2) what does 'mutual recognition' of rationality mean? While there seems to be agreement in the literature that 'mutual recognition' of rationality is to be interpreted as 'common belief' of rationality, the issue of what it means to say that a player is rational is not settled. Everybody agrees that the notion of rationality involves two ingredients: choice and beliefs. However, the precise nature of their relationship involves subtle issues which will be discussed below, with a focus on dynamic games. We shall restrict attention to situations of complete information, which are defined as situations where the game being played is common knowledge among the players.[2]

There is a bewildering collection of claims in the literature concerning the implications of rationality in dynamic games with perfect information: [4] proves that common *knowledge* of rationality implies the backward induction solution, [11] and [50] prove that common *belief/certainty* of rationality is *not* sufficient for backward induction, [45] proves that what is needed for backward induction is common *hypothesis* of rationality, [31] shows that common *confidence* of rationality logically contradicts the knowledge implied by the structure of the game, etc. The purpose of this chapter is not to review this literature[3] but to highlight some of the conceptual issues that have emerged.

In Sect. 2 we start with a brief exposition of one of the essential components of a definition of rationality, namely the concept of belief, and we review the notions of a model of a game and of rationality in the context of simultaneous games. We also discuss the role of counterfactuals in the analysis of simultaneous games. In the context of dynamic games there is a new issue that needs to be addressed, namely what it means to choose a strategy and what the proper interpretation of strategies is. This is addressed in Sect. 3 where we also discuss the subtle issues that arise when attempting to define rationality in dynamic games.[4] In Sect. 4 we turn to the topic of belief revision in dynamic games and explore the use of subjective counterfactuals in the analysis of dynamic games with perfect information. Section 5 concludes.

The formalism is introduced gradually throughout the chapter and only to the extent that is necessary to give precise content to the concepts discussed.

---

[2] On the other hand, in a situation of *incomplete* information at least one player lacks knowledge of some of the aspects of the game, such as the preferences of her opponents, or the actions available to them, or the possible outcomes, etc.

[3] Surveys of the literature on the epistemic foundations of game theory can be found in [8,25,30,39,40].

[4] The notion of rationality in dynamic games is also discussed in [41].

For the reader's convenience a table in the Appendix summarizes the notation used and the corresponding interpretation.

The analysis is carried out entirely from a semantic perspective.[5]

2   Belief, Common Belief and Models of Games

For simplicity, we shall restrict attention to a qualitative notion of belief, thus avoiding the additional layer of complexity associated with probabilistic or graded beliefs.

Definition 1. *An* interactive belief structure *(or* multi-agent Kripke structure*) is a tuple* $\langle N, \Omega, \{\mathcal{B}_i\}_{i \in N} \rangle$ *where* N *is a finite set of* players, Ω *is a set of* states *and, for every player* $i \in N$, $\mathcal{B}_i$ *is a binary relation on* Ω *representing* doxastic accessibility: *the interpretation of* $\omega \mathcal{B}_i \omega'$ *is that at state* ω *player* i *considers state* ω' *possible.*

We denote by $\mathcal{B}_i(\omega)$ the set of states that are compatible with player i's beliefs at state ω,[6] that is,

$$\mathcal{B}_i(\omega) = \{\omega' \in \Omega : \omega \mathcal{B}_i \omega'\}. \tag{1}$$

We assume that each $\mathcal{B}_i$ is serial ($\mathcal{B}_i(\omega) \neq \varnothing$, $\forall \omega \in \Omega$), transitive (if $\omega' \in \mathcal{B}_i(\omega)$ then $\mathcal{B}_i(\omega') \subseteq \mathcal{B}_i(\omega)$) and euclidean (if $\omega' \in \mathcal{B}_i(\omega)$ then $\mathcal{B}_i(\omega) \subseteq \mathcal{B}_i(\omega')$). Seriality captures the notion of consistency of beliefs, while the last two properties correspond to the notions of positive and negative introspection of beliefs.[7]

Subsets of Ω are called *events*. We shall use E and F as variables for events. Associated with the binary relation $\mathcal{B}_i$ is a *belief operator* on events $\mathbb{B}_i : 2^\Omega \to 2^\Omega$ defined by

$$\mathbb{B}_i E = \{\omega \in \Omega : \mathcal{B}_i(\omega) \subseteq E\}. \tag{2}$$

Thus $\mathbb{B}_i E$ is the event that player i believes E.[8]

Figure 1 shows an interactive belief structure with two players, where each relation $\mathcal{B}_i$ is represented by arrows: $\omega' \in \mathcal{B}_i(\omega)$ if and only if there is an arrow, for player i, from ω to ω'. Thus, in Fig. 1, we have that $\mathcal{B}_1 = \{(\alpha, \alpha), (\beta, \gamma), (\gamma, \gamma)\}$ and $\mathcal{B}_2 = \{(\alpha, \alpha), (\beta, \alpha), (\gamma, \gamma)\}$, so that, for example, $\mathcal{B}_1(\beta) = \{\gamma\}$ while $\mathcal{B}_2(\beta) =$

---

[5] For a syntactic analysis see [12,17,22,27–29]. See also [37].

[6] Thus $\mathcal{B}_i$ can also be viewed as a function from Ω into 2^Ω (the power set of Ω). Such functions are called *possibility correspondences* (or information functions) in the game-theoretic literature.

[7] For more details see the survey in [8].

[8] In modal logic belief operators are defined as syntactic operators on formulas. Given a (multi-agent) Kripke structure, a model based on it is obtained by associating with every state an assignment of truth value to every atomic formula (equivalently, by associating with every atomic formula the set of states where the formula is true). Given an arbitrary formula ϕ, one then stipulates that, at a state ω, the formula $B_i\phi$ (interpreted as 'agent i believes that ϕ') is true if and only if ϕ is true at every state $\omega' \in \mathcal{B}_i(\omega)$ (that is, $\mathcal{B}_i(\omega)$ is a subset of the truth set of ϕ). If event E is the truth set of formula ϕ then the event $\mathbb{B}_i E$ is the truth set of the formula $B_i\phi$.

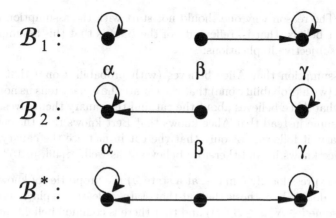

Fig. 1. An interactive belief structure

$\{\alpha\}$. In terms of belief operators, in this structure we have that, for instance, $\mathbb{B}_1\{\gamma\} = \{\beta, \gamma\}$, that is, at both states β and γ Player 1 believes event $\{\gamma\}$, while $\mathbb{B}_2\{\gamma\} = \{\gamma\}$, so that Player 2 believes event $\{\gamma\}$ only at state γ.

Let $\mathcal{B}^*$ be the transitive closure of $\bigcup_{i \in N} \mathcal{B}_i$[9] and define the corresponding operator $\mathbb{B}^* : 2^{\Omega} \to 2^{\Omega}$ by

$$\mathbb{B}^* E = \{\omega \in \Omega : \mathcal{B}^*(\omega) \subseteq E\}. \tag{3}$$

$\mathbb{B}^*$ is called the *common belief* operator and when $\omega \in \mathbb{B}^* E$ then at state ω every player believes E and every player believes that every player believes E, and so on, *ad infinitum*.

Figure 1 shows the relation $\mathcal{B}^*$ (the transitive closure of $\mathcal{B}_1 \cup \mathcal{B}_2$): in this case we have that, for example, $\mathbb{B}^*\{\gamma\} = \{\gamma\}$ and thus $\mathbb{B}_1\mathbb{B}^*\{\gamma\} = \{\beta, \gamma\}$, that is, event $\{\gamma\}$ is commonly believed only at state γ, but at state β Player 1 erroneously believes that it is common belief that $\{\gamma\}$ is the case.[10]

When the relations $\mathcal{B}_i$ ($i \in N$) are also assumed to be reflexive ($\omega \in \mathcal{B}_i(\omega)$, $\forall \omega \in \Omega$), then they become equivalence relations and thus each $\mathcal{B}_i$ gives rise to a partition of Ω. In partitional models, beliefs are necessarily correct and one can speak of *knowledge* rather than belief. As [49] points out, it is methodologically preferable to carry out the analysis in terms of (possibly erroneous) beliefs and then - if desired - add further conditions that are sufficient to turn beliefs into

---

[9] That is, $\omega' \in \mathcal{B}^*(\omega)$ if and only if there is a sequence $\langle \omega_1, ..., \omega_m \rangle$ in Ω and a sequence $\langle j_1, ..., j_{m-1} \rangle$ in N such that (1) $\omega_1 = \omega$, (2) $\omega_m = \omega'$ and (3) for all $k = 1, ..., m-1$, $\omega_{k+1} \in \mathcal{B}_{j_k}(\omega_k)$.

[10] As can be seen from Fig. 1, the common belief relation $\mathcal{B}^*$ is not necessarily euclidean, despite the fact that the $\mathcal{B}_i$'s are euclidean. In other words, in general, the notion of common belief does not satisfy negative introspection (although it does satisfy positive introspection). It is shown in [24] that negative introspection of common belief holds if and only if no agent has erroneous beliefs about what is commonly believed.

knowledge. The reason why one should not start with the assumption of necessarily correct beliefs (that is, reflexivity of the $\mathcal{B}_i$'s) is that this assumption has strong intersubjective implications:

> "The assumption that Alice believes (with probability one) that Bert believes (with probability one) that the cat ate the canary tells us nothing about what Alice believes about the cat and the canary themselves. But if we assume instead that Alice knows that Bert knows that the cat ate the canary, it follows, not only that the cat in fact ate the canary, but that Alice knows it, and therefore believes it as well." ([49], p. 153.)

One can express locally (that is, at a state ω) the properties of knowledge by means of the double hypothesis that, at that state, at least one player has correct beliefs (for some $i \in N$, $\omega \in \mathcal{B}_i(\omega)$) and that there is common belief that nobody has erroneous beliefs (for all $\omega' \in \mathcal{B}^*(\omega)$ and for all $i \in N$, $\omega' \in \mathcal{B}_i(\omega')$).[11] Adding such hypotheses introduces strong forms of agreements among the players (see [23]) and is, in general, not realistic.

Interactive belief structures can be used to model particular contexts in which a game is played. Let us take, as a starting point, strategic-form games (also called normal-form games), where players make their choices simultaneously (an example is a sealed-bid auction).[12]

Definition 2. *A strategic-form game with ordinal payoffs is a tuple* $\langle N, \{S_i, \succsim_i\}_{i \in N} \rangle$ *where N is a set of players and, for every $i \in N$, S_i is a set of choices or strategies available to player i and $\succsim_i$ is i's preference relation over the set of strategy profiles $S = \underset{i \in N}{\times} S_i$.*[13]

---

[11] This is a local version of knowledge (defined as true belief) which is compatible with the existence of other states where some or all players have erroneous beliefs (see [23], in particular Definition 2 on page 9 and the example of Fig. 2 on page 6). Note that philosophical objections have been raised to defining knowledge as true belief; for a discussion of this issue see, for example, [52].

[12] Strategic-form games can also be used to represent situations where players move sequentially, rather than simultaneously. This is because, as discussed later, strategies in such games are defined as complete, contingent plans of action. However, the choice of a strategy in a dynamic game is thought of as being made before the game begins and thus the strategic-form representation of a dynamic game can be viewed as a simultaneous game where all the players choose their strategies simultaneously before the game is played.

[13] A preference relation over a set S is a binary relation $\succsim$ on S which is complete or connected (for all $s, s' \in S$, either $s \succsim s'$ or $s' \succsim s$, or both) and transitive (for all $s, s', s'' \in S$, if $s \succsim s'$ and $s' \succsim s''$ then $s \succsim s''$). We write $s \succ s'$ as a short-hand for $s \succsim s'$ and $s' \not\succsim s$ and we write $s \sim s'$ as a short-hand for $s \succsim s'$ and $s' \succsim s$. The interpretation of $s \succsim_i s'$ is that player i considers s to be at least as good as s', while $s \succ_i s'$ means that player i prefers s to s' and $s \sim_i s'$ means that she is indifferent between s and s'. The interpretation is that there is a set Z of possible outcomes over which every player has a preference relation. An outcome function $o : S \to Z$ associates an outcome with every strategy profile, so that the preference relation over Z induces a preference relation over S.

We shall throughout focus on ordinal preferences (rather than cardinal preferences with associated expected utility comparisons)[14] for two reasons: (1) since the game is usually hypothesized to be common knowledge among the players, it seems far more realistic to assume that each player knows the ordinal rankings of her opponents rather than their full attitude to risk (represented by a cardinal utility function) and (2) our aim is to point out some general conceptual issues, which are independent of the notion of expected utility.

The definition of a strategic-form game specifies the choices available to the players and what motivates those choices (their preferences over the possible outcomes); however, it leaves out an important factor in the determination of players' choices, namely what they believe about the other players. Adding a specification of the players' beliefs determines the context in which a particular game is played and this can be done with the help of an interactive belief structure.

Definition 3. *Fix a strategic-form game $G = \langle N, \{S_i, \succsim_i\}_{i \in N} \rangle$. A model of G is a tuple $\langle N, \Omega, \{\mathcal{B}_i\}_{i \in N}, \{\sigma_i\}_{i \in N} \rangle$, where $\langle N, \Omega, \{\mathcal{B}_i\}_{i \in N} \rangle$ is an interactive belief structure (see Definition 1) and, for every $i \in N$, $\sigma_i : \Omega \to S_i$ is a function that assigns to each state ω a strategy $\sigma_i(\omega) \in S_i$ of player i.*

Let $\sigma(\omega) = (\sigma_i(\omega))_{i \in N}$ denote the strategy profile associated with state ω. The function $\sigma : \Omega \to S$ gives content to the players' beliefs. If $\omega \in \Omega$, $x \in S_i$ and $\sigma_i(\omega) = x$ then the interpretation is that at state ω player i "chooses" strategy x. The exact meaning of 'choosing' is not elaborated further in the literature: does it mean that player i *has actually played* x, or that she is *committed to playing* x, or that x is the *output of her deliberation process*? Whatever the answer, the assumption commonly made in the literature is that player i has correct beliefs about her chosen strategy, that is, she chooses strategy x if and only if she believes that her chosen strategy is x. This can be expressed formally as follows. For every $x \in S_i$, let $[\sigma_i = x]$ be the event that player i chooses strategy x, that is, $[\sigma_i = x] = \{\omega \in \Omega : \sigma_i(\omega) = x\}$. Then the assumption is that

$$[\sigma_i = x] = \mathbb{B}_i [\sigma_i = x]. \tag{4}$$

We will return to this assumption later on, in our discussion of dynamic games. Figure 2 shows a strategic-form game in the form of a table, where the preference relation $\succsim_i$ of player i is represented numerically by an ordinal *utility function* $u_i : S \to \mathbb{R}$, that is, a function satisfying the property that $u_i(s) \geq u_i(s')$ if and only if $s \succsim_i s'$. In each cell of the table the first number is the utility of Player 1 and the second number the utility of Player 2. A model of this game can be obtained by adding to the interactive belief frame of Fig. 1 the following strategy assignments:

$$\sigma_1(\alpha) = b, \quad \sigma_1(\beta) = \sigma_1(\gamma) = t$$
$$\sigma_2(\alpha) = \sigma_2(\beta) = r, \quad \sigma_2(\gamma) = l. \tag{5}$$

---

[14] Cardinal utility functions are also called Bernoulli utility functions or von Neumann-Morgenstern utility functions.

Player 2

		l	r
Player	t	2 , 1	0 , 0
1	b	1 , 2	1 , 2

Fig. 2. A strategic form game

How can rationality be captured in a model? Consider the following - rather weak - definition of rationality: player i is rational at state $\hat{\omega}$ if - given that she chooses the strategy $\hat{s}_i \in S_i$ at state $\hat{\omega}$ (that is, given that $\sigma_i(\hat{\omega}) = \hat{s}_i$) - there is no other strategy $s_i \in S_i$ which player i believes, at state $\hat{\omega}$, to be better (that is, to yield a higher payoff) than $\hat{s}_i$. This can be stated formally as follows. First of all, for every state ω, denote by $\sigma_{-i}(\omega)$ the strategy profile of the players other than i, that is, $\sigma_{-i}(\omega) = (\sigma_1(\omega), ..., \sigma_{i-1}(\omega), \sigma_{i+1}(\omega), ..., \sigma_n(\omega))$ (where n is the number of players). Then (recall that - since $\sigma_i(\hat{\omega}) = \hat{s}_i$ - by (4) $\sigma_i(\omega) = \hat{s}_i$, for all $\omega \in \mathcal{B}_i(\hat{\omega})$):

> Player i is *rational at* $\hat{\omega}$ if, $\forall s_i \in S_i$, it is not the case
> that, $\forall \omega \in \mathcal{B}_i(\hat{\omega})$, $u_i(s_i, \sigma_{-i}(\omega)) > u_i(\hat{s}_i, \sigma_{-i}(\omega))$
> (where $\hat{s}_i = \sigma_i(\hat{\omega})$). $\qquad$ (6)

Equivalently, let $[u_i(s_i) > u_i(\hat{s}_i)] = \{\omega \in \Omega : u_i(s_i, \sigma_{-i}(\omega)) > u_i(\hat{s}_i, \sigma_{-i}(\omega))\}$. Then

> Player i is *rational at* $\hat{\omega}$ if, $\forall s_i \in S_i$, $\hat{\omega} \notin \mathbb{B}_i[u_i(s_i) > u_i(\hat{s}_i)]$
> (where $\hat{s}_i = \sigma_i(\hat{\omega})$). $\qquad$ (7)

For example, in the model of the strategic-form game of Fig. 2 obtained by adding to the interactive belief structure of Fig. 1 the strategy assignments given above in (5), we have that both players are rational at every state and thus there is common belief of rationality at every state. In particular, there is common belief of rationality at state β, even though the strategy profile actually chosen there is (t, r) (with payoffs $(0, 0)$) and each player would do strictly better with a different choice of strategy. Note also that, in this model, at every state it is common belief between the players that each player has correct beliefs,[15] although at state β neither player does in fact have correct beliefs.

It is well known that, in any model of any finite strategic-form game, a strategy profile $s = (s_i)_{i \in N}$ is compatible with common belief of rationality if and only if, for every player i, the strategy s_i survives the iterated deletion of strictly dominated strategies.[16]

---

[15] That is, $\forall \omega \in \Omega$, $\forall \omega' \in \mathcal{B}^*(\omega)$, $\omega' \in \mathcal{B}_1(\omega')$ and $\omega' \in \mathcal{B}_2(\omega')$.

[16] Thus, if at a state ω there is common belief of rationality then, for every player i, $\sigma_i(\omega)$ survives the iterated deletion of strictly dominated strategies. For more details on this result, which originates in [13] and [38], and relevant references, see [8, 22, 30, 40].

What is the conceptual content of the definition given in (7)? It is widely claimed that the notion of rationality involves the use of counterfactual reasoning. For example, Aumann writes:

> "[O]ne really cannot discuss rationality, or indeed decision making, without substantive conditionals and counterfactuals. Making a decision means choosing among alternatives. Thus one must consider hypothetical situations - what would happen if one did something different from what one actually does. [...] In interactive decision making - games - you must consider what other people would do if you did something different from what you actually do." ([4], p. 15)

Yet the structures used so far do not incorporate the tools needed for counterfactual reasoning. The definition of rationality given in (7) involves comparing the payoff of a strategy different from the one actually chosen with the payoff of the chosen strategy. Can this counterfactual be made explicit?

First we review the standard semantics for counterfactuals.[17]

Definition 4. *Given a set of states Ω and a set $\mathcal{E} \subseteq 2^{\Omega} \setminus \varnothing$ of events, interpreted as admissible hypotheses, a* counterfactual selection function *is a function $f : \Omega \times \mathcal{E} \to 2^{\Omega}$ that satisfies the following properties: $\forall \omega \in \Omega$, $\forall E, F \in \mathcal{E}$,*

$$1. f(\omega, E) \neq \varnothing.$$
$$2. f(\omega, E) \subseteq E.$$
$$3. \text{If } f\omega \in E \text{ then } f(\omega, E) = \{\omega\}.$$
$$4. \text{If } E \subseteq F \text{ and } f(\omega, F) \cap E \neq \varnothing \text{ then } f(\omega, E) = f(\omega, F) \cap E. \qquad (8)$$

The event $f(\omega, E)$ is interpreted as "the set of states closest to ω where E is true". Condition 1 says that there indeed exist states closest to ω where E is true (recall that if $E \in \mathcal{E}$ then $E \neq \varnothing$). Condition 2 is a consistency condition that says that the states closest to ω where E is true are indeed states where E is true. Condition 3 says that if E is true at ω then there is only one state closest to ω where E is true, namely ω itself. Condition 4 says that if E implies F and some closest F-states to ω are in E, then the closest E-states to ω are precisely those states in E that are also the closest F-states to ω.[18]

Given a hypothesis $E \in \mathcal{E}$ and an event $F \subseteq \Omega$, a counterfactual statement of the form "if E were the case then F would be the case", which we denote by $E \Rightarrow F$, is considered to be true at state ω if and only if $f(\omega, E) \subseteq F$, that is,

---

[17] For an extensive discussion see [34]. In the game-theoretic literature (see, for example [16] and [56]) a simpler approach is often used (originally introduced by [48]) where $f(\omega, E)$ is always a singleton.

[18] When $\mathcal{E}$ coincides with $2^{\Omega} \setminus \varnothing$, Condition 4 implies that, for every $\omega \in \Omega$, there exists a complete and transitive "closeness to ω" binary relation $\preceq_\omega$ on Ω such that $f(\omega, E) = \{\omega' \in E : \omega' \preceq_\omega x, \forall x \in E\}$ (see Theorem 2.2 in [54]) thus justifying the interpretation suggested above: $\omega_1 \preceq_\omega \omega_2$ is interpreted as 'state ω_1 is closer to ω than state ω_2 is' and $f(\omega, E)$ is the set of states in E that are closest to ω.

if F is true in the closest states to ω where E is true. Thus, one can define the operator $\Rrightarrow\ :\mathcal{E}\times 2^{\Omega}\to 2^{\Omega}$ as follows:

$$E \Rrightarrow F = \{\omega \in \Omega : f(\omega, E) \subseteq F\}. \qquad (9)$$

Adding a counterfactual selection function to an interactive belief structure allows one to consider complex statements of the form "if E were the case then player i would believe F " (corresponding to the event $E \Rrightarrow \mathbb{B}_i F$), or "player i believes that if E were the case then F would be the case" (corresponding to $\mathbb{B}_i(E \Rrightarrow F)$), or "Player 1 believes that if E were the case then Player 2 would believe F" (corresponding to $\mathbb{B}_1(E \Rrightarrow \mathbb{B}_2 F)$), etc.

Now, returning to models of strategic-form games and the definition of rationality given in (7), the addition of a counterfactual selection function to a model allows one to compare player i's payoff at a state $\hat{\omega}$, where she has chosen strategy $\hat{s}_i$, with her payoff at the states closest to $\hat{\omega}$ where she chooses a strategy $s_i \neq \hat{s}_i$. Implicit in (7) is the assumption that in those counterfactual states player i's beliefs about her opponents' choices are the same as in $\hat{\omega}$. This is an assumption: it may be a sensible one to make (indeed Stalnaker [50,51] argues that it would be conceptually wrong *not* to make this assumption) but nonetheless it may be worthwhile bringing it to light in a more complete analysis where counterfactuals are explicitly modeled. Within the context of strategic-form games, this is done in [16] and [56], where counterfactuals are invoked explicitly in the definition of rationality.[19]

3 Models of Dynamic Games

In dynamic games (also called extensive-form games) players make choices sequentially, having some information about the moves previously made by their opponents. If information is partial, the game is said to have *imperfect information*, while the case of full information is referred to as *perfect information*. We shall focus on perfect-information games, which are defined as follows. If A is a set, we denote by A^* the set of finite sequences in A. If $h = \langle a_1, ..., a_k\rangle \in A^*$ and $1 \leq j \leq k$, the sequence $\langle a_1, ..., a_j\rangle$ is called a *prefix* of h. If $h = \langle a_1, ..., a_k\rangle \in A^*$ and $a \in A$, we denote the sequence $\langle a_1, ..., a_k, a\rangle \in A^*$ by ha.

Definition 5. *A finite dynamic game with perfect information and ordinal payoffs is a tuple $\langle A, H, N, \iota, \{\succsim_i\}_{i\in N}\rangle$ whose elements are:*

- *A finite set of actions A.*
- *A finite set of histories $H \subseteq A^*$ which is closed under prefixes (that is, if $h \in H$ and $h' \in A^*$ is a prefix of h, then $h' \in H$). The null history $\langle\rangle$, denoted by $\emptyset$, is an element of H and is a prefix of every history. A history $h \in H$ such that, for every $a \in A$, $ha \notin H$, is called a terminal history. The set of*

---

[19] As remarked in Footnote 17, both authors use the less general definition of selection function where $f : \Omega \times \mathcal{E} \to \Omega$, that is, for every state ω and event E, there is a unique state closest to ω where E is true.

terminal histories is denoted by Z. $D = H \backslash Z$ denotes the set of non-terminal or decision histories. For every decision history $h \in D$, we denote by $A(h)$ the set of actions available at h, that is, $A(h) = \{a \in A : ha \in H\}$.
- *A finite set N of players.*
- *A function $\iota : D \to N$ that assigns a player to each decision history. Thus $\iota(h)$ is the player who moves at history h. For every $i \in N$, let $D_i = \iota^{-1}(i)$ be the set of histories assigned to player i.*
- *For every player $i \in N$, $\succsim_i$ is an ordinal ranking of the set Z of terminal histories.*

The ordinal ranking of player i is normally represented by means of an ordinal *utility* (or *payoff*) *function* $U_i : Z \to \mathbb{R}$ satisfying the property that $U_i(z) \geq U_i(z')$ if and only if $z \succsim_i z'$.

Histories will be denoted more succinctly by listing the corresponding actions, without angled brackets and without commas; thus instead of writing $\langle \emptyset, a_1, a_2, a_3, a_4 \rangle$ we simply write $a_1 a_2 a_3 a_4$.

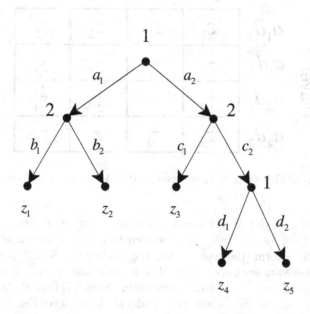

Fig. 3. A perfect information game

An example of a perfect-information game is shown in Fig. 3 in the form of a tree. Each node in the tree represents a history of prior moves and is labeled with the player whose turn it is to move. For example, at history $a_2 c_2$ it is Player 1's turn to move (after his initial choice of a_2 followed by Player 2's choice of c_2) and he has to choose between two actions: d_1 and d_2. The terminal histories (the leaves of the tree, denoted by z_j, $j = 1, ..., 5$) represent the possible outcomes and each player i is assumed to have a preference relation $\succsim_i$ over the set of terminal histories (in Fig. 3 the players' preferences over the terminal histories have been omitted).

In their seminal book, [55] showed that a dynamic game can be reduced to a normal-form (or strategic-form) game by defining strategies as complete, contingent plans of action. In the case of perfect-information games a strategy for a player is a function that associates with every decision history assigned to that player one of the choices available there. For example, a possible strategy of Player 1 in the game of Fig. 3 is (a_1, d_2). A profile of strategies (one for each player) determines a unique path from the null history (the root of the tree) to a terminal history (a leaf of the tree). Figure 4 shows the strategic-form corresponding to the extensive form of Fig. 3.

Player 2

	b_1c_1	b_1c_2	b_2c_1	b_2c_2
a_1d_1	z_1	z_1	z_2	z_2
a_1d_2	z_1	z_1	z_2	z_2
a_2d_1	z_3	z_4	z_3	z_4
a_2d_2	z_3	z_5	z_3	z_5

(left label: Player 1)

Fig. 4. The strategic form corresponding to the game of Fig. 3

How should a model of a dynamic game be constructed? One approach in the literature (see, for example, [4]) has been to consider models of the corresponding strategic-form (the type of models considered in Sect. 2: see Definition 3). However, there are several conceptual issues that arise in this context. Recall that the interpretation of $s_i = \sigma_i(\omega)$ suggested in Sect. 2 is that at state ω player i "chooses" strategy s_i. Now consider a model of the game of Fig. 3 and a state ω where $\sigma_1(\omega) = (a_1, d_2)$. What does it mean to say that Player 1 "chooses" strategy (a_1, d_2)? The first part of the strategy, namely a_1, can be interpreted as a description of Player 1's actual choice to play a_1, but the second part of the strategy, namely d_2, has no such interpretation: if Player 1 in fact plays a_1 then he knows that he will not have to make any further choices and thus it is not clear what it means for him to "choose" to play d_2 in a situation that is made impossible by his decision to play a_1.[20] Thus it does not seem to make sense to interpret $\sigma_1(\omega) = (a_1, d_2)$ as 'at state ω Player 1 chooses (a_1, d_2)'. Perhaps the correct interpretation is in terms of a more complex sentence such as 'Player 1 chooses to play a_1 and if - contrary to this - he were to play a_2 and Player 2 were to follow with c_2, then Player 1 would play d_2'. Thus while in a simultaneous game the association of a strategy of player i to a state can be interpreted as a description of player i's actual behavior at that state, in the case of dynamic games this interpretation is no longer valid, since one would end up describing not only the actual behavior of player i but also his counterfactual behavior. Methodologically, this is not satisfactory: if it is considered to be necessary to specify what a player would do in situations that do not occur in the state under consideration, then one should model the counterfactual explicitly. But why should it be necessary to specify at state ω (where Player 1 is playing a_1) what he would do at the counterfactual history $a_2 c_2$? Perhaps what matters is not so much what Player 1 would actually do there but what Player 2 believes that Player 1 would do: after all, Player 2 might not know that Player 1 has decided to play a_1 and needs to consider what to do in the eventuality that Player 1 actually ends up playing a_2. So, perhaps, the strategy of Player 1 is to be interpreted as having two components: (1) a description of Player 1's behavior and (2) a conjecture in the mind of Player 2 about what Player 1 would do.[21] If this is the correct interpretation, then one could object - from a methodological point of view - that it would be preferable to disentangle the two components and model them explicitly.

In order to clarify these issues it seems that, in the case of dynamic games, one should not adopt the models of Sect. 2 and instead consider a more general notion of model, where states are described in terms of players' *actual behavior* and any relevant counterfactual propositions are modeled explicitly.

We shall first consider models obtained by adding a counterfactual selection function (see Definition 4) to an interactive belief structure (see Definition 1) and show that such models are not adequate.

Fix a dynamic game Γ with perfect information and consider the following candidate for a definition of a model of Γ: it is a tuple $\langle N, \Omega, \{\mathcal{B}_i\}_{i \in N}, f, \zeta \rangle$ where $\langle N, \Omega, \{\mathcal{B}_i\}_{i \in N} \rangle$ is an interactive belief structure, $f : \Omega \times \mathcal{E} \to 2^\Omega$ is a counterfactual selection function and $\zeta : \Omega \to Z$ is a function that associates

---

[20] For this reason, some authors (see, for example, [40]), instead of using strategies, use the weaker notion of "plan of action" introduced by [44]. A plan of action for a player only contains choices that are not ruled out by his earlier choices. For example, the possible plans of action for Player 1 in the game of Fig. 3 are $a_1, (a_2, d_1)$ and (a_2, d_2). However, most of the issues raised below apply also to plans of action. The reason for this is that a choice of player i at a later decision history of his may be counterfactual at a state because of the choices of *other* players (which prevent that history from being reached).

[21] This interpretation of strategies has in fact been put forward in the literature for the case of mixed strategies (which we do not consider in this chapter, given our non-probabilistic approach): see, for example, [6] and the references given there in Footnote 7.

with every state $\omega \in \Omega$ a terminal history (recall that Z denotes the set of terminal histories in Γ).[22] Given a history h in the game, we denote by $[h]$ the set of states where h is reached, that is, $[h] = \{\omega \in \Omega : h$ is a prefix of $\zeta(\omega)\}$. We take the set of admissible hypotheses $\mathcal{E}$ (the domain of $f(\omega, \cdot)$) to be the set of propositions of the form "history h is reached", that is, $\mathcal{E} = \{[h] : h \in H\}$ (where H is the set of histories in the game). We now discuss a number of issues that arise in such models.

In the models of Sect. 2 it was assumed that a player always knows his own strategy (see (4) above). Should a similar assumption be made within the context of dynamic games? That is, suppose that at state ω player i takes action a; should we assume that player i believes that she takes action a? For example, consider a model of the game of Fig. 3 in which there are two states, ω and ω', such that $\mathcal{B}_2(\omega) = \{\omega, \omega'\}$ and $\zeta(\omega) = a_1 b_1$. Then at state ω Player 2 takes action b_1. Should we require that Player 2 take action b_1 also at ω' (since $\omega' \in \mathcal{B}_2(\omega)$)? The answer is negative: the relation $\mathcal{B}_2$ represents the prior or *initial* beliefs of Player 2 (that is, her beliefs before the game begins) and Player 2 may be uncertain as to whether Player 1 will play a_1 or a_2 and plan to play herself b_1 in the former case and c_1 in the latter case. Thus it makes perfect sense to have $\zeta(\omega') = a_2 c_1$. If we want to rule out uncertainty by a player about her action at a decision history of hers, then we need to impose the following restriction:

> If h is a decision history of player i, a an action available to i at h
>
> and ha a prefix of $\zeta(\omega)$ then, $\forall \omega' \in \mathcal{B}_i(\omega)$,
>
> if h is a prefix of $\zeta(\omega')$ then ha is a prefix of $\zeta(\omega')$. (10)

The above definition can be stated more succinctly in terms of events. If E and F are two events, we denote by $E \to F$ the event $\neg E \cup F$ (we use the negation symbol $\neg$ to denote the set-theoretic complement, that is, $\neg E$ is the complement of event E). Thus $E \to F$ captures the material conditional. Recall that, given a history h in the game, $[h] = \{\omega \in \Omega : h$ is a prefix of $\zeta(\omega)\}$; recall also that D_i denotes the set of decision histories of player i and $A(h)$ the set of choices available at h. Then (10) can be stated as follows:

$$\forall h \in D_i, \forall a \in A(h),$$
$$[ha] \subseteq \mathbb{B}_i([h] \to [ha]). \tag{11}$$

In words: if, at a state, player i takes action a at her decision history h, then she believes that if h is reached then she takes action a.[23]

A more subtle issue is whether we should require (perhaps as a condition of rationality) that a player have correct beliefs about what she would do in a situation that she believes will not arise. Consider, for example, the (part of

---

[22] [45] was the first to propose models of perfect-information games where states are described not in terms of strategies but in terms of terminal histories.

[23] Note that, if at state ω player i believes that history h will *not* be reached ($\forall \omega' \in \mathcal{B}_i(\omega)$, $\omega' \notin [h]$) then $\mathcal{B}_i(\omega) \subseteq \neg[h] \subseteq [h] \to [ha]$, so that $\omega \in \mathbb{B}_i([h] \to [ha])$ and therefore (11) is trivially satisfied (even if $\omega \in [h]$).

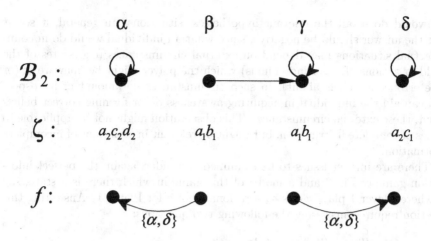

Fig. 5. Part of a model of the game of Fig. 3

a) model of the game of Fig. 3 illustrated in Fig. 5. The first line gives $\mathcal{B}_2$, the doxastic accessibility relation of Player 2, the second line the function ζ (which associates with every state a terminal history) and the third line is a partial illustration of the counterfactual selection function: the arrow from state β to state α labeled with the set $\{\alpha, \delta\}$ represents $f(\beta, \{\alpha, \delta\}) = \{\alpha\}$ and the arrow from γ to δ labeled with the set $\{\alpha, \delta\}$ represents $f(\gamma, \{\alpha, \delta\}) = \{\delta\}$.[24] Note that the event that Player 1 plays a_2 is the set of states ω where a_2 is a prefix of $\zeta(\omega)$: $[a_2] = \{\alpha, \delta\}$. Recall that $E \Rightarrow F$ denotes the counterfactual conditional 'if E were the case then F would be the case'. Now, $[a_2] \Rightarrow [a_2c_1] = \{\gamma, \delta\}$ and $[a_2] \Rightarrow [a_2c_2] = \{\alpha, \beta\}$.[25] Thus $\beta \in [a_2] \Rightarrow [a_2c_2]$ and also $\beta \in \mathbb{B}_2([a_2] \Rightarrow [a_2c_1])$.[26] That is, at state β it is actually the case that if Player 1 were to play a_2 then Player 2 would respond with c_2, but Player 2 erroneously believes that (if Player 1 were to play a_2) she would respond with c_1.

As a condition of rationality, should one rule out situations like the one illustrated in Fig. 5? Shouldn't a rational player have introspective access to what

---

[24] On the other hand, we have not represented the fact that $f(\alpha, \{\alpha, \delta\}) = \{\alpha\}$, which follows from point 3 of Definition 4 (since $\alpha \in \{\alpha, \delta\}$) and the fact that $f(\delta, \{\alpha, \delta\}) = \{\delta\}$, which also follows from point 3 of Definition 4. We have also omitted other values of the selection function f, which are not relevant for the discussion below.

[25] Recall that, by Definition 4, since $\alpha \in [a_2]$, $f(\alpha, [a_2]) = \{\alpha\}$, so that, since $\alpha \in [a_2c_2]$ (because a_2c_2 is a prefix of $\zeta(\alpha) = a_2c_2d_2$), $\alpha \in [a_2] \Rightarrow [a_2c_2]$. Furthermore, since $f(\beta, [a_2]) = \{\alpha\}$, $\beta \in [a_2] \Rightarrow [a_2c_2]$. There is no other state ω where $f(\omega, [a_2]) \subseteq [a_2c_2]$. Thus $[a_2] \Rightarrow [a_2c_2] = \{\alpha, \beta\}$. The argument for $[a_2] \Rightarrow [a_2c_1] = \{\gamma, \delta\}$ is similar.

[26] Since $\mathcal{B}_2(\beta) = \{\gamma\}$ and $\gamma \in [a_2] \Rightarrow [a_2c_1]$, $\beta \in \mathbb{B}_2([a_2] \Rightarrow [a_2c_1])$. Recall that the material conditional 'if E is the case then F is the case' is captured by the event $\neg E \cup F$, which we denote by $E \to F$. Then $[a_2] \to [a_2c_1] = \{\beta, \gamma, \delta\}$ and $[a_2] \to [a_2c_2] = \{\alpha, \beta, \gamma\}$, so that we also have, trivially, that $\beta \in \mathbb{B}_2([a_2] \to [a_2c_1])$ and $\beta \in \mathbb{B}_2([a_2] \to [a_2c_2])$.

she would do in all the relevant hypothetical situations? In general, it seems that the answer should be negative, since what an individual would do in counterfactual situations may depend on external circumstances (e.g. states of the world or actions of other individuals) which the player might be unaware of (or have erroneous beliefs about). In such circumstances no amount of introspection can aid the individual in acquiring awareness of, or forming correct beliefs about, these external circumstances. This observation might not be applicable to games of complete information, but might be relevant in situations of incomplete information.[27]

There are further issues to be examined. Consider, again, the perfect information game of Fig. 3 and a model of this game in which there is a state, say α, where Player 1 plays a_2. Is a_2 a rational choice for Player 1? Answering this question requires answering the following two questions:

Q1. What *will* Player 2 do next?

Q2. What *would* Player 2 do if, instead, a_1 had been chosen?

Let us start with Q1. Consider a model (different from the one described in Fig. 5) where at state α the play of the game is $a_2c_2d_1$ (that is, $\zeta(\alpha) = a_2c_2d_1$). If there is "common recognition" of rationality, Player 1 will ask himself how a rational Player 2 will respond to his initial choice of a_2. In order to determine what is rational for Player 2 to do at state α, we need to examine Player 2's beliefs at α. Suppose that Player 2 mistakenly believes that Player 1 will play a_1 ($\alpha \in \mathbb{B}_2[a_1]$); for example, $\mathcal{B}_2(\alpha) = \{\beta\}$ and $\beta \in [a_1]$. Furthermore, suppose that $f(\beta, [a_2]) = \{\gamma\}$ and $\gamma \in [a_2c_2d_2]$. Then at α Player 2 believes that if it were the case that Player 1 played a_2 then the play of the game would be $a_2c_2d_2$ ($\alpha \in \mathbb{B}_2([a_2] \rightrightarrows [a_2c_2d_2])$), in particular, she believes that *Player 1 would play* d_2. Since, at state α, Player 1 in fact plays a_2, Player 2 will be surprised: she will be informed that Player 1 played a_2 and that she herself has to choose between c_1 and c_2. What choice she will make depends on her beliefs after she learns that (contrary to her initial expectation) Player 1 played a_2, that is, on her *revised beliefs*. In general, no restrictions can be imposed on Player 2's revised beliefs after a surprise: for example, it seems perfectly plausible to allow Player 2 to become convinced that the play of the game will be $a_2c_2d_1$; in particular, that *Player 1 will play* d_1. The models that we are considering do not provide us with the tools to express such a change of mind for Player 2: if one takes as her revised beliefs her initial beliefs about counterfactual statements that have a_2 as an antecedent, then - since $\alpha \in \mathbb{B}_2([a_2] \rightrightarrows [a_2c_2d_2])$ - one is forced to rule out the possibility that after learning that Player 1 played a_2 Player 2 will believe that the play of the game will be $a_2c_2d_1$. Stalnaker argues that imposing such

---

[27] Recall that a game is said to have complete information if the game itself is common knowledge among the players. On the other hand, in a situation of incomplete information at least one player lacks knowledge of some of the aspects of the game, such as the preferences of her opponents, or the actions available to them, or the possible outcomes, etc.

restrictions is conceptually wrong, since it is based on confounding causal with epistemic counterfactuals:

> "Player 2 has the following initial belief: Player 1 would choose d_2 on his second move [after his initial choice of a_2] if he had a second move. This is a causal 'if' – an 'if' used to express 2's opinion about 1's disposition to act in a situation that she believes will not arise. [...] But to ask what Player 2 would believe about Player 1 if she learned that she was wrong about 1's first choice is to ask a completely different question – this 'if' is epistemic; it concerns Player 2's belief revision policies, and not Player 1's disposition to act." ([50], p. 48; with small changes to adapt the quote to the game of Fig. 3.)

Let us now turn to question Q2. Suppose that, as in the previous example, we are considering a model of the game of Fig. 3 and a state α in that model where

$$\alpha \in [a_2 c_2 d_1] \cap \mathbb{B}_1[a_2] \cap \mathbb{B}_2[a_1 b_1] \cap \mathbb{B}_1 \mathbb{B}_2[a_1 b_1] \tag{12}$$

(for example, (12) is satisfied if $\mathcal{B}_1(\alpha) = \{\alpha\}, \mathcal{B}_2(\alpha) = \{\beta\}$ and $\beta \in [a_1 b_1]$). Thus at α Player 1 plays a_2. Is this a rational choice? The answer depends on how Player 2 would respond to the alternative choice of a_1. However, since the rationality of playing a_2 has to be judged relative to Player 1's beliefs, what matters is not what Player 2 would actually do (at state α) if a_1 were to be played, but what Player 1 believes that Player 2 would do. How should we model such beliefs of Player 1? Again, one possibility is to refer to Player 1's beliefs about counterfactuals with $[a_1]$ as antecedent. If we follow this route, then we restrict the possible beliefs of Player 1; in particular, it cannot be the case that Player 1 believes that if he were to play a_1 then Player 2 would play b_2, that is, we cannot have $\alpha \in \mathbb{B}_1([a_1] \rightrightarrows [a_1 b_2])$. Intuitively, the reason is as follows (the formal proof will follow). The counterfactual selection function is meant to capture causal relationships between events. As Stalnaker points out, in the counterfactual world where a player makes a choice different from the one that he is actually making, the prior beliefs of the other players must be the same as in the actual world (by changing his choice he cannot cause the prior beliefs of his opponents to change):

> "I know, for example, that it would be irrational to cooperate in a one-shot prisoners' dilemma because I know that in the counterfactual situation in which I cooperate, my payoff is less than it would be if I defected. And while I have the capacity to influence my payoff (negatively) by making this alternative choice, I could not, by making this choice, influence your prior beliefs about what I will do; that is, your prior beliefs will be the same, in the counterfactual situation in which I make the alternative choice, as they are in the actual situation." ([52], p. 178)

The formal proof that it cannot be the case that $\alpha \in \mathbb{B}_1([a_1] \rightrightarrows [a_1 b_2])$ goes as follows. Suppose that $\alpha \in \mathbb{B}_1([a_1] \rightrightarrows [a_1 b_2])$ and fix an arbitrary $\omega \in \mathcal{B}_1(\alpha)$.

By (12), since $\alpha \in \mathbb{B}_1[a_2]$, $\omega \in [a_2]$. Fix an arbitrary $\delta \in f(\omega, [a_1])$. Since $\alpha \in \mathbb{B}_1([a_1] \rightrightarrows [a_1 b_2])$, and $\omega \in \mathcal{B}_1(\alpha)$, $\omega \in [a_1] \rightrightarrows [a_1 b_2]$, that is, $f(\omega, [a_1]) \subseteq [a_1 b_2]$. Thus

$$\delta \in [a_1 b_2]. \tag{13}$$

Since $\omega \in \mathcal{B}_1(\alpha)$ and $\alpha \in \mathbb{B}_1 \mathbb{B}_2([a_1 b_1])$, $\omega \in \mathbb{B}_2[a_1 b_1]$. By the above remark, at δ the initial beliefs of Player 2 must be the same as at ω.[28] Hence $\delta \in \mathbb{B}_2[a_1 b_1]$. By definition, $\delta \in \mathbb{B}_2[a_1 b_1]$ if and only if $\mathcal{B}_2(\delta) \subseteq [a_1 b_1]$. Thus, since $[a_1 b_1] \subseteq \neg[a_1] \cup [a_1 b_1] = [a_1] \rightarrow [a_1 b_1]$, $\mathcal{B}_2(\delta) \subseteq [a_1] \rightarrow [a_1 b_1]$, that is, $\delta \in \mathbb{B}_2([a_1] \rightarrow [a_1 b_1])$. Now, (11) requires that, since $\delta \in [a_1 b_2]$, $\delta \in \mathbb{B}_2([a_1] \rightarrow [a_1 b_2])$. Hence, since $\delta \in \mathbb{B}_2[a_1]$, $\delta \in \mathbb{B}_2[a_1 b_2]$, contradicting (13).

In words, since $\alpha \in \mathbb{B}_1 \mathbb{B}_2[a_1 b_1]$, at every state ω that Player 1 considers possible at α ($\omega \in \mathcal{B}_1(\alpha)$) Player 2 believes that the play of the game is $a_1 b_1$, that is, that she herself will play b_1. If $\alpha \in \mathbb{B}_1([a_1] \rightrightarrows [a_1 b_2])$ then $\omega \in [a_1] \rightrightarrows [a_1 b_2]$; thus, if δ is a state closest to ω where Player 1 plays a_1, then (by the second property of counterfactual selection functions) at δ Player 2 will actually play b_2. Since Player 1, by changing his choice, cannot cause the initial beliefs of Player 2 to change, Player 2 must have at δ the same beliefs that she has at ω, namely that she will play b_1. Thus at state δ Player 2 believes that she will take action b_1 at her decision history a_1 while in fact she will take action b_2, contradicting the requirement expressed in (11).

Thus we have shown that adding a counterfactual selection function to an interactive belief structure does not provide an adequate notion of model of a dynamic game. The approach followed in the literature[29] has been to do without an "objective" counterfactual selection function f and to introduce in its place "subjective" counterfactual functions f_i (one for each player $i \in N$) representing the players' dispositions to revise their beliefs under various hypotheses.[30] This is the topic of the next section.

4   Belief Revision

We will now consider models of dynamic games defined as tuples $\langle N, \Omega, \{\mathcal{B}_i\}_{i \in N}, \{\mathcal{E}_i, f_i\}_{i \in N}, \zeta \rangle$ where - as before - $\langle N, \Omega, \{\mathcal{B}_i\}_{i \in N} \rangle$ is an interactive belief structure and $\zeta : \Omega \to Z$ is a function that associates with every state $\omega \in \Omega$ a terminal history. The new element is $\{\mathcal{E}_i, f_i\}$ (for every player $i \in N$), which is a subjective counterfactual selection function, defined as follows.

---

[28] As shown above, at state ω Player 1 chooses a_2; $f(\omega, [a_1])$ is the set of states closest to ω where Player 1 chooses a_1; in these states Player 2's prior beliefs must be the same as at ω, otherwise by switching from a_2 to a_1 Player 1 would cause a change in Player 2's prior beliefs.

[29] See, for example, [2, 7, 9, 14, 19, 28, 33, 45].

[30] In [28] there is also an objective counterfactual selection function, but it is used only to encode the structure of the game in the syntax.

Definition 6. *For every $i \in N$, let $\mathcal{E}_i \subseteq 2^{\Omega}\backslash\varnothing$ be a set of events representing potential items of information or admissible hypotheses for player i.*[31] *A subjective counterfactual selection function is a function $f_i : \Omega \times \mathcal{E}_i \to 2^{\Omega}$ that satisfies the following properties: $\forall\omega \in \Omega, \forall E, F \in \mathcal{E}_i$,*

> *1. $f_i(\omega, E) \neq \varnothing$,*
>
> *2. $f_i(\omega, E) \subseteq E$,*
>
> *3. if $\mathcal{B}_i(\omega) \cap E \neq \varnothing$ then $f_i(\omega, E) = \mathcal{B}_i(\omega) \cap E$,*
>
> *4. if $E \subseteq F$ and $f_i(\omega, F) \cap E \neq \varnothing$ then $f_i(\omega, E) = f_i(\omega, F) \cap E$.*

The event $f_i(\omega, E)$ is interpreted as the set of states that player i would consider possible, at state ω, under the supposition that (or if informed that) E is true. Condition 1 requires these suppositional beliefs to be consistent. Condition 2 requires that E be indeed considered true. Condition 3 says that if E is compatible with the initial beliefs then the suppositional beliefs coincide with the initial beliefs conditioned on event E.[32] Condition 4 is an extension of 3: if E implies F and E is compatible (not with player i 's prior beliefs but) with the *posterior* beliefs that she would have if she supposed (or learned) that F were the case (let's call these her posterior F-beliefs), then her beliefs under the supposition (or information) that E must coincide with her posterior F-beliefs conditioned on event E.[33]

Remark 1. If $\mathcal{E}_i = 2^{\Omega}\backslash\varnothing$ then Conditions 1–4 in Definition 6 imply that, for every $\omega \in \Omega$, there exists a "plausibility" relation Q_i^{ω} on Ω which is complete ($\forall\omega_1, \omega_2 \in \Omega$, either $\omega_1 Q_i^{\omega}\omega_2$ or $\omega_2 Q_i^{\omega}\omega_1$ or both) and transitive ($\forall\omega_1, \omega_2, \omega_3 \in \Omega$, if $\omega_1 Q_i^{\omega}\omega_2$ and $\omega_2 Q_i^{\omega}\omega_3$ then $\omega_1 Q_i^{\omega}\omega_3$) and such that, for every non-empty $E \subseteq \Omega$, $f_i(\omega, E) = \{x \in E : xQ_i^{\omega}y, \forall y \in E\}$. The interpretation of $\alpha Q_i^{\omega}\beta$ is that - at state ω and according to player i - state α is at least as plausible as state β. Thus $f_i(\omega, E)$ is the set of most plausible states in E (according to player i at state ω). If $\mathcal{E}_i \neq 2^{\Omega}\backslash\varnothing$ then Conditions 1–4 in Definition 6 are necessary but not sufficient for the existence of such a plausibility relation. The existence of a plausibility relation that rationalizes the function $f_i(\omega, \cdot) : \mathcal{E}_i \to 2^{\Omega}$ is necessary and sufficient for the belief revision policy encoded in $f_i(\omega, \cdot)$ to be compatible with the theory of belief revision introduced in [1], known as the AGM theory (see [18]).

---

[31] For example, in a perfect-information game one can take $\mathcal{E}_i = \{[h] : h \in D_i\}$, that is, the set of propositions of the form "decision history h of player i is reached" or $\mathcal{E}_i = \{[h] : h \in H\}$, the set of propositions corresponding to all histories (in which case $\mathcal{E}_i = \mathcal{E}_j$ for any two players i and j).

[32] Note that it follows from Condition 3 and seriality of $\mathcal{B}_i$ that, for every $\omega \in \Omega$, $f_i(\omega, \Omega) = \mathcal{B}_i(\omega)$, so that one could simplify the definition of model by dropping the relations $\mathcal{B}_i$ and recovering the initial beliefs from the set $f_i(\omega, \Omega)$. We have chosen not to do so in order to maintain continuity in the exposition.

[33] Although widely accepted, this principle of belief revision is not uncontroversial (see [42] and [53]).

One can associate with each function f_i an operator $\Rightarrow_i : \mathcal{E}_i \times 2^\Omega \to 2^\Omega$ as follows:

$$E \Rightarrow_i F = \{\omega \in \Omega : f_i(\omega, E) \subseteq F\}. \tag{14}$$

Possible interpretations of the event $E \Rightarrow_i F$ are "according to player i, if E were the case, then F would be true" [33] or "if informed that E, player i would believe that F" [50] or "under the supposition that E, player i would believe that F" [2].[34]

Thus the function f_i can be used to model the full epistemic state of player i; in particular, how player i would revise her prior beliefs if she contemplated information that contradicted those beliefs. However, as pointed out by Stalnaker,

> "It should be noted that even with the addition of the belief revision structure to the epistemic models [...], they remain static models. A model of this kind represents only the agent's beliefs at a fixed time [before the game is played], together with the policies or dispositions to revise her beliefs that she has at that time. The model does not represent any actual revisions that are made when new information is actually received."([52], p. 198.)[35]

Condition (11) rules out the possibility that a player may be uncertain about her own choice of action at decision histories of hers that are not ruled out by her initial beliefs. Does a corresponding restriction hold for revised beliefs? That is, suppose that at state ω player i erroneously believes that her decision history h will not be reached ($\omega \in [h]$ but $\omega \in \mathbb{B}_i\neg[h]$); suppose also that a is the action that she will choose at h ($\omega \in [ha]$). Is it necessarily the case that, according to her revised beliefs on the suppositions that h is reached, she believes that she takes action a? That is, is it the case that $\omega \in [h] \Rightarrow_i [ha]$? In general, the answer is negative. For example, consider a model of the game of Fig. 3 in which there are states α, β and γ such that $\alpha \in [a_1 b_1]$, $\mathcal{B}_2(\alpha) = \{\beta\}$, $\beta \in [a_2 c_1]$, $f_2(\alpha, [a_1]) = \{\gamma\}$ and $\gamma \in [a_1 b_2]$. Then we have that at state α Player 2 will in fact take action b_1 (after being surprised by Player 1's choice of a_1) and yet, according to her revised beliefs on the supposition that Player 1 plays a_1, she does not believe that she would take action b_1 (in fact she believes that she

---

[34] Equivalently, one can think of $\Rightarrow_i$ as a conditional belief operator $\mathbb{B}_i(\cdot|\cdot)$ with the interpretation of $\mathbb{B}_i(F|E)$ as 'player i believes F given information/supposition E' (see, for example, [15] who uses the notation $\mathbb{B}_i^E(F)$ instead of $\mathbb{B}_i(F|E)$).

[35] The author goes on to say that "The models can be enriched by adding a temporal dimension to represent the dynamics, but doing so requires that the knowledge and belief operators be time indexed..." For a model where the belief operators are indeed time indexed and represent the actual beliefs of the players when actually informed that it is their turn to move, see [20].

would take action b_2): $\alpha \notin [a_1] \Rightarrow_i [a_1 b_1]$. In order to rule this out we need to impose the following strengthening of (11):[36]

$$\forall h \in D_i, \ \forall a \in A(h),$$

$$[ha] \subseteq ([h] \Rightarrow_i [ha]). \tag{15}$$

Should (15) be considered a necessary component of a definition of rationality? Perhaps so, if the revised beliefs were the actual beliefs of player i when she is actually informed (to her surprise) that her decision history h has been reached. In that case it may be reasonable to assume that - as the player makes up her mind about what to do - she forms correct beliefs about what she is going to do. However, we stressed above that the models we are considering are static models: they represent the initial beliefs and disposition to revise those beliefs at the beginning of the game. Given this interpretation of the revised beliefs as hypothetical beliefs conditional on various suppositions, it seems that violations of (15) might be perfectly rational. To illustrate this point, consider the above example with the following modification: $f_2(\alpha, [a_1]) = \{\alpha, \gamma\}$. It is possible that if Player 1 plays a_1 , Player 2 is indifferent between playing b_1 or b_2 (she gets the same payoff). Thus she can coherently form the belief that if - contrary to what she expects - Player 1 were to play a_1, then she might end up choosing either b_1 or b_2: $\alpha \in [a_1] \Rightarrow_i ([a_1 b_1] \cup [a_1 b_2])$. Of course, when actually faced with the choice between b_1 and b_2 she will have to break her indifference and pick one action (perhaps by tossing a coin): in the example under consideration (where $\alpha \in [a_1 b_1]$) she will pick b_1 (perhaps because the outcome of the coin toss is Heads: something she will know then but cannot know at the beginning).

How can rationality of choice be captured in the models that we are considering? Various definitions of rationality have been suggested in the literature, most notably *material rationality* and *substantive rationality* [4,5]. The former notion is weaker in that a player can be found to be irrational only at decision histories of hers that are actually reached. The latter notion, on the other hand, is more stringent since a player can be judged to be irrational at a decision history h of hers even if she knows that h will not be reached. We will focus on the weaker notion of material rationality. We want to define a player's rationality as a proposition, that is, an event. Let $u_i : Z \to \mathbb{R}$ be player i's ordinal utility function (representing her preferences over the set of terminal histories Z) and define $\pi_i : \Omega \to \mathbb{R}$ by $\pi_i(\omega) = u_i(\zeta(\omega))$. For every $x \in \mathbb{R}$, let $[\pi_i \leq x]$ be the event that

---

[36] (15) is implied by (11) whenever player i's initial beliefs do not rule out h. That is, if $\omega \in \neg \mathbb{B}_i \neg [h]$ (equivalently, $\mathcal{B}_i(\omega) \cap [h] \neq \varnothing$) then, for every $a \in A(h)$,

$$\text{if } \omega \in [ha] \text{ then } \omega \in ([h] \Rightarrow_i [ha]). \quad (F1)$$

In fact, by Condition 3 of Definition 6 (since, by hypothesis, $\mathcal{B}_i(\omega) \cap [h] \neq \varnothing$),

$$f_i(\omega, [h]) = \mathcal{B}_i(\omega) \cap [h]. \quad (F2)$$

Let $a \in A(h)$ be such that $\omega \in [ha]$. Then, by (11), $\omega \in \mathbb{B}_i([h] \to [ha])$, that is, $\mathcal{B}_i(\omega) \subseteq \neg [h] \cup [ha]$. Thus $\mathcal{B}_i(\omega) \cap [h] \subseteq (\neg [h] \cap [h]) \cup ([ha] \cap [h]) = \varnothing \cup [ha] = [ha]$ (since $[ha] \subseteq [h]$) and therefore, by (F2), $f_i(\omega, [h]) \subseteq [ha]$, that is, $\omega \in [h] \Rightarrow_i [ha]$.

player i's payoff is not greater than x, that is, $[\pi_i \leq x] = \{\omega \in \Omega : \pi_i(\omega) \leq x\}$ and, similarly, let $[\pi_i > x] \stackrel{\text{def}}{=} \{\omega \in \Omega : \pi_i(\omega) > x\}$. Then we say that player i is *materially rational* at a state if, for every decision history h of hers that is actually reached at that state and for every real number x, it is not the case that she believes – under the supposition that h is reached – that (1) her payoff from her actual choice would not be greater than x and (2) her payoff would be greater than x if she were to take an action different from the one that she is actually taking (at that history in that state).[37]

Formally this can be stated as follows (recall that D_i denotes the set of decision histories of player i and $A(h)$ the set of actions available at h):

> Player i is *materially rational* at $\omega \in \Omega$ if , $\forall h \in D_i, \forall a \in A(h)$
> if ha is a prefix of $\zeta(\omega)$ then, $\forall b \in A(h), \forall x \in \mathbb{R}$,
> $$([ha] \Rrightarrow_i [\pi_i \leq x]) \rightarrow \neg ([hb] \Rrightarrow_i [\pi_i > x]). \tag{16}$$

Note that, in general, we cannot replace the antecedent $[ha] \Rrightarrow_i [\pi_i \leq x]$ with $\mathbb{B}_i([ha] \rightarrow [\pi_i \leq x])$, because at state ω player i might initially believe that h will not be reached, in which case it would be trivially true that $\omega \in \mathbb{B}_i([ha] \rightarrow [\pi_i \leq x])$. Thus, in general, her rationality is judged on the basis of her *revised* beliefs on the supposition that h is reached. Note, however, that if $\omega \in \neg\mathbb{B}_i\neg[h]$, that is, if at ω she does not rule out the possibility that h will be reached and $a \in A(h)$ is the action that she actually takes at ω ($\omega \in [ha]$), then, for every event F, $\omega \in \mathbb{B}_i([ha] \rightarrow F)$ if and only if $\omega \in ([ha] \Rrightarrow_i F)$.[38] Note also that, according to (16), a player is trivially rational at any state at which she does not take any actions.

The solution concept which is normally used for perfect-information games is the backward-induction solution, which is obtained as follows. Start from a

---

[37] This is a "local" definition in that it only considers, for every decision history of player i, a change in player i's choice at that decision history and not also at later decision histories of hers (if any). One could make the definition of rationality more stringent by simultaneously considering changes in the choices at a decision history and subsequent decision histories of the same player (if any).

[38] Proof. Suppose that $\omega \in [ha] \cap \neg\mathbb{B}_i\neg[h]$. As shown in Footnote 36 (see (F2)),

$$\mathcal{B}_i(\omega) \cap [h] = f_i(\omega, [h]). \quad (G1)$$

Since $[ha] \subseteq [h]$,

$$\mathcal{B}_i(\omega) \cap [h] \cap [ha] = \mathcal{B}_i(\omega) \cap [ha]. \quad (G2)$$

As shown in Footnote 36, $f_i(\omega, [h]) \subseteq [ha]$ and, by Condition 1 of Definition 6, $f_i(\omega, [h]) \neq \emptyset$. Thus $f_i(\omega, [h]) \cap [ha] = f_i(\omega, [h]) \neq \emptyset$. Hence, by Condition 4 of Definition 6,

$$f_i(\omega, [h]) \cap [ha] = f_i(\omega, [ha]). \quad (G3)$$

By intersecting both sides of (G1) with $[ha]$ and using (G2) and (G3) we get that $\mathcal{B}_i(\omega) \cap [ha] = f_i(\omega, [ha])$.

decision history followed only by terminal histories (such as history a_1a_2 in the game of Fig. 6) and pick an action there that is payoff-maximizing for the corresponding player; delete the selected decision history, turn it into a terminal history and associate with it the payoff vector corresponding to the selected choice; repeat the procedure until all the decision histories have been exhausted. For example, the backward-induction solution of the game of Fig. 6 selects actions d_3 and d_1 for Player 1 and d_2 for Player 2, so that the corresponding outcome is d_1.

Does initial common belief that all the players are materially rational (according to (16)) imply backward induction in perfect-information games? The answer is negative.[39] To see this, consider the perfect-information game shown in Fig. 6 and the model of it shown in Fig. 7.[40] First of all, note that the common belief relation $\mathcal{B}^*$ is obtained by adding to $\mathcal{B}_2$ the pair (β, β); thus, in particular, $\mathcal{B}^*(\beta) = \{\beta, \gamma\}$. We want to show that both players are materially rational at both states β and γ, so that at state β it is common belief that both players are materially rational, despite that fact that the play of the game at β is $a_1a_2d_3$, while the outcome associated with the backward-induction solution is d_1 (furthermore, there is no Nash equilibrium whose associated outcome is $a_1a_2d_3$). Clearly, Player 1 is materially rational at state β (since he obtains his largest possible payoff); he is also rational at state γ because he knows that he plays d_1, obtaining a payoff of 1, and believes that if he were to play a_1 Player 2 would respond with d_2 and give him a payoff of zero: this belief is encoded in $f_1(\gamma, [a_1]) = \{\delta\}$ (where $[a_1] = \{\alpha, \beta, \delta\}$) and $\zeta(\delta) = a_1d_2$. Player 2 is trivially materially rational at state γ since she does not take any actions there. Now consider state β. Player 2 initially erroneously believes that Player 1 will end the game by playing d_1; however, Player 1 is in fact playing a_1 and thus Player 2 will be surprised. Her initial disposition to revise her beliefs on the supposition that Player 1 plays a_1 is such that she would believe that she herself would play a_2 and Player 1 would follow with a_3, thus giving her the largest possible payoff (this belief is encoded in $f_2(\beta, [a_1]) = \{\alpha\}$ and $\zeta(\alpha) = a_1a_2a_3$). Hence she is rational at state β, according to (16).

In order to obtain the backward-induction solution, one needs to go beyond common initial belief of material rationality. Proposals in the literature include the notions of epistemic independence [50], strong belief [10], stable belief [7],

---

[39] In fact, common belief of material rationality does not even imply a Nash equilibrium outcome. A *Nash equilibrium* is a strategy profile satisfying the property that no player can increase her payoff by unilaterally changing her strategy. A Nash equilibrium *outcome* of a perfect-information game is a terminal history associated with a Nash equilibrium. A backward-induction solution of a perfect-information game can be written as a strategy profile and is always a Nash equilibrium.

[40] In Fig. 6, for every terminal history, the top number associated with it is Player 1's utility and the bottom number is Player 2's utility. In Fig. 7 we have only represented parts of the functions f_1 and f_2, namely that $f_1(\gamma, \{\alpha, \beta, \delta\}) = \{\delta\}$ and $f_2(\beta, \{\alpha, \beta, \delta\}) = f_2(\gamma, \{\alpha, \beta, \delta\}) = \{\alpha\}$ (note that $[a_1] = \{\alpha, \beta, \delta\}$). Similar examples can be found in [15, 28, 43, 50].

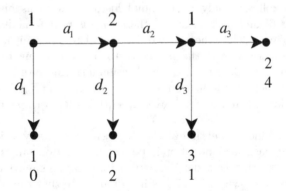

Fig. 6. A perfect information game

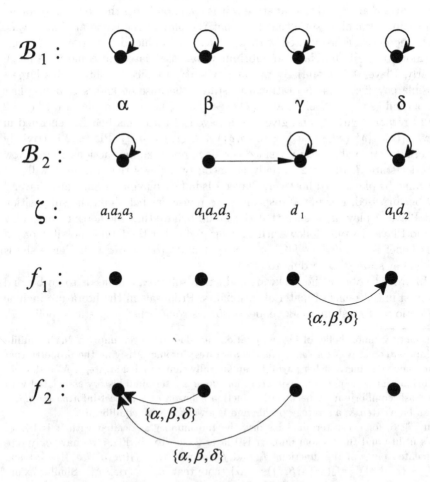

Fig. 7. A model of the game of Fig. 6

substantive rationality [4, 35]. For an overview of this literature the reader is referred to [25] and [39].

It is worth stressing that *in the models considered above, strategies do not play any role*: states are described in terms of the players' actual behavior along a play of the game.[41] One could view a player's strategy as her (conditional) beliefs about what she would do under the supposition that each of her decision histories is reached. However, the models considered so far do not guarantee that a player's revised beliefs select a unique action at each of her decision histories. For example, consider a model of the game of Fig. 3 in which there are states α, β and γ such that $\alpha \in [a_2 c_1]$, $\mathcal{B}_2(\alpha) = \{\alpha\}$, $\beta \in [a_1 b_1]$, $\gamma \in [a_1 b_2]$ and $f_2(\alpha, [a_1]) = \{\beta, \gamma\}$. Then, at state α, Player 2 knows that she will take action c_1 and, according to her revised beliefs on the supposition that Player 1 plays a_1, she is uncertain as to whether she would respond to a_1 by playing b_1 or b_2 (perhaps she is indifferent between b_1 and b_2, because she would get the same payoff in either case). One could rule this possibility out by imposing the following restriction:

$$\forall h \in D_i, \forall a, b \in A(h), \forall \omega, \omega', \omega'' \in \Omega, if \omega', \omega'' \in f_i(\omega, [h])$$

and ha is a prefix of $\zeta(\omega')$ and hb is a prefix of $\zeta(\omega'')$ then $a = b$.   (17)

If (17) is imposed then one can associate with every state a unique strategy for every player. However, as [45] points out, in this setup strategies would be cognitive constructs rather than objective counterfactuals about what a player would actually do at each of her decision histories.

5   Conclusion

Roughly speaking, a player's choice is rational if, according to what the player believes, there is no other choice which is better for her. Thus, in order to be able to assess the rationality of a player, one needs to be able to represent both the player's choices and her beliefs. The notion of a model of a game does precisely this. We have discussed a number of conceptual issues that arise in attempting to represent not only the actual beliefs but also the counterfactual or hypothetical beliefs of the players. These issues highlight the complexity of defining the notion of rationality in dynamic games and of specifying an appropriate interpretation of the hypothesis that there is "common recognition" of rationality.

A strategy of a player in a dynamic game with perfect information, according to the definition first proposed by von Neumann and Morgenstern [55], is a complete contingent plan specifying a choice of action for every decision history that belongs to that player.[42] We have argued that using the notion of strategy

---

[41] For an example of epistemic models of dynamic games where strategies do play a role see [41].

[42] In general dynamic games, a strategy specifies a choice for every information set of the player.

in models of dynamic games is problematic, since it implicitly introduces counterfactual considerations, both objective (in terms of statements about what a
player would do in situations that do not arise) and subjective (in terms of the
hypothetical or conditional beliefs of the players). Such counterfactuals ought
to be modeled explicitly. We first considered the use of objective counterfactuals in models of dynamic games, but concluded that such counterfactuals are
inadequate, since they express causal relationships, while it is epistemic counterfactuals that seem to be relevant in terms of evaluating the rationality of choices.
We then considered models that make exclusive use of subjective (or epistemic)
counterfactuals and showed that in these models strategies do not play any role
and can thus be dispensed with.

The models of dynamic games considered above, however, are not the only
possibility. Instead of modeling the epistemic states of the players in terms of
their prior beliefs and prior dispositions to revise those beliefs in a static framework, one could model the actual beliefs that the players hold at the time at
which they make their choices. In such a framework the players' initial belief
revision policies (or dispositions to revise their initial beliefs) can be dispensed
with: the analysis can be carried out entirely in terms of the actual beliefs at
the time of choice. This alternative approach is put forward in [20], where an
epistemic characterization of backward induction is provided that does not rely
on (objective or subjective) counterfactuals.[43,44]

Acknowledgments. I am grateful to Sonja Smets for presenting this chapter at the
Workshop on Modeling Strategic Reasoning (Lorentz Center, Leiden, February 2012)
and for offering several constructive comments. I am also grateful to two anonymous
reviewers and to the participants in the workshop for many useful comments and
suggestions.

---

[43] [20] uses a dynamic framework where the set of "possible worlds" is given by state-
instant pairs (ω, t). Each state ω specifies the entire play of the game (that is, a
terminal history) and, for every instant t, (ω, t) specifies the history that is reached
at that instant (in state ω). A player is said to be active at (ω, t) if the history
reached in state ω at date t is a decision history of his. At every state-instant pair
(ω, t) the beliefs of the active player provide an answer to the question "what will
happen if I take action a?", for every available action a. A player is said to be rational
at (ω, t) if either he is not active there or the action he ends up taking at state ω is
optimal given his beliefs at (ω, t). Backward induction is characterized in terms of
the following event: the first mover (at date 0) (i) is rational and has correct beliefs,
(ii) believes that the active player at date 1 is rational and has correct beliefs, (iii)
believes that the active player at date 1 believes that the active player at date 2 is
rational and has correct beliefs, etc.

[44] The focus of this chapter has been on the issue of modeling the notion of rationality
and "common recognition" of rationality in dynamic games with perfect information.
Alternatively one can use the AGM theory of belief revision to provide foundations
for refinements of Nash equilibrium in dynamic games. This is done in [19,21] where
a notion of perfect Bayesian equilibrium is proposed for general dynamic games
(thus allowing for imperfect information). Perfect Bayesian equilibria constitute a
refinement of subgame-perfect equilibria and are a superset of sequential equilibria.
The notion of sequential equilibrium was introduced by [36].

A Summary of Notation

The following table summarizes the notation used in this chapter.

Notation	Interpretation
Ω	Set of states
$\mathcal{B}_i$	Player i's binary "doxastic accessibility" relation on Ω. The interpretation of $\omega \mathcal{B}_i \omega'$ is that at state ω player i considers state ω' possible: see Definition 1
$\mathcal{B}_i(\omega) = \{\omega' \in \Omega : \omega \mathcal{B}_i \omega'\}$	Belief set of player i at state ω
$\mathbb{B}_i : 2^\Omega \to 2^\Omega$	Belief operator of player i. If $E \subseteq \Omega$ then $\mathbb{B}_i E$ is the set of states where player i believes E, that is, $\mathbb{B}_i E = \{\omega \in \Omega : \mathcal{B}_i(\omega) \subseteq E\}$
$\mathcal{B}^*$	Common belief relation on the set of states Ω (the transitive closure of the union of the $\mathcal{B}_i$'s)
$\mathbb{B}^* : 2^\Omega \to 2^\Omega$	Common belief operator
$\langle N, \{S_i, \succsim_i\}_{i \in N}\rangle$	Strategic-form game: see Definition 2
$f : \Omega \times \mathcal{E} \to 2^\Omega$	Objective counterfactual selection function. The event $f(\omega, E)$ is interpreted as "the set of states closest to ω where E is true": see Definition 4
$E \Rightarrow F = \{\omega \in \Omega : f(\omega, E) \subseteq F\}$	The interpretation of $E \Rightarrow F$ is "the set of states where it is true that if E were the case then F would be the case."
$\langle A, H, N, \iota, \{\succsim_i\}_{i \in N}\rangle$	Dynamic game with perfect information. See Definition 5
$f_i : \Omega \times \mathcal{E}_i \to 2^\Omega$	Subjective counterfactual selection function. The event $f_i(\omega, E)$ is interpreted as the set of states that player i would consider possible, at state ω, under the supposition that (or if informed that) E is true: see Definition 6
$E \Rightarrow_i F = \{\omega \in \Omega : f_i(\omega, E) \subseteq F\}$	The event $E \Rightarrow_i F$ is interpreted as "the set of states where, according to player i, if E were the case, then F would be true"

References

1. Alchourrón, C., Gärdenfors, P., Makinson, D.: On the logic of theory change: Partial meet contraction and revision functions. J. Symbolic Logic **50**, 510–530 (1985)
2. Arló-Costa, H., Bicchieri, C.: Knowing and supposing in games of perfect information. Stud. Logica **86**, 353–373 (2007)

3. Aumann, R.: What is game theory trying to accomplish? In: Arrow, K., Honkapo-hja, S. (eds.) Frontiers in Economics, pp. 28–76. Basil Blackwell, Oxford (1985)

4. Aumann, R.: Backward induction and common knowledge of rationality. Games Econ. Behav. **8**, 6–19 (1995)

5. Aumann, R.: On the centipede game. Games Econ. Behav. **23**, 97–105 (1998)

6. Aumann, R., Brandenburger, A.: Epistemic conditions for Nash equilibrium. Econometrica **63**, 1161–1180 (1995)

7. Baltag, A., Smets, S., Zvesper, J.: Keep 'hoping' for rationality: A solution to the backward induction paradox. Synthese **169**, 301–333 (2009)

8. Battigalli, P., Bonanno, G.: Recent results on belief, knowledge and the epistemic foundations of game theory. Res. Econ. **53**, 149–225 (1999)

9. Battigalli, P., Di-Tillio, A., Samet, D.: Strategies and interactive beliefs in dynamic games. In: Acemoglu, D., Arellano, M., Dekel, E. (eds.) Advances in Economics and Econometrics. Theory and Applications: Tenth World Congress. Cambridge University Press, Cambridge (2013)

10. Battigalli, P., Siniscalchi, M.: Strong belief and forward induction reasoning. J. Econ. Theor. **106**, 356–391 (2002)

11. Ben-Porath, E.: Nash equilibrium and backwards induction in perfect information games. Rev. Econ. Stud. **64**, 23–46 (1997)

12. van Benthem, J.: Logical Dynamics of Information and Interaction. Cambridge University Press, Cambridge (2011)

13. Bernheim, D.: Rationalizable strategic behavior. Econometrica **52**, 1002–1028 (1984)

14. Board, O.: Belief revision and rationalizability. In: Gilboa, I. (ed.) Theoretical Aspects of Rationality and Knowledge (TARK VII). Morgan Kaufman, San Francisco (1998)

15. Board, O.: Dynamic interactive epistemology. Games Econ. Behav. **49**, 49–80 (2004)

16. Board, O.: The equivalence of Bayes and causal rationality in games. Theor. Decis. **61**, 1–19 (2006)

17. Bonanno, G.: A syntactic approach to rationality in games with ordinal payoffs. In: Bonanno, G., van der Hoek, W., Wooldridge, M. (eds.) Logic and the Foundations of Game and Decision Theory (LOFT 7). Texts in Logic and Games, vol. 3, pp. 59–86. Amsterdam University Press, Amsterdam (2008)

18. Bonanno, G.: Rational choice and AGM belief revision. Artif. Intell. **173**, 1194–1203 (2009)

19. Bonanno, G.: AGM belief revision in dynamic games. In: Apt, K. (ed.) Proceedings of the 13th Conference on Theoretical Aspects of Rationality and Knowledge, TARK XIII, pp. 37–45. ACM, New York (2011)

20. Bonanno, G.: A dynamic epistemic characterization of backward induction without counterfactuals. Games Econ. Behav. **78**, 31–45 (2013)

21. Bonanno, G.: AGM-consistency and perfect Bayesian equilibrium. Part I: definition and properties. Int. J. Game Theor. **42**, 567–592 (2013)

22. Bonanno, G.: Epistemic foundations of game theory. In: van Ditmarsch, H., Halpern, J., van der Hoek, W., Kooi, B. (eds.), Handbook of Logics for Knowledge and Belief, pp. 411–450. College Publications (2015)

23. Bonanno, G., Nehring, K.: Assessing the truth axiom under incomplete information. Math. Soc. Sci. **36**, 3–29 (1998)

24. Bonanno, G., Nehring, K.: Common belief with the logic of individual belief. Math. Logic Q. **46**, 49–52 (2000)

25. Brandenburger, A.: The power of paradox: some recent developments in interactive epistemology. Int. J. Game Theor. **35**, 465–492 (2007)
26. Camerer, C.: Behavioral Game Theory: Experiments in Strategic Interaction. Princeton University Press, Princeton (2003)
27. Clausing, T.: Doxastic conditions for backward induction. Theor. Decis. **54**, 315–336 (2003)
28. Clausing, T.: Belief revision in games of perfect information. Econ. Philos. **20**, 89–115 (2004)
29. de Bruin, B.: Explaining Games: The Epistemic Programme in Game Theory. Springer, The Netherlands (2010)
30. Dekel, E., Gul, F.: Rationality and knowledge in game theory. In: Kreps, D., Wallis, K. (eds.) Advances in Economics and Econometrics, pp. 87–172. Cambridge University Press, Cambridge (1997)
31. Feinberg, Y.: Subjective reasoning - dynamic games. Games Econ. Behav. **52**, 54–93 (2005)
32. Gerstung, M., Nakhoul, H., Beerenwinkel, N.: Evolutionary games with affine fitness functions: applications to cancer. Dyn. Games Appl. **1**, 370–385 (2011)
33. Halpern, J.: Hypothetical knowledge and counterfactual reasoning. Int. J. Game Theor. **28**, 315–330 (1999)
34. Halpern, J.: Set-theoretic completeness for epistemic and conditional logic. Ann. Math. Artif. Intell. **26**, 1–27 (1999)
35. Halpern, J.: Substantive rationality and backward induction. Games Econ. Behav. **37**, 425–435 (2001)
36. Kreps, D., Wilson, R.: Sequential equilibrium. Econometrica **50**, 863–894 (1982)
37. Pacuit, E.: Dynamic Models of Rational Deliberation in Games. In: van Benthem, J., Ghosh, S., Verbrugge, R. (eds.) Models of Strategic Reasoning. LNCS, vol. 8972, pp. 3–33. Springer, Heidelberg (2015)
38. Pearce, D.: Rationalizable strategic behavior and the problem of perfection. Econometrica **52**, 1029–1050 (1984)
39. Perea, A.: Epistemic foundations for backward induction: An overview. In: van Benthem, J., Gabbay, D., Löwe, B. (eds.) Interactive logic. Proceedings of the 7th Augustus de Morgan Workshop. Texts in Logic and Games, vol. 1, pp. 159–193. Amsterdam University Press, Amsterdam (2007)
40. Perea, A.: Epistemic Game Theory: Reasoning and Choice. Cambridge University Press, Cambridge (2012)
41. Perea, A.: Finite reasoning procedures for dynamic games. In: van Benthem, J., Ghosh, S., Verbrugge, R. (eds.) Models of Strategic Reasoning. Lecturer Notes in Computer Science, vol. 8972, pp. 63–90. Springer, Heidelberg (2015)
42. Rabinowicz, W.: Stable revision, or is preservation worth preserving? In: Fuhrmann, A., Rott, H. (eds.) Logic, Action and Information: Essays on Logic in Philosophy and Artificial Intelligence, pp. 101–128. de Gruyter, Berlin (1996)
43. Rabinowicz, W.: Backward induction in games: On an attempt at logical reconstruction. In: Rabinowicz, W. (ed.) Value and Choice: Some Common Themes in Decision Theory and Moral Philosophy, pp. 243–256. Lund Philosophy Reports, Lund (2000)
44. Rubinstein, A.: Comments on the interpretation of game theory. Econometrica **59**, 909–924 (1991)
45. Samet, D.: Hypothetical knowledge and games with perfect information. Games Econ. Behav. **17**, 230–251 (1996)
46. Shoham, Y., Leyton-Brown, K.: Multiagent Systems: Algorithmic, Game-theoretic, and Logical Foundations. Cambridge University Press, Cambridge (2008)

47. Maynard Smith, J.: Evolution and the Theory of Games. Cambridge University Press, Cambridge (1982)
48. Stalnaker, R.: A theory of conditionals. In: Rescher, N. (ed.) Studies in Logical Theory, pp. 98–112. Blackwell, Oxford (1968)
49. Stalnaker, R.: Knowledge, belief and counterfactual reasoning in games. Econ. Philos. **12**, 133–163 (1996)
50. Stalnaker, R.: Belief revision in games: Forward and backward induction. Math. Soc. Sci. **36**, 31–56 (1998)
51. Stalnaker, R.: Extensive and strategic forms: Games and models for games. Res. Econ. **53**, 293–319 (1999)
52. Stalnaker, R.: On logics of knowledge and belief. Philos. Stud. **128**, 169–199 (2006)
53. Stalnaker, R.: Iterated belief revision. Erkenntnis **128**, 189–209 (2009)
54. Suzumura, K.: Rational Choice, Collective Decisions and Social Welfare. Cambridge University Press, Cambridge (1983)
55. von Neumann, J., Morgenstern, O.: Theory of Games and Economic Behavior. Princeton University Press, Princeton (1944)
56. Zambrano, E.: Counterfactual reasoning and common knowledge of rationality in normal form games. Topics Theor. Econ. 4, Article 8 (2004)

Finite Reasoning Procedures
for Dynamic Games

Andrés Perea[(⊠)]

EpiCenter and Department of Quantitative Economics, Maastricht University,
Maastricht, The Netherlands
a.perea@maastrichtuniversity.nl

Abstract. In this chapter we focus on the epistemic concept of *common belief in future rationality* (Perea [37]), which describes a backward induction type of reasoning for general dynamic games. It states that a player always believes that his opponents will choose rationally now and in the future, always believes that his opponents always believe that their opponents choose rationally now and in the future, and so on, *ad infinitum*. It thus involves infinitely many conditions, which might suggest that this concept is too demanding for real players in a game. In this chapter we show, however, that this is not true. For finite dynamic games we present a *finite* reasoning procedure that a player can use to reason his way towards common belief in future rationality.

Keywords: Epistemic game theory · Reasoning · Dynamic games · Beliefs

1 Introduction

If you make a choice in a game, then you must realize that the final outcome does not only depend on your own choice, but also on the choices of your opponents. It is therefore natural that you first *reason* about your opponents in order to form a *plausible belief* about their choices, before you make your own choice. Now, how can we formally model such reasoning procedures about your opponents? And how do these reasoning procedures affect the choice you will eventually make in the game? These questions naturally lead to *epistemic game theory*– a modern approach to game theory which takes seriously the fact that the players in a game are *human beings* who reason before they reach their final decision.

In our view, the most important idea in epistemic game theory is *common belief in rationality* ([43], see also [12]). It states that a player, when making his choice, chooses *optimally* given the belief he holds about the opponents' choices. Moreover, the player also believes that his opponents will choose optimally as well, and that their opponents believe that the other players will also choose optimally, and so on, *ad infinitum*. This idea really constitutes the basis for epistemic game theory, as most – if not all – concepts within epistemic game theory can be viewed as some variant of *common belief in rationality*. See [36] for

© Springer-Verlag Berlin Heidelberg 2015
J. van Benthem et al. (Eds.): Models of Strategic Reasoning, LNCS 8972, pp. 63–90, 2016.
DOI: 10.1007/978-3-662-48540-8_3

a textbook that gives a detailed overview of most of these concepts in epistemic game theory.

For dynamic games there is a backward induction analogue to common belief in rationality, namely *common belief in future rationality* [37]. This concept states that a player, at each of his information sets, believes that his opponents will choose rationally *now and in the future*. Here, by an information set we mean a stage in the game where this player has to make a choice. However, *common belief in future rationality* does not require a player to believe that his opponents have chosen rationally in the past! On top of this, the concept states that a player also always believes that his opponents, at each of their information sets, believe that their opponents will choose rationally now and in the future, and so on, *ad infinitum*.

For dynamic games with perfect information, various authors have used some variant of the idea of *common belief in future rationality* as a possible foundation for backward induction. See [2,5,19,40]. Among these contributions, the concept of *stable belief in dynamic rationality* in [5] matches completely the idea of *common belief in future rationality*, although they restrict attention to non-probabilistic beliefs. Perea [32] provides an overview of the various epistemic foundations for backward induction that have been offered in the literature.

Some people have criticized *common belief in rationality* because it involves *infinitely* many conditions, and hence – they argue – it will be very difficult for a player to meet each of these infinitely many conditions. The same could be said about *common belief in future rationality*. The main purpose of this chapter will be to show that this critique is actually not justified, provided we stick to *finite* games. We will show, namely, that in dynamic games with finitely many information sets, and finitely many choices at every information set, *common belief in future rationality* can be achieved by reasoning procedures that use *finitely* many steps only!

Let us be more precise about this statement. Suppose a player in a dynamic game holds not only conditional beliefs about his opponents' strategies, but also conditional beliefs about his opponents' conditional beliefs about the other players' strategies, and so on, *ad infinitum*. That is, this player holds a full *belief hierarchy* about his opponents – an object that is needed in order to formally define *common belief in future rationality*. Such belief hierarchies can be efficiently encoded within an *epistemic model with types*. This is a model in which for every player there is a set of so-called "types", and where there is a function that assigns to every type of player i a string of conditional beliefs about the opponents' strategies *and types* – one conditional belief for every information set. Within such an epistemic model, we can then *derive* for every type a *full hierarchy of conditional beliefs* about the opponents' strategies and beliefs. So, the "types" in this epistemic model, together with the functions that map types to conditional beliefs on the opponents' strategies and types, can be viewed as encodings of the conditional belief hierarchies that we are eventually interested in. This construction is based on Harsanyi's [21] seminal way of encoding belief hierarchies for games with incomplete information. If a belief hierarchy can be derived from an epistemic model with *finitely many types* only, we say that this belief hierarchy is *finitely generated.* Such finitely generated belief hierarchies will play a central role in this chapter, as we will show that they are "sufficient" when studying *common belief in future rationality* in finite dynamic games.

Let us now come back to the question whether *common belief in future rationality* can be achieved by finite reasoning procedures. As a first step, we show in Sect. 3 that for a *finitely generated* belief hierarchy, it only takes *finitely* many steps to verify whether this given belief hierarchy expresses *common belief in future rationality* or not. So, although *common belief in future rationality* involves infinitely many conditions, checking these conditions can be reduced to a *finite* procedure whenever we consider belief hierarchies that are finitely generated. This procedure can thus be viewed as an *ex-post* procedure which can be used to *evaluate* a given belief hierarchy, but it does not explain *how* a player arrives at such a belief hierarchy.

In Sect. 4 we go one step further by asking *how* a player can reason his way towards *common belief in future rationality.* To that purpose, we present a *finite* reasoning procedure such that (a) this procedure will always lead the player, within finitely many steps, to belief hierarchies that express *common belief in future rationality,* and (b) for every strategy that is possible under *common belief in future rationality* the procedure generates a belief hierarchy supporting this strategy. So, in a sense, the reasoning procedure yields an *exhaustive* set of belief hierarchies for *common belief in future rationality.* This reasoning procedure can be viewed as an *ex-ante* procedure, as it describes how a player may reason *before* forming his eventual belief hierarchy, and *before* making his eventual choice. The reasoning procedure we present in Sect. 4 is based on the *backward dominance procedure* [37], which is a recursive elimination procedure that delivers all strategies that can rationally be made under *common belief in future rationality.*

So far, the epistemic game theory literature has largely focused on *ex-post* procedures, but not so much on *ex-ante* procedures. Indeed, most concepts within epistemic game theory can be viewed as *ex-post* procedures that can be used to judge a given belief hierarchy on its reasonability, but do not explain *how* a player could reason his way towards such a belief hierarchy. A notable exception is Pacuit [28] – another chapter within this volume that also explicitly investigates how people may reason before arriving at a given belief hierarchy. A lot of work remains to be done in this area, and in my view this may constitute one of the major challenges for epistemic game theory in the future: to explore *how* people may reason their way towards a plausible belief hierarchy. I hope that this volume will make a valuable contribution to this line of research.

Overall, our main contribution in this chapter is thus to (a) describe a reasoning process that a player can use to reason his way towards (an exhaustive set of) belief hierarchies expressing *common belief in future rationality* and (b) to show that this reasoning process only involves finitely many steps. Hence, we see that in finite dynamic games the concept of *common belief in future rationality* can be characterized by *finite* reasoning procedures. *Static* games are just a special case of dynamic games, where every player only makes a choice once, and where all players choose simultaneously. It is clear that in static games, the

Table 1. Overview of epistemic concepts and their recursive procedures

Epistemic concept	Recursive procedure
Common belief in rationality (Tan and Werlang [43])	Iterated elimination of strictly Dominated choices (based on Pearce [30], Tan and Werlang [43])
Permissibility (Brandenburger [11], Börgers [10])	Dekel-Fudenberg procedure (Dekel and Fudenberg [17])
Proper rationalizability (Schuhmacher [41], Asheim [2])	Iterated addition of preference restrictions (Perea [35])
Common assumption of rationality (Brandenburger, Friedenberg and Keisler [14])	Iterated elimination of weakly dominated choices
Common belief in future rationality (Perea [37])	Backward dominance procedure (Perea [37])
Common strong belief in rationality (Battigalli and Siniscalchi [8])	Iterated conditional dominance procedure (Shimoji and Watson [42], Based on Pearce [30], Battigalli [6])

concept of *common belief in future rationality* reduces to the basic concept of *common belief in rationality*. As such, the results in this chapter immediately carry over to *common belief in rationality* as well. Hence, also the concept of *common belief in rationality* in finite static games can be characterized by *finite* reasoning procedures, just by applying the reasoning procedures in this chapter to the special case of static games.

This chapter can therefore be seen as an answer to the critique that epistemic concepts like *common belief in rationality* and *common belief in future rationality* would be too demanding because of the infinitely many conditions. We believe this critique is not justified.

Similar conclusions can be drawn for various *other* epistemic concepts in the literature, like *permissibility* [10, 11], *proper rationalizability* [2, 41] and *common assumption of rationality* [14] for static games with lexicographic beliefs, and *common strong belief in rationality* [8] for dynamic games. For each of these epistemic concepts there exists a *finite* recursive procedure that yields all choices (or strategies, if we have a dynamic game) that can rationally be chosen under the concept. We list these procedures, with their references, in Table 1. An overview of these epistemic concepts and their associated recursive procedures can be found in my textbook [36].

Among these procedures, iterated elimination of weakly dominated choices is an old algorithm with a long tradition in game theory, and it is not clear where this procedure has been described for the first time in the literature. The procedure already appears in early books by Luce and Raiffa [23] and Farquharson [18].

The concept of *common strong belief in rationality* by Battigalli and Siniscalchi [8] can be seen as a counterpart to *common belief in future rationality*, as it establishes a *forward induction* type of reasoning, whereas *common belief in future rationality* constitutes a *backward induction* type of reasoning.

More precisely, *common strong belief in rationality* requires a player to believe that his opponent has chosen rationally *in the past* whenever this is possible, whereas *common belief in future rationality* does not require this. On the other hand, *common belief in future rationality* requires a player to *always* believe that his opponent will choose rationally in the future, whereas *common strong belief in rationality* does not require this if the player concludes that his opponent has made mistakes in the past. A more detailed comparison between the two concepts can be found in [34].

The outline of the chapter is as follows. In Sect. 2 we formally define the idea of *common belief in future rationality* within an epistemic model. Section 3 presents a finite reasoning procedure to verify whether a finitely generated belief hierarchy expresses *common belief in future rationality* or not. In Sect. 4 we present a finite reasoning procedure which yields, for *every* strategy that can rationally be chosen under *common belief in future rationality*, some belief hierarchy expressing *common belief in future rationality* which supports that strategy. We conclude the chapter with a discussion in Sect. 5. For simplicity, we stick to two-player games throughout this chapter. However, all ideas and results can easily be extended to games with more than two players.

2   Common Belief in Future Rationality

In this section we present the idea of *common belief in future rationality* [37] and show how it can be formalized within an epistemic model with types.

2.1   Main Idea

Common belief in future rationality [37] reflects the idea that you believe, at each of your information sets, that your opponent will choose rationally *now* and in the *future*, but not necessarily that he chose rationally in the *past*. Here, by an *information set* for player i we mean an instance in the game where player i must make a choice. In fact, in some dynamic games it is simply *impossible* to believe, at certain information sets, that your opponent has chosen rationally in the past, as this information set can only be reached through a suboptimal choice by the opponent. But it is *always* possible to believe that your opponent will choose rationally now and in the future. On top of this, *common belief in future rationality* also states that you always believe that your opponent reasons in precisely this way as well. That is, you always believe that your opponent, at each of his information sets, believes that you will choose rationally *now* and in the *future*. By iterating this thought process *ad infinitum* we eventually arrive at *common belief in future rationality*.

2.2   Dynamic Games

We now wish to formalize the idea of *common belief in future rationality*. As a first step, we formally introduce *dynamic games*. As already announced in the introduction, we will restrict attention to two-player games for simplicity, although everything in this chapter can easily be generalized to games with more than two players. At the same time, the model of a dynamic game presented here is a bit more general than usual, as we explicitly allow for *simultaneous* choices by players at certain stages of the game.

Definition 1 (Dynamic Game). *A **dynamic game** is a tuple* $\Gamma = (I, X, Z, (X_i, C_i, H_i, u_i)_{i \in I})$ *where*

(a) $I = \{1, 2\}$ *is the set of players;*
(b) X *is the set of non-terminal histories. Every non-terminal history* $x \in X$ *represents a situation where one or more players must make a choice;*
(c) Z *is the set of terminal histories. Every terminal history* $z \in Z$ *represents a situation where the game ends;*
(d) $X_i \subseteq X$ *is the set of histories at which player i must make a choice. At every history* $x \in X$ *at least one player must make a choice, that is, for every* $x \in X$ *there is at least some i with* $x \in X_i$. *However, for a given history x there may be various players i with* $x \in X_i$. *This models a situation where various players simultaneously choose at x. For a given history* $x \in X$, *we denote by* $I(x) := \{i \in I : x \in X_i\}$ *the set of active players at x;*
(e) C_i *assigns to every history* $x \in X_i$ *the set of choice s $C_i(x)$ from which player i can choose at x;*
(f) H_i *is the collection of information sets for player i. Formally,* $H_i = \{h_i^1, ..., h_i^K\}$ *where* $h_i^k \subseteq X_i$ *for every k, the sets h_i^k are mutually disjoint, and* $X_i = \cup_k h_i^k$. *The interpretation of an information set* $h \in H_i$ *is that at h player i knows that some history in h has been realized, without knowing precisely which one;*
(g) u_i *is player i's utility function, assigning to every terminal history* $z \in Z$ *some utility $u_i(z)$ in* $\mathbb{R}$.

Throughout this chapter we assume that all sets above are finite. The histories in X and Z consist of finite sequences of choice-combinations

$$((c_i^1)_{i \in I^1}, (c_i^2)_{i \in I^2}, ..., (c_i^K)_{i \in I^K}),$$

where $I^1, ..., I^K$ are nonempty subsets of players, such that

(a) $\emptyset$ (the empty sequence) is in X,
(b) if $x \in X$ and $(c_i)_{i \in I(x)} \in \prod_{i \in I(x)} C_i(x)$, then $(x, (c_i)_{i \in I(x)}) \in X \cup Z$,
(c) if $z \in Z$, then there is no choice combination $(c_i)_{i \in \hat{I}}$ such that $(z, (c_i)_{i \in \hat{I}}) \in X \cup Z$,
(d) for every $x \in X \cup Z$, $x \neq \emptyset$, there is a unique $y \in X$ and $(c_i)_{i \in I(y)} \in \prod_{i \in I(y)} C_i(y)$ such that $x = (y, (c_i)_{i \in I(y)})$.

Hence, a history $x \in X \cup Z$ represents the sequence of choice-combinations that have been made by the players until this moment.

Moreover, we assume that the collections H_i of information sets are such that

(a) two histories in the same information set for player i have the same set of available choices for player i. That is, for every $h \in H_i$, and every $x, y \in h$, it holds that $C_i(x) = C_i(y)$. This condition must hold since player i is assumed to know his set of available choices at h. We can thus speak of $C_i(h)$ for a given information set $h \in H_i$;

(b) two histories in the same information set for player i must pass through exactly the same collection of information sets for player i, and must hold exactly the same past choices for player i. This condition guarantees that player i has *perfect recall*, that is, at every information set $h \in H_i$ player i remembers the information he possessed before, and the choices he made before.

Say that an information set h *follows* some other information set h' if there are histories $x \in h$ and $y \in h'$ such that $x = (y, (c_i^1)_{i \in I^1}, (c_i^2)_{i \in I^2}, ..., (c_i^K)_{i \in I^K})$ for some choice-combinations $(c_i^1)_{i \in I^1}, (c_i^2)_{i \in I^2}, ..., (c_i^K)_{i \in I^K}$. The information sets h and h' are called *simultaneous* if there is some history x with $x \in h$ and $x \in h'$. Finally, we say that information set h *weakly follows* h' if either h follows h', or h and h' are simultaneous.

Note that the game model is quite similar to *coalition logic* in [29], and the *Alternating-Time Temporal Logic* in [1]. See also the chapter by Bulling, Goranko and Jamroga [24] in this volume, which uses the *Alternating-Time Temporal Logic*.

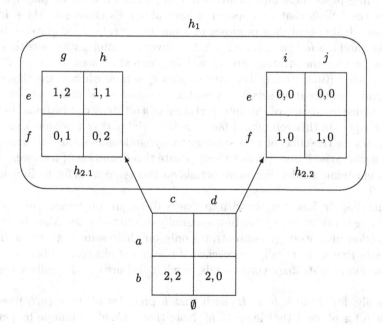

Fig. 1. Example of a dynamic game Here, $\emptyset$ and h_1 are information sets for player 1, and $\emptyset, h_{2.1}$ and $h_{2.2}$ are information sets for player 2

To illustrate the concepts defined above, let us have a look at the example in Fig. 1. At the beginning of the game, $\emptyset$, player 1 chooses between a and b, and player 2 simultaneously chooses between c and d. So, $\emptyset$ is an information set that belongs to both players 1 and 2. If player 1 chooses b, the game ends, and the utilities are as depicted. If he chooses a, then the game moves to information set $h_{2.1}$ or information set $h_{2.2}$, depending on whether player 2 has chosen c or d. Player 1, however, does not know whether player 2 has chosen c or d, so player 1 faces information set h_1 after choosing a. Hence, $h_{2.1}$ and $h_{2.2}$ are information sets that belong only to player 2, whereas h_1 is an information set that belongs only to player 1. Note that information sets $h_1, h_{2.1}$ and $h_{2.2}$ follow $\emptyset$, and that player 2's information sets $h_{2.1}$ and $h_{2.2}$ are simultaneous with player 1's information set h_1. At $h_1, h_{2.1}$ and $h_{2.2}$, players 1 and 2 simultaneously make a choice, after which the game ends.

2.3 Strategies

In the literature, a *strategy* for player i in a dynamic game is usually defined as a complete choice plan that specifies a choice for player i at *each* of his information sets – also at those information sets that cannot be reached if player i implements this strategy. Indeed, this is the original definition introduced by Von Neumann [27] which has later become the standard definition of a strategy in game theory. There is however a conceptual problem with this classical definition of a strategy, namely how to interpret the specification of choices at information sets that cannot be reached under this same strategy. Rubinstein [39] interprets these latter choices not as planned choices by player i, but rather as the beliefs that i's opponents have about i's choices at these information sets. Rubinstein thus proposes to separate a strategy for player i into a *choice part* and a *belief part*: the choices for player i at information sets that *can* be reached under the strategy are viewed as planned choices by player i, and constitute what Rubinstein calls player i's *plan of action*, whereas the choices at the remaining information sets are viewed as the opponents' beliefs about these choices. A nice discussion of this interpretation of a strategy can be found in [9] – another chapter in this volume. In fact, a substantial part of Bonanno's chapter concentrates on the concept of a strategy in dynamic games, and explores the subtleties that arise if one wishes to incorporate this definition of a strategy into a formal epistemic model. For more details on this issue we refer to Bonanno's chapter [9].

In this chapter, however, we wish to clearly distinguish between *choices* and *beliefs*, as we think these are two fundamentally distinct objects. More precisely, our definition of a strategy concentrates only on choices for player i at information sets that can actually be reached if player i sticks to his plan. That is, our definition of a strategy corresponds to what Rubinstein [39] calls a *plan of action*.

Formally, for every $h, h' \in H_i$ such that h precedes h', let $c_i(h, h')$ be the choice at h for player i that leads to h'. Note that $c_i(h, h')$ is unique by perfect recall. Consider a subset $\hat{H}_i \subseteq H_i$, not necessarily containing all information sets for player i, and a function s_i that assigns to every $h \in \hat{H}_i$ some choice $s_i(h) \in C_i(h)$. We say that s_i *possibly reaches* an information set h if at every $h' \in \hat{H}_i$ preceding h we have that $s_i(h') = c_i(h', h)$. By $H_i(s_i)$ we denote the collection of player i information sets that s_i possibly reaches. A *strategy* for player i is a function s_i, assigning to every $h \in \hat{H}_i \subseteq H_i$ some choice $s_i(h) \in C_i(h)$, such that $\hat{H}_i = H_i(s_i)$.

For a given information set h, denote by $S_i(h)$ the set of strategies for player i that possibly reach h. By $S(h)$ we denote the set of strategy profiles $(s_i)_{i \in I}$ that reach some history in h.

In the game of Fig. 1, the strategies for player 1 are (a, e), (a, f) and b, whereas the strategies for player 2 are (c, g), (c, h), (d, i) and (d, j). Note that within our terminology, b is a complete strategy for player 1 as player 1, by choosing b, will make sure that his subsequent information set h_1 cannot be reached, and hence we do not have to specify what player 1 would do if h_1 would be reached. Note also that player 1 cannot make his choice dependent on whether $h_{2.1}$ or $h_{2.2}$ is reached, since these are information sets for player 2 only, and player 1 does not know which of these information sets is reached. As such, (a, e) is a complete strategy for player 1. For player 2, (c, g) is a complete strategy as by choosing c player 2 will make sure that $h_{2.2}$ cannot be reached, and hence we do not have to specify what player 2 would do if $h_{2.2}$ would be reached. Similarly for his other three strategies.

In this example, the sets of strategies that possibly reach the various information sets are as follows:

$$S_1(\emptyset) = S_1, \qquad S_2(\emptyset) = S_2,$$
$$S_1(h_1) = S_1(h_{2.1}) = S_1(h_{2.2}) = \{(a, e), (a, f)\},$$
$$S_2(h_1) = S_2, \qquad S_2(h_{2.1}) = \{(c, g), (c, h)\}, \qquad S_2(h_{2.2}) = \{(d, i), (d, j)\}.$$

2.4   Epistemic Model

We say that a strategy is *rational* for you at a certain information set if it is optimal at that information set, *given your conditional belief there* about the opponent's strategy choice. In order to believe that your *opponent* chooses rationally at a certain information set, you must therefore not only hold conditional beliefs about the opponent's strategy choice, but also conditional beliefs about the opponent's conditional beliefs about your strategy choice. This is what we call a *second-order* belief. Moreover, if we go one step further and want to model the event that you believe that your opponent believes that you choose rationally, we need not only your belief about the opponent's beliefs about your strategy choice, but also your belief about the opponent's beliefs about your beliefs about the opponent's strategy choice – that is, your *third-order* belief. Consequently, formally defining the idea of *common belief in future rationality* requires us to consider *infinite belief hierarchies,* specifying your conditional beliefs about the opponent's strategy choice, your conditional beliefs about the opponent's conditional beliefs about your strategy choice, and so on *ad infinitum.*

A problem with infinite belief hierarchies is that writing them down explicitly is an impossible task, since we would need to write down infinitely many beliefs.

So is there a way to efficiently *encode* such infinite belief hierarchies without writing too much? The answer is "yes", as we will see right now. Note that your belief hierarchy specifies first-order beliefs about the opponent's strategy choice, second-order beliefs about the opponent's first-order beliefs about your strategy choice, third-order beliefs about the opponent's second-order beliefs, and so on. Hence we conclude that your belief hierarchy specifies conditional beliefs about the opponent's strategy choice *and the opponent's belief hierarchy.* Now let us call every belief hierarchy a *type.* Then, every type can be identified with its conditional beliefs about the opponent's strategy choice *and the opponent's type.* This elegant and powerful idea goes back to Harsanyi (1967–1968), who used it to model infinite belief hierarchies in games with incomplete information.

Let us now implement this idea of encoding infinite belief hierarchies formally. Fix some finite dynamic game Γ with two players.

Definition 2 (Finite Epistemic Model). *A finite epistemic model for the game Γ is a tuple $M = (T_1, T_2, b_1, b_2)$ where*

(a) T_i *is the finite set of types for player i, and*
(b) b_i *assigns to every type $t_i \in T_i$ and every information set $h \in H_i$ some probabilistic belief $b_i(t_i, h) \in \Delta(S_j(h) \times T_j)$ about opponent j's strategy-type pairs.*

Remember that $S_j(h)$ denotes the set of strategies for opponent j that possibly reach h. By $\Delta(S_j(h) \times T_j)$ we denote the set of probability distributions on $S_j(h) \times T_j$. So, within an epistemic model every type holds at each of his information sets a conditional belief about the opponent's strategy choice and the opponent's type, as we discussed above. For every type $t_i \in T_i$ we can now *derive* its complete belief hierarchy from the belief functions b_i and b_j. Namely, type t_i holds at information set $h \in H_i$ a conditional belief $b_i(t_i, h)$ on $S_j(h) \times T_j$. By taking the marginal of $b_i(t_i, h)$ on $S_j(h)$ we obtain t_i's *first-order* belief at h on j's strategy choice. Moreover, t_i holds at information set $h \in H_i$ a conditional belief about j's possible types. As each of j's types t_j holds first-order conditional beliefs on i's strategy choices, we can thus derive from b_i and b_j the *second-order* conditional belief that t_i holds at $h \in H_i$ about j's first-order beliefs about i's strategy choice. By continuing this procedure we can thus deduce, for every type t_i in the model, each of its belief levels by making use of the belief functions b_i and b_j. In this way, the epistemic model above can be viewed as a short and convenient way to *encode* the infinite belief hierarchy of a player.

By means of this epistemic model we can in particular model the *belief revision* of players during the game. Consider two different information sets h and h' for player i, where h' comes after h. Note that type t_i's conditional belief at h' about j's strategy choice may be different from his conditional belief at h, and hence a type t_i may *revise* his belief about j's strategy choice as the game moves from h to h'. Moreover, t_i's conditional belief at h' about j's *type* may be different from his conditional belief at h, and hence a type t_i may *revise* his belief about j's *type* – and hence about j's conditional beliefs – as the game moves from h to h'. So, all different kinds of belief revisions – about the opponent's strategy, but also about the opponent's beliefs – can be captured within this epistemic model.

Table 2. An epistemic model for the game in Fig. 1

Types	$T_1 = \{t_1, t_1'\}, T_2 = \{t_2\}$
Beliefs for player 1	$b_1(t_1, \emptyset) = ((c, h), t_2)$ $b_1(t_1, h_1) = ((c, h), t_2)$ $b_1(t_1', \emptyset) = ((d, i), t_2)$ $b_1(t_1', h_1) = ((d, i), t_2)$
Beliefs for player 2	$b_2(t_2, \emptyset) = (b, t_1)$ $b_2(t_2, h_{2.1}) = ((a, f), t_1')$ $b_2(t_2, h_{2.2}) = ((a, f), t_1')$

As an illustration, consider the epistemic model in Table 2, which is an epistemic model for the game in Fig. 1. So, we consider two possible types for player 1, t_1 and t_1', and one possible type for player 2, t_2. Player 2's type t_2 believes at the beginning of the game that player 1 chooses b and is of type t_1, whereas at $h_{2.1}$ and $h_{2.2}$ this type believes that player 1 chooses strategy (a, f) and is of type t_1'. In particular, type t_2 revises his belief about player 1's strategy choice if the game moves from $\emptyset$ to $h_{2.1}$ or $h_{2.2}$. Note that player 1's type t_1 believes that player 2 chooses strategy (c, h), whereas his other type t_1' believes that player 2 chooses strategy (d, i). So, type t_2 believes at $\emptyset$ that player 1 believes that player 2 chooses (c, h), whereas t_2 believes at $h_{2.1}$ and $h_{2.2}$ that player 1 believes that player 2 chooses (d, i). Hence, player 2's type t_2 also revises his belief about player 1's *belief* if the game moves from $\emptyset$ to $h_{2.1}$ or $h_{2.2}$. By continuing in this fashion, we can derive the full belief hierarchy for type t_2. Similarly for the other types in this model.

Note that in our definition of an epistemic model we require the sets of types to be *finite*. This imposes a restriction on the possible belief hierarchies we can encode, since not every belief hierarchy can be derived from a type within an epistemic model with *finite* sets of types. For some belief hierarchies we would need *infinitely* many types to encode them. Belief hierarchies that *can* be derived from a *finite* epistemic model will be called *finitely generated*.

Definition 3 (Finitely Generated Belief Hierarchy). *A belief hierarchy* β_i *for player i is **finitely generated** if there is some finite epistemic model* $M = (T_1, T_2, b_1, b_2)$, *and some type $t_i \in T_i$ in that model, such that β_i is the belief hierarchy induced by t_i within M.*

Throughout this chapter we will restrict attention to *finite* epistemic models, and hence to *finitely generated* belief hierarchies. We will see in Sect. 4 that this is not a serious restriction within the context of *common belief in future rationality*, as every strategy that is optimal for *some* belief hierarchy – not necessarily finitely generated – that expresses *common belief in future rationality*, is also optimal for some *finitely generated* belief hierarchy that expresses *common belief in future rationality*. Moreover, finitely generated belief hierarchies are much easier to work with than those that are not finitely generated.

2.5   Common Belief in Future Rationality: Formal Definition

Remember that *common belief in future rationality* states that you always believe that the opponent chooses rationally now and in the future, you always believe that the opponent always believes that you choose rationally now and in the future, and so on, *ad infinitum*. Within an epistemic model we can state these conditions formally.

We first define what it means for a strategy s_i to be optimal for a type t_i at a given information set h. Consider a type t_i, a strategy s_i and an information set $h \in H_i(s_i)$ that is possibly reached by s_i. By $u_i(s_i, t_i \mid h)$ we denote the expected utility from choosing s_i under the conditional belief that t_i holds at h about the opponent's strategy choice.

Definition 4 (Optimality at a Given Information Set). *Consider a type t_i, a strategy s_i and a history $h \in H_i(s_i)$. Strategy s_i is optimal for type t_i at h, if $u_i(s_i, t_i \mid h) \geq u_i(s'_i, t_i \mid h)$ for all $s'_i \in S_i(h)$.*

Remember that $S_i(h)$ is the set of player i strategies that possibly reach h. So, not only do we require that player i's single choice at h is optimal at this information set, but we require that player i's *complete future choice plan* from h on is optimal, given his belief at h about the opponent's strategies. That is, optimality refers both to player i's choice at h and all of his future choices following h.

Bonanno [9] uses a different definition of optimality in his chapter, as he only requires the choice at h to be optimal at h, without requiring optimality for the future choices following h. Hence, Bonanno's definition can be seen as a *local* optimality condition, whereas we use a *global* optimality condition here.

Note that, in order to verify whether strategy s_i is optimal for the type t_i at h, we only need to look at t_i's *first-order* conditional belief at h about j's strategy choice, not at t_i's higher-order beliefs about j's beliefs. In particular, it follows that every strategy s_i that is optimal at h for *some* type t_i – possibly not finitely generated – is also optimal for a *finitely generated* type t'_i. Take, namely, any finitely generated type t'_i that has the same first-order beliefs about j's strategy choices as t_i. We can now define belief in the opponent's future rationality.

Definition 5 (Belief in the Opponent's Future Rationality). *Consider a type t_i and an information set $h \in H_i$. Type t_i believes at h in j's future* rationality if $b_i(t_i, h)$ only assigns positive probability to j's strategy-type pairs (s_j, t_j) where s_j is optimal for t_j at every $h' \in H_j(s_j)$ that weakly follows h. Type t_i believes in the opponent's future rationality if he does so at every information set $h \in H_i$.

So, to be precise, a type that believes in the opponent's future rationality believes that the opponent chooses rationally now (if the opponent makes a choice at a simultaneous information set), and at every information set that follows. As such, the correct terminology would be "belief in the opponent's *present* and future rationality", but we stick to "belief in the opponent's future rationality" so as to keep the name short.

Note also that *belief in the opponent's future rationality* means that a player *always* believes – at each of his information sets – that his opponent will choose rationally in the future. This corresponds exactly to what Baltag, Smets and Zvesper [5] call *stable belief in dynamic rationality*, although they restrict to non-probabilistic beliefs in games with perfect information. In their terminology, *stable belief* means that a player believes so at every information set in the game, whereas *dynamic rationality* means that at a given information set, a player chooses rationally from that moment on – hence mimicking our condition of optimality at an information set. So, when we say *belief* in *belief in the opponent's future rationality* we actually mean *stable belief* in the sense of [5].

We can now formally define the other conditions in common belief in future rationality in an inductive manner.

Definition 6 (Common Belief in Future Rationality). *Consider a finite epistemic model $M = (T_1, T_2, b_1, b_2)$.*

(Induction start) *A type $t_i \in T_i$ is said to express 1-fold belief in future rationality if t_i believes in j's future rationality.*

(Induction step) *For every $k \geq 2$, a type $t_i \in T_i$ is said to express k-fold belief in future rationality if at every information set $h \in H_i$, the belief $b_i(t_i, h)$ only assigns positive probability to j's types t_j that express $(k-1)$-fold belief in future rationality.*

Type $t_i \in T_i$ is said to express **common belief in future rationality** if it expresses k-fold belief in future rationality for all k.

Finally, we define those strategies that can rationally be chosen under *common belief in future rationality*. We say that a strategy s_i is *rational* for a type t_i if s_i is optimal for t_i at every $h \in H_i(s_i)$. In the literature, this is often called *sequential rationality*. We say that strategy s_i can *rationally be chosen under common belief in future rationality* if there is some epistemic model $M = (T_1, T_2, b_1, b_2)$, and some type $t_i \in T_i$, such that t_i expresses *common belief in future rationality*, and s_i is rational for t_i.

3   Checking Common Belief in Future Rationality

Some people have criticized the concept of *common belief in rationality*, because one has to verify *infinitely many* conditions in order to conclude that a given belief hierarchy expresses *common belief in rationality*. The same could be said about *common belief in future rationality*. We will show in this section that this is *not* true for *finitely generated* belief hierarchies. Namely, verifying whether a *finitely generated* belief hierarchy expresses *common belief in future rationality* or not only requires checking *finitely* many conditions, and can usually be done very quickly. To that purpose we present a reasoning procedure with finitely many steps which, for a given finitely generated belief hierarchy, tells us whether that belief hierarchy expresses *common belief in future rationality* or not.

Consider an epistemic model $M = (T_1, T_2, b_1, b_2)$ with finitely many types for both players. For every type $t_i \in T_i$, let $T_j(t_i)$ be the set of types for player j that type t_i deems possible at some of his information sets. That is, $T_j(t_i)$ contains all types $t_j \in T_j$ such that $b_i(t_i, h)(c_j, t_j) > 0$ for some $h \in H_i$ and some $c_j \in C_j$. We recursively define the sets of types $T_j^k(t_i)$ and $T_i^k(t_i)$ as follows.

Algorithm 1 (Relevant Types for t_i) *Consider a finite dynamic game Γ with two players, and a finite epistemic model $M = (T_1, T_2, b_1, b_2)$ for Γ. Fix a type $t_i \in T_i$.*

(Induction start) *Let $T_i^1(t_i) := \{t_i\}$.*
(Induction step) *For every even round $k \geq 2$, let $T_j^k(t_i) := \cup_{t_i \in T_i^{k-1}(t_i)} T_j(t_i)$.*
For every odd round $k \geq 3$, let $T_i^k(t_i) := \cup_{t_j \in T_j^{k-1}(t_i)} T_i(t_j)$.

So, $T_j^2(t_i)$ contains all the opponent's types that t_i deems possible, $T_i^3(t_i)$ contains all types for player i which are deemed possible by some type t_j that t_i deems possible, and so on. This procedure eventually yields the sets of types $T_i^*(t_i) = \cup_k T_i^k(t_i)$ and $T_j^*(t_i) = \cup_k T_j^k(t_i)$. These sets $T_i^*(t_i)$ and $T_j^*(t_i)$ contain precisely those types that enter t_i's belief hierarchy in some of its levels, and we will call these the *relevant* types for t_i. Since there are only finitely many types in M, there must be some round K such that $T_j^*(t_i) = T_j^K(t_i)$, and $T_i^*(t_i) = T_i^{K+1}(t_i)$. That is, this procedure must stop after finitely many rounds.

If we would allow for *infinite* epistemic models, then the algorithm above could be extended accordingly through the use of higher ordinals and transfinite induction. But since we restrict our attention to finite epistemic models here, usual induction will suffice for our purposes.

Now, suppose that type t_i expresses *common belief in future rationality*. Then, in particular, t_i must believe in j's future rationality. Moreover, t_i must only consider possible opponent's types t_j that believe in i's future rationality, that is, every type in $T_j^2(t_i)$ must believe in the opponent's future rationality. Also, t_i must only consider possible types for j that only consider possible types for i that believe in j's future rationality. In other words, all types in $T_i^3(t_i)$ must believe in the opponent's future rationality. By continuing in this fashion, we conclude that all types in $T_i^*(t_i)$ and $T_j^*(t_i)$ believe in the opponent's future rationality. So, we see that every type t_i that expresses *common belief in future rationality*, must have the property that all types in $T_i^*(t_i)$ and $T_j^*(t_i)$ believe in the opponent's future rationality.

However, we can show that the opposite is also true! Consider, namely, a type t_i within a finite epistemic model $M = (T_1, T_2, b_1, b_2)$ for which all types in $T_i^*(t_i)$

and $T_j^*(t_i)$ believe in the opponent's future rationality. Then, in particular, every type in $T_i^1(t_i)$ believes in j's future rationality. As $T_i^1(t_i) = \{t_i\}$, it follows that t_i believes in j's future rationality. Also, every type in $T_j^2(t_i)$ believes in the opponent's future rationality. As $T_j^2(t_i)$ contains exactly those types for j that t_i deems possible, it follows that t_i only deems possible types for j that believe in i's future rationality. By continuing in this way, we conclude that t_i expresses *common belief in future rationality*. The two insights above lead to the following theorem.

Theorem 1 (Checking Common Belief in Future Rationality). *Consider a finite dynamic game Γ with two players, and a finite epistemic model $M = (T_1, T_2, b_1, b_2)$ for Γ. Then, a type t_i expresses common belief in future rationality, if and only if, all types in $T_i^*(t_i)$ and $T_j^*(t_i)$ believe in the opponent's future rationality.*

Note that checking whether all types in $T_i^*(t_i)$ and $T_j^*(t_i)$ believe in the opponent's future rationality can be done within finitely many steps. We have seen above, namely, that the sets of relevant types for t_i – that is, the sets $T_i^*(t_i)$ and $T_j^*(t_i)$ – can be derived within finitely many steps, and only contain finitely many types. So, within a finite epistemic model, checking for *common belief in future rationality* only requires finitely many reasoning steps. Consequently, if we take a finitely generated belief hierarchy, then it only takes finitely many steps to verify whether it expresses *common belief in future rationality* or not.

4   Reasoning Towards Common Belief in Future Rationality

In this section our goal is more ambitious, in that we wish to explore *how* a player can reason his way towards a belief hierarchy that expresses *common belief in future rationality*. More precisely, we offer a reasoning procedure that generates a finite set of belief hierarchies such that, for *every* strategy that can rationally be chosen under *common belief in future rationality*, there will be a belief hierarchy in this set which supports that strategy. In that sense, the reasoning procedure yields an *exhaustive* set of belief hierarchies.

The reasoning procedure will be illustrated in the second part of this section by means of an example. The reader should feel free to jump back and forth between the description of the procedure and the example while reading the various steps of the reasoning procedure. This could certainly help to clarify the different steps of the procedure. On purpose, we have separated the example from the description of the procedure, so as to enhance readability.

4.1   Procedure

To see how this reasoning procedure works, let us start with exploring the consequences of "believing in the opponent's future rationality". For that purpose, we will heavily make use of the following lemma, which appears in [30].

Lemma 1 (Pearce's Lemma (1984)). *Consider a static two-person game* $\Gamma = (S_1, S_2, u_1, u_2)$, *where* S_i *is player* i's *finite set of strategies, and* u_i *is player* i's *utility function. Then, a strategy* s_i *is optimal for some probabilistic belief* $b_i \in \Delta(S_j)$, *if and only if,* s_i *is not strictly dominated by a randomized strategy.*

Here, a *randomized strategy* r_i for player i is a probability distribution on i's strategies, that is, i selects each of his strategies s_i' with probability $r_i(s_i')$. And we say that the strategy s_i is *strictly dominated* by the randomized strategy r_i if r_i always yields a higher expected utility than s_i against any strategy s_j of player j.

One way to prove Pearce's lemma is by using linear programming techniques. More precisely, one can formulate the question whether s_i is optimal for some probabilistic belief as a linear program. Subsequently, one can write down the dual program, and show that this dual program corresponds to the question whether s_i is strictly dominated by a randomized strategy. By the duality theorem of linear programming, which states that the original linear program and the dual program have the same optimal value (see, for instance [16]), it follows that s_i is optimal for some probabilistic belief, if and only if, it is not strictly dominated by a randomized strategy.

Now, suppose that within a dynamic game, player i believes at some information set $h \in H_i$ that opponent j chooses rationally now and in the future. Then, player i will at h only assign positive probability to strategies s_j for player j that are optimal, at every $h' \in H_j$ weakly following h, for *some* belief that j can hold at h' about i's strategy choice.

Consider such a future information set $h' \in H_j$; let $\Gamma^0(h') = (S_j(h'), S_i(h'))$ be the *full decision problem* for player j at h', at which he can only choose strategies in $S_j(h')$ that possibly reach h', and believes that player i can only choose strategies in $S_i(h')$ that possibly reach h'. From Lemma 1 we know that a strategy s_j is optimal for player j at h' for some belief about i's strategy choice, if and only if, s_j is *not strictly dominated* within the full decision problem $\Gamma^0(h') = (S_j(h'), S_i(h'))$ by a *randomized* strategy r_j.

Putting these things together, we see that if i believes at h in j's future rationality, then i assigns at h only positive probability to j's strategies s_j that are not strictly dominated within any full decision problem $\Gamma^0(h')$ for player j that weakly follows h. Or, put differently, player i assigns at h probability zero to any opponent's strategy s_j that *is* strictly dominated at some full decision problem $\Gamma^0(h')$ for player j that weakly follows h. That is, we eliminate any such opponent's strategy s_j from player i's full decision problem $\Gamma^0(h) = (S_i(h), S_j(h))$ at h.

We thus see that, if player i believes in j's future rationality, then player i eliminates, at each of his full decision problems $\Gamma^0(h)$, those opponent's strategies s_j that are strictly dominated within some full decision problem $\Gamma^0(h')$ for player j that weakly follows h. Let us denote by $\Gamma^1(h)$ the reduced decision problem for player i at h that remains after eliminating such opponent's strategies s_j from $\Gamma^0(h)$.

Next, suppose that player i does not only believe in j's future rationality, but also believes that j believes in i's future rationality. Take an information set h for player i, and an arbitrary information set h' for player j that weakly follows h. As i believes that j believes in i's future rationality, player i believes that player j, at information set h', believes that player i will only choose strategies from $\Gamma^1(h')$. Moreover, as i believes in j's future rationality, player i believes that j will choose rationally at h'. Together, these two insights imply that player i believes at h that j will only choose strategies s_j that are not strictly dominated within $\Gamma^1(h')$. Or, equivalently, player i eliminates from his decision problem $\Gamma^1(h)$ all strategies s_j for player j that are strictly dominated within $\Gamma^1(h')$. As this holds for every player j information set h' that weakly follows h, we see that player i will eliminate, from each of his decision problems $\Gamma^1(h)$, all opponent's strategies s_j that are strictly dominated within some decision problem $\Gamma^1(h')$ for player j that weakly follows h.

Hence, if player i expresses up to 2-fold belief in future rationality, then he will eliminate, from each of his decision problems $\Gamma^1(h)$, all opponent's strategies s_j that are strictly dominated within some decision problem $\Gamma^1(h')$ for player j that weakly follows h. Let us denote by $\Gamma^2(h)$ the reduced decision problem for player i that remains after eliminating such opponent's strategies s_j from $\Gamma^1(h)$.

By continuing in this fashion, we conclude that if player i expresses up to k-fold belief in future rationality – that is, expresses 1-fold, 2-fold, ... until k-fold belief in future rationality – then he believes at every information set $h \in H_i$ that opponent j will only choose strategies from the reduced decision problem $\Gamma^k(h)$. This leads to the following reasoning procedure, known as the *backward dominance procedure* [37]. The procedure is closely related to Penta's [31] *backwards rationalizability* procedure, and is equivalent to Chen and Micali's [15] *backward robust solution*.

Algorithm 2 (Backward Dominance Procedure). *Consider a finite dynamic game Γ with two players.*

(Induction start) *For every information set h, let $\Gamma^0(h) = (S_1(h), S_2(h))$ be the full decision problem at h.*

(Induction step) *For every $k \geq 1$, and every information set h, let $\Gamma^k(h) = (S_1^k(h), S_2^k(h))$ be the reduced decision problem which is obtained from $\Gamma^{k-1}(h)$ by eliminating, for both players i, those strategies s_i that are strictly dominated at some decision problem $\Gamma^{k-1}(h')$ weakly following h at which i is active.*

Suppose that h is an information set at which player i is active. Then, the interpretation of the reduced decision problem $\Gamma^k(h) = (S_1^k(h), S_2^k(h))$ is that at round k of the procedure, player i believes at h that opponent j chooses some strategy in $S_j^k(h)$. As the sets $S_j^k(h)$ become smaller as k becomes bigger, the procedure thus puts more and more restrictions on player i's conditional beliefs about j's strategy choice. However, since in a finite dynamic game there are only finitely many information sets and strategies, this procedure must stop after finitely many rounds! Namely, there must be some round K such that

$S_1^{K+1}(h) = S_1^K(h)$ and $S_2^{K+1}(h) = S_2^K(h)$ for all information sets h. But then, $S_j^k(h) = S_j^K(h)$ for all information sets h and every $k \geq K + 1$, and hence the procedure will not put more restrictions on i's conditional beliefs about j's strategy choice after round K. This reasoning procedure is therefore a *finite* procedure, guaranteed to end within finitely many steps.

Above we have argued that if player i reasons in accordance with *common belief in future rationality*, then his belief at information set h about j's strategy choice will only assign positive probability to strategies in $S_j^K(h)$. As a consequence, he can only rationally choose a strategy s_i that is optimal, at every information set $h \in H_i$, for such a conditional belief that only considers j's strategy choices in $S_j^K(h)$. But then, by Lemma 1, strategy s_i must not be strictly dominated at any information set $h \in H_i$ if we restrict to j's strategy choices in $S_j^K(h)$. That is, s_i must be in $S_i^K(\emptyset)$, where $\emptyset$ denotes the beginning of the game. We can thus conclude that every strategy s_i that can rationally be chosen under *common belief in future rationality* must be in $S_i^K(\emptyset)$ – that is, must survive the backward dominance procedure at the beginning of the game.

We can show, however, that the converse is also true! That is, every strategy in $S_i^K(\emptyset)$ can be supported by a belief hierarchy that expresses *common belief in future rationality*. Suppose, namely, that player i has performed the backward dominance procedure in his mind, which has left him with the strategies $S_i^K(h)$ and $S_j^K(h)$ at every information set h of the game. Then, by construction, every strategy $s_i \in S_i^K(h)$ is not strictly dominated on $S_j^K(h')$, for every information set h' weakly following h at which i is active. Thus, by Lemma 1, every strategy $s_i \in S_i^K(h)$ is optimal, at every $h' \in H_i$ weakly following h, for some probabilistic belief $b_i^{s_i,h}(h') \in \Delta(S_j^K(h'))$. Similarly, every strategy $s_j \in S_j^K(h)$ will be optimal, at every $h' \in H_j$ weakly following h, for some probabilistic belief $b_j^{s_j,h}(h') \in \Delta(S_i^K(h'))$.

First, we define the sets of types

$$T_i = \{t_i^{s_i,h} : h \in H \text{ and } s_i \in S_i^K(h)\} \text{ and}$$
$$T_j = \{t_j^{s_j,h} : h \in H \text{ and } s_j \in S_j^K(h)\},$$

where H denotes the collection of all information sets in the game. The superscript s_i, h in $t_i^{s_i,h}$ indicates that, by our construction of the beliefs that we will give in the next paragraph, the strategy s_i will be optimal for the type $t_i^{s_i,h}$ at all player i information sets weakly following h.

Subsequently, we define the conditional beliefs of the types about the opponent's strategy-type pairs to be

$$b_i(t_i^{s_i,h}, h')(s_j, t_j) = \begin{cases} b_i^{s_i,h}(h')(s_j), & \text{if } t_j = t_j^{s_j,h'} \\ 0, & \text{otherwise} \end{cases}$$

for every $h' \in H_i$, and

$$b_j(t_j^{s_j,h}, h')(s_i, t_i) = \begin{cases} b_j^{s_j,h}(h')(s_i), & \text{if } t_i = t_i^{s_i,h'} \\ 0, & \text{otherwise} \end{cases}$$

for all $h' \in H_j$.

This yields an epistemic model M. Hence, every type $t_i^{s_i,h}$ for player i, at every information set $h' \in H_i$, only considers possible strategy-type pairs $(s_j, t_j^{s_j,h'})$ where $s_j \in S_j^K(h')$, and his conditional belief at h' about j's strategy choice is given by $b_i^{s_i,h}(h')$. By construction, strategy $s_i \in S_i^K(h)$ is optimal for $b_i^{s_i,h}(h')$ at every $h' \in H_i$ weakly following h. As a consequence, strategy $s_i \in S_i^K(h)$ is optimal for type $t_i^{s_i,h}$ at every $h' \in H_i$ weakly following h. The same holds for player j. Since type $t_i^{s_i,h}$, at every information set $h' \in H_i$, only considers possible strategy-type pairs $(s_j, t_j^{s_j,h'})$ where $s_j \in S_j^K(h')$, it follows that type $t_i^{s_i,h}$, at every information set $h' \in H_i$, only considers possible strategy-type pairs $(s_j, t_j^{s_j,h'})$ where strategy s_j is optimal for $t_j^{s_j,h'}$ at every $h'' \in H_j$ weakly following h'. That is, type $t_i^{s_i,h}$ believes in the opponent's future rationality.

Since this holds for every type $t_i^{s_i,h}$ in this epistemic model M, it follows directly from Theorem 1 that every type in the epistemic model M above expresses *common belief in future rationality*.

Now, take some strategy $s_i \in S_i^K(\emptyset)$, which survives the backward dominance procedure at the beginning of the game. Then, we know from our insights above that s_i is optimal for the type $t_i^{s_i,\emptyset}$ at every $h \in H_i$ weakly following $\emptyset$ – that is, at *every* $h \in H_i$ in the game. As the type $t_i^{s_i,\emptyset}$ expresses *common belief in future rationality*, we thus see that every strategy $s_i \in S_i^K(\emptyset)$ can rationally be chosen by some type $t_i^{s_i,\emptyset}$ that expresses *common belief in future rationality*. In other words, for every strategy $s_i \in S_i^K(\emptyset)$ that survives the backward dominance procedure at $\emptyset$, there is a belief hierarchy expressing *common belief in future rationality* – namely the belief hierarchy induced by $t_i^{s_i,\emptyset}$ in the epistemic model M – for which s_i is optimal. This insight thus leads to the following theorem.

Theorem 2 (Reasoning Towards Common Belief in Future Rationality). *Consider a finite dynamic game Γ with two players. Suppose we apply the backward dominance procedure until it terminates at round K. That is, $S_1^{K+1}(h) = S_1^K(h)$ and $S_2^{K+1}(h) = S_2^K(h)$ for all information sets h. For every information set h, both players i, every strategy $s_i \in S_i^K(h)$, and every information set $h' \in H_i$ weakly following h, let $b_i^{s_i,h}(h') \in \Delta(S_j^K(h'))$ be a probabilistic belief on $S_j^K(h')$ for which s_i is optimal. For both players i, define the set of types*

$$T_i = \{t_i^{s_i,h} : h \in H \text{ and } s_i \in S_i^K(h)\},$$

and for every type $t_i^{s_i,h}$ and every $h' \in H_i$ define the conditional belief

$$b_i(t_i^{s_i,h}, h')(s_j, t_j) = \begin{cases} b_i^{s_i,h}(h')(s_j), & \text{if } t_j = t_j^{s_j,h'} \\ 0, & \text{otherwise} \end{cases}$$

about j's strategy-type pairs. Then, all types in this epistemic model M express common belief in future rationality. Moreover,

(1) *for every strategy $s_i \in S_i^K(\emptyset)$ that survives the backward dominance procedure at $\emptyset$ there is a belief hierarchy in M expressing common belief in future rationality for which s_i is optimal at all $h \in H_i$ possibly reached by s_i – namely the belief hierarchy induced by $t_i^{s_i,\emptyset}$;*

(2) *for every strategy $s_i \notin S_i^K(\emptyset)$ that does not survive the backward dominance procedure at $\emptyset$, there is no belief hierarchy whatsoever expressing common belief in future rationality for which s_i is optimal at all $h \in H_i$ possibly reached by s_i.*

So, whenever a strategy s_i *is* optimal for some belief hierarchy that expresses *common belief in future rationality*, this reasoning procedure generates one. In that sense, we can say that this reasoning procedure yields an "exhaustive" set of belief hierarchies. Note also that this is a reasoning procedure with *finitely* many steps, as the backward dominance procedure terminates after finitely many rounds, after which we only have to construct finitely many types – one for each information set h and each surviving strategy $s_i \in S_i^K(h)$ at h.

The theorem above also shows that *finitely generated* belief hierarchies are sufficient when it comes to exploring *common belief in future rationality* within a finite dynamic game. Suppose, namely, that some strategy s_i is optimal, at all $h \in H_i$ possibly reached by s_i, for *some* belief hierarchy – not necessarily finitely generated – that expresses *common belief in future rationality*. Then, according to part (2) in the theorem, strategy s_i must be in $S_i^K(\emptyset)$. But in that case, the procedure above generates a finitely generated belief hierarchy for which the strategy s_i is optimal – namely the belief hierarchy induced by the type $t_i^{s_i,\emptyset}$ within the finite epistemic model M. So we see that, whenever a strategy s_i is optimal for *some* belief hierarchy – not necessarily finitely generated – that expresses *common belief in future rationality*, then it is also optimal for a *finitely generated* belief hierarchy that expresses *common belief in future rationality*.

Corollary 1 (Finitely Generated Belief Hierarchies are Sufficient). *Consider a finite dynamic game Γ with two players. If a strategy s_i is optimal for* **some** *belief hierarchy – not necessarily finitely generated – that expresses common belief in future rationality, then it is also optimal for a* **finitely generated** *belief hierarchy that expresses common belief in future rationality.*

Here, whenever we say that s_i is optimal for some belief hierarchy, we mean that it is optimal for this belief hierarchy at every information set $h \in H_i$ possibly reached by s_i. This corollary thus states that, if we wish to verify which strategies can rationally be chosen under common belief in future rationality, then it is sufficient to stick to *finite* epistemic models. In that sense, the corollary bears a close resemblance to the *finite model property* in modal logic (see, for instance, [20]).

4.2 Example

We shall now illustrate the reasoning procedure above by means of an example. Consider the dynamic game in Fig. 2. At the beginning, player 1 can choose

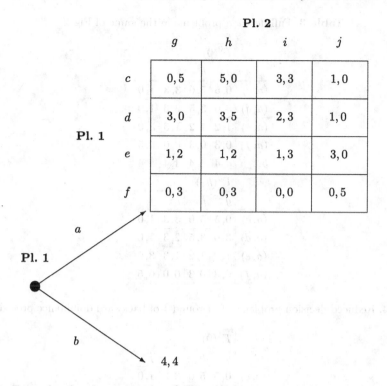

Fig. 2. Example of a dynamic game $\emptyset$ denotes the beginning of the game, and h_1 denotes the information set that follows the choice a

between a and b. If he chooses b, the game ends, and the utilities for players 1 and 2 will be $(4, 4)$. If he chooses a, the game continues, and players 1 and 2 must simultaneously choose from $\{c, d, e, f\}$ and $\{g, h, i, j\}$, respectively. The utilities for both players in that case can be found in the table following choice a. Let us denote the beginning of the game by $\emptyset$, and the information set following choice a by h_1. Hence, $\emptyset$ and h_1 are the two information sets in the game. At $\emptyset$ only player 1 makes a choice, whereas both players 1 and 2 are active at h_1.

We will first run the backward dominance procedure for this example, and then build an epistemic model on the basis of that procedure, following the construction in Theorem 2.

There are two information sets in this game, namely $\emptyset$ and h_1. The full decision problems at both information sets are given in Table 3.

We will now start the backward dominance procedure. In round 1, we see that within the full decision problem $\Gamma^0(\emptyset)$ at the beginning of the game, the strategies $(a, d), (a, e)$ and (a, f) are strictly dominated for player 1 by b. So, we eliminate $(a, d), (a, e)$ and (a, f) from $\Gamma^0(\emptyset)$, but not – yet – from $\Gamma^0(h_1)$, as h_1 follows $\emptyset$. Moreover, within the full decision problem $\Gamma^0(h_1)$ at h_1, player 1's strategy (a, f) is strictly dominated by (a, d) and (a, e), and hence we eliminate (a, f) from $\Gamma^0(h_1)$ and $\Gamma^0(\emptyset)$. Note, however, that we already eliminated (a, f) at

Table 3. Full decision problems in the game of Fig. 2

	$\Gamma^0(\emptyset)$			
	g	h	i	j
(a,c)	$0,5$	$5,0$	$3,3$	$1,0$
(a,d)	$3,0$	$3,5$	$2,3$	$1,0$
(a,e)	$1,2$	$1,2$	$1,3$	$3,0$
(a,f)	$0,3$	$0,3$	$0,0$	$0,5$
b	$4,4$	$4,4$	$4,4$	$4,4$
	$\Gamma^0(h_1)$			
	g	h	i	j
(a,c)	$0,5$	$5,0$	$3,3$	$1,0$
(a,d)	$3,0$	$3,5$	$2,3$	$1,0$
(a,e)	$1,2$	$1,2$	$1,3$	$3,0$
(a,f)	$0,3$	$0,3$	$0,0$	$0,5$

Table 4. Reduced decision problems after round 1 of backward dominance procedure

	$\Gamma^1(\emptyset)$			
	g	h	i	j
(a,c)	$0,5$	$5,0$	$3,3$	$1,0$
b	$4,4$	$4,4$	$4,4$	$4,4$
	$\Gamma^1(h_1)$			
	g	h	i	j
(a,c)	$0,5$	$5,0$	$3,3$	$1,0$
(a,d)	$3,0$	$3,5$	$2,3$	$1,0$
(a,e)	$1,2$	$1,2$	$1,3$	$3,0$

$\Gamma^0(\emptyset)$, so we only need to eliminate (a,f) from $\Gamma^0(h_1)$ at that step. For player 2, no strategy is strictly dominated within $\Gamma^0(\emptyset)$ or $\Gamma^0(h_1)$, so we cannot yet eliminate any strategy for player 2. This leads to the reduced decision problems $\Gamma^1(\emptyset)$ and $\Gamma^1(h_1)$ in Table 4.

We now turn to round 2. Within $\Gamma^1(h_1)$, player 2's strategy j is strictly dominated by i. Hence, we can eliminate strategy j from $\Gamma^1(h_1)$, but also from $\Gamma^1(\emptyset)$, as h_1 follows $\emptyset$. No other strategies can be eliminated at this round. This leads to the reduced decision problems $\Gamma^2(\emptyset)$ and $\Gamma^2(h_1)$ in Table 5.

In round 3, player 1's strategy (a,e) is strictly dominated by (a,d) within $\Gamma^2(h_1)$, and hence we can eliminate (a,e) from $\Gamma^2(h_1)$. This leads to the final decision problems in Table 6, from which no further strategies can be eliminated. Note, for instance, that strategy i is not strictly dominated for player 2 within $\Gamma^3(h_1)$, as it is optimal for the belief that assigns probability 0.5 to (a,c) and (a,d).

Table 5. Reduced decision problems after round 2 of backward dominance procedure

	g	h	i
$\Gamma^2(\emptyset)$			
(a,c)	$0,5$	$5,0$	$3,3$
b	$4,4$	$4,4$	$4,4$
$\Gamma^2(h_1)$			
(a,c)	$0,5$	$5,0$	$3,3$
(a,d)	$3,0$	$3,5$	$2,3$
(a,e)	$1,2$	$1,2$	$1,3$

Table 6. Final decision problems in the backward dominance procedure

	g	h	i
$\Gamma^3(\emptyset)$			
(a,c)	$0,5$	$5,0$	$3,3$
b	$4,4$	$4,4$	$4,4$
$\Gamma^3(h_1)$			
(a,c)	$0,5$	$5,0$	$3,3$
(a,d)	$3,0$	$3,5$	$2,3$

We will now build an epistemic model on the basis of the final decision problems $\Gamma^3(\emptyset)$ and $\Gamma^3(h_1)$, using the construction in Theorem 2. At $\emptyset$, the surviving strategies are (a,c) and b for player 1, and g,h and i for player 2. That is, $S_1^3(\emptyset) = \{(a,c),b\}$ and $S_2^3(\emptyset) = \{g,h,i\}$. Moreover, at h_1 the surviving strategies are given by $S_1^3(h_1) = \{(a,c),(a,d)\}$ and $S_2^3(h_1) = \{g,h,i\}$. These strategies are optimal, at $\emptyset$ and/or h_1, for the following beliefs:

– strategy $(a,c) \in S_1^3(\emptyset)$ is optimal, at $\emptyset$, for the belief $b_1^{(a,c),\emptyset}(\emptyset) \in \Delta(S_1^3(\emptyset))$ that assigns probability 1 to h;
– strategy $(a,c) \in S_1^3(\emptyset)$ is optimal, at h_1 following $\emptyset$, for the belief $b_1^{(a,c),\emptyset}(h_1) \in \Delta(S_1^3(h_1))$ that assigns probability 1 to h;
– strategy $b \in S_1^3(\emptyset)$ is optimal, at $\emptyset$, for the belief $b_1^{b,\emptyset}(\emptyset) \in \Delta(S_1^3(\emptyset))$ that assigns probability 1 to g;
– strategy $(a,d) \in S_1^3(h_1)$ is optimal, at h_1, for the belief $b_1^{(a,d),h_1}(h_1) \in \Delta(S_1^3(h_1))$ that assigns probability 1 to g;
– strategy $g \in S_2^3(\emptyset)$ is optimal, at h_1 following $\emptyset$, for the belief $b_2^{g,\emptyset}(h_1) \in \Delta(S_1^3(h_1))$ that assigns probability 1 to (a,c);
– strategy $h \in S_2^3(\emptyset)$ is optimal, at h_1 following $\emptyset$, for the belief $b_2^{h,\emptyset}(h_1) \in \Delta(S_1^3(h_1))$ that assigns probability 1 to (a,d);

– strategy $i \in S_2^3(\emptyset)$ is optimal, at h_1 following $\emptyset$, for the belief $b_2^{i,\emptyset}(h_1) \in \Delta(S_1^3(h_1))$ that assigns probability 0.5 to (a,c) and probability 0.5 to (a,d).

On the basis of these beliefs we can now construct an epistemic model as in Theorem 2. So, for both players i, both information sets h, and every strategy $s_i \in S_i^3(h)$, we construct a type $t_i^{s_i,h}$, resulting in the type sets

$$T_1 = \{t_1^{(a,c),\emptyset}, t_1^{b,\emptyset}, t_1^{(a,c),h_1}, t_1^{(a,d),h_1}\} \text{ and } T_2 = \{t_2^{g,\emptyset}, t_2^{h,\emptyset}, t_2^{i,\emptyset}, t_2^{g,h_1}, t_2^{h,h_1}, t_2^{i,h_1}\}.$$

The conditional beliefs for the types about the opponent's strategy-type pairs can then be based on the beliefs above. By using the construction in Theorem 2, this yields the following beliefs for the types:

$$b_1(t_1^{(a,c),\emptyset}, \emptyset) = (h, t_2^{h,\emptyset}), \quad b_1(t_1^{(a,c),\emptyset}, h_1) = (h, t_2^{h,h_1}),$$
$$b_1(t_1^{b,\emptyset}, \emptyset) = (g, t_2^{g,\emptyset}), \quad b_1(t_1^{b,\emptyset}, h_1) = (g, t_2^{g,h_1}),$$
$$b_1(t_1^{(a,c),h_1}, \emptyset) = (h, t_2^{h,\emptyset}), \quad b_1(t_1^{(a,c),h_1}, h_1) = (h, t_2^{h,h_1}),$$
$$b_1(t_1^{(a,d),h_1}, \emptyset) = (g, t_2^{g,\emptyset}), \quad b_1(t_1^{(a,d),h_1}, h_1) = (g, t_2^{g,h_1}),$$

$$b_2(t_2^{g,\emptyset}, h_1) = ((a,c), t_1^{(a,c),h_1}),$$
$$b_2(t_2^{g,h_1}, h_1) = ((a,c), t_1^{(a,c),h_1}),$$
$$b_2(t_2^{h,\emptyset}, h_1) = ((a,d), t_1^{(a,d),h_1}),$$
$$b_2(t_2^{h,h_1}, h_1) = ((a,d), t_1^{(a,d),h_1}),$$
$$b_2(t_2^{i,\emptyset}, h_1) = (0.5) \cdot ((a,c), t_1^{(a,c),h_1}) + (0.5) \cdot ((a,d), t_1^{(a,d),h_1}),$$
$$b_2(t_2^{i,h_1}, h_1) = (0.5) \cdot ((a,c), t_1^{(a,c),h_1}) + (0.5) \cdot ((a,d), t_1^{(a,d),h_1}).$$

Here, $b_2(t_2^{i,\emptyset}, h_1) = (0.5) \cdot ((a,c), t_1^{(a,c),h_1}) + (0.5) \cdot ((a,d), t_1^{(a,d),h_1})$ means that type $t_2^{i,\emptyset}$ assigns at h_1 probability 0.5 to the event that player 1 chooses (a,c) while being of type $t_1^{(a,c),h_1}$, and assigns probability 0.5 to the event that player 1 chooses (a,d) while being of type $t_1^{(a,d),h_1}$.

By Theorem 2 we know that all types so constructed express *common belief in future rationality*, and that for every strategy that can rationally be chosen under *common belief in future rationality* there is a type in this model for which that strategy is optimal. Indeed, the backward dominance procedure delivers the strategies $(a,c), b, g, h$ and i at $\emptyset$, and hence we know from [37] that these are exactly the strategies that can rationally be chosen under *common belief in future rationality*. Note that

– strategy (a,c) is optimal, at $\emptyset$ and h_1, for the type $t_1^{(a,c),\emptyset}$;
– strategy b is optimal, at $\emptyset$, for the type $t_1^{b,\emptyset}$;
– strategy g is optimal, at h_1, for the type $t_2^{g,\emptyset}$;
– strategy h is optimal, at h_1, for the type $t_2^{h,\emptyset}$; and
– strategy i is optimal, at h_1, for the type $t_2^{i,\emptyset}$.

So, for every strategy that can rationally be chosen under *common belief in future rationality*, we have constructed – by means of the epistemic model above – a finitely generated belief hierarchy that expresses *common belief in future rationality*, and that supports this strategy.

Note, however, that there is some redundancy in the epistemic model above. Namely, it is easily seen that the types $t_1^{(a,c),\emptyset}$ and $t_1^{(a,c),h_1}$ have identical belief hierarchies, and so do $t_1^{b,\emptyset}$ and $t_1^{(a,d),h_1}$. The same holds for $t_2^{g,\emptyset}$ and t_2^{g,h_1}, for $t_2^{h,\emptyset}$ and t_2^{h,h_1}, and also for $t_2^{i,\emptyset}$ and t_2^{i,h_1}. Hence, we can substitute $t_1^{(a,c),\emptyset}$ and $t_1^{(a,c),h_1}$ by a single type $t_1^{(a,c)}$, and we can substitute $t_1^{b,\emptyset}$ and $t_1^{(a,d),h_1}$ by a single type t_1^b. Similarly, we can substitute $t_2^{g,\emptyset}$ and t_2^{g,h_1} by a single type t_2^g, we can substitute $t_2^{h,\emptyset}$ and t_2^{h,h_1} by a single type t_2^h, and $t_2^{i,\emptyset}$ and t_2^{i,h_1} by t_2^i. This eventually leads to the smaller – yet equivalent – epistemic model with type sets

$$T_1 = \{t_1^{(a,c)}, t_1^b\} \text{ and } T_2 = \{t_2^g, t_2^h, t_2^i\}$$

and beliefs

$$b_1(t_1^{(a,c)}, \emptyset) = b_1(t_1^{(a,c)}, h_1) = (h, t_2^h)$$
$$b_1(t_1^b, \emptyset) = b_1(t_1^b, h_1) = (g, t_2^h)$$

$$b_2(t_2^g, h_1) = ((a,c), t_1^{(a,c)}),$$
$$b_2(t_2^h, h_1) = ((a,d), t_1^b),$$
$$b_2(t_2^i, h_1) = (0.5) \cdot ((a,c), t_1^{(a,c)}) + (0.5) \cdot ((a,d), t_1^b).$$

This redundancy is typical for the construction of the epistemic model in Theorem 2. In most games, the epistemic model constructed in this way will contain types that are "duplicates" of each other, as they generate the same belief hierarchy.

5   Discussion

5.1   Algorithms as Reasoning Procedures

In this chapter we have presented an algorithm that leads to belief hierarchies expressing *common belief in future rationality*, and it is based on the backward dominance procedure proposed in [37]. The difference is that in this chapter we interpret this algorithm not as a computational tool for the analyst, but rather as a finite reasoning procedure that some player *inside* the game can use (a) to verify which strategies he can rationally choose under *common belief in future rationality*, and (b) to support each of these strategies by a belief hierarchy expressing *common belief in future rationality*.

Hence, one of the main messages in this chapter is that the algorithm above for *common belief in future rationality* does not only serve as a computational tool for the analyst, but can also be used by a player inside the game as an intuitive reasoning procedure. Compare this to the concepts of Nash equilibrium [25, 26] for static games, and sequential equilibrium [22] for dynamic games. There is no easy, finite iterative procedure to find one Nash equilibrium – let alone *all* Nash equilibria – in a game. In particular, there is no clear reasoning procedure that a player inside the game can use to reason his way towards a Nash equilibrium. Besides, we believe that Nash equilibrium imposes some implausible conditions on a player's belief hierarchy, as it requires a player to believe that his opponent is *correct* about the actual beliefs he holds (see [4, 13, 33, 38] and [3, p.5]). In view of all this, we think that Nash equilibrium is not a very appealing concept if we wish to describe the reasoning of players about their opponents. The same actually holds for the concept of sequential equilibrium.

5.2   Finitely Generated Belief Hierarchies

In this chapter we have restricted our attention to *finitely generated* belief hierarchies – that is, belief hierarchies that can be derived from an epistemic model with *finitely* many types. By doing so we actually exclude some belief hierarchies, as not every belief hierarchy can be generated within a finite epistemic model. If we wish to include *all* possible belief hierarchies in our model, then we must necessarily look at *complete* type spaces for dynamic games as constructed in [7].

But for our purposes here it is actually sufficient to concentrate on finitely generated belief hierarchies. Theorem 2 implies, namely, that whenever a strategy s_i is optimal for *some* belief hierarchy – not necessarily finitely generated – that expresses *common belief in future rationality*, then s_i is also optimal for some *finitely generated* belief hierarchy that expresses *common belief in future rationality*. Moreover, finitely generated belief hierarchies have the advantage that they are particularly easy to work with, and that checking for *common belief in future rationality* can be done within finitely many steps, as is shown in Theorem 1.

Acknowledgments. I would like to thank the participants at the Workshop on Modeling Strategic Reasoning in Leiden (2012) for many useful comments. I am also grateful to two anonymous referees for valuable suggestions.

References

1. Alur, R., Henzinger, T.A., Kupferman, O.: Alternating-time temporal logic. J. ACM **49**(5), 672–713 (2002)
2. Asheim, G.B.: Proper rationalizability in lexicographic beliefs. Int. J. Game Theor. **30**(4), 453–478 (2002)
3. Asheim, G.B.: The Consistent Preferences Approach to Deductive Reasoning in Games. Theory and decision library, vol. 37. Springer Science & Business Media, Dordrecht (2006)
4. Aumann, R., Brandenburger, A.: Epistemic conditions for Nash equilibrium. Econometrica **63**, 1161–1180 (1995)

5. Baltag, A., Smets, S., Zvesper, J.: Keep 'hoping' for rationality: A solution to the backward induction paradox. Synthese **169**, 301–333 (2009)
6. Battigalli, P.: On rationalizability in extensive games. J. Econ. Theor. **74**, 40–61 (1997)
7. Battigalli, P., Siniscalchi, M.: Hierarchies of conditional beliefs and interactive epistemology in dynamic games. J. Econ. Theor. **88**(1), 188–230 (1999)
8. Battigalli, P., Siniscalchi, M.: Strong belief and forward induction reasoning. J. Econ. Theor. **106**, 356–391 (2002)
9. Bonanno, G.: Reasoning about strategies and rational play in dynamic games. In: van Benthem, J., Ghosh, S., Verbrugge, R. (eds.) Models of Strategic Reasoning. LNCS, vol. 8972, pp. 34–62. Springer, Heidelberg (2015)
10. Börgers, T.: Weak dominance and approximate common knowledge. J. Econ. Theor. **64**(1), 265–276 (1994)
11. Brandenburger, A.: Lexicographic probabilities and iterated admissibility. In: Dasgupta, P., et al. (eds.) Economic Analysis of Markets and Games, pp. 282–290. MIT Press, Cambridge (1992)
12. Brandenburger, A., Dekel, E.: Rationalizability and correlated equilibria. Econometrica: J. Econ. Soc. **55**(6), 1391–1402 (1987)
13. Brandenburger, A., Dekel, E.: The role of common knowledge assumptions in game theory. In: Hahn, F. (ed.) The Economics of Missing Markets. Information and Games, pp. 46–61. Oxford University Press, Oxford (1989)
14. Brandenburger, A., Friedenberg, A., Keisler, H.J.: Admissibility in games. Econometrica **76**(2), 307–352 (2008)
15. Chen, J., Micali, S.: The robustness of extensive-form rationalizability. Working paper (2011)
16. Dantzig, G.B., Thapa, M.N.: Linear Programming 1: Introduction. Springer, Heidelberg (1997)
17. Dekel, E., Fudenberg, D.: Rational behavior with payoff uncertainty. J. Econ. Theor. **52**(2), 243–267 (1990)
18. Farquharson, R.: Theory of Voting. Yale University Press, New Haven (1969)
19. Feinberg, Y.: Subjective reasoning - dynamic games. Games Econ. Behav. **52**, 54–93 (2005)
20. Goranko, V., Otto, M.: Model theory of modal logics. In: Blackburn, P., van Benthem, J., Wolter, F. (eds.) Handbook of Modal Logic. Elsevier, Amsterdam (2006)
21. Harsanyi, J.C.: Games with incomplete information played by "Bayesian" players. Manag. Sci. Parts i, ii, iii,**14**, 159–182, 320–334, 486–502 (1967, 1968)
22. Kreps, D., Wilson, R.: Sequential equilibria. Econometrica **50**, 863–894 (1982)
23. Luce, R.D., Raiffa, H.: Games and Decisions: Introduction and Critical Survey. Wiley, New York (1957)
24. Bulling, N., Goranko, V., Jamroga, W.: Logics for reasoning about strategic abilities in multi-player game. In: van Benthem, J., Ghosh, S., Verbrugge, R. (eds.) Models of Strategic Reasoning Logics. LNCS, vol. 8972, pp. 93–136. Springer, Heidelberg (2015)
25. Nash, J.F.: Equilibrium points in n-person games. Proc. Nat. Acad. Sci. **36**, 48–49 (1950)
26. Nash, J.F.: Non-cooperative games. Ann. Math. **54**, 286–295 (1951)
27. von Neumann, J.: Zur Theorie der Gesellschaftsspiele. Mathematische Annalen **100**(1), 295–320 (1928). Translated by Bargmann, S.: On the theory of games of strategy. In: Tucker, A.W., Luce, R.D. (eds.) Contributions to the Theory of Games, vol. IV, pp. 13–43. Princeton University Press, Princeton (1959)

28. Pacuit, E.: Dynamic models of rational deliberation in games. In: van Benthem, J., Ghosh, S., Verbrugge, R. (eds.) Models of Strategic Reasoning. LNCS, vol. 8972, pp. 3–33. Springer, Heidelberg (2015)

29. Pauly, M.: Logic for Social Software. Ph.D. thesis, University of Amsterdam (2001)

30. Pearce, D.G.: Rationalizable strategic behavior and the problem of perfection. Econometrica **52**(4), 1029–1050 (1984)

31. Penta, A.: Robust dynamic mechanism design. Technical report, working paper, University of Pennsylvania (2009)

32. Perea, A.: Epistemic foundations for backward induction: An overview. In: van Benthem, J., Gabbay, D., Löwe, B. (eds.) Interactive logic. Proceedings of the 7th Augustus de Morgan Workshop, Texts in Logic and Games, vol. 1, pp. 159–193. Amsterdam University Press (2007)

33. Perea, A.: A one-person doxastic characterization of Nash strategies. Synthese **158**(2), 251–271 (2007)

34. Perea, A.: Backward induction versus forward induction reasoning. Games **1**(3), 168–188 (2010)

35. Perea, A.: An algorithm for proper rationalizability. Games Econ. Behav. **72**(2), 510–525 (2011)

36. Perea, A.: Epistemic Game Theory: Reasoning and Choice. Cambridge University Press, Cambridge (2012)

37. Perea, A.: Belief in the opponents' future rationality. Games Econ. Behav. **83**, 231–254 (2014)

38. Polak, B.: Epistemic conditions for Nash equilibrium, and common knowledge of rationality. Econometrica **67**(3), 673–676 (1999)

39. Rubinstein, A.: Comments on the interpretation of game theory. Econometrica **59**, 909–924 (1991)

40. Samet, D.: Hypothetical knowledge and games with perfect information. Games Econ. Behav. **17**, 230–251 (1996)

41. Schuhmacher, F.: Proper rationalizability and backward induction. Int. J. Game Theor. **28**(4), 599–615 (1999)

42. Shimoji, M., Watson, J.: Conditional dominance, rationalizability, and game forms. J. Econ. Theor. **83**(2), 161–195 (1998)

43. Tan, T.C.-C., da Costa Werlang, S.R.: The Bayesian foundations of solution concepts of games. J. Econ. Theor. **45**(2), 370–391 (1988)

Formal Frameworks for Strategies

Logics for Reasoning About Strategic Abilities in Multi-player Games

Nils Bulling[1][(✉)], Valentin Goranko[2,3], and Wojciech Jamroga[4,5]

[1] Department of Intelligent Systems, TU Delft, Delft, The Netherlands
n.bulling@tudelft.nl
[2] Department of Philosophy, Stockholm University, Stockholm, Sweden
valentin.goranko@philosophy.su.se
[3] Department of Mathematics, University of Johannesburg,
Johannesburg, South Africa
[4] Institute of Computer Science, Polish Academy of Sciences, Warszawa, Poland
[5] Computer Science and Communication Research Unit and Interdisc.
Centre on Security, Reliability and Trust, University of Luxembourg,
Luxembourg City, Luxembourg
w.jamroga@ipipan.waw.pl

Abstract. We introduce and discuss basic concepts, ideas, and logical formalisms used for reasoning about strategic abilities in multi-player games. In particular, we present concurrent game models and the alternating time temporal logic ATL* and its fragment ATL. We discuss variations of the language and semantics of ATL* that take into account the limitations and complications arising from incomplete information, perfect or imperfect memory of players, reasoning within dynamically changing strategy contexts, or using stronger, constructive concepts of strategy. Finally, we briefly summarize some technical results regarding decision problems for some variants of ATL.

Keywords: Logics · Game theory · Strategic reasoning · Strategic logic · Multi-agent systems · Automated reasoning

1   Introduction: Strategic Reasoning

Strategic reasoning is ubiquitous in the modern world. Our entire lives comprise a complex flux of diverse yet interleaved games that we play in different social contexts with different sets of other players, different rules, objectives and preferences. The outcomes of these games determine not only our sense of success (winning) or failure (losing) in life but also what games we engage to play further, and how. In this process we adopt, consciously or not, and follow, commit, abandon, modify and re-commit again to a stream of local strategies. Thus, we are gradually composing and building a big strategy which, together with all

© Springer-Verlag Berlin Heidelberg 2015
J. van Benthem et al. (Eds.): Models of Strategic Reasoning, LNCS 8972, pp. 93–136, 2016.
DOI: 10.1007/978-3-662-48540-8_4

that happens in the surrounding environment and the 'butterfly effects' coming from the rest of the world, determines a unique play called Life...[1]

After this lyrical-philosophical overture, let us make some more analytic introductory notes on our view of strategic reasoning.

To begin with, one can distinguish two, related yet different, perspectives on strategic reasoning depending on the position of the reasoner[2]:

- Reasoning of the agents (players) *from within the game* on what strategy to adopt in order to best achieve their objectives. This starts with 'zero-order' reasoning from the player's own perspective, but not taking into account the other players' strategic reasoning. Then it evolves into 'first-order' reasoning by only taking into account the other players' zero-order strategic reasoning; then likewise second-, third-, etc. higher-order strategic reasoning, eventually converging to the concept of 'common belief/knowledge of rationality', fundamental in game theory.
- Reasoning of an external observer, *from outside the game*, on what strategies the playing agents can *objectively* adopt in trying to achieve their objectives. This reasoning can again be stratified into conceptual layers by taking into account the players' observational, informational, memory, and reasoning limitations in the game, but also their knowledge or ignorance about the other players' limitations, their objectives, etc. Eventually, a complex hierarchy of levels of 'objective' or 'external' strategic reasoning emerges, that essentially embeds the 'internal' one above.

One can also distinguish different threads of strategic reasoning depending on the rationality assumptions, both for the proponents and the opponents. As we noted, the game-theoretic tradition emphasizes reasoning about *rational players'* strategic behaviour *under the assumption of common belief or knowledge of rationality*. Depending on how this assumption is perceived various solution concepts emerge, describing or prescribing the players' rational strategic behaviour. For the epistemic and doxastic foundations of strategic behaviour of rational agents, focusing on the internal perspective of strategic reasoning, we refer to other chapters in this volume: Bonanno [18], Perea [74] and Pacuit [68]. Another active and promising direction of current research on strategic reasoning, presented in this chapter, does not consider players taking into account any assumptions about the rationality of the other players but analyzes, from an external observer's perspective, the players' *objective abilities* to adopt and to apply strategies that guarantee the achievement of their goals *regardless of the rationality level and strategic behaviour of the opponents*. Thus, when assessing objectively the strategic abilities of individual players or coalitions of players – generically called the 'proponents' – to achieve a specific goal we essentially assume that the remaining

---

[1] While 'strategy' is commonly defined as a complete conditional plan, we cannot resist noting here John Lennon's famous quote: "Life is what happens while you are busy making other plans".

[2] Roughly corresponding to 'first-person deliberation' vs. 'third-person assessment of strategic action in games' in van Benthem [16].

players – the 'opponents' – play a collective adversary in a strictly competitive game between the proponents and the opponents.

One can also regard the framework presented in this chapter as analyzing the objective strategic abilities of players – possibly impaired by imperfect or incomplete knowledge about the game – to achieve qualitative goals using zero-order reasoning only in concurrent extended multi-player games[3].

2   Concurrent Game Models and Strategic Abilities

Logics of strategic reasoning build upon several fundamental concepts from game theory, the most important being that of a 'strategy'. The notion of strategy adopted in this chapter is classical: a conditional plan that prescribes what action a given agent (or, a coalition of agents) should take in every possible situation that may arise in the system (game) in which they act. This notion will be made mathematically more precise in this chapter, where strategies will be used to provide formal logical semantics.

We start with a technical overview of the basic game-theoretic concepts used later on in this chapter. For more details we refer the reader to e.g. [51,65].

Throughout this chapter we use the terms 'agent' and 'player' as synonyms and consider an arbitrarily fixed nonempty finite[4] set of players/agents Agt. We also fix a nonempty set of atomic propositions *Prop* that encode basic properties of game states.

2.1   One-Round Multi-player Strategic Games

The abstract games studied in traditional non-cooperative game theory are usually presented either in *extensive* or in *strategic* form (also known as *normal form*). We first focus on the latter type of games here.

Strategic Games

Definition 1 (Strategic Game Forms and Strategic Games). *A* strategic game form *is a tuple* $(\text{Agt}, \{\text{Act}_a \mid a \in \text{Agt}\}, \text{Out}, \text{out})$ *that consists of a nonempty finite set of players* Agt, *a nonempty set of* actions *(also known as* moves *or* choices*)* Act_a *for each player* $a \in \text{Agt}$, *a nonempty set of* outcomes Out, *and an outcome function* $\text{out} : \prod_{a \in \text{Agt}} \text{Act}_a \to \text{Out}$, *that associates an outcome with every action profile; that is, tuple of actions, one for each player[5].*

A strategic game *is a strategic game form endowed with* preference orders $\leq_a$ *on the set of outcomes, one for each player. Often, players' preferences are*

---

[3] We do, however, discuss briefly in Sect. 5.2 how some concepts of rationality can be expressed in logical languages considered here.

[4] We have no strong reason for this finiteness assumption, other than common sense and technical convenience.

[5] We assume that there is an ordering on Agt which is respected in the definition of tuples etc.

expressed by payoff functions $u_a : \mathsf{Out} \to \mathbb{R}$. *Then, the preference relations are implicitly defined as follows:* $o \leq_a o'$ *iff* $u_a(o) \leq u_a(o')$. *Thus, strategic games can be represented either as tuples* $(\mathsf{Agt}, \{\mathsf{Act}_a \mid a \in \mathsf{Agt}\}, \mathsf{Out}, \mathsf{out}, (\leq_a)_{a \in \mathsf{Agt}})$ *or* $(\mathsf{Agt}, \{\mathsf{Act}_a \mid a \in \mathsf{Agt}\}, \mathsf{Out}, \mathsf{out}, (u_a)_{a \in \mathsf{Agt}})$.

In traditional game theory outcomes are usually characterized quantitatively by real values called *utilities* or *payoffs*. More generally, outcomes can be abstract objects, ordered by relations $\leq_a$ which represent preferences of players, as in the definition above. Here we abstract from the actual preferences between outcomes and focus on the players' powers to enforce particular properties (sets) of outcome states. Thus, we will use the terms "strategic game" and "strategic game form" interchangeably, assuming that game forms come equipped with some preference orders that have no direct bearing on our discussion.

The intuition behind a strategic game is simple: each player chooses an action from her set of possible actions. All actions are performed *independently and simultaneously*. Thus, all players perform a collective action based on which the outcome function determines the (unique) outcome. Hence, a strategic game typically represents a one-shot interaction.

$1\backslash 2$	*coop*	*defect*
coop	$(3, 3)$	$(0, 5)$
defect	$(5, 0)$	$(1, 1)$

Fig. 1. Prisoner's Dilemma.

Example 1 (Prisoner's Dilemma as a Strategic Game). We will use a version of the well-known Prisoner's Dilemma game, given in Fig. 1, to illustrate the basic concepts introduced in this section. Each of the two players in the game can choose to cooperate (play action *coop*) or to defect (play action *defect*). Formally, the game is defined as $(\{1, 2\}, \{\mathsf{Act}_1, \mathsf{Act}_2\}, \{o_1, o_2, o_3, o_4\}, \mathsf{out}, (\leq_1, \leq_2))$ with $\mathsf{Act}_1 = \mathsf{Act}_2 = \{coop, defect\}$, $\mathsf{out}(coop, coop) = o_1$, $\mathsf{out}(coop, defect) = o_2$, $\mathsf{out}(defect, coop) = o_3$, and $\mathsf{out}(defect, defect) = o_4$. Moreover, we define $\leq_1$ and $\leq_2$ as the smallest transitive relations with $o_2 \leq_1 o_4 \leq_1 o_1 \leq_1 o_3$ and $o_3 \leq_2 o_4 \leq_2 o_1 \leq_2 o_2$. In the figure we have shown the value of the payoff functions u_1 and u_2 defined as follows: $u_1(o_1) = u_2(o_1) = 3$, $u_1(o_4) = u_2(o_4) = 1$, $u_1(o_2) = u_2(o_3) = 0$, and $u_1(o_3) = u_2(o_2) = 5$.

2.2 Effectivity Functions and Models for Strategic Games

It is important to note that in strategic games none of the players knows in advance the actions chosen by the other players, and therefore has no definitive control on the outcome of the game. So, what power does an individual player or a coalition of players have to influence the outcome in such a game? We will address this fundamental question below in terms of *effectivity functions*, first introduced in cooperative[6] game theory in Moulin and Peleg [64] and in social choice theory in Abdou and Keiding [1], to provide an abstract representation of powers of players and coalitions.

Definition 2 (Effectivity Functions and Models). *Given a set of players* Agt *and a set of outcomes* Out, *a (coalitional) effectivity function (EF) over* Agt *and* Out *is a mapping* $E : \mathcal{P}(Agt) \to \mathcal{P}(\mathcal{P}(Out))$ *that associates a family of sets of outcomes with each coalition of players.*

A (coalitional) effectivity model (EM) is a coalitional effectivity function endowed with a labelling $V :$ Out $\to \mathcal{P}(Prop)$ *of outcomes with sets of atomic propositions from Prop. The labeling prescribes which atomic propositions are true in a given outcome state.*

Intuitively, for a group of agents $A \subseteq$ Agt every element of $E(A)$ is the set of all possible outcomes that can result from a given joint action of players in A, depending on how the remaining players from Agt decide to act. In other words, for every set X in $E(A)$ the coalition A has a collective action that is guaranteed to yield an outcome in X, regardless of the actions taken by the players in $\overline{A} =$ Agt $\setminus A$. Therefore, every element of $E(A)$ can be regarded as representing a possible joint action of coalition A.

Every strategic game G naturally defines an effectivity function called the α-effectivity function of G and denoted by E_G^α, which is defined as follows.

Definition 3 (Effectivity in Strategic Games, Pauly [71]). *For a strategic game* G, *the* α-*effectivity function* $E_G^\alpha : \mathcal{P}(Agt) \to \mathcal{P}(\mathcal{P}(Out))$ *is defined as follows:* $X \in E_G^\alpha(A)$ *if and only if there exists a joint action* σ_A *for* A *such that for every joint action* $\sigma_{\overline{A}}$ *of* $\overline{A}$ *we have* out$(\sigma_A, \sigma_{\overline{A}}) \in X$.

Respectively, the β-*effectivity function for* G *is* $E_G^\beta : \mathcal{P}(Agt) \to \mathcal{P}(\mathcal{P}(Out))$, *defined as follows:* $X \in E_G^\beta(A)$ *if and only if for every joint action* $\sigma_{\overline{A}}$ *of* $\overline{A}$ *there exists a joint action* σ_A *of* A *(generally, depending on* $\sigma_{\overline{A}}$*) such that* out$(\sigma_A, \sigma_{\overline{A}}) \in X$.

Intuitively, α-effectivity functions describe the powers of coalitions to *guarantee* outcomes satisfying desired properties while β-effectivity functions describe the abilities of coalitions to *prevent* outcomes satisfying undesired properties.

Since strategic games are determined, α-effectivity and β-effectivity of coalitions are dual to each other in a sense that for every coalition A and $X \subseteq$ Out:

$$X \in E_G^\alpha(A) \text{ iff } \overline{X} \notin E_G^\beta(\overline{A})$$

where $\overline{X} =$ Out$\setminus X$. That is, a coalition A can guarantee an outcome with a property X precisely when its complementary coalition $\overline{A}$ cannot prevent it.

---

[6] Coalitional effectivity can be regarded as a concept of cooperative game theory from the internal perspective of the coalition, but from the external perspective of the other players it becomes a concept of non-cooperative game theory. We will not dwell into this apparent duality here.

Example 2 (Prisoner's Dilemma as Effectivity Model). The Prisoner's Dilemma from Example 1 can also be represented by the following effectivity function over $(\{1,2\}, \{o_1, \ldots, o_4\})$: $E(\emptyset) = \{\mathsf{Out}\}$, $E(\{1\}) = \{\{o_1, o_2\}, \{o_3, o_4\}\} \cup \{X \subseteq \{o_1, \ldots, o_4\} \mid \{o_1, o_2\} \subseteq X$ or $\{o_3, o_4\} \subseteq X\}$, $E(\{2\}) = \{\{o_1, o_3\}, \{o_2, o_4\}\} \cup \{X \subseteq \{o_1, \ldots, o_4\} \mid \{o_1, o_3\} \subseteq X$ or $\{o_2, o_4\} \subseteq X\}$, and $E(\{1,2\}) = \{\{o_1\}, \{o_2\}, \{o_3\}, \{o_4\}\} \cup \{\exists i \in \{1,2,3,4\}$ s.t. $o_i \in X\} = \mathcal{P}(\{o_1, o_2, o_3, o_4\}) \setminus \{\emptyset\}$.

Let us adopt atomic propositions representing the payoff values for each agent $\{\mathsf{p}_\mathsf{a}^j \mid \mathsf{a} \in \mathsf{Agt}, j \in \{0,1,3,5\}\}$ and label the outcomes appropriately. Then, for example, we have $V(o_1) = \{\mathsf{p}_1^3, \mathsf{p}_2^3\}$ and $V(o_2) = \{\mathsf{p}_1^0, \mathsf{u}_2^5\}$.

2.3 Characterization of Effectivity Functions of Strategic Games

Clearly, not every abstract effectivity function defined as above corresponds to strategic games. The following notion captures the properties required for such correspondence.

Definition 4 (True Playability (Pauly [71], Goranko et al. [45]). *An effectivity function* $\mathsf{E} : \mathcal{P}(\mathsf{Agt}) \to \mathcal{P}(\mathcal{P}(\mathsf{Out}))$ *is truly playable iff the following conditions hold:*

Outcome monotonicity: $X \in \mathsf{E}(A)$ *and* $X \subseteq Y$ *implies* $Y \in \mathsf{E}(A)$;
Liveness: $\emptyset \notin \mathsf{E}(A)$;
Safety: $\mathsf{St} \in \mathsf{E}(A)$;
Superadditivity: *if* $A_1 \cap A_2 = \emptyset$, $X \in \mathsf{E}(A_1)$ *and* $Y \in \mathsf{E}(A_2)$, *then* $X \cap Y \in \mathsf{E}(A_1 \cup A_2)$;
Agt-maximality: $\overline{X} \notin \mathsf{E}(\emptyset)$ *implies* $X \in \mathsf{E}(\mathsf{Agt})$;
Determinacy: *if* $X \in \mathsf{E}(\mathsf{Agt})$ *then* $\{x\} \in \mathsf{E}(\mathsf{Agt})$ *for some* $x \in X$.

It is easy to see that every α-effectivity function of a strategic game is truly playable. The converse holds too as stated below.

Representation theorem for effectivity functions.[7] An effectivity function E for $(\mathsf{Agt}, \mathsf{Out})$ is truly playable if and only if there exists a strategic game $G = (\mathsf{Agt}, \{\mathsf{Act}_i \mid i \in \mathsf{Agt}\}, \mathsf{Out}, \mathsf{out})$ such that $\mathsf{E}_G^\alpha = \mathsf{E}$, see [45,71].

Actual α-effectivity in Strategic Games. The notion of effectivity in game G can be refined to the "actual" α-effectivity function of G that collects *precisely* the sets of outcomes of collective actions available to the coalition without closing the sets under outcome monotonicity. Formally, given a strategic game $G = (\mathsf{Agt}, \{\mathsf{Act}_i \mid i \in \mathsf{Agt}\}, \mathsf{Out}, \mathsf{out})$, a coalition A and a joint action σ_A we define outcome_states(σ_A) as the set of all possible outcomes that can result from σ_A:

$$\text{outcome\_states}(\sigma_A) = \{\mathsf{out}(\sigma_A, \sigma_{\overline{A}}) \mid \sigma_{\overline{A}} \text{ is a joint action for } \overline{A}\}.$$

---

[7] This representation theorem was first proved in Pauly [71] for so called "playable" effectivity functions, without the *Determinacy* requirement. It has been recently shown in [45] that, for games with infinite outcome spaces, "playability" is not sufficient. The *Determinacy* condition was identified and added to define "truly playable" effectivity functions and prove a correct version of the representation theorem.

We define the *actual α-effectivity function* $\widehat{\mathsf{E}}_G : \mathcal{P}(\mathsf{Agt}) \to \mathcal{P}(\mathcal{P}(\mathsf{Out}))$ as the family of all outcome sets effected by possible joint actions of A:

$$\widehat{\mathsf{E}}_G(A) = \{\mathsf{outcome\_states}(\sigma_A) \mid \sigma_A \text{ is a joint action for } A\}.$$

Clearly, the standard α-effectivity function for G can now be obtained by closure under outcome-monotonicity:

$$\mathsf{E}_G(A) = \{Y \mid X \subseteq Y \text{ for some } X \in \widehat{\mathsf{E}}_G(A)\}.$$

Conversely, obtaining $\widehat{\mathsf{E}}_G$ from E_G for games with infinite outcome states is not so straightforward because $\widehat{\mathsf{E}}_G$ may not be uniquely determined by E_G, so the notion of actual effectivity is at least as interesting and perhaps more important than "standard", outcome-monotone effectivity. We refer the interested reader for further discussion and details to [44].

2.4   Strategic Abilities in Concurrent Game Models

Extensive game forms allow to model turn-based games, where at every non-terminal position only one player is allowed to make a move. In this section we discuss more general (as we explain further) "concurrent" games, where at every position all players make their moves simultaneously.

Extensive Games meet Repeated Games: Concurrent Game Structures. Strategic games are usually interpreted as one-step games. Especially in evolutionary game theory, they are often considered in a repeated setting: game G is played a number of times, and the payoffs from all rounds are aggregated. Concurrent game structures from [8], which are essentially equivalent to multi-player game frames from [71] (see Goranko [42]), generalize the setting of repeated games by allowing *different* strategic games to be played at different stages. This way we obtain multi-step games that are defined on some state space, in which every state is associated with a strategic game with outcomes being states again. The resulting game consists of successive rounds of playing one-step strategic games where the outcome of every round determines the successor state, and therefore the strategic game to be played at the next round. Alternatively, one can see concurrent game structures as a generalization of extensive game forms where simultaneous moves of different players are allowed, as well as loops to previously visited states.

Definition 5 (Concurrent Game Structures and Models). *A concurrent game structure (CGS) is a tuple*

$$\mathcal{S} = (\mathsf{Agt}, \mathsf{St}, \mathsf{Act}, \mathsf{act}, \mathsf{out})$$

which consists of a non-empty finite set of players $\mathsf{Agt} = \{1, \ldots, \mathsf{k}\}$, *a non-empty set of states[8]* St, *a non-empty set of atomic actions* Act, *a function* act :

---

[8] The set of states is assumed finite in [8] but that restriction is not necessary for our purposes. In Sect. 6.3 we even rely on the fact that the set of states can be infinite.

$\mathsf{Agt} \times \mathsf{St} \to \mathcal{P}(\mathsf{Act}) \setminus \{\emptyset\}$ *that defines the set of actions available to each player at each state, and a (deterministic) transition function* out *that assigns a unique successor (outcome) state* $\mathsf{out}(q, \alpha_1, \ldots, \alpha_k)$ *to each state* q *and each tuple of actions* $\langle \alpha_1, \ldots, \alpha_k \rangle$ *such that* $\alpha_a \in \mathsf{act}(a, q)$ *for each* $a \in \mathsf{Agt}$ *(i.e., each* α_a *that can be executed by player* a *in state* q*).*

A concurrent game model *(CGM) over a set of atomic propositions Prop is a CGS endowed with a labelling* $V : \mathsf{St} \to \mathcal{P}(Prop)$ *of game states with subsets of Prop, thus prescribing which atomic propositions are true at a given state.*

Thus, all players in a CGS execute their actions synchronously and the combination of these actions together with the current state determines the transition to a successor state in the CGS.

Note that turn-based extensive form games can be readily represented as concurrent game structures by assigning at each non-leaf state the respective set of actions to the player whose turn it is to move from that state, while allowing a single action 'pass' to all other players at that state. At leaf states all players are only allowed to 'pass' and the result of such collective pass action is the same state, thus looping there forever.

Example 3 (Prisoner's Escape). A CGM $\mathcal{M}_{esc}$ is shown in Fig. 2 modeling the following scenario. A prison has two exits: the rear exit guarded by the guard Alex and the front exit guarded by the guard Bob. The prison is using the following procedure for exiting (e.g., for the personnel): every person authorized to exit the prison is given secret passwords, one for every guard. When exiting

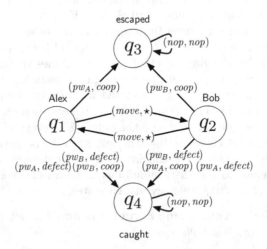

Fig. 2. Prisoner's escape modelled as CGM $\mathcal{M}_{esc}$. An action tuple (a_1, a_2) consists of an action of Frank (a_1) and Charlie (a_2). $\star$ is a placeholder for any action available at the very state; e.g., the tuple $(move, \star)$ leading from state q_1 to q_2 is a shortcut for the tuples $(move, defect)$ and $(move, coop)$. Loops are added to the "final states" q_3 and q_4 where action nop is the only available action for both players. We leave the formal definition to the reader.

the prison the guard must be given the password associated with him/her. If a person gives a wrong password to any guard, he is caught and arrested. Now, Frank is a prisoner who wants to escape, of course. Somehow Frank has got a key for his cell and has learned the passwords for each of the guards. Charlie is an internal guard in the prison and can always see when Frank is going to any of the exits. Frank has bribed Charlie to keep quiet and not to warn the other guards. Charlie can cooperate (actions *coop*), by keeping quiet, or can defect (action *defect*), by alerting the guards. Thus, the successful escape of Frank depends on Charlie's cooperation.

Global Coalition Effectivity Functions and Models. Every CGS $\mathcal{S}$ can be associated with a *global effectivity function* $\mathsf{E} : \mathsf{St} \times \mathcal{P}(\mathbb{A}\mathsf{gt}) \to \mathcal{P}(\mathcal{P}(\mathsf{St}))$ that assigns a (local) α-effectivity function $\mathsf{E}_q = \mathsf{E}(q, \cdot)$ to every state $q \in \mathsf{St}$, generated by the strategic game associated with q in $\mathcal{S}$. These can be accordingly extended to *global effectivity models* by adding valuation of the atomic propositions.

Global effectivity functions and models have been introduced abstractly in [71–73] (called there 'effectivity frames and models'). The global effectivity functions generated by concurrent game structures are characterized in [45,71] by the true playability conditions listed in Sect. 2.3, applied to every E_q.

The idea of effectivity functions has also been extended to *path effectivity functions* in [44]. They will not be discussed here; the reader is referred to that paper for more details.

2.5 Strategies and Strategic Ability

Strategies in Concurrent Game Models. A *path* in a CGS/CGM is an infinite sequence of states that can result from subsequent transitions in the structure/model. A *strategy* of a player a in a CGS/CGM $\mathcal{M}$ is a conditional plan that specifies what a should do in each possible situation. Depending on the type of memory that we assume for the players, a strategy can be *memoryless* (alias *positional*), formally represented with a function $\mathsf{s}_\mathsf{a} : \mathsf{St} \to \mathsf{Act}$, such that $\mathsf{s}_\mathsf{a}(q) \in \mathsf{act}_\mathsf{a}(q)$, or *memory-based* (alias *perfect recall*), represented by a function $\mathsf{s}_\mathsf{a} : \mathsf{St}^+ \to \mathsf{Act}$ such that $\mathsf{s}_\mathsf{a}(\langle \ldots, q \rangle) \in \mathsf{act}_\mathsf{a}(q)$, where St^+ is the set of *histories*, i.e., finite sequences of states in $\mathcal{M}$. The latter corresponds to players with perfect recall of the past states; the former corresponds to players whose memory, if any, is entirely encoded in the current state of the system. Intermediate options, where agents have bounded memory, have been studied by Ågothes and Walther [5], but will not be discussed here.

A *joint strategy* of a group of players $A = \{\mathsf{a}_1, ..., \mathsf{a}_r\}$ is simply a tuple of strategies $\mathsf{s}_A = \langle \mathsf{s}_{\mathsf{a}_1}, ..., \mathsf{s}_{\mathsf{a}_r} \rangle$, one for each player from A. We denote player a's component of the joint strategy s_A by $\mathsf{s}_A[\mathsf{a}]$. Then, in the case of positional joint strategy s_A, the action that $\mathsf{s}_A[\mathsf{a}]$ prescribes to player a at state q is $\mathsf{s}_A[\mathsf{a}](q)$; respectively, $\mathsf{s}_A[\mathsf{a}](\pi)$ is the action that a memory-based joint strategy s_A prescribes to a from the finite path (i.e., history) π. By a slight abuse of notation, we will use $\mathsf{s}_A(q)$ and $\mathsf{s}_A(\pi)$ to denote the joint actions of A in state q and history π, respectively.

Outcomes of Strategies and Strategic Abilities. The outcome set function outcome_states can be naturally extended from joint actions to all strategy profiles applied at a given state (respectively, history) in a given CGS (or CGM). Then outcome_states(q, s_A) (respectively, outcome_states(π, s_A)) returns the set of all possible successor states that can result from applying a given positional (respectively, memory-based) joint strategy s_A of the coalition A at state q (respectively, at history π). Formally,

$$\text{outcome\_states}(q, \mathsf{s}_A) = \{\text{out}(q, \mathsf{s}_A(q), \mathsf{s}_{\overline{A}}(q)) \mid \mathsf{s}_{\overline{A}} \text{ is a joint strategy of } \overline{A}\}.$$

The local actual effectivity function $\widehat{\mathsf{E}}_{\mathcal{S}}$, defining the coalitional powers at every state q in $\mathcal{S}$, is defined explicitly as

$$\widehat{\mathsf{E}}_{\mathcal{S}}(q, A) = \{\text{outcome\_states}(q, \mathsf{s}_A) \mid \mathsf{s}_A \text{ is a memoryless joint strategy of } A\}.$$

As before, the standard α-effectivity functions for $\mathcal{S}$ can be obtained by closure under outcome-monotonicity:

$$\mathsf{E}_{\mathcal{S}}(q, A) = \{Y \mid X \subseteq Y \text{ for some } X \in \widehat{\mathsf{E}}_{\mathcal{S}}(q, A)\}.$$

Likewise for outcome_states(π, s_A), $\widehat{\mathsf{E}}_{\mathcal{S}}(\pi, A)$, and $\mathsf{E}_{\mathcal{S}}(\pi, A)$ which we will not further discuss here.

Example 4 (Prisoner's Escape Continued). $\widehat{\mathsf{E}}_{\mathcal{S}}(q_1, \{\text{Frank}\}) = \{\{q_2\}, \{q_4\}, \{q_3, q_4\}\}$, where $\mathcal{S}$ denotes the underlying CGS of $\mathcal{M}_{esc}$.

We extend the function outcome_states to a function outcome_plays that returns the set of all *plays*, i.e., all paths $\lambda \in \mathsf{St}^\omega$ that can be realised when the players in A follow strategy s_A from a given state q (respectively, history π) onward. Formally, for memoryless strategies this is defined as:

outcome_plays$(q, \mathsf{s}_A) = \{\lambda = q_0, q_1, q_2... \mid q_0 = q$ and for each $j \in \mathbb{N}$ there exists an action profile for all players $\langle \alpha_1^j, ..., \alpha_k^j \rangle$ such that $\alpha_{\mathsf{a}}^j \in \text{act}_{\mathsf{a}}(q_j)$ for every $\mathsf{a} \in \text{Agt}$, $\alpha_{\mathsf{a}}^j = \mathsf{s}_A[\mathsf{a}](q_j)$ for every $\mathsf{a} \in A$, and $q_{j+1} = \text{out}(q_j, \alpha_{\mathsf{a}_1}^j, ..., \alpha_{\mathsf{a}_k}^j)\}.$

The definition for memory-based strategies is analogous: outcome_plays(q, s_A) consists of all plays of the game that start in q and can be realised as a result of each player in A following its individual memory-based strategy in s_A, while the remaining players act in any way that is admissible by the game structure.

Example 5 (Prisoner's Escape Continued). Suppose the guard Charlie, who is a friend with the guard Bob and does not want to cause him trouble, adopts the *memoryless strategy* to cooperate with Frank if he goes to the rear exit (i.e., at state q_1) by not warning Alex, but to defect and warn Bob if Frank decides to go to the front exit, i.e. at state q_2. Naturally, Frank does not know that. The set of possible outcome plays enabled by this strategy and starting from state q_1 is:

$$\{(q_1 q_2)^\omega, q_1(q_2 q_1)^n q_3^\omega, (q_1 q_2)^n q_4^\omega \mid n \in \mathbb{N}\}.$$

Suppose now being at q_1 Frank decides, for his own reasons, to try to escape through the front exit. Frank's strategy is to move at q_1 and to give the password to the guard at q_2. The resulting play from that strategy profile is the play $q_1 q_2 q_4^\omega$.

Memory-based strategies are more flexible. For instance, a memory-based strategy for Charlie could be one where he defects *the first time* Frank appears at any given exit, but thereafter cooperates at the rear exit (say, because he was then given more money by Frank) and defects at the front exit. That strategy enables the following set of plays from q_1:

$$\{(q_1 q_2)^\omega, q_1 q_4^\omega, (q_1 q_2)^n q_4^\omega, q_1 (q_2 q_1)^{n+1} q_3^\omega \mid n \in \mathbb{N}\}.$$

So, if Frank tries to escape as soon as possible with Charlie's support, he will fail; however, if he decides to first move to the front exit (and to pay Charlie extra money) and tries to escape the second time he appears at the front exit, he may succeed.

Note that there is no *memoryless strategy* that would allow Frank to escape if Charlie adopts the strategy specified above. This is because Frank's memoryless strategy must specify *the same action* in each state every time he is at that state, regardless of the history of the game up to that point. Thus, either Frank tries to escape through one of the exits right away, or he executes *move* forever, or gets caught.

A fundamental question regarding a concurrent game model is: *what can a given player or coalition achieve in that game?* So far the objectives of players and coalitions are not formally specified, but a typical objective would be to reach a state satisfying a given property, e.g. a winning state. Generally, an objective is a property of plays, for instance one can talk about winning or losing plays for the given player or coalition. More precisely, if the current state of the game is q we say that a coalition of players A can (is sure to) achieve an objective O from that state if there is a joint strategy $\mathbf{s}_A$ for A such that every play from outcome_plays$(q, \mathbf{s}_A)$ satisfies the objective O. The central problem that we discuss in the rest of this chapter is *how to use logic to formally specify strategic objectives of players and coalitions and how to formally determine their abilities to achieve such objectives.*

3   Logics for Strategic Reasoning and Coalitional Abilities

Logic and game theory have a long and rich history of interaction which we will not discuss here and refer the reader to e.g. [15]. Here, we will focus on the role of logic in formalizing and structuring reasoning about strategic abilities in multi-player games.

3.1   Expressing Local Coalitional Powers: Coalition Logic

The concept of α-effectivity in strategic games (Definition 3) has the distinct flavour of a *non-normal modal operator with neighbourhood semantics*, see [33], and this observation was utilized by Pauly who introduced in [71,73] a multi-modal logic capturing coalitional effectiveness in strategic games, called *Coalition Logic* (CL). CL extends classical propositional logic with a family of modal operators [A] parameterized with coalitions, i.e. subsets of the set of agents Agt. Intuitively, the formula $[A]\varphi$ says that *coalition A has, at the given game state, the power to guarantee an outcome satisfying* φ. Formally, operator [A] is interpreted in global effectivity models $\mathcal{M} = (E, V)$ as follows:

$$\mathcal{M}, q \models [A]\varphi \text{ iff } \|\varphi\|_{\mathcal{M}} \in E_q(A),$$

where $\|\varphi\|_{\mathcal{M}} := \{s \in St \mid \mathcal{M}, s \models \varphi\}$.

This implicitly defines the semantics of CL in every concurrent game model $\mathcal{M}$, in terms of the generated global α-effectivity function $E_{\mathcal{M}}$.

Coalition logic is a very natural language to express *local* strategic abilities of players and coalitions; that is, their powers to guarantee desired properties in the *successor states*.

Example 6 In the following we state some properties expressed in CL.

1. *"If Player 1 has an action to guarantee a winning successor state, then Player 2 cannot prevent reaching a winning successor state."*

    $$[1]\,Win1 \rightarrow \neg[2]\neg\,Win1.$$

2. *"Player 1 has an action to guarantee a successor state where she is rich, and has an action to guarantee a successor state where she is happy, but has no action to guarantee a successor state where she is both rich and happy."*

    $$[1]Rich \wedge [1]Happy \wedge \neg[1](Rich \wedge Happy).$$

3. *"None of players 1 and 2 has an action ensuring an outcome state satisfying Goal, but they have a collective action ensuring such an outcome state."*

    $$\neg[1]\,Goal \wedge \neg[2]\,Goal \wedge [1,2]\,Goal.$$

Example 7 (Prisoner's Escape: Example 3 Continued). Let us denote hereafter Frank by f and Charlie by c. Then we have $\mathcal{M}_{esc}, q_1 \models \neg[f]\text{escaped}$ and $\mathcal{M}_{esc}, q_1 \models [f, c]\text{escaped}$.

3.2   Expressing Long-Term Strategic Abilities in the Logic ATL*

While CL is suitable for expressing local properties and immediate abilities, it cannot capture *long-term* strategic abilities of players and coalitions. For these, we need to extend the language of CL with more expressive temporal operators. That was done in [71,72] where Pauly introduced the *Extended Coalition Logic* ECL, interpreted essentially (up to notational difference) on concurrent game models. Independently, a more expressive logical system called *Alternating-Time Temporal Logic*, ATL* (and its syntactic fragment ATL) was introduced and studied by Alur, Henzinger and Kupferman in a series of papers, see [6–8] as a logic for reasoning about open systems. The main syntactic construct of ATL* is a formula of type $\langle\langle A \rangle\rangle \gamma$, intuitively meaning:

> *"The coalition A has a collective strategy to guarantee the satisfaction of the objective γ on every play enabled by that strategy"*[9].

As shown in [42,43] Pauly's ECL is directly embeddable into ATL, so we will not discuss ECL further, but will focus on ATL and ATL* interpreted over concurrent game models.

ATL* and its Fragment ATL: Syntax and Semantics. Formally, the alternating-time temporal logic ATL* is a multimodal logic extending the linear time temporal logic LTL– comprising the temporal operators $\mathcal{X}$ ("at the next state"), $\mathcal{G}$ ("always from now on") and $\mathcal{U}$ ("until") – with *strategic path quantifiers* $\langle\!\langle A \rangle\!\rangle$ indexed with coalitions A of players. There are two types of formulae of ATL*: *state formulae* that constitute the logic, and which are evaluated at game states, and *path formulae*, which are evaluated on game plays. These are respectively defined by the following grammars, where $A \subseteq \mathbb{A}\mathrm{gt}, \mathsf{p} \in Prop$:

State formulae: $\varphi :: = \mathsf{p} \mid \neg\varphi \mid \varphi \wedge \varphi \mid \langle\!\langle A \rangle\!\rangle\gamma$,
Path formulae: $\gamma :: = \varphi \mid \neg\gamma \mid \gamma \wedge \gamma \mid \mathcal{X}\gamma \mid \mathcal{G}\gamma \mid \gamma\mathcal{U}\gamma$.

The formal semantics of ATL* was initially based on *alternating transition systems* in [6,7], and subsequently reworked for concurrent game models, as follows[10]. Let $\mathcal{M}$ be a CGM, q a state in $\mathcal{M}$, and $\lambda = q_0q_1\ldots$ be a path in $\mathcal{M}$. For every $i \in \mathbb{N}$ we define $\lambda[i] = q_i$, and denote by $\lambda[0..i]$ the prefix $q_0q_1\ldots q_i$, and by $\lambda[i..\infty]$ the suffix $q_iq_{i+1}\ldots$ of λ. The semantics of ATL* is given as follows (cf. [8]). For state formulae:

$\mathcal{M}, q \models \mathsf{p}$ iff $q \in V(\mathsf{p})$, for $\mathsf{p} \in Prop$;
$\mathcal{M}, q \models \neg\varphi$ iff $\mathcal{M}, q \not\models \varphi$;
$\mathcal{M}, q \models \varphi_1 \wedge \varphi_2$ iff $\mathcal{M}, q \models \varphi_1$ and $\mathcal{M}, q \models \varphi_2$;
$\mathcal{M}, q \models \langle\!\langle A \rangle\!\rangle\gamma$ iff there is a joint strategy $\mathbf{s}_A$ for A such that $\mathcal{M}, \lambda \models \gamma$ for every play $\lambda \in \mathsf{outcome\_plays}(q, \mathbf{s}_A)$;

and for path formulae:
$\mathcal{M}, \lambda \models \varphi$ iff $\mathcal{M}, \lambda[0] \models \varphi$ for any state formula φ;
$\mathcal{M}, \lambda \models \neg\gamma$ iff $\mathcal{M}, \lambda \not\models \gamma$;
$\mathcal{M}, \lambda \models \gamma_1 \wedge \gamma_2$ iff $\mathcal{M}, \lambda \models \gamma_1$ and $\mathcal{M}, \lambda \models \gamma_2$;
$\mathcal{M}, \lambda \models \mathcal{X}\gamma$ iff $\mathcal{M}, \lambda[1, \infty] \models \gamma$;
$\mathcal{M}, \lambda \models \mathcal{G}\gamma$ iff $\mathcal{M}, \lambda[i, \infty] \models \gamma$ for every $i \geq 0$; and
$\mathcal{M}, \lambda \models \gamma_1\mathcal{U}\gamma_2$ iff there is i such that $\mathcal{M}, \lambda[i, \infty] \models \gamma_2$ and $\mathcal{M}, \lambda[j, \infty] \models \gamma_1$ for all $0 \leq j < i$.

The other Boolean connectives and constants $\top$ and $\bot$ are defined as usual. The operator $\mathcal{F}$ ("sometime in the future") is defined as $\mathcal{F}\varphi \equiv \top\mathcal{U}\varphi$.[11]

---

[9] We use the terms *objective* and *goal* of a coalition A as synonyms, to indicate the subformula γ of the formula $\langle\!\langle A \rangle\!\rangle\gamma$. In doing so, we ignore the issue of whether agents may have (common) goals, how these goals arise, etc.

[10] As proved in [42,43], under natural assumptions the two semantics are equivalent.

[11] Of course, $\mathcal{G}$ is definable as $\neg\mathcal{F}\neg$, but keeping it as a primitive operator in the language is convenient when defining the sublanguage ATL.

The logic ATL* is very expressive, often more than necessary. This expressiveness comes at a high computational price which can be avoided if we settle for a reasonably designed fragment which is still sufficient in many cases. The key idea is to restrict *the combination of temporal operators* in the language. That can be achieved by imposing a syntactic restriction on the construction of formulae: occurrences of temporal operators must be immediately preceded by strategic path quantifiers. The result is the logic ATL defined by the following grammar, for $A \subseteq \mathbb{A}gt, \mathsf{p} \in Prop$:

$$\varphi ::= \mathsf{p} \mid \neg\varphi \mid \varphi \wedge \varphi \mid \langle\langle A \rangle\rangle \mathcal{X}\varphi \mid \langle\langle A \rangle\rangle \mathcal{G}\varphi \mid \langle\langle A \rangle\rangle(\varphi \mathcal{U} \varphi).$$

For example, $\langle\langle A \rangle\rangle \mathcal{G} \mathcal{F} \mathsf{p}$ is an ATL* formula but not an ATL formula whereas $\langle\langle A \rangle\rangle \mathcal{G} \langle\langle B \rangle\rangle \mathcal{F} \mathsf{p}$ is also an ATL formula. Thus, the coalitional objectives in ATL formulae are quite simple. As a consequence, it turns out that for the formulae of ATL the two notions of strategy, memoryless and memory-based, yield the same semantics [8,47].

Note that CL can be seen as the fragment of ATL involving only Booleans and operators $\langle\langle A \rangle\rangle \mathcal{X}$, whereas ECL also involves the operator $\langle\langle A \rangle\rangle \mathcal{G}$ (denoted in [71,72] by $[A^*]$). Both logics inherit the semantics of ATL on concurrent game models.

Example 8 (Prisoner's Escape Continued). We express some properties of the escape scenario from Example 3 in ATL*. (We recall that we denote Frank by f and Charlie by c.) We remark that all but the last formula belong to ATL.

1. $\mathcal{M}_{esc}, q_1 \models \neg\langle\langle f \rangle\rangle \mathcal{F}$ escaped: Frank cannot guarantee to escape on his own (from q_1).
2. $\mathcal{M}_{esc}, q_1 \models \langle\langle f, c \rangle\rangle \mathcal{F}$ escaped: if Frank and Charlie cooperate then they can ensure that Frank eventually escapes.
3. $\mathcal{M}_{esc}, q_1 \models \langle\langle c \rangle\rangle \mathcal{G} \neg$escape: Charlie can guarantee that Frank never escapes.
4. $\mathcal{M}_{esc}, q_1 \models \neg\langle\langle c \rangle\rangle \mathcal{F}$ caught: Charlie cannot guarantee that Frank is caught.
5. $\mathcal{M}_{esc}, q_1 \models \langle\langle f \rangle\rangle \mathcal{X}$ (Bob $\wedge \langle\langle f, c \rangle\rangle \mathcal{X}$ escaped): Frank has a strategy to reach the front exit guarded by Bob in the next step and then escape with the help of Charlie.
6. $\mathcal{M}_{esc}, q_1 \models \langle\langle f \rangle\rangle \mathcal{G} \mathcal{F}$ Alex: Frank can guarantee to reach the rear exit guarded by Alex infinitely many times.

3.3 From Branching-Time Temporal Logics to ATL*

We have introduced ATL* from a game-theoretic perspective as a logic for reasoning about players' strategic abilities. An alternative approach, in fact the one adopted by its inventors in [8], is to introduce ATL/ATL* as a generalization of the branching-time temporal logic CTL/CTL* to enable reasoning about open systems. Indeed, CTL/CTL* can be regarded as a 1-player version of ATL/ATL* where – assuming the singleton set of agents is $\{i\}$ – the existential path quantifier E is identified with $\langle\langle i \rangle\rangle$ and the universal path quantifier A is identified with $\langle\langle \emptyset \rangle\rangle$. Indeed, we leave it to the reader to check that the semantics of $\langle\langle i \rangle\rangle \varphi$

and $\langle\!\langle\emptyset\rangle\!\rangle\varphi$ in any single-agent CGM $\mathcal{M}$ coincide with the semantics of $\mathsf{E}\,\varphi$ and $\mathsf{A}\,\varphi$ in $\mathcal{M}$ regarded as a transition system with transitions determined by the possible actions of the agent i, respectively.

ATL/ATL* can be regarded – at least formally, but see a discussion further – as a multi-agent extension of CTL/CTL* resulting into a more refined quantification scheme over the paths, respectively computations, enabled by some collective strategy of the given coalition.

4   Variations in Reasoning About Strategies

In this section, we discuss two interesting and important directions of extending the basic pattern of reasoning about agents' strategies and abilities. First, we investigate limitations and inadequacies stemming from the compositionality of the semantics of CL and ATL* that seem to be in conflict with the concept of strategy commitment. We discuss variant notions of strategic ability that attempt to resolve these problems. Then, we briefly summarize some attempts at reasoning about outcomes of *particular strategies*, rather than the mere existence of suitable plans.

4.1   Persistence of Strategic Committments

Strategic Commitment and Persistence in the Semantics of ATL*. Agents in actual multi-agent systems commit to strategies and relinquish their commitments in pursuit of their individual and collective goals in a dynamic, pragmatic, and often quite subtle way. While the semantics of ATL* is based on the standard notion of strategy, it appears that it does not capture adequately all aspects of strategic behaviour. For instance, the meaning of the ATL* formula $\langle\!\langle A\rangle\!\rangle\gamma$ is that the coalition A has a collective strategy, say s_A, to bring about the truth of γ *if the agents in A follow that strategy*. However, according to the formal semantics of ATL*, as introduced in [8], the evaluation of γ in the possible plays of the system enabled by s_A *does not take that strategy into account anymore*. That is, if γ contains a subformula $\langle\!\langle B\rangle\!\rangle\psi$, then in the evaluation of $\langle\!\langle B\rangle\!\rangle\psi$ the agents in $A \cap B$ are free to choose *any (other)* strategy as part of the collective strategy of B claimed to exist to justify the truth of ψ. Thus, the semantics of ATL* *does not commit the agents in A to the strategies they adopt in order to bring about the truth of the formula* $\langle\!\langle A\rangle\!\rangle\gamma$. This is in agreement with the semantics of path quantifiers in CTL*, where it is natural to express claims like $\mathsf{E}\mathcal{G}\,\mathsf{E}\varphi$ read as "there is a path, such that from any state of that path the system can deviate to another path which satisfies φ". One may argue that this feature disagrees with the game-theoretic view of a strategy as a full conditional plan that *completely specifies the agent's future behavior*. To see the problem more explicitly, consider the ATL formula $\langle\!\langle i\rangle\!\rangle\mathcal{G}\,(\gamma \wedge \langle\!\langle i\rangle\!\rangle\mathcal{X}\,\neg\gamma)$. Depending on how orthodoxly or liberally one adopts the concept of strategic commitment, the requirement expressed – that agent i has a strategy to ensure both that γ holds forever and that it can always alter that strategy to reach a

non-γ state – may be considered satisfiable or not. This issue has been independently addressed in different ways in [3,4,19,75,81], where various proposals
have been made in order to incorporate strategic commitment and persistent
strategies in the syntax and semantics of ATL*.

Paradoxes of Non-persistence. We continue with two more similar examples
to argue that non-persistent strategies can lead to apparently counterintuitive
descriptions of strategic ability.

Example 9 (Non-renewable Resource). Consider a system with a shared resource,
where we are interested in reasoning about whether agent a has access to the
resource. Let p denote the fact that agent a controls the resource. The ATL
formula $\langle\langle a \rangle\rangle \mathcal{X} p$ expresses the claim that a is able to obtain control of the resource
in the next moment, if it chooses to. Now imagine that agent a does not need
to access the resource all the time, but it would like to be able to control the
resource any time it needs it. Intuitively, this is expressed in ATL by the formula
$\langle\langle a \rangle\rangle \mathcal{G} \langle\langle a \rangle\rangle \mathcal{X} p$, saying that a has a strategy which guarantees that, in any future
state of the system, a can always force the next state to be one where a controls
the resource.

Now, consider the single-agent system $\mathcal{M}_0$ from Fig. 3. We have that
$\mathcal{M}_0, q_1 \models \langle\langle a \rangle\rangle \mathcal{X} p$: a can choose action α_2, which guarantees that p is true next.
But we also have that $\mathcal{M}_0, q_1 \models \langle\langle a \rangle\rangle \mathcal{G} \langle\langle a \rangle\rangle \mathcal{X} p$: a's strategy in this case is to
always choose α_1, which guarantees that the system will stay in q_1 forever and,
as we have seen, $\mathcal{M}_0, q_1 \models \langle\langle a \rangle\rangle \mathcal{X} p$. However, this system does not have exactly
the property we had in mind because by following that strategy, agent a dooms
itself to *never access the resource* – in which case it is maybe counter-intuitive
that $\langle\langle a \rangle\rangle \mathcal{X} p$ should be true. In other words, a can ensure that it is forever *able*
to access the resource, but only by never *actually* accessing it.[12] Indeed, while a
can force the *possibility* of achieving p to be true forever, the actual achievement
of p destroys that possibility.

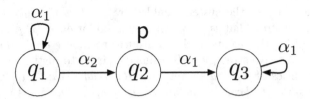

Fig. 3. Having the cake *or* eating it: model $\mathcal{M}_0$ with a single agent a. The transitions
between states are labeled by the actions chosen by agent a.

Example 10 (Nested Strategic Operators). Non-persistence of strategic commit-
ments in nested strategic formulas (like in $\langle\langle a \rangle\rangle \mathcal{G} \langle\langle a \rangle\rangle \mathcal{X} p$) also contradicts the

---

[12] This is the famous "have the cake or eat it" dilemma. One can keep *being able to
eat the cake*, but only by never eating the cake.

observation that a player's choice constrains the outcomes that can be achieved by other players. Consider the ATL* formula $\langle\!\langle A \rangle\!\rangle \langle\!\langle B \rangle\!\rangle \gamma$. It is easy to see that, according to the semantics of ATL*, the formula is equivalent to $\langle\!\langle B \rangle\!\rangle \gamma$ for any pair A, B of coalitions (intersecting or not). Thus, none of A's strategy can influence the outcome of B's play, which is opposite to what we typically assume in strategic reasoning.

Alternative Semantics of Strategic Play. What are the alternatives? Let us analyze them using the example formula $\langle\!\langle 1, 2 \rangle\!\rangle \mathcal{G} \langle\!\langle 2, 3 \rangle\!\rangle \mathcal{X} p$.

1. **Irrevocable Strategies.** At the point of evaluation of $\langle\!\langle 1, 2 \rangle\!\rangle \mathcal{G} \langle\!\langle 2, 3 \rangle\!\rangle \mathcal{X} p$ the strategies of agents 1 and 2 are selected and fixed. When evaluating the subformula $\langle\!\langle 2, 3 \rangle\!\rangle \mathcal{X} p$ only the strategy of agent 3 can vary. A natural, straightforward way of obtaining this semantics with minimal change to the standard semantics of ATL* is to *update* the model when agents choose a strategy, so that their future choices must be consistent with that strategy, but otherwise keeping semantics (definition of strategies, etc.) as is. We call these *irrevocable strategies* (see [3]), since a commitment to a strategy can never be revoked in this semantics, and denote by IATL the version of ATL adopting (memoryless) irrevocable strategies in its semantics.

2. **Strategy Contexts.** At the point of evaluation of $\langle\!\langle 1, 2 \rangle\!\rangle \mathcal{G} \langle\!\langle 2, 3 \rangle\!\rangle \mathcal{X} p$ the strategies of agents 1 and 2 are selected and fixed, but when evaluating the subformula $\langle\!\langle 2, 3 \rangle\!\rangle \mathcal{X} p$ agent 2 is granted the freedom to *change its strategy in order to achieve the current goal*, i.e. $\mathcal{X} p$. Thus, both agents 2 and 3 can choose new strategies, and moreover they can do that under the assumption that agent 1 remains committed to his strategy selected at the point of evaluation of $\langle\!\langle 1, 2 \rangle\!\rangle \mathcal{G} \langle\!\langle 2, 3 \rangle\!\rangle \mathcal{X} p$. This is a simple case of what we will later call *strategy contexts*.

ATL with Irrevocable Strategies. A strategy in game theory is usually understood as a plan that completely prescribes the player's behaviour, in all conceivable situations and for all future moments. An alternative semantics for strategic quantifiers takes this into account by adopting *irrevocable* strategies, implemented through the mechanism of *model update*.

Definition 6 (Model Update). *Let $\mathcal{M}$ be a CGM, A a coalition, and s_A a strategy for A. The* update *of $\mathcal{M}$ by s_A, denoted $M \dagger s_A$, is the model $\mathcal{M}$ where the choice of each agent $i \in A$ is fixed by the strategy $s_A[i]$; that is, $d_i(q) = \{s_i(q)\}$ for each state q.*

The semantics of ATL* *with irrevocable strategies* (IATL*) is now defined as follows, where q is a state in a CGS $\mathcal{M}$:

$[\mathcal{M}, q \models \langle\!\langle A \rangle\!\rangle \gamma$ iff there is a joint strategy s_A such that for every path $\lambda \in$ outcome_plays$_{\mathcal{M}}(q, s_A)$ we have $\mathcal{M} \dagger s_A, \lambda \models \gamma$.

Depending on whether memory-based strategies, or only memoryless strategies, are allowed two different versions of ATL with irrevocable strategies emerge: MATL and IATL. For further details on these, we refer the reader to [3,4].

ATL with Strategy Contexts. A somewhat different and more flexible app-roach has been proposed by Brihaye et al. [19]. Instead of a "hard" model update that transforms the CGM according to the chosen strategy, the model is kept intact and the strategy is only added to the *strategy context*. The context collects strategies being currently executed, and hence influences the outcome paths that can occur. On the other hand, since the model itself does not change, each strategy can be revoked – in particular when an agent chooses another strategy in a nested cooperation modality. Formally, let s_A be a joint strategy of agents A (the current strategy context), and let t_B be a new joint strategy of agents B. We define the *context update* $s_A \circ t_B$ as the joint strategy f for agents in $A \cup B$ such that $f[i] = t_B[i]$ for $i \in B$ and $f[i] = s_A[i]$ for $i \in A \setminus B$. That is, the new strategies from t_B are added to the context, possibly replacing some of the previous ones. The semantic rule for strategic modalities becomes:

$\mathcal{M}, q, f \models \langle\!\langle A \rangle\!\rangle \gamma$ iff there is a joint strategy s_A for the agents in A such that for every path $\lambda \in$ outcome_plays$(q, f \circ s_A)$ we have that $\mathcal{M}, \lambda, f \circ s_A \models \gamma$.

Additionally, $\mathcal{M}, q \models \varphi$ iff $\mathcal{M}, q, f_\emptyset \models \varphi$ where $f_\emptyset$ is the only joint strategy of the empty coalition (i.e., the empty tuple).

For more details and a thorough analysis of the model checking problem for ATL with strategy contexts, we refer the reader to [19]. A proof of the undecid-ability of the satisfiability problem for ATL with strategy contexts can be found in [79].

4.2 Making Strategies Explicit

In this section, we discuss several proposed variations of ATL with explicit references to strategies in the logical language.

Counterfactual ATL (CATL), proposed by van der Hoek et al. [52], extends ATL with operators of "counterfactual commitment" $\mathcal{C}_i(\sigma, \varphi)$ where i is an agent, σ is a term symbol standing for a strategy, and φ is a formula. The informal reading of $\mathcal{C}_i(\sigma, \varphi)$ is: "*if it were the case that agent i committed to strategy σ, then φ would hold*". The semantics is based on model updates, like the IATL semantics presented in Sect. 4.1:

$$\mathcal{M}, q \models \mathcal{C}_i(\sigma, \varphi) \text{ iff } \mathcal{M} \dagger [\![\sigma]\!]_i, q \models \varphi$$

where $[\![\sigma]\!]_i$ is the strategy of agent i denoted by the strategy term σ.

ATL *with intentions* (ATLI), proposed by Jamroga et al. [59], is similar to CATL, but its counterfactual operators have a different flavour: $(\mathbf{str}_i\sigma)\varphi$ reads as "*suppose that agent i intends to play strategy σ, then φ holds*". An intention is a kind of commitment – it persists – but it can be revoked by switching to another intention. Semantically, this is done by an additional "marking" of the intended actions in the concurrent game model. Moreover, strategies can be nondeterministic, which provides semantic tools for e.g. partial strategies as well as explicit release of commitments. Thus, Jamroga et al. [59] provide in fact the semantics of ATL based on strategy contexts (here called intentions).

However, ATLI does not allow to quantify over intentions, and hence allows only for limited context change. ATLI and its richer variant called ATLP ("ATL with plausibility" see [29]) have been used to e.g. characterize game-theoretic solution concepts and outcomes that can be obtained by rational agents. We discuss this and show some examples in Sect. 5.

Alternating-time temporal logic with explicit strategies (ATLES), see [81], is a revised version of CATL which dispenses with the counterfactual operators. Instead, strategic modalities are subscripted by *commitment functions* which are partial functions of the form $\rho = \{a_1 \mapsto \sigma_1, \ldots, a_l \mapsto \sigma_l\}$ where each a_j is an agent and σ_j is a strategy term. The meaning of a formula such as $\langle\!\langle A \rangle\!\rangle_\rho \mathcal{G} \varphi$ is that there exists a strategy for $A \cup \{a_1, \ldots, a_l\}$ where each a_j is required to play $[\![\sigma_j]\!]$ such that φ will hold. Note, that ATLES formulae also involve strategy commitment. Consider, for instance, formula $\langle\!\langle A \rangle\!\rangle_\rho \mathcal{G} \langle\!\langle A \rangle\!\rangle_\rho \mathcal{F} \varphi$. If A is a subset of the domain of ρ then in the evaluation of the subformula $\langle\!\langle A \rangle\!\rangle_\rho \mathcal{F} \varphi$, A is bound to play the same joint strategy it selected for the outer modality $\langle\!\langle A \rangle\!\rangle_\rho \mathcal{G}$.

Alternating-time temporal epistemic logic with actions (ATEL − A), proposed by Ågotnes [2], enables reasoning about the interplay between explicit strategies of bounded length and agents' knowledge.

Strategy Logic, introduced by Chatterjee et al. [31,32], treats strategies in two-player turn-based games as explicit first-order objects and enables specifying important properties of non-zero-sum games in a simple and natural way. In particular, the one-alternation fragment of strategy logic subsumes ATL* and is strong enough to express the existence of Nash equilibria and secure equilibria.

The idea of treating strategies explicitly in the language and quantifying over them is subsequently followed up in a series of papers, e.g. in [61–63] where strategy logic is extended and generalized to concurrent games, and a decidable fragment (as complex as ATL*) of it is identified and studied.

5   Reasoning About Games

ATL* and its variations are closely related to basic concepts in game theory. Firstly, their models are derived from those used in game theory. Secondly, their semantics are based on the notions of *strategies* and their *outcomes*, central in a game-theoretic analysis. In this section we give a brief overview of how to relate game theory and strategic logics. We begin with the relation between games (as viewed and analyzed in game theory) and concurrent game models. Then, we present logics which can be used to *characterize* solution concepts and logics which can *use* such solution concepts to reason about the outcome of games and the ability of rational players. For a more substantial treatment on solution concepts we refer the reader to the chapters by Bonanno [18], Pacuit [68], and Perea [74] in this book.

5.1   Representing Games as Concurrent Games Models

Standard models of modal logics correspond to strategic games, as shown in [9,52]. Moreover, concurrent game models have a close relationship to strategic and

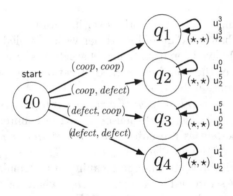

Fig. 4. Prisoner's Dilemma modelled as CGM $\mathcal{M}_{pris}$.

extensive form games, cf. [59]. We illustrate the correspondence with two examples of how strategic and extensive game frames compare to concurrent game models. The major difference is that CGMs lack the notion of payoff/outcome. However, we recall after [9,59] that CGMs can embed strategic games (cf. Example 11) and extensive games with perfect information (cf. Example 12) in a natural way. This can be done, e.g., by adding auxiliary propositions to the leaf nodes of tree-like CGMs that describe the payoffs of agents. Under this perspective, concurrent game structures can be seen as a strict generalisation of extensive form games.

In formal terms, consider first any strategic game and let U be the set of all possible utility values in it. For each value $v \in U$ and agent $a \in \text{Agt}$, we introduce a proposition u_a^v and put $u_a^v \in V(q)$ iff a gets a payoff v in state q.

Example 11 (Prisoner's Dilemma as CGM). The Prisoner's Dilemma (Example 1) can also be represented by the following CGM:

$$(\{1,2\}, \{q_0, \ldots, q_4\}, \{defect, coop\}, \text{Act}, \text{out}, V)$$

with $\text{Act}(a, q) = \{defect, coop\}$ for all players a and states q, $\text{out}(q_0, coop, coop) = q_1$, $\text{out}(q_0, coop, defect) = q_2$, $\text{out}(q_0, defect, coop) = q_3$, $\text{out}(q_0, defect, defect) = q_4$, and $\text{out}(q_i, a_1, a_2) = q_i$ for $i = 1, \ldots, 4$ and $a_1, a_2 \in \{defect, coop\}$. The CGM is shown in Fig. 4 where the labeling function V is defined over $Prop = \{\text{start}\} \cup \{u_a^v \mid a \in \text{Agt}, v \in \{0,1,3,5\}\}$ as shown in the figure; e.g., we have $V(q_2) = \{u_1^0, u_2^5\}$ representing that players 1 and 2 receive utility of 0 and 5, respectively, if strategy profile $(coop, defect)$ is played.

Example 12 (Bargaining). This example shows that CGMs are also rich enough to model (possibly infinite) extensive form games. Consider bargaining with time discount (cf. [65,76]). Two players, a_1 and a_2, bargain over how to split goods worth initially $w_0 = 1$ euro. After each round without agreement, the subjective worth of the goods reduces by *discount rates* δ_1 (for player a_1) and δ_2 (for player a_2). So, after t rounds the goods are worth $\langle \delta_1^t, \delta_2^t \rangle$, respectively. Subsequently, a_1 (if t is even) or a_2 (if t is odd) makes an offer to split the goods in proportions

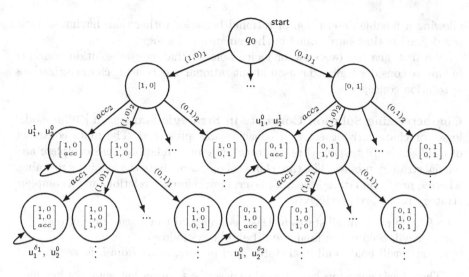

Fig. 5. CGM $\mathcal{M}_{barg}$ modeling the bargaining game.

$\langle x, 1 - x \rangle$, and the other player accepts or rejects it. If the offer is accepted, then a_1 takes $x\delta_1^t$, and a_2 gets $(1 - x)\delta_2^t$; otherwise the game continues.

The CGM corresponding to this extensive form game is shown in Fig. 5. Note that the model has a tree-like structure with infinite depth and an infinite branching factor. Nodes represent various states of the negotiation process, and arcs show how agents' moves change the state of the game. A node label refers to the history of the game for better readability. For instance, $\begin{bmatrix} 0,1 \\ 1,0 \\ acc \end{bmatrix}$ has the meaning that in the first round 1 offered $\langle 0, 1 \rangle$ which was rejected by 2. In the next round 2's offer $\langle 1, 0 \rangle$ has been accepted by 1 and the game has ended.

5.2 Characterization of Solution Concepts and Abilities

Rationality can be approached in different ways. Research within game theory understandably favours work on the *characterization* of various types of rationality (and defining most appropriate solution concepts). Applications of game theory, also understandably, tend toward *using* the solution concepts in order to predict the outcome in a given game; in other words, to "solve" the game. In this section we discuss logics which address both aspects. A natural question is *why* we need logics for describing and using solution concepts. In our opinion there are at least three good reasons: (i) Logical descriptions of solution concepts help for better understanding of their inner structures; e.g. interrelations can be proven by means of logical reasoning. (ii) Model checking provides an automatic way to verify properties of games and strategy profiles; e.g. whether a given profile is a Nash equilibrium in a given game or whether there is a Nash equilibrium at all. (iii) Often, the logical characterization of solution concepts is a necessary first step for using them to reason about rational agents in a flexible way, i.e. for allowing a flexible description of rational behavior rather than having a static pre-defined notion, hard-coded in the semantics of a logic.

We first give an overview of logics able to characterize solution concepts before we consider logics to reason about rational agents using characterizations of solution concepts.

Characterizing Solution Concepts in Strategic Games. In [50], a modal logic for characterizing solution concepts was presented. The main construct of the logic is $[\beta]\varphi$ where β ranges over preference relations, and complete and partial strategy profiles. The three kinds of operators have the following meaning, where i, $pref_i$, and σ, represent a player, her preference relation, and a complete strategy profile, respectively:

$[pref_i]\varphi$: φ holds in all states at least as preferred to i as the current one.
$[\sigma]\varphi$: φ will hold in the final state if all players follow σ.
$[\sigma_{-i}]\varphi$: φ will hold in all final states if all players, apart from i, follow σ.

These basic operators can be used to describe solution concepts. For instance, the formula $BR_i(\sigma) \equiv (\neg[\sigma_{-i}]\neg[pref_i]\varphi) \rightarrow [\sigma]\varphi$ expresses that σ_i is a *best response* to σ_{-i} with respect to φ: if there is a strategy for i (note that σ_{-i} does not fix a strategy for i) such that the reachable state satisfies φ and is among the most preferred ones for player i; then, the strategy σ_i (which is included in σ) does also bring about φ. Then, the property that σ is a Nash equilibrium can be captured with the formula $NE(\sigma) \equiv \bigwedge_{i \in \text{Agt}} BR_i(\sigma)$.

The above characterization of Nash equilibrium illustrates that, in order to assign properties to specific strategies, the strategies (or better: associated syntactic symbols) must be explicit in the object language. In Sect. 4.2 we have discussed some ATL-like logics of this kind that allow to reason about the outcome of specific strategies.

In ATLI, proposed by Jamroga et al. [59] (cf. Sect. 4.2) for example, best response strategies can be characterized as follows (where U is assumed to be a *finite* set of utility values, and $u_a^{\geq v} \equiv \bigvee_{v \in U} u_a^v$ expresses that agent a gets a utility value of at least v):

$$BR_a(\sigma) \equiv (\mathbf{str}_{\text{Agt} \setminus \{a\}} \sigma[\text{Agt} \setminus \{a\}]) \bigwedge_{v \in U} \left((\langle\!\langle a \rangle\!\rangle \mathcal{F} u_a^v) \rightarrow ((\mathbf{str}_a \sigma[a]) \langle\!\langle \emptyset \rangle\!\rangle \mathcal{F} u_a^{\geq v}) \right).$$

$BR_a(\sigma)$ refers to $\sigma[a]$ being a best response strategy for a against $\sigma[\text{Agt} \setminus \{a\}]$. The first counterfactual operator occurring in $BR_a(\sigma)$ fixes the strategies for all players except a. Then, each conjunct corresponds to a utility value v and expresses that if player a has a strategy to eventually achieve v (given the fixed strategies of the other players); then, a's strategy $\sigma[a]$ does eventually guarantee at least v. That is, $\sigma[a]$ is at least as good as any other strategy of a against the other players' strategies $\sigma[\text{Agt} \setminus \{a\}]$. The best response strategy allows to characterize Nash equilibria and subgame perfect Nash equilibria:

$$NE(\sigma) \equiv \bigwedge_{a \in \text{Agt}} BR_a(\sigma) \quad \text{and} \quad SPN(\sigma) \equiv \langle\!\langle \emptyset \rangle\!\rangle \mathcal{G} \, NE(\sigma).$$

Example 13 (Prisoner's Dilemma Continued). We continue Example 11. Suppose the strategy term σ represents the strategy profile in which both players execute *coop* in q_0 and an arbitrary action in the "final" states q_1, q_2, q_3, q_4. Let us now justify $\mathcal{M}_{dil}, q_0 \models BR_1(\sigma)$. The first operator ($\mathbf{str}_{\mathrm{Agt}\setminus\{1\}}\sigma[\mathrm{Agt} \setminus \{1\}]$) fixes the strategy of player 2, i.e. to cooperate. Then, player 1 has a strategy to obtain payoff u_1^3 and u_1^0 (expressed by $\langle\!\langle 1 \rangle\!\rangle \mathcal{F} u_1^v$) by playing *coop* and *defect* in q_0, respectively. Hence, player 1's strategy contained in σ also guarantees a payoff of u_1^3 (expressed by $(\mathbf{str}_1\sigma[1])\langle\!\langle \emptyset \rangle\!\rangle \mathcal{F} u_1^{\geq v}$). This shows that player 1's strategy contained in σ is indeed a best response to player 2's strategy contained in σ.

We have another look at the given characterization of a best response strategy; in particular, at the temporal operator $\mathcal{F}$ used in the characterization. The antecedent $\langle\!\langle a \rangle\!\rangle \mathcal{F} u_a^v$ requires that player a achieves v somewhere along every resulting path; it is true for the *greatest* value v along the path. In contrast, if we replace $\mathcal{F}$ by $\mathcal{G}$ the antecedent is only satisfied for the smallest value v; for, it has to be true in *every* state along a path. In general, we can use any of the *unary* temporal operators $\mathcal{X}, \mathcal{G}, \mathcal{F}, \_\mathcal{U}\psi, \psi\mathcal{U}\_$ and define variants BR_a^T, NE^T, SPN^T where T stands for any of these temporal operators and replaces $\mathcal{F}$ everywhere in the characterizations above. We refer to them as T-best response etc., each corresponding to a *different temporal pattern* of utilities. For example, we may assume that *agent a gets v* if a utility of at least v is guaranteed for every time moment ($T = \mathcal{G}$), or if it is eventually achieved ($T = \mathcal{F}$), and so on. In [59] it is shown that the $\mathcal{F}$-Nash equilibrium corresponds to its game-theoretic counterpart. This is obvious from the way games were encoded into CGMs: utility values were added to terminal states.

In Bulling et al. [29], these concepts are further generalized to *general solution concepts.* They evaluate strategies with respect to path formulae: the utility of a strategy depends on the truth of specific path formula. Furthermore, ATL *with plausibility* is introduced which extends ATL with intentions in several respects.

Further approaches for characterizing solution concepts, which we cannot discuss in detail due to lack of space, are proposed in [9, 14, 52].

Reasoning about the Outcome of Rational Play. The logics discussed in the previous paragraph allow to characterize game-theoretic solution concepts. It is also interesting to *use* game-theoretic solution concepts to reason about rational players. Although players have limited ability to predict the future often some lines of action seem more sensible or realistic than others. If a rationality criterion is available, we obtain means to focus on a proper subset of possible plays and to reason about the abilities of players.

Game logic with preferences (GLP), proposed by van Otterloo et al. [53], was designed to address the *outcome* of rational play in extensive form games with perfect information. The central idea of GLP is facilitated by the *preference operator* $[A : \varphi]$, interpreted as follows: If the truth of φ can be enforced by group A, then we remove from the model all the actions of A that do *not* enforce it and evaluate ψ in the resulting model. Thus, the evaluation of GLP formulae is underpinned by the assumption that *rational agents satisfy their preferences whenever they can.* This is a way of *using* solution concepts to reason about rational outcome.

The ideas behind ATLI and GLP were combined and extended in ATL *with plausibility* (ATLP), proposed by Bulling et al. [29]. The logic allows to reason about various rationality assumptions of agents in a flexible way. For this purpose, sets of rational strategy profiles can be specified in the object language in order to analyze agents' play if only these strategy profiles were allowed. For example, if we again consider the Prisoner's Dilemma CGM from Example 13, a typical formula has the following form: **set - pl** $\sigma.NE^{\mathcal{F}}(\sigma)$**Pl** $\langle\!\langle\{1\}\rangle\!\rangle\mathcal{X}((u_1^3 \wedge u_2^3) \vee (u_1^1 \wedge u_2^1))$. The formula expresses that if it is supposed to be rational to follow $\mathcal{F}$-Nash equilibrium strategy profiles; then, player 1 can guarantee that the players will both get a payoff of 1 or both get a payoff of 3. Similar to ATLI, $NE^{\mathcal{F}}(\sigma)$ describes all Nash equilibrium strategies. The term $\sigma.NE^{\mathcal{F}}(\sigma)$ collects all these strategy profiles and the operator **set - pl·** assumes that they describe rational behavior. Finally, operator **Pl** assumes that all agents play indeed rationally, and restricts their choices to rational ones; that is, Nash equilibria in this example. The restriction to rational behavior rules out all other alternatives. The logic also allows to characterize generalized versions of classical solution concepts through the characterization of patterns of payoffs by temporal formulae and quantification over strategy profiles. For further details, we refer to [24,29]. In [26] ATLP was enriched with an epistemic dimension, more precisely combined with the logic CSL discussed in Sect. 6.4, to reason about rational players under incomplete information.

Game Logic (GL) from Parikh [69] is another logic to reason about games, more precisely about determined two-player games. It builds upon propositional dynamic logic (PDL) and extends it with new operators. The work in [53,66,67] commits to a particular view of rationality (Nash equilibria, undominated strategies etc.). Finally, we would also like to mention the related work in [14] on rational dynamics and in [17] on modal logic and game theory.

6 Strategic Reasoning Under Incomplete Information

6.1 Incomplete Information Models and Uniform Strategies

The decision making capabilities and abilities of strategically reasoning players are influenced by the knowledge they possess about the world, other players, past actions, etc. So far we have considered structures of *complete and (almost) perfect information* in the sense that players are completely aware of the rules and structure of the game system and of the current state of the play. The only information they lack is the choice of actions of the other players at the current state. However, in reality this is rarely the case: usually players have only partial information about the structure and the rules of the game, as well as the precise history and the current state of the game. It is important to note that strategic ability crucially depends on the players' knowledge. In the following we are concerned with the following question: *What can players achieve in a game if they are only partially informed about its structure and the current state?*

Following the tradition of epistemic logic, we model the players' incomplete information[13] by *indistinguishability relations* $\sim \subseteq \mathsf{St} \times \mathsf{St}$ on the state space. We write $q \sim_a q'$ to describe player a's inability to discern between states q and q'. Both states appear identical from a's perspective. The indistinguishability relations are traditionally assumed to be equivalence relations. The knowledge of a player is then determined as follows: a player *knows* a property O in a state q if O is the case in all states indistinguishable from q for that player.

How does the incomplete information, modelled by an indistinguishability relation, affect the abilities of players? In the case of ATL^* with complete information, abilities to achieve goals were modeled by strategies defined on states or (play) histories, i.e. memoryless and memory-based strategies. A basic assumption in the case of incomplete information is that *a player has the same choices in indistinguishable states*, otherwise he/she would have a way to discern between these states.

Formally, a concurrent game with incomplete information is modelled by a *concurrent epistemic game structure* (CEGS), which is a tuple

$$\mathcal{S} = (\mathsf{Agt}, \mathsf{St}, \{\sim_a \mid a \in \mathsf{Agt}\}, \mathsf{Act}, \mathsf{act}, \mathsf{out})$$

where $(\mathsf{Agt}, \mathsf{St}, \mathsf{Act}, \mathsf{act}, \mathsf{out})$ is a CGS (cf. Definition 5) and $\sim_a$ is the indistinguishability relation of player a over St, one per agent in Agt, such that if $q \sim_a q'$ then $\mathsf{act}_a(q) = \mathsf{act}_a(q')$.

Just like a CGM, a *concurrent epistemic game model* (CEGM) is defined by adding to a CEGS a labeling of game states with sets of atomic propositions. Note that models of perfect information (CGMs) can be seen as a special case of CEGMs where each $\sim_a$ is the smallest reflexive relation (i.e., such that $q \sim_a q'$ iff $q = q'$).

Example 14 (Prisoner's Escape with Incomplete Information). We now explore the consequences of incomplete information in the Prisoner's escape scenario from Example 3. Recall that Frank knows the two passwords but suppose now that he does not know which one is for which guard. Equivalently, we can assume that he does not know how the guards look and which guard is at which exit. Hence, Frank does not know which password to use where. Surely, Charlie knows the guards and who is at which exit. In this setting, Frank is still able to escape with Charlie's active help. That is, Frank asks Charlie about the guards, which we now model explicitly with the action *ask*. When asked, Charlie replies by telling the truth. But at states q_1 and q_2 Charlie still has the choice of cooperating by keeping quiet or defecting by warning the guards when he sees Frank going to the respective exit. A CEGM $\mathcal{M}'_{esc}$ modelling this scenario is shown in Fig. 6.

---

[13] Traditionally in game theory two different terms are used to indicate lack of information: "incomplete" and "imperfect". Usually, the former refers to uncertainties about the game structure and rules, while the latter refers to uncertainties about the history, current state, etc. of the specific *play of the game*. Here we will use the latter term in about the same sense, whereas we will use "incomplete information" more loosely, to indicate any possible relevant lack of information.

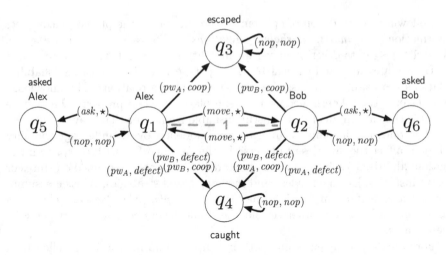

Fig. 6. Prisoner's escape with incomplete information.

The relation $q_1 \sim_1 q_2$ represents that player 1 (Frank), does not know which guard is at which entrance.

How do these perceptual limitations affect the agents' abilities? Under the assumption of complete information, Frank and Charlie can guarantee that Frank will eventually escape from q_1 and q_2 by a simple memoryless strategy for both: $s_{\{1,2\}}(q_1) = (pw_A, coop)$, $s_{\{1,2\}}(q_2) = (pw_B, coop)$, and arbitrarily defined for the other states in $\mathcal{M}_{esc}$. This strategy, however, is *not* feasible if Frank's incomplete information is taken into account because it prescribes to him different actions in the indistinguishable states q_1 and q_2. Actually, it is easy to see that in that sense there is no feasible *memoryless* strategy which achieves the property from q_1 or q_2. This is so because a strategy must be successful from all epistemic alternatives for the player (Frank). For example, his action prescribed by the strategy at q_2 must also be successful from q_1 and vice versa. This claim will become precise later, when we present the formal semantics.

However, Frank has a feasible *memory-based* strategy which guarantees that he can eventually escape, again in cooperation with Charlie. Firstly, from state q_1 or q_2 Frank asks Charlie about the guards, thus *learns* about the environment, and then goes back to use the correct password and to escape if Charlie cooperates. Formally, the reason for a successful memory-based strategy is that the *histories* $q_1 q_5 q_1$ and $q_2 q_6 q_2$ can be distinguished by Frank.

We will analyze the interaction between memory and information more formally in Sect. 6.3.

The above example indicates that the notion of strategy must be refined in order to be consistent with the incomplete information setting. An executable strategy must assign the same choices to indistinguishable situations. Such strategies are called *uniform*, e.g. see [58].

Definition 7 (Uniform Strategies). *Let $\mathcal{M}$ be a CEGM over sets of states St. A memoryless strategy s_a (over $\mathcal{M}$) is uniform if the following condition is satisfied:*

$$\text{for all states } q, q' \in \text{St}, \text{ if } q \sim_a q' \text{ then } s_a(q) = s_a(q').$$

For memory-based *strategies we lift the indistinguishability between states to indistinguishability between (play) histories. Two histories $\pi = q_0 q_1 \ldots q_n$ and $\pi' = q'_0 q'_1 \ldots q'_{n'}$ are said to be indistinguishable for agent a, denoted by $\pi \approx_a \pi'$, if and only if, $n = n'$ and $q_i \sim_a q'_i$ for $i = 0, \ldots, n$.[14]*
A memory-based strategy s_a is uniform if the following condition holds:

$$\text{for all histories } \pi, \pi' \in \text{St}^+, \text{ if } \pi \approx_a \pi' \text{ then } s_a(\pi) = s_a(\pi').$$

Analogously to perfect information, a uniform joint strategy for a group A is a tuple of individual uniform strategies, one per member of A.[15]

6.2 Expressing Strategic Ability Under Uncertainty in ATL*

Agents' incomplete information and use of memory can be incorporated into ATL* in different ways, see e.g. [8,56–58,78]. In [78] a natural taxonomy of four strategy types was proposed: I (respectively i) stands for *complete* (respectively *incomplete*) *information*, and R (respectively r) refers to *perfect recall* (respectively *no recall*). The approach of Schobbens et al. [78] was syntactic in the sense that cooperation modalities were extended with subscripts: $\langle\!\langle A \rangle\!\rangle_{xy}$ where x indicates the use of memory in the strategies (memory-based if $x = R$ / memoryless if $x = r$) and y indicates the information setting (complete information if $y = I$ and incomplete information if $y = i$).

Here, we take a semantic approach. We assume that the object language of ATL/ATL* stays the same, but the semantics is parameterized with the strategy type – yielding four different semantic variants of the logic, labeled accordingly (ATL$_{IR}$, ATL$_{Ir}$, ATL$_{iR}$, ATL$_{ir}$). As a consequence, we obtain the following semantic relations:

$\models_{IR}$: complete information and memory-based strategies;
$\models_{Ir}$: complete information and memoryless strategies;
$\models_{iR}$: incomplete information and memory-based strategies;
$\models_{ir}$: incomplete information and memoryless strategies.

Given a CEGM $\mathcal{M}$, the two complete information semantic variants are obtained by updating the main semantic clause from Sect. 3.2 as follows:

---

[14] This corresponds to the notion of synchronous perfect recall according to [41].

[15] Note that uniformity of a joint strategy is based on individual epistemic relations, rather than any collective epistemic relation (representing, e.g., A's common, mutual, or distributed knowledge, cf. Sect. 6.4). This is because executability of agent a's choices within strategy s_A should only depend on what a can observe and deduce.

Alternative semantics where uniformity of joint strategies is defined in terms of knowledge of the group as a whole have been discussed in [36,48].

$\mathcal{M}, q \models_{IR} \langle\!\langle A \rangle\!\rangle \gamma$ iff there is a *memory-based* joint strategy s_A for A such that $\mathcal{M}, \lambda \models \gamma$ for every play $\lambda \in$ outcome_plays(q, s_A);

$\mathcal{M}, q \models_{Ir} \langle\!\langle A \rangle\!\rangle \gamma$ iff there is a *memoryless* joint strategy s_A for A such that $\mathcal{M}, \lambda \models \gamma$ for every play $\lambda \in$ outcome_plays(q, s_A).

For the imperfect information variants we have:

$\mathcal{M}, q \models_{iR} \langle\!\langle A \rangle\!\rangle \gamma$ iff there is a *uniform memory-based* joint strategy s_A for A such that $\mathcal{M}, \lambda \models \gamma$ for every play $\lambda \in \bigcup_{q' \in \mathsf{St} \text{ s.t. } q \sim_A q'}$ outcome_plays(q', s_A);

$\mathcal{M}, q \models_{ir} \langle\!\langle A \rangle\!\rangle \gamma$ iff there is a *uniform memoryless* joint strategy s_A for A such that $\mathcal{M}, \lambda \models \gamma$ for every play $\lambda \in \bigcup_{q' \in \mathsf{St} \text{ s.t. } q \sim_A q'}$ outcome_plays(q', s_A);

where $\sim_A := \bigcup_{a \in A} \sim_a$ is used to capture the *collective knowledge of coalition* A. It is clear from the definition that this particular notion of collective knowledge refers to what everybody in A knows, e.g. [41]. For a discussion of other possibilities, we refer the reader to Sect. 6.4.

Example 15 (Prisoner's Escape: Example 14 Continued). We formalize some properties from Example 14.

1. For all $q \in \mathsf{St} \setminus \{q_4\}$ we have $\mathcal{M}'_{esc}, q \models_{Ir} \langle\!\langle f, c \rangle\!\rangle \mathcal{F}$ escaped: under the assumption of complete information coalition $\{f, c\}$ can guarantee that Frank can escape by using a memoryless strategy.
2. $\mathcal{M}'_{esc}, q_1 \not\models_{ir} \langle\!\langle f, c \rangle\!\rangle (\neg\text{asked}) \mathcal{U}$ escaped: under the assumption of incomplete information Frank and Charlie cannot guarantee that Frank will eventually escape without asking Charlie about the identity of the guards. This is true even in the case of memory-based strategies:
   $\mathcal{M}'_{esc}, q_1 \not\models_{iR} \langle\!\langle f, c \rangle\!\rangle (\neg\text{asked}) \mathcal{U}$ escaped.
3. $\mathcal{M}'_{esc}, q_1 \models_{iR} \langle\!\langle f, c \rangle\!\rangle \mathcal{F}$ escaped: under the assumption of incomplete information Frank and Charlie can guarantee that Frank will eventually escape by using a uniform memory-based strategy.

In [28] incomplete information has been additionally classified according to *objective* and *subjective* ability. Here, we only consider *subjective* ability; that is, $\langle\!\langle A \rangle\!\rangle \gamma$ means that A is not only able to execute the right strategy but A can also identify the strategy. The mere existence of a winning strategy (without A being able to find it) is not sufficient under this interpretation. This is why, when evaluating $\langle\!\langle A \rangle\!\rangle \gamma$ in state q, all epistemic alternatives of q with respect to $\sim_A$ are taken into account. Again, we will discuss some other possibilities in Sect. 6.4.

Finally, we would like to add a note on the treatment of nested strategic modalities in ATL. When a nested strategic modality is interpreted, the new strategy does not take into account the previous sequence of events: Agents are effectively forgetting what they have observed before. This can lead to counter-intuitive behaviors in the presence of perfect recall and incomplete information. To overcome this, just recently a "no-forgetting semantics" for ATL has been proposed in Bulling et al. [30].

6.3 Comparing Semantics of Strategic Ability

Semantic variants of ATL are derived from different assumptions about agents' capabilities. Can the agents "see" the current state of the system, or only a part of it? Can they memorize the whole history of observations in the game? Different answers to these questions induce different semantics of strategic ability, and they clearly give rise to different analysis of a given game model. However, it is not entirely clear to what extent they give rise to different *logics*. One natural question that arises is whether the semantic variants generate different sets of valid (and dually satisfiable) sentences. In this section, we show a comparison of the validity sets for ATL* with respect to the four semantic variants presented in the previous section. A detailed analysis and technical results can be found in [28].

The comparison of the validity sets is important for at least two reasons. Firstly, many logicians identify a logic with the set of sentences that are valid in the logic. Thus, by comparing validity sets we compare the respective logics in the traditional sense. Perhaps more importantly, validities of ATL capture general properties of games under consideration: if, e.g., two variants of ATL generate the same valid sentences then the underlying notions of ability induce the same kind of games. All the variants studied here are defined over the same class of models (CEGS). The difference between games "induced" by different semantics lies in available strategies and the winning conditions for them.

We recall that we use superscripts (e.g., '$*$') to denote the syntactic variant of ATL, and subscripts to denote the semantic variant being used. For example, ATL$^*_{ir}$ denotes the language of ATL* interpreted with the semantic relation $\models_{ir}$, that is, the one which assumes incomplete information and memoryless strategies. Moreover, we will use $Valid(L)$ to denote the set of validities of logic L, and $Sat(L)$ to denote the set of satisfiable formulas in L.

Perfect vs. Incomplete Information. We begin by comparing properties of games with limited information to those where players can always recognize the current state of the world. Firstly, we recall that complete information can be seen as a special case of incomplete information: each CGM can be seen as a CEGM in which each indistinguishability relation is taken as the smallest reflexive relation. Hence, every valid formula of ATL$^*_{ir}$ is also a validity of ATL$^*_{Ir}$: if there were a CEGM $\mathcal{M}$ with $\mathcal{M} \not\models_{Ir} \varphi$ then also $\mathcal{M} \not\models_{ir} \varphi$ would be the case. On the other hand, the formula $\langle\!\langle A \rangle\!\rangle \mathcal{F} \varphi \leftrightarrow \varphi \vee \langle\!\langle A \rangle\!\rangle \mathcal{X} \langle\!\langle A \rangle\!\rangle \mathcal{F} \varphi$ is a validity of ATL$_{Ir}$ but not of ATL$_{ir}$, which shows that the containment is strict even in the limited syntactic fragment of ATL.[16]

The argument for ATL$_{iR}$ vs. ATL$_{IR}$ is analogous. Thus, we get that $Valid(ATL_{ir}) \subsetneq Valid(ATL_{Ir})$ and $Valid(ATL_{iR}) \subsetneq Valid(ATL_{IR})$, and the same for the broader language of ATL*.

---

[16] The equivalence between $\langle\!\langle A \rangle\!\rangle \mathcal{F} \varphi$ and $\varphi \vee \langle\!\langle A \rangle\!\rangle \mathcal{X} \langle\!\langle A \rangle\!\rangle \mathcal{F} \varphi$ is extremely important since it provides a fixpoint characterization of $\langle\!\langle A \rangle\!\rangle \mathcal{F} \varphi$. The fact that $\langle\!\langle A \rangle\!\rangle \mathcal{F} \varphi \leftrightarrow \varphi \vee \langle\!\langle A \rangle\!\rangle \mathcal{X} \langle\!\langle A \rangle\!\rangle \mathcal{F} \varphi$ is not valid under incomplete information is one of the main reasons why constructing verification and satisfiability checking algorithms is so difficult for incomplete information strategies.

Memory-based vs. Memoryless Strategies. The comparison of memory-based and memoryless strategies is technically more involved. Firstly, we observe that for any *tree-like* CGM $\mathcal{M}$ the sets of memory-based and memoryless strategies coincide. Secondly, one can show that every CGM $\mathcal{M}$ and state q in $\mathcal{M}$ can be unfolded into an equivalent (more precisely, bisimilar) tree-like CGM $T(\mathcal{M}, q)$ as in [3]. These two observations imply that $\mathsf{ATL}^*_{\mathsf{Ir}} \subseteq \mathsf{ATL}^*_{\mathsf{IR}}$; for, if $\mathcal{M}, q \not\models_{IR} \varphi$ then $T(\mathcal{M}, q), q \not\models_{IR} \varphi$ (by the latter observation) and $T(\mathcal{M}, q), q \not\models_{Ir} \varphi$ (by the first observation). Moreover, the formula $\varphi \equiv \langle\langle A \rangle\rangle(\mathcal{F}\varphi_1 \wedge \mathcal{F}\varphi_2) \leftrightarrow \langle\langle A \rangle\rangle\mathcal{F}((\varphi_1 \wedge \langle\langle A \rangle\rangle\mathcal{F}\varphi_2) \vee (\varphi_2 \wedge \langle\langle A \rangle\rangle\mathcal{F}\varphi_1))$ is a validity of $\mathsf{ATL}^*_{\mathsf{IR}}$ but not of $\mathsf{ATL}^*_{\mathsf{Ir}}$, which shows that the inclusion is strict.[17] Note, however, that φ is *not* a formula of ATL. Indeed, it is well known that the semantics given by $\models_{IR}$ and $\models_{Ir}$ coincide in ATL, cf. [8,78]. As a consequence, we obtain that $Valid(\mathsf{ATL}^*_{\mathsf{Ir}}) \subsetneqq Valid(\mathsf{ATL}^*_{\mathsf{IR}})$ and $Valid(\mathsf{ATL}_{\mathsf{Ir}}) = Valid(\mathsf{ATL}_{\mathsf{IR}})$.

We observe that strict subsumption holds already for the language of ATL^+ which allows cooperation modalities to be followed by a Boolean combination of simple path formulae.

Finally, we consider the effect of memory in the incomplete information setting. The idea is the same as for perfect information, but the unfolding of a CEGM into an equivalent tree-like CEGM is technically more complex, as one has to take into account the indistinguishability relations (see [28] for details). To show that the inclusion is strict, we use $\langle\langle A \rangle\rangle\mathcal{X}\,\langle\langle A \rangle\rangle\mathcal{F}\varphi \rightarrow \langle\langle A \rangle\rangle\mathcal{F}\varphi$ which is valid in $\mathsf{ATL}_{\mathsf{iR}}$ but not in $\mathsf{ATL}_{\mathsf{ir}}$.[18] Thus, we get that $Valid(\mathsf{ATL}_{\mathsf{ir}}) \subsetneqq Valid(\mathsf{ATL}_{\mathsf{iR}})$, and analogously for the broader language of ATL^*.

Summary. We have obtained above the following hierarchy of logics:

$$Valid(\mathsf{ATL}^*_{\mathsf{ir}}) \subsetneqq Valid(\mathsf{ATL}^*_{\mathsf{iR}}) \subsetneqq Valid(\mathsf{ATL}^*_{\mathsf{Ir}}) \subsetneqq Valid(\mathsf{ATL}^*_{\mathsf{IR}}),$$
$$\text{and } Valid(\mathsf{ATL}_{\mathsf{ir}}) \subsetneqq Valid(\mathsf{ATL}_{\mathsf{iR}}) \subsetneqq Valid(\mathsf{ATL}_{\mathsf{Ir}}) = Valid(\mathsf{ATL}_{\mathsf{IR}}).$$

Equivalently, we can observe the following pattern in the sets of *satisfiable* sentences:

$$Sat(\mathsf{ATL}^*_{\mathsf{IR}}) \subsetneqq Sat(\mathsf{ATL}^*_{\mathsf{Ir}}) \subsetneqq Sat(\mathsf{ATL}^*_{\mathsf{iR}}) \subsetneqq Sat(\mathsf{ATL}^*_{\mathsf{ir}}),$$
$$\text{and } Sat(\mathsf{ATL}_{\mathsf{IR}}) = Sat(\mathsf{ATL}_{\mathsf{Ir}}) \subsetneqq Sat(\mathsf{ATL}_{\mathsf{iR}}) \subsetneqq Sat(\mathsf{ATL}_{\mathsf{ir}}).$$

The first, and most important, conclusion is that all four semantic variants of ability are different with respect to the properties of games they induce. Moreover, the results capture formally the usual intuition: complete information is a particular case of incomplete information, memory-based games are special

---

[17] The formula expresses decomposability of conjuctive goals: being able to achieve $\varphi_1 \wedge \varphi_2$ must be equivalent to having a strategy that achieves first φ_1 and φ_2, or vice versa. It is easy to see that the requirement holds for agents with perfect memory, but not for ones bound to use memoryless strategies (and hence to play the same action whenever the game comes back to a previously visited state).

[18] The formula states that, if A has an opening move and a follow-up strategy to achieve eventually φ, then both strategies can be combined into a single strategy enforcing eventually φ already from the initial state.

cases of memoryless games, and information is a more distinguishing factor than memory.

On a more general level, the results show that what agents can achieve is more sensitive to the strategic model of an agent (and a precise notion of achievement) than it was generally realized. No less importantly, the study reveals that some natural properties – usually taken for granted when reasoning about actions – may cease to be universally true if we change the strategic setting. Examples include fixpoint characterizations of temporal/strategic operators (that enable incremental synthesis and iterative execution of strategies), decomposability of conjunctive goals, and the duality between necessary and obtainable outcomes in a game (cf. [28] for an example). The first kind of property is especially important for practical purposes, since fixpoint equivalences provide the basis for most model checking and satisfiability checking algorithms. Last but not least, the results show that the language of ATL* is sufficiently expressive to distinguish the main notions of ability.

6.4 Epistemic Extensions of ATL

Reasoning about Knowledge. In this section we consider how the language of ATL can be combined with that of *epistemic logic*, in order to reason about the interplay of knowledge and ability more explicitly. The basic epistemic logic involves modalities for individual agent's knowledge K_i, with $K_i\varphi$ interpreted as "agent i knows that φ". Additionally, one can consider modalities for collective knowledge of groups of agents: *mutual knowledge* ($E_A\varphi$: "everybody in group A knows that φ"), *common knowledge* ($C_A\varphi$: "all the agents in A know that φ, and they know that they know it etc."), and *distributed knowledge* ($D_A\varphi$: "if the agents could share their individual information, they would be able to recognize that φ").

The formal semantics of epistemic operators is defined in terms of indistinguishability relations $\sim_1, ..., \sim_k$, given for instance in a concurrent epistemic game model:

$$\mathcal{M}, q \models K_i\varphi \text{ iff } \mathcal{M}, q' \models \varphi \text{ for all } q' \text{ such that } q \sim_i q'.$$

The accessibility relation corresponding to E_A is defined as $\sim_A^E = \bigcup_{i \in A} \sim_i$, and the semantics of E_A becomes

$$\mathcal{M}, q \models E_A\varphi \text{ iff } \mathcal{M}, q' \models \varphi \text{ for all } q' \text{ such that } q \sim_A^E q'.$$

Likewise, common knowledge C_A is given semantics in terms of the relation $\sim_A^C$ defined as the transitive closure of $\sim_A^E$:

$$\mathcal{M}, q \models C_A\varphi \text{ iff } \mathcal{M}, q' \models \varphi \text{ for all } q' \text{ such that } q \sim_A^C q'.$$

Finally, distributed knowledge D_A is based on the relation $\sim_A^D = \bigcap_{i \in A} \sim_i$, with the semantic clause defined analogously. For a more extensive exposition of epistemic logic, we refer the reader to [41,49,54].

Bringing Strategies and Knowledge Together: ATEL. The *alternating-time temporal epistemic logic* ATEL was introduced in [55,56] as a straightforward combination of the multi-agent epistemic logic and ATL in order to formalize reasoning about the interaction of knowledge and abilities of agents and coalitions. ATEL enables specification of various modes and nuances of interaction between knowledge and strategic abilities, e.g.: $\langle\!\langle A\rangle\!\rangle\varphi \to E_A\langle\!\langle A\rangle\!\rangle\varphi$ (if group A can bring about φ then everybody in A knows that they can), $E_A\langle\!\langle A\rangle\!\rangle\varphi \wedge \neg C_A\langle\!\langle A\rangle\!\rangle\varphi$ (the agents in A have mutual knowledge but not common knowledge that they can enforce φ); $\langle\!\langle i\rangle\!\rangle\varphi \to K_i\neg\langle\!\langle \mathsf{Agt} \setminus \{i\}\rangle\!\rangle\neg\varphi$ (if i can bring about φ then she knows that the rest of agents cannot prevent it), etc.

Models of ATEL are *concurrent epistemic game models* (CEGM): $\mathcal{M} = (\mathsf{Agt}, \mathsf{St}, \mathsf{Act}, \mathsf{act}, \mathsf{out}, V, \sim_1, ..., \sim_k)$ combining the CGM-based models for ATL and the multi-agent epistemic models. That is, the same models are used for ATEL and the Schobbens' ATL_{xy} variants of ATL as those presented in Sect. 6.2. The semantics of ATEL simply combines the semantic clauses from ATL and those from epistemic logic.

While ATEL extends both ATL and epistemic logic, it also raises a number of conceptual problems. Most importantly, one would expect that an agent's ability to achieve property φ should imply that the agent has enough control and knowledge to *identify* and *execute* a strategy that enforces φ. Unfortunately, neither of these can be expressed in ATEL.[19] A number of approaches have been proposed to overcome this problem. Most of the solutions agree that only *uniform* strategies (i.e., strategies that specify the same choices in indistinguishable states) are really executable, cf. our exposition of ATL variants for incomplete information in Sect. 6.2. However, in order to identify a successful strategy, the agents must consider not only the courses of action, starting from the current state of the system, but also from states that are indistinguishable from the current one. There are many cases here, especially when group epistemics is concerned: the agents may have common, ordinary, or distributed knowledge about a strategy being successful, or they may be hinted the right strategy by a distinguished member (the "leader"), a subgroup ("headquarters committee") or even another group of agents ("consulting company").

Epistemic Levels of Strategic Ability. There are several possible interpretations of A's ability to bring about property γ, formalized by formula $\langle\!\langle A\rangle\!\rangle\gamma$, under imperfect information:

1. There exists a behavior specification σ_A (not necessarily executable!) for agents in A such that, for every execution of σ_A, γ holds;
2. There is a uniform strategy s_A such that, for every execution of s_A, γ holds *(A has objective ability to enforce γ)*;
3. A knows that there is a uniform s_A such that, for every execution of s_A, γ holds *(A has a strategy "de dicto" to enforce γ)*;
4. There is a uniform s_A such that A knows that, for every execution of s_A, γ holds *(A has a strategy "de re" to enforce γ)*.

---

[19] For a formal argument, see [2,57].

Note that the above interpretations form a sequence of increasingly stronger levels of ability – each next one implies the previous ones.

Case 4 is arguably most interesting, as it formalizes the notion of agents in A *knowing how to play in order to enforce* γ. However, the statement "A knows that every execution of s_A satisfies γ" is precise only if A consists of a single agent a. Then, we take into account the paths starting from states indistinguishable from the current one according to a (i.e., $\bigcup_{q' \text{ with } q \sim_a q'}$ outcome_plays(q', s_a)). In case of multiple agents, there are several different "modes" in which they can know the right strategy. That is, given strategy s_A, coalition A can have:

- *Common knowledge* that s_A is a winning strategy. This requires the least amount of additional communication when coordinating a joint strategy: it is sufficient that agents in A agree upon a total order over their collective strategies before the game; then, during the game, they always choose the maximal strategy (with respect to this order) out of all the strategies that they commonly identify as winning;
- *Mutual knowledge* that s_A is a winning strategy: everybody in A knows that s_A is winning;
- *Distributed knowledge* that s_A is a winning strategy: if the agents share their knowledge at the current state, they can identify the strategy as winning;
- *"Leader"*: the strategy can be identified by an agent $a \in A$;
- *"Headquarters committee"*: the strategy can be identified by a subgroup $A' \subseteq A$;
- *"Consulting company"*: the strategy can be identified by another group B;
- ...other cases are also possible.

Expressing Levels of Ability: Constructive Knowledge. The issue of expressing various knowledge-related levels of ability through a suitable combination of strategic and epistemic logics has attracted significant attention. Most extensions (or refinements) of ATL, proposed as solutions, cover only some of the possibilities, albeit in an elegant way [2, 66, 78]. Others, such as [58, 60], offer a more general treatment of the problem at the expense of an overblown logical language. *Constructive Strategic Logic* (CSL), proposed by Jamroga and Ågotnes [57], aims at a solution which is both general and elegant. However, there is a price to pay. In CSL, formulae are interpreted over *sets of states* rather than single states. We write $\mathcal{M}, Q \models \langle\!\langle A \rangle\!\rangle \varphi$ to express the fact that A must have a strategy which is successful for all "opening" states from Q. New epistemic operators $\mathbb{K}_i, \mathbb{E}_A, \mathbb{C}_A, \mathbb{D}_A$ for "practical" or "constructive" knowledge yield the set of states for which a single evidence (i.e., a successful strategy) should be presented (instead of checking if the required property holds in each of the states separately, like standard epistemic operators do).

Formally, the semantics of CSL (in its broadest syntactic variant CSL*) over concurrent epistemic game models is defined by the following clauses:

$\mathcal{M}, Q \models p$ iff $p \in \pi(q)$ for every $q \in Q$;
$\mathcal{M}, Q \models \neg\varphi$ iff $\mathcal{M}, Q \not\models \varphi$;
$\mathcal{M}, Q \models \varphi \wedge \psi$ iff $\mathcal{M}, Q \models \varphi$ and $\mathcal{M}, Q \models \psi$;

$\mathcal{M}, Q \models \langle\!\langle A \rangle\!\rangle \varphi$ iff there is a uniform strategy s_A such that $\mathcal{M}, \lambda \models \varphi$ for every $\lambda \in \bigcup_{q \in Q}$ outcome_plays(q, s_A);

$\mathcal{M}, Q \models \mathbb{K}_i \varphi$ iff $\mathcal{M}, \{q' \mid \exists_{q \in Q} \ q \sim_i q'\} \models \varphi$;
$\mathcal{M}, Q \models \mathbb{C}_A \varphi$ iff $\mathcal{M}, \{q' \mid \exists_{q \in Q} \ q \sim_A^C q'\} \models \varphi$;
$\mathcal{M}, Q \models \mathbb{E}_A \varphi$ iff $\mathcal{M}, \{q' \mid \exists_{q \in Q} \ q \sim_A^E q'\} \models \varphi$;
$\mathcal{M}, Q \models \mathbb{D}_A \varphi$ iff $\mathcal{M}, \{q' \mid \exists_{q \in Q} \ q \sim_A^D q'\} \models \varphi$.

The semantic clauses for path subformulae are the same as in ATL*. Additionally, we define that $\mathcal{M}, q \models \varphi$ iff $\mathcal{M}, \{q\} \models \varphi$.

A nice feature of CSL is that standard knowledge operators can be defined using constructive knowledge, e.g., as $K_a \varphi \equiv \mathbb{K}_a \langle\!\langle \emptyset \rangle\!\rangle \varphi \mathcal{U} \varphi$[20]. It is easy to see that $\mathcal{M}, q \models \mathbb{K}_a \langle\!\langle \emptyset \rangle\!\rangle \varphi \mathcal{U} \varphi$ iff $\mathcal{M}, q' \models \varphi$ for every q' such that $q \sim_a q'$.

We point out that in CSL:

1. $\mathbb{K}_a \langle\!\langle a \rangle\!\rangle \varphi$ refers to agent a having a strategy *"de re"* to enforce φ (i.e. having a successful uniform strategy and knowing the strategy);
2. $K_a \langle\!\langle a \rangle\!\rangle \varphi$ refers to agent a having a strategy *"de dicto"* to enforce φ (i.e. knowing only that *some* successful uniform strategy is available);
3. $\langle\!\langle a \rangle\!\rangle \varphi$ expresses that agent a has a uniform strategy to enforce φ *from the current state* (but not necessarily even knows about it).

Thus, $\mathbb{K}_a \langle\!\langle a \rangle\!\rangle \varphi$ captures the notion of a's knowing *how to play* to achieve φ, while $K_a \langle\!\langle a \rangle\!\rangle \varphi$ refers to knowing only *that a successful play is possible*. This extends naturally to abilities of coalitions, with $\mathbb{C}_A \langle\!\langle A \rangle\!\rangle \varphi, \mathbb{E}_A \langle\!\langle A \rangle\!\rangle \varphi, \mathbb{D}_A \langle\!\langle A \rangle\!\rangle \varphi$ formalizing common, mutual, and distributed knowledge how to play, $\mathbb{K}_a \langle\!\langle A \rangle\!\rangle \varphi$ capturing the "leader" scenario, and so on (and similarly for different levels of knowledge "de dicto"). We conclude this topic with the following example.

Example 16 (Market Scenario). Consider an industrial company that wants to start production, and looks for a good strategy when and how it should do it. The market model is depicted in Fig. 7. The economy is assumed to run in simple cycles: after the moment of bad economy (bad-market), there is always a good time for small and medium enterprises (s&m), after which the market tightens and an oligopoly emerges. At the end, the market gets stale, and we have stagnation and bad economy again.

The company c is the only agent whose actions are represented in the model. The company can wait (action *wait*) or decide to start production: either on its own (*own-production*), or as a subcontractor of a major company (*subproduction*). Both decisions can lead to either loss or success, depending on the current market conditions. However, the company management cannot recognize the market conditions: bad market, time for small and medium enterprises, and oligopoly market look the same to them, as the epistemic links for c indicate.

The company can call the services of two marketing experts. Expert 1 is a specialist on oligopoly, and can recognize oligopoly conditions (although she cannot

---

[20] We cannot replace $\varphi \mathcal{U} \varphi$ by φ when the latter is a path formula, as then $\langle\!\langle \emptyset \rangle\!\rangle \varphi$ would not be a formula of CSL.

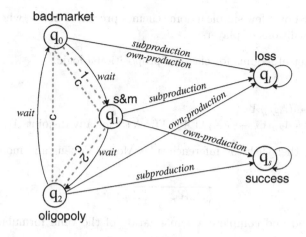

Fig. 7. Simple market: model $\mathcal{M}_{mark}$

distinguish between bad economy and s&m market). Expert 2 can recognize bad economy, but he cannot distinguish between other types of market. The experts' actions have no influence on the actual transitions of the model, and are omitted from the graph in Fig. 7. It is easy to see that the company cannot identify a successful strategy on its own: for instance, for the small and medium enterprises period, we have that $\mathcal{M}_{mark}, q_1 \models \neg \mathbb{K}_c \langle\!\langle c \rangle\!\rangle \mathcal{F}$ success. It is not even enough to call the help of a single expert: $\mathcal{M}_{mark}, q_1 \models \neg \mathbb{K}_1 \langle\!\langle c \rangle\!\rangle \mathcal{F}$ success $\wedge \neg \mathbb{K}_2 \langle\!\langle c \rangle\!\rangle \mathcal{F}$ success, or to ask the experts to independently work out a common strategy: $\mathcal{M}_{mark}, q_1 \models \neg \mathbb{E}_{\{1,2\}} \langle\!\langle c \rangle\!\rangle \mathcal{F}$ success. Still, the experts can propose the right strategy if they join forces and share available information: $\mathcal{M}_{mark}, q_1 \models \mathbb{D}_{\{1,2\}} \langle\!\langle c \rangle\!\rangle \mathcal{F}$ success.

This is not true anymore for bad market, i.e., $\mathcal{M}_{mark}, q_0 \models \neg \mathbb{D}_{\{1,2\}} \langle\!\langle c \rangle\!\rangle \mathcal{F}$ success, because c is a memoryless agent, and it has no uniform strategy to enforce success from q_0 at all. However, the experts can suggest a more complex scheme that involves consulting them once again in the future, as evidenced by $\mathcal{M}_{mark}, q_0 \models \mathbb{D}_{\{1,2\}} \langle\!\langle c \rangle\!\rangle \mathcal{X} \ \mathbb{D}_{\{1,2\}} \langle\!\langle c \rangle\!\rangle \mathcal{F}$ success.

7   Deductive Systems and Logical Decision Problems

7.1   Validity and Satisfiability in **ATL** and **ATL***

Characterizing the valid and, dually, the satisfiable formulae of a given logic by means of sound and complete deductive systems is a fundamental logical problem. Few such deductive systems have been developed so far for the logics discussed here, and these are mostly axiomatic systems. We will briefly present the one for ATL.

Axiomatic Systems for CL and ATL. In Pauly [71–73] it was shown that the conditions of liveness, safety, superadditivity, and Agt-maximality in Definition 4 can be captured by a few simple axiom schemes presented below, where $A_1, A_2 \subseteq$ Agt are any coalitions of players:

1. Complete set of axioms for classical propositional logic.
2. $\langle\!\langle \text{Agt} \rangle\!\rangle \mathcal{X} \top$
3. $\langle\!\langle A \rangle\!\rangle \mathcal{X} \bot$
4. $\neg \langle\!\langle \emptyset \rangle\!\rangle \mathcal{X} \varphi \rightarrow \langle\!\langle \text{Agt} \rangle\!\rangle \mathcal{X} \neg\varphi$
5. $\langle\!\langle A_1 \rangle\!\rangle \mathcal{X} \varphi \wedge \langle\!\langle A_2 \rangle\!\rangle \mathcal{X} \psi \rightarrow \langle\!\langle A_1 \cup A_2 \rangle\!\rangle \mathcal{X}(\varphi \wedge \psi)$ for any disjoint $A_1, A_2 \subseteq \text{Agt}$

These, together with the inference rules Modus Ponens and monotonicity:

$$\frac{\varphi \rightarrow \psi}{\langle\!\langle A \rangle\!\rangle \mathcal{X} \varphi \rightarrow \langle\!\langle A \rangle\!\rangle \mathcal{X} \psi}$$

provide a sound and complete axiomatization of the valid formulae of CL, see [71,73].

The temporal operators $\mathcal{G}$ and $\mathcal{U}$ satisfy the following validities in ATL that define them recursively as fixed points of certain monotone operators:

$(\mathbf{FP}_\mathcal{G})\ \langle\!\langle A \rangle\!\rangle \mathcal{G}\varphi \leftrightarrow \varphi \wedge \langle\!\langle A \rangle\!\rangle \mathcal{X} \langle\!\langle A \rangle\!\rangle \mathcal{G}\varphi,$
$(\mathbf{GFP}_\mathcal{G})\ \langle\!\langle \emptyset \rangle\!\rangle \mathcal{G}(\theta \rightarrow (\varphi \wedge \langle\!\langle A \rangle\!\rangle \mathcal{X}\theta)) \rightarrow \langle\!\langle \emptyset \rangle\!\rangle \mathcal{G}(\theta \rightarrow \langle\!\langle A \rangle\!\rangle \mathcal{G}\varphi),$
$(\mathbf{FP}_\mathcal{U})\ \langle\!\langle A \rangle\!\rangle \psi \mathcal{U} \varphi \leftrightarrow \varphi \vee (\psi \wedge \langle\!\langle A \rangle\!\rangle \mathcal{X} \langle\!\langle A \rangle\!\rangle \psi \mathcal{U} \varphi),$
$(\mathbf{LFP}_\mathcal{U})\ \langle\!\langle \emptyset \rangle\!\rangle \mathcal{G}((\varphi \vee (\psi \wedge \langle\!\langle A \rangle\!\rangle \mathcal{X}\theta)) \rightarrow \theta) \rightarrow \langle\!\langle \emptyset \rangle\!\rangle \mathcal{G}(\langle\!\langle A \rangle\!\rangle \psi \mathcal{U} \varphi \rightarrow \theta).$

It was proved in Goranko and van Drimmelen [47] that these axioms added to Pauly's axioms for CL, plus the rule $\langle\!\langle \emptyset \rangle\!\rangle \mathcal{G}$-*Necessitation*:

$$\frac{\varphi}{\langle\!\langle \emptyset \rangle\!\rangle \mathcal{G}\varphi}.$$

provide a sound and complete axiomatization for the validities of ATL.

No explicit complete axiomatizations for ATL*, nor for any of the variations of ATL with incomplete information, are known yet.

Decidability and Decision Methods for ATL and ATL*. A fundamental algorithmic problem in logic is whether a given logical formula is satisfiable in any model for the given logic, or dually, whether its negation is valid in the given semantics. A constructive procedure for testing satisfiability is of practical importance because it can be used to construct (to synthesize) models from formal logical specifications. Sound and complete axiomatic systems provide only semi-decision methods for testing validity, respectively non-satisfiability, while complete algorithmic decision methods exist only for logics with a decidable validity/satisfiability problem. The decidability of that problem in ATL, with **EXPTIME**-complete worst-case complexity of the decision algorithm, was first proved in van Drimmelen [39] (see also Goranko and van Drimmelen [47] for detailed proofs) by proving a bounded-branching tree-model property and using alternating tree automata, under the assumption that the number of agents is fixed. The **EXPTIME**-completeness of ATL satisfiability was later re-proved in Walther et al. [80] without the assumption of fixed number of agents. An optimal and practically implementable tableau-based constructive decision method for testing satisfiability in ATL was developed in Goranko and Shkatov [46]. Later, the decidability and **2EXPTIME**-complete complexity of the satisfiability problem for ATL* was proved in Schewe [77] using alternating tree automata.

7.2   Model Checking of ATL and ATL*

Model checking is another fundamental logical decision problem. It calls for a procedure that determines whether a given formula is true in a given model. For such procedures to be algorithmically implementable, the model must be finite, or effectively (finitely) presented. We briefly discuss model checking ATL and ATL* under the different semantic variants considered in this chapter. We focus on the main technical issues that arise in that area, namely the computational complexity of the model checking algorithms, as a measure of the inherent complexity of the underlying semantics of the logic. The relevant complexity results are summarized in Fig. 8.

	Ir	IR	ir	iR
ATL	**P**	**P**	Δ_2^P	Undecidable[†]
ATL*	**PSPACE**	**2EXPTIME**	**PSPACE**	Undecidable

Fig. 8. Overview of the exact complexity results for model checking in explicit models of formulae from the logic in the respective row with the semantics given in the column.

A deterministic polynomial-time model checking algorithm for ATL_{ir} (and thus ATL_{iR}) is presented in Alur et al. [8]. The algorithm is based on the fixpoint characterizations of strategic-temporal modalities:

$$\langle\!\langle A \rangle\!\rangle \mathcal{G} \, \varphi \leftrightarrow \varphi \wedge \langle\!\langle A \rangle\!\rangle \mathcal{X} \, \langle\!\langle A \rangle\!\rangle \mathcal{G} \, \varphi$$

$$\langle\!\langle A \rangle\!\rangle \varphi_1 \, \mathcal{U} \, \varphi_2 \leftrightarrow \varphi_2 \vee (\varphi_1 \wedge \langle\!\langle A \rangle\!\rangle \mathcal{X} \, \langle\!\langle A \rangle\!\rangle \varphi_1 \, \mathcal{U} \, \varphi_2).$$

The perfect information assumption allows to compute a winning strategy step-by-step (if it exists). In the case of $\langle\!\langle A \rangle\!\rangle \mathcal{G} \, \varphi$, for example, the procedure starts with all states in which φ holds and subsequently removes states in which there is no joint action for team A to guarantee to end up in one of the states in which φ holds. Let us refer to the resulting set of states as Q_1. In the next step it is checked whether for each state in Q_1 there is a joint action of team A which guarantees to remain in Q_1. States in which such a joint action does not exist are removed from Q_1. This procedure is applied recursively until a fixed point is reached. The formula $\langle\!\langle A \rangle\!\rangle \mathcal{G} \, \varphi$ is true in all the remaining states.

The deterministic **2EXPTIME** algorithm for model checking ATL_{IR}^* makes use of a sophisticated tree automaton construction, see [8].

Algorithms for the the remaining settings based on memoryless strategies employ model checking algorithms for CTL and CTL* (model checking is **P**-complete and **PSPACE**-complete, respectively, see Clarke et al. [35]). The key observation is that there are only finitely many *memoryless* strategies and that a strategy can be guessed in non-deterministic polynomial time. Then, all transitions not possible given the guessed strategy profile are removed from the model and the resulting *temporal* model checking problem is solved (cf. [78]). For illustration, consider ATL_{iR} and the formula $\langle\!\langle A \rangle\!\rangle \mathcal{G}\,\varphi$. First, we guess a memoryless uniform strategy s_A of coalition A. It is easy to see that the validation whether the strategy profile is uniform or not can be done in deterministic polynomial-time. Afterwards, all transitions not possible according to s_A are removed from the model as well as all transition labels. It remains to check whether $\mathcal{G}\,\varphi$ holds on *all* possible behaviors/paths in the resulting purely temporal model. The latter corresponds to CTL model checking of $\mathsf{A}\mathcal{G}\,\varphi$. However, since φ may contain *nested* cooperation modalities we need to proceed *bottom-up* which shows that the problem is contained in $\mathbf{P}^{\mathbf{NP}^{\mathbf{P}}} = \boldsymbol{\Delta}_2^{\mathbf{P}}$. Similarly, we obtain **PSPACE** algorithms for ATL_{Ir}^* and ATL_{ir}^*: guess strategies and solve the CTL* model checking problem, which can be done in $\mathbf{P}^{\mathbf{NP}^{\mathbf{PSPACE}}} = \mathbf{PSPACE}$.

We note that model checking of ATL in the case of imperfect information and memory-based strategy is undecidable, cf. [8, 37].

For a more detailed overview of the complexities of model checking of these logics we refer the reader to [8, 25] for ATL and ATL*, [27] for ATL$^+$, a computationally better behaved fragment of ATL*, and to [32, 61–63] for more powerful and recent extensions of ATL*.

8 Concluding Remarks: Brief Parallels with Other Logical Approaches to Strategic Reasoning

While strategic reasoning is a highly involved and complex form of reasoning, requiring strong logical and analytic skills, its seems rather surprising that until the 1980 s formal logic was seldom employed to either analyze or facilitate strategic reasoning. However, with the ongoing invasion of logic into game theory and multi-agent systems over the past 20 years, its role in both doing and analyzing strategic reasoning has become increasingly more instrumental and recognized. Logic has been successfully applied to several rather different aspects of strategic reasoning and the variety of logical systems presented and discussed here gives a good overall picture of only one of the logical approaches to strategic reasoning, viz. reasoning *about objective strategic abilities of players and coalitions pursuing a specific goal, in competitive concurrent multi-player games where the remaining players are regarded as (temporary) adversaries as far as achieving of that goal is concerned*. As mentioned in the introduction, there are several other related logic-based approaches to strategic reasoning and most of them are treated in other chapters of this book.

– *Logics of agencies, abilities and actions.* Philosophical approaches to developing logics of agency and ability, include early works of von Wright and Kanger and more recent ones by Brown [23], Belnap and Perloff [13], and Chellas

[34]. In particular, Brown [23] proposes a modal logic with non-normal modalities formalising the idea that the modality for ability has a more complex, existential-universal meaning (the agent has *some* action or choice, such that *every* outcome from executing that action (making that choice) achieves the aim), underlying the approaches to formalizing agents' ability presented here.

– STIT *logics.* These originate from the work of Belnap [13] introducing the operator *seeing to it that,* abbreviated to "STIT". The approach to strategic reasoning taken in the STIT family of logics of agency, discussed in Broersen and Herzig [21], is the closest to the one presented in this chapter and we will provide a more detailed parallel with it now. To begin with, both the STIT-based and the ATL-based approaches assume that agents act simultaneously and independently. The main conceptual difference between the family of STIT logics of agency and ATL-like logics is that the former delve into more philosophical issues of agency and emphasize the *intentional aspect* of the agents' strategies, whereas the latter take a more pragmatic view on agents and focus on the *practical effects* of their strategic abilities and choices, disregarding desires, intentions, and other less explicit attitudes. The basic STIT operator is similar to the one-step strategic modality of CL while the intended meaning of the "strategic" version of the STIT operator, SSTIT, comes very close to the intended meaning of the strategic operator $\langle\!\langle\rangle\!\rangle$ in ATL. The main technical difference between these logics is in the semantics, which is rather more general and abstract in the case of STIT as compared to ATL. Strategies in ATL models are explicit rules mapping possible game configurations to prescribed actions, whereas strategies in STIT models are implicit and essentially represented by the respective plays ('histories') that they can enable. More precisely, the formal semantics of the SSTIT operator defines 'histories' as abstract objects representing the possible courses of events. Agents' strategies are abstract sets of histories satisfying some requirements, of which the most essential one is that every strategy profile of the set of all agents intersects in a single history. This semantics essentially extends the original semantics for ATL based on "alternating transition systems", subsequently replaced by the more concrete and – in our view – more realistic semantics based on concurrent game models, presented here[21]. Due to the expressiveness of the language of STIT/SSTIT and the generality of its semantics, it naturally embeds ATL* with complete information, as well as a number of its variations considered here, as demonstrated in [20,22]. The price to pay for that expressiveness, as it should be expected, is the generally intractable and usually undecidable complexity of STIT logics.

– *Logics for compositional reasoning about strategies,* initiated by Parikh [69] and discussed and extended in this book by Paul, Ramanujam and Simon [70], is another approach, conceptually close to the present, where strategies are treated as first-class citizens to which an endogenous, structural view is

---

[21] Yet, the SSTIT semantic structures relate quite naturally to path effectivity models introduced and characterized in [44], and these could provide a more feasible semantics for SSTIT.

applied, and "the study of rationality in extensive form games largely takes a functional view of strategies". In a way, this approach relates to the ATL-based one like the Propositional Dynamic Logic PDL relates to the temporal logics LTL and CTL as alternative approaches to reasoning about programs.

- *Logics of knowledge and beliefs.* As we have noted repeatedly, strategic reasoning is intimately related to players' knowledge and information. One of the deepest and most successful manifestations of logical methods in strategic reasoning is the doxastic-epistemic treatment of the concepts of individual and common rationality in game theory. This approach is treated in-depth and from different perspectives in the chapters by Bonanno [18], Pacuit [68] and Perea [74] of this book, as well as in Baltag, Smets et al. [11,12], etc. As stated in the chapter by Pacuit [68], this approach is not so focused on strategies and strategic abilities per se, but rather on the process of rational deliberation that leads players to their strategic choices and the latter are crucially dependent on the players' mutual rationality assumptions, rather than on demand for success against any – rational, adversarial, or simply random – behaviour of the others.
- *Logics for social choice theory*, discussed in the chapter by van Eijck [40] of this book, focuses on logical modeling of specific strategic abilities that arise on social choice scenarios such as voting.
- *Dynamic epistemic logic.* The relation of the ATL-based family of logics with Dynamic epistemic logic (DEL) [10,38] is more distant and implicit. DEL does not purport to reason explicitly about strategic abilities of agents, but it does provide a framework for such reasoning, in terms of which *epistemic objectives* agents can achieve by performing various epistemic actions, represented by action models.
- Lastly, for broader and more conceptual perspectives on the subject we refer the reader to the rest of this book and to van Benthem [15].

Acknowledgments. We are grateful to the participants in the Workshop on *Modelling Strategic Reasoning* held in February 2012 in the Lorentz Center, Leiden, and particularly to Nicolas Troquard and Dirk Walther, as well as to the anonymous reviewers, for their valuable comments and suggestions. Wojciech Jamroga acknowledges the support of the National Research Fund (FNR) Luxembourg under the project GALOT (INTER/DFG/12/06), as well as the support of the 7th Framework Programme of the European Union under the Marie Curie IEF project ReVINK (PIEF-GA-2012-626398). The final work of Valentin Goranko on this chapter was done while he was an invited visiting professor at the Centre International de Mathématiques et Informatique de Toulouse.

References

1. Abdou, J., Keiding, H.: Effectivity Functions in Social Choice Theory. Kluwer, Netherlands (1991)
2. Ågotnes, T.: Action and knowledge in alternating-time temporal logic. Synthese **149**(2), 377–409 (2006). Section on Knowledge, Rationality and Action

3. Ågotnes, T., Goranko, V., Jamroga, W.: Alternating-time temporal logics with irrevocable strategies. In: Samet, D. (ed.) Proceeding of TARK XI, pp. 15–24. ACM, New York (2007)
4. Ågotnes, T., Goranko, V., Jamroga, W.: Strategic commitment and release in logics for multi-agent systems (extended abstract). Technical report IfI-08-01, Clausthal University of Technology (2008)
5. Ågotnes, T., Walther, D.: A logic of strategic ability under bounded memory. J. Logic Lang. Inform. 18(1), 55–77 (2009)
6. Alur, R., Henzinger, T.A., Kupferman, O.: Alternating-time temporal logic. In: Proceedings of the FOCS 1997, pp. 100–109. IEEE Computer Society Press (1997)
7. Kupferman, O., Alur, R., Henzinger, T.A.: Alternating-time temporal logic. In: de Roever, W.-P., Pnueli, A., Langmaack, H. (eds.) COMPOS 1997. LNCS, vol. 1536, pp. 23–60. Springer, Heidelberg (1998)
8. Alur, R., Henzinger, T.A., Kupferman, O.: Alternating-time temporal logic. J. ACM 49, 672–713 (2002)
9. Baltag, A.: A logic for suspicious players. Bull. Econ. Res. 54(1), 1–46 (2002)
10. Baltag, A., Moss, L.S., Solecki, S.: The logic of public announcements, common knowledge and private suspicions. Technical report SEN-R9922, CWI, Amsterdam (1999)
11. Baltag, A., Smets, S.: A qualitative theory of dynamic interactive belief revision. In: Bonanno, G., van der Hoek, W., Wooldridge, M. (eds.) Logic and the Foundation of Game and Decision Theory (LOFT7), volume 3 of Texts in Logic and Games, pp. 13–60. Amsterdam University Press, Amsterdam (2008)
12. Baltag, A., Smets, S., Zvesper, J.A.: Keep 'hoping' for rationality: A solution to the backward induction paradox. Synthese 169(2), 301–333 (2009)
13. Belnap, N., Perloff, M.: Seeing to it that: a canonical form for agentives. Theoria 54, 175–199 (1988)
14. van Benthem, J.: Rational dynamics and epistemic logic in games. In: Vannucci, S. (ed.) Logic, Game Theory and Social Choice III, pp. 19–23. ILLC, Amsterdam (2003)
15. van Benthem, J.: Logic in Games. MIT Press, Cambridge (2013)
16. van Benthem, J.: Logic of strategies: What and how? In: van Benthem, J., Ghosh, S., Verbrugge, R. (eds.) Models of Strategic Reasoning. LNCS, vol. 8972, pp. 321–332. Springer, Heidelberg (2015)
17. Bonanno, G.: Modal logic and game theory: two alternative approaches. Risk Decis. Policy 7, 309–324 (2002)
18. Bonanno, G.: Reasoning about strategies and rational play in dynamic games. In: van Benthem, J., Ghosh, S., Verbrugge, R. (eds.) Models of Strategic Reasoning. LNCS, vol. 8972, pp. 34–62. Springer, Heidelberg (2015)
19. Brihaye, T., Da Costa, A., Laroussinie, F., Markey, N.: ATL with strategy contexts and bounded memory. Technical report LSV-08-14, ENS Cachan (2008)
20. Broersen, J.: CTL.STIT: enhancing ATL to express important multi-agent system verification properties. In: Proceedings of the AAMAS 2010, pp. 683–690 (2010)
21. Broersen, J., Herzig, A.: Using STIT theory to talk about strategies. In: van Benthem, J., Ghosh, S., Verbrugge, R. (eds.) Models of Strategic Reasoning. Lecturer Notes in Computer Science, vol. 8972, pp. 137–173. Springer, Heidelberg (2015)
22. Broersen, J., Herzig, A., Troquard, N.: Embedding alternating-time temporal logic in strategic STIT logic of agency. J. Log. Comput. 16(5), 559–578 (2006)
23. Brown, M.A.: On the logic of ability. J. Philos. Logic 17, 1–26 (1988)
24. Bulling, N.: Modelling and Verifying Abilities of Rational Agents. Ph.D. thesis, Clausthal University of Technology (2010)

25. Bulling, N., Dix, J., Jamroga, W.: Model checking logics of strategic ability: Complexity. In: Dastani, M., Hindriks, K.V., Meyer, J.-J.C. (eds.) Specification and Verification of Multi-Agent Systems, pp. 125–159. Springer, New York (2010)

26. Bulling, N., Jamroga, W.: Rational play and rational beliefs under uncertainty. In: Proceedings of AAMAS 2009, pp. 257–264. ACM Press, Budapest, May 2009

27. Bulling, N., Jamroga, W.: Verifying agents with memory is harder than it seemed. AI Commun. **23**(4), 389–403 (2010)

28. Bulling, N., Jamroga, W.: Comparing variants of strategic ability: How uncertainty and memory influence general properties of games. Auton. Agent. Multi-Agent Syst. **28**(3), 474–518 (2014)

29. Bulling, N., Jamroga, W., Dix, J.: Reasoning about temporal properties of rational play. Ann. Math. Artif. Intell. **53**(1–4), 51–114 (2009)

30. Bulling, N., Jamroga, W., Popovici, M.: ATL* with truly perfect recall: Expressivity and validities. In: Proceedings of the 21st European Conference on Artificial Intelligence (ECAI 2014), pp. 177-182. IOS Press, Prague, August 2014

31. Chatterjee, K., Piterman, N., Henzinger, T.A.: Strategy logic. In: Caires, L., Vasconcelos, V.T. (eds.) CONCUR 2007. LNCS, vol. 4703, pp. 59–73. Springer, Heidelberg (2007)

32. Chatterjee, K., Henzinger, T.A., Piterman, N.: Strategy logic. Inf. Comput. **208**(6), 677–693 (2010)

33. Chellas, B.: Modal Logic: An Introduction. Cambridge University Press, Cambridge (1980)

34. Chellas, B.: On bringing it about. J. Philos. Logic **24**(6), 563–571 (1995)

35. Clarke, E.M., Emerson, E.A., Sistla, A.P.: Automatic verification of finite-state concurrent systems using temporal logic specifications. ACM Trans. Program. Lang. Syst. **8**(2), 244–263 (1986)

36. Diaconu, R., Dima, C.: Model-checking alternating-time temporal logic with strategies based on common knowledge is undecidable. Appl. Artif. Intell. **26**(4), 331–348 (2012)

37. Dima, C., Tiplea, F.L.: Model-checking ATL under imperfect information and perfect recall semantics is undecidable (2011). CoRR, abs/1102.4225

38. van Ditmarsch, H., van der Hoek, W., Kooi, B.: Dynamic Epistemic Logic. Springer, Dordecht (2008)

39. van Drimmelen, G.: Satisfiability in alternating-time temporal logic. In: Proceedings of LICS 2003, pp. 208–217. IEEE Computer Society Press (2003)

40. van Eijck, J.: Strategies in social software. In: van Benthem, J., Ghosh, S., Verbrugge, R. (eds.) Models of Strategic Reasoning. LNCS, vol. 8972, pp. 292–317. Springer, Heidelberg (2015)

41. Fagin, R., Halpern, J.Y., Moses, Y., Vardi, M.Y.: Reasoning about Knowledge. MIT Press, London (1995)

42. Goranko, V.: Coalition games and alternating temporal logics. In: van Benthem, J. (ed.) Proceedings of TARK VIII, pp. 259–272. Morgan Kaufmann, San Francisco (2001)

43. Goranko, V., Jamroga, W.: Comparing semantics of logics for multi-agent systems. Synthese **139**(2), 241–280 (2004)

44. Goranko, V., Jamroga, W.: State and path coalition effectivity models for logics of multi-player games. In: Proceedings of AAMAS 2012 (2012)

45. Goranko, V., Jamroga, W., Turrini, P.: Strategic games and truly playable effectivity functions. In: Proceedings of AAMAS 2011, pp. 727–734 (2011)

46. Goranko, V., Shkatov, D.: Tableau-based decision procedures for logics of strategic ability in multiagent systems. ACM Trans. Comput. Log. **11**(1), 1–48 (2009)

47. Goranko, V., van Drimmelen, G.: Complete axiomatization and decidability of alternating-time temporal logic. Theoret. Comput. Sci. **353**(1), 93–117 (2006)
48. Guelev, D.P., Dima, C., Enea, C.: An alternating-time temporal logic with knowledge, perfect recall and past: axiomatisation and model-checking. J. Appl. Non-Class. Logics **21**(1), 93–131 (2011)
49. Halpern, J.Y.: Reasoning about knowledge: a survey. In: Gabbay, D.M., Hogger, C.J., Robinson, J.A. (eds.) Handbook of Logic in Artificial Intelligence and Logic Programming, vol. 4: Epistemic and Temporal Reasoning, pp. 1–34. Oxford University Press, Oxford (1995)
50. Harrenstein, B.P., van der Hoek, W., Meyer, J.-J.C., Witteveen, C.: A modal characterization of nash equilibrium. Fundam. Informaticae **57**(2–4), 281–321 (2003)
51. Hart, S.: Games in extensive and strategic forms. In: Aumann, R.J., Hart, S. (eds.) Handbook of Game Theory with Economic Applications, vol. 1, pp. 19–40. Elsevier, North-Holland (1992)
52. van der Hoek, W., Jamroga, W., Wooldridge, M.: A logic for strategic reasoning. In: Proceedings of AAMAS 2005, pp. 157–164 (2005)
53. van der Hoek, W., van Otterloo, S., Wooldridge, M.: Preferences in game logics. In: Proceedings of AAMAS-04 (2004)
54. van der Hoek, W., Verbrugge, R.: Epistemic logic: A survey. Game Theory Appl. **8**, 53–94 (2002)
55. van der Hoek, W., Wooldridge, M.: Tractable multiagent planning for epistemic goals. In: Castelfranchi, C., Johnson, W.L. (eds.) Proceeding of AAMAS-02, pp. 1167–1174. ACM Press, New York (2002)
56. van der Hoek, W., Wooldridge, M.: Cooperation, knowledge and time: Alternating-time temporal epistemic logic and its applications. Stud. Logica **75**(1), 125–157 (2003)
57. Jamroga, W., Ågotnes, T.: Constructive knowledge: What agents can achieve under incomplete information. J. Appl. Non-Class. Logics **17**(4), 423–475 (2007)
58. Jamroga, W., van der Hoek, W.: Agents that know how to play. Fundamenta Informaticae **63**(2–3), 185–219 (2004)
59. Jamroga, W., Wooldridge, M.J., van der Hoek, W.: Intentions and strategies in game-like scenarios. In: Bento, C., Cardoso, A., Dias, G. (eds.) EPIA 2005. LNCS (LNAI), vol. 3808, pp. 512–523. Springer, Heidelberg (2005)
60. Jonker, G.: Feasible strategies in Alternating-time Temporal Epistemic Logic. Master thesis, University of Utrecht (2003)
61. Mogavero, F., Murano, A., Perelli, G., Vardi, M.Y.: What makes ATL* decidable? a decidable fragment of strategy logic. In: Ulidowski, I., Koutny, M. (eds.) CONCUR 2012. LNCS, vol. 7454, pp. 193–208. Springer, Heidelberg (2012)
62. Mogavero, F., Murano, A., Vardi, M.Y.: Reasoning about strategies. In: Lodaya, K., Mahajan, M. (eds.) Proceedings of FSTTCS 2010, LIPIcs, pp. 133–144. Atlantis Press, Schloss Dagstuhl - Leibniz-Zentrum fuer Informatik (2010)
63. Vardi, M.Y., Murano, A., Mogavero, F.: Relentful strategic reasoning in alternating-time temporal logic. In: Voronkov, A., Clarke, E.M. (eds.) LPAR-16 2010. LNCS, vol. 6355, pp. 371–386. Springer, Heidelberg (2010)
64. Moulin, H., Peleg, B.: Cores of effectivity functions and implementation theory. J. Math. Econ. **10**(1), 115–145 (1982)
65. Osborne, M., Rubinstein, A.: A Course in Game Theory. MIT Press, Cambridge (1994)
66. van Otterloo, S., Jonker, G.: On epistemic temporal strategic logic. Electron. Notes Theoret. Comput. Sci. **126**, 35–45 (2004)

67. van Otterloo, S., Roy, O.: Verification of voting protocols. Working paper, University of Amsterdam (2005)
68. Pacuit, E.: Dynamic models of rational deliberation in games. In: van Benthem, J., Ghosh, S., Verbrugge, R. (eds.) Models of Strategic Reasoning. LNCS, vol. 8972, pp. 3–33. Springer, Heidelberg (2015)
69. Parikh, R.: The logic of games and its applications. Ann. Discrete Math. **24**, 111–140 (1985)
70. Paul, S., Ramanujam, R., Simon, S.: Automata and compositional strategies in extensive form games. In: van Benthem, J., Ghosh, S., Verbrugge, R. (eds.) Models of Strategic Reasoning. LNCS, vol. 8972, pp. 174–201. Springer, Heidelberg (2015)
71. Pauly, M.: Logic for Social Software. Ph.D. thesis, University of Amsterdam (2001)
72. Pauly, M.: A logical framework for coalitional effectivity in dynamic procedures. Bull. Econ. Res. **53**(4), 305–324 (2001)
73. Pauly, M.: A modal logic for coalitional power in games. J. Logic Comput. **12**(1), 149–166 (2002)
74. Perea, A.: Finite reasoning procedures for dynamic games. In: van Benthem, J., Ghosh, S., Verbrugge, R. (eds.) Models of Strategic Reasoning. LNCS, vol. 8972, pp. 63–90. Springer, Heidelberg (2015)
75. Pinchinat, S.: A generic constructive solution for concurrent games with expressive constraints on strategies. In: Okamura, Y., Yoneda, T., Higashino, T., Namjoshi, K.S. (eds.) ATVA 2007. LNCS, vol. 4762, pp. 253–267. Springer, Heidelberg (2007)
76. Sandholm, T.W.: Distributed rational decision making. In: Weiss, G. (ed.) Multiagent Systems: A Modern Approach to Distributed Artificial Intelligence, pp. 201–258. The MIT Press, Cambridge (1999)
77. Schewe, S.: ATL* satisfiability is 2EXPTIME-Complete. In: Walukiewicz, I., Goldberg, L.A., Halldórsson, M.M., Damgård, I., Ingólfsdóttir, A., Aceto, L. (eds.) ICALP 2008, Part II. LNCS, vol. 5126, pp. 373–385. Springer, Heidelberg (2008)
78. Schobbens, P.Y.: Alternating-time logic with imperfect recall. Electron. Notes Theoret. Comput. Sci. **85**(2), 82–93 (2004)
79. Troquard, N., Walther, D.: On satisfiability in ATL with strategy contexts. In: del Cerro, L.F., Herzig, A., Mengin, J. (eds.) JELIA 2012. LNCS, vol. 7519, pp. 398–410. Springer, Heidelberg (2012)
80. Walther, D., Lutz, C., Wolter, F., Wooldridge, M.: ATL satisfiability is indeed EXPTIME-complete. J. Logic Comput. **16**(6), 765–787 (2006)
81. Walther, D., van der Hoek, W., Wooldridge, M.: Alternating-time temporal logic with explicit strategies. In: Samet, D. (ed.) Proceedings of the TARK XI, pp. 269–278. Presses Universitaires de Louvain, New York (2007)

Using STIT Theory to Talk About Strategies

Jan Broersen[1]([✉]) and Andreas Herzig[2]

[1] Department of Philosophy and Religious Studies, Universiteit Utrecht,
Utrecht, The Netherlands
J.M.Broersen@uu.nl

[2] Institut de Recherche en Informatique de Toulouse, Université Paul Sabatier,
Toulouse, France
Andreas.Herzig@irit.fr

Abstract. This chapter gives an overview of logical theories of 'seeing-to-it-that', commonly abbreviated *stit*, and focusses on the notion of 'strategy' as used in their semantics. The chapter covers both 'one-step' strategies (i.e., atomic actions) and long-term strategies and explains how they give semantics to different *stit* languages. Furthermore, the chapter discusses how extensions with epistemic operators can be used to clarify the problem of uniform strategies. Finally, it is shown how strategic *stit* theories disambiguate some seemingly paradoxical observations recently made in the context of logics of strategic ability (ATL).

Keywords: Logics of agency · Extensive form games · Theory of action · Processes and strategies

1 Introduction

The theory of 'seeing-to-it-that', abbreviated *stit*, is one of the main theories in the philosophy of action. There is no single monolithic *stit* theory but rather a variety of theories that differ in logical language and semantics. The most well-known are the *Chellas stit*, the *deliberative stit*, the *achievement stit*, and the *strategic (Chellas) stit*. All of them can be built on very different views on time; for instance, time may be *discrete* or not.

Stit theories are relevant for the analysis of strategies, both at the short-term (one-step) level and on the long-term (extensive) level. For instance, in the strategic (extensive) variants of *stit* theory one may express that an agent has a strategy ensuring that some property is eventually true, is henceforth true, or is true until some other property is obtained. Here, the agent has a *strategy* if there exists a 'plan' of appropriate future choices guaranteeing that a given outcome obtains independent of what other agents do if the plan is executed. In short-term versions of *stit* formalisms, e.g., versions based on a temporal 'next' operator or instantaneous versions, one reasons about one-step strategies, alias (atomic) actions.

The relation with strategies in game theory is somewhat confusing. The semantics of *stit*-logics that concern one-step actions (e.g., 'turning the switch to

© Springer-Verlag Berlin Heidelberg 2015
J. van Benthem et al. (Eds.): Models of Strategic Reasoning, LNCS 8972, pp. 137–173, 2015.
DOI: 10.1007/978-3-662-48540-8_5

put on the light') is based on situations that in game theory are called 'strategic': an agent performs a one step action that guarantees a condition independent of the actions of other agents at the same moment. So, in *stit*-theory we can view the one-step actions of agents as 'winning' strategic moves these agents play against the non-determinism in their world; the non-determinism resulting from choices of other agents and from 'nature' performing moves concurrently (in the turning on the light scenario: maybe more switches, agents or non-deterministic components are involved). To add to the confusion, the *strategic* versions of *stit*-theory concern operators that are given semantics by what in game theory are called 'extensive game forms'.

This chapter is organised as follows. We start by giving a brief overview of the different *stit* theories (Sect. 2) that are aimed at the modelling of one-step agency. After that we examine extensive strategies within the strategic Chellas *stit*; in particular we shall clarify the relation with other strategic logics by embedding Alternating-time Temporal Logic (ATL and ATL*) into the logic of the strategic Chellas *stit* operator (Sect. 3). We then investigate micro level strategies within a discrete version of the Chellas *stit*; we show that if one extends *stit* theories by an epistemic operator one can elegantly reason about uniform strategies (Sect. 4). Finally (Sect. 5), we briefly discuss some problems with the interpretation of nested strategic ability operators and show that by a translation to strategic *stit* formulas, the conceptual problems disappear.

2   A Brief Introduction to *Stit* Theory

Consider a simple scenario where there is an agent i in a room with a light bulb. Our agent may either do nothing or toggle the light switch. Toggling the switch will switch the light on if it was off before, and will switch the light off if it was on before. Suppose the light is off and i toggles the switch. We may describe what i does by saying "i brings it about that the light is on at the next time step". Moreover, regardless whether i decides to toggle the switch or not, we may also say that i *has a strategy* to ensure that the light in the room is on: it simply consists in toggling the switch. The strategy gets a bit more complex if we suppose that i is standing outside the room and is able to enter it. Then i's strategy gets: first enter, then toggle. Can we say that i still has a strategy if i is blind and does not know whether the light is on or not? Well, one could then say that the agent has a strategy *but does not know this*: he does not have what is called a uniform strategy. We may also consider multiple agents, such as a blind and a lame agent outside the room, or we may consider multiway switching where each of the two agents has his own toggle switch each of which is connected to the light bulb. In both cases, neither agent has a strategy to ensure an outcome independent of what the other agent does. However, the coalition of the two agents together has a (joint) strategy guaranteeing that the light is on.

In the literature we can find different kinds of formal action theories that can represent scenarios like these. In this section we introduce a theory that is firmly rooted in a non-deterministic world-view: the theory of *seeing-to-it-that*, abbreviated *stit*.

One view on agency is that an action can be identified with an *event* that is brought about by an *agent* [20,39]. The philosophical literature describes this as an agent being *agentive* for an event. Examples of such events are an arm being raised, a computer starting, a person being killed, etc. So, my action of switching the computer on is identified with me bringing about the event that the computer starts. The literature gives several semantical accounts of the event-based view. The most prominent one in computer science is the one associated with dynamic logic. In dynamic logic events (or, to be more precise, 'event types') are associated with a *binary relation between possible worlds*, also called a 'transition relation'. Transition relations for atomic events can be combined by operations of relation algebra such as sequential or nondeterministic composition in order to build transition relations for complex events (event types).

The *stit* view on agency does not depart from a metaphysics involving events. One can even argue that it was developed in opposition to Davidson's event-based view on agency (see the comments on this in [5])[1]. In *stit* logic the relation between agents and the effects these agents bring about are central; if there are events that somehow are responsible for this relation, then this process of 'agentive causation' is abstracted away from entirely. According to Belnap and Perloff's *stit-thesis*, every agentive sentence can be transformed into a sentence of the form "*i* sees to it that φ", where *i* is an agent and φ is a proposition. In other words, an action is characterized as the relation between an agent and the effect (proposition) the agent brings about by performing that action. This modelling choice results in the sentence "agent *i* sees to it that φ" also being a proposition.

The two views on the semantics of agency described above characterise two traditions for logics of action. Dynamic logics were introduced and studied in theoretical computer science, but were also investigated by philosophers [37]. The logics of 'seeing-to-it-that' (stit) [4,5] and the logics of 'bringing-it-about-that' [21,22,35] are two closely related sub-families in the other tradition. These logics are studied in philosophy of action and more recently in multi-agent systems; for a recent overview, see [27]. The logics of the *stit* operator have in common that they are built on *branching-time structures* and that they make the hypothesis that *agents act independently*. This distinguishes them from the bringing-it-about logics.

In the rest of the present section we briefly recall the four classical *stit* operators and their models. Throughout this chapter $p, q, \ldots$ denote propositional variables from a countable set $\mathcal{P}$ and $\varphi, \psi, \ldots$ denote formulas; natural numbers $1, 2, 3, \ldots, n$ are used to denote agents[2] (individuals) populating the world, while arbitrary agents are referred to by agent variables $i, j, \ldots$ that range over this set. The agent set as a whole is denoted by Ags. Finally, we use $A_1, A_2 \ldots$ as variables over sets of agents, often also called 'groups' or 'coalitions' (we drop

---

[1] Here we will not elaborate on the relation between Davidson's event-based theory and dynamic logic's event-type-based view.

[2] Of course, not any natural number in the paper denotes an agent; numbers are also used in their standard interpretation.

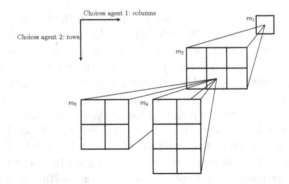

Fig. 1. visualisation of a two-agent BT+AC structure (histories are not pictured, but they run from the back to the front, within the boundaries of the game forms)

the index and write A if the context is such that we only need to refer to one group).

2.1 Branching-Time Models with Agents' Choices: The Basics

The semantics of the various *stit* operators is in terms of branching-time (BT) models that are equipped with information about the agents' choices (AC). Figure 1 gives a visualisation of a two agent BT+AC structure where at any moment m_i agent 1 choses between the columns and agent 2 choses between the rows. Agents are allowed to choose simultaneously. This contrasts with extensive form game trees where agents act in turns.

Branching-time models inherit the Ockhamist view of time [41] where the truth of statements is evaluated with respect to a moment that is situated on a particular history through time [5,31,32]. A *BT structure* is a tree whose vertices are called *moments*. The edges of the tree correspond to the course of time. A *history* is a maximal path in the tree. In our example scenarios from the beginning of this section where there is only one agent i, the possible histories are the different sequences of moments that can be obtained by i performing some sequences of actions from his repertoire. When a moment belongs to a history we say that the history passes through that moment. So the world evolves non-deterministically, and the possible futures of a given moment are represented by the histories passing through it.

Indeterminism of time is partially due to the agents' choices: at every moment m, each agent has a repertoire of choices, and each of these choices consists in selecting a subset of the set of histories passing through m. In Fig. 1 the choices of agent 1 are visualised as the columns of the game forms representing moments; agent 2 can choose between the rows in the game forms. Note that at moment m_2, whether m_3 or m_4 will occur is not under control of any agent and also not under the combined control of the two agents involved; whether one of these moments occurs is in the hands of nature. Figure 1 does not picture histories, but they are easily imagined to run through the moments within the boundaries of the cells in the game forms. Also Fig. 1 gives a very 'partial' view: for every moment only the continuation relative to one particular choice profile of the two agents is pictured.

In the initial version of our example scenario where the light is off at m, by choosing to toggle i selects the set of histories passing through m where the light is on at the next time point, and by choosing to do nothing i selects the set of histories passing through m where the light remains off. It is understood that for each of his choices, the agent can guarantee the future to be in the subset he selects. It is also understood that the agents choose independently: whatever each of the agents chooses, the intersection of all the agents' choices must be non-empty. This is the *independence constraint*, and Belnap et al. assume that independence is always appropriate.[3]

Formally, a *branching time structure* (*BT structure*) is a couple $\langle \mathsf{Mom}, < \rangle$ where:

- Mom is a non-empty set of moments;
- $<$ is an irreflexive tree-like partial order[4].

Note that Mom is an arbitrary set; in particular it may be infinite, and if so it might be countable or not. Depending on that, the ordering $<$ may be discrete, dense, or even continuous.

A *history* is a maximal linearly ordered set of moments complying with the $<$ ordering. We use H to denote the set of all histories, and we use H_m to denote the set of histories passing through the moment m, i.e., the set of histories h such that $m \in h$. Two histories $h_1, h_2 \in H_m$ are *undivided* at m if and only if there is some m' such that $m < m'$ and m' belongs to both h_1 and h_2.

A *model of branching time and agents' choices* (for short: a *BT+AC model*) is a 4-tuple of the form $\mathcal{M} = \langle \mathsf{Mom}, <, \mathcal{C}, \pi \rangle$ where

- $\langle \mathsf{Mom}, < \rangle$ is a BT structure;
- $\mathcal{C}$ is a function from $Ags \times \mathsf{Mom}$ to $2^{H \times H}$ such that each $\mathcal{C}(i, m)$ is an equivalence relation on H_m, where $\mathcal{C}(i, m)$ is agent i's set of choices at m; the elements of $\mathcal{C}(i, m)$ are called i's *choice cells at* m;[5]

---

[3] The same independence assumption is made in games in strategic form where the outcomes of the agents' actions are represented by a matrix. The independence constraint was questioned by researchers in the tradition of bringing-it-about-that logics, who have argued that it is too strong.

[4] A tree-like partial order is a relation such that
- if $m_1 \le m_2$ and $m_2 \le m_3$ then $m_1 \le m_3$;
- if $m_1 \le m_2$ and $m_2 \le m_1$ then $m_1 = m_2$;
- if $m_1 \le m_3$ and $m_2 \le m_3$ then $m_1 \le m_2$ or $m_2 \le m_1$;
- for every m_1 and m_2 there is a m_0 such that $m_0 \le m_1$ and $m_0 \le m_2$.
where $\le$ is defined by $m_1 \le m_2$ if either $m_1 < m_2$ or $m_1 = m_2$.

[5] The original definition in [5] is equivalent: there, $\mathcal{C}$ is function from $Ags \times \mathsf{Mom}$ to 2^{2^H} mapping each agent and each moment into a partition of H_m.

– π is a function from $\mathsf{Mom} \times H$ to $2^{\mathcal{P}}$ associating to every propositional variable $p \in \mathcal{P}$ the set of moment-history pairs where p is true.[6]

It is assumed that $\mathcal{C}$ satisfies the following constraints of *independence of agents* and of *no choice between undivided histories*.

1. for every moment m and for every mapping H_m associating agents i with one of their choice cells $H_m(i) \subseteq \mathcal{C}(i,m)$ we have $\bigcap_{i \in Ags} H_m(i) \neq \emptyset$;
2. if two histories h_1 and h_2 are undivided at m then $\langle h_1, h_2 \rangle \in \mathcal{C}(i,m)$ for every agent i.

The constraint of independence of agents says that any individual choice is compatible with the other agents' choices: if at m, agent i chooses $H_m(i)$ and agent j chooses $H_m(j)$, then these choices do not conflict, in the sense that there is at least one history in the intersection $H_m(i) \cap H_m(j)$ of these choices. The constraint of no choice between undivided histories says that if two histories h_1 and h_2 are undivided at m, then no possible choice for any agent at m distinguishes between the two histories: for each agent i, the histories h_1 and h_2 must belong to the same choice cell at m.

The above BT+AC models are just what is needed to interpret the so-called Chellas *stit* operator in the individual case and without the temporal 'next'. In the next section we list the various items to be added in order to account for the other operators.

2.2 Branching-Time Models with Agents' Choices: Various Extensions

Up to now we have only interpreted operators of individually seeing-to-it-that. One can as well extend choice functions from agents to *groups of agents* by stipulating the following:

$$\mathcal{C}(A, m) = \bigcap_{i \in A} \mathcal{C}(i, m)$$

Note that this is in line with the assumption of independence of agents. Note also that with this definition the above 'no choice between undivided histories' constraint can be formulated as: if $m \in h_1 \cap h_2$ and $m_0 < m$ then $\langle h_1, h_2 \rangle \in \mathcal{C}(Ags, m_0)$.

If the language has a *temporal 'next' operator* then the ordering $<$ has to be discrete. Recall that an ordering $<$ is discrete if and only if for every $m \in \mathsf{Mom}$ there is a set of closest moments $\text{succ}(m)$ such that for every $m' \in \text{succ}(m)$, $m < m'$ and there is no $m'' \in \mathsf{Mom}$ with $m < m'' < m'$. The successor function can be extended to moment-history pairs: $\text{succ}(m, h)$ is the moment m' such that $\text{succ}(m) \cap h = \{m'\}$. Then the constraint of independence of agents can

---

[6] So p's truth value at a given moment m may differ depending on the history. This allows a natural evaluation of statements about the future.

be formulated equivalently as: for every moment m and for all sets of agents A_1, A_2 such that $A_1 \cap A_2 = \emptyset$, if $U_1 \in \mathcal{C}(A_1, m)$ and $U_2 \in \mathcal{C}(A_2, m)$ then if $U_1 \cap U_2 \in \mathcal{C}(A_1 \cup A_2, m)$. This constraint is called superadditivity [34].

In order to interpret the *achievement stit* operator $[i \text{ AStit}]$ we have to add further temporal information to BT structures: we have to suppose that every moment is situated at a particular *instant in time*. Formally, this is achieved by a function mapping the set of moments Mom into a totally ordered set of instants. This enables comparison of moments that are not on the same history: it enables us to say that two moments in the future of m are at the same instant. Moreover, it is assumed that an agent does not perform an infinite number of non-vacuous choices during a finite interval of time (known as the absence of 'busy choosers'). This allows to validate a principle saying that *refraining from refraining is doing*, see below.

In order to interpret the *strategic Chellas stit* operator $[i \text{ sstit}]$ we have to add to our BT+AC structures information about the agents' strategies. This is what we will do in Sect. 3.

2.3 Various Modal Operators and Some Fused Versions

In the literature the sentence "agent i sees to it that φ" is formally written $[i : \text{stit } \varphi]$. We here prefer to write this as $[i \text{ Stit}]\varphi$ in order to be more in line with standard modal logic notation. We shall use that notation when we talk about general properties that are shared by all the *stit* operators. When we write down principles that are specifically satisfied by the Chellas *stit* then we use the modal operator $[i \text{ CStit}]$. Similarly, we use $[i \text{ DStit}]$ for the deliberative *stit*, $[i \text{ AStit}]$ for the achievement *stit*, and $[i \text{ sstit}]$ for the strategic Chellas *stit*.

The achievement *stit* is the original *stit* modality as proposed by Belnap and Perloff [4]. Its semantics was rather complex and was modified and simplified later by Horty and Belnap [32], resulting in a different *stit* modality that is called the deliberative *stit*. In the case of the achievement *stit*, the decisive choice of the action is in the past, while in the case of the deliberative *stit*, the decisive choice of the action is at the current moment. So the idea of deliberativeness resides in that an agent is currently seeing to something but could as well see to something else. While the achievement *stit* operator is perhaps most satisfactory from a backwards looking perspective on agency and responsibility for outcomes, the other forms of *stit* take a more decision theoretic and forward looking stance.

Some *stit* theories allow not only individual agents as arguments of *stit* operators, but also sets of agents. They have operators $[A \text{ Stit}]$, one per subset A of the set of agents *Ags*.

Stit theories come also with an operator of *historical possibility* $\Diamond$. The formula $\Diamond\varphi$ reads "there is a possible history passing through the current moment such that φ". We can define the dual modal operator $\Box$ by stipulating $\Box\varphi \overset{\text{def}}{=} \neg\Diamond\neg\varphi$. The formula $\Box\varphi$ reads "φ is settled true at the current moment".

We moreover use the temporal operators 'henceforth' G, 'eventually' F, and 'next' X. We take F as basic and stipulate that the dual $G\varphi$ abbreviates $\neg F\neg\varphi$.

In some *stit* logics, the grammar of the language is constrained in a way such that the different modal operators cannot be nested arbitrarily: the *stit* operator must be immediately followed by a temporal operator; and the other way round, the temporal operator must always be preceded by the *stit* operator. For example, formulas such as $[i \text{ sstit}]p$ or Xp are forbidden. We say that in these languages, the *stit* operator and the temporal operators are *fused*. The logic of the strategic Chellas *stit* operator moreover fuses historical possibility with the operators $[A \text{ sstit}]$. Anticipating a bit we note that such fused operators are also found in the language of other temporal logics with branching-time such as Alternating-time Temporal Logic ATL (see [17] in this volume) and Computation Tree Logic CTL, where the operator of quantification over branches has to be followed by a temporal operator. Actually ATL operators such as $\langle\langle A \rangle\rangle X$ can be understood as the fusion of the the strategic Chellas *stit* operator $[A \text{ sstit}]$ and the temporal operator X. We will explain this in detail in the next section (Sect. 3.2).

Just as in every modal logic, the *stit* operators can be nested: $[i \text{ Stit}][j \text{ Stit}]\varphi$ says that agent i makes agent j see to it that φ. However, it will turn out that for each *stit* logic such nestings are trivial (and are so in different ways). This is due to a fundamental hypothesis underlying all *stit* theories: the agents are independent, so there can be no coercion.

2.4   Various Truth Conditions

A significant variety of modalities of agency has been studied within *stit* theories. We are going to introduce here four of them that have rather different properties: the Chellas *stit* operator $[i \text{ CStit}]$, the deliberative *stit* operator $[i \text{ DStit}]$, the achievement *stit* operator $[i \text{ AStit}]$, and the strategic Chellas *stit* operator $[i \text{ sstit}]$.

Formulas are evaluated in a BT+AC model $\mathcal{M}$ with respect to moment-history pairs (m, h) such that m is on h.

Let us start with the simple cases. The operator of historical possibility $\Diamond$ and the temporal operators are interpreted as follows:

$\mathcal{M}, h, m \models \Diamond\varphi$ iff $\mathcal{M}, h', m \models \varphi$ for some history h' such that $m \in h'$;

$\mathcal{M}, h, m \models F\varphi$ iff $\mathcal{M}, h, m' \models \varphi$ for some moment m' such that $m \leq m'$;

$\mathcal{M}, h, m \models X\varphi$ iff $\mathcal{M}, h, \text{succ}(m, h) \models \varphi$.

The latter operator requires discrete BT+AC models.

Among the *stit* operators it is Chellas's $[A \text{ CStit}]$ that has the simplest truth condition:

$\mathcal{M}, h, m \models [A \text{ CStit}]\varphi$ iff $\mathcal{M}, h', m \models \varphi$ for every h' such that $\langle h, h' \rangle \in \mathcal{C}(A, m)$.

Hence the formula $[i \text{ CStit}]\varphi$ is true at a moment-history pair (m, h) if and only if φ is true at every (m, h') such that h' and h are in the same choice of i at m. So the Chellas *stit* operator amounts to a simple quantification over the histories that the current choice of the agent allows.

The deliberative *stit* operator $[A \text{ DStit}]$ adds a negative condition to the truth condition for the Chellas *stit* operator:

$\mathcal{M}, h, m \models [A \text{ DStit}]\varphi$ iff $\mathcal{M}, h', m \models \varphi$ for every h' such that $\langle h, h' \rangle \in \mathcal{C}(A, m)$
and there is a h'' such that $m \in h''$ and $\mathcal{M}, h'', m \not\models \varphi$.

As the reader may have observed, $[A \text{ DStit}]\varphi$ has the same truth condition as $[A \text{ CStit}]\varphi \wedge \Diamond\neg\varphi$. The other way round, the Chellas *stit* operator can be expressed with $[i \text{ DStit}]$ as $[i \text{ DStit}]\varphi \vee \Box\varphi$.

The achievement *stit* operator $[i \text{ AStit}]$ is about a choice in the past. For ease of exposition we do not consider coalitions of agents. An agent i sees to it that φ if a previous choice of i made sure that φ is true at the current instant, and φ could have been false at this instant had i done otherwise. We state the truth condition in a rather informal way in order to make it easier to understand. The precise definition requires to spell out what it means that two moments are at the same instant.

$\mathcal{M}, h, m \models [i \text{ AStit}]\varphi$ iff there is a moment m_0 preceding m on h such that
(1) $\mathcal{M}, h', m' \models \varphi$ for every h' and m' such that
    (i) $\langle h, h' \rangle \in \mathcal{C}(i, m_0)$,
    (ii) m' is on h' at the same instant as m;
(2) there is a history h'' and a moment m'' at the
    same instant as m with $\mathcal{M}, h'', m'' \not\models \varphi$.

We recall that $\langle h, h' \rangle \in \mathcal{C}(i, m_0)$ means that h and h' are in the same choice cell of i at m_0.

2.5 Principles Common to All Three *Stit* Operators

We start by formulating several principles that the logics of each of the *stit* operators satisfy. Table 1 summarises them.

Axiom schema 1 says that the modal operator of historical necessity is a normal modal 'box' operator, moreover satisfying the T axiom schema $\Box\varphi \to \varphi$, the 4 axiom schema $\Box\varphi \to \Box\Box\varphi$, and the 5 axiom schema $\neg\Box\varphi \to \Box\neg\Box\varphi$.

As to the operators of agency, first, a bringing-about-of-a-proposition is not sensitive to the syntactical formulation of that proposition. This is the *principle of equivalents for actual agency* (rule 2).

Table 1. Principles valid for of all three *stit* operators

$$\text{the S5 axioms for } \Box \tag{1}$$

$$\frac{\varphi \leftrightarrow \psi}{[i \text{ Stit}]\varphi \leftrightarrow [i \text{ Stit}]\psi} \tag{2}$$

$$[i \text{ Stit}]\varphi \to \varphi \tag{3}$$

$$([i \text{ Stit}]\varphi \wedge [i \text{ Stit}]\psi) \to [i \text{ Stit}](\varphi \wedge \psi) \tag{4}$$

$$[i \text{ Stit}]\varphi \to [i \text{ Stit}][i \text{ Stit}]\varphi \tag{5}$$

$$[i \text{ Stit}]\varphi \leftrightarrow [i \text{ Stit}]\neg[i \text{ Stit}]\neg[i \text{ Stit}]\varphi \tag{6}$$

$$(\Diamond[1 \text{ Stit}]\varphi_1 \wedge \ldots \wedge \Diamond[n \text{ Stit}]\varphi_n) \to \Diamond([1 \text{ Stit}]\varphi_1 \wedge \ldots \wedge [n \text{ Stit}]\varphi_n) \tag{7}$$

Second, if we view agentive sentences as propositions then it is natural to require that the set of worlds where φ is true contains the set of worlds where i is agentive for φ. This is a *principle of success* (axiom schema 3): the proposition "i sees to it that φ" should imply the proposition φ. In other words, it should be valid that if i sees to it that φ then φ is true. Note that it follows from this principle that an agent can never see to a contradiction.

Third, the different approaches agree about the *principle of aggregation* (axiom schema 4): "if i sees to it that φ and i sees to it that ψ then i sees to it that $\varphi \wedge \psi$".

Fourth, all versions of the *stit* operator satisfy that if i sees to it that φ then i sees to it that i sees to it that φ (axiom schema 5).

Fifth, the Chellas *stit* operator, the deliberative *stit* operator, and the achievement *stit* all satisfy (axiom schema 6): "refraining from refraining from seeing to is seeing to" [5]; for the case of the achievement *stit* the validity relies on the assumption that an agent does not perform an infinite number of non-vacuous choices during a finite interval of time.

Finally, the feature distinguishing *stit* theory from bringing-it-about theory is that the agents' choices are *independent*. Independence between pairs of agents can be written as:

$$(\Diamond[i \, \text{Stit}]\varphi \wedge \Diamond[j \, \text{Stit}]\psi) \rightarrow \Diamond([i \, \text{Stit}]\varphi \wedge [j \, \text{Stit}]\psi), \text{ for } i \neq j \qquad (8)$$

It follows that when i and j are different then $\Diamond[i \, \text{Stit}]\varphi \wedge \Diamond[j \, \text{Stit}]\neg\varphi$ is unsatisfiable (because by the success principle $[i \, \text{Stit}]\varphi \rightarrow \varphi$ is valid and because $\Diamond$ is a normal modal diamond). This axiom schema can straightforwardly be extended from pairs of agents i, j to the set of all n agents, yielding the axiom schema 7 of Table 1. A version of the independence axiom is central in Xu's axiomatisation of the Chellas *stit* operator ([5, Chap. 17]).

Finally, the Chellas *stit* and the deliberative *stit* are mutually reducible:

$$[A \, \text{DStit}]\varphi \leftrightarrow [A \, \text{CStit}]\varphi \wedge \Diamond\neg\varphi \qquad (9)$$

$$[i \, \text{CStit}] \leftrightarrow [i \, \text{DStit}]\varphi \vee \Box\neg\varphi \qquad (10)$$

Beyond these principles common to all the *stit* operators there are quite some differences between the respective logics. We shall overview these in the rest of the section.

2.6   The Logic of the Individual Chellas *Stit* Operator

The Chellas *stit* operator is interpreted as 'truth at all moment-history pairs in the same choice cell'. Such a truth condition makes the Chellas *stit* operator a normal modal operator. Such operators enjoy the rule of equivalents (rule 2), the aggregation axiom (schema 4), and the axiom of normality $[i \, \text{CStit}]\top$ and moreover the axiom of monotony $[i \, \text{CStit}](\varphi \wedge \psi) \rightarrow ([i \, \text{CStit}]\varphi \wedge [i \, \text{CStit}]\psi)$. The normality axiom says that agents are agentive for a tautology. The aggregation axiom tells us that the implication of the monotony axiom is actually an

Table 2. Complete axiomatisation of the individual Chellas *stit* operator [5]

$$\text{the common principles of Table 1} \tag{11}$$

$$[i\ \mathsf{CStit}]\top \tag{12}$$

$$[i\ \mathsf{CStit}](\varphi \wedge \psi) \rightarrow ([i\ \mathsf{CStit}]\varphi \wedge [i\ \mathsf{CStit}]\psi) \tag{13}$$

$$\neg[i\ \mathsf{CStit}]\varphi \rightarrow [i\ \mathsf{CStit}]\neg[i\ \mathsf{CStit}]\varphi \tag{14}$$

$$\Box\varphi \rightarrow [i\ \mathsf{CStit}]\varphi \tag{15}$$

equivalence. None of the latter two axioms is valid for the deliberative and the achievement *stit* operator.

As 'being in the same choice cell' is an equivalence relation, every operator $[i\ \mathsf{CStit}]$ obeys the principles of modal logic S5: the two common axiom schemas $\top$ and 4 (schemas 3 and 5 of Table 1) and axiom schema 5 (schema 15 of Table 2).

Another principle of the Chellas *stit* not shared by the other operators is: $\Box\varphi \rightarrow [i\ \mathsf{CStit}]\varphi$ (schema 14 of Table 2). In words, an agent cannot avoid what is settled; in particular he brings about every tautology.

In Table 2 we give Xu's complete axiomatisation of the logic of the individual Chellas *stit* operator and the operator of historical necessity (but without any temporal operator) [5]. Decidability of that logic follows from completeness together with the finite model property. It was proved in [3] that the satisfiability problem is NExpTime complete.

A somewhat surprising consequence of the independence of agents in the logic of the Chellas *stit* is the validity of the following 'make do implies settled' principle:

$$[i\ \mathsf{CStit}][j\ \mathsf{CStit}]\varphi \rightarrow \Box\varphi, \text{ for } i \neq j \tag{16}$$

In words, i can make j see to it that φ only if φ is settled. This highlights that unlike in the logic of bringing it about, in *stit* logics we cannot reason about the power of agents over others. While this principle may be felt to be unfortunate from the point of view of common sense, it accommodates well with social choice theory and game theory. In [3] it is shown that the axiom schema 16 is actually equivalent to axiom schema 8 and that its generalisation to any finite number of agents can substitute Xu's axiom of independence in the axiomatisation. Based on this and the above observation that the modal logic of both the Chellas *stit* operator $[i\ \mathsf{CStit}]$ and the historical necessity operator $\Box$ is S5, an equivalent Kripke-style semantics is defined there, where the modal operators $[i\ \mathsf{CStit}]$ and $\Box$ are interpreted by means of equivalence relations R_i and $R_\Box$. These relations are not independent: we have for instance $R_i \subseteq R_\Box$, ensuring that axiom schema 15 is valid.

2.7 The Logic of the Group Chellas *Stit* Operator

The logic of the group version of the Chellas *stit* operator was investigated in [15,16,28]. That logic inherits all the principles of the Chellas *stit* setting.

A quite straightforward property of the group version is coalition monotony, viz. that a supergroup sees to at least as much as any of its subgroups sees to:

$$[A_1 \text{ CStit}]\varphi \rightarrow [A_1 \cup A_2 \text{ CStit}]\varphi \tag{17}$$

The *stit* counterpart of the superadditivity principle of coalition logic [34] is:

$$(\Diamond[A_1 \text{ CStit}]\varphi_1 \wedge \Diamond[A_2 \text{ CStit}]\varphi_2) \rightarrow \Diamond[A_1 \cup A_2 \text{ CStit}](\varphi_1 \wedge \varphi_2), \quad \text{for } A_1 \cap A_2 = \emptyset \tag{18}$$

So disjoint coalitions can combine their forces.

This principle follows from a more general principle of coalitional interaction:

$$[A_1 \text{ CStit}][A_2 \text{ CStit}]\varphi \leftrightarrow [A_1 \cap A_2 \text{ CStit}]\varphi \tag{19}$$

The above principles are not complete. This follows from the proof in [28] that the logic of the group Chellas *stit* operator is non-axiomatisable. Moreover, it was proved there that the satisfiability problem is undecidable. The temporal dimension plays no role in these results. The proof is by reduction of the group *stit* satisfiability problem to the satisfiability problem of the product logic $S5^n$. For the strategic *stit* setting an analogous proof will be given in Sect. 3.4.

2.8   The Logic of the Deliberative *Stit* Operator

It has been a source of disagreement in the literature whether an agent may bring about a logical tautology. The logic of the deliberative *stit* operator rules it out:

$$\neg[i \text{ DStit}]\top \tag{20}$$

is valid. That is, no agent is agentive for a tautology.

Somewhat surprisingly, the axiom of monotony $[i \text{ Stit}](\varphi \wedge \psi) \rightarrow ([i \text{ Stit}]\varphi \wedge [i \text{ Stit}]\psi)$ is invalid: i may bring it about that $\varphi \wedge \psi$ without necessarily bringing it about that φ. $[i \text{ Stit}]$ is therefore not a normal modal 'box' operator.

While for the Chellas *stit* operator we had that $[i \text{ CStit}][j \text{ CStit}]\varphi$ implies that φ is settled —alias historically necessary—, for the deliberative *stit* operator $[i \text{ DStit}][j \text{ DStit}]\varphi$ can never be the case: we have the validity

$$[i \text{ DStit}][j \text{ DStit}]\varphi \rightarrow \bot, \quad \text{for } i \neq j \tag{21}$$

The logic of the deliberative *stit* was not specifically investigated in the literature. Note that axiomatisability results for (the individual and group version of) the Chellas *stit* immediately transfer to the deliberative *stit* via the reduction principle of axiom schema 10.

2.9   The Logic of the Achievement *Stit* Operator

The idea of achievement is conveyed by the principle of success (axiom schema 3 of Table 1) and by the following principle that no agent sees to a tautology (that is shared by the deliberative *stit*):

$$\neg[i \text{ AStit}]\top \tag{22}$$

Xu axiomatised the logic of the achievement *stit* for the case of a single agent, without the operator of historical possibility and without temporal operators. His axiomatisation comprises the common principles of Table 1 (in particular the much emphasised "refraining from refraining" axiom, which is in the focus of his work), the above schema 22, plus some rather complex principles [40] that we do not render here.

3   The Generalisation to Strategic *Stit*

The *stit* formalisms discussed so far all departed from the idea that an agentive effort is something that requires only one choice, one step. However, we now want to apply the idea of agency to full strategies for which the outcomes do not necessarily depend on one choice but possibly on a series of choices (steps) to be taken successively. In this section we discuss a general setup for a semantics that achieves this goal.

3.1   Stit Theory Applied to Strategies: G.STRAT

In Sect. 2 we used BT+AC structures that for each moment m determine a set of choices each corresponding to separate sets of histories running through that moment. We used this choice information in the structures to give semantics to agency operators that model what can be achieved through the execution of individual choices. In this section we will basically use the same structures[7] to define the semantics of agency operators that model what can be achieved through successive executions of choices. An immediate consequence of this change in focus is that the type of properties an agent can achieve is broadened. For instance, by performing a sequence of choices, it may be possible for an agent to guarantee a safety property (a certain condition is preserved over time, by continuously making the right choices along the way). Or, by performing the right strategy it may be possible for an agent to guarantee, independently of choices made by other agents along the way, that a condition is eventually guaranteed. Such a situation would be an example of an agent performing a winning strategy.

Over the past 10 years, finding a good semantics for strategic *stit* turned out to be a difficult task. The quest for such a semantics began with part V of 'Facing the Future' [5], and Horty provided some valuable suggestions in his book [31], without giving much details or worked out definitions[8]. One main problem for defining a semantics is to decide against what elements of choice structures

---

[7] One difference is that instead of trees we will use bundles of histories. The difference is that in a tree-based semantics histories are defined relative to trees (see Sect. 2.1) whereas in a bundled semantics tree-like structures are built from histories. So in tree semantics the trees are the elementary constituent objects whereas in bundled semantics the histories are. Both views are largely compatible; only for rather strong temporal languages the difference becomes expressible.

[8] Horty does provide worked-out definitions for the notion of strategic ability, but that is not the notion we are looking for here.

to evaluate the truth of formulas. For the standard *stit* theories we defined in Sect. 2 truth is evaluated against moment-history pairs. As Horty points out [31] this is not correct for a strategic version of *stit* theory. One and the same history can be the result of many different possible strategies. This means that a single history cannot provide the evaluation context for assessing what strategy an agent or a group of agents performs. So, a semantics that evaluates truth of formulas against moment-history pairs, as in Sect. 2, cannot be correct for a logic of strategic action; we need to be able to evaluate against complete strategies. In [14] we have tried to define a strategic *stit* semantics where we took strategy-state pairs for the units of evaluation. Although this semantics is correct (for instance, it embeds ATL), it is both technically and conceptually complicated. The reason for this lack of clarity is that the strategies in the strategy-state pairs of the units of evaluation are strategies of arbitrary coalitions A. This means it has to be defined how strategic formulas containing coalitions different from A are to be evaluated against a context where the coalition A performs a given fixed strategy. This is possible, as the paper shows, but the definitions are complex.

The crucial step was taken in [9], where it was proposed to evaluate against tuples of the form $\langle s, h, \alpha_1, \alpha_2, \ldots \alpha_n \rangle$, where s is a state, h a history, and $\alpha_1, \alpha_2, \ldots \alpha_n$ a strategy profile (s is on h and h is part of any strategy α_i). To be consistent with the terminology in Sect. 2 we will slightly correct the terminology of [9] and speak of 'moments' instead of 'states'. So the evaluation context for the formulas of our strategic *stit* logic will be provided by profiles $\langle m, h, \alpha_1, \alpha_2, \ldots \alpha_n \rangle$, where m is a moment, h a history, and $\alpha_1, \alpha_2, \ldots \alpha_n$ a strategy profile. The history h is the history currently under consideration (like in the semantics of temporal logics). This should not be interpreted as h being the unique 'actual' history; we might be evaluating a formula as part of a bigger and more complex formula involving quantifiers or epistemic operators, and within such a context it is inappropriate to call h 'actual'. The strategy profile records what strategies are performed relative to the current m and the current h. We need this information to evaluate truths concerning the current execution of strategies by arbitrary groups of agents. A strategy profile $\vec{\alpha} = \alpha_1, \alpha_2, \ldots \alpha_n$ encodes the strategies of individual agents as bundles of histories through time. The bundle of strategy α for agent i at moment m represents the choice the agent makes according to strategy α at that moment. The range of histories allowed by the bundle at m represents non-determinism of i's choice; separate histories in the bundle reflecting i's α-choice at m can be linked to simultaneous influence of other agents and nature at that moment. Note that this conceptualisation of strategies as bundles of histories $\vec{\alpha}$ does not make explicit what the strategy actually achieves or what names are given to the choices and actions taken according to the strategy in the moments along the way. What the strategy *achieves* depends on what properties it ensures along the way (that is, the temporal properties that hold on the intersection of all the histories in a profile, and in particular, on the history h). Furthermore, whether or not the strategy can be encoded as a little finite state machine or regular action expression, depends on the action names we might be able to give to the choices and the relation between those actions and their effects in the states along the way. The advantage (or disadvantage, depending on the perspective and application domain) of this *stit* view on strategies is that it abstracts away from all this detail, enabling an appropriate abstract view on reasoning about strategies.

Below we present the formal syntax and semantics of G.STRAT, a logic that was first presented in [9][9]. The G in the acronym G.STRAT stands for 'Group' and STRAT stands for 'strategic'.

Definition 1 (Syntax). *Well-formed formulas of the language $\mathcal{L}_{G.STRAT}$ are defined by:*

$$\varphi := p \mid \neg\varphi \mid \varphi \wedge \varphi \mid [A \text{ sstit}]\varphi \mid X\varphi \mid \varphi U \varphi$$

The p are elements from a countable infinite set of propositional symbols $\mathcal{P}$, and A is a subset of a finite set of agents Ags. We will often use natural numbers as agent names, and sometimes use i to refer to an arbitrary agent in this set. We use the notation $\overline{A}$ to refer to the complementary agent set $Ags \backslash A$. We use $\varphi, \psi, \ldots$ to represent arbitrary well-formed formulas. We use the standard propositional abbreviations, the standard notation for the duals of modal boxes (i.e., diamonds) and the following:

Definition 2 (Syntactic abbreviations).

$$F\varphi \equiv_{def} \top U \varphi$$
$$G\varphi \equiv_{def} \neg F \neg \varphi$$
$$\Box\varphi \equiv_{def} [\emptyset \text{ sstit}]\varphi$$

We now go on to define the semantic structures for G.STRAT. In the literature [2,25], strategies are most often defined as mappings from states to choices in states. The choices can have names (multi-player game models), or not (alternating transition systems) [25]. Here we take an equivalent, though slightly different viewpoint: strategies *are* sets of histories obeying certain structural properties. This is nothing more than a convenient shift of viewpoint and does not result in a fundamentally new type of strategies. If we define strategies as mappings from states/moments to choices, we have to define 'compliance' of a history to a strategy as a secondary concept. By defining strategies as sets of histories with a certain structure there is no need anymore to define a notion of 'compliance'.

As explained above we introduce 'profiles' as the units of evaluation. A 'profile' records the dynamic aspects of a system of agents. The profiles of our semantics take a moment, a history and a strategy profile (a list of strategies, one for each agent in the system) as components. So, the formulas of G.STRAT are evaluated against tuples $\langle m, h, \alpha_1, \alpha_2, \ldots \alpha_n \rangle$, where m is a moment, h a history, and $\alpha_1, \alpha_2, \ldots \alpha_n$ a strategy profile. Then, the truth of formulas is evaluated against the background of a *current* moment, a *current* history, and a *current* strategy-profile. If, under this semantics, we want to consider truths that do *not*

---

[9] Here we make minor modifications to the presentation of the semantics.

epend on dynamic aspects as represented by the histories and the strategies, we can use the historical necessity operator $\Box$. In particular, if $\Box\varphi$ holds, φ can be said to hold 'statically'. In *stit*-theory, one says that φ is 'moment determinate'. We also say that φ is 'settled'[10], which refers to the fact that it is completely independent of any action currently taken by any agent in the system.

We now first give the definition of the modal frames. Then afterwards, we explain the different items of the definition using the frame visualisation in Fig. 1.

Definition 3 (Strategic frames). *A frame is a tuple* $\mathcal{F} = \langle M, H, \{St(i) \mid i \in Ags\}, \{R_A \mid A \subseteq Ags\}\rangle$ *such that:*

1. *M is a non-empty set of moments. Elements of M are denoted $m, m', \ldots$*
2. *H is a non-empty set of 'backwards bundled' histories. A history $h \in H$ is a sequence $\ldots m, m', m'' \ldots$ of mutually different elements from M. For m appearing strictly before m' on the history h we write $m <_h m'$. To denote that m' succeeds m on h we use a successor function succ and write $m' = succ(m, h)$. Histories $h \in H$ and successor functions succ are isomorphic with $(\mathbb{Z}, +1)$ by a bijective function $f : M \times H \mapsto \mathbb{Z}$ that ensures that $m' = succ(m, h)$ and $f(m, h) = x$ if and only if $f(m', h) = y$ and $y = x + 1$. Furthermore, let $H_n = \{h \mid h \in H \text{ and } n \text{ on } h\}$ (as in Sect. 2.1). The following constraint on the set H ensures a deterministic past:*
   a. *for all $h \in H$, if $m = succ(n, h)$ then $H_m \subseteq H_n$*
3. *$St(i)$ yields for each $i \in Ags$ a non-empty set of strategies. Strategies are non-empty sets of histories obeying properties that follow from the constraints a., b., c., d. and e. below. For agent 1, the strategies $St(1)$ are denoted α_1, β_1, etc. A strategy profile[11] relative to $St(i)$ is a list of strategies $\alpha_1, \alpha_2, \ldots \alpha_n$, where $\{1, 2, \ldots, n\} = Ags$ and $\alpha_i \in St(i)$ for any i. For strategy profiles we will use the vector notation '$\vec{\alpha}$' when we need to be more concise. Tuples $\langle m, h, \alpha_1, \alpha_2, \ldots \alpha_n\rangle$ such that m belongs to h and for all $i \in Ags$, $h \in \alpha_i$ we call 'profiles'. Profiles of the form $\langle m, h, \alpha_1, \alpha_2, \ldots \alpha_n\rangle$ will be the units of evaluation (possible worlds) of our modal semantics. We impose the following constraints on profiles (and, implicitly, the strategies in them).*
   a. *for all $m \in M$, there is a profile $\langle m, h, \alpha_1, \alpha_2, \ldots \alpha_n\rangle$*
   b. *for any $i \in Ags$, if $\langle m, h, \alpha_1, \ldots, \alpha_i, \ldots, \alpha_n\rangle$ is a profile at m, and if for a history $h' \in H$ through m and the strategy α_i in the profile it holds that for all x on h' there is a $h'' \in \alpha_i$ such that x is on h'', then $h' \in \alpha_i$*

---

[10] Settledness does *not* necessarily mean that a property is *always* true in the future (as often thought). Settledness may also apply to the condition that φ occurs 'some' time in the future, now, or indeed any condition expressible as linear time temporal formula. So, settledness is a universal quantification over the *branching* dimension of time, and *not* over the dimension of duration.

[11] In the game forms of game theory strategy profiles are referred to by means of names associated with the choices of agents in states. Here we abstract from names of choices, as explained.

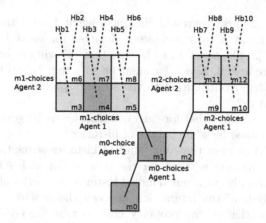

Fig. 2. Visualisation (from [10]) of a strategy profile in a partial two agent G.STRAT structure. The choices each agent performs are shown in light grey. The unique pattern of joint choices determined by the joint strategy is shown in dark grey.

c. *for any* $i \in Ags$, *if* $\langle m, h, \alpha_1, \ldots, \alpha_i, \ldots, \alpha_n \rangle$ *is a profile at* m, *and there is a profile* $\langle n, h', \beta_1, \ldots, \beta_i, \ldots, \beta_n \rangle$ *at* n *such that* $n = succ(h, m)$, *then there is a profile* $\langle m, h'', \alpha_1, \ldots, \gamma_i, \ldots, \alpha_n \rangle$ *at* m *such that* $\gamma_i = (\alpha_i \backslash H_n) \cup (\beta_i \cap H_n)$

d. *if* $\langle m, h, \alpha_1, \alpha_2, \ldots, \alpha_n \rangle$ *and* $\langle m, h', \beta_1, \beta_2, \ldots, \beta_n \rangle$ *are profiles at* m, *then any* $\langle m, h'', \gamma_1, \gamma_2, \ldots, \gamma_n \rangle$ *such that for any* i, $\gamma_i = \alpha_i$ *or* $\gamma_i = \beta_i$, *is also a profile at* m

e. *if* $\langle m, h, \alpha_1, \alpha_2, \ldots \alpha_n \rangle$ *is a profile at* m *and for some* h', *for all* $i \in Ags$, $h' \in \alpha_i$ *then* $h' = h$

4. *The relations* R_A *are 'effectivity' equivalence classes over profiles such that* $\langle m, h, \alpha_1, \alpha_2, \ldots \alpha_n \rangle R_A \langle m', h', \beta_1, \beta_2, \ldots \beta_n \rangle$ *if and only if* $m = m'$, *and for all* $i \in A, \alpha_i = \beta_i$

Item **1** gives the basic elements of the frames: the set of moments M.

Item **2** defines histories to be linearly ordered sets of moments. Also it defines a bundling structure for the set H of all histories: histories that come together when going in the past direction will stay together in that direction. This implies that in the future direction, once bundles have separated they will never come together again.

Item **3** defines strategies. Strategies are sets of histories with certain properties. A strategy profile is a choice of strategy for each agent in the system. Figure 2 visualises a (partial) frame and a strategy profile in it, from the viewpoint of moment $m0$. Note that there is an important difference with Fig. 1: in the present picture moments are no longer associated with game forms but with the cells inside game forms. This is not an essential difference: we can say that in the present picture the partitioning of histories into choices is pictured at subsequent moments. Formally there is no difference: the difference is only in the visualisation.

Columns that are grey represent choices of agent 1, rows that are grey represent choices of agent 2. No $m2$-choice is depicted for agent 1, because in the pictured strategy profile, agent 1 can be sure that $m2$ will not be reached as the result of his choice at $m0$. Agent 1 cannot be sure that this is this case, so his strategy (his strategy contribution to the strategy profile in the picture) does specify a choice at $m2$.

Condition **3(a)** ensures that for each moment, for each agent, its strategy at that moment is defined by some bundle of histories.

Condition **3(b)** ensures that our bundled histories semantics behaves as a tree semantics on aspects relevant for the comparison with ATL. We need to impose this condition because our bundled histories semantics allows for a more fine grained analysis of the interaction between choice and time than a tree semantics[12]. In particular, the property ensures that G.STRAT obeyes ATL's induction axiom.

Condition **3(c)** ensures that if an agent has two different strategies in his repertoire, recombinations of these strategies where first one strategy is followed and later on (next) the other, are always also in the repertoire of that agent[13].

Condition **3(d)** ensures that we can always recombine strategies of individual agents contributing to a group strategy into a new joint strategy. This implements the *stit*-requirement of *independence of agency* (no agent can choose in such a way that some other agent is deprived of one of its choices). Note that independence is not a local property of strategies but a global one. This corresponds to the notion of independence in ATL (Sect. 3.2 below).

Condition **3(e)** ensures that there is *exactly one* history complying to all strategies of a strategy profile. This reflects the idea, also assumed in ATL (Alternating Time Temporal Logic, see Sect. 3.2) and CL (Coalition Logic [34]), that a choice of strategy for each agent in the system completely determines the entire future. This means that, strictly speaking, we do not have to introduce h here as an independent element of the evaluation context, since we can define it as the intersection of the strategies in the strategy profile. The reason that we do this anyway is that it facilitates an easy definition of the semantics and leaves open the possibility to drop condition **3(e)** and allow for non-determinism introduced by the agents' environment. In Fig. 1 the bundle of histories $Hb3$ through the darker grey little squares is the bundle of histories containing the unique history through $m0$ that is determined by the intersection of the strategies of agents 1 and 2 in the profile. Note that if we view these frames as a setup for the dynamics of the world we live in, we have to buy in to the idea that non-determinism is *only* due to choices of agents, and that the rest of nature is deterministic. This is exactly why we may want to drop the constraint **3(e)**.

We could have added the following extra constraint on strategies. To formulate the constraint we need some extra notation. Let $C(m, \alpha)$ denote the

---

[12] There are infinite sets of histories that cannot be characterised as the histories running through an infinite tree; the condition ensures that such infinite sets are excluded.

[13] We thank Hein Duijf for pointing us to this constraint.

choice specified by strategy α at moment m, that is $C(m, \alpha) = \{m' \mid m' = succ(m, h), h \in \alpha\}^{14}$. The extra constraint we could impose is:

3(f) For two different strategies α_i and β_i of an agent i for any moment m we always have that $C(m, \alpha_i) \cap C(m, \beta_i) = \emptyset$.

This expresses that different choices of an agent at a moment m do not 'overlap'. However, since modal truth is invariant under bisimulation [6] (see the proof sketch of Theorem 1), this constraint has no effect on the logic, and we do not add it.

Finally, item **4** defines the basic units of evaluation and the agency relation over them. Note that the difference with classical multi-agent or group *stit*-models [5] is that moments are not partitioned by one-shot actions, but by strategies. This generalisation is the essential step for defining our *strategic* version of the *stit*-operator. Now **4** defines R_A to be a relation reaching all profiles that only deviate from the current profile in the sense that agents not among A perform a choice different from the current one. This reflects the basic idea of agency saying that acting or choosing is ensuring a condition irrespective of what other agents do or choose.

Now we are ready to define the formal semantics of the language $\mathcal{L}_{\mathsf{G.STRAT}}$. The semantics is multi-dimensional, and the truth conditions are quite standard. First we define models based on the frames of the previous definition.

Definition 4 (Strategic models). *A frame* $\mathcal{F} = \langle M, H, \{St(a) \mid a \in Ags\}, \{R_A \mid A \subseteq Ags\}\rangle$ *is extended to a model* $\mathcal{M} = \langle M, H, \{St(a) \mid a \in Ags\}, \{R_A \mid A \subseteq Ags\}, \pi\rangle$ *by adding a valuation* π *of atomic propositions:*

- π *is a valuation function* $\pi : P \longrightarrow 2^{M \times H \times St(a)}$ *assigning to each atomic proposition the set of evaluation tuples (or 'profiles', see Definition 3) in which they are true.*

Definition 5 (Truth, validity, logic). *Truth* $\mathcal{M}, \langle m, h, \vec{\alpha}\rangle \models \varphi$, *of a G.STRAT-formula* φ *in a profile* $\langle m, h, \vec{\alpha}\rangle$ *of a model* $\mathcal{M} = \langle M, H, \{St(a) \mid a \in Ags\}, \{R_A \mid A \subseteq Ags\}, \pi\rangle$ *is defined as (suppressing the model denotation '$\mathcal{M}$'):*

$\langle m, h, \vec{\alpha}\rangle \models p \qquad \Leftrightarrow \langle m, h, \vec{\alpha}\rangle \in \pi(p)$

$\langle m, h, \vec{\alpha}\rangle \models \neg\varphi \qquad \Leftrightarrow not \ \langle m, h, \vec{\alpha}\rangle \models \varphi$

$\langle m, h, \vec{\alpha}\rangle \models \varphi \wedge \psi \qquad \Leftrightarrow \langle m, h, \vec{\alpha}\rangle \models \varphi \ and \ \langle m, h, \vec{\alpha}\rangle \models \psi$

$\langle m, h, \vec{\alpha}\rangle \models [A \ \mathsf{sstit}]\varphi \Leftrightarrow for \ all \ h', \vec{\beta} \ such \ that$
$\qquad\qquad\qquad\qquad \langle m, h, \vec{\alpha}\rangle R_A \langle m, h', \vec{\beta}\rangle$
$\qquad\qquad\qquad\qquad it \ holds \ that \ \langle m, h', \vec{\beta}\rangle \models \varphi$

$\langle m, h, \vec{\alpha}\rangle \models \mathsf{X}\varphi \qquad \Leftrightarrow for \ all \ m' \ such \ that \ m' = succ(m, h)$
$\qquad\qquad\qquad\qquad it \ holds \ that \ \langle m', h, \vec{\alpha}\rangle \models \varphi$

$\langle m, h, \vec{\alpha}\rangle \models \psi \mathsf{U}\varphi \qquad \Leftrightarrow there \ is \ a \ m' \ such \ that$
$\qquad\qquad\qquad\qquad (1) \ m \leq_h m' \ and$
$\qquad\qquad\qquad\qquad (2) \ \langle m', h, \vec{\alpha}\rangle \models \varphi \ and$
$\qquad\qquad\qquad\qquad (3) \ for \ all \ m'' \ with \ m \leq_h m'' <_h m' \ we \ have \ \langle m'', h, \vec{\alpha}\rangle \models \psi$

---

[14] Note that choices of a strategy can be empty at a given moment m.

Validity on a G.STRAT-model $\mathcal{M}$ *is defined as truth in all profiles of the G.STRAT-model. General validity of a formula* φ *is defined as validity on all possible G.STRAT-models. The logic G.STRAT is the subset of all general validities of* $\mathcal{L}_{G.STRAT}$ *over the class of G.STRAT-models.*

One important class of properties expressible in G.STRAT are properties of strategies that are conditional on the execution of other strategies. For instance, we can express that a strategy of agent 2 for guaranteeing a certain interesting position with Chess is only possible if the opponent, agent 1, plays the Sicilian opening: [1 sstit]G*Sicilian* → ◊[2 sstit]F*Position I* (where we may think of the proposition *Sicilian* as a set of condition-choice rules specifying the moves that constitute the Sicilian opening). The consequence of this implication is also expressible in ATL (to be discussed in the next section) but the antecedent is not. Properties like these have the same structure as 'assumption-guarantee' properties which are known from the compositional formal verification of concurrent systems (see [10]). Also G.STRAT enables one to zoom in and specify abstract strategies by filling in their details. If we want to specify that the Sicilian defence always answers the move e4 with c5, we may specify: [1 sstit]G*Sicilian* → ([2 sstit]X@*e4* → [1 sstit]XX@*c5*).

We do not have an axiomatic way yet to characterise the validities of this logic. Such a characterisation would be more than welcome, since it would shed light on the axiomatisation of many related formalisms (see Sect. 3.5). One point where the absence of an axiomatisation comes to the fore quite clearly is in Sect. 5 where we see examples of formulas that are valid and invalid for G.STRAT; it would have been good to show this using an axiomatisation.

3.2 Embedding ATL

In this section we show that G.STRAT embeds ATL [2,17] and thus also CTL [23] and CL [34]. Also we mention validities for G.STRAT that do not hold for ATL. Let us first give a brief exposition of ATL in its most common form defined on concurrent game structures (CGSs). The syntax of ATL formulas is:

Definition 6. *Given that p ranges over P, and that A ranges over* 2^{Ags}, *the language of ATL is defined by:*

$$\varphi ::= p \mid \neg\varphi \mid \varphi \wedge \varphi \mid \langle\langle A \rangle\rangle X\varphi \mid \langle\langle A \rangle\rangle G\varphi \mid \langle\langle A \rangle\rangle\varphi U \varphi$$

The intended reading of $\langle\langle A \rangle\rangle \eta$, with η a temporal formula as allowed by the above syntax, is that "group A *can* perform a strategy that ensures η whatever agents in $Ags \backslash A$ do". In other words: group A has some winning strategy for η. The syntax of ATL is constrained such that cooperation modalities $\langle\langle A \rangle\rangle$ are always followed by a standard temporal operator: X (next), G (always), U (until). Most commonly, the semantics of ATL is defined in terms of transition systems where transitions are labeled with combinations of action names, one for each agent acting at that transition. These structures are called 'concurrent game structures'. Formally, a concurrent game structure (CGS) is a tuple

$\mathcal{M} = \langle Ag, S, V, Act, d, o \rangle$ where $Ag = \{1, ..., k\}$ is the nonempty finite set of all agents, S a nonempty set of states, $V : Prop \mapsto 2^S$ a valuation of atomic propositions, and Act a nonempty set of (atomic) actions[15]. A function $d : Ag \times S \mapsto 2^{Act}$ defines nonempty sets of actions agents can opt to choose at a given state, and o is a (deterministic) transition function that assigns a unique outcome state $q' = o(q, a_1, ..., a_k)$ to state q and a tuple of actions $\langle a_1, ..., a_k \rangle$ with $a_i \in d(i, q)$ that can be executed by Ag in q. A strategy of agent i is a conditional plan that for each state specifies what i is going to do in that state. Thus, a strategy of agent i is represented by a function $s_i : S \mapsto Act$, such that $s_i(q) \in d(i, q)$. A collective strategy for a group of agents $C = \{1, ..., r\}$ is a tuple of strategies $s_C = \langle s_1, ..., s_r \rangle$, one for each agent from C. C's set of collective strategies is denoted by Σ_C. Also, by $s_C[i]$, we denote agent i's contribution to the collective strategy s_C. The function $out(q, s_C)$ yields the set of all paths that are allowed by the execution in state q of strategy s_C by coalition C. With these provisions we can now semantically define the logic ATL using concurrent game structures.

In ATL truth is defined relative to states. Strategic *stit*, as defined in the previous section, defines truth relative to profiles. This reflects two crucial differences. The states featuring in the semantics of ATL are different from the moments taken up as part of the profiles that form the evaluation context of strategic *stit* formulas. The difference between states and moments is that states may occur more than once on a history, while moments may not. The second, more fundamental difference is the one between evaluation relative to states and evaluation relative to profiles; the first is what Arthur Prior called the Peircean solution to the temporal logic conceptual problem of future contingencies, the second is a suitable generalisation of the *stit* solution to this same problem. Before explaining that despite these differences, ATL can be embedded in strategic *stit*, we give the formal semantics of ATL.

Definition 7 (Truth, validity ATL). *Truth* $\mathcal{M}, q \models \varphi$, *of an ATL-formula* φ *at a state* q *of a concurrent game structure* $\mathcal{M} = \langle Ag, S, V, Act, d, o \rangle$ *is defined as:*

$\mathcal{M}, q \models \langle\langle C \rangle\rangle \mathbf{X}\varphi$ *iff there is a* $s_C \in \Sigma_C$ *such that, for each path* $\lambda \in out(s_C, q)$, *we have*
         $\mathcal{M}, \lambda[1] \models \varphi$

$\mathcal{M}, q \models \langle\langle C \rangle\rangle \mathbf{G}\varphi$ *iff there is a* $s_C \in \Sigma_C$ *such that, for each* $\lambda \in out(s_C, q)$, *we have*
         $\mathcal{M}, \lambda[i] \models \varphi$ *for every* $i \geq 0$

$\mathcal{M}, q \models \langle\langle C \rangle\rangle \varphi \mathbf{U} \psi$ *iff there is a* $s_C \in \Sigma_C$ *such that, for each* $\lambda \in out(s_C, q)$, *there is an* $i \geq 0$
         for which $\mathcal{M}, \lambda[i] \models \psi$, *and* $\mathcal{M}, \lambda[j] \models \varphi$ *for each* $0 \leq j \leq i$

General ATL *validity of a formula* φ *is defined as validity in all states of all possible concurrent game structures. The logic* ATL *is the subset of all general validities of* $\mathcal{L}_{ATL}$ *over the class of concurrent game structures.*

We now define a translation from ATL formulas to G.STRAT formulas. This translation determines an embedding of ATL in G.STRAT, as we will show.

---

[15] It would be more correct to call these 'action types'.

Definition 8 (Mapping ATL to G.STRAT [9]**).** *We define a mapping T from ATL formulas to G.STRAT formulas. The central modalities are mapped as follows:*

$$\langle\langle A\rangle\rangle \mathrm{X}\varphi \text{ maps to } \Diamond[A \text{ sstit}]\mathrm{X}\varphi,$$
$$\langle\langle A\rangle\rangle \mathrm{G}\varphi \text{ maps to } \Diamond[A \text{ sstit}]\mathrm{G}\varphi,$$
$$\langle\langle A\rangle\rangle(\varphi \mathrm{U}\, \psi) \text{ maps to } \Diamond[A \text{ sstit}](\varphi \mathrm{U}\, \psi).$$

Modality-free formula parts of ATL formulas are mapped to identical modality-free formula parts of G.STRAT formulas.

Theorem 1. *The mapping of Definition 8 embeds the logic ATL in the logic G.STRAT.*

Proof Sketch. We need to prove that the mapping of Definition 8 preserves the logic in both directions. We will take the most straightforward approach of showing that an ATL formula φ is satisfiable on some concurrent game structure if an only if the related G.STRAT formula $T(\varphi)$ is satisfiable on a strategic model. For the 'only if' direction we map a satisfying concurrent game structure to a strategic model. For this we take the following steps.

(1) From the state s which satisfies the ATL formula φ unravel the concurrent game structure into a tree. By the unravelling, unique states of the concurrent game structures are possibly mapped to multiple moments in the tree. The tree determines a set of histories H satisfying the backwards bundling constraint of item 2 in Definition 3. For each moment m in the unravelled tree we will build a profile $\langle m, h, \vec{\alpha}\rangle$ in the next step.

(2) For each agent i construct the set of all its possible strategies $St(i)$ by collecting the right histories as determined by the functions d and o in the concurrent game structure. It is not too difficult to assess that this construction guarantees that the conditions on strategies and profiles as defined for strategy frames (Definition 3, conditions 3.a, 3.b, 3.c, 3.d and 3.e) are met (but, see e.g. footnote 12). After this step in the construction, we no longer need the names for actions. They can be discarded. With $St(i)$ we know all the possible strategy profiles relative to a moment m in the tree. We construct all the possible profiles $\langle m, h, \vec{\alpha}\rangle$ relative to m by considering all the possible profiles and by taking h to be the unique intersection of a profile. Uniqueness is guaranteed by the output function o of the originating concurrent game structure. Given the structure of profiles, item 4 of Definition 3 defines the relations R_A.

(3) For all profiles $\langle m, h, \vec{\alpha}\rangle$ in the constructed frame make the valuation of atomic propositions P identical to the valuation in the unique state s in the originating concurrent game structure that is associated to the moment m.

The above steps make clear what the differences and similarities between concurrent game structures and strategic models are. Now we can prove preservation of satisfiability by this mapping by induction over the general structure of formulas. However, the crucial element to be checked is the equivalence of the truth conditions of the ATL operators and the combined truth conditions of the combination of G.STRAT operators we translate to (Definition 8). But it is quite clear that they are just two different ways of writing exactly the same conditions.

For the 'if' direction we make a similar construction; we map a strategic model to a concurrent game structure. This construction encompasses the following steps.

(1) From the moment m where the G.STRAT formula φ is satisfied, look at the strategies in $St(i)$ and give all different bundles of histories through the moment m appearing in one of the strategies an arbitrary but unique action name (however, names may be reused at other moments, and it does not matter at all for which bundles). This constructs the set Act of actions. If it happens to be that there is a history through m that belongs to more than one named bundle relative to m (note that this is not disallowed for strategy models; see the remark in the discussion of the set $St(i)$ after the definition of the strategic frames), make a copy of the subtree pointed at by that history, and assign a separate copy to each of the two named bundles (actions). From this point on, refer to the moments as 'states'. Now construct the functions d and o based on the action names given to the bundles relative to the states. That the function d exists and can be constructed is guaranteed by condition 3.a in Definition 3. That the (infinite) set of histories allowed by an ATL strategy is closed under recomposition of histories using the first parts of other histories is guaranteed by 3.b. That the set of possible ATL strategies available to an agent in an ATL model is closed under switching to other possible strategies in a next state is guaranteed by condition 3.c. That o yields an outcome for every combination of actions (any action profile) is guaranteed by 3.d. That o maps to a single output state is guaranteed by condition 3.e.

(2) For the construction of the valuation function V in states s we look at the valuation π of atoms in profiles $\langle m, h, \vec{\alpha} \rangle$ of the originating strategic model. The problem is that these might be different for different histories and different strategies relative to the same moment m. But if that is the case, we can make different copies s and s' associated with the moment m for any two profiles based on m having different valuations of atomic propositions and accordingly add branches to the state associated with the moment preceding m. Making copies of states in this way blows up the branching factor of the game structures, but does not affect truth or validity on structures because modal logic truth is invariant under bisimulation.

This procedure results in a concurrent game structure that is a tree. It might be that the tree can be made finite by identifying bisimilar states, but that is not important for showing satisfiability. Again, by inspection of the truth conditions, we establish that satisfiability is preserved under this mapping from strategy models to concurrent game structures. ∎

As a corollary we get that the translation of the Hilbert style axioms and derivation rules of the ATL axiomatisation [26] results in sound axioms and sound rules for G.STRAT. It will be instructive to check this for ATL's maximality axiom: (N) $\neg\langle\langle\emptyset\rangle\rangle X\neg\varphi \rightarrow \langle\langle Ags\rangle\rangle X\varphi$. In the translation to G.STRAT we get $\neg\Diamond[\emptyset \text{ sstit}]X\neg\varphi \rightarrow \Diamond[Ags \text{ sstit}]X\varphi$. This is equivalent with $\Box\langle\emptyset \text{ sstit}\rangle X\varphi \rightarrow \Diamond[Ags \text{ sstit}]X\varphi$. The $\Box$ operator is an abbreviation in G.STRAT and it is interpreted by the equivalence class $R_\emptyset$. Therefore the schema is equivalent to $\Diamond X\varphi \rightarrow \Diamond[Ags \text{ sstit}]X\varphi$. Now this is only true for every φ on strategy models if the strategy frames obey the property that the intersection of all strategies in a profile contains exactly one history (condition 3.e in Definition 3). If we drop that condition of the frames, the maximality condition would not hold and ATL would not be a fragment. However, we would still have an interesting logic of strategies; one that allows for non-determinism of a non-agentive source.

It is clear that we cannot have an embedding of G.STRAT in ATL: satisfiability is undecidable for G.STRAT (see Sect. 3.4) while it is not for ATL.

3.3   Embedding ATL*

The logic ATL* generalizes ATL by partly breaking the syntactic connection between the ability operator $\langle\langle A\rangle\rangle$ and the temporal operators: within the scope of $\langle\langle A\rangle\rangle$ operators, temporal operators may occur nested, without being immediately preceded by another $\langle\langle A\rangle\rangle$ operator. Note however that we are still two steps removed from the more general syntax of G.STRAT: temporal operators are not yet allowed to occur outside the scope of an $\langle\langle A\rangle\rangle$ operator and $\langle\langle A\rangle\rangle$ is not decomposed into $\Diamond[A \text{ sstit}]\varphi$.

Definition 9. *Given that p ranges over P, and that A ranges over 2^{Ags}, the language of ATL* is defined by:*

$$\varphi ::= p \mid \neg\varphi \mid \varphi \wedge \varphi \mid \langle\langle A\rangle\rangle\sigma$$
$$\sigma ::= \varphi \mid \neg\sigma \mid \sigma \wedge \sigma \mid X\sigma \mid \sigma U \sigma$$

Since the temporal operators still only occur in the scope of a strategy operator, which means that the context of temporal operators is always one where there is a quantification over histories (the Peircean solution to the problem of future contingencies [36]), the formulas σ are commonly referred to as path formulas. Also in the semantics the two types of formulas are treated separately.

We can reuse the concurrent game structures defined for ATL, but we have to make one generalisation concerning the strategies. In ATL a strategy can be a function $s_i : S \mapsto Act$, such that $s_i(q) \in d(i,q)$. For ATL* we have to generalise this to a function $ms_i : S^+ \mapsto Act$, such that $s_i(q) \in d(i,q)$. A strategy ms is said to be a strategy with memory. Accordingly we will use ms_C to denote a strategy with memory for coalition C and $m\Sigma_C$ to denote all such strategies for C. Now the truth conditions are as follows.

Definition 10 (Truth, validity ATL*). *Truth $\mathcal{M}, q \models \varphi$, of an ATL*-formula φ at a state q of concurrent game structure $\mathcal{M} = \langle Ag, S, V, Act, d, o\rangle$ is defined as:*

$\mathcal{M}, q \models \langle\langle C \rangle\rangle\varphi$ iff there is an $ms_C \in m\Sigma_C$ such that, for each path $\lambda \in out(ms_C, q)$, we have
   $\mathcal{M}, \lambda \models \varphi$
$\mathcal{M}, \lambda \models \varphi$ iff $\mathcal{M}, \lambda[0] \models \varphi$, for φ a state formula
$\mathcal{M}, \lambda \models \neg\varphi$ iff not $\mathcal{M}, \lambda \models \varphi$
$\mathcal{M}, \lambda \models \varphi \wedge \psi$ iff $\mathcal{M}, \lambda \models \varphi$ and $\mathcal{M}, \lambda \models \psi$
$\mathcal{M}, \lambda \models \mathrm{X}\varphi$ iff $\mathcal{M}, \lambda[1] \models \varphi$
$\mathcal{M}, \lambda \models \varphi\mathrm{U}\psi$ iff there is an $i \geq 0$ for which $\mathcal{M}, \lambda[i] \models \psi$, and $\mathcal{M}, \lambda[j] \models \varphi$ for each $0 \leq j \leq i$

General ATL* validity of a formula φ is defined as validity in all states of all possible concurrent game structures. The logic ATL* is the subset of all general validities of $\mathcal{L}_{ATL*}$ over the class of concurrent game structures.

Definition 11 (Mapping ATL* to G.STRAT). We define a mapping from ATL* formulas to G.STRAT formulas. The central ATL*-modality is mapped as follows:

$$\langle\langle A \rangle\rangle\varphi \text{ maps to } \Diamond[A \text{ sstit}]\varphi$$

Other modal and non-modal logic operators of ATL* are mapped to their identical G.STRAT companion.

Theorem 2. The mapping of Definition 11 embeds the logic ATL* in the logic G.STRAT.

Proof Sketch. The proof deviates only marginally from the one for ATL. We only need to pay attention to the generalised form of strategies in ATL*. In the mapping that proves preservation of satisfiability from ATL* formulas to G.STRAT formulas, the first step is to unravel the satisfying concurrent game structure. After unravelling, the structure is a tree. Now, for trees the distinction between strategies with memory and strategies without memory is irrelevant since the information that is thought to have been stored in the 'memory' of states (i.e., the states that have been visited before) can now be thought to be encoded in the moments of the tree (each moment in a tree has a unique past in the tree). If in the originating concurrent game structure there is a strategy *with* memory (choices depend on which states have been visited before), then by unraveling, this strategy is transformed into an equivalent strategy *without* memory (choices do not depend on past moments, because those moments are uniquely determined by the present moment). This means that exactly the same proof strategy works for ATL*[16].   ∎

As mentioned in the proof sketch above, any ATL* strategy with memory within a non-tree model can be related to an ATL* strategy without memory on the associated unravelled tree model. So, if for ATL* we would stick to trees as the structures of interpretation, the issue of memory (and other issues) is avoided. However, much effort has been spent on studying ATL* and endogenous epistemic versions of ATL (versions talking about epistemic indistinguishability, but without introducing separate epistemic modalities in the object language) where

---

[16] We are neglecting here the possibility of a significant difference resulting from the difference between bundle semantics and tree semantics; it will always be possible to find a condition on G.STRAT frames that eliminates this difference relative to ATL*.

the structures are not necessarily trees. And then it makes a difference what type of strategies are used for the semantics: strategies with or without memory. The resulting semantics can be seen to consist of two layers. For instance, if we want to check satisfiability of an ATL* formula for a semantics where strategies do not come with a memory, we have to perform two steps: first find a concurrent game structure where loops can be used to represent infinite paths, and second, check if within this structure the formula can be satisfied by strategies that forget if they have have been in some state before and ignorantly do the same action again each time they come to the same state after completing a loop. Much is known about the complexity of model checking of such semantics, however, there are no axiomatisations of the logics. We believe the non-standard, two layered structure of the semantics in combination with the slightly contrived syntax is to blame for this.

3.4   Embedding Chellas Group *Stit*

In Sect. 2.7 we discussed Chellas group *stit*. Here we show that it is embedded in G.STRAT. Group *stit* does not encompass any temporal operators, so we may directly map the group *stit* operator to the strategic *stit* operator and leave the temporal operators out of the discussion.

Definition 12 (Mapping GroupSTIT to G.STRAT). *We define a mapping from GroupSTIT formulas to G.STRAT formulas. The central GroupSTIT modality is mapped as follows:*

$$[A \, \mathrm{CStit}]\varphi \text{ maps to } [A \, \mathrm{sstit}]\varphi$$

Modality-free (sub)formulas of GroupSTIT formulas are mapped to identical modality-free (sub)formulas of G.STRAT formulas.

Theorem 3. *The mapping of Definition 12 embeds the logic GroupSTIT in the logic G.STRAT.*

Proof Sketch. Again we consider two mappings. The mapping from GroupSTIT structures to G.STRAT structures maps moment-history indexes m, h of group $BT{+}AC$ structures (Sect. 2.2) to profiles $\langle m, h, \vec{\alpha} \rangle$ of strategy structures by making up arbitrary strategies $\vec{\alpha}$ with the only precaution that we ensure that the first 'step' of strategies corresponds to the choice cells in the originating $BT{+}AC$ structure (that $BT{+}AC$ structures are based on a tree ordering, while strategic structures are based on backwards bundled sets of histories, is not an essential difference). The mapping from G.STRAT structures to GroupSTIT structures simply discards all the structure encoded for the strategies and reduces profiles $\langle m, h, \vec{\alpha} \rangle$ to moment-history indexes m, h and associates choice cells with the initial steps of the strategies. Both directions preserve satisfiability since strategy structures obey all the conditions specified for $BT{+}AC$ *structures* as defined in Sect. 2.1. ∎

As discussed in the introduction, satisfiability checking for Chellas group *stit* logic formulas is undecidable and also a finite axiomatisation is not possible [28]. The reason is that Chellas group *stit* itself embeds S5 product logics [24] where the number of members in the product corresponds with the number of agents of the logic. It will be instructive to point to this fragment also in G.STRAT.

Definition 13 (the sub-logic AIV^{atemp} [9,28]). AIV^{atemp} *is the logic such that $AIV^{atemp} \subset G.STRAT$ that results from restricting the syntax of Definition 1 by (1) dropping the until and next operators ('atemp' stands for 'atemporal'), and (2) restricting the set of operators $[A \text{ sstit}]\varphi$ with $A \subseteq Ags$, to the set $\{[P \text{ sstit}]\varphi \mid P = Ags\backslash\{a\} \text{ and } a \in Ags\}$. The groups P are called 'anti-individuals' in [28], hence the acronym 'AIV' in the name of this fragment.*

Theorem 4. *For $|Ags| \geq 3$, the satisfiability problem of the fragment AIV^{atemp} is undecidable, and there is no standard finite Hilbert-style axiomatisation.*

Proof Sketch. To give semantics the fragment AIV^{atemp} we can ignore most interaction conditions on strategies in profiles $\langle m, h, \vec{\alpha} \rangle$. We can even ignore all of the temporal structure in profiles. Now item 4 in Definition 3 defines the relations R_A as equivalence classes over profiles, which leads to S5 also for the logics of the modalities $[P \text{ sstit}]\varphi$. Furthermore, with Definition 3 item 4 we can recognize a standard multi-dimensional product of S5 logics where the modalities $[P \text{ sstit}]\varphi$ form the dimensions of the product. Now the properties of the theorem are standard results for such logics. See e.g. [24].   ∎

The implication of the theorem is that reasoning about agency of groups is not feasible without restrictions of some kind. Of course, if we go to smaller fragments, we can expect better properties. For instance, following [28], we conclude that the complexity of the fragment determined by the operators "$[a \text{ sstit}]\varphi$ with $a \in Ags$" is NEXPTIME-complete. Another fragment, called CTL.STIT, was considered in [10]. The logic CTL.STIT is in between G.STRAT and ATL. It links agency operators to temporal operators, thereby avoiding the undecidable group *stit* fragment discussed above. But, it generalizes ATL by allowing talking about agency explicitly, where ATL only talks about ability (i.e., in ATL also the $\Diamond$ operator is not separable from the agency operators). We believe that CTL.STIT is decidable and axiomatisable, but proofs still have to be provided.

3.5 An Overview of Fragments of G.STRAT

In this section we discuss Fig. 3 that gives an overview of fragments of G.STRAT. The figure emphasises that the semantics of G.STRAT unifies all the well known logics appearing in the figure: the only differences between the logics are due to language restrictions on the general G.STRAT syntax.

It will be interesting to see which logics cannot be brought under the same picture. First of all there are the variants of ATL* (and ATEL) interpreted on structures that are not necessarily trees and where the 'memory' of strategies is limited [18]. These do not fall into the same picture, since they concern a genuinely different semantics. So, they embody a move to a different semantics

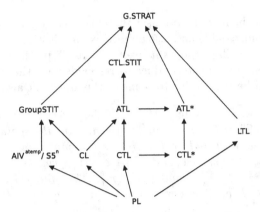

Fig. 3. Simultaneous language/logic inclusions under the G.STRAT semantics

for the same language, while the picture of Fig. 3 shows moves to sublanguages over the same semantics.

The logic XSTIT [8,11] also does not fit into the scheme. We get its syntax by restricting G.STRAT's temporal operators to only the next operator, and by applying the restriction that it is always preceded by a collective *stit* modality. If XSTIT would be a fragment under the same semantics, in Fig. 3 it would appear as a separate link between PL and CTL.STIT. The reason that XSTIT does not fit in is that it does not obey the maximality axiom $\Box \langle \emptyset$ sstit$\rangle$X$\varphi \rightarrow \Diamond[Ags$ sstit$]$Xφ. In stead, XSTIT obeys the weaker axiom $\langle \emptyset$ sstit$\rangle$X$\Box\varphi \rightarrow \Diamond[Ags$ sstit$]$Xφ. Actually we feel that maximality is a very strong property, since it leaves no room for non-determinism of a non-agentive source. The weaker XSTIT property is more cautious and does leave room for conditions whose coming about is not due to the involvement of agents. However, without assuming maximality for G.STRAT, the inclusions in the figure could not have been made.

Finally there is the version of *stit* logic that is central in Horty's book on deontic *stit* [31]. This version encompasses both future and past temporal modalities, which means that irrespective of its semantics, it does not fit into the picture sketched here. However, if in Horty's version of *stit* we leave out the past modality, we are left with a syntax that combines GroupSTIT with a subset of the temporal LTL operators. On the basis of these syntactic characteristics it would form a link between GroupSTIT and G.STRAT. With this provision to its syntax we conjecture that Horty's *stit* logic can indeed be seen as a fragment of G.STRAT. To assess the truth of this conjecture, we would have to study mappings from Horty's models to G.STRAT models.

4   Epistemic Extensions and Uniform Strategies

One may express that agent i has the *capability* to achieve φ by the formula $\Diamond[i$ CStit$]\varphi$.[17] When an agent does not have perfect knowledge of his

---

[17] Actually Chellas's original version of his logic was only about capabilities.

environment then it might happen that he has the capability to achieve φ but does not know this. The dedicated term in the game theory literature is that the agent does not have a *uniform strategy* to achieve φ (although he has a strategy *tout court* to do so). In Castelfranchi's terms, the agent does not have the power to achieve φ [19,33]. In this section we sketch an epistemic extension of the logic of the Chellas *stit* that allows to account for uniform strategies, following a proposal in [15,16,29].

In order to distinguish what an agent can do from what an agent knows he can do we add epistemic operators Know_i to the language. We first show that the resulting logic allows distinguishing the *de re* $\Diamond\text{Know}_i[i\ \text{CStit}]\varphi$ ("there is a strategy of which i knows that it achieves φ") from the weaker *de dicto* $\text{Know}_i\Diamond[i\ \text{CStit}]\text{X}\varphi$ ("i knows that there is a strategy achieving φ"). We then argue that other logics of strategic ability such as ATL and CL—or rather, their epistemic extensions—do not have enough linguistic resources in order to account for the above distinction.

The problem of uniform strategies can be explained for a single individual agent and on the one-step level. The latter means that we do not need the temporal operators G and U, but only the temporal 'next' operator X.

4.1   An Epistemic Extension of the Logic of the Chellas *Stit*

Consider a language with the historical possibility operator $\Diamond$, the temporal operator X, and the Chellas *stit* operators $[i\ \text{CStit}]$ and the epistemic operators Know_i, one per agent i. How should one interpret the epistemic operator Know_i in BT+AC structures? The question boils down to the question of how to define a relation of indistinguishability $\overset{i}{\sim}$ in BT+AC structures. We basically have two choices: either $\overset{i}{\sim}$ relates moments, or it relates moment-history pairs. We choose the latter; that the former is not a good choice will become clear later on when we are going to discuss uniform strategies in CL and ATL.

An *epistemic BT+AC model* is a 5-tuple of the form $\mathcal{M} = \langle\text{Mom}, <, \mathcal{C}, \sim, \pi\rangle$ where $\langle\text{Mom}, <, \mathcal{C}, \pi\rangle$ is a discrete BT+AC model and where $\sim$ is a function from *Ags* to $(\text{Mom} \times H) \times (\text{Mom} \times H)$.[18]

Let us come back to our scenario where there is an agent i in some room with a switch and a light bulb. Let us suppose the light is on but that the agent

---

[18]   In the papers [15,16,29] it is supposed that models satisfy the following constraints.

- If $h_1, h_2 \in H_m$ and $\langle m, h_1\rangle \overset{i}{\sim} \langle m', h_1'\rangle$ then there is $h_2' \in H_{m'}$ such that $\langle m, h_2\rangle \overset{i}{\sim} \langle m', h_2'\rangle$.
- If $\langle m, h_1\rangle \overset{i}{\sim} \langle m', h_1'\rangle$ and $h_1', h_2' \in H_{m'}$ then there is $h_2 \in H_m$ such that $\langle m, h_2\rangle \overset{i}{\sim} \langle m', h_2'\rangle$.
- If $\text{succ}(m_1, h) = m_2$ and $\langle m_2, h\rangle \overset{i}{\sim} \langle m_2', h'\rangle$ then there is a moment m_1' such that $\langle m_1, h\rangle \overset{i}{\sim} \langle m_1', h'\rangle$ and $\text{succ}(m_1', h) = m_2'$ (no forgetting).

However, they are not needed in order to explain the solution the epistemic extension of the Chellas *stit* provides to the problem of uniform strategies.

is blind and does not know whether this is the case or not. Intuitively, the agent has a strategy to ensure that the light is on next (viz. to do nothing) but does not know this. He therefore does not have a uniform strategy to ensure that the light is on in the next state.

Our BT+AC structure is $\langle \mathsf{Mom}, < \rangle$ where $\mathsf{Mom} = \{\mathsf{on}, \mathsf{off}\}^+$ is the set of all finite sequences of on and off and where $<$ is the prefix relation. So there are two roots of our BT+AC structure: $\langle \mathsf{on} \rangle$ and $\langle \mathsf{off} \rangle$. The set $\mathcal{C}(i, \mathsf{on})$ of i's choices at on is $\{H_{\mathsf{on},\mathsf{skip}}, H_{\mathsf{on},\mathsf{toggle}}\}$ where $H_{\mathsf{on},\mathsf{skip}}$ is the set of all histories of the form $\langle \mathsf{on}, \langle \mathsf{on}, \mathsf{on} \rangle, \dots \rangle$ and where $H_{\mathsf{on},\mathsf{toggle}}$ is the set of all histories of the form $\langle \mathsf{on}, \langle \mathsf{on}, \mathsf{off} \rangle, \dots \rangle$. The set $\mathcal{C}(i, \mathsf{off}) = \{H_{\mathsf{off},\mathsf{skip}}, H_{\mathsf{off},\mathsf{toggle}}\}$ of i's choices at off is defined similarly. Suppose the propositional variable light stands for "the light is on". The valuation is such that $\pi(m, h)$ is empty if the last element of the sequence m is off and is $\{light\}$ if the last element of the sequence m is on.

The above makes up a BT+AC model, and it remains to define the indistinguishability relation. We model that i is aware of the action he is going to do next (but not beyond) by stipulating that $\overset{i}{\sim}$ is the reflexive and symmetric closure of the following relation:

$$(\{\langle \mathsf{on}, h \rangle, \langle \mathsf{off}, g \rangle : h^1 \neq g^1 \text{ and } (h^2)^2 \neq (g^2)^2\}\}$$

where h^1 is the first element of the sequence h, h^2 is its second element (which is itself a sequence), $(h^2)^2$ is the second element of the latter, etc. For example we have

$$\langle \mathsf{on}, \langle \mathsf{on}, \langle \mathsf{on}, \mathsf{on} \rangle, \dots \rangle \rangle \overset{i}{\sim} \langle \mathsf{off}, \langle \mathsf{off}, \langle \mathsf{off}, \mathsf{off} \rangle, \dots \rangle \rangle$$

$$\langle \mathsf{on}, \langle \mathsf{on}, \langle \mathsf{on}, \mathsf{off} \rangle, \dots \rangle \rangle \overset{i}{\sim} \langle \mathsf{off}, \langle \mathsf{off}, \langle \mathsf{off}, \mathsf{on} \rangle, \dots \rangle \rangle$$

In the first line the agent knows that he will do nothing and in the second line he knows that he will toggle.

Let $\mathcal{M} = \langle \mathsf{Mom}, <, \mathcal{C}, \sim, \pi \rangle$ be the epistemic BT+AC model defined in that way. As the reader may check, we have

$$\mathcal{M}, \langle \mathsf{on} \rangle, h \models \mathsf{Know}_i \Diamond [i\ \mathsf{CStit}]\mathsf{X}light$$

for every history h: the agent knows that there is a strategy to achieve that the light is on next. But we also have

$$\mathcal{M}, \langle \mathsf{on} \rangle, h \not\models \Diamond \mathsf{Know}_i [i\ \mathsf{CStit}]\mathsf{X}light$$

which expresses that no such strategy is uniform.

4.2 Uniform Strategies and **ATEL**

Other logics of agent capability exist. Most prominent are Coalition Logic (CL) and Alternating-time Temporal Logic (ATL) (see Sect. 3.2). We also refer to the chapter on ATL in this volume [17] for an introduction to CL and ATL. We just recall here that both have modal operators of capability $\langle\langle i \rangle\rangle\mathsf{X}$ that allow to talk about what i is capable to achieve in the next state: $\langle\langle i \rangle\rangle X\varphi$ reads "agent i is able to achieve that φ holds next, whatever the other agents do". This is a non-normal modal operator (neither the necessity nor the aggregation axiom schemas are valid). It was shown in [25] that CL is a fragment of ATL: the concept of capability of a coalition A to achieve φ of Coalition Logic CL can be expressed by the ATL formula $\langle\langle A \rangle\rangle X\varphi$.

It was also shown that CL can be embedded into the discrete version of the logic of the Chellas *stit* [13] and that ATL can be embedded into a strategic version of the latter [12]. Also in Sect. 3.2 we have provided an embedding into a variant of BT+AC structures.

ATL has been extended with epistemic operators $Know_i$, yielding Alternating-time Epistemic Temporal Logic ATEL [30]. In terms of BT+AC structures, the indistinguishability relation in ATEL models is between moments, and not between moment-history pairs. However, the latter was crucial in our 'stit-based' solution to the problem of uniform strategies. It is a consequence of this limitation that in ATEL one can only reason about formulas of the form $Know_i \Diamond [i \; CStit] X light$, written $Know_i \langle\langle i \rangle\rangle X light$ in the language of ATEL. However, in the language of ATEL there is no counterpart for the formula $\Diamond Know_i [i \; CStit] X light$.

5 Strategy Contexts, Commitments, and Bindings

In this section we discuss how the embedding of ATL and ATL* sheds light on some possible problems in the interpretation of nested ATL and ATL* formulas. Our main claim will be that in the more general and expressive context of G.STRAT the conceptual problems concerning 'committing' to strategies, and reasoning in 'strategy contexts' disappear.

5.1 Having a Strategy Not to Have a Strategy

In relation to recent discussions on ATL [1,7,38], objections have been raised concerning the interpretation of nested strategic ability formulas. Let us for instance consider the following formula that expresses that i has a strategy such that in the next state it does not have a strategy for p:

$$\langle\langle i \rangle\rangle X \neg \langle\langle i \rangle\rangle X p$$

It is tempting to believe there is a conceptual problem in the interpretation of this formula[19]. It may seem to express something that is impossible: one cannot have a strategy for not to have that *same* strategy. It seems that such strategies would bite their own tail, so to speak. However, if it would be true that indeed this formula would constitute a strategic situation that is logically impossible, then it should be logically inconsistent and its negation should be a validity of

---

[19] For instance, such claims have been made in discussions during workshops connected to this volume.

ATL. But, that is not the case. The formula is satisfiable in ATL. And the models satisfying the formula constitute possible strategic situations an agent can be in. An example is from Greek mythology: Ulysses can have a strategy *now* not to have a strategy *later* (next) to give in to the seductive song of the Sirens: he ties himself to the mast of his boat. Or, one can have a strategy *now* not to have a strategy *tomorrow* (next) to keep ones promise of giving a talk, by sabotaging the projector.

So a strategy witness to the truth of $\langle\langle i\rangle\rangle X\neg\langle\langle i\rangle\rangle Xp$ does not bite its own tail, since there is a temporal separation between the validity time of the first $\langle\langle i\rangle\rangle$-operator (that is, 'now') and the validity time of the second $\langle\langle i\rangle\rangle$-operator (that is, 'next'). For the strategies being witness to the validity of the first $\langle\langle i\rangle\rangle$-operator, all that counts is that the first step in such a strategy ensures a situation where it is true what is expressed by the second $\langle\langle i\rangle\rangle$-operator: that there is no winning strategy to ensure p one step further down the road. Note that the quantifications over strategies in the two states (the initial state where the first $\langle\langle i\rangle\rangle$-operator is evaluated, and the second state where the second $\langle\langle i\rangle\rangle$-operator is evaluated) are entirely independent.

One may suspect however, that things go wrong after all if one uses temporal operators other than the next operator. But that is not true. Even the suspiciously looking formula $\langle\langle i\rangle\rangle G\neg\langle\langle i\rangle\rangle Gp$ is satisfiable and admits intuitive interpretations. Again, the scopes of both $\langle\langle i\rangle\rangle$-operators are not the same. The scope of the first is the tree as it stretches out from the current state. The scope of the second operator is the tree as it stretches out from any of the states somewhere in the future of the current state.

The ATL formula discussed above admits intuitive interpretations because strategy operators $\langle\langle i\rangle\rangle$ are always followed by a temporal operator X, or G, which ensure that the validity time of the first occurrence of the $\langle\langle i\rangle\rangle$-operator is different from the validity time of the second occurrence of the $\langle\langle i\rangle\rangle$-operator. But what would happen if we go to ATL* where temporal operators are not strictly preceded by strategy operators? It seems that this gives us an opportunity to write formulas where a temporal separation of the validity times of both strategy operators is absent. The following are examples of such formulas:

$$\langle\langle i\rangle\rangle\neg\langle\langle i\rangle\rangle Xp \quad \langle\langle i\rangle\rangle\neg\langle\langle i\rangle\rangle Fp \quad \langle\langle i\rangle\rangle\neg\langle\langle i\rangle\rangle Gp$$

If we carefully look at the semantics of ATL*, as given in Definition 10, we see that also in these examples the quantifications over strategies for both strategy operators in the formulas are independent. This means that, for instance, the following schemas are valid for ATL*

$$\langle\langle i\rangle\rangle\neg\langle\langle i\rangle\rangle Xp \leftrightarrow \neg\langle\langle i\rangle\rangle Xp$$

$$\neg\langle\langle i\rangle\rangle\neg\langle\langle i\rangle\rangle Xp \leftrightarrow \langle\langle i\rangle\rangle Xp$$

We may recognise here that the $\langle\langle i\rangle\rangle$ operator behaves as an S5 operator, which means that any number of nested strategy operators is reducible to a single strategy operator[20]. For the single operator there are no interpretation problems. This reduction also makes intuitive sense. A strategy for not having a strategy for p at the current state should indeed be the same as simply not having a strategy for p in the current state, since if the validity time of both operators is indeed the current state, the agent simply has no time for his strategy not to have the strategy. The only way then to satisfy $\langle\langle i\rangle\rangle\neg\langle\langle i\rangle\rangle Xp$, is to already not have the strategy for p, that is $\neg\langle\langle i\rangle\rangle Xp$.

In the *stit* literature, for the related concept of 'refraining', questions like these are discussed already quite some time. In particular it is discussed whether refraining from refraining to see to it that p is the same as seeing to it that p. Modeling refraining is essential to any theory of agency. We can describe agency as the theory that defines the difference between (1) pure events and (2) actions. Now this difference comes out most clearly in case of the absence of anything happening; in the theory of events that is just absence of any event. But in a theory of agency it must be more than that; the agent chooses actively to refrain from doing something, and somehow this 'effort', how ever little it is, has to be accounted for in the theory.

5.2 Having a Strategy in the Context of Commitment to Another Strategy

But let us now complicate things a little further. In the previous section we talked about strategies for not having a strategy. Here we will discuss having a strategy in the context of another strategy. In such a case it can be that the contextual strategy specifies conditions that seem to conflict with the strategy considered within that context. An example is given by the following formula:

$$\langle\langle i\rangle\rangle G(p \wedge \langle\langle i\rangle\rangle X\neg p)$$

This says that i has a strategy such that globally p while at the same time, also globally, it has a strategy for not p in the next state. This seems to complicate things because some temporal conflict may be suspected between p and $\neg p$. Formulas like these have recently triggered several investigations [1,7,38] based on the idea that the strategy that is witness to the truth of the second operator in the formula is somehow restricted or partly/fully determined by the strategy being witness to the truth of the first operator appearing in the formula. But there is no reason whatsoever to assume such a conflict. The formula is satisfiable and the quantifications over strategies in the first operator are completely independent of the quantifications over strategies in the second operator. Things become clearer, we suspect, if we switch to the G.STRAT representation of the formula. That representation is $\Diamond[i \text{ sstit}]G(p \wedge \Diamond[i \text{ sstit}]X\neg p)$. If we see $\neg p$ as

---

[20] Note that similar formulas can be formulated in plain CTL*. Take for instance the CTL* formula $A\neg AXp$, where the A's are universal path quantifiers. For both occurrences of A in the formula, the quantification scope is the same. The only sensible interpretation is to treat the quantifiers as S5 modalities, which then gives rise to, for instance, the following logical equivalence: $A\neg AXp \leftrightarrow \neg AXp$ for CTL*.

the possibility to 'escape from p', we can describe this is having a strategy that guards p in any future state, but at the same time guards that there is always the escape route $\neg p$. Guarding that there is an escape route does not imply that the strategy actually prescribes to *take* the escape route. So, guaranteeing globally that p and at the same time guaranteeing globally a *possibility* for $\neg p$ is perfectly consistent.

Now we believe that when other authors mention that the second (translated) $\langle\langle i \rangle\rangle$-operator could be interpreted differently, namely, under the commitment already made by the choices specified by the strategy being witness to the first (translated) $\langle\langle i \rangle\rangle$-operator in the formula, they can mean only one thing. And what they mean is expressed, we believe, by the formula $\Diamond[i \text{ sstit}]\mathsf{G}(p \wedge [i \text{ sstit}]\mathsf{X}\neg p)$. The difference with the formula $\Diamond[i \text{ sstit}]\mathsf{G}(p \wedge \Diamond[i \text{ sstit}]\mathsf{X}\neg p)$ is that there is no existential quantification over strategies in the second part. So, indeed, the second part of the formula should be evaluated under the choice of strategy for satisfying the first part. The problem with this is that it indeed gives conflicting semantic requirements. We can see that the formula $\Diamond[i \text{ sstit}]\mathsf{G}(p \wedge [i \text{ sstit}]\mathsf{X}\neg p)$ is inconsistent in G.STRAT: there cannot be a model satisfying it because of the conflicting semantic demands about strategies. In terms of p: agent i cannot guard that p is true henceforth and at the same time guard that it does that by a strategy that forces it to take the escape route $\neg p$.

This shows how strategic *stit* disambiguates the seemingly problematic formula $\langle\langle i \rangle\rangle\mathsf{G}(p \wedge \langle\langle i \rangle\rangle\mathsf{X}\neg p)$. And we also see why attempts to solve the problem by *not* decomposing the ATL operators have to take refuge to giving the same $\langle\langle i \rangle\rangle$-operator a different meaning depending on whether or not it appears in the context of another occurrence of the $\langle\langle i \rangle\rangle$-operator. Let us indeed assume that we want to interpret the first occurrence of the $\langle\langle i \rangle\rangle$-operator in the formula as a $\Diamond[i \text{ sstit}]$ combination while our view on the interpretation of the second occurrence of the $\langle\langle i \rangle\rangle$-operator is that it corresponds with $[i \text{ sstit}]$. Now, if we commit ourselves to not decomposing the $\langle\langle i \rangle\rangle$-operator, the only thing we can do is to give the $\langle\langle i \rangle\rangle$-operator another *meaning* if it occurs in the context of another $\langle\langle i \rangle\rangle$-operator. So, this leads to non-uniformity of the semantics, such as in the work of Brihaye et al. [7].

Since the truth in G.STRAT is evaluated relative to (strategy) profiles, a context or commitment is simply expressible as a standard conditional using the material implication: for two G.STRAT formulas φ and ψ, the conditional $\varphi \to \psi$ expresses that strategic property ψ holds in the strategic context φ. We already saw an example of this at the end of Sect. 3.1.

6 Conclusion

In this chapter we started by giving a brief overview of traditional *stit* logics as applied to one step strategies/actions. Then we discussed a semantics that generalised the *stit* ideas to the truly strategic setting where reaching or guaranteeing a condition may take more than one step. We have shown that the semantics embeds well known logics such as ATL and ATL*. More in particular we have explained how a whole range of well-known temporal logic and logics for agency and ability can all be seen as fragments of strategic *stit* under one uniform semantics. Then we discussed how the strategic *stit* semantics sheds light on the issue of uniform strategies, and finally, how the general semantics for strategic *stit* explains the conceptual difficulties recently encountered in the semantics of ATL concerning the interpretation of strategic ability and strategic action within a context of other strategies already committed to.

We believe that strategic *stit* is a valuable addition to the range of formalisms available for reasoning about strategies. Strategic *stit* enables one to specify properties of agentive strategy performance without explicitly representing the programs or processes by which an agentive strategic effort achieves or ensures certain conditions. Furthermore, we believe that strategic *stit* can function as a basis to clarify further conceptual problems in the interpretation of epistemic strategic logics. We have seen some of this potential already in Sects. 4 and 5 where we showed how to shed light on the problem of uniformity of strategies and the problems induced by the interpretation of nestings of strategic formulas. But, we believe that this is only the start of further and more detailed investigations into complex concepts such as 'knowing how' and 'knowingly performing a strategy' that require careful further analysis.

Acknowledgements. Thanks are due to the two reviewers of the present chapter as well as to Valentin Goranko and Hein Duijf for careful readings that helped to improve the chapter. Jan Broersen gratefully acknowledges financial support from the ERC-2013-CoG project REINS, nr. 616512.

References

1. Ågotnes, T., Goranko, V., Jamroga, W.: Alternating-time temporal logics with irrevocable strategies. In: Samet, D. (ed.) Proceedings of the Theoretical Aspects of Rationality and Knowledge (TARK), pp. 15–24 (2007)
2. Alur, R., Henzinger, T.A., Kupferman, O.: Alternating-time temporal logic. J. ACM **49**(5), 672–713 (2002)
3. Balbiani, P., Herzig, A., Troquard, N.: Alternative axiomatics and complexity of deliberative STIT theories. J. Philos. Logic **37**(4), 387–406 (2008)
4. Belnap, N., Perloff, M.: Seeing to it that: A canonical form for agentives. Theoria **54**(3), 175–199 (1988)
5. Belnap, N., Perloff, M., Xu, M.: Facing the Future: Agents and Choices in Our Indeterminist World. Oxford University Press, Oxford (2001)
6. Blackburn, P., de Rijke, M., Venema, Y.: Modal Logic. Cambridge Tracts in Theoretical Computer Science, vol. 53. Cambridge University Press, Cambridge (2001)
7. Brihaye, T., Da Costa, A., Laroussinie, F., Markey, N.: ATL with strategy contexts and bounded memory. In: Artemov, S., Nerode, A. (eds.) LFCS 2009. LNCS, vol. 5407, pp. 92–106. Springer, Heidelberg (2008)
8. Broersen, J.: A complete STIT logic for knowledge and action, and some of its applications. In: Baldoni, M., Son, T.C., van Riemsdijk, M.B., Winikoff, M. (eds.) DALT 2008. LNCS (LNAI), vol. 5397, pp. 47–59. Springer, Heidelberg (2009)

9. Broersen, J.: A stit-logic for extensive form group strategies. In: WI-IAT 2009: Proceedings of the 2009 IEEE/WIC/ACM International Joint Conference on Web Intelligence and Intelligent Agent Technology, Washington, DC, USA, pp. 484–487. IEEE Computer Society (2009)

10. Broersen, J.: CTL.STIT: enhancing ATL to express important multi-agent system verification properties. In: Proceedings of the Ninth International Joint Conference on Autonomous Agents and Multiagent Systems (AAMAS 2010). ACM, New York (2010)

11. Broersen, J.: Deontic epistemic stit logic distinguishing modes of mens rea. J. Appl. Logic 9(2), 127–152 (2011)

12. Broersen, J., Herzig, A., Troquard, N.: Embedding Alternating-time Temporal Logic in strategic STIT logic of agency. J. Logic Comput. 16(5), 559–578 (2006)

13. Broersen, J., Herzig, A., Troquard, N.: From coalition logic to STIT. Electron. Notes Theor. Comput. Sci. 157(4), 23–35 (2006). Proceedings of the Logic and Communication in Multi-Agent Systems (LCMAS 2005)

14. Broersen, J., Herzig, A., Troquard, N.: A STIT-extension of ATL. In: Fisher, M., van der Hoek, W., Lisitsa, A., Konev, B. (eds.) JELIA 2006. LNCS (LNAI), vol. 4160, pp. 69–81. Springer, Heidelberg (2006)

15. Broersen, J., Herzig, A., Troquard, N.: A normal simulation of coalition logic and an epistemic extension. In: Samet, D. (ed.) Proceedings of the Theoretical Aspects Rationality and Knowledge (TARK XI), Brussels, pp. 92–101. ACM Digital Library (2007)

16. Broersen, J., Herzig, A., Troquard, N.: What groups do, can do, and know they can do: An analysis in normal modal logics. J. Appl. Non-Class. Logics 19(3), 261–289 (2009)

17. Bulling, N., Goranko, V., Jamroga, W.: Logics for reasoning about strategic abilities in multi-player games. In: van Benthem, J., Ghosh, S., Verbrugge, R. (eds.) Models of Strategic Reasoning. LNCS, vol. 8972, pp. 93–136. Springer, Heidelberg (2015)

18. Bulling, N., Jamroga, W.: Verifying agents with memory is harder than it seemed. AI Commun. 23(4), 389–403 (2010)

19. Castelfranchi, C.: The micro-macro constitution of power. Protosociology 18–19, 208–265 (2003)

20. Chisholm, R.M.: The descriptive element in the concept of action. J. Philos. 61, 613–624 (1964)

21. Elgesem, D.: Action theory and modal logic. Ph.D. thesis, Department of Philosophy, University of Oslo (1993)

22. Elgesem, D.: The modal logic of agency. Nord. J. Philos. Logic 2(2), 1–46 (1997)

23. Emerson, E.A.: Temporal and modal logic. In: van Leeuwen, J. (ed.) Handbook of Theoretical Computer Science, Volume B: Formal Models and Semantics, chapter 14, pp. 996–1072. Elsevier Science, Amsterdam (1990)

24. Gabbay, D.M., Kurucz, A., Wolter, F., Zakharyachev, M.: Many-Dimensional Modal Logics: Theory and Applications. Elsevier, Amsterdam (2003)

25. Goranko, V., Jamroga, W.: Comparing semantics of logics for multi-agent systems. Synthese 139(2), 241–280 (2004)

26. Goranko, V., van Drimmelen, G.: Complete axiomatization and decidability of alternating-time temporal logic. Theor. Comput. Sci. 353(1–3), 93–117 (2006)

27. Herzig, A., Lorini, E., Troquard, N.: Action theories. In: Hansson, S.O., Hendricks, V.F. (eds.) Handbook of Formal Philosophy. Springer (2014)

28. Herzig, A., Schwarzentruber, F.: Properties of logics of individual and group agency. In: Areces, C., Goldblatt, R. (eds.) Advances in Modal Logic, vol. 7, pp. 133–149. College Publications, London (2008)

29. Herzig, A., Troquard, N.: Knowing how to play: Uniform choices in logics of agency. In: Weiss, G., Stone, P. (eds.) 5th International Joint Conference on Autonomous Agents & Multi-Agent Systems (AAMAS 2006), Hakodate, Japan, 8–12 Mai 2006, pp. 209–216. ACM Press

30. van der Hoek, W., Wooldridge, M.: Cooperation, knowledge, and time: Alternating-time temporal epistemic logic and its applications. Stud. Logica 75(1), 125–157 (2003)

31. Horty, J.F.: Agency and Deontic Logic. Oxford University Press, Oxford (2001)

32. Horty, J.F., Belnap, N.: The deliberative STIT: A study of action, omission, ability and obligation. J. Philos. Logic 24(6), 583–644 (1995)

33. Lorini, E., Troquard, N., Herzig, A., Broersen, J.: Grounding power on actions and mental attitudes. Logic J. IGPL 21, 311–331 (2012)

34. Pauly, M.: A modal logic for coalitional power in games. J. Logic Comput. 12(1), 149–166 (2002)

35. Pörn, I.: Action Theory and Social Science: Some Formal Models. Synthese Library 120. D. Reidel, Dordrecht (1977)

36. Prior, A.N.: Past, Present, and Future. Clarendon Press, Oxford (1967)

37. Segerberg, K. (ed.): Logic of Action, Special issue of Studia Logica, vol. 51:3/4. Springer, Dordrecht (1992)

38. Troquard, N., Walther, D.: On satisfiability in ATL with strategy contexts. In: Herzig, A., Mengin, J., del Cerro, L.F. (eds.) JELIA 2012. LNCS, vol. 7519, pp. 398–410. Springer, Heidelberg (2012)

39. von Wright, G.H.: Norm and Action. International Library of Philosophy and Scientific Method. A Logical Enquiry. Routledge & Kegan Paul, London (1963)

40. Xu, M.: On the basic logic of STIT with a single agent. J. Symbolic Logic 60(2), 459–483 (1995)

41. Zanardo, A.: Branching-time logic with quantification over branches: The point of view of modal logic. J. Symbolic Logic 61, 1–39 (1996)

Automata and Compositional Strategies in Extensive Form Games

Soumya Paul[1], R. Ramanujam[2](✉), and Sunil Simon[3]

[1] IRIT, Université Paul Sabatier, Toulouse, France
[2] Institute of Mathematical Sciences, Chennai, India
jam@imsc.res.in
[3] Indian Institute of Technology, Kanpur, India

Abstract. We study automata as memory structure for "online" strategizing in extensive form games. By online strategizing we mean a model in which players start with potential (partial) strategies that are generic plans for (local) subgames and dynamically compose and switch between them. We consider such startegizing to be relevant for a theory of play. We suggest that for sufficiently large games and resource limited players, the game is better modelled as an infinite horizon game, and thus the study is carried out in games of infinite duration on finite game arenas. We show how strategy switching can be realised by finite state transducers and how they can be used to answer questions on stability of strategies.

Keywords: Memory in strategies · Strategy specifications · Strategy switching · Infinite games on finite graphs

1 Overview

The seminal paper of John von Neumann [45] begins with a section titled Great Simplification. In it, he brilliantly lays down a rationale that has dominated game theory: there is no loss of generality in assuming that a rational player chooses his strategy before the game begins, since a strategy lets him specify a choice for every possible historical situation he might find himself in during the game. So von Neumann concludes that each player must choose his strategy *without being informed of the other players' strategic choices*. Indeed this is the great simplification[1] that led to normal form game representations and much of game theory as we know it.

In the case of finite extensive form games, this abstraction works very nicely. Even if the game is one of imperfect information, such an abstraction helps us to ignore the extensive temporal structures of games and concentrate on outcome based analysis. Equilibrium theory helps us predict how a rational player would choose; in a prescriptive sense, the theory tries to give good advice to the decision maker. The strategy in an equilibrium profile can be seen as such an advice.

---

[1] due originally to Émile Borel [11]; von Neumann was only developing the idea.

© Springer-Verlag Berlin Heidelberg 2015
J. van Benthem et al. (Eds.): Models of Strategic Reasoning, LNCS 8972, pp. 174–201, 2015.
DOI: 10.1007/978-3-662-48540-8_6

Difficulties arise in the case of games with multiple equilibria, and this has been extensively discussed in the literature [35]. An entirely different kind of trouble arises when computational considerations matter. In particular, suppose that the advice oracle that the strategy represents is to be a computer program, then the notion of strategy as any complete plan for all player moves needs re-examination. To take an admittedly ridiculous example, consider a game in which a player has a binary choice, and the strategy defined by: when it's the player's turn to move and the game position is node n (under some fixed ordering of tree nodes), play 1 if the nth Turing machine (under a fixed enumeration of Turing machines) halts on empty input, and play 0 otherwise. This would indeed be a strategy, and may even survive elimination of dominated strategies for particular outcomes, but not only does this function lacks reason, it is also unimplementable (as a computer program). The space of functions from player nodes to available choices is indeed too rich. Taking implementability as a criterion, we can look for algorithms that compute equilibrium strategies and such an *algorithmic game theory* [34] is being developed by computer scientists.

On the other hand, *epistemic game theory* [38] attempts to study the rationale underlying a strategy, examining the reasons that underlie the choice made by a player at a game position. Such a viewpoint refuses the offer made by the great simplification and delves into the temporal extensive game structure. This is particularly important when a player finds the history of play on an off-equilibrium path. Given that an opponent has deviated from a choice dictated by an optimal strategy, how should the player expect the opponent to play in future? Several solutions have been proposed in the literature, such as forward induction [38] but the main point is that such solutions involve *online* strategizing, during course of play, rather than the offline strategies given by the great simplification.

Aumann and Dreze [3] make a strong case for the focus of game theory to shift from the existence of equilibria to a prescriptive theory that would advise a player how to play in any particular situation, in light of the history that led to the situation. In a series of articles, van Benthem [6–9] has called for a *theory of play*, which includes not only the deliberative aspects of pre-game strategizing but also reasoning in the game. This involves consideration of a range of events that occur during play: players' observations, information received about other players, etc.; these cause a revision of player beliefs and expectations and affect strategizing.

It is this thread, that of online strategizing that takes into account the temporal extensive structure, that we take up in this article, with an emphasis on computational considerations as suggested above. That is, we move away from pre-game selection of strategies to strategies constructed during course of play by an automaton. This leads us to a study of compositional structure in strategies. The restriction to finite state devices highlights the *memory* needed by a computationally limited player who must select observations to record during play and can see only a part of the future, as opposed to an agent with unbounded memory who has access to the entire past and future.

When the game is given as a finite tree, it seems pointless to talk of an agent with limited memory, since any finite state device can code up the tree in its memory. However, if the game tree is sufficiently large, such as in the game of Chess, the player would see only an abstraction of the tree. In general, if the temporal extensive structure of the game is large relative to the memory capability of players, strategizing by the player is affected by the abstraction of the future. Indeed, as van Benthem [8] argues, in any game where we only know top-level structure, a 'fuzzy' view of the future is unavoidable. In the study of game playing programs in Artificial Intelligence, it is customary to work with local game analysis, along with general heuristic values for unanalyzed later parts of the game [25].

The remark about abstracting the future raises an important question: how should such a game be represented, and how can the player strategize in such a game? The answer we provide is in the spirit of Rubinstein [43]: a game with a "very long horizon" is best modelled as a game with *infinite horizon*. According to Rubinstein [43], a game should be seen as a description of relevant factors as perceived by the players, and not as a presentation of the physical rules of the game. If a player strategizes in a game as if it has an unbounded horizon, an infinite tree represents the game better.[2] Therefore we present the game arena as a finite graph and the game as an infinite tree obtained by unfolding the graph. The game arena can be seen as a finite presentation of a set of rules; players look for patterns, and based on the occurrence of patterns and past information (recorded selectively), they make choices. Such a consideration leads us to the realm of regular infinite games.

In our model, a player enters the game arena with information on the game structure and on other players' skills, as well as an initial set of possible strategies to employ. As the play progresses, she makes observations and accordingly revises strategies, *switches* from one to another, perhaps even devises new strategies that she hadn't considered before. The dynamics of such interaction eventually leads to some strategies being eliminated, and some becoming stable. It is this process that we wish to study using automata.

This chapter continues the line of work initiated in [42] on a compositional structure in strategies realised by automata. Strategy switching is emphasized here, and the rationale for why a player following a strategy might switch to another one online. We study another form of switching as well: a player who cannot decide between two strategies may, rather than committing to one or the other, choose to go back and forth between the two, following either of the two nondeterministically. This can be seen as a nondeterministic analogue of *mixed strategies*, without specifying a probability distribution. In the end, the player is not following either of the two strategies but a nondeterministic mix of both. Thus the central premise of this chapter is that exploring structure in strategies is worthwhile from a logical perspective, and that automata theory is helpful in this regard.

---

[2] Indeed the considerations of online strategizing and compositional structure seem more relevant for such temporally large games. Arguably, for sufficiently small games, pre-game deliberation might suffice.

Infinite games have a long history, and their study has led to some beautiful set theory and topology. Regular infinite games have received attention from theoretical computer science in the last two decades, principally due to their relevance to game models of reactive system design and verification. Notions such as determinacy of win/lose games, equilibria, and computation of equilibrium strategies have been worked out for these games [22]. A central thread of this research is the adequacy of *finite memory* strategies for standard solution concepts.

What we discuss in this article is the realisation of compositional strategies, involving switching and response to other players' behaviour, as finite state transducers, thus explicating their memory structure. In itself, this is not surprising, given the limited expressive power of the specification language of strategies. However, the construction is interesting since it shows ways by which strategies may be combined algorithmically.

What questions can one study in such a model? Once player objectives and preferences are specified, natural questions relate to existence of best response, synthesis of such strategies etc., and for a logical analysis, axiomatic characterizations of formulas specifying how a strategy may ensure an outcome for a player. These questions are addressed in [40] and [42] and not taken up here. Instead we focus only on implications of strategy switching. When players may switch from one strategy to another, there is an associated *dynamics* of strategies and patterns in game evolution. Is it the case that, after online exploration of opponents' behaviour, a player settles down to a specific strategy and does not switch any further? This can be seen as a form of stability in strategizing.

In fact, when a player no longer considers a strategy at all after a point in game evolution, this may have consequences as well. When all players stop considering a strategy similarly, it may simply get eliminated from the game, leading to a new game. When all strategies available to a player are eliminated, a player may be forced out of the game. Such questions are especially relevant in the context of bargaining and negotiations, as evidenced in many political contexts. Questions of this nature were studied in [36]. We do not study such dynamic game forms, but merely point out that strategy switching can lead to many interesting stability questions and that realization of strategies by finite state transducers can be used to answer such questions.

In what follows, we give a brief introduction to infinite games, and since they need to be finitely specified, finite graph representation of (regular) infinite games. Then we discuss the structure of strategy specifications, and we see that switching introduces some conceptual difficulty. We then show how strategy specifications can be implemented using automata. We discuss related work at the end of the article.

2   Infinite Games

In this section we give an introduction to infinite games on finite graphs. The main aim here is to set up the preliminaries and point to the rich literature on automata as strategies in regular infinite games. These automata, in turn, provide us a tool for strategy composition that we take up later on. *Automata, Logics and Infinite Games* [22] is a good source for an introduction to infinite games on finite graphs, as well as strategies as finite state automata.

2.1   Game Model

When we consider games of unbounded duration, a natural question is how such a game is presented. While this question is generally not easy to answer, in the special case of *regular* infinite games, we can conceive of the game tree as an unfolding of a finite graph with cycles. Thus games on finite graphs give a finite presentation for games of unbounded duration: we call these game arenas.

Game Arena. A game arena is a structure $\mathcal{G} = (W, \rightarrow, w_0, \lambda)$ over a finite set of moves (or actions) Σ, where:

- W is a finite set of game positions.
- $\rightarrow : W \times \Sigma \times W$ is an edge relation which satisfies the condition: if $(w, a, w') \in \rightarrow$ and $(w, a, w'') \in \rightarrow$ then $w' = w''$.
- $w_0 \in W$ is the initial game position.
- $\lambda : W \rightarrow N$ is the turn function which associates each game position with a player.

We often denote $(w, a, v) \in \rightarrow$ by $w \xrightarrow{a} v$. For a node w, let $\vec{w} = \{v \in W \mid w \xrightarrow{a} v$ for some $a \in \Sigma\}$. For technical convenience, we assume that for all $w \in W$, $\vec{w} \neq \emptyset$, that is, there are no 'dead-ends'. For $i \in N$, let $W^i = \{w \in W \mid \lambda(w) = i\}$. A play in the game arena $\mathcal{G}$ starts by placing a token on w_0 and proceeds as follows: at any stage if the token is at a position w and $\lambda(w) = i$ then player i picks an action which is enabled for her at w, and the token is moved to v where $w \xrightarrow{a} v$. Formally, a play in $\mathcal{G}$ is an infinite path $\rho = w_0 a_0 w_1 a_1 \ldots$ such that for all $j \geq 0$, $w_j \xrightarrow{a_j} w_{j+1}$. Let $Plays(\mathcal{G})$ denote the set of all plays in $\mathcal{G}$. A history h is a finite path in the arena. For a history $h = w_0 a_0 w_1 a_1 \ldots w_k$ we denote by $last(h)$ the last element of h that is $last(h) = w_k$.

A subarena of $\mathcal{G}$ is a subgraph of $\mathcal{G}$ with no dead-ends.

Extensive Form Game. The (infinite) extensive form game tree $T_{\mathcal{G}}$ associated with $\mathcal{G}$ is obtained by the tree unfolding of $\mathcal{G}$ which we define below.

Given a game arena $\mathcal{G} = (W, \rightarrow, w_0, \lambda)$, the tree unfolding of $\mathcal{G}$ is the least tree structure $T_{\mathcal{G}} = (S, \Rightarrow, s_0, \widehat{\lambda})$ where $S \subseteq (W \times \Sigma)^* W$ and $\Rightarrow : S \times \Sigma \rightarrow S$ satisfies the condition:

- $w_0 \in S$.
- If $s = (w_0, a_0) \ldots w_k \in S$ and $w_k \xrightarrow{a} w'$ then $s' = (w_0, a_0) \ldots (w_k, a) w' \in S$ and $s \xrightarrow{a} s'$.

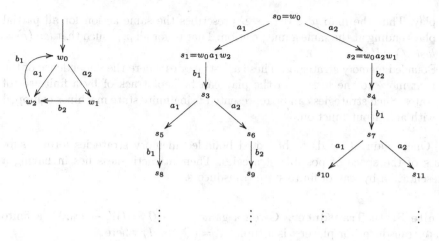

Fig. 1. Game arena and tree unfolding

Further, for a node $s = (w_0, a_0) \ldots w_k \in S$, $\widehat{\lambda}(s) = \lambda(w_k)$.

Figure 1 illustrates a game arena and its tree unfolding. A node s in $T_{\mathcal{G}}$ denotes a finite partial play in the arena. Thus $s = w_0 a_0 w_1 a_1 \ldots w_k$ and $last(s) = w_k$. Note that for any node s, $last(s) \in W$. The prefix relation $s \sqsubseteq s'$ specifies that the node s' is reachable from s in the tree. For $i \in N$, let $S^i = \{s \in S \mid \widehat{\lambda}(s) = i\}$.

2.2 Strategies

A strategy μ^i for player i specifies for each partial play ending in a game position of player i which action to choose. Thus μ^i is a map $\mu^i : (W \times \Sigma)^* W^i \to \Sigma$. A play $\rho : w_0 a_0 w_1 \cdots$ is said to be consistent with a strategy μ^i if for all $j, 0 \leq j$, we have $\lambda(w_j) = i$ implies $\mu^i(\rho) = a_j$. A strategy μ^i can also be viewed as a labelled tree $T_{\mathcal{G}}^{\mu^i} = (T_{\mathcal{G}}, m)$ where $m : S^i \to \Sigma$ such that for all $s \in S^i$, $m(s) = \mu^i(s)$. Let $Strat^i$ denote the set of all strategies of player i in $\mathcal{G}$.

A strategy profile $\overline{\mu}$ consists of a tuple of strategies, one for each player. For $i \in N$, let $\mu^{-i} = (\mu^1, \ldots, \mu^{i-1}, \mu^{i+1}, \ldots, \mu^n)$. A play ρ is consistent with a strategy profile $\overline{\mu}$ if ρ is consistent with μ^i for all $i \in N$. It is easy to check that for a strategy profile $\overline{\mu}$, there exists a unique play in $\mathcal{G}$ which is consistent with $\overline{\mu}$. This can be thought of as the play generated by $\overline{\mu}$. We denote this play by $\rho_{\overline{\mu}}$.

Note that according to the definition, a strategy can in principle depend on the complete history of play and in general need not be computable. For computationally bounded players it is not possible to implement or even choose to play such an arbitrarily defined strategy. In this context, the following two types of strategies are of particular interest:

- Memoryless (positional) strategies: These are strategies for which the next move depends only on the current game position and not on the history of play. Thus the map $\mu^i : W^i \to \Sigma$ prescribes the same action for all partial plays ending at the same game position. That is, for all ρ, ρ' such that $last(\rho) = last(\rho')$, $\mu^i(\rho) = \mu^i(\rho')$.

– **Bounded memory strategies:** These are strategies where the dependence of the next move to the history of the play can be kept track of by a finite set of states. Such strategies can be represented using finite state machines equipped with an output function.

Once again, it needs to be noted bounded memory strategies form a subclass of the space of possible strategies. Their attractiveness lies in having a presentation by way of finite state transducers.

Finite State Transducer. Given a game arena $\mathcal{G} = (W, \to, w_0, \lambda)$, a finite state transducer for player i is a tuple $\mathcal{A}^i = (Q, \delta, o, I)$ where

– Q is a finite set of states.
– $\delta : Q \times W \times \Sigma \to 2^Q$ is a nondeterministic transition function.
– $o : Q \times W^i \to \Sigma$ is the output function of the transducer.
– $I \subseteq Q$ is the set of initial states.

Let μ^i be a strategy of player i and $T_{\mathcal{G}}^{\mu^i} = (T_{\mathcal{G}}, m)$ be the corresponding strategy tree. A run of $\mathcal{A}^i$ on $T_{\mathcal{G}}^{\mu^i}$ is a Q labelled tree $T = (S, \Rightarrow, s_0, m, f)$, where $f : S \to Q$ is a map defined as follows: $f(s_0) = q_0$, and for any s_k where $s_k \overset{a}{\Rightarrow} s'_k$, we have $f(s'_k) \in \delta(f(s_k), last(s_k), a_k)$. A Q labelled tree T is accepted by $\mathcal{A}^i$ if for every tree node $s \in S$ where $s \in S^i$, $m(s) = a$ implies $o(f(s), last(s)) = a$.

We say a strategy tree $T_{\mathcal{G}}^{\mu^i}$ is accepted by $\mathcal{A}^i$ if $\mathcal{A}^i$ has an accepting run on $T_{\mathcal{G}}^{\mu^i}$. For a state q and a tree node s, we often use the notation $o(q, s)$ to denote $o(q, last(s))$. If the transition function of $\mathcal{A}^i$ is deterministic then it is easy to see that the strategy generated by $\mathcal{A}^i$ is unique.

Given a history $s = w_0 a_0 w_1 \ldots w_k$, a strategy $\mu^i[s]$ for player i after s is a map $\mu^i[s] : s(W \times \Sigma)^* W^i \to \Sigma$. Let $T_{\mathcal{G}}^{\mu^i[s]}$ be the strategy tree corresponding to $\mu^i[s]$. We denote the set of all strategies for player i after s by $Strat^i(s)$. A run of $\mathcal{A}^i$ on $T_{\mathcal{G}}^{\mu^i[s]}$ is a Q labelled tree $T[s]$ as defined earlier, with root node s. We say that the Q labelled tree $T[s]$ is accepted by $\mathcal{A}^i$ if for every tree node s' where $s \sqsubseteq s'$ and $\widehat{\lambda}(s') = i$, if $m(s') = a$ then $o(f(s'), last(s')) = a$. We denote by $Lang(\mathcal{A}^i, s)$ the set of all strategy trees $T_{\mathcal{G}}^{\mu^i[s]}$ which are accepted by $\mathcal{A}^i$.

2.3 Objectives

Players' Objectives. In games where the outcome is binary and every player either wins or loses, a natural way of specifying players' objectives is to associate with each player $i \in N$ a set $\Phi_i \subseteq Plays(\mathcal{G})$ with the interpretation that a play ρ is winning for player i iff $\rho \in \Phi_i$. Note that the objectives could be overlapping, i.e., for player i and j it is possible to have $\Phi_i \cap \Phi_j \neq \emptyset$. A game is then specified as the pair $G = (\mathcal{G}, \{\Phi_i\}_{i \in N})$.

Given a game $G = (\mathcal{G}, \{\Phi_i\}_{i \in N})$, we call a strategy μ^i for player i winning if for all plays ρ conforming to μ^i, $\rho \in \Phi_i$. In other words, a strategy μ^i is winning if for every profile μ^{-i} of the other players, the play ρ generated by $\bar{\mu}$, we have: $\rho \in \Phi_i$.

Two player games are games in which the number of players are restricted to two, i.e. the set of players $N = \{1, 2\}$. For such games, we often use the notation i and $\bar{\imath}$ to denote the players where $\bar{\imath} = 2$ when $i = 1$ and $\bar{\imath} = 1$ when $i = 2$. Two player game in which the players' objectives are strictly complementary are called zero sum games. Formally, these are games where the set of plays can be partitioned into disjoint sets Φ_1 and Φ_2. This implies that when a play ρ is winning for player i, it is not winning for player $\bar{\imath}$.

In general, when games are not strictly winning or losing for players, we have a preference order $\preceq^i \subseteq (Plays(\mathcal{G}) \times Plays(\mathcal{G}))$ for each player $i \in N$. Note that this generalizes winning sets, since a winning set Φ_i defines a preference in the obvious manner: player i prefers plays in Φ_i over those in $Plays(\mathcal{G}) \setminus \Phi_i$.

Note that the specification of objectives is infinite, and we are interested in *finitely presented* objectives, to be described below.

Solution Concepts. In the case of win/lose games the natural notion of solving a game is to determine whether a player has a winning strategy. A two player zero sum game G is said to be **determined** if there exists a player $i \in \{1, 2\}$ such that i has a winning strategy in G.

One of the early results which helped highlight the relationship between determinacy and the topological properties of the winning set Φ is the Gale-Stewart theorem [17]. Here the game arena is understood to be an infinite graph, but the other notions remain the same. The theorem asserts that every game where Φ is an open set is determined. This result was later improved by Martin [30] to show determinacy for games with Borel objectives: a large class of subsets of topological spaces, of importance to mathematical analysis. The important consequence for games on finite arenas is that all regular objectives to be considered below are determined.

For games with overlapping objectives, a popular solution concept is that of the Nash equilibrium.

- Given a profile $\bar{\mu}$, the strategy μ^i of player i is a best response to μ^{-i} if $\forall \nu^i \in Strat^i$, $\rho_{(\nu^i, \mu^{-i})} \preceq^i \rho_{\bar{\mu}}$.
- A strategy profile $\bar{\mu}$ is said to be in equilibrium if for all $i \in N$, μ^i is a best response to μ^{-i}.

Existence of Nash equilibria in infinite games is much less studied. Indeed, it is unclear whether other notions of equilibria might be more appropriate for games of unbounded duration.

Finitely Presented Objectives. Since we are interested in resource limited players, the preference orders themselves need to be finitely presented. A player's decision to prefer one play over another is limited by her observations of the two plays. With finite resources, a player can observe either only a finite prefix of the infinite play, or repetitive behaviour (if any). When the game arena is finite, every infinite play must settle down eventually within a strongly connected component of the arena, and hence preferences over plays can be presented as an ordering over connected components. In general, player's preferences are associated with loops or cycles in the arena. Since a player records her observations as play proceeds she may remember how play arrived at a specific loop as well, or how many times a particular loop was traversed before entering another. However, these observations and counting are limited by the player's resources.

These observations lead us to the notion of an evaluation automaton for each player. We present this for winning sets: a play is in the winning set of player i only if it is accepted by the evaluation automaton for player i.

A finite deterministic evaluation automaton over the input alphabet $W \times \Sigma$ is a tuple $\mathbb{A} = (Q, \Delta, r_0, Acc)$ where

- Q is a finite set of states.
- $\Delta : (Q \times W \times \Sigma) \to Q$ is the transition function.
- $r_0 \in Q$ is the initial state.
- Acc specifies the acceptance condition.

The run of $\mathbb{A}$ on an infinite sequence $\rho : w_0 a_0 w_1 \ldots$ is a sequence of states $\varphi_\rho : r_0 r_1 \ldots$ such that for all $j \geq 0$, $r_{j+1} = \Delta(r_j, w_j, a_j)$. Let $Inf(\varphi_\rho)$ denote the set of states occurring infinitely often in φ. The most commonly used acceptance conditions are the following requirements on $Inf(\varphi)$:

- Reachability condition: For a set of designated states $R \subseteq Q$, $\Phi_i = \{\rho = w_0 a_0 w_1 a_1 \ldots \mid \exists k \text{ with } w_k \in R\}$.
- Büchi condition [12]: For a set of "good states" $B \subseteq Q$, $Inf(\varphi_\rho) \cap B \neq \emptyset$. In other words, some final state occurs infinitely often in the run φ_ρ.
- Muller condition [33]: For a family $\mathcal{F} \subseteq 2^Q$, $\bigvee_{F \in \mathcal{F}} Inf(\varphi_\rho) = F$. This requires that the set of states occurring infinitely often in the run φ_ρ forms a set in $\mathcal{F}$.
- Parity condition: Let $c : Q \to \{1, \ldots, k\}$ (where $k \in \mathbb{N}$). The run ρ is accepting iff $\min\{c(r) \mid r \in Inf(\varphi_\rho)\}$ is even.

In terms of expressiveness it is known that a Parity condition can be translated to a Muller condition and vice-versa but this can lead to a blow-up in the size of the arena. The deterministic Büchi condition is strictly less expressive than the Muller or the Parity condition and the Reachability condition is strictly less expressive than the Büchi condition.

Algorithmic Questions. Now that we have finite game arenas and finite presentation of objectives, we can ask algorithmic questions on them.

- Verification question: Given a game $G = (\mathcal{G}, \{\Phi_i\}_{i \in N})$ and player i, does player i have a winning strategy in G?

– Synthesis question: Given a game $G = (\mathcal{G}, \{\Phi_i\}_{i \in N})$ and player i, is it possible to construct a winning strategy for player i (when it exists)?

The determinacy of two player zero sum games with regular objectives follows from Martin's theorem since regular objectives fall in the second level of the Borel hierarchy. However, this result does not suffice for algorithmic purposes since the winning strategies employed depends on the complete history of the play, and therefore require infinite memory. The seminal result of Büchi and Landweber [13] showed that when players' objectives are presented as Muller conditions, the winner can be determined and that the winning strategy can be effectively synthesised in bounded memory strategies. For parity games on the other hand, memoryless strategies suffice for winning [16,31]. In other words, these results showed that it is possible to solve the verification and synthesis questions for games with regular objectives.

The existence of Nash equilibrium for games with regular win-lose objectives follows from the result of [15]. The main idea here is the effective use of threat strategies whereby a player deviating from the equilibrium profile is punished by others to receive the outcome which she can guarantee on her own. The existence of sub-game perfect equilibrium [44] for games with binary objectives was shown in [23]. When we consider games with overlapping objectives, existence of Nash equilibrium for games with Muller conditions was shown by [37].

Note that these solution concepts raise the question of *existence* of optimal strategies: either winning strategies or equilibrium profiles, and perhaps realising these (offline) strategies by automata. Returning to the motivation we presented earlier, a natural question to consider is: given a game arena and a finite presentation of player objectives, how can a player select and compose strategies online, to achieve an outcome? This requires us to look for structure in strategies, which is what we take up next.

The use of finite state automata to study strategies in games of unbounded duration underlies this entire body of work, and [22] is a good source for an introduction to this methodology. However, the literature focusses largely on win/lose games, as the intended applications are for system and design and verification: the system being designed is in a game situation against a hypothetical environment, and behaviour according to intended specification constitutes a win for the system. Extensions to multi-player games typically consider a coordination game: a multi-component system where all components coordinate against the hypothetical environment.

Our departure here is the use of automata to represent the process of strategizing by bounded memory players in games of unbounded duration. In a theory of play, we need to describe how players observe play, record their observations and strategize on-line. Automata provide a representation of this process.

3 Strategizing by Players

We now shift our focus to studying the game from the players' viewpoint, and look for a theory in which players start the game with an initial set of strategies and compose from them by switching between them depending on their interpretation of course of play. In the process they generate more and more complex strategies. We use tools from logic and automata theory for this study.

3.1 Partial Strategies

Not only do resource-bounded players strategise dynamically, their strategies are also partial, consisting of partial plans. Players, in general, cannot conceive of every possible situation right at the beginning of the game and hence plan only partially. A partial strategy specifies a subset of the available moves for every history, or in other words, it restricts some of the available moves. Formally, given a game $\mathcal{G} = (W, \rightarrow, w_0, \lambda)$ a partial strategy is a function $\nu : (W \times \Sigma)^* W^i \rightarrow (2^\Sigma \setminus \emptyset)$. Let $Pstrat^i$ denote the set of all partial strategies of player i. A partial strategy ν of player i can also be viewed as a labelled tree $T_\mathcal{G}^\nu = (T_\mathcal{G}, m^\nu)$ where $m^\nu : S^i \rightarrow 2^\Sigma$ such that, for every node $s \in S^i$, we have $m^\nu(s) = \nu(s)$.

A partial strategy tree $T_\mathcal{G}^\nu = (T_\mathcal{G}, m^\nu)$ for player i may .be viewed as a set $\mathcal{T}_\mathcal{G}^\nu$ of total strategy trees where a total strategy tree $T = (T_\mathcal{G}, m) \in \mathcal{T}_\mathcal{G}^\nu$ if and only if for every $s \in S^i$, $m(s) \in m^\nu(s)$. It is easy to see that a finite memory partial strategy can thus be presented in terms of a transducer $\mathcal{A}^\nu$ such that $Lang(\mathcal{A}^\nu) = \mathcal{T}_\mathcal{G}^\nu$.

Given a history s, it is also convenient to define a partial strategy ν "after" s, denoted $\nu[s]$ which is formally a map $\nu[s] : s(W \times \Sigma)^* W^i \rightarrow (2^\Sigma \setminus \emptyset)$. Let $Pstrat^i(s)$ denote the set of all partial strategies after s of player i. The corresponding partial strategy tree is denoted by $T_\mathcal{G}^{\nu[s]}$.

3.2 Switching from One Strategy to Another

Suppose there are two players 1 and 2 and their set of actions are $\{a, b\}$ and $\{c, d\}$ respectively. Consider two strategies of Player 1, μ_a and μ_b. μ_a specifies the action a at every game node and μ_b specifies the action b at every game node. Now suppose Player 1 plays strategy μ_a for the first move and then plays strategy μ_b on the subtree from her next move. The resulting prescription μ (say) is thus also a strategy for player 1. See Fig. 2.

Suppose μ_1 and μ_2 are two strategies of player i and suppose that she follows μ_1 for at most k moves of the game (here, by convention, a move can be either a Player 1 move or a Player 2 move) and then switches to μ_2. We denote the resulting set of strategies by $\mu_1^k \mu_2$ and the resulting set of strategy trees by $T_\mathcal{G}^{\mu_1 k} T_\mathcal{G}^{\mu_2}$. Every tree T in the set $T_\mathcal{G}^{\mu_1 k} T_\mathcal{G}^{\mu_2}$ can be viewed to have been constructed as follows. Let $T_\mathcal{G}^{\mu_1}(k)$ be a finite subtree of $T_\mathcal{G}^{\mu_1}$ such that every branch of $T_\mathcal{G}^{\mu_1}(k)$ is of depth at most k. Let $leaves(T_\mathcal{G}^{\mu_1}(k))$ denote the set of leaves of this tree. For every $s \in leaves(T_\mathcal{G}^{\mu_1}(k))$, we attach $T_\mathcal{G}^{\mu_2(s)}$ to s. The operation can also be lifted to an arbitrary set of strategy trees, $\mathcal{T}_1$ and $\mathcal{T}_2$ (say). We denote the resulting set of trees as $\mathcal{T}_1^k \mathcal{T}_2$.

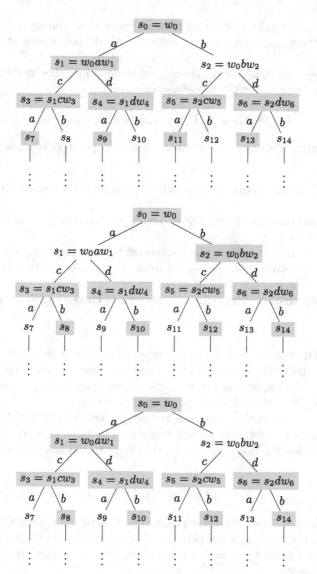

Fig. 2. The strategy μ_a; the strategy μ_b; and $\mu_a{}^2\mu_b$. Note that, by definition, since the second move is by Player 2, $\mu_a{}^2\mu_b$ and $\mu_a\mu_b$ define the same strategies

3.3 Specification of Strategy Composition

To talk about the outcomes of the game, we introduce a countable set of propositions $\mathcal{P}_i$ for every player i and a valuation function val_i which are evaluated on the vertices of the arena. These propositions code up the outcomes of the game in the lines of [10]. val_i is lifted on the nodes of the game tree $T_{\mathcal{G}}$ in the usual manner.

Syntax. By an 'atomic strategy' of player i we mean a strategy which dictates her to play the same action at all positions. We denote atomic strategies by ϕ_a, $a \in \Sigma_i$.

The strategy set Φ_i of player i is obtained by combining her atomic strategies using some operators. Let Φ_i^- be defined as:

$$\Phi_i^- ::= \phi_a, \ a \in \Sigma_i \mid \phi_1 \cup \phi_2 \mid \phi_1 {}^\frown \phi_2 \mid \phi_1 + \phi_2$$

The intuitive meaning of the strategy building operators is explained as follows:

- ϕ_a, $a \in \Sigma_i$ is the atomic strategy where player i plays the action a at each move.
- $\phi_1 \cup \phi_2$ means that the player plays according to the strategy ϕ_1 or the strategy ϕ_2.
- $\phi_1 {}^\frown \phi_2$ means that the player plays according to the strategy ϕ_1 and then after some history, switches to playing according to ϕ_2. The position at which she makes the switch is not fixed in advance.
- $\phi_1 + \phi_2$ says that at every point, the player can choose to follow either ϕ_1 or ϕ_2.

The Test Operator. Let Φ_i be the strategies built from player i's atomic strategies applying the operators of Φ_i^- and also the *test operator* $\psi?\phi$. Intuitively, $\psi?\phi$ says that at every history, the player tests if the property ψ holds of that history. If it does then she plays according to ϕ.

What is the observable condition ψ that player i checks for? We think of these conditions as past time formulas of a simple tense logic over the atomic set of observables $\mathcal{P}_i$. More specifically, ψ belongs to the following syntax:

$$\Psi_i ::= p \in \mathcal{P}_i \mid \neg\psi \mid \psi_1 \vee \psi_2 \mid \langle a \rangle^- \psi \mid \langle a \rangle^+ \psi \mid \psi_1 \mathcal{S} \psi_2 \mid j?\phi, j \neq i, \ \phi \in \Phi_j^-$$

Intuitively, $j?\phi$ is the test where player i checks if player j is playing according to ϕ. Now as the observables of player j, $\mathcal{P}_j$ and their combinations are private to her, player i cannot reason based on them. Hence ϕ comes from Φ_j^- rather than the entire Φ_j.

The usual operators $\ominus\psi$ (previous), $\bigcirc\psi$ (next), $\Diamond\psi$ (sometime in the past) and $\boxminus\psi$ (throughout the past) are defined as $\ominus\psi \equiv \bigvee_{a \in \Sigma} \langle a \rangle^- \psi, \bigcirc\psi \equiv \bigvee_{a \in \Sigma} \langle a \rangle^+ \psi$, $\Diamond\psi \equiv \top \mathcal{S}\psi$ and $\boxminus\psi \equiv \neg\Diamond\neg\psi$.

An observable $\psi \in \Psi_i$ is interpreted over the nodes of the game tree. Formally, for a node $s \in T_\mathcal{G}$, $s \models \psi$ is defined inductively as:

- $s \models p$ iff $p \in val_i(s)$.
- $s \models \neg\psi$ iff $s \not\models \psi$.
- $s \models \psi_1 \vee \psi_2$ iff $s \models \psi_1$ or $s \models \psi_2$.
- $s \models \langle a \rangle^- \psi$ iff $s = s'a$ and $s' \models \psi$.
- $s \models \langle a \rangle^+ \psi$ iff for all $sa \in T$, $sa \models \psi$.

- $s \models \psi_1 S \psi_2$ iff $\exists s' \sqsubset s$ such that $s' \models \psi_2$ and $\forall s'' : s' \sqsubset s'' \sqsubseteq s, s'' \models \psi_1$.
- $s \models j?\phi$ iff there exists T' such that $T' \in [\![\phi, \epsilon]\!]_{T_\mathcal{G}}$ and $s \in T'$.

where $[\![\phi, \epsilon]\!]_{T_\mathcal{G}}$ will be defined shortly.

Note that in the syntax of Ψ_i, we do not have the corresponding indefinite future time operator $\mathcal{U}$. This is to reflect our view of strategizing as memory limited observations of the past, with bounded lookahead, as expressed by the operator $\langle a \rangle^+ \psi$.

Semantics. We now give the formal semantics of the strategy specifications. Given the game tree $T_\mathcal{G} = (S, \Rightarrow, s_0)$, the semantics of a strategy specification $\phi \in \Phi_i$ is a function $[\![\cdot]\!]_{T_\mathcal{G}} : \Phi_i \times S \to 2^{Strat_i}$. That is, each specification at a node s of the game tree is associated with a set of total strategy trees after history s.

For any $s \in S$, $[\![\cdot]\!]_{T_\mathcal{G}}$ is defined inductively as follows:

- $[\![\phi_a, s]\!]_{T_\mathcal{G}} = T^{\phi_a[s]}$ where for all $s' \in S$ such that $s \sqsubseteq s'$ and $\widehat{\lambda}(s') = i$, we have $\phi_a[s](s') = a$.
- $[\![\phi_1 \cup \phi_2, s]\!]_{T_\mathcal{G}} = [\![\phi_1, s]\!]_{T_\mathcal{G}} \cup [\![\phi_2, s]\!]_{T_\mathcal{G}}$.
- $[\![\phi_1 \widehat{\ } \phi_2, s]\!]_{T_\mathcal{G}} = [\![\phi_1, s]\!]_{T_\mathcal{G}} \cup \bigcup_{l \geq |s|} ([\![\phi_1, s]\!]_{T_\mathcal{G}}{}^l [\![\phi_2, \epsilon]\!]_{T_\mathcal{G}})$.
- $[\![(\phi_1 + \phi_2), s]\!]_{T_\mathcal{G}}$: $T = (T_\mathcal{G}, m) \in [\![(\phi_1 + \phi_2), s]\!]_{T_\mathcal{G}}$ if and only if there exists $T^1 = (T_\mathcal{G}, m_1) \in [\![\phi_1, s]\!]_{T_\mathcal{G}}$ and $T^2 = (T_\mathcal{G}, m_2) \in [\![\phi_2, s]\!]_{T_\mathcal{G}}$ such that the following condition is satisfied:
  - for all $s' \in S$ such that $s \sqsubseteq s'$ and $\widehat{\lambda}(s') = i$, $m(s') = m_1(s')$ or $m(s') = m_2(s')$.
- $[\![\psi?\phi, s]\!]_{T_\mathcal{G}}$: $T = (T_\mathcal{G}, m) \in [\![\psi?\phi, s]\!]_{T_\mathcal{G}}$ if and only if $s \in T$ and there exists $T' = (T_\mathcal{G}, m') \in [\![\phi, s]\!]_{T_\mathcal{G}}$ such that the following condition is satisfied:
  - for all $s' \in S$ such that $s \sqsubseteq s'$ and $\widehat{\lambda}(s') = i$, if ψ holds at s' then $m(s') = m'(s')$ and if ψ does not hold at s' then $m(s') = \overrightarrow{w}$ where $w = last(s')$.

A crucial difference between the two kinds of switching operators needs emphasis. $\phi_1 \widehat{\ } \phi_2$ specified a one-time nondeterministic switching from following ϕ_1 to following ϕ_2 whereas $\phi_1 + \phi_2$ specifies switching nondeterministically back and forth between the two. The latter can be seen as a qualitative specification of a *mixed strategy* for extensive form games: a player mixes the two strategies nondeterministically during course of play. The crucial difference is the lack of any probability distribution; however, such an extension is easy to conceive of: let $\phi_1 +_r \phi_2$ specify that at any point of time, if the player is playing ϕ_i, she switches to ϕ_{3-i} with probability r (and continues playing ϕ_i with probability $1 - r$). This suggests that we can build compositional structure in mixed strategies as well.

3.4   An Example

Consider the game of tennis. A player, poised to serve, considers for a moment: Should I serve wide, or down the 'T'? Should I serve deep, or short? When I last served deep and wide, he hit it onto the net. Should I try it again, or has he learnt now? The opponent, on his part, considers as he takes his stance: if he serves short, should I go for a cross-court shot and reveal my strength off that flank? If I do it too often, he will not serve such balls at all. Should I play it safe?

Let the player's set of atomic strategies be given as $\Sigma_{player} = \{\sigma_{short},$ $\sigma_{deep}, \sigma_{wide}, \sigma_T\}$ which corresponds to serving short, deep, wide and down-the-T respectively.

Let $p_{(short,net)}$ be the observable which says that the outcome of short serve is a return into the net. Then the following specification says that the player keeps serving short and wide till the opponent is able to return (does not hit into the net).

$$- \ \neg\Diamond p_{(short,shot)}?(\sigma_{short} \cap \sigma_{wide})$$

The specification $\sigma_{short}{}^\frown\sigma_{wide}{}^\frown\sigma_{deep}$ for the player says that he starts by serving short and after some point he switches to serving wide and again switches but this time to serving deep.

The simple specification $\sigma_{short} + \sigma_{deep}$ is yet most natural and indicative of a mixed strategy, that of occasionally serving short and serving deep but in no fixed pattern.

3.5   Logic

Note that we have only presented a syntax for strategy composition and not a logic for reasoning about games and strategies. Our idea is that such strategy specifications can be embedded into modal and temporal logics, and in our contention, without altering their flavour. Consider a modal logic with the modal operator $\langle i, \sigma \rangle \alpha$, interpreted at s to mean that player i has a strategy σ from that point on to ensure the outcome α [6]. Here σ need not be a specific functional strategy and can be a compositional specification. A presentation on these lines is carried out in [39].

Similarly a dynamic game logic, in which we have the operator $\langle i, g, \sigma \rangle \alpha$ which asserts that in game g player i has a strategy σ to ensure α [18]. Again, these can be compositional strategies, and this is discussed in [41].

Consider a temporal logic for games such as ATL with explicit strategies. However, since we are speaking of long term strategic abilities of players and coalitions, we are in the context of ATL* [14]. We can again consider a modality such as $\langle\langle C, f \rangle\rangle \alpha$, where f specifies a strategy σ_i for each player $i \in C$. The intended meaning is that the coalition C, has a collective strategy given by f to ensure α. While such explicit strategies have been studied in alternating temporal logics, the use of structured strategies constraining the paths is the departure advocated here. This can be seen in the spirit of extensions of temporal logic currently used in the industry such as PSL [20] in which the until operator is indexed: $\alpha \mathcal{U}_\pi \beta$, where π is a regular expression, and asserts the existence of an instant reachable by π at which β holds, and until then α holds.

However, such embeddings of structured strategies in modalities would not in themselves lead to reasoning as envisaged by us. For instance, in the case of game logic, strategy composition critically depends on game composition and reasoning about them separately glosses over this. Similarly, in the context of alternating temporal logic, in $\langle\!\langle C, f \rangle\!\rangle \alpha$, more than the function f, we are interested in the interdependence between $f(i)$ and $f(j)$, where both i and j are in C. Such analysis opens up interesting avenues for exploration.

4   Transducer Lemma

In this section we prove a result that shows the correspondence between the strategy specifications introduced in the previous section with finite state transducers. This helps us to do algorithmic analysis of the games.

Lemma 1. *Given a strategy specification $\phi \in \Phi_i$, we can construct a finite state transducer $\mathcal{A}_\phi$ such that for all histories s, for all $\nu[s] \in Pstrat_i(s)$ and for all strategy trees $T_\mathcal{G}^{\mu[s]} \in T_\mathcal{G}^{\nu[s]}$, we have $T_\mathcal{G}^{\mu[s]} \in [\![\phi, s]\!]_{T_\mathcal{G}}$ iff $T_\mathcal{G}^{\mu[s]} \in Lang(\mathcal{A}_\phi, s)$.*

Proof Idea. The proof proceeds in two steps. In the first step we construct the transducer $\mathcal{A}_\phi$ and in the second step we show that for all s, for all $\nu[s] \in Pstrat_i(s)$ and for all strategy trees $T_\mathcal{G}^{\mu[s]} \in T_\mathcal{G}^{\nu[s]}$, $T_\mathcal{G}^{\mu[s]} \in [\![\phi, s]\!]_{T_\mathcal{G}}$ iff $T_\mathcal{G}^{\mu[s]} \in Lang(\mathcal{A}_\phi, s)$. $\mathcal{A}_\phi$ is constructed inductively. $\mathcal{A}_{\phi_a}$ is just a one state transducer that outputs a at every turn of player i. $\mathcal{A}_{\phi_1 \cup \phi}$ is constructed as the union of $\mathcal{A}_{\phi_1}$ and $\mathcal{A}_{\phi_2}$. $\mathcal{A}_{\phi_1 \cup \phi_2}$ nondeterministically chooses either $\mathcal{A}_{\phi_1}$ or $\mathcal{A}_{\phi_2}$ right at the beginning and then simulates it, mirroring its output. $\mathcal{A}_{\phi \frown \phi_2}$ and $\mathcal{A}_{\phi_1 + \phi_2}$ are constructed as products of $\mathcal{A}_{\phi_1}$ and $\mathcal{A}_{\phi_2}$. Both $\mathcal{A}_{\phi_1}$ and $\mathcal{A}_{\phi_2}$ are simulated in parallel. In the former case, $\mathcal{A}_{\phi \frown \phi_2}$ switches from mirroring the output of $\mathcal{A}_{\phi_1}$ to that of $\mathcal{A}_{\phi_2}$ nondeterministically at some point. Whereas, $\mathcal{A}_{\phi_1 + \phi_2}$ switches back and forth between mirroring the outputs of $\mathcal{A}_{\phi_1}$ and $\mathcal{A}_{\phi_2}$ nondeterministically. $\mathcal{A}_{\psi ? \phi'}$ has to check, at each step, if ψ holds at that history. If so then it mirrors the output of $\mathcal{A}_{\phi'}$ and if not it outputs any move. This is achieved by taking the states of $\mathcal{A}_{\psi ? \phi'}$ to be the product of $\mathcal{A}_{\phi'}$ with "logical states" (atoms of ψ) that tell us whether a subformula of ψ holds at that history.

Step 2 is proved again by an induction on the structure of ϕ. The idea is to show that a strategy tree T is in the semantics of ϕ iff T is in the language defined by $\mathcal{A}_\phi$. The base case for ϕ_a follows from the definition. For $\phi_1 \cup \phi_2$ we show that T is a strategy tree of $\phi_1 \cup \phi_2$ iff it is in the language defined by either $\mathcal{A}_{\phi_1}$ or $\mathcal{A}_{\phi_2}$. For $\phi_1 \frown \phi_2$ we know that T is a strategy tree iff it can be obtained by pruning a tree T_1 at some finite depth and attaching a trees T_m to every leaf of the resulting tree where T_1 is a strategy tree of ϕ_1 and the T_ms are strategy trees of T_2. By the induction hypothesis, this holds iff T_1 is in the language defined by $\mathcal{A}_{\phi_1}$ and the T_ms are in the language defined by $\mathcal{A}_{\phi_2}$. Finally, for $\psi ? \phi'$, we know that a tree T is a strategy tree of $\psi ? \phi'$ iff on every branch of T if for a finite path, ψ holds then the move of player i corresponds to the strategy ϕ'. The check for ψ is done using the 'atom graph' of ψ and the move corresponding to ϕ' is verified using the transducer $\mathcal{A}_{\phi'}$ which exists by the induction hypothesis.   □

We now present the proof in detail.

Proof. **Step 1:** The construction of the transducer $\mathcal{A}_\phi$ is done inductively on the structure of ϕ. Fix the input and output alphabets to be Σ.

$\phi \equiv \phi_a$: The transducer consists of a single state and outputs the action a at every turn for player i. Formally, $\mathcal{A}_\phi = (\{q_0\}, \delta, o, \{q_0\})$ where

- $\delta = \{(q, b, q) \mid b \in \Sigma\}$.
- $o(q, w) = a$ for all w such that $\lambda(w) = i$.

$\phi \equiv \phi_1 \cup \phi_2$: The transducer $\mathcal{A}_{\phi_1 \cup \phi_2}$ should nondeterministically choose either $\mathcal{A}_{\phi_1}$ or $\mathcal{A}_{\phi_2}$ right at the beginning and then simulate it, mirroring its output. By the induction hypothesis we have transducers $\mathcal{A}_{\phi_1} = (Q_1, \delta_1, o_1, I_1)$ and $\mathcal{A}_{\phi_2} = (Q_2, \delta_2, o_2, I_2)$. We define $\mathcal{A}_{\phi_1 \cup \phi_2} = (Q, \delta, o, I)$ where

- $Q = Q_1 \cup Q_2$,
- $\delta = \delta_1 \cup \delta_2$,
- $I = I_1 \cup I_2$, and
- $o = o_1 \cup o_2$.

$\phi \equiv \phi_1 {}^\frown \phi_2$: The state space of $\mathcal{A}_{\phi_1 {}^\frown \phi_2}$ is the product space of the states of the transducers $\mathcal{A}_{\phi_1}$ and $\mathcal{A}_{\phi_2}$. $\mathcal{A}_{\phi_1 {}^\frown \phi_2}$ simulates both these transducers and switches from mirroring the output of $\mathcal{A}_{\phi_1}$ to that of $\mathcal{A}_{\phi_2}$ nondeterministically at some point. By the induction hypothesis, we have transducers $\mathcal{A}_{\phi_1} = (Q_1, \delta_1, o_1, I_1^0)$ and $\mathcal{A}_{\phi_2} = (Q_2, \delta_2, o_2, I_2^0)$. We define $\mathcal{A}_{\phi_1 {}^\frown \phi_2} = (Q, \delta, o, I^0)$ where

- $Q = Q_1 \times Q_2 \times \{1, 2\}$,
- $\delta = \{(q_1, q_2, 1) \xrightarrow{a} (q_1', q_2', 1), (q_1, q_2, 2) \xrightarrow{a} (q_1', q_2', 2),$
  $\quad (q_1, q_2, 1) \xrightarrow{a} (q_1', q_2', 2) \mid q_1 \xrightarrow{a}_1 q_1', q_2 \xrightarrow{a}_2 q_2'\}$,
- $I^0 = I_1^0 \times I_2^0 \times \{1\}$ and
- $o : Q \times W \to \Sigma$ such that $o((q_1, q_2, 1), w) = o_1(q_1, w)$, $o((q_1, q_2, 2), w) = o_2(q_2, w)$.

$\phi \equiv \phi_1 + \phi_2$: The construction of $\mathcal{A}_{(\phi_1 + \phi_2)}$ is similar to that of $\mathcal{A}_{\phi_1 {}^\frown \phi_2}$. It simulates both $\mathcal{A}_{\phi_1}$ and $\mathcal{A}_{\phi_2}$ and keeps switching nondeterministically between the outputs of both. By the induction hypothesis we have transducers $\mathcal{A}_{\phi_1} = (Q_1, \delta_1, o_1, I_1^0)$ and $\mathcal{A}_{\phi_2} = (Q_2, \delta_2, o_2, I_2^0)$. We define $\mathcal{A}_{(\phi_1 + \phi_2)} = (Q, \delta, o, I^0)$ where

- $Q = Q_1 \times Q_2 \times \{1, 2\}$,
- $\delta = \{(q_1, q_2, 1) \xrightarrow{a} (q_1', q_2', 1), (q_1, q_2, 2) \xrightarrow{a} (q_1', q_2', 2),$
  $\quad (q_1, q_2, 1) \xrightarrow{a} (q_1', q_2', 2), (q_1, q_2, 2) \xrightarrow{a} (q_1', q_2', 1) \mid$
  $q_1 \xrightarrow{a}_1 q_1', q_2 \xrightarrow{a}_2 q_2'\}$,
- $I^0 = I_1^0 \times I_2^0 \times \{1, 2\}$ and

– $o : Q \times W \to \Sigma$ such that $o((q_1, q_2, 1), w) = o_1(q_1, w)$, $o((q_1, q_2, 2), w) = o_2(q_2, w)$.

$\phi \equiv \psi?\phi'$: At each step $\mathcal{A}_{\psi?\phi'}$ has to check if ψ holds at that history. We achieve this by taking the states of $\mathcal{A}_{\psi?\phi'}$ to be the product of $\mathcal{A}_{\phi'}$ with "logical states" that tell us whether a subformula of ψ holds at that tree node.

First, some preliminaries. Let SF_ψ be the least set containing ψ and closed under subformulas: if $\alpha \in SF_\psi$ and β is a subformula of α then $\beta \in SF_\psi$. Further we assume that SF_ψ is closed under negation: $\beta \in SF_\psi$ iff $\neg\beta \in SF_\psi$ where we treat $\neg\neg\alpha$ to be the same as α; moreover, if $\alpha\mathcal{S}\beta \in SF_\psi$, we have that $\ominus\alpha\mathcal{S}\beta \in SF_\psi$ as well. Such a set is called the Fischer - Ladner closure and we denote this set by $CL(\psi)$.

Now let $v \subseteq CL(\psi)$. We call v an *atom* if it is 'locally' consistent and complete: that is, for every $\psi' \in CL(\psi)$, $\neg\psi' \in v$ iff $\psi' \notin v$; for every $\psi_1 \vee \psi_2 \in CL(\psi)$, $\psi_1 \vee \psi_2 \in v$ iff $\psi_1 \in v$ or $\psi_2 \in v$; for every $\psi_1\mathcal{S}\psi_2 \in CL(\psi)$, we have: if $\psi_2 \in v$ then $\psi_1\mathcal{S}\psi_2 \in v$; otherwise $\{\psi_1, \psi_1\mathcal{S}\psi_2, \ominus\psi_1\mathcal{S}\psi_2\} \subseteq v$. Let V_ψ denote the set of ψ-atoms. $v \in V_\psi$ is said to be an *initial* atom if it satisfies the conditions: $\psi_1\mathcal{S}\psi_2 \in v$ iff $\psi_2 \in v$ and there is no formula of the form $\langle a \rangle^-\alpha$ in v.

Define a relation $\to_\psi \subseteq (V_\psi \times \Sigma \times V_\psi)$ as follows: $v \xrightarrow{a} v'$ iff the following conditions hold: for every $\langle a \rangle^-\alpha$ in $CL(\psi)$, if $\alpha \in v$ then $\langle a \rangle^-\alpha \in v'$ and for every $\langle a \rangle^+\alpha$ in $CL(\psi)$, if $\alpha \in v'$ then $\langle a \rangle^-\alpha \in v$. This relation gives us $G_\psi = (V_\psi, \to_\psi)$, the atom graph of ψ.

We can now define the transducer for this case. Let $\mathcal{A}_{\phi'} = (Q', \delta', o', I')$ which exists by the induction hypothesis. We define $\mathcal{A}_{\psi?\phi'} = (Q, \delta, o, I)$ where

– $Q \subseteq Q' \times V_\psi$,
– $I \subseteq Q$ such that $(q, v) \in I$ iff $q \in I'$ and v is an initial atom,
– $(q, v) \xrightarrow{a} (q', v')$ iff $q \xrightarrow{a} q'$ and $v \xrightarrow{a} v'$, and
– $o((q, v), w) = o(q, w)$ iff $\psi \in v$. Otherwise $o((q, v), w) = \Sigma$.

Note that $o((q, v), w) = \Sigma$ means that the transducer outputs 'any' action that is available at w.

Step 2: We now show that for all s, for all $\nu[s] \in Pstrat_i(s)$ and for all strategy trees $T_\mathcal{G}^{\mu[s]} \in T_\mathcal{G}^{\nu[s]}$, $T_\mathcal{G}^{\mu[s]} \in [\![\phi, s]\!]_{T_\mathcal{G}}$ iff $T_\mathcal{G}^{\mu[s]} \in Lang(\mathcal{A}_\phi, s)$. The proof is by induction on the structure of ϕ.

$\phi = \phi_a$: By construction $\mathcal{A}_\phi$ has just one state q and all transitions out of q lead to q itself. The output function is the constant output function $o(q, w) = a$ for all w such that $\lambda(w) = i$. Hence by the definition of $[\![\phi_a, s]\!]_{T_\mathcal{G}}$ we have, $T_\mathcal{G}^{\mu[s]} \in [\![\phi_a, s]\!]_{T_\mathcal{G}}$ if and only if $T_\mathcal{G}^{\mu[s]} \in Lang(\mathcal{A}_{\phi_a}, s)$ for all s.

$\phi = \phi_1 \cup \phi_2$: By the semantics, $T_\mathcal{G}^{\mu[s]} \in [\![\phi_1 \cup \phi_2, s]\!]_{T_\mathcal{G}}$ iff $T_\mathcal{G}^{\mu[s]} \in [\![\phi_1, s]\!]_{T_\mathcal{G}} \cup [\![\phi_2, s]\!]_{T_\mathcal{G}}$ iff $T_\mathcal{G}^{\mu[s]} \in [\![\phi_1, s]\!]_{T_\mathcal{G}}$ or $T_\mathcal{G}^{\mu[s]} \in [\![\phi_2, s]\!]_{T_\mathcal{G}}$. By induction hypothesis, $T_\mathcal{G}^{\mu[s]} \in Lang(\mathcal{A}_{\phi_1}, s)$ or $T_\mathcal{G}^{\mu[s]} \in Lang(\mathcal{A}_{\phi_2}, s)$. Since $Lang(\mathcal{A}_{\phi_1 \cup \phi_2}, s) =$

$Lang(\mathcal{A}_{\phi_1}, s) \cup Lang(\mathcal{A}_{\phi_2}, s)$ by the construction of $\mathcal{A}_{\phi_1 \cup \phi_2}$, we have $T_{\mathcal{G}}^{\mu[s]} \in$ $Lang(\mathcal{A}_{\phi_1}, s) \cup Lang(\mathcal{A}_{\phi_2}, s)$ iff $T_{\mathcal{G}}^{\mu[s]} \in Lang(\mathcal{A}_{\phi_1 \cup \phi_2}, s)$.

$\phi = \phi_1 {}^\frown \phi_2$: The labelled tree $T_{\mathcal{G}}^{\mu[s]} \in [\![\phi_1{}^\frown\phi_2, s]\!]_{T_{\mathcal{G}}}$ implies by definition of $[\![\phi_1{}^\frown\phi_2, s]\!]_{T_{\mathcal{G}}}$ that there exists a labelled tree $T_{\mathcal{G}}^{\mu'[s]} \in [\![\phi_1, s]\!]_{T_{\mathcal{G}}}$ and a finite subtree $T_{\mathcal{G}}^{\mu'[s]}(k)$ of $T_{\mathcal{G}}^{\mu'[s]}$ such that $T_{\mathcal{G}}^{\mu'[s]}(k)$ is also a subtree of $T_{\mathcal{G}}^{\mu'[s]}$ and every branch of $T_{\mathcal{G}}^{\mu'[s]}(k)$ is of depth at most k. Also by definition, for every leaf node s' of $T_{\mathcal{G}}^{\mu'[s]}(k)$, there exists $T_{\mathcal{G}}^{\mu''[s']} \in [\![\phi_2, s']\!]_{T_{\mathcal{G}}}$ such that the labelled subtree of $T_{\mathcal{G}}^{\mu[s]}$ rooted at s' is the same as $T_{\mathcal{G}}^{\mu''[s']}$. By the induction hypothesis, $T_{\mathcal{G}}^{\mu'[s]} \in Lang(\mathcal{A}_{\phi_1}, s)$ and $T_{\mathcal{G}}^{\mu''[s']} \in Lang(\mathcal{A}_{\phi_2}, s')$. Thus the run of $\mathcal{A}_{\phi_1{}^\frown\phi_2}$ where the transducer makes a switch from the output of $\mathcal{A}_{\phi_1}$ to that of $\mathcal{A}_{\phi_2}$ at $leaves(T_{\mathcal{G}}^{\mu'[s]}(k))$ is the accepting run for $T_{\mathcal{G}}^{\mu[s]}$.

Conversely, suppose $T_{\mathcal{G}}^{\mu[s]} \in Lang(\mathcal{A}_{\phi_1{}^\frown\phi_2})$. Let r be an accepting run of $\mathcal{A}_{\phi_1{}^\frown\phi_2}$. Then there exists a $k \geq 0$ such that $\mathcal{A}_{\phi_1{}^\frown\phi_2}$ switches from mirroring the output of $\mathcal{A}_{\phi_1}$ to that of $\mathcal{A}_{\phi_2}$ in at most k steps on all branches of r. Let $T_{\mathcal{G}}(k)$ be the finite tree on which r is a valid run till it makes the switch. We have that there exists a labelled tree $T_{\mathcal{G}}^{\mu'[s]} \in Lang(\mathcal{A}_{\phi_1}, s)$ such that $T_{\mathcal{G}}(k)$ is a subtree of $T_{\mathcal{G}}^{\mu'[s]}$. Also, for all leaf nodes $s' \in leaves(T_{\mathcal{G}}(k))$, there exist $T_{\mathcal{G}}^{\mu''[s']}$ where $\in Lang(\mathcal{A}_{\phi_2}, s')$ such that $\mu[s](s'') = \mu'[s](s'')$ for all s'' with $|s''| \leq |s'|$ and $\mu[s](s'') = \mu''[s'](s''')$ where $ss'' = s's'''$ for all s'' with $|s''| > |s'|$. By induction hypothesis, $T_{\mathcal{G}}^{\mu'[s]} \in [\![\phi_1, s]\!]_{T_{\mathcal{G}}}$ and $T_{\mathcal{G}}^{\mu''[s']} \in [\![\phi_2, s']\!]_{T_{\mathcal{G}}}$. Hence the labelled tree $T_{\mathcal{G}}^{\mu[s]}$ obtained by pasting $T_{\mathcal{G}}^{\mu''[s']}$ at all leaf nodes s' of $T_{\mathcal{G}}^k$ belongs to $[\![\phi_1{}^\frown\phi_2, s]\!]_{T_{\mathcal{G}}}$ by the definition of $[\![\phi_1{}^\frown\phi_2, s]\!]_{T_{\mathcal{G}}}$.

$\phi = (\phi_1 + \phi_2)$: Suppose $T_{\mathcal{G}}^{\mu[s]} = (T, m) \in [\![\phi_1 + \phi_2, s]\!]_{T_{\mathcal{G}}}$. By semantics, $s \in T_{\mathcal{G}}^{\mu[s]}$ and there exists $(T_1, m_1) \in [\![\phi_1, s]\!]_{T_{\mathcal{G}}}$ and $(T_2, m_2) \in [\![\phi_2, s]\!]_{T_{\mathcal{G}}}$ such that for all $s' \in T_{\mathcal{G}}^{\mu[s]}$, $m(s') = m_1(s')$ or $m(s') = m_2(s')$. By induction hypothesis $(T_1, m_1) \in Lang(\mathcal{A}_{\phi_1}, s)$ and $(T_2, m_2) \in Lang(\mathcal{A}_{\phi_2}, s)$. By construction, at every node s', the transducer $\mathcal{A}_{\phi_1+\phi_2}$ mirrors the output of either $\mathcal{A}_{\phi_1}$ or $\mathcal{A}_{\phi_2}$. Therefore we have that $T_{\mathcal{G}}^{\mu[s]} \in Lang(\mathcal{A}_{\phi_1+\phi_2}, s)$.

Conversely, suppose $T_{\mathcal{G}}^{\mu[s]} = (T, m) \in Lang(\mathcal{A}_{\phi_1+\phi_2}, s)$. For all $s \in T_{\mathcal{G}}^{\mu[s]}$, $\mathcal{A}_{\phi_1+\phi_2}$ mirrors the the output of either $\mathcal{A}_{\phi_1}$ or $\mathcal{A}_{\phi_2}$. Therefore, by construction of $\mathcal{A}_{\phi_1+\phi_2}$, there exists $(T_1, m_1) \in Lang(\mathcal{A}_{\phi_1}, s)$ and $(T_2, m_2) \in Lang(\mathcal{A}_{\phi_2}, s)$ such that for all s' we have $m(s') = m_1(s')$ or $m(s') = m_2(s')$. By induction hypothesis, $(T_1, m_1) \in [\![\phi_1, s]\!]_{T_{\mathcal{G}}}$ and $(T_2, m_2) \in [\![\phi_2, s]\!]_{T_{\mathcal{G}}}$. By semantics, $T_{\mathcal{G}}^{\mu[s]} \in [\![\phi_1 + \phi_2, s]\!]_{T_{\mathcal{G}}}$.

$\phi = \psi ? \phi'$: Let $\mathcal{A}_\phi = (Q, \delta, o, I)$, let r be a run of $\mathcal{A}_\phi$ on $T_{\mathcal{G}}^{\mu[s]}$.

Claim 1. For all $s' \in T_{\mathcal{G}}^{\mu[s]}$ and for all $\alpha \in CL(\psi)$, $\alpha \in r(s')$ iff $s' \models \alpha$. where $CL(\psi)$ is the subformula closure of ψ. Assume Claim 1 and suppose that $T_{\mathcal{G}}^{\mu[s]} = (T, m) \in [\![\phi, s]\!]_{T_{\mathcal{G}}}$. By semantics, there exists $(T', m') \in$

$[\![\phi', s]\!]_{T_{\mathcal{G}}}$ such that for all $s' \in T_{\mathcal{G}}^{\nu[s]}$, if $s' \models \psi$ then $m(s') = m'(s')$. And if $s' \not\models \psi$ then $m(s') \in \Sigma$. By induction hypothesis, $T_{\mathcal{G}}^{\mu'[s]} \in Lang(\mathcal{A}_{\phi'}, s)$ and by Claim 1 we have $s' \models \psi$ implies $\psi \in r(s')$. By construction of $\mathcal{A}_\phi$, we then have that $T_{\mathcal{G}}^{\mu[s]} \in Lang(\mathcal{A}_\phi, s)$.

Conversely, assume Claim 1 and suppose that $T_{\mathcal{G}}^{\mu[s]} = (T, m) \in Lang(\mathcal{A}_\phi, s)$. For a node $s' \in T_{\mathcal{G}}^{\mu[s]}$, let $r(s') = (q', v')$. If $\psi \in v'$ then $\mathcal{A}_\phi$ mirrors the output of $\mathcal{A}_{\phi'}$ and if $\psi \notin v'$ then the transducer outputs an arbitrary action available in Σ. Therefore, by construction of $\mathcal{A}_\phi$, there exits $(T', m') \in Lang(\mathcal{A}_{\phi'}, s)$ such that for all s', if $\psi \in v'$ then $m(s) = m'(s')$. By induction hypothesis, $T_{\mathcal{G}}^{\mu[s]} \in [\![\phi', s]\!]_{T_{\mathcal{G}}}$ and by Claim 1 if $\psi \in v'$ then $s' \models \psi$. By the semantics we then have that $T_{\mathcal{G}}^{\mu[s]} \in [\![\phi, s]\!]_{T_{\mathcal{G}}}$.

It now remains to prove Claim 1. We do so by a second induction on the structure of α.

$\alpha = p \in \mathcal{P}_i$: Follows from definition since in the construction we ensured that $(q, v) \in Q$ iff $q \cap \mathcal{P}_i = v \cap \mathcal{P}_i$.

$\alpha = \neg\beta$: $s' \models \neg\beta$ iff $s' \not\models \beta$ iff $\beta \notin r(s') = (q, v)$ iff $\neg\beta \in (q, v)$ (since v is an atom).

$\alpha = \alpha_1 \vee \alpha_2$: $s' \models \alpha$ iff $s' \models \alpha_1$ or $s' \models \alpha_2$ iff $\alpha_1 \in r(s')$ or $\alpha_2 \in r(s')$ where $r(s') = (q, v)$ iff $\alpha_1 \vee \alpha_2 \in r(s')$ (since v is an atom).

$\alpha = \langle a \rangle^- \beta$: $s' \models \langle a \rangle^- \beta$ iff $s' = s''aw$ and $s'' \models \beta$ iff $\beta \in r(s'') = (q', v')$ iff $\langle a \rangle^- \beta \in r(s) = (q, v)$ since v is an atom and $(q', v') \xrightarrow{a} (q, v)$ iff $q' \xrightarrow{a} q$ and $v' \xrightarrow{a} v$ by construction.

$\alpha = \langle a \rangle^+ \beta$: Similar to the case for $\alpha = \langle a \rangle^- \beta$.

$\alpha = \alpha_1 \mathcal{S} \alpha_2$: $s' \models \alpha_1 \mathcal{S} \alpha_2$ iff there exists s_1, $s_1 \sqsubset s'$ such that $s_1 \models \alpha_2$ and for all s_2, $s_1 \sqsubset s_2 \sqsubseteq s'$ and $s_2 \models \alpha_1$. We do an induction on $|s'| - |s_1|$. When $|s'| - |s_1| = 0$, $s' \models \alpha_2$ iff $\alpha \in r(s')$ by induction hypothesis where $r(s') = (q, v)$ iff $\alpha_1 \mathcal{S} \alpha_2 \in r(s')$ (since v is an atom). When $|s'| - |s_1| = k + 1$, $s_2 \models \alpha_1 \mathcal{S} \alpha_2$ and either s' in which case we are done (by definition of initial atom), or $s' \models \ominus(\alpha_1 \mathcal{S} \alpha_2)$ where $s' = s_2 a w$ iff $\alpha_1 \mathcal{S} \alpha_2 \in r(s_2)$ iff $\alpha_1 \mathcal{S} \alpha_2 \in r(s') = (q, v)$ (since v is an atom).

$j?\phi$: $s' \models j?\phi$ iff there exists T^ϕ such that $T^\phi \in [\![\phi, \epsilon]\!]_{T_{\mathcal{G}}}$ and $s' \in T^\phi$ iff $T^\phi \in Lang(\mathcal{A}_\phi, \epsilon)$ by the main induction hypothesis, iff $j?\phi \in r(s') = (q, v)$ since by construction, $j?\phi \in v$ and $q \in \delta'(q_0, last(s'))$ where q_0 is an initial state of $\mathcal{A}_\phi$.

5   Applications

The Transducer Lemma provides us with a tool to talk about eventual outcomes in games and eventual behaviour of players given that they play according to strategy specifications given in our syntax. We formalise this below.

Given a game arena, and strategy specifications for players, we are interested in studying long-range outcomes. The strategy specifications are akin to player types; based on observations during play, they constrain player actions at game positions. We would then like to know whether a given outcome is achieved. Since these are infinite games, the natural such notion is that of **stable** outcomes.

5.1 Stable Outcome

Let $\mathcal{G} = (W, \rightarrow, w_0, \lambda)$ be a game arena and let there be n players. Suppose the strategies of the players are given as $\phi_1, \phi_2, \ldots \phi_n$ respectively where each ϕ_i is from the syntax Φ_i as described in Sect. 3. Suppose α is a property from the following syntax:

$$\alpha := p \in \mathcal{P} \mid \neg\alpha \mid \alpha_1 \vee \alpha_2 \mid \langle a \rangle^+ \alpha$$

where $\mathcal{P}$ is a set of 'global' propositions and $val : W \rightarrow 2^{\mathcal{P}}$ gives their valuation at the nodes of the arena. We want to check if it is the case that eventually the property α always holds given that the players play according to their strategy specifications. In other words, we wish to check if α becomes 'stable' in the game, where we define stability as: Given a subarena $\mathcal{G}'$ of $\mathcal{G}$, α is said to be **stable** in $\mathcal{G}'$ if $s \models \alpha$ for every $s \in T_{\mathcal{G}'}$.

We do this as follows. We first construct transducers $\mathcal{A}_{\phi_i}$, as described in Sect. 4, for the strategy specification of each player i. We then take the 'restriction' of the arena $\mathcal{G}$ with respect to each of these transducers which results in a new arena $\mathcal{G}'$. The restriction of $\mathcal{G}$ with respect to a transducer $\mathcal{A}_{\phi_i} = (Q, \delta, o, q_0)$ is denoted as $\mathcal{G} \restriction \mathcal{A}_{\phi_i}$ and is defined as $\mathcal{G} \restriction \mathcal{A}_{\phi_i} = (W', \rightarrow', w_0', \lambda')$ where

- $W' \subseteq W \times Q$ such that $w' = (w, q) \in W'$ iff $p \in val(w) \Leftrightarrow p \in val_i(q)$ for all $p \in \mathcal{P} \cap \mathcal{P}_i$.
- For every $w_1', w_2' \in W'$ where $w_1' = (w_1, q_1)$ and $w_2' = (w_2, q_2)$ $w_1' \xrightarrow{a}' w_2'$ iff $w_1 \xrightarrow{a} w_2$ and $q_1 \xrightarrow{a} q_2$.
- $w_0' = (w_0, q_0)$.
- $\lambda'(w', q') = \lambda(w)$.

Thus the final restricted arena is $\mathcal{G}' = (((\mathcal{G} \restriction \mathcal{A}_{\phi_1}) \restriction \ldots) \restriction \mathcal{A}_{\phi_n})$. Note that the Transducer Lemma ensures that in the restricted arena $\mathcal{G}'$, for every node $w' \in \mathcal{G}'$ the outgoing edges are exactly the moves prescribed by the strategy specification ϕ_i for player i where $\lambda'(w') = i$. Finally, to check whether α becomes eventually stable, we check the stability of α in $\mathcal{G}'$. This can be done by a simple marking procedure on the nodes of $\mathcal{G}'$ with the subformulae of α. We thus have proved the following theorem:

Theorem 1. *Given a game arena $\mathcal{G} = (W, \rightarrow, w_0, \lambda)$ with n players and given that the players play according to strategy specifications $\phi_1, \phi_2, \ldots \phi_n$ respectively where each $\phi_i \in \Phi_i$, we can effectively decide if a property α becomes eventually stable in the game.*

5.2   Solution Concepts

Apart from achieving logically specified outcomes as above, there are other applications of the transducer construction. In the study of (offline) strategies in game theory, the standard questions relate to best response, equilibria etc. In the case of structured strategies, similar questions can be answered using automata.

However, since a strategy specification denotes a set of strategies satisfying certain properties, notions like strategy comparison and best response with respect to strategy specifications need to be redefined. When we have functional strategies μ_1 and μ_2 for a player i, we can consider μ_1 to dominate μ_2 if for every opponent strategy profile μ^{-i}, the play (μ_1, μ^{-i}) is preferred by i over the play (μ_2, μ^{-i}). But when does a set of strategies dominate another set? This is not clear.

One notion we can define says that σ is better than σ' if for any outcome α if there is a strategy conforming to the specification σ' which ensures α, then there also exists a strategy conforming to σ which ensures α as well.

But then it's equally reasonable to define comparison somewhat differently. According to this, σ is better than σ' if for any outcome α whenever there is a strategy conforming to σ which cannot guarantee α, there also exists a strategy conforming to σ' which cannot guarantee α either. This can be thought of as a soundness condition. A risk averse player might prefer this way of comparison.

We do not want to fix any comparison notion here, but merely point out that there are different and interesting notions of comparison. But once we fix such a notion, we can consider algorithmic questions relating to players' best response.

- Does player i have a strategy conforming to σ to ensure outcome α as long as the other players play according to the specifications τ^{-i}?
- Do all strategies for player i conforming to σ constitute a best reponse against τ^{-i} for α?
- Given specifications τ^{-i} for the other players, synthesize a best response for player i as an automaton.

Now, all these questions can be answered algorithmically using the transducer construction for strategy specifications, for appropriately defined outcomes. [40] presents some results in that direction. In general, we can study questions like whether a given tuple of strategy specifications constitutes a Nash equilibrium (with respect to fixed strategy comparison notions). In some sense, the main idea is that all the difficulties related to online strategy switching are modularised into the transducer construction.

5.3   Game Logics

As indicated earlier, we expect strategy specifications to be embedded in logics with assertions of the form "playing a strategy conforming to σ ensures outcome α for player i". The decision procedures for model checking such logics are naturally constructed by tree automata that run over game trees, with transducers running in parallel for strategy specifications in subformulas. Thus the construction offers a generic way of algorithmically constructing strategies on the fly for logically specified outcomes. [42] presents some results in that direction.

A more general remark would be that in any logics for reasoning about extensive form games, if the embedded specifications admit a transducer construction such as the one outlined here, the model checking algorithm for the logic constitutes strategy construction in the sense envisaged in our motivation. [41] constitutes one such example, but this style of automata based reasoning about strategies needs to be expanded much further, especially for Alternating Temporal Logics. An interesting challenge would be to introduce *belief structure* into automata so that the considerable body of logical work on epistemic reasoning about strategies ([8]) can be addressed. As long as epistemic assertions relate only to the past, automaton construction seems extendable. When beliefs about future need to be considered, the issues become indeed complex.

6 Discussion

We have presented a syntax of strategy specifications involving strategy switching and showed their realization as automata. This be seen as making a *prima facie* case for considering online strategizing and the use of automata for studying memory structure in such strategies.

Related Work

As remarked in the introduction, the motivation for considering online strategizing at all comes from the felt need for a 'theory of play' on the lines of [6,8,9]. The motivation for considering games as infinite trees for such a study is akin to the discussion on games with memory in [43]. The model itself and the representation of strategies as finite state transducers, is based on the study of regular infinite games, as in [22].

An important line of work in game theory about strategy switching is that of Lipman and Wang in [28,29]. The framework is that of finite and infinite repeated games, and players switch strategies during periods of the repeated game. They look at how equilibria change when players incur a cost on every strategy switch they make. The critical difference for our work is that switching is not based on previous game outcomes but observations by players in the course of play.

In general, dynamic learning has been extensively studied in game theory: for instance, Young ([47,48]) considers a model in which each player chooses an optimal strategy based on a sample of information about what other players have done in the past. Similar analyses have been carried out in the context of cooperative game theory as well: here players decide dynamically which coalition to join. One asks how coalition structures change over time, and which coalition players will eventually arrive at ([2]). Evolutionary game theory ([46]) studies how players observe payoffs of other players in their neighbourhood and accordingly change strategies to maximise fitness. However, these studies again use offline strategies and deliberation between periods of repeated games rather than online strategizing in games which is the focus here.

We have used a syntax for strategy specifications that is logical, using formulas of a simple modal logic for observations of players but otherwise using operators that can be seen as algebraic, their semantics given by operations on trees. Note the absence of negation in strategy specifications; thus, they are closer to programs in propositional dynamic logic (PDL) rather than logical assertions in themselves. Indeed, like in the case of PDL, where programs are embedded in an assertion language that speaks of postconditions, strategy specifications would be embedded in a logical language that speaks of preferences and outcomes, so that one can speak of σ ensuring the "best" outcome α for a player. A programme of this sort is carried out for a more restricted class of strategy specifications in [42] and a complete axiomatization is given. In general, we do not see the language of specifications as a logical means rather than as an end, and our purpose here has been to show their realization as automata.

In this context, we note that there exist a variety of logics in which strategy specifications may be embedded in the sense above. In general, any logic that speaks of a player (or a set of players) having a strategy to ensure an outcome would be appropriate. Notable among these is the work on alternating temporal logic (ATL) [1], a logic on trees with just these kind of assertions. Various extensions of ATL ([26,27]) have been proposed to incorporate knowledge of players and strategies explicitly into the logic. In particular, the logic ATL* ([14]) is powerful enough to include changing strategy contexts and constructive concepts of strategy as well. However, in our presentation, we focus not on reasoning about games as in ATL but only on strategy switching and composition.

In [4,5,8] van Benthem uses dynamic logic to describe games as well as strategies. In fact, PDL can be seen as a language for strategy specifications as well. However, it is unclear whether the switching operator, being a kind of 'interval' operator, or the mixing operator +, are definable in PDL at all. Note that these operators are much closer to those of *process logic* ([24]). A form of ⌒ operator, called 'chop' is extensively used in interval logics ([32]) but these are over linear orders and similar operations on trees seem to be difficult to define.

Ghosh [18] presents a complete axiomatisation of a logic describing both games and strategies in a dynamic logic framework where assertions are made about atomic strategies. Our earlier work [39] studies a logic in which not only are games structured, but so also are strategies. [19] enriches strategy specifications with an interleaving based parallel composition operator. All these logics are closely related and automata constructions can be given for the strategy specifications in these logics. Typically, logics like PDL correspond to automata on sequences whereas strategy logics involve automata that accept trees or act as tree to word transducers, and hence the constructions tend to be more complex. Strategy switching makes essential use of transductions which has been the emphasis here.

Further work

We have advocated a programme of working with 'online constructible' strategy spaces in large extensive form games, but what we have provided is a mere illustration of possibilities that such constructions can be carried out within the framework of simple modal logics and automata. However, the programme requires a precise delineation of such a strategy space within that of the classical offline strategy space, or even within the computable strategy space. The work presented here does not provide any basis for such a characterization.

The notion of strategies as constraining relations rather than functions is in itself worthy of deeper study, and characterizing the class of relations that can be realised as programs seems to be an interesting question. Partial strategies are akin to heuristics that can apply to a variety of game situations. The study here suggests that we can consider access to a library of such partial strategies and online composition, much like software.

While we have focused on one particular aspect of online strategizing, namely that of composition and switching, a number of aspects need incorporation for building a theory of play. Critically, the belief structure of players about other players' strategies and their mutual beliefs and expectations critically affects strategizing ([8]). While strategy specifications presented here can be viewed in themselves as player types, the latter crucially incorporate beliefs as well, and this needs further exploration.

The expressiveness of the specification language for strategies that we have presented is unclear. Since the automata considered recognize regular tree languages, and hence (presumably) are equivalent to some monadic second order logic on trees, one expects that there must be strategies implementable as automata but not definable in this limited specification language. However, note that switching involves taking an 'initial fragment' of one subtree and a 'final fragment' of another subtree and gluing them together. The logical status of such tree operations is unclear. Is this first-order definable, and if yes, with what vocabulary? Note that characterizing first order definability on (unranked) trees is difficult in general. What is an expressively complete set of strategy composition operators with respect to finite state transducers? This seems to be an interesting question to answer.

Another important dimension is the algebraic structure of strategy composition ([21]). What is a natural notion of equivalence on strategies, and reductions between them? Switching imposes an interval-like substructure on trees, and the interaction of such structure with other operators seems worthy of further study.

Acknowledgments. The authors would like to thank Dietmar Berwanger and Sujata Ghosh for many interesting discussions on this theme and the editors of the volume for their patience and encouragement.

References

1. Alur, R., Henzinger, T.A., Kupferman, O.: Alternating-time temporal logic. J. ACM **49**(5), 672–713 (2002)
2. Arnold, T., Schwalbe, U.: Dynamic coalition formation and the core. J. Econ. Behav. Organ. **49**, 363–380 (2002)
3. Aumann, R.J., Dreze, J.H.: When all is said and done, how should you play and what should you expect? (2005). http://www.ma.huji.ac.il/raumann/pdf/dp_387. pdf
4. van Benthem, J.: Games in dynamic epistemic logic. Bull. Econ. Res. **53**(4), 219–248 (2001)
5. van Benthem, J.: Extensive games as process models. J. Logic Lang. Inform. **11**, 289–313 (2002)
6. van Benthem, J.: In praise of strategies. In: van Eijck, J., Verbrugge, R. (eds.) Foundations of Social Software, Studies in Logic, pp. 283–317. College Publications (2007)
7. van Benthem, J.: Exploring a theory of play. In: Apt, K.R. (ed.) Proceedings of the 13th Conference on Theoretical Aspects of Rationality and Knowledge, pp. 12–16. ACM (2011)
8. van Benthem, J.: Logic in Games. MIT Press, Cambridge (2014)
9. van Benthem, J., Pacuit, E., Roy, O.: Toward a theory of play: a logical perspective on games and interaction. Games **2**, 52–86 (2011)
10. Bonanno, G.: Modal logic and game theory: two alternative approaches. Risk Decis. Policy **7**, 309–324 (2002)
11. Borel, E.: La théorie du jeu et les equations intégrales à noyau symétrique gauche. C. R. Acad. Sci. **173**, 1304–1308 (1921)
12. Büchi, J.R.: On a decision method in restricted second-order arithmetic. In: Proceedings of the 1960 International Congress for Logic, Methodology and Philosophy of Science, pp. 1–11. Stanford University Press (1962)
13. Büchi, J.R., Landweber, L.H.: Solving sequential conditions by finite-state strategies. Trans. Americal Math. Soc. **138**, 295–311 (1969)
14. Bulling, N., Goranko, V., Jamroga, W.: Logics for reasoning about strategic abilities in multi-player games. In: van Benthem, J., Ghosh, S., Verbrugge, R. (eds.) Models of Strategic Reasoning. LNCS, vol. 8972, pp. 93–136. Springer, Heidelberg (2015)
15. Majumdar, R., Jurdziński, M., Chatterjee, K.: On nash equilibria in stochastic games. In: Tarlecki, A., Marcinkowski, J. (eds.) CSL 2004. LNCS, vol. 3210, pp. 26–40. Springer, Heidelberg (2004)
16. Emerson, A., Jutla, C.: Tree automata, mu-calculus and determinacy. In: Proceedings of the 32nd IEEE Symposium on Foundations of Computer Science, pp. 368–377. IEEE Computer Society Press (1991)
17. Gale, D., Stewart, F.: Infinite games with perfect information. Ann. Math. Stud. **28**, 245–266 (1953)
18. Ghosh, S.: Strategies made explicit in dynamic game logic. In: Proceedings of the Workshop on Logic and Intelligent Interaction, ESSLLI 2008, pp. 74–81 (2008)
19. Ghosh, S., Simon, S., Ramanujam, R.: Playing extensive form games in parallel. In: Dix, J., Governatori, G., Leite, J., Jamroga, W. (eds.) CLIMA XI. LNCS, vol. 6245, pp. 153–170. Springer, Heidelberg (2010)

20. Glazberg, Z., Moulin, M., Orni, A., Ruah, S., Zarpas, E.: PSL: Beyond hardware verification. In: Ramesh, S., Sampath, P. (eds.) Next Generation Design and Verification Methodologies for Distributed Embedded Control Systems, pp. 245–260. Springer, Netherlands (2007)

21. Goranko, V.: The basic algebra of game equivalences. Stud. Logica 75(2), 221–238 (2003)

22. Farwer, B.: ω-automata. In: Grädel, E., Thomas, W., Wilke, T. (eds.) Automata, Logics, and Infinite Games. LNCS, vol. 2500, pp. 3–21. Springer, Heidelberg (2002)

23. Grädel, E., Ummels, M.: Solution concepts and algorithms for infinite multiplayer games. In: New Perspectives on Games and Interaction. Texts in Logic and Games, vol. 4, pp. 151–178. Amsterdam University Press (2008)

24. Harel, D., Kozen, D., Parikh, R.: Process logic: expressiveness, decidability, completeness. J. Comput. Syst. Sci. 25(2), 144–170 (1982)

25. van den Herik, J., Schaeffer, J.: Games, computers, and artificial intelligence. Artif. Intell. 134, 1–7 (2001)

26. van der Hoek, W., Jamroga, W., Wooldridge, M.: A logic for strategic reasoning. In: Proceedings of the Fourth International Joint Conference on Autonomous Agents and Multi-Agent Systems, pp. 157–164 (2005)

27. van der Hoek, W., Wooldridge, M.: Cooperation, knowledge, and time: alternating-time temporal epistemic logic and its applications. Stud. Logica 75(1), 125–157 (2003)

28. Lipman, B.L., Wang, R.: Switching costs in frequently repeated games. Working Papers 955, Queen's University, Department of Economics, September 1997

29. Lipman, B.L., Wang, R.: Switching costs in infinitely repeated games. Games Econ. Behav. 66(1), 292–314 (2009)

30. Martin, D.A.: Borel determinacy. Ann. Math. 102, 363–371 (1975)

31. Mostowski, A.W.: Games with forbidden positions. Technical Report 78, Instytut Matematyki, Uniwersytet Gdański, Poland (1991)

32. Moszkowski, B.C., Manna, Z.: Reasoning in interval temporal logic. In: Clarke, E.M., Kozen, D. (eds.) Logic of Programs. Lecture Notes in Computer Science, vol. 164, pp. 371–382. Springer, Heidelberg (1983)

33. Muller, D.E.: Infinite sequences and finite machines. In: Proceedings of the 4th IEEE Symposium on Switching Circuit Theory and Logical Design, pp. 3–16 (1963)

34. Nisan, N., Roughgarden, T., Tardos, E., Vazirani, V.V.: Algorithmic Game Theory. Cambridge University Press, New York (2007)

35. Osborne, M.J., Rubinstein, A.: A Course in Game Theory. MIT Press, Cambridge (1994)

36. Paul, S., Ramanujam, R., Simon, S.: Stability under strategy switching. In: Löwe, B., Merkle, W., Ambos-Spies, K. (eds.) CiE 2009. LNCS, vol. 5635, pp. 389–398. Springer, Heidelberg (2009)

37. Paul, S., Simon, S.: Nash equilibrium in generalised Muller games. In: Proceedings of the Conference on Foundation of Software Technology and Theoretical Computer Science, FSTTCS, Leibniz International Proceedings in Informatics (LIPIcs), vol. 4, pp. 335–346. Schloss Dagstuhl-Leibniz-Zentrum für Informatik (2009)

38. Perea, A.: Epistemic Game Theory: Reasoning and Choice. Cambridge University Press, Cambridge (2012)

39. Ramanujam, R., Simon, S.: Axioms for composite strategies. In: Proceedings of the 7th Conference on Logic and the Foundations of Game and Decision Theory (LOFT 2006) pp. 189–198 (2006)

40. Ramanujam, R., Simon, S.: Structured strategies in games on graphs. In: Flum, J., Grädel, E., Wilke, T. (eds.) Logic and Automata: History and Perspectives. Texts in Logic and Games, vol. 2, pp. 567–587. Amsterdam University Press (2007)

41. Ramanujam, R., Simon, S.: Dynamic logic on games with structured strategies. In: Proceedings of the 11th International Conference on Principles of Knowledge Representation and Reasoning (KR-2008), pp. 49–58. AAAI Press (2008)

42. Ramanujam, R., Simon, S.: A logical structure for strategies. In: Logic and the Foundations of Game and Decision Theory (LOFT 7), Texts in Logic and Games, vol. 3, pp. 183–208. Amsterdam University Press (2008)

43. Rubinstein, A.: Comments on the interpretation of game theory. Econometrica **59**, 909–924 (1991)

44. Selten, R.: Spieltheoretische Behandlung eines Oligopolmodells mit Nachfrageträgheit. Zeitschrift für die Gesamte Staatswissenschaft **121**, 301–324 (1965)

45. von Neumann, J.: Zur Theorie der Gesellschaftsspiele. Math. Ann. **100**, 295–328 (1928)

46. Weibull, J.W.: Evolutionary Game Theory. MIT Press, Cambridge, MA (1997)

47. Young, H.P.: The evolution of conventions. Econometrica **61**, 57–84 (1993). Blackwell Publishing

48. Young, H.P.: The diffusion of innovations in social networks. Economics Working Paper Archive 437, The Johns Hopkins University, Department of Economics (2000)

Languages for Imperfect Information

Gabriel Sandu$^{(\boxtimes)}$

Theoretical Philosophy, University of Helsinki, Helsinki, Finland
sandu@mappi.helsinki.fi

Abstract. This chapter gives a self-contained introduction to game-theoretical semantics (GTS) both for classical first-order logic and for one of its extensions, Independence-Friendly Logic (IF logic). The games used for the interpretation of IF logic are 2-player win-lose extensive games of imperfect information. Several game-theoretical phenomena will be discussed in this context, including signaling and indeterminacy. To overcome indeterminacy, we introduce mixed strategies and apply Von Neumann's Minimax Theorem. This results in a probabilistic interpretation of IF sentences (equilibrium semantics). We shall use IF logic and its equilibrium semantics to model some well known examples which involve games with imperfect information: Lewis' signaling games and Monty Hall.

Keywords: Game-theoretical semantics · IF logic · Nash equilibrium · Signalling games · Monty Hall

1 Introduction

Evaluation games for first-order logic have arisen from the work of Hintikka in the 1970s. They led to various applications to natural language phenomena (e.g., pronominal anaphora) in a single framework which is now known as game-theoretical semantics (GTS). Van Benthem [6] is right in emphasizing that these games analyze the 'logical skeleton' of sentence construction: connectives, quantifiers, and anaphoric referential relationships, with logic being the driver of the analysis here. Hintikka and Kulas [29,30] and Hintikka and Sandu [31–34] synthesize some of the work done in this area. This paradigm was amplified in the years that followed but since the late 1980s and during the 1990s there was a switch of interest: logic was still the driving force but the emphasis was on the role of evaluation games for the foundations of mathematics. Drawing on some earlier work by Henkin [26], Hintikka [27] observed that the connection between quantifier dependence and choice functions could be naturally extended to go beyond the patterns allowed by traditional first-order logic. Hintikka and Sandu [31] sketch the general lines of the programme and Hintikka [28] explores the connections between quantifier-independence, choice functions, games of imperfect information and expressive power (descriptive completeness) in the foundations of mathematics. Since the very beginning, Hintikka conceived evaluation games as a challenge to the more traditional compositional paradigm which arose from

© Springer-Verlag Berlin Heidelberg 2015
J. van Benthem et al. (Eds.): Models of Strategic Reasoning, LNCS 8972, pp. 202–251, 2015.
DOI: 10.1007/978-3-662-48540-8_7

the work of Tarski and Montague and constituted the underlying methodology in the model-theoretical tradition. The seminal paper by Hodges [35] showed, nevertheless, that compositional and game-theoretical methods can go hand in hand. Hodges' compositional interpretation has stimulated much of the recent work where quantifier-dependence and independence are replaced with dependence and independence between terms [1,21,23,50].

The present contribution focuses on the interpretation of quantifier-dependence and independence by games of imperfect information. Imperfect information gives rise to two phenomena well known to game theorists: indeterminacy and signaling. As we will see, the former should not be regarded as pathological in logic: we follow a suggestion by Ajtai (reported in [10]) and apply Von Neumann's Minimax Theorem to the underlying games. We will see how the resulting "equilibrium semantics" replaces logic with game theory as the driving force of the analysis. We give several applications (Lewis signaling games, Monty Hall) which show how the value of the corresponding IF sentences are obtained through the iterative elimination of dominated strategies. We also compare the game-theoretical solution to the Monty Hall puzzle to solutions which conditionalize on propositions and actions (update product models with probabilities [7,9]). The chapter will be structured as follows. In Sect. 2 we discuss some of the motivations for introducing patterns of quantifier dependence and independence that go beyond those allowed by ordinary first-order logic (Independence-Friendly Logic, or IF logic, for short). Section 3 contains a short introduction to the semantics of ordinary first-order logic. Section 4 contains a self-contained introduction to the game-theoretical semantics for ordinary first-order logic (semantical games of perfect information). We also discuss alternative frameworks (Skolem semantics). Section 5 introduces the game-theoretical semantics for IF logic (semantical games of imperfect information). In Sect. 6 we discuss some typical examples of game-theoretical phenomena with imperfect information, like signaling, coordination and indeterminacy. Section 7 considers mixed strategies and mixed strategy equilibria which lead to an "equilibrium semantics" for indetermined IF sentences. In Sect. 8 we return to Lewis' signaling games and re-analyse them in IF logic with equilibrium semantics. Section 9 considers some meta-properties of IF strategic games related to expressive power and complexity of finding equilibria. Section 10 contains an analysis of Monty Hall and its modeling in IF logic. Section 11 discusses IF languages as specification languages for games of imperfect information. Finally Sect. 12 mentions some open problems and discusses some of the items on the agenda of future research.

2 Dependence and Independence of Quantifiers

In a seminal paper, Goldfarb tells us that

> "The connection between quantifiers and choice functions or, more precisely, between quantifier-dependence and choice functions, is at the heart of how classical logicians in the twenties viewed the nature of quantification" [22].

A typical illustration is the so-called epsilon-delta definition of a continuous function. A function f is continuous at a point x_0 if given any $\varepsilon > 0$ one can choose $\delta > 0$ so that for all y, when x_0 is within distance δ from y, then $f(x_0)$ is within distance ε from $f(y)$. Ignoring the restrictions on the quantifiers, this definition states the dependence of δ on both x_0 and ε and its independence of y. It is standardly rendered in the logical symbolism by

$$\forall x_0 \forall \varepsilon \exists \delta \forall y [|x_0 - y| < \delta \rightarrow |f(x_0) - f(y)| < \varepsilon].$$

It sometimes turns out that one can find a δ which works no matter what x_0 is. In this case the choice of δ depends only on ε but is independent of x_0. This is known in mathematics as uniform continuity. To express it in the logical formalism we have to rearrange the four quantifiers in a different way:

$$\forall \varepsilon \exists \delta \forall x_0 \forall y [|x_0 - y| < \delta \rightarrow |f(x_0) - f(y)| < \varepsilon].$$

However, there are patterns of quantifiers for which this kind rearrangement does not work any longer. One of them, known to logicians for more than half a century is the following:

1. For every x and x', there exists a y depending only on x and a y' depending only on x' such that $Q(x, x', y, y')$ is true.

Several formalisms have been invented to cope with this limitation. In Henkin [26], (1) is represented by a block of *branching (Henkin) quantifiers*

$$\begin{pmatrix} \forall x & \exists y \\ \forall x' & \exists y' \end{pmatrix} Q(x, x', y, y')$$

whose truth-conditions are given by:

$$\begin{pmatrix} \forall x & \exists y \\ \forall x' & \exists y' \end{pmatrix} Q(x, x', y, y') \Leftrightarrow \exists f \exists g \forall x \forall x' Q(x, x', f(x), g(x')).$$

Here f and g range over unary functions of the universe.

Ehrenfeucht noticed that the "Ehrenfeucht sentence" φ_{eh}

$$\exists w \begin{pmatrix} \forall x & \exists y \\ \forall x' & \exists y' \end{pmatrix} R(x, x', y, y', w)$$

where $R(x, x', y, y', w)$ is the formula

$$w \neq y \wedge (x = x' \leftrightarrow y = y')$$

defines (Dedekind) infinity. Indeed, the truth-conditions of the branching quantifiers render φ_{eh} equivalent with

$$\exists w \exists f \exists g \forall x \forall x' (w \neq f(x) \wedge x = x' \leftrightarrow f(x) = g(y)).$$

Notice that the formula $x = x' \rightarrow f(x) = g(x)$ states that $f = g$ whereas the other direction asserts that f is injective. Thus φ_{eh} asserts that there is an injective function f whose range is not the whole universe, i.e., the universe is infinite. Enderton [15] and Walkoe [53] collect the basic results about Henkin quantifiers and its variants. Krynicki and Mostowski [39] collect the basic results on Henkin quantifiers up to 1995.

Hintikka [27] discusses natural languages examples which match the structure of the branching quantifier, like

2. Some relative of each villager and some relative of each townsman hate each other.

3. Some book by every author is referred to in some essay by every critic.

His conclusion is that one needs a more expressive logic than ordinary first-order logic to serve as a framework of regimentation for natural language. The issue of whether Hintikka's sentences provide genuine examples of branching quantification which exceed the expressive power of first-order logic has been extensively debated. Barwise [5] discusses these matters in details.

Sandu and Hintikka [31] replaced branching quantifiers with a more general linear formalism capable to express arbitrary patterns of quantifier dependence and independence in logic. In the resulting logic, *Independence-friendly logic*, (IF logic for short), (1) is regimented by making explicit the independence of y from x' and that of y' from both x and y:

$$\forall x \forall x' (\exists y / \{x'\})(\exists y' / \{x, y\}) Q(x, x', y, y').$$

IF logic has a game-theoretical semantics which makes it tailor-made for expressing signaling phenomena typically associated with games of imperfect information. It has also been given an alternative compositional interpretation due to Hodges [35] which has recently stimulated various formalisms for expressing dependencies and independencies between variables. One such formalism is Väänänen's *Dependence logic* [50]. It keeps the linear ordering of the first-order quantifiers intact but introduces new atomic formulas which expresses the relevant dependencies at the level of terms, e.g.

$$\forall x \forall x' \exists y \exists y' (= (x, y) \wedge = (x', y') \wedge Q(x, x', y, y')).$$

Here $= (x, y)$ means: y functionally depends on x.

In this chapter we shall focus on Independence-friendly logic and its interpretation in terms of semantical games of imperfect information. We start by shortly reviewing Hintikka's game-theoretical interpretation (GTS) for standard first-order logic.

3 First-Order Languages

Our presentation here will follow quite closely [42]. We recall that a vocabulary is a set of relation symbols and constant symbols, each endowed with a natural number (arity) which indicates the number of arguments the symbol accepts. Function symbols of arity 0 are called individual constants. In addition to the vocabulary, we have a countably infinite set $\{x_0, x_1, \ldots\}$ of variables. Function symbols combine with variables and individual constants to form more complex terms in the usual way. Relation symbols combine with terms to form atomic formulas which, in turn, combine with the quantifiers $\exists x$ and $\forall x$ and with the connectives $\neg$, $\vee$ and $\wedge$ to form compound formulas. A first-order formula is thus always defined relatively to an underlying vocabulary L that we shall often leave unspecified. Formulas of the form $t_1 = t_2$ or $R(t_1, \ldots, t_n)$ are called atomic. A literal is either an atomic formula or its negation.

A particular occurrence of a variable x is free in the formula φ if it does not lie within the scope of any quantifier of the form $\exists x$ or $\forall x$. This can be made more precise through an inductive definition. For atomic formulas φ, all its variables are free. For compound formulas we have:

$$
\begin{aligned}
Free(\neg\varphi) &= Free(\varphi) \\
Free(\varphi \wedge \psi) = Free(\varphi \vee \psi) &= Free(\varphi) \cup Free(\psi) \\
Free(\exists x\varphi) = Free(\forall x\varphi) &= Free(\varphi) - \{x\}.
\end{aligned}
$$

An occurrence of a variable is bound if it is not free. Notice that a variable is bound by the innermost quantifier in whose scope it lies. A formula with no free variables is called a sentence. A formula is in negation normal form if all occurrences of the negation symbol $\neg$ are infront of atomic formulas.

3.1   Models

First-order formulas receive an interpretation through models. A model $\mathbb{M}$ for a vocabulary $L = \{R, \ldots, f, \ldots c, \ldots\}$, or an L-model, has the form

$$
\mathbb{M} = (M; R^{\mathbb{M}}, \ldots, f^{\mathbb{M}}, \ldots, c^{\mathbb{M}}, \ldots)
$$

where M is a non-empty set called the universe of $\mathbb{M}$. If R is an n-ary relation symbol, then its interpretation R^M is an n-ary relation on M; if f is an n-ary function symbol, then its interpretation f^M is an n-ary function on M; and if c is an individual constant, then its interpretation c^M is a member (0-place function) of M. Let $\mathbb{M}$ be an L-model, $\mathbb{M}'$ an L'-model, and $L \subseteq L'$. If $\mathbb{M}$ and $\mathbb{M}'$ have the same universe, and in addition, for every relation symbol R in L, $R^{\mathbb{M}} = R^{\mathbb{M}'}$, for every function symbol f in L, $f^{\mathbb{M}} = f^{\mathbb{M}'}$, then $\mathbb{M}'$ is called an expansion of $\mathbb{M}$ to L'.

3.2   Assignments

A model gives an interpretation for the relation and function symbols of a given vocabulary, but not for variables. This job is done by assignments. Let $\mathbb{M}$ be a model. An assignment in $\mathbb{M}$ is a partial function from a (finite) set of variables to M. If s is an assignment in $\mathbb{M}$, and $a \in M$, then $s(x_i/a)$ is the assignment with domain $dom(s) \cup \{x_i\}$ defined by: $s(x_i/a)(x_j) = s(x_j)$ if $i \neq j$; and $s(x_i/a)(x_j) = a$ if $i = j$. That is, $s' = s(x/a)$ is exactly like s except that $s'(x) = a$. Notice that if $x \in dom(s)$, then the value that s assigns to x is overwritten when we assign it a new value.

3.3   Satisfaction of Atomic Formulas

Once an assignment s in a model $\mathbb{M}$ is fixed, every term t in the underlying language receives an interpretation $s(t)$ under that assignment:

$$s(c) \quad = \quad c^{\mathbb{M}}$$
$$s(f(t_1,\ldots,t_n)) = f^{\mathbb{M}}(s(t_1),\ldots,s(t_n)).$$

We are now ready for the definition of satisfaction in a model $\mathbb{M}$ of an atomic formula relative to an assignment s to its free variables:

Definition. Let L be a vocabulary, M an L-model, and s an assignment in M. Then

$$\mathbb{M}, s \models t_1 = t_2 \quad \textit{iff} \quad s(t_1) = s(t_2)$$
$$\mathbb{M}, s \models R(t_1,\ldots,t_n) \textit{ iff } (s(t_1),\ldots,s(t_n)) \in R^{\mathbb{M}}.$$

It may be useful to give an example at this stage. Let $\mathbb{N} = \{\omega; +^{\mathbb{N}}, \cdot^{\mathbb{N}}, \leq^{\mathbb{N}}\}$ be the standard model of the language of arithmetics, i.e., its universe ω is the set of natural numbers, $+^{\mathbb{N}}$ and $\cdot^{\mathbb{N}}$ are the usual operations of multiplication and addition on the natural numbers and $\leq^{\mathbb{N}}$ is the standard ordering relation. Let s be an assignment such that $s(x) = 2$ and $s(y) = 5$. Then

$$\mathbb{N}, s \models x \leq y \qquad\qquad \mathbb{N}, s \nvDash y \leq x$$
$$\mathbb{N}, s \models x + y = y + x \quad \mathbb{N}, s \nvDash (x \cdot y) + x = (x + y) \cdot x$$

4   Game-Theoretical Semantics

A semantical game is played by two players, $\exists$ (Eloise) and $\forall$ (Abelard). They consider a first-order formula φ in negation normal form, model $\mathbb{M}$, which interprets the vocabulary of φ, and an assignment s in $\mathbb{M}$ which includes the free variables of φ. $\exists$ tries to show that φ is true in $\mathbb{M}$ (relative to the assignment s), and $\forall$ tries to show that φ is false in $\mathbb{M}$. The game starts from the initial position (φ, s), and after each move the players reach a position (ψ, r), where ψ is a subformula of φ and r is an assignment which eventually extends or modify s. Here are the rules of the game:

1. (ψ, r), where ψ is a literal. The game stops. If $\mathbb{M}, r \models \psi$ then $\exists$ wins. Otherwise $\forall$ wins. Notice that the notion $\mathbb{M}, r \models \psi$ has been defined in Sect. 3.3.
2. $(\psi \vee \psi', r)$: $\exists$ chooses $\theta \in \{\psi, \psi'\}$ and players move to (θ, r).
3. $(\psi \wedge \psi', r)$: $\forall$ chooses $\theta \in \{\psi, \psi'\}$ and players move to (θ, r).
4. $(\exists x \psi, r)$: $\exists$ chooses $a \in M$ and players move to $(\psi, r(x/a))$.
5. $(\forall x \psi, r)$: $\forall$ chooses $a \in M$ and players move to $(\psi, r(x/a))$.

We denote this game by $G(\mathbb{M}, s, \varphi)$. It may be easily reformulated as a finite two-player, win-lose extensive game with perfect information,

$$G(\mathbb{M}, s, \varphi) = (N, H, Z, P, (u_p)_{p \in N})$$

where

- N is the set of players, $N = \{\exists, \forall\}$,
- H is the set of histories of the game,
- Z is the set of maximal histories (plays),
- $P : H \setminus Z \to N$ is the player function which tells whose player's turn is to move, and finally
- $u_p \colon Z \to \{0, 1\}$ is the payoff function for player p such that for each $h \in Z$: $u_p(h) = 0$ or $u_p(h) = 1$ (but not both).

The last condition makes the win-lose property of the game explicit. When $u_p(h) = 1$ we say that p wins the play h; and when $u_p(h) = 0$, we say that p loses h.

Example. Let φ be the sentence $\forall x \exists y \; x = y$ and $\mathbb{M} = \{a, b\}$. In the initial position $(\varphi, \varnothing)$ ($\varnothing$ is the empty assignment), Abelard can choose either a or b which generates the histories

$$h_a = ((\varphi, \varnothing), (\psi, \{(x, a)\}))$$
$$h_b = ((\varphi, \varnothing), (\psi, \{(x, b)\})).$$

Each of them is a choice point for Eloise, who can choose either a or b. This results in four maximal histories (plays):

$$h_{aa} = ((\varphi, \varnothing), (\exists y \; x = y, \{(x, a)\}), (x = y, \{(x, a), (y, a)\}))$$
$$h_{ab} = ((\varphi, \varnothing), (\exists y \; x = y, \{(x, a)\}), (x = y, \{(x, a), (y, b)\}))$$
$$h_{ba} = ((\varphi, \varnothing), (\exists y \; x = y, \{(x, b)\}), (x = y, \{(x, b), (y, a)\}))$$
$$h_{bb} = ((\varphi, \varnothing), (\exists y \; x = y, \{(x, b)\}), (x = y, \{(x, b), (y, b)\}))$$

Eloise wins both h_{aa} and h_{bb}, that is, $u_\exists(h_{aa}) = u_\exists(h_{bb}) = 1$ (and thereby $u_\forall(h_{aa}) = u_\forall(h_{bb}) = 0$); on the other side, Abelard wins both h_{ab} and h_{ba}. In the game-theoretical literature, it is customary to represent extensive games in the form of a tree: the initial history (φ, s) is the root of the tree and a play proceeds down the branches. An extensive game has finite horizon if each of its histories is finite. The extensive game in our example can be presented in a tree form, as shown in Fig. 1.

Here the payoffs of the payers are indicated by the corresponding quantifiers: e.g. the existential quantifier indicates the payoff $(1,0)$, etc.

4.1 Game-Theoretical Truth and Falsity

When making choices as prescribed by the rules of the game, each player follows a (deterministic) strategy which gives him or her the next move to make. A strategy for player p in the game $G(\mathbb{M}, s, \varphi)$ is a function σ defined on all (non-maximal) histories h where p is to move; $\sigma(h)$ is the next position to be reached in the game. The strategy σ is winning for p if p wins every maximal history (play) where he or she follows σ. In the last example there are four strategies for Eloise, but only one is winning, σ_{ab} defined by (Fig. 1):

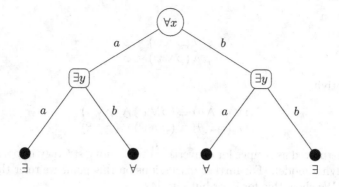

Fig. 1. The semantic game for $\forall x \exists y (x = y)$ in the structure $\mathbb{M} = \{a, b\}$

$$\sigma_{ab}(h_a) = (y, a) \text{ and } \sigma_{ab}(h_b) = (y, b)$$

Eloise follows it in h_{aa} and h_{bb} that she both wins. On the other side, Abelard has two possible strategies, τ_a and τ_b,

$$\tau_a(\varphi, \varnothing) = (x, a) \text{ and } \tau_a(\varphi, \varnothing) = (x, b)$$

He follows the former in h_{aa} and h_{ab} and the latter in h_{ba} and h_{bb}. None of them is winning.

We are now ready to define game-theoretical truth, $\mathbb{M}, s \models_{GTS}^{+} \varphi$, and game-theoretical falsity, $\mathbb{M}, s \models_{GTS}^{-} \varphi$.

Definition. Let φ be a first-order L-formula, $\mathbb{M}$ an L-model and s an assignment in M whose domain contains $Free(\varphi)$. Then

- $\mathbb{M}, s \models_{GTS}^{+} \varphi$ iff there is a winning strategy for Eloise in $G(\mathbb{M}, s, \varphi)$
- $\mathbb{M}, s \models_{GTS}^{-} \varphi$ iff there is a winning strategy for Abelard in $G(\mathbb{M}, s, \varphi)$.

The principle of determinacy, stated below and known as Zermelo Theorem, ensures us that the principle of bivalence holds:

Theorem (Zermelo [54]). Every win-lose game with finite horizon and one initial root is determinate.

An advantage of rephrasing truth and falsity in game-theoretical terms is that many of the logical equivalences of ordinary first-order logic like

- Commutativity

$$\varphi \wedge \psi \equiv \psi \wedge \varphi$$

- Associativity

$$\varphi \vee (\psi \vee \theta) \equiv (\varphi \vee \psi) \vee \theta$$
$$\varphi \wedge (\psi \wedge \theta) \equiv (\varphi \wedge \psi) \wedge \theta$$

– Absorption

$$\varphi \vee (\varphi \wedge \psi) \equiv \varphi$$
$$\varphi \wedge (\varphi \vee \psi) \equiv \varphi$$

– Distributivity

$$\varphi \vee (\psi \wedge \theta) \equiv (\varphi \vee \psi) \wedge (\varphi \vee \theta)$$
$$\varphi \wedge (\psi \vee \theta) \equiv (\varphi \wedge \psi) \vee (\varphi \wedge \theta)$$

may be interpreted as recipes for converting one winning strategy into another in any underlying model. (For further discussions on this point we refer the reader to [8, 42]). We show this for distributivity [42].

Suppose Eloise has a winning strategy σ in the game $G(\mathbb{M}, s, \varphi \vee (\psi \wedge \theta))$. Suppose the first choice of Eloise according to σ is φ. Define a winning strategy τ for Eloise in $G(\mathbb{M}, s, (\varphi \vee \psi) \wedge (\varphi \vee \theta))$ as follows. If Abelard chooses $\varphi \vee \psi$, then let τ pick up φ and then mimic σ for the rest of the game in φ. If Abelard chooses $\varphi \vee \theta$, then let τ pick up φ and mimic σ for the rest of the game in φ.

Suppose now that the first choice of Eloise according to σ is $(\psi \wedge \theta)$. Then σ must be a winning strategy in both ψ and θ. Define a winning strategy τ for Eloise in $G(\mathbb{M}, s, (\varphi \vee \psi) \wedge (\varphi \vee \theta))$ as follows. If Abelard chooses $\varphi \vee \psi$, then let τ pick up ψ and mimic σ for the rest of the game in ψ. If Abelard chooses $\varphi \vee \theta$, then let τ pick up θ and mimic σ for the rest of the game in θ. The converse is shown in a similar way.

4.2   Game-Theoretical Negation

We relax the assumption that negation occurs only in front of atomic formulas. Then we need a game-rule for negation. It will be given in terms of the players "switching roles". This in turn justifies the need for introducing roles for the two players.

– At the beginning of the game $\exists$ is (has the role of) the Verifier (V) and $\forall$ is the Falsifier (F)

The rules of the game $G(\mathbb{M}, s, \varphi)$ are now restated as:

– $(P(t_1, \ldots, t_n), r)$: The game stops. If r satisfies $P(t_1, \ldots, t_n)$, then V wins. Otherwise F wins.
– $(\neg \psi, r)$: Players move to (B, r) with roles inversed.
– $(\psi \vee \psi', r)$: V chooses $\theta \in \{\psi, \psi'\}$ and players move to (θ, r).
– $(\psi \wedge \psi', r)$: F chooses $\theta \in \{\psi, \psi'\}$ and players move to (θ, r).
– $(\exists x \psi, r)$: V chooses $a \in M$ and players move to $(\psi, r(x/a))$.
– $(\forall x \psi, r)$: F chooses $a \in M$ and players move to $(\psi, r(x/a))$.

Obviously we are still inside the class of finite, 2-player, win-lose extensive games of perfect information. The notion of strategy for a player p is defined exactly as before, as are game-theoretical truth and falsity. Zermelo's theorem still applies. The switching role interpretation of negation justifies the following fact:

Proposition. Let φ be a first-order L-formula, $\mathbb{M}$ an L-model and s an assignment in $\mathbb{M}$ whose domain contains $Free(\varphi)$. Then

$$\mathbb{M}, s \models^+_{GTS} \neg\varphi \text{ iff } \mathbb{M}, s \models^-_{GTS} \varphi$$
$$\mathbb{M}, s \models^-_{GTS} \neg\varphi \text{ iff } \mathbb{M}, s \models^+_{GTS} \varphi.$$

It follows from Zermelo's theorem that for first-order logic game-theoretical negation is contradictory negation [42].

Proposition. Let φ be a first-order L-formula, $\mathbb{M}$ an L-model and s an assignment in $\mathbb{M}$ whose domain contains $Free(\varphi)$. Then

$$\mathbb{M}, s \models^+_{GTS} \neg\varphi \text{ iff } \mathbb{M}, s \not\models^+_{GTS} \varphi.$$

Proof. Suppose that $\mathbb{M}, s \models^+_{GTS} \neg\varphi$. By the previous proposition, Abelard has a winning strategy in $G(\mathbb{M}, s, \varphi)$. But then Eloise cannot have one ($G(\mathbb{M}, s, \varphi)$ is a win-lose game). Conversely, suppose that Eloise does not have a winning strategy in $G(\mathbb{M}, s, \varphi)$. Then by Zermelo's theorem, Abelard has one, i.e. $\mathbb{M}, s \models^-_{GTS} \varphi$ which by the previous proposition implies $\mathbb{M}, s \models^+_{GTS} \neg\varphi$.

There is another property of game-theoretical negation that is worth mentioning: it is dual negation, that is, it travels through the quantifiers and connectives in its scope, changes them into their duals (i.e. it changes $\exists x$, $\forall x$, $\vee$, and $\wedge$ into $\forall x$, $\exists x$, $\wedge$, and $\vee$ respectively) until it reaches an atomic formula. Instead of giving a formal definition we prefer an example:

$$\mathbb{M}, s \models^\pm_{GTS} \neg\exists x\forall y\exists z\forall w R(x,y,z,w) \text{ iff } \mathbb{M}, s \models^\pm_{GTS} \forall x\exists y\forall z\exists w\neg R(x,y,z,w).$$

4.3 Decomposing Strategies: Skolem Functions and Kreisel Counterexamples

Strategies in extensive games are "global": they are defined for every history which is a choice point for the relevant player. Every such strategy can be decomposed into "local" strategies, one for every move of the given player. Local strategies are completely determined by the syntax of the given formula and the underlying model [42].

Definition. Let φ be an ordinary first-order formula in negation normal form in a given vocabulary L. The skolemized form or skolemization of φ, with free variables in the set U, $Sk_U(\varphi)$, is given by the following clauses:

1. $Sk_U(\psi) = \psi$, for ψ a literal
2. $Sk_U(\psi \circ \theta) = Sk_U(\psi) \circ Sk_U(\theta)$, for $\circ \in \{\vee, \wedge\}$
3. $Sk_U(\forall x\psi) = \forall x Sk_{U\cup\{x\}}(\psi)$
4. $Sk_U(\exists x\psi) = Sub(Sk_{U\cup\{x\}}(\psi), x, f(y_1, \ldots, y_n))$,

where $y_1, \ldots, y_n$ are all the variables in U and f is a new function symbol of appropriate arity. Here $Sub(Sk_{U\cup\{x\}}(\psi), x, f(y_1, \ldots, y_n))$ denotes the formula which is the result of the substitution of the Skolem term $f(y_1, \ldots, y_n)$ for the variable x in the formula ψ. We abbreviate $Sk_\varnothing(\varphi)$ by $Sk(\varphi)$.

Skolemizing a first-order sentence makes explicit the dependencies of variables, as Goldfarb pointed out. We obtain an alternative definition of truth.

Definition. Let φ be a first-order L-formula, $\mathbb{M}$ an L-model and s an assignment in $\mathbb{M}$ whose domain contains $Free(\varphi)$. Then $\mathbb{M}, s \models^+_{Sk} \varphi$ if and only if there exist functions $g_1, \ldots, g_n$ of appropriate arity in $\mathbb{M}$ to be the interpretations of the new function symbols in $Sk_U(\varphi)$ such that

$$\mathbb{M}, g_1, \ldots, g_n, s \models Sk_{dom(s)}(\varphi)$$

where U is the domain of s and $\mathbb{M}, g_1, \ldots, g_n$ is the expansion of $\mathbb{M}$ to the new vocabulary which includes the new function symbols in $Sk_U(\varphi)$. The functions $g_1, \ldots, g_n$ are called Skolem functions.

Global strategies can be converted into local ones and vice versa.

Theorem. Let φ be a first-order sentence in negation normal form. Then for any model $\mathbb{M}$:

$$\mathbb{M} \models^+_{GTS} \varphi \text{ iff } \mathbb{M} \models^+_{Sk} \varphi$$

Proof. A model-theoretical proof for particular first-order games is given in Mann et al. (2011). For game theorists this is a dejà vu result. First-order games $G(\mathbb{M}, s, \varphi)$ are extensive 2-player win-lose games with perfect information. Look at the associated strategic game. After deleting all the weakly dominated strategies one gets the solution of the game. This observation follows from Ewerhart [16, 17] who shows that any perfect information extensive-form strictly competitive game with n different payoffs can be solved in $n - 1$ rounds. Thus first-order games, having two distinct payoffs, are solvable in one round. The notions of strategic game and weakly dominated strategy will be introduced in Sect. 7.1.

We now define the dual procedure of Skolemization.

Definition. Let φ be an ordinary first-order formula in negation normal form in a given vocabulary L with free variables in U. The Kreisel form $Kr_U(\varphi)$ of φ is defined by:

1. $Kr_U(\psi) = \neg \psi$, for ψ a literal
2. $Kr_U(\psi \vee \theta) = Kr_U(\psi) \wedge Kr_U(\theta)$,
3. $Kr_U(\psi \wedge \theta) = Kr_U(\psi) \vee Kr_U(\theta)$
4. $Kr_U(\exists x \psi) = \forall x Kr_{U \cup \{x\}}(\psi)$
5. $Kr_U(\forall x \psi) = Sub(Kr_{U \cup \{x\}}(\psi), x, g(y_1, \ldots, y_m))$

where $y_1, \ldots, y_m$ are all the variables in U.

Definition. Let φ be a first-order L-formula, $\mathbb{M}$ an L-model and s an assignment in $\mathbb{M}$ whose domain contains $Free(\varphi)$. Then $\mathbb{M}, s \models^-_{Sk} \varphi$ if and only if there exist $h_1, \ldots, h_m$ in M to be the interpretations of the new function symbols in $Kr(\varphi)$ such that

$$\mathbb{M}, h_1, \ldots, h_m, s \models Kr_{dom(s)}(\varphi)$$

where U is the domain of s. We call $h_1, \ldots, h_m$ Kreisel counterexamples.

The illustrate the relation between Skolem functions and Kreisel's counterexamples, let's look at the following example [49, p. 224]. Let φ be the first-order formula

$$\exists x \forall y \exists z \forall w R(x, y, z, w).$$

The Kreisel form of φ is $\forall x \forall z \neg R(x, f(x), z, g(x, f(x), z))$. We pointed out in Sect. 4.2 that $\neg \varphi$ is game-theoretically equivalent to $\forall x \exists y \forall z \exists w \neg R(x, y, z, w)$. The Skolem form $Sk(\neg \varphi)$ is $\forall x \forall z \neg R(x, f(x), z, g(x, f(x), z))$ (actually in first-order logic, φ is equivalent to $\forall x \forall z \neg R(x, f(x), z, g(x, z)))$. In addition, from the first proposition in Sect. 4.2 we know that for any model $\mathbb{M}$ we have

$$\mathbb{M} \models^{+}_{GTS} \neg \varphi \text{ iff } \mathbb{M} \models^{-}_{GTS} \varphi.$$

It follows that $\mathbb{M} \models^{-}_{GTS} \varphi$ if and only if $\mathbb{M} \models^{+}_{GTS} \neg \varphi$ if and only if $\mathbb{M} \models^{+}_{GTS} \forall x \exists y \forall z \exists w \neg R(x, y, z, w)$. The last statement is equivalent, by the definition of truth under Skolem semantics and its equivalence with game-theoretical truth, to the existence of appropriate Skolem functions h, k such that

$$M, h, k \models \forall x \forall z \neg R(x, f(x), z, g(x, f(x), z)).$$

We have abusively followed Shoenfield and called h and k (Kreisel) counterexamples (to φ). We see that the falsity of φ amounts to the existence of certain counterexamples to φ which in turn become the appropriate Skolem functions witnessing the truth of $\neg \varphi$. By the second proposition of Sect. 4.2. we also know that

$$\mathbb{M} \models^{+}_{GTS} \neg \varphi \text{ iff } \mathbb{M} \not\models^{+}_{GTS} \varphi.$$

Then $\mathbb{M} \models^{+}_{GTS} \varphi$ if and only if $\mathbb{M} \not\models^{-}_{GTS} \varphi$. In other words, φ is true if and only if there are no counterexamples h and k to φ. (Shoenfield's main interest is in Kreisel's No Counterexample Interpretation: the connection between the non-existence of counterexamples to φ and the existence of higher-order functionals $F(f, g)$ and $G(f, g)$ useful in proving the consistency of arithmetic. That has not been our concern here).

One can show, as in the Skolemization case, that global strategies for Abelard can be converted into Kreisel counterexamples and vice versa.

Theorem ([42]). Let φ be a first-order sentence in negation normal form. Then for every model $\mathbb{M}$:

$$\mathbb{M} \models^{-}_{GTS} \varphi \text{ iff } \mathbb{M} \models^{-}_{Sk} \varphi.$$

The game-theoretical semantics and the alternative Skolem semantics for first-order logic that we presented in this section have natural extensions when we switch to Independence-Friendly Logic in the next section.

5   Independence-Friendly Logic (IF Logic)

Independence-Friendly Logic (IF logic) will turn out to offer a handy tool for modeling various phenomena of imperfect information. After presenting its syntax, we shall present a game-theoretical interpretation (games of imperfect information) and alternative Skolem semantics we will follow the presentation in [42].

5.1   The Syntax

The independence-friendly language IF_L is obtained from a basic vocabulary L through the following rules:

- If t_1 and t_2 are L-terms, then $(t_1 = t_2) \in IF_L$ and $\neg(t_1 = t_2) \in IF_L$.
- If R is an n-ary relation symbol in L and $t_1, \ldots, t_n$ are L-terms, then
  $R(t_1, \ldots, t_n) \in IF_L$ and $\neg R(t_1, \ldots, t_n) \in IF_L$.
- If $\varphi, \psi \in IF_L$ and W is a finite set of variables, then $(\varphi (\vee/W) \psi) \in IF_L$ and
  $(\varphi (\wedge/W) \psi) \in IF_L$.
- If $\varphi \in IF_L$, x is a variable and W is a finite set of variables, then
  $(\exists x/W)\varphi \in IF_L$ and $(\forall x/W)\varphi \in IF_L$.

The interpretation of e.g. $(\exists x/W)$ is: "the choice of x is independent of the values of the variables in W". When $W = \varnothing$, we recover the standard quantifiers and connectives. Notice that we restrict attention to IF formulas in negation normal form. In this chapter we shall consider only standard disjunctions and conjunctions.

The set of free variables of an IF formula φ is defined as in ordinary first-order logic, except for the clauses for the quantifiers which are now replaced by:

$$Free((\exists x/W)\varphi) = Free(\forall x/W)\varphi) = (Free(\varphi) - \{x\}) \cup W.$$

5.2   Semantical Games: Extensive Games of Imperfect Information

The notions of models, assignments and the satisfaction clauses for atomic formulas are the same as for ordinary first-order languages. The game-theoretical interpretation of the latter naturally extends to the present case: the assumption of the players' information in finite 2-player, win-lose extensive games is now relaxed to imperfect information.

The rules of a semantical game $G(\mathbb{M}, s, \varphi)$ where φ is an IF formula in negation normal form, $\mathbb{M}$ is a model which interprets the vocabulary of φ, and s is an assignment in $\mathbb{M}$ which includes the free variables of φ are identical with the five rules given earlier: in the last two clauses $(\exists x\psi, r)$ and $(\forall x\psi, r)$ are replaced with $((\exists x/W)\psi, r)$ and $((\forall x/W)\psi, r)$, respectively. The changes will affect only the information sets and thereby the strategies of the players. The imperfect information comes in the form of the players' restricted access to the current assignment in the game.

Let W be a set of finite variables, s and s' be two assignments in a model $\mathbb{M}$ with the same domain which includes W. We say that that s and s' are W-equivalent, $s \approx_W s'$, if for every variable $x \in dom(s) \setminus W$ we have $s(x) = s'(x)$.

Every history h in $G(\mathbb{M}, s, \varphi)$ induces an assignment s_h in the model $\mathbb{M}$, which extends or modifies the initial assignment s. We are going to define two indistinguishable relations $\sim_\exists$ and $\sim_\forall$ on the set of non-maximal histories of the game.

For $\sim_\exists$ there are two cases:

- It is Eloise's turn to move corresponding to a disjunction $\psi \vee \psi'$. In the context of the extensive game, let h and h' be two histories in the game where such a move is supposed to happen. Then we stipulate that

$$h \sim_\exists h' \Leftrightarrow s_h = s_{h'}.$$

- It is Eloise's turn to move corresponding to $(\exists x / W)\psi$. Then for any two histories h, h' where such a move is about to happen, we stipulate:

$$h \sim_\exists h' \Leftrightarrow s_h \approx_W s_{h'}.$$

The relation $\sim_\forall$ is specified completely analogously.

The relations $\sim_\exists$ and $\sim_\forall$ specify exactly how much information the players have at their disposal at a given decision point.

A strategy σ_p for player p in the semantical game $G(\mathbb{M}, s, \varphi)$ is defined exactly as in the games of perfect information, except for the requirement of uniformity: for every h, h'

$$h \sim_p h' \Rightarrow \sigma_p(h) = \sigma_p(h').$$

5.3 Game-Theoretical Truth and Falsity

Truth and falsity of an IF formula in a model are defined exactly as before, keeping in mind, of course, that strategies are now uniform:

Definition. Let φ be an IF formula, $\mathbb{M}$ a model and s an assignment in $\mathbb{M}$ whose domain includes $Free(\psi)$. Then

- $\mathbb{M}, s \models^+_{GTS} \psi$ iff there is a winning strategy for $\exists$ in $G(\mathbb{M}, s, \psi)$
- $\mathbb{M}, s \models^-_{GTS} \psi$ iff there is a winning strategy for $\forall$ in $G(\mathbb{M}, s, \psi)$.

Imperfect information introduces indeterminacy into the logic, as the next example shows.

Example (Matching Pennies). This is a well known game played by two players, who turn secretly a coin to Heads or Tails. The coins are revealed simultaneously. The first player wins if the outcomes match; the second player wins if they differ. We can express this game in IF logic using a variant φ_{MP} of our earlier example, $\varphi_{MP} = \forall x (\exists y / \{x\}) \, x = y$ interpreted in a two element

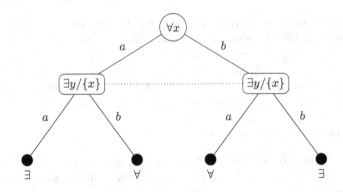

Fig. 2. The semantic game for $\forall x(\exists y/\{x\})x = y$ in the structure $\mathbb{M} = \{a, b\}$

model $\mathbb{M} = \{a, b\}$. The extensive game can be represented in a tree form (Fig. 2)
where the dots indicate that the two histories

$$h_a = ((\varphi_{MP}, \varnothing), ((\exists y/\{x\})\, x = y, \{(x, a)\}))$$
$$h_b = ((\varphi_{MP}, \varnothing), ((\exists y/\{x\})\, x = y, \{(x, b)\}))$$

are equivalent for Eloise, i.e., $h_a \sim_\exists h_b$. (Note that the corresponding assignments $\{(x, a)\}$ and $\{(x, b)\}$ are trivially $\{x\}$-equivalent). Let σ be a strategy for Eloise. Given the uniformity requirement, Eloise must choose the same value c for y in both cases:

$$\sigma(h_a) = \sigma(h_b) = (y, c).$$

There are two maximal plays

$$((\varphi_{MP}, \varnothing), ((\exists y/\{x\})\, x = y, \{(x, a)\}), (x = y, \{(x, a), (y, c)\}))$$
$$((\varphi_{MP}, \varnothing), ((\exists y/\{x\})\, x = y, \{(x, b)\}), (x = y, \{(x, b), (y, c)\}))$$

where this strategy is followed, of which Eloise wins only one. Let τ be a strategy for Abelard such that $\tau(\varphi_{MP}, \varnothing) = (x, c)$. Then τ is a winning strategy iff Abelard wins both maximal plays

$$((\varphi_{MP}, \varnothing), ((\exists y/\{x\})\, x = y, \{(x, c)\}), (x = y, \{(x, c), (y, a)\}))$$
$$((\varphi_{MP}, \varnothing), ((\exists y/\{x\})\, x = y, \{(x, c)\}), (x = y, \{(x, c), (y, b)\}))$$

which is again impossible. Thus neither Eloise nor Abelard has a winning strategy in the game.

5.4   Skolem Semantics

As in the case of first-order logic, we give also an alternative interpretation in terms of Skolem functions and Kreisel counterexamples which will turn out to be useful later on. The Skolem form of an IF formula in negation normal form is defined exactly as in the first-order case, except for the clauses:

$$Sk_U((\forall x/W)\psi) = \forall x Sk_{U \cup \{x\}}(\psi)$$
$$Sk_U((\exists x/W)\psi) = Sub(Sk_{U \cup \{x\}}(\psi), x, f(y_1, \ldots, y_n))$$

where $y_1, \ldots, y_n$ are all the variables in $U \setminus W$ and f is a new function symbol of appropriate arity.

In a similar spirit, the Kreisel form is defined exactly as in the first-order case, except for the clauses:

$$Kr_U((\exists x/W)\psi) = \forall x Kr_{U \cup \{x\}}(\psi)$$
$$Kr_U((\forall x/W)\psi) = Sub(Kr_{U \cup \{x\}}(\psi), x, g(y_1, \ldots, y_m))$$

where $y_1, \ldots, y_m$ are all the variables in $U \setminus W$.

Truth and falsity in the Skolem semantics is defined analogously with the first-order case.

Definition. Let φ be an IF formula in negation normal form, $\mathbb{M}$ a model, and s an assignment in $\mathbb{M}$ whose domain includes the free variables of φ. Then

(i) $\mathbb{M}, s \vDash^+_{Sk} \varphi$ if and only if there exist functions $g_1, \ldots, g_n$ of appropriate arity in $\mathbb{M}$ to be the interpretations of the new function symbols in $Sk_{dom(s)}(\varphi)$ such that

$$\mathbb{M}, g_1, \ldots, g_n, s \vDash Sk_{dom(s)}(\varphi)$$

(ii) $\mathbb{M}, s \vDash^-_{Sk} \varphi$ if and only if there exist functions $g_1, \ldots, g_m$ of appropriate arity in $\mathbb{M}$ to be the interpretations of the new function symbols in $Kr_{dom(s)}(\varphi)$ such that

$$\mathbb{M}, g_1, \ldots, g_m, s \vDash Kr_{dom(s)}(\varphi).$$

Like in the first-order case, global strategies can be converted into local ones and vice versa.

Theorem ([42]). Let φ be an IF sentence in negation normal form. Then for any model $\mathbb{M}$:
 (i) $\mathbb{M} \vDash^+_{GTS} \varphi$ if and only if $\mathbb{M} \vDash^+_{Sk} \varphi$.
 (ii) $\mathbb{M} \vDash^-_{GTS} \varphi$ if and only if $\mathbb{M} \vDash^-_{Sk} \varphi$.

Proof. This is Theorem 4.13 in [42]. The proof exploits the fact that the uniformity of the strategies of e.g. Eloise in the extensive game of imperfect information has a clear counterpart in the relevant Skolem functions taking as arguments only the values of those quantified variables that she "sees". We shall give several examples.

Example. Hodges [35] discusses the following sentence φ_H (Hodges sentence)

$$\forall x \exists z (\exists y / \{x\}) x = y$$

which is formed from the Matching Pennies sentence φ_{MP} by inserting the dummy quantifier $\exists z$. Surprisingly Eloise has a winning strategy (on any model M with at least two elements) whereas she does not have one in the game $G(M, \varnothing, \varphi_{MP})$, as shown earlier. For convenience, let ψ abbreviate the subformula $\exists z (\exists y / \{x\}) x = y$ and χ abbreviate the subformula $(\exists y / \{x\}) x = y$. Note that corresponding to $\exists z$ there are two histories where Eloise is to move

$$h_a = ((\varphi_{MP}, \varnothing), (\psi, \{(x, a)\}))$$
$$h_b = ((\varphi_{MP}, \varnothing), (\psi, \{(x, b)\})).$$

and corresponding to $(\exists y / \{x\})$ there are four histories where she is to move:

$$h_{aa} = ((\varphi_{MP}, \varnothing), (\psi, \{(x, a)\}), (\chi, \{(x, a), (z, a)\}))$$
$$h_{ba} = ((\varphi_{MP}, \varnothing), (\psi, \{(x, b)\}), (\chi, \{(x, b), (z, a)\}))$$
$$h_{ab} = ((\varphi_{MP}, \varnothing), (\psi, \{(x, a)\}), (\chi, \{(x, a), (z, b)\}))$$
$$h_{bb} = ((\varphi_{MP}, \varnothing), (\psi, \{(x, b)\}), (\chi, \{(x, b), (z, b)\})).$$

We can represent the game in the following tree form (Fig. 3):

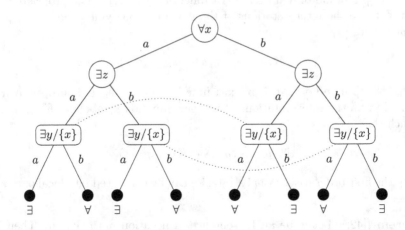

Fig. 3. The semantic game for $\forall x \exists z (\exists y / \{x\}) x = y$ in $M = \{a, b\}$

We observe that the corresponding assignments are such that $s_a \sim_\varnothing s_a$, and $s_b \sim_\varnothing s_b$. In addition, $s_{aa} \approx_{\{x\}} s_{ba}$, and $s_{ab} \approx_{\{x\}} s_{bb}$, hence $h_{aa} \sim_\exists h_{ba}$ and $h_{ab} \sim_\exists h_{bb}$. Therefore by the uniformity requirement, Eloise's strategies σ must be such that $\sigma(h_{aa}) = \sigma(h_{ba})$ and $\sigma(h_{ab}) = \sigma(h_{bb})$. Here is a winning strategy:

$$\sigma(h_a) = (y, a) \text{ and } \sigma(h_{aa}) = \sigma(h_{ba}) = (y, a)$$
$$\sigma(h_b) = (y, b) \text{ and } \sigma(h_{ab}) = \sigma(h_{bb}) = (y, b).$$

There are two maximal histories in which Eloise follows this strategy

$$(\varphi_{MP}, \varnothing), (\psi, \{(x, a)\}), (\chi, \{(x, a), (z, a)\}), (x = y, \{(x, a), (z, a), (y, a)\}))$$
$$(\varphi_{MP}, \varnothing), (\psi, \{(x, b)\}), (\chi, \{(x, b), (z, b)\}), (x = y, \{(x, b), (z, b), (y, b)\}))$$

and she wins both of them. The Skolem form of φ_H is obtained in the following steps:

$$Sk_{\{x,y,z\}}(x = y) = (x = y)$$
$$Sk_{\{x,z\}}((\exists y/\{x\})\, x = y) = (x = g(z))$$
$$Sk_{\{x\}}(\exists z(\exists y/\{x\})\, x = y) = (x = g(f(x))$$
$$Sk_{\varnothing}(\forall x \exists z(\exists y/\{x\})\, x = y) = \forall x(x = g(f(x)).$$

Note that the $\{x\}$-uniformity of σ corresponds to the interpretation of f being a unary function. It is straightforward do find two functions $h, k : M \to M$ to be the interpretation of f and g such that $M, h, k \models \forall x(x = g(f(x)))$: let $h(a) = k(a) = a$. For comparison, the Skolem form of the Matching Pennies sentence φ_{MP} is

$$Sk(\varphi_{MP} = \forall x(\exists y/\{x\})\, x = y) = \forall x\, x = c.$$

Example (Dedekind Infinity). We prefer to use the following IF sentence φ_{inf} for defining (Dedekind) infinity:

$$\exists w \forall x(\exists y/\{w\})(\exists z/\{w, x\})(w \neq y \wedge z = x).$$

It may be checked that $Sk(\varphi_{inf})$ is

$$\forall x\, [g(f(x)) = x \wedge f(x) \neq c]$$

where f and g are new unary function symbols and c is a new constant symbol. This sentence asserts that f is an injection whose range is not the entire universe. Thus $Sk(\varphi_{inf})$ is true in an expansion $\mathbb{M}$ of a given model if and only if the universe of $\mathbb{M}$ is (Dedekind) infinite.

5.5   Signaling and Coordination

We have considered the sentences:

(φ_{MP}) $\forall x(\exists y/\{x\})x = y$
(φ_H) $\forall x \exists z(\exists y/\{x\})x = y.$

We pointed out that φ_{MP} is logically indeterminate, unlike the Hodges sentence φ_H which is logically true. It makes sense in the second case, as suggested by Hodges [35], to think of Eloise as a team consisting of two existential players: $\exists z$ copies Abelard's move (that she sees) and the second player $\exists y$ copies her partner's choice (that she sees).

The successful coordination of the two existential players in this case may be seen as a case of signaling: Any convention of play whereby one partner properly informs the other of his holdings or desires [43].

Signaling in IF logic has been extensively discussed [3,4,13,35,37,42]. Here we give one more example of a logical falsehood which involves signaling among the players in Abelard's team (a variation of an example from [37]). Consider the sentence

$$\exists x \exists y \exists z [x = y \wedge \forall v (\forall u / \{x\})(u \neq x \vee v \neq z)]$$

played on an arbitrary model $\mathbb{M}$ which contains at least two elements. We may think of $\wedge$, $\forall v$ and $\forall u$ as a team of universal players. Here is a winning strategy for this team for any choices $a, b, c \in M$ of Eloise as the values of x, y, and z, respectively:

- If $a \neq b$ then $\forall_1$ chooses Left; If $a = b$ then $\forall_1$ chooses Right. After this $\forall_2$ chooses c to be the value of v; finally $\forall_3$ chooses b to be the value of u.

Note that $\forall_2$ "sees" the value of x; and $\forall_3$ sees the value of y. The Kreisel form of this sentence

$$\forall x \forall y \forall z [x \neq y \vee (f(y, z) = x \wedge g(x, y, z) = z)]$$

makes the above strategy explicit.

5.6   Independence from Existential Quantifiers

Perhaps surprisingly, the sentence

$$\exists x (\exists y / \{x\}) x = y$$

is game-theoretically strongly equivalent (both truth and falsity equivalent) with the sentence

$$\exists x \exists y x = y.$$

For another example, notice also that the IF formulas

(a) $\forall x (\exists z / \{x\})(\exists y / \{x, z\}) x = y$

and

(b) $\forall x (\exists z / \{x\})(\exists y / \{x\}) x = y$

are strongly equivalent (both indeterminate on all structures with at least two elements). The question legitimately arises whether this is always the case, i.e. whether one can always remove the independence from an existential quantifier without affecting the truth-conditions of a given sentence. The answer is negative, as the following example [41] shows:

(c) $\forall x \exists z (\exists y / \{x, z\}) x = y.$

This sentence is logically indeterminate, but removing the independence from z leads to the Hodges sentence

(d) $\forall x \exists z (\exists y / \{x\}) x = y$

which is, as pointed out earlier, logically true.

Now it is interesting to compare the two pairs of examples: (a) and (b) on one side, with (b) and (c) on the other. Removing the independence of y from z in (c) creates the possibility of signaling the value of x in (d). On the other side, the same move in (a) still blocks the signaling of the value of x in (b). Barbero [3] investigates systematically the conditions in which the removal of the independence from an existential quantifier matters for the truth-value of a given sentence.

5.7 Lewis' Signaling Systems

The property of IF logic to express signaling phenomena opens the door to the definability of signaling problems in this logic. In fact for a very restricted variant of Lewis' signaling problems, this may be achieved by a variant of the Hodges' sentence as we will show now.

Lewis [40] defines a *signaling problem* as a situation which involves a communicator (C) and an audience (A). C observes one of several states m which he tries to communicate or "signal" to A, who does not see m. After receiving the signal, A performs one of several alternative actions, called responses. For every situation m there is a corresponding best response $b(m)$. This is primitive information which comes with the specification of the system. Lewis argues that a word acquires its meaning in virtue of its role in the solution of various signaling problems.

To model a Lewisian coordination problem we fix the following elements:

- A set W of situations or states of affairs, a set Σ of signals, and a set R of responses.
- A function $b : W \to R$ which maps each situation to its best response.
- An encoding function $f : W \to \Sigma$ employed by C to choose a signal for every situation
- A decoding function $g : \Sigma \to R$ employed by A to decide which action to perform in response to the signal it receives.

A *signaling system* is a pair (f, g) of encoding and decoding functions such that $g \circ f = b$.

The standard example of a signaling problem is that of a driver who is trying to back into a parking space. She has an assistant who gets out of the car and stands in a location where she can simultaneously see how much space there is behind the car and be seen by the driver. There are two states of affairs the assistant wishes to communicate, i.e., whether there is enough space behind the car for the driver to continue to back up. The assistant has two signals at her disposal: she can stand palms facing in or palms facing out. The driver has two possible responses: she can back up or she can stop.

There are two solutions to this signaling problem. The assistant can stand palms facing in when there is space, and palms facing out when there is no space, and *vice versa*. In the first case, the driver should continue backing up when she sees the assistant stand palms facing in, and back up when the assistant stands palms facing out. In the second case, the driver should stop when he sees the assistant stands palms facing in, and back up when the assistant stands palms facing out. Both systems work equally well in the sense that the composition of the two communicating and responding strategies realize the best response: the driver backs up when there is space, and he stops when there is not.

We express a Lewisian signaling system in IF logic using the following variant of the Hodges sentence:

$$\forall x \exists z (\exists y / \{x\}) \{(W(x) \rightarrow (\Sigma(z) \wedge R(y) \wedge y = b(x)))\}.$$

The symbolism is self-explanatory: W stands for the set of states, Σ for the set of signals, R for the set of responses, and b for the best action function.

We prefer yet another variant of this sentence which expresses the fact that A's task is not to do the best action, but simply to identify the situation from which the message was sent:

$$\varphi_{sig} = \forall x \exists z (\exists y / \{x\}) \{(W(x) \rightarrow (\Sigma(z) \wedge R(y) \wedge y = x))\}$$

We consider the class of models of the form

$$M = (M, W^M, \Sigma^M, R^M)$$

where

$$M = \{s_1, \ldots, s_n, t_1, \ldots, t_m\}$$
$$W^M = R^M = \{s_1, \ldots, s_n\}$$
$$\Sigma^M = \{t_1, \ldots, t_m\}$$

Lewis considered only signaling systems in which the number m of signals equals the number n of states. In this case, there is a simple way for the two existential players to achieve successful coordination: The first existential player (C) uses the signal t_i to signal the state s_i; and the second existential player (A) decodes the signal t_i back into the state s_i. The pair of functions $h(s_i) = t_i$ and $k(t_i) = s_i$ (the other values do not matter) serve as verifying instances for the Skolem form of φ_{sig}

$$Sk(\varphi_{sig}) = \forall x \{(W(x) \rightarrow (\Sigma(f(x)) \wedge R(g(f(x))) \wedge g(f(x)) = x)\}.$$

6   Indeterminacy

Imperfect information introduces indeterminacy into the games. Our favourite example was the Matching Pennies sentence $\varphi_{MP} = \forall x (\exists y / \{x\}) x = y$ which is logically indeterminate (we exclude one-element models). It will turn out to be useful to look at the indeterminacy of this sentence by considering its Skolem $\forall x\, x = c$ and Kreisel form $\forall y\, d \neq y$. There is no way to interpret the constant c (d) in such a way that $\forall x\, x = c$ $(\forall y\, d \neq y)$ is true. It is interesting to compare this example with another logically indeterminate sentence, the "Inverted Matching Pennies" φ_{IMP}

$$\forall x(\exists y/\{x\})x \neq y$$

whose Skolem and Kreisel forms are $\forall xx \neq c$ and $\forall yd = y$, respectively.

Another example of an indeterminate sentence is the signaling sentence φ_{sig}. We pointed out that this sentence is determinate (true) in all models $\mathbb{M} = (M, W^{\mathbb{M}}, \Sigma^{\mathbb{M}}, R^{\mathbb{M}})$ where the number m of signals equals the number of states, that is, $\mid W^{\mathbb{M}} \mid = n = \mid \Sigma^{\mathbb{M}} \mid = m$. This sentence is false when there are no signals, i.e. $\Sigma^{\mathbb{M}} = \varnothing$ (hence there are at least two states in W^M): it is enough to consider $Kr(\varphi_{sig})$

$$Kr(\varphi_{sig}) = \forall z \forall y\{(W(c) \land \neg(\Sigma(z) \land R(y) \land y = x)\}$$

and take the interpretation of c to be one of the states. All the objects in M are states, and each of them renders $Kr(\varphi_{sig})$ true.

Fact. Let $\mathbb{M} = (M, W^{\mathbb{M}}, \Sigma^{\mathbb{M}}, R^{\mathbb{M}})$ be such that the number m of signals is strictly less than the number of states, that is, $0 < m < n$. Then φ_{sig} is indeterminate.

Proof. Suppose, for a contradiction, that $\mathbb{M} \vDash^+ \varphi$, that is, $\mathbb{M}, h, k \vDash Sk(\varphi_{sig})$ for some functions $h, k : M \to M$ to be the interpretations of the new function symbols f, g in $Sk(\varphi_{sig})$. Given that $m < n$ and for every $s \in W^M$ it holds that $h(s) \in \Sigma^M$, there must exist distinct s_i, s_j such that $h(s_i) = h(s_j) = t$, for some $t \in \Sigma^M$. But then we must also have $k(h(s_i)) = s_i$ and $k(h(s_j)) = s_j$, a contradiction. Suppose now that $\mathbb{M} \vDash^- \varphi$, that is, $M, a \vDash Kr(\varphi_{sig})$ for some individual $a \in M$ to be the interpretation of the new constant symbol c in $Kr(\varphi_{sig})$. Pick up $z = t_i \in \Sigma^M$ and $y = a$. Then we have $t_i \in \Sigma^M$, $a \in R^M$ and $y = a$, again a contradiction. Note that for φ_{sig} to be indeterminate, M has to have at least three elements: at least one signal and at least two states.

Although Eloise (the existential team) does not have a winning strategy when $m < n$, it is easy to see that the pair of functions (h, k) defined as above gives Eloise a win in m cases. We will see later on that this is the "best" result she can achieve.

Fact. The sentence φ_{inf}

$$\exists w \forall x (\exists y/\{w\})(\exists z/\{w, x\})(w \neq y \land z = x)$$

which defines infinity in IF logic is indeterminate on all finite models.

Proof. Recall that $Sk(\varphi_{inf})$

$$\forall x\, [g(f(x)) = x \land f(x) \neq c]$$

asserts that f is an injection whose range is not the entire universe. Thus $Sk(\varphi_{inf})$ cannot be true in a finite model. On the other side, $Kr(\varphi_{inf})$

$$\forall w \forall y \forall z (w = y \lor z \neq h(w))$$

where h is a new function symbol can be true in a model $\mathbb{M}$ only if the universe of $\mathbb{M}$ has one element. As we excluded one element models, $Kr(\varphi_{inf})$ is false on all finite models.

7   Equilibrium Semantics

7.1   From Extensive to Strategic Games

There is a way to resolve the indeterminacy of IF sentences by following a suggestion due to Ajtai (reported in [10]) in the context of branching quantifiers:

> ... a formula might neither hold nor fail; that is, there might be no winning strategy for either player. The simplest example of this phenomenon is given by
>
> $$\begin{pmatrix} \forall x \\ \exists y \end{pmatrix} x = y$$
>
> in any structure with at least two elements. Although unpleasant, this lack of determinacy should not be viewed as pathological; it is the usual situation for games of imperfect information. Miklos Ajtai has suggested applying the Von Neumann minimax theorem to these games ... In this approach, formulas which neither hold nor fail have intermediate truth values; the example
>
> $$\begin{pmatrix} \forall x \\ \exists y \end{pmatrix} x = y$$
>
> has truth value $1/n$ in structures of cardinality n.

Given the representation of the sentence $\begin{pmatrix} \forall x \\ \exists y \end{pmatrix} x = y$ in the IF formalism as the Matching Pennies sentence φ_{MP}, the above suggestion amounts to taking the value of this sentence on a finite model $\mathbb{M}$ of cardinality n to be $1/n$. The suggestion has been worked out in details for the first time in [47], and generalized in [42, 48]. We sketch its main lines, using Ajtai's example.

In the extensive game $G(\mathbb{M}, \varphi_{MP})$, with $\mathbb{M} = \{1, \ldots, n\}$, let $S_\exists$ and $S_\forall$ denote the set of strategies of Eloise and Abelard, respectively. The members of $S_\exists$ are completely determined by $\mathbb{M}$ and $Sk(\varphi_{MP})$, which is $\forall x \; x = c$. Likewise, the composition of $S_\forall$ is completely determined by $\mathbb{M}$ and $Kr(\varphi_{MP})$ which is $\forall y \neg d = y$. Thus $S_\exists$ consists of all the possible values in $\mathbb{M}$ of the constant c, i.e., $S_\exists = \mathbb{M}$; and $S_\forall$ consists of all the possible values in $\mathbb{M}$ of the constant d, i.e. $S_\forall = \mathbb{M}$. The outcome of playing any strategy $s \in S_\exists$ against any strategy $t \in S_\forall$ is a play (maximal history) of $G(\mathbb{M}, \varphi_{MP})$, which results in a win for Eloise or a win for Abelard. In other words,

- We let $u_\exists$, the utility function of player $\exists$, be defined by: $u_\exists(s,t) = 1$ if playing $s \in S_\exists$ against $t \in S_\forall$ in $G(\mathbb{M}, \varphi_{MP})$ yields a win for $\exists$; and $u_\exists(s,t) = 0$, otherwise.
- $u_\forall$ is defined analoguously.

We have converted the extensive game $G(\mathbb{M}, \varphi_{MP})$ into a strategic game

$$\Gamma(\mathbb{M}, \varphi_{MP}) = (S_\exists, S_\forall, u_\exists, u_\forall).$$

It may be displayed, as usual, in a matrix form:

	1	2	$\cdots$	n
1	$(1,0)$	$(0,1)$	$\cdots$	$(0,1)$
2	$(0,1)$	$(1,0)$	$\cdots$	$(0,1)$
$\vdots$	$\vdots$	$\vdots$	$\ddots$	$(0,1)$
n	$(0,1)$	$(0,1)$	$\cdots$	n

The same procedure can be used to convert any extensive semantical game $G(\mathbb{M}, \varphi)$ into a strategic IF game $\Gamma(\mathbb{M}, \varphi)$ for an arbitrary IF sentence φ and finite model $\mathbb{M}$.

Obviously strategic IF games are 2-player, finite win-lose games. One can then define the notion of equilibrium in the standard way.

We can check that in the IF strategic games $\Gamma(\mathbb{M}, \varphi_{MP})$ and $\Gamma(\mathbb{M}, \varphi_{IMP})$ with $\mathbb{M} = \{1, \ldots, n\}$, there is no equilibrium. Actually this is just another facet of the indeterminacy of the semantical games $G(\mathbb{M}, \varphi_{MP})$ and $G(\mathbb{M}, \varphi_{IMP})$.

7.2 Mixed Strategy Equilibria in Two Player Win-Lose Finite Strategic Games

After converting semantical games into strategic games, we are ready to implement Ajtai's suggestion. It is based on a procedure well known to game theorists: mixed strategy equilibria and Von Neumann's Theorem. We give a short presentation of the basic definitions and results [42, 48]. Let

$$\Gamma(\mathbb{M}, \varphi) = (S_\exists, S_\forall, u_\exists, u_\forall)$$

be a two player finite strategic game. A mixed strategy ν for player p is a probability distribution over S_p, that is, a function $\nu : S_p \to [0,1]$ such that $\sum_{\tau \in S_p} \nu(\tau) = 1$. ν is uniform over $S_p' \subseteq S_p$ if it assigns equal probability to all strategies in S_p' and zero probability to all the strategies in $S_p - S_p'$. The support of ν is the set of strategies to which ν assigns non-zero probability. Obviously we can simulate a pure strategy σ with a mixed strategy ν such that ν assigns σ probability 1. Given a mixed strategy μ for player $\exists$ and a mixed strategy ν for player $\forall$, the expected utility for player p is given by:

$$U_p(\mu, \nu) = \sum_{\sigma \in S_\exists} \sum_{\tau \in S_\forall} \mu(\sigma)\nu(\tau)u_p(\sigma, \tau)$$

When $\sigma \in S_\exists$ and ν is a mixed strategy for player $\forall$, we let

$$U_p(\sigma, \nu) = \sum_{\tau \in S_\forall} \nu(\tau) u_p(\sigma, \tau)$$

Similarly if $\tau \in S_\forall$ and μ is a mixed strategy for player $\exists$, we let

$$U_p(\mu, \tau) = \sum_{\sigma \in S_\exists} \mu(\sigma) u_p(\sigma, \tau)$$

The notion of mixed strategy equilibrium is defined exactly as in the pure strategies case.

The following two results are well known.

Theorem (Von Neuman's Minimax Theorem [52]). Every finite, two-person, constant-sum game has an equilibrium in mixed strategies.

Corollary. Let (μ, ν) and (μ', ν') be two mixed strategy equilibria in a constant sum game. Then $U_p(\mu, \nu) = U_p(\mu', \nu')$.

These two results guarantee that we can talk about the value $V(\Gamma)$ of a strategic IF game Γ: it is the expected utility returned to player $\exists$ by any equilibrium in the relevant strategic game.

The next result will help us to identify equilibria.

Proposition. Let μ^* be a mixed strategy for player $\exists$ and ν^* a mixed strategy for player $\forall$ in a finite strategic, two player win-lose game Γ. The pair (μ^*, ν^*) is an equilibrium in Γ if and only if the following conditions hold:

1. $U_\exists(\mu^*, \nu^*) = U_\exists(\sigma, \nu^*)$ for every $\sigma \in S_\exists$ in the support of μ^*
2. $U_\forall(\mu^*, \nu^*) = U_\forall(\mu^*, \tau)$ for every $\tau \in S_\forall$ in the support of ν^*
3. $U_\exists(\mu^*, \nu^*) \geq U_\exists(\sigma, \nu^*)$ for every $\sigma \in S_\exists$ outside the support of μ^*
4. $U_\forall(\mu^*, \nu^*) \geq U_\forall(\mu^*, \tau)$ for every $\tau \in S_\forall$ outside the support of ν^*.

Proof. (See [44], p. 116)

Example. We apply this proposition to calculate the values of the strategic games $\Gamma(\mathbb{M}, \varphi_{MP})$ and $\Gamma(\mathbb{M}, \varphi_{IMP})$ on a model $\mathbb{M}$ which contains n elements. The picture below illustrates the case in which $n = 4$:

	1	2	3	4		1	2	3	4
1	(1,0)	(0,1)	(0,1)	(0,1)	1	(0,1)	(1,0)	(1,0)	(1,0)
2	(0,1)	(1,0)	(0,1)	(0,1)	2	(1,0)	(0,1)	(1,0)	(1,0)
3	(0,1)	(1,0)	(1,0)	(0,1)	3	(1,0)	(1,0)	(0,1)	(1,0)
4	(0,1)	(0,1)	(0,1)	(1,0)	4	(1,0)	(1,0)	(1,0)	(0,1)

The above proposition can be applied to show that the strategy pair (μ^*, ν^*) where both μ^* and ν^* are uniform strategies with support $M = \{1, ..., n\}$, forms an equilibrium in both games which returns to Eloise an expected utility of $1/n$ in the first game and $n-1/n$ in the second.

Our new framework guarantees a probabilistic value for any IF sentence φ on any given finite structure $\mathbb{M}$. Actually we can introduce a satisfaction relation $\models_\varepsilon$ between IF sentences φ and models $\mathbb{M}$, with ε such that $0 \leq \varepsilon \leq 1$ defined by:

– $\mathbb{M} \models_\varepsilon \varphi$ iff the value of the strategic game $\Gamma(\mathbb{M}, \varphi)$ is ε.

It can be shown that the new interpretation is a conservative extension over the GTS interpretation, in the following sense:

Proposition ([42], Proposition 7.4). Let φ be an arbitrary IF sentence and $\mathbb{M}$ a finite model. Then:

(i) $\mathbb{M} \models^+ \varphi$ iff $\mathbb{M} \models_1 \varphi$
(ii) $\mathbb{M} \models^- \varphi$ iff $\mathbb{M} \models_0 \varphi$.

To identify equilibria we shall make use of few other well known results.

Definition. Let $\Gamma(\mathbb{M}, \varphi)$ be a strategic IF game. For $\sigma, \sigma' \in S_\exists$, we say that σ' weakly dominates σ if the following two conditions hold:

(i) For every $\tau \in S_\forall : u_\exists(\sigma', \tau) \geq u_\exists(\sigma, \tau)$
(ii) For some $\tau \in S_\forall : u_\exists(\sigma', \tau) > u_\exists(\sigma, \tau)$.

A similar notion is defined for Abelard.
   The following result enables us to eliminate weakly dominated strategies.

Proposition. Let $\Gamma(\mathbb{M}, \varphi)$ be a strategic IF game. Then Γ has an equilibrium $(\sigma_\exists, \sigma_\forall)$ such that for each player p none of the strategies in the support of σ_p is weakly dominated in Γ.

Proof See [44]. An anonymous referee has pointed out that this result is an immediate consequence of Selten [46] who proved that every finite game has an undominated equilibrium (so in particular our IF games have this property). The proof requires the finiteness of the game.

Definition. Let $\Gamma(\mathbb{M}, \varphi)$ be a strategic IF game. For $\sigma, \sigma' \in S_\exists$, we say that σ' is payoff equivalent to σ if for every $\tau \in S_\forall : u_\exists(\sigma', \tau) = u_\exists(\sigma, \tau)$.

A similar notion is defined for Abelard.
   We list another result which allows the elimination of payoff equivalent strategies.

Proposition. Let $\Gamma(\mathbb{M}, \varphi)$ be a strategic IF game. Then Γ has equilibrium $(\sigma_\exists, \sigma_\forall)$ such that for each player p there are no strategies in the support of σ_p which are payoff equivalent.

Proof. An anonymous referee pointed out that this is a well known result in game theory (it follows from interchangeability in Nash (1951). Mann et al. ([42]; Proposition 7.22) proves this result in the context of IF logic.

We now apply the framework developed so far to two case studies.

8   Lewis' Signaling Problem Revisited

It is known that (i) every win-lose game has a value in $\mathbb{Q}$ (the rational numbers) and that, conversely, (ii) for every $q \in \mathbb{Q}$, there is a win-lose game with value q [45]. We will use the Lewis signaling sentence and its models to show that the class of IF games, which is only a subclass of the of the class of winn-lose two-player games, realize also precisely the rationals in $[0, 1]$.

Recall the game $G(\mathbb{M}, \varphi_{sig})$ associated with the sentence φ_{sig} and a given structure $\mathbb{M} = (M, S^M, \Sigma^M, R^M)$ as specified in Sect. 5.7. Let

$$\Gamma(\mathbb{M}, \varphi_{sig}) = (S_\exists, S_\forall, u_\exists, u_\forall)$$

be the corresponding IF game. (Note that the set of states S^M here is the same as the set W in Sect. 5.7). From the Skolem form of φ_{sig}, we gather that $S_\exists$ consists of all pairs (h, k) of functions $h, k : M \to M$. On the basis of the Kreisel form of φ_{sig} we take $S_\forall$ to be the entire universe $M = \{s_1, \ldots, s_n, t_1, \ldots, t_m\}$. The strategic game may be displayed in the matrix form:

	s_1	$\cdots$	s_n	t_1	$\cdots$	t_m
(h_1, k_1)				$(1,0)$	$\cdots$	$(1,0)$
(h_2, k_2)				$(1,0)$	$\cdots$	$(1,0)$
$\vdots$				$\vdots$	$\vdots$	$\vdots$
(h_p, k_p)				$(1,0)$	$\cdots$	$(1,0)$

The first observation is that any strategy of Abelard that chooses from outside S^M is weakly dominated by every strategy that chooses from S^M. Thus the value of the game is the same as that of the smaller game:

	s_1	$\cdots$	s_n
(h_1, k_1)			
(h_2, k_2)			
$\vdots$			
(h_p, k_p)			

In this game, let $\mathbb{B} = \{B \subseteq S^M \text{ and } \mid B \mid = m\}$. Given that $m < n$, then for every $B \subseteq \mathbb{B}$, there must exist at least one pair (h, k) of functions such that

A1 $h \upharpoonright B : B \to \Sigma^M$ is one-one and onto
A2 $k(h(s)) = s$, for every $s \in B$.

Obviously when (h, k) is played against $s \in S^M$, the payoffs are $(1, 0)$ whenever $s \in B$, and $(0, 1)$ when $s \notin B$.

For any $B \subseteq \mathbb{B}$, let T_B be the collection of all pairs (h, k) that satisfy conditions (A1) and (A2). Every strategy that violates conditions A1 and A2 is weakly dominated by all strategies in some T_B. Thus the value of the game is the same as the value of the smaller game in which the strategies of Eloise are restricted to those in the sets T_B. All the strategies in the same set T_B are payoff equivalent for Eloise. Thus we can further reduce the game to a smaller one in which the strategies of Eloise are limited to one arbitrarily chosen member $(h, k)_B$ from each T_B. Let collect all of them into the class $T_{\mathbb{B}}$.

We now compute the value of the game. Let μ be the uniform probability distribution with support $T_{\mathbb{B}}$ and ν the uniform probability distribution with support S^M. We claim that the pair (μ, ν) is an equilibrium with value m/n.

First we observe that

$$U_{\exists}(\mu, \nu) = \sum_{s \in S^M} \sum_{B \in \mathbb{B}} \nu(s) \mu((h, k)_B) u_{\exists}((h, k)_B, s) = \sum_{B \in \mathbb{B}_s} \nu((h, k)_B)$$

where $\mathbb{B}_s = \{B \subseteq \mathbb{B} : s \in B\}$, for any $s \in S^M$.

Second observe that $\sum_{B \in \mathbb{B}_s} \nu((h, k)_B)$ denotes the probability m/n that a randomly drawn set B of m objects contains s.

Our analysis of the Lewis games can be stated in the form of the following theorem.

Theorem [4]. Let $\mathbb{M} = (M, S^M, \Sigma^M, R^M)$ be a structure as specified earlier, $0 \leq m < n$ be integers and $q = m/n$. The sentence φ_{sig} has the value q on the structure $\mathbb{M}$.

One remark is in order. Our earlier fact established the indeterminacy of φ_{sig} in every model with at least three elements $(0 < m < n)$. But we noticed earlier that when $m = 0$ then φ_{sig} is false, hence its value is 0 in conformity with the statement of the theorem.

9   Strategic IF Games Realize All Rationals

We aim to show that the expressive power of IF logic under the equilibrium semantics is independent from the threshold operator ϵ, roughly in the sense that if $\varepsilon, \varepsilon'$ are rational numbers (satisfying some constraints), then for every IF sentence φ there is another IF sentence φ' in the same vocabulary such that for all models $\mathbb{M}$, φ has the value ε on $\mathbb{M}$ iff φ' has the value ε' on $\mathbb{M}$. For this we need to consider another proof of the fact that IF logic realize all rationals. This result will turn ut to be important for some complexity results.

Theorem [48]. Let $0 \leq m < n$ be integers and $q = m/n$. There exists an IF sentence that has value q on every model with at least two elements.

Proof. The IF sentence φ_{rat} used to prove this theorem is in the empty vocabulary but varies with the numbers m and n:

$$\forall x_1 (\forall x_2 / \{x_1\}) \ldots (\forall x_m / \{x_1, \ldots, x_{m-1}\}) (\exists y / \{x_1, \ldots, x_m\}) [\beta_1 \vee \beta_2 \vee \beta_3]$$

where β_1 is

$$\bigvee_{i \in \{1, \ldots, m\}} \bigvee_{j \in \{1, \ldots, m\} - \{i\}} x_i = x_j$$

β_2 is

$$\bigvee_{i\in\{1,\ldots,m\}}\bigwedge_{j\in\{1,\ldots,n\}} x_i \neq c_j$$

and β_3 is

$$\bigvee_{i\in\{1,\ldots,m\}} x_i = y.$$

This sentence describes the following game, where M is is a finite set consisting of at least n elements and C is a subset of M of cardinality n (whose elements are named by the constants c_j) :

- Abelard picks up m elements from the universe.
- Eloise picks up one element without knowing the elements chosen by Abelard.
- Eloise wins if: (a) Abelard chose twice the same element; or (b) Abelard chose an element outside the set $C = \{c_1, \ldots, c_n\}$; or (c) Eloise chose one of the elements chosen by Abelard.

The first two conditions force Abelard to choose m distinct objects from C.

This game is resolved in very much the same way as we resolved the Lewis signaling game $G(\mathbb{M}, \varphi_{sig})$. Note first that any strategy of Eloise that chooses c from outside C is weakly dominated by every strategy that chooses from C. So we reduce the game to the smaller one in which the set of strategies of Eloise is C. Let $\mathbb{B} = \{B \subseteq C$ and $\mid B \mid = m\}$ and T_B be the set of strategies of Abelard that pick the objects in B in any order. All the strategies in the same T_B are payoff equivalent. Any strategy that is not in some set T_B violates one of the conditions (a) and (b) (or both) and will result in a loss for Abelard. Every such strategy is weakly dominated by a strategy in some T_B. Pick up arbitrarily one strategy τ_B from each set T_B. Collect all of them into a set T^*. We reduce the game to the smaller one in which Abelard chooses from T^*. Let μ be a uniform mixed strategy with support C and ν a uniform mixed strategy with support T^*. We claim that (μ, ν) is an equilibrium with value m/n. As in the Lewis signaling game, we observe that

$$U_\exists(\mu, \nu) = \sum_{c\in C}\sum_{B\in\mathbb{B}} \mu(c)\nu(\tau_B)u_\exists(c, \tau_B) = \sum_{B\in\mathbb{B}_c} \nu(\tau_B)$$

where $\mathbb{B}_c = \{B \subseteq \mathbb{B} : c \in B\}$, for any $c \in C$. The expression $\sum_{B\in\mathbb{B}_c} \nu(\tau_B)$ denotes the probability m/n that a randomly drawn set B of m objects contains c.

The proof has assumed that $\mid M \mid \geq n$ and that we have available n distinct objects at our disposal. In [48] it is shown that we can drop both assumptions so that at the end we need only two dedicated letters which can also be chosen by Eloise.

Notice that the sentence produced by this theorem varies with the numbers m and n. In the previous theorem we showed that there is a single IF sentence which, for every m, n such that $0 \leq m \leq n$, it gets value $q = m/n$. The result of the present theorem has been also proved independently in [20].

In the next result we use the "rationals game" to obtain new IF games with a desired value.

Proposition [48]. Let φ be an arbitrary IF sentence and let $0 \leq q \leq 1$ be a rational number. Then
1. There is an IF sentence ψ such that for every structure $\mathbb{M}$ we have:
   $V(\Gamma') = q + (1 - q)V(\Gamma)$.
2. There is an IF sentence ψ such that for every structure $\mathbb{M}$ we have:
   $V(\Gamma') = qV(\Gamma)$.
where Γ is the strategic game $\Gamma(\mathbb{M}, \varphi)$ and $\Gamma' = \Gamma(\mathbb{M}, \psi)$.

Proof. Let $v = V(\Gamma)$. Consider the following variation of the "rationals" game. We let the play from the last theorem be played (on $\mathbb{M}$) until all the quantifiers moves have been handled. Then Eloise is shown all objects which have been chosen so far, and she is offered a choice between: (a) continuing to play that game to the end, or, (b) playing instead the game of φ on $\mathbb{M}$. Notice that in any play of the game, either the selected assignment satisfies $\gamma = \beta_1 \vee \beta_2 \vee \beta_3$ in which case Eloise will get payoff 1 by choosing (a). Or the selected assignment makes γ false in which case Eloise would get payoff 0 if she chose (a). So if the first alternative occurs, let Eloise choose (a) and get payoff 1. If the second alternative occurs, let her choose (b) and get payoff v. By the reasoning of the previous theorem, Eloise will get payoff 1 in q cases, and payoff v in $(1 - q)$ cases. Hence the value of this game is $q + (1 - q)v$. The IF sentence ψ we are looking for is

$$\forall x_1 (\forall x_2 / \{x_1\}) \ldots (\forall x_m / \{x_1, \ldots, x_{m-1}\})(\exists y / \{x_1, \ldots, x_m\}) \{[\beta_1 \vee \beta_2 \vee \beta_3] \vee \phi\}$$

(2) is proved in the same way using the IF sentence

$$\forall x_1 (\forall x_2 / \{x_1\}) \ldots (\forall x_m / \{x_1, \ldots, x_{m-1}\})(\exists y / \{x_1, \ldots, x_m\}) \{[\beta_1 \vee \beta_2 \vee \beta_3] \wedge \phi\}.$$

Theorem [48]. Let $0 < \varepsilon, \varepsilon' \leq 1$ be rationals such that if ε' is 1 then $\varepsilon = 1$. Then for every IF sentence φ in the vocabulary L there is an IF sentence ψ in the same vocabulary such that for every L-model $\mathbb{M}$, φ has the value ε on $\mathbb{M}$ iff ψ has the value ε' on $\mathbb{M}$.

Proof. There are two cases. For the case $\varepsilon < \varepsilon' \leq 1$ we let q be the rational $\varepsilon' - \varepsilon / 1 - \varepsilon$. By the previous Proposition (1) we know there is an IF sentence in the same vocabulary for which for every model $\mathbb{M}$ we have: $V(\Gamma') = q + (1 - q)V(\Gamma)$. An elementary algebraic argument shows that $\mathbb{M} \models_\varepsilon \varphi$ iff $\mathbb{M} \models_{\varepsilon'} \psi$. For the case $\varepsilon > \varepsilon'$ it is enough to take $q = \varepsilon' / \varepsilon$.

9.1   Complexity of Finding Equilibria

The satisfaction relation $\models_\varepsilon$ between IF sentences φ and finite models $\mathbb{M}$ introduces a new form of definability: we let

$$Mod_\varepsilon(\varphi) = \{\mathbb{M} : \mathbb{M} \models_\varepsilon \varphi\}$$

and IF_ε to be the class of all $Mod_\varepsilon(\varphi)$ where φ is an IF sentence.

In the classical framework in which a logic is associated with the class $Str(\varphi)$ of models in which a sentence φ is true, Fagin has shown that $NP = \Sigma_1^1$, that is, every NP-solvable problem is definable in Σ_1^1 and conversely, every Σ_1^1-definable property is solvable in NP. Here Σ_1^1 denotes the existential subfragment of second-order logic.

The previous results give a lower bound for IF_ε.

Fact. [48] Let $0 < \varepsilon \le 1$ be rational. Then $NP \subseteq IF_\varepsilon$.

Proof. The result $NP = IF_1$ follows from Fagin's result mentioned above together with the fact that Σ_1^1 coincides in expressive power with IF logic and our earlier proposition to the effect that $\mathbb{M} \models_{GTS}^+ \varphi$ iff $\mathbb{M} \models_1 \varphi$ on any finite model $\mathbb{M}$. To show that $NP \subseteq IF_\varepsilon$ for any ε satisfying the above constraints, it is enough to show that for every $Mod_1(\varphi) \in IF_1$ there is a $Mod_\varepsilon(\varphi') \in IF_\varepsilon$ such that $Mod_1(\varphi) = Mod_\varepsilon(\varphi')$. This is implied by our last theorem.

For an upper bound, see [42, Sect. 7].

10   Monty Hall

10.1   Formulation of the Problem

There are various formulations of the problem. Here is one of them:

> Suppose you are on a Monty Hall's *Let's Make a Deal*! You are given the choice of three doors, behind one door is a car, the others goats. You pick up a door, say 1, Monty Hall opens another door, say 3, which has a goat. Monty says to you "Do you want to pick door 2?" Is it to your advantage to switch your choice of doors? [24, Example 4.6, p. 136],

This formulation should be compared to the following one:

> We say that C is using the "stay" strategy if she picks a door, and, if offered a chance to switch to another door, declines to do so (i.e., he stays with his original choice). Similarly, we say that C is using the "switch" strategy if he picks a door, and, if offered a chance to switch to another door, takes the offer. Now suppose that C decides in advance to play the "stay" strategy. Her only action in this case is to pick a door (and decline an invitation to switch, if one is offered). What is the probability that she wins a car? The same question can be asked about the "switch" strategy (Idem, p. 137).

Grinstead and Snell [24] remark that the first formulation of the problem "asks for the conditional probability that C wins if she switches doors, *given that* she has chosen door 1 and that Monty Hall has chosen door 3" whereas the second formulation is about the comparative probabilities of two kinds of strategies for C, the "switch" strategy and the "stay" strategy:

Using the "stay" strategy, a contestant will win the car with probability
1/3, since 1/3 of the time the door he picks will have the car behind it.
On the other hand, if C plays the "switch" strategy, then he will win
whenever the door he originally picked does not have the car behind it,
which happens 2/3 of the time (Idem, p. 137).

A similar formulation of the general problem and its solution may be found also
in [36].

10.2   Solution: Conditional Probabilities

We give the solution to the first formulation of the problem as described in [24].
It is formulated in terms of trees and it is easily comparable the other two
approaches we will be considering. Here is the tree that represents all the possible
sequences of choices of MH and C (Fig. 4):

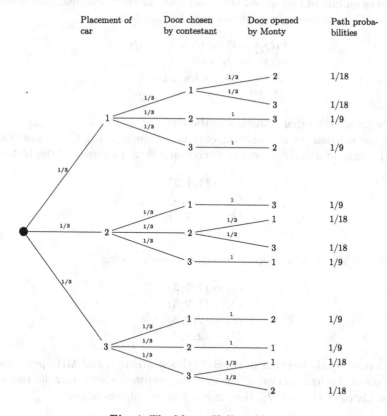

Fig. 4. The Monty Hall problem

Each maximal branch has the form (x, y, z), where x stands for the door where the prize is hidden, y for the door chosen be C, and z for the door open by MH. From the description of the game it is clear that if $x = y$, then z takes two possible values; and if $x \neq y$, then z can take only one value. Thus there are all in all 12 maximal branches. In this setting the event D_1 of the prize being hidden behind door 1 is to be identified with the subtree (set) consisting of the histories:

$$O_1 = (1, 1, 2)$$
$$O_2 = (1, 1, 3)$$
$$O_3 = (1, 2, 3)$$
$$O_4 = (1, 3, 2).$$

It is assumed that the events of the car being hidden behind door 1, door 2, and door 3 are equiprobable and so are the events of C's choosing door 1, door 2, or door 3. Likewise, it is reasonable to assume that whenever Monty Hall has a choice to open one of two doors, the two events are equiprobable; and when he can open only one door, the probability is 1. Thus

$$P(O_1) = 1/3 \times 1/3 \times 1/2 = 1/18$$
$$P(O_2) = 1/3 \times 1/3 \times 1/2 = 1/18$$
$$P(O_3) = 1/3 \times 1/3 \times 1 = 1/9$$
$$P(O_4) = 1/3 \times 1/3 \times 1 = 1/9.$$

Similarly for all the other branches in the tree.

Now the original puzzle concerns only the event in which C chooses door 1, and MH opens door 3. The event of C choosing door 1 consists of the histories:

$$O_1 = (1, 1, 2)$$
$$O_2 = (1, 1, 3)$$
$$O_5 = (2, 1, 3)$$
$$O_9 = (3, 1, 2).$$

The event of MH opening door 3 consists of the histories:

$$O_2 = (1, 1, 3)$$
$$O_3 = (1, 2, 3)$$
$$O_5 = (2, 1, 3)$$
$$O_7 = (2, 2, 3).$$

Let us denote by B the event in which C chooses door 1, and MH opens door 3. It consists of the intersection of the two events listed above, that is, the set of histories histories O_5 and O_2. Here is a list of our abbreviations:

B for "C chooses door 1 and Monty Hall opens door 3"
D_1 for "the prize is behind Door 1"
D_2 for "the prize is behind Door 2"
D_3 for "the prize is behind Door 3".

We can check that $P(O_5) = 1/19$ and $P(O_2) = 1/18$. Hence

$$P(B) = P(\{O_2, O_5\}) = P(O_2) + P(O_5) = 1/6.$$

We are now in a position to compute the conditional probabilities. We apply Bayes' law which says that the probability of an event A conditional on an event E is the probability of the event A and E divided by the probability of the event E. In our case this means:

$$P(D_1/B) = P(O_2)/P(B) = 1/18/1/6 = 1/3$$
$$P(D_2/B) = P(O_5)/P(B) = 1/9/1/6 = 2/3.$$

Thus the answer to the original question is: Yes, it is in C's interest to switch doors.

10.3   Product Updates and Dynamic Logic

Information models for groups of agents G are Kripke structures M consisting of a universe W of possible worlds and equivalence relations R_i between these worlds which indicate the uncertainty of agents $i \in G$. The language contains an epistemic operator K_i, one for each individual agent $i \in G$ [18].

New information obtained through public actions such as truthful public announcement change such models by removing all worlds from the current model which are incompatible with the new information. The state elimination is the simplest update procedure. Atomic facts are 'persistent' under update, retaining their truth but the truth value of epistemic assertions may change because we have to re-evaluate formulas with epistemic operators in the new smaller models [14].

The update mechanism has two components. An epistemic multiagent model M as described above, and an action model A consisting of the set of all actions and the action indistinguishable relations A_i between them, one for each agent i. Compared to the epistemic models, action models have one additional particularity: they indicate, for each action a, its precondition PRE_a, that is, the set of possible worlds where a can be performed.

The product models $M \times A$ is a Kripke model whose universe is

$$\{(s, a) : s \in W, a \text{ is an action in } A, (M, s) \vDash PRE_a\}$$

and whose accessibility relations are obtained through the principle:

$R_i(s, a)(t, b)$ iff both $R_i st$ (in M) and $A_i ab$ (in A).

In other words, the uncertainty among new states can only come from existing uncertainty via indistinguishable actions.

After these preliminaries we can turn to the particular version of Monty Hall in which C chooses door 1 [7,38]. In the tree approach we have seen that this version corresponds to the four branches $\{O_1, O_2, O_5, O_9\}$ tree we analyzed in the previous section. In update logic this tree is reconceptualized as a series of product updates:

- First MH put the prize behind one of the three doors. This generates an epistemic model M_1
- M_1 is then updated with C's action a_1: C chooses door 1. The result is the product model M_2
- Finally MH publicly opens some door. This updates M_2 with two possible actions, a_2 (MH opens door 2), and a_3 (MH opens door 3). The result is the product model M_3.

C's and MH's actions are governed by the following principles which determine their preconditions:

1. C may choose any of the three doors.
2. MH can open only a door that C did not choose, and where the car is not hidden.

Now, some of the details.

The epistemic model $M_1 = (W_1, R_C^1, R_{MH}^1)$ corresponds to the tree (Fig. 5):

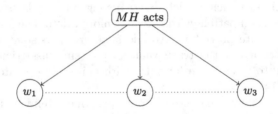

Fig. 5.

Here $W_1 = \{w_1, w_2, w_3\}$, (w_1 represents the world where the car is behind door 1, etc.) and the accessibility relations are obvious: MH's actions are accessible to himself, but not to the contestant C (the dots indicate the accessibility relations of C).

M_1 is updated with the action model $A_1 = (V_1, Q_C^1, Q_{MH}^1)$, where $V_1 = \{a_1\}$ and the accessibility relations Q_C^1 and Q_{MH}^1 are $V_1 \times V_1$ reflecting the fact that a_1 is a public action. From condition (1) we know that $Pre(a_1) = W$. The product model (Fig. 6)

$$M_2 = M_1 \times A_1 = (W_2, R_C^2, R_{MH}^2)$$

can be represented as the tree with three possible worlds

$$v_1 = (w_1, a_1)$$
$$v_2 = (w_2, a_1)$$
$$v_3 = (w_3, a_1).$$

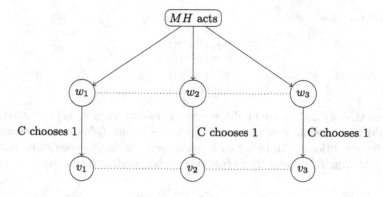

Fig. 6.

All the worlds in W_2 remain indistinguishable to C, i.e. $R_C^2 = W_2 \times W_2$ whereas Monty Hall knows exactly where she is.

Finally M_2 is updated with the action model $A_2 = (V_2, Q_C^2, Q_{MH}^2)$ where $V_2 = \{a_2, a_3\}$, (a_2: MH opens door 2, etc.) and

$$Q_C^2 = Q_{MH}^2 = \{(a_2, a_2), (a_3, a_3)\}.$$

From condition (2) we know that $Pre(a_2) = \{v_1, v_3\}$ and $Pre(a_3) = \{v_1, v_2\}$. The result of this update is the product model

$$M_3 = M_2 \times A_2 = (W_3, R_C^3, R_{MH}^3)$$

which can be represented as the tree (Fig. 7):

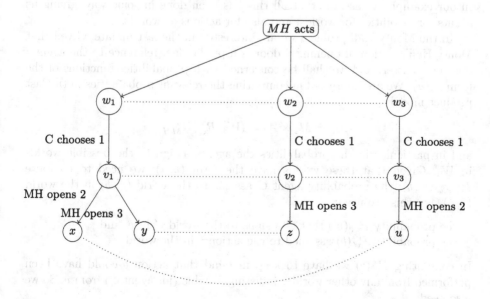

Fig. 7.

with four possible worlds:

$$x = (v_1, a_2)$$
$$y = (v_1, a_3)$$
$$z = (v_2, a_3)$$
$$u = (v_3, a_2).$$

Given that a_2 and a_3 are public actions, C knows, after a_2 is performed, that she could be either in x or in u, i.e. $R_C^3 xu$ and $R_C^3 ux$ (plus the corresponding reflexivity conditions). And after a_3 is performed, she knows she can be either in y or in z, that is, $R_C^3 yz$ and $R_C^3 zy$ (plus the corresponding reflexivity conditions).

Product Updates with Probabilities. We follow [7] and show how product update models may be endowed with a probability structure.

For epistemic models M, we consider, for each agent i, the equivalence classes $D_{i,s} = \{t : R_i st\}$. Probability functions $P_{i,s}$ are then defined over the probability space $D_{i,s}$. For simplicity, it is assumed that these functions are the same for every world in the set $D_{i,s}$. We simplify matters even more in finite models and assume that the functions $P_{i,s}$ assign probabilities $P_{i,s}(w)$ to single worlds w. We can then use sums of these values to assign probabilities to propositions, viewed as the set of worlds where they are true. Then we can interpret $P_{i,s}(\varphi)$ as assigning a probabilistic value ϕ. In case this value is 1, this will correspond to the assertion $K_i \varphi$.

Next, we assign probabilities to actions in the universe of the action models A. This is done relatively to a state s. The basic notion is:

– $P_{i,s}(a)$, the probability that the agent i assigns to action a in the world s.

In our example we assume that all this has been done in some way, giving us agents' probabilities for worlds, and also for actions at worlds.

In the Monty Hall problem we are interested in the last update. Given that Monty Hall's action of opening a door is a public one, reference to the agent i does not matter, and we shall be concerned with probabilities functions of the form $P_s(a)$. We are interested in computing the relevant probabilities in the last product model

$$M_3 = M_2 \times A_2 = (W_3, R_C^3, R_{MH}^3)$$

and in particular in the probabilities the agents assign to the possible worlds in W_3. Given that these worlds have the form (v, a), we need to compute $P_{c,(v,a)}(v', b)$: the probability agent C assigns to the world (v', b) in the world (v, a). For this, we need:

– the probability $P_{i,v}(v')$ that C assigns to the world v' in v, and
– the probability $P_{v'}(b)$ assigned to the action b in the world v'.

In computing $P_{v'}(b)$ we have to keep in mind that action b could have been performed from any other world u indistinguishable (for agent C) from v. So we also need:

– the probabilities $P_{C,v}(u)$ for every u such that $R_C v u$ together with the probabilities $P_u(b)$.

To compute $P_{c,(v,a)}(v',b)$ we use the formula:

$$P_{c,(v,a)}(v',b) = \frac{P_{i,v}(v') \times P_{v'}(b)}{\sum_{R_C v u} P_{C,v}(u) \times P_u(b)}$$

Skipping over some details, we obtain as expected

$$P_{C,v_1}(v_1) = P_{c,(w_1,a_1)}(w_1,a_1) = 1/3$$
$$P_{C,v_1}(v_2) = P_{c,(w_1,a_1)}(w_2,a_1) = 1/3.$$

Finally we use the same formula to compute

$$P_{c,x}(y) = P_{c,(v_1,a_3)}(v_1,a_3) = 1/3$$
$$P_{c,x}(z) = P_{c,(v_1,a_3)}(v_2,a_3) = 2/3.$$

To understand where the difference lies, notice that $P_{c,(v_1,a_3)}(v_1,a_3)$ is obtained by dividing

$$P_{C,v_1}(v_1) \times P_{v_1}(a_3)$$

by

$$P_{C,v_1}(v_1) \times P_{v_1}(a_3) + P_{C,v_1}(v_2) \times P_{v_2}(a_3)$$

whereas $P_{c,(v_1,a_3)}(v_2,a_3)$ is obtained by dividing

$$P_{C,v_1}(v_2) \times P_{v_2}(a_3)$$

by

$$P_{C,v_1}(v_1) \times P_{v_1}(a_3) + P_{C,v_1}(v_2) \times P_{v_2}(a_3).$$

What makes the difference is that $P_{v_1}(a_3) = 1/2$ and $P_{v_2}(a_3) = 1$.

This result tells us that the probability $P_{c,(v_1,a_3)}(v_2,a_3)$ that C assigns in the actual world (v_1,a_3) to the world (v_2,a_3) in which the car is behind door 2 is $2/3$ whereas the probability $P_{c,(v_1,a_3)}(v_1,a_3)$ that C assigns in the actual world to the car being hidden behind door 1 is $1/3$. So it is rational for C to switch these two doors.

10.4 A Game-Theoretical Solution

Monty Hall as an Extensive Game of Imperfect Information. We give a game-theoretical analysis of the puzzle [51]. For other game-theoretical solutions the reader is referred to ⟨http://leeps.ucsc.edu/misc/page/monty-hall-puzzle/ and Friedman, [19]⟩. We represent the puzzle in the form of a finite win-lose game of imperfect information played by two players. C (the counterpart of

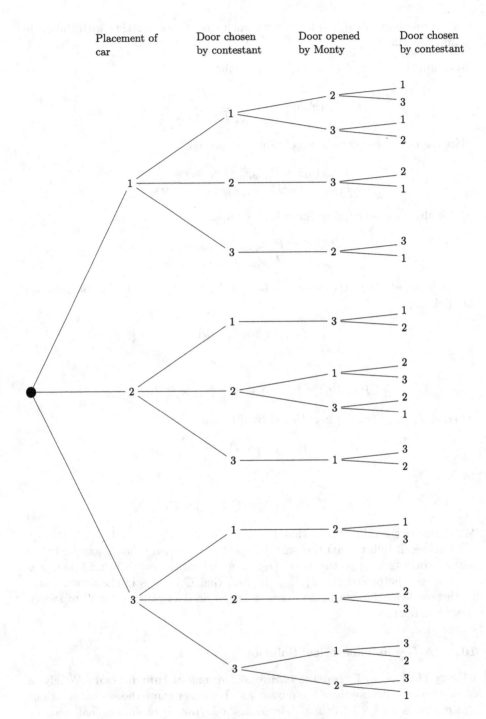

Fig. 8. The Monty Hall problem

Eloise) tries to identify the door with the prize whereas her opponent MH (the counterpart of Abelard) tries to deceive her. The tree which constitutes the extensive form of the game is identical with the tree in the previous section, except for containing one more layer of representations (Fig. 8).

Maximal branches represent possible plays of the game, and have the form (x, y, z, t) with a new extra term t to stand for the final choice of C.

The rules of the game dictate that z must be distinct from x and y and that t is either y or, otherwise, it must be distinct from z. Thus the sequence $(1, 1, 2, 1)$ represents the possible play:

> MH hides the prize behind door 1; C chooses door 1; MH opens door 2; C chooses door 1.

Thus there are 24 plays. C wins every play in which she identifies the door which hides the prize. MH wins the remaining ones.

The imperfect information of the game is manifest in some of its histories being indistinguishable (equivalent). This holds only for player C. The indistinguishable histories are determined by the following two clauses:

C1   Any two histories (x) and (x') are equivalent for player C.
C2   Any histories (x, y, z) and (x', y', z') such that $y = y'$ and $z = z'$ are equivalent for player C.

(C1) expresses the fact that C does not know the door where the prize is hidden when making her first choice. And (C2) expresses the fact that she does not know the door where the prize is hidden, when she makes her second choice.

Strategies. A strategy for player C is any function F which gives her a choice for any history where she is to move. Thus F will give her, for every choice of x, a value for y and for every sequence (x, y, z), a value for t. Imperfect information will impose the following restriction (uniformity) on any strategy F:

– If the histories h and h' are equivalent, then $F(h) = F(h')$.

We prefer to decompose any F into two "local" strategies, that is, two functions f and f' such that f yields a value for y and f' yields a value for t. Given (C1), f will be have to be a constant function, that is, a door i. Given (C2), f' will take only y and z as arguments.

To conclude, player C's set S_C of strategies will consist of pairs (i, h_i), where i stands for a door and h_i for a function of two arguments (y, z). A strategy (i, h_i) is winning if C wins every play where she follows it. The notion of "following a strategy" is standard in game theory and could be given a formal definition. It will become, however, clear from examples.

We focus on two kinds of strategies for player C.

– The "stay" strategy, S_C^{Stay}: choose a door, then stick to the initial guess no matter what MH does.

It is encoded by three strategy pairs, i.e.,

$$S_C^{Stay} = \{(i, h_i) : i = 1, 2, 3\},$$

where

$$h_i(y, z) = i$$

Each strategy (i, h_i) is followed in the play

$$(x, i, z, h_i(i, z))$$

for any x and z. It is winning whenever C's initial guess is correct (i.e., $i = x$) and losing, otherwise. Obviously none of these strategies is winning *simpliciter* (i.e., against any move of the opponent).

– The "switch" strategy, S_C^{Switch}: choose a door, and then after MH opens a door, switch doors.

Thus

$$S_C^{Switch} = \{(1, f_1), (2, f_2), (3, f_3)\}$$

where

$$f_1(1, 2) = 3 \; f_1(1, 3) = 2$$
$$f_2(2, 3) = 1 \; f_2(2, 1) = 3$$
$$f_3(3, 2) = 1 \; f_3(3, 1) = 2.$$

Each of the three strategies wins in two cases in which the initial choice is incorrect, $i \neq x$, and loses in the remaining case.

MH's strategies consists also of pairs (j, g): the first corresponds to a value for x; the function g associates to each argument (x, y) a value for z.

The only strategy available to MH (given the rules of the game) is: "hide the prize behind a door, and after C chooses a door, open any other door". Thus S_{MH} is encoded by the following strategy pairs:

$(1, g_1) : g_1(1, 1) = 2 \; g_1(1, 2) = 3 \; g_1(1, 3) = 2$
$(1, g_1') : g_1'(1, 1) = 3 \; g_1'(1, 2) = 3 \; g_1'(1, 3) = 2$
$(2, g_2) : g_2(2, 1) = 3 \; g_2(2, 2) = 1 \; g_2(2, 3) = 1$
$(2, g_2') : g_2'(2, 1) = 3 \; g_2'(2, 2) = 3 \; g_2'(2, 3) = 1$
$(3, g_3) : g_3(3, 1) = 2 \; g_3(3, 2) = 1 \; g_3(3, 3) = 1$
$(3, g_3') : g_3'(3, 1) = 2 \; g_3'(3, 2) = 1 \; g_3'(3, 3) = 2$

Each of the strategy pair (j, g_j) is followed in every play of the form

$$(j, y, g_j(j, y), t)$$

for any y and t. It is winning whenever $j \neq t$ and losing otherwise. None of these strategies is winning *simpliciter*.

The Monty Hall game is indeterminate: this should come as no surprise, for imperfect information often introduces indeterminacy in games. To resolve it, we apply the same technique as above by moving to the strategic form of the game. Afterwards we find an equilibrium in mixed strategies.

Whenever MH follows one of his strategies in S_{MH}, and C follows one of her strategies in S_C, a play of the extensive game is generated which is a win for either one of the players. For instance, when MH follows $(3, g_3)$ and C follows $(1, h_1)$, the result is the play $(3, 1, 2, 1)$ which is a win for MH.

The following table registers the payoffs of the players for all the strategy pairs the players might play:

	$(1, g_1)$	$(1, g_1')$	$(2, g_2)$	$(2, g_2')$	$(3, g_3)$	$(3, g_3')$
$(1, h_1)$	$(1, 0)$	$(1, 0)$	$(0, 1)$	$(0, 1)$	$(0, 1)$	$(0, 1)$
$(2, h_2)$	$(0, 1)$	$(0, 1)$	$(1, 0)$	$(1, 0)$	$(0, 1)$	$(0, 1)$
$(3, h_3)$	$(0, 1)$	$(0, 1)$	$(0, 1)$	$(0, 1)$	$(1, 0)$	$(1, 0)$
$(1, f_1)$	$(0, 1)$	$(0, 1)$	$(1, 0)$	$(1, 0)$	$(1, 0)$	$(1, 0)$
$(2, f_2)$	$(1, 0)$	$(1, 0)$	$(0, 1)$	$(0, 1)$	$(1, 0)$	$(1, 0)$
$(3, f_3)$	$(1, 0)$	$(1, 0)$	$(1, 0)$	$(1, 0)$	$(0, 1)$	$(0, 1)$

This matrix is nothing else but the Monty Hall puzzle represented as a finite, two players, win-loss *strategic* game

$$\Gamma_{MH} = (S_C, S_{MH}, u_C, u_{MH})$$

where u_{MH} and u_C are the payoffs of the two players as depicted in the matrix. We notice that each strategy (i, h_i) is weakly dominated by some strategy (j, f_j), and that the strategies (i, g_i') and (i, g_i) are payoff equivalent for Abelard. We apply the last two propositions of the sect. 7.2 and reduce the game to the smaller one:

	$(1, g_1)$	$(2, g_2)$	$(3, g_3)$
$(1, f_1)$	$(0, 1)$	$(1, 0)$	$(1, 0)$
$(2, f_2)$	$(1, 0)$	$(0, 1)$	$(1, 0)$
$(3, f_3)$	$(1, 0)$	$(1, 0)$	$(0, 1)$

Let μ be the uniform probability distribution $\mu(1, f_i) = \dfrac{1}{3}$ and ν the uniform probability distribution $\nu(j, g_j) = \dfrac{1}{3}$. It is straightforward to check that this is an equilibrium using the Proposition in Sect. 7.3. The expected utility of player C for this equilibrium is 2/3.

Notice that μ assigns an equal probability to each of the pure strategies which implement the "switch" strategy. The important thing is not that it returns to player C an expected utility of $2/3$ but rather that it weakly dominates the "stay" strategy. If we want to compute the expected utility returned to C by the latter strategy, we should return to the bigger game in the above table where both the "switch" and the "stay" strategies are listed. We know that the value of the game described in the table is the same as that delivered by the equilibrium pair (μ, ν). In the game of the table, let ν^* be the same as ν, and let μ^* be the probability distribution such that: $\mu^*(i, f_i) = \frac{1}{3}$ and $\mu^*(i, h_i) = 0$. The pair (μ^*, ν^*) is an equilibrium in this larger game. We compute $U_p((i, h_i), \nu^*)$:

$$U_p((i, h_i), \nu^*) = \sum_{tau \in S_{MH}} \nu^*(\tau) u_p((i, h_i), t) = 2 \times \frac{1}{6} \times 1 = \frac{1}{3}$$

In other words, the "stay" strategy returns an expected utility of $\frac{1}{3}$.

Monty Hall in IF Logic. The Monty Hall game is expressed in IF logic by the sentence

$$\forall x (\exists y / \{x\}) \forall z [x \neq z \wedge y \neq z \rightarrow (\exists t / \{x\}) x = t]$$

or equivalently by the sentence φ_{MH}

$$\forall x (\exists y / \{x\}) \forall z [x = z \vee y = z \vee (\exists t / \{x\}) x = t].$$

We can think of the Contestant, C, as the existential quantifier and disjunction, and of Monty Hall as the universal quantifier. We do not want to push the formalization too far. The intuitive reading of our sentence should be clear: For any door x where the prize is hidden by Monty Hall, for every door y guessed by C, for every door z opened by Monty Hall, if z is distinct from x and from y, then C has one more choice to identify the door where the prize is.

We can also represent explicitly the variant in which C uses the "stay" strategy by the IF sentence φ^1_{MH}

$$\forall x (\exists y / \{x\}) \forall z [x = z \vee y = z \vee (\exists t / \{x\})(x = t \wedge t = y)]$$

as well as the variant in which C uses the "switch" strategy by φ^2_{MH}

$$\forall x (\exists y / \{x\}) \forall z [x = z \vee y = z \vee (\exists t / \{x\})(x = t \wedge t \neq y)].$$

Under the equilibrium semantics the value of φ^1_{MH} turns out to be $1/3$ and that of φ^2_{MH} turns out to be $2/3$. We have thus recovered in IF logic both Isaacs's and Grinstead and Snell's solution to the general version of the puzzle expressed in the earlier quotation. Still the game-theoretical conceptualization of the puzzle and its representation as φ_{MH} goes beyond their analysis. It is a "qualitative solution": the "switch" weakly dominates the "stay" strategy.

We take stock. The updated account gave the same solution to the Monty Hall problem as the classical account based on conditional probabilities. Both approaches conditionalize, the former on actions, the second on propositions and yield two posterior probabilities. I take both approaches to provide a solution to a *particular, local, decision theoretical* problem, that of explaining why a particular action is more rational than another in certain particular circumstances. The reader is referred to [7] for the differences between the two approaches.

I take the game-theoretical account to provide an explanation to a general, global problem: why it is rational for an agent to play one strategy against another. The relevant notion of rationality is game - not decision - theoretical: one strategy weakly dominates another. There is no need for conditionalization and no need for prior probabilities. Velica and Sandu [51] provides a detailed game-theoretical analysis of the puzzle and comparisons to other approaches.

11   IF Logic and Game Specification

(I am very grateful to Pietro Galliani for this section). As we saw, IF Logic can be used to represent games (such as the Monty Hall game, or the signaling games) and reason about their properties. From this point of view, IF Logic can be thought of as a *Game Specification Language*. Indeed, the methodology displayed in the above examples has been the following:

1. First, we selected a "target" game G_0 of independent interest, such as Matching Pennies, a signaling game or the Monty Hall puzzle;
2. Then we encoded this game in terms of a first-order structure M and a IF Logic formula φ such that $\Gamma(M, \varphi) = G_0$.

Of course, this is certainly not the only possible motivation for the study of IF Logic; however, as one possible area of application, game specification can be thought of as a useful testbed for the development and study of variants and extensions of this framework. I am following closely Galliani's suggestions here.

A first, easy observation is that a game specification language can be naturally coupled with a *game query* language. As an example, consider the following (extremely simple) game query language:

$$\gamma ::= \mathbf{WS}(\varphi) \mid \mathbf{NE}(\varphi) = r \mid \mathbf{NE}(\varphi) = \mathbf{NE}(\varphi) \mid \neg\gamma \mid \gamma \vee \gamma$$

where v ranges over all variable symbols, φ ranges over all IF Logic sentences and r ranges over the interval $[0, 1]$.

The semantic conditions for the **WS** and **NE** operators are of course

- $M \models \mathbf{WS}(\varphi)$ if and only if the existential player has a winning strategy in the strategic two-player game $\Gamma(M, \varphi)$;
- $M \models \mathbf{NE}(\varphi) = r$ if and only if the Nash equilibria of the game $\Gamma(M, \varphi)$ have value r.
- $M \models \mathbf{NE}(\varphi_1) = \mathbf{NE}(\varphi_2)$ if and only if the values of the Nash equilibria for the games $\Gamma(M, \varphi_1)$ and $\Gamma(M, \varphi_2)$ are the same.

Clearly, both game-theoretic semantics and equilibrium semantics can be interpreted in this formalism. Moreover, we can use it to describe fairly complex statements concerning the properties of games. For example, in the Monty Hall puzzle, the "switch" strategy is the optimal one for the contestant. This corresponds precisely to the validity of the formula

$$\mathbf{NE}(\forall x(\exists y/x)\forall z(x = z \vee y = z \vee (\exists t/x)x = t)) = \mathbf{NE}(\forall x(\exists y/x)\forall z(x = z \vee \\ y = z \vee (\exists t/x)(x = t \wedge t \neq y))).$$

The left hand of this equality describes the Monty Hall puzzle, as before; the right one, on the other hand, describes a *solution* of this puzzle. The additional condition "$t \neq y$" constrains Eloise's second choice to be different from her first one; and the fact that these two expressions have the same value means precisely that Eloise obtains her maximum possible average payoff when she adopts this strategy.

The "game query language" that we described is of extremely limited interest, of course, and will not be examined any further in this work. What we want to emphasize here is that IF Logic and its variants can indeed be thought of as languages for describing games. In this spirit, we will now present a simple extension of IF Logic which allows for the specification of some interesting variants of the games seen so far. I am talking about *probabilistic quantifiers*.

The idea is as follows: let M be a finite model, and let $\mu : M \to [0,1]$ be a probability distribution over its domain. Then the quantifier $\mu x(\varphi)$ corresponds to a move in which the value of the variable x is selected according to the distribution μ. (The same idea appears, in a different context, in [2,25,39], among others.) It is unproblematic to extend our definition of semantic games to this case: the resulting games are still zero-sum, but now the payoffs may be between 0 and 1, as they represent the *expected* outcome of the game for the players' choices of strategies. As a simple example, consider the following variant of φ_{MP}:

$$\varphi_{lot} = (\mu x)(\exists y/\{x\})(x = t).$$

This formula expresses a *lottery*: the value of x is selected according to a fixed distribution μ, then Eloise selects the value of y without examining the value of x, and wins the game only if $x = y$. Clearly, if M has n elements and μ stands for the uniform distribution, the value of the semantic game is still $1/n$; and if μ is not uniform, the value of the game is precisely $\max\{\mu(a) : a \in M\}$ and the optimal strategy for Eloise consists in selecting the most likely element.

So far so good. What else can we do with these probabilistic quantifiers? Let us reconsider the signaling game sentence

$$\varphi_{sig} = \forall x \exists z (\exists y/\{x\})(S(x) \to (\Sigma(z) \wedge R(y) \wedge y = x)).$$

In its semantic game Abelard represents the source of the signal and Eloise represents both the encoder and the decoder of the signal. Hence, the source is assumed to be *adversarial*, and to aim to cause as much difficulty as possible to the encoder/decoder. This form of worst-case analysis has its uses, of course; but not all sources of data need to behave in this way. What if some of the states are less likely, or more likely, than others? If we want to use IF Logic to modeling signaling games in a more general setting, and to connect it to the vast amount of work done on such topics within Information and Coding Theory, this is easily of the first questions which we should ask.

Using probabilistic quantifiers, this variant of the signaling game may be represented as

$$(\mu x)\exists z(\exists y/\{x\})(S(x) \to (\Sigma(z) \wedge R(y) \wedge y = x)).$$

Given a model M for which $S^M = R^M = \{s_1 \ldots s_n\}$, $\Sigma^M = \{t_1 \ldots t_m\}$, and $m < n$, and given a distribution μ such that $\mu(a) > 0 \Rightarrow a \in \{s_1 \ldots s_n\}$, it is easy to see that the value of the formula is

$$\max \left\{ \sum_{a \in A} \mu(a) : A \subseteq \{s_1 \ldots s_n\}, |A| = m \right\}$$

corresponding to the strategy of the existential player in which she attempts to encode and decode faithfully the m most likely possible states; and a special case of this, we have that if $\mu(a) = 1/n$ for all $a \in \{s_1 \ldots s_n\}$, the value of the formula is m/n.

Finally, let us reconsider the Monty Hall game. Its analysis in terms of IF Logic represents, faithfully, the case in which Monty Hall personally chooses where to place the prize before the start of the game; but as we said, there also exist variants of the puzzle in which the prize is assumed to have been placed behind each door according to a specific distribution (generally, the uniform one). This, of course, can be modeled by the expression

$$(\mu_U x)(\exists y/\{x\})\forall z[x = z \vee y = z \vee (\exists t/\{x\})x = t]$$

As these two simple examples show, adding probabilistic quantifiers to the language of IF Logic radically increases its potential as a game specification language. We will not discuss this example further here; but we present it as one of the possible avenues for the development of variants and extensions of IF Logic.

12   Some Open Problems

– *IF quantifiers and natural language.* The connection between IF logic and scope phenomena in natural language has not been systematically investigated. Some promising new lines are Brasoveanu and Farkas [12] who propose a novel account of "selective" covariation (imperfect information) involving universal quantifiers and indefinites in natural language. The authors use the syntax of IF logic to mark the constraints on the choice of indefinites and use a semantical mechanism that relies on sets of variable assignments.

- *Interpretation of the probabilistic values.* What does it actually mean to say that an IF sentence φ has the value ε on a model $\mathbb{M}$? It would be worthwhile to connect this notion to other notions which seem to belong to the same family such as many-valued logics.
- *Motivation of the framework.* The way we combine logic and games is different from the mainstream combination which brings logic in (e.g. epistemic logic) in order to make explicit and characterize implicit assumptions about the players' knowledge and behaviour. We use IF logic to attain greater expressive power, for instance, to express certain games (Matching Pennies, Lewis signaling games, Monty Hall, etc.). As in the rise of the "semantic tradition" in the old times, we aim at finding a logical language in which games, strategies, etc. may be precisely expressed. But once we have done that, it would be of course desirable to derive some of the solutions to different puzzles by exploiting some syntactical properties of the formalism.
- *The relation with coordination games.* (I am grateful to an anonymous referee for suggesting this.) We have provided an independence-friendly game-theoretic formalization of Lewis' signaling problem. There is also a well-known game-theoretic formalization of this problem as coordination games. Is there a deeper connection between the two? Can we associate with every coordination game an independence-friendly game the solution of which relates to the solution of the coordination game as in the Lewis example?
- *Toolkits for computing values.* So far all our examples have been relatively simple: they involve only the identity relation and/or unary predicates. The underlying problem is that it is too hard, not only practically but also computationally, to compute the values of a given IF game in a more complex vocabulary with relation symbols with 2 or higher arity.
- *Uniform strategies.* In all our examples, all equilibrium strategies are uniform. This statement cannot be generalized to arbitrary games: The games of the formula $\forall x(\exists y/\{x\})R(x,y)$ span the entire space of win-lose zero-sum two player games, which includes games that do not have equilibria in uniform strategies. However, it would be interesting to know whether such a theorem could be proved for IF sentences with restricted vocabulary, e.g., only sentences with the identity symbol.
- *Computational aspects.* Equilibria presuppose that we have a "source of randomness" available. It would be interesting if we could show somehow that this source of randomness can be used to simulate random computations. In the computer science literature such algorithms are well known (e.g., Monte Carlo algorithms).
- *Definability results.* Given a value $0 < \varepsilon < 1$ and an IF sentence φ, what kind of classes of models $\mathbb{M}$ can be defined by the property "φ has value ε in $\mathbb{M}$"? We have seen earlier in Sect. 9 that there are IF sentences which assume all the values in $\mathbb{Q}$ as the model varies. It could be interesting to see which other subsets of $\mathbb{Q}$ could be defined in this sense by an IF sentence.
- *Philosophical aspects.* An anonymous referee pointed out that we have not given any justification for the selection of equilibria among strategies which are not weakly dominated. In other words, there are no further explicit

theoretical assumptions from which this selection principle could follow. In standard game theory such principle codifies implicit assumptions about the behaviour of the players. They are made explicit in epistemic game theory. According to the referee, weak dominance is motivated by trembles, which in turn are made explicit by lexicographic expected utility [11]. A player has a sequence of beliefs (over the strategies of the other player). He employs his first-order belief unless hypothetically contradicted, then his second-order belief, etc. The union of support of these beliefs cover the entire space. I agree that weak dominance can be made explicit but I do not think it can be justified, but this is something which requires further thought. The referee has an interesting suggestion: one would expect Abelard (the universal quantifier) and Eloise (the existential quantifier) to display the same kind of rationality when they play IF games as when they play ordinary first-order games. Or, as the referee pointed out (Sect. 4.4), first-order logic games are solvable by one round of weak dominance. Hence weak dominance (relativized to preferences over lotteries) should be a guiding principle in IF logic too.

Acknowledgments. I am very much indebted to the Department of Logic at the Institute of Philosophy of the Academy of Sciences of the Czech Republic, which has hosted me for three months during the spring of 2013 and has provided stimulating conditions and discussions for the completion of this work. I am also indebted to Pietro Galliani and to two anonymous referees for excellent suggestions.

References

1. Abramsky, S., Väänänen, J.: From IF to BI: a tale of dependence and separation. CoRR abs/1102 (2011)
2. Bacchus, F.: A logic for representing and reasoning with statistical knowledge. Comput. Intell. **6**, 209–231 (1990)
3. Barbero, F.: On existential declarations of independence in IF logic. Rev. Symb. Log. **6**(02), 254–280 (2013)
4. Barbero, F., Sandu, G.: Signaling in independence-friendly logic. Log. J. IGPL **22**, 638–664 (2014)
5. Barwise, J.: On branching quantifiers in English. J. Philos. Log. **8**, 47–80 (1979)
6. van Benthem, J.F.A.K.: Games that make sense. In: Apt, K.R., van Rooij, R. (eds.) New Perspectives on Games and Interaction. Texts in Logic and Games, vol. 4, pp. 197–209. Amsterdam University Press, Amsterdam (2008)
7. van Benthem, J.F.A.K.: Conditional probability meets update logic. J. Log. Lang. Inform. **12**, 409–421 (2003)
8. van Benthem, J.F.A.K.: Logic in Games. MIT Press, Cambridge (2014)
9. van Benthem, J.F.A.K., Gerbrandy, J., Kooi, B.: Dynamic update with probabilities. Stud. Logica. **93**, 67–96 (2009)
10. Blass, A., Gurevich, Y.: Henkin quantifiers and complete problems. Ann. Pure Appl. Log. **32**, 1–16 (1986)
11. Blume, L., Brandenburger, A., Dekel, E.: Lexicographic probabilities and choice under uncertainty. Econometrica J. Econometric Soc. **59**, 61–79 (1991)
12. Brasoveanu, A., Farkas, D.F.: How indefinites choose their scope. Linguist. Philos. **34**(1), 1–55 (2011)

13. Caicedo, X., Dechesne, F., Janssen, T.M.V.: Equivalence and quantifier rules for logic with imperfect information. Log. J. IGPL **17**, 91–129 (2009)
14. van Ditmarsch, H., van der Hoek, W., Kooi, B.: Dynamic Epistemic Logic. Springer, Dordrecht (2007)
15. Enderton, H.B.: Finite partially ordered quantifiers. Zeitschrift für Mathematische Logik und Grundlagen der Mathematik **16**, 393–397 (1970)
16. Ewerhart, C.: Chess-like games are dominance solvable in at most two steps. Games Econ. Behav. **33**(1), 41–47 (2000)
17. Ewerhart, C.: Iterated weak dominance in strictly competitive games of perfect information. J. Econ. Theor. **107**(2), 474–482 (2002)
18. Fagin, R., Halpern, J., Moses, Y., Vardi, M.: Reasoning About Knowledge. MIT Press, Cambridge, MA (1995)
19. Friedman, D.: Monty Hall's three doors: construction and deconstruction of a choice anomaly. Am. Econ. Rev. **88**, 933–946 (1998)
20. Galliani, P.: Game values and equilibria for undetermined sentences of dependence logic. M.Sc. thesis, Universiteit van Amsterdam (2008). Master of Logic Series 2008-08
21. Galliani, P.: Inclusion and exclusion dependencies in team semantics - on some logics of imperfect information. Ann. Pure Appl. Log. **163**, 68–84 (2012)
22. Goldfarb, W.: Logic in the twenties: the nature of the quantifier. J. Symb. Log. **44**, 351–368 (1979)
23. Grädel, E., Väänänen, J.: Dependence and independence. Stud. Logica. **101**(2), 399–410 (2013)
24. Grinstead, C.M., Snell, L.: Introduction to Probabilities, 2nd edn. American Mathematical Society, Providence (1998)
25. Halpern, J.: An analysis of first-order logics of probability. Artif. Intell. **46**, 311–350 (1990)
26. Henkin, L.: Some remarks on infinitely long formulas. In: Bernays, P. (ed.) Intuitionistic Methods: Proceedings of the Symposium on Foundations of Mathematics, pp. 167–183. Pergamon Press, Oxford (1961)
27. Hintikka, J.: Quantifiers vs. quantification theory. Linguist. Inq. **5**, 153–174 (1974)
28. Hintikka, J.: The Principles of Mathematics Revisited. Cambridge University Press, Cambridge (1996)
29. Hintikka, J., Kulas, J.: The Game of Language. D. Reidel, Dordrecht (1983)
30. Hintikka, J., Kulas, J.: Anaphora and Definite Descriptions: Two Applications of Game-Theoretical Semantics. D. Reidel, Dordrecht (1985)
31. Hintikka, J., Sandu, G.: Informational independence as a semantical phenomenon. In: Frolov, I.T., Fenstad, J.E., Hilpinen, R. (eds.) Logic, Methodology and Philosophy of Science VIII. Studies in Logic and the Foundations of Mathematics, pp. 571–589. North-Holland, Amsterdam (1989)
32. Hintikka, J., Sandu, G.: On the Methodology of Linguistics: A Case Study. Basil Blackwell, Oxford (1991)
33. Hintikka, J., Sandu, G.: Game-theoretical semantics. In: van Benthem, J., ter Meulen, A. (eds.) Handbook of Logic and Language, pp. 361–410. Elsevier, Amsterdam (1997)
34. Hintikka, J., Sandu, G.: Game-theoretical semantics. In: van Benthem, J., ter Meulen, A. (eds.) Handbook of Logic and Language, 2nd edn, pp. 415–466. Elsevier, Amsterdam (2010)
35. Hodges, W.: Compositional semantics for a language of imperfect information. Log. J. IGPL **5**, 539–563 (1997)

36. Isaac, R.: The Pleasures of Probabilities. Springer, New York (1995)
37. Janssen, T.M.V., Dechesne, F.: Signalling in IF games: a tricky business. In: Rebuschi, M., van Benthem, J., Heinzmann, G., Visser, H. (eds.) The Age of Alternative Logics: Assessing Philosophy of Logic and Mathematics Today, pp. 221–241. Springer, Berlin (2006)
38. Kooi, B.P.: Probabilistic dynamic epistemic logic. J. Log. Lang. Inform. **12**(4), 381–408 (2003)
39. Krynicki, M., Mostowski, M.: Ambiguous quantifiers. In: Orlowska, E. (ed.) Logic at Work, pp. 548–565. Springer, Heidelberg (1999)
40. Lewis, D.: Convention: A Philosophical Study. Harvard University Press, Cambridge (1969)
41. Mann, A.L.: Workshop on dependence and independence logic. In: ESSLLI (2010)
42. Mann, A.L., Sandu, G., Sevenster, M.: Independence-Friendly Logic: A Game-Theoretic Approach. London Mathematical Society Lecture Note Series, vol. 386. Cambridge University Press, Cambridge (2011)
43. Morehead, A.H., Frey, R.L., Mott-Smith, G.: The New Complete Hoyle Revised. Doubleday, New York (1991)
44. Osborne, J.M.: An Introduction to Game Theory. Oxford University Press, Oxford (2003)
45. Raghavan, T.E.S.: Zero-sum two person games. In: Aumann, R.J., Hart, S. (eds.) Handbook of Game Theory with Economic Applications, vol. 2, pp. 736–759. Elsevier, Amsterdam (1994)
46. Selten, R.: Reexamination of the perfectness concept for equilibrium points in extensive games. Int. J. Game Theory **4**(1), 25–55 (1975)
47. Sevenster, M.: Branches of Imperfect Information: Logic, Games, and Computation. Ph.D. thesis, University of Amsterdam (2006)
48. Sevenster, M., Sandu, G.: Equilibrium semantics of languages of imperfect information. Ann. Pure Appl. Log. **161**, 618–631 (2010)
49. Shoenfield, J.R.: Mathematical Logic. Addison-Wesley, Reading (1967)
50. Väänänen, J.: Dependence Logic: A New Approach to Independence Friendly Logic. Cambridge University Press, Cambridge (2007)
51. Velica, S., Sandu, G.: Monty Hall: a game-theoretical solution. In: Başkent, C., Moss, L., Ramanujam, R. (eds.) Rohit Parikh on Logic, Language and Society, Springer
52. von Neumann, J.: Zur Theorie der Gesellschaftsspiele. Mathematische Annalen **100**, 295–320 (1928)
53. Walkoe, W.: Finite partially-ordered quantification. J. Symb. Log. **35**, 535–555 (1970)
54. Zermelo, E.: Über eine Anwendung der Mengenlehre auf die Theorie des Schachspiels. In: Love, A.E.H. (ed.) Proceedings of the Fifth International Congress of Mathematicians, II, pp. 501–504. Cambridge University Press, Cambridge (1913)

Strategies in Social Situations

Strategies of Persuasion, Manipulation and Propaganda: Psychological and Social Aspects

Michael Franke[1](✉) and Robert van Rooij[2]

[1] Department of Linguistics, University of Tübingen, Tübingen, Germany
mchfranke@gmail.com
[2] Institute for Logic, Language and Computation (ILLC),
University of Amsterdam, Amsterdam, The Netherlands
R.A.M.vanRooij@uva.nl

Abstract. How can one influence the behavior of others? What is a good persuasion strategy? It is obviously of great importance to determine *what* information best to provide and also *how* to convey it. To delineate how and when manipulation of others can be successful, the first part of this chapter reviews basic findings of decision and game theory on models of strategic communication. But there is also a social aspect to manipulation, concerned with determining *who we should address* so as best to promote our opinion in a larger group or society as a whole. The second half of this chapter therefore looks at a novel extension of DeGroot's [19] classical model of opinion dynamics that allows agents to strategically influence some agents more than others. This side-by-side investigation of psychological and social aspects enables us to reflect on the general question what a good manipulation strategy is. We submit that successful manipulation requires exploiting critical weaknesses, such as limited capability of strategic reasoning, limited awareness, susceptibility to cognitive biases or to potentially indirect social pressure.

Keywords: Pragmatic reasoning · Bounded rationality · Opinion dynamics · Persuasion · Heuristics

You might be an artist, politician, banker, merchant, terrorist, or, what is likely given that you are obviously reading this, a scientist. Whatever your profession or call of heart, your career depends, whether you like it or not, in substantial part on your success at influencing the behavior and opinions of others in ways favorable to you (but not necessarily favorable to them). Those who aspire to be successful manipulators face two major challenges. The first challenge is the most fundamental and we shall call it *pragmatic* or *one-to-one*: a single manipulator faces a single decision maker whose opinion or behavior the former seeks to influence. The one-to-one challenge is mostly, but not exclusively, about *rhetoric*, i.e., the proper use of logical arguments and other, less normatively compelling, but perhaps even more efficiently persuasive communication strategies (e.g. [80]).

© Springer-Verlag Berlin Heidelberg 2015
J. van Benthem et al. (Eds.): Models of Strategic Reasoning, LNCS 8972, pp. 255–291, 2015.
DOI: 10.1007/978-3-662-48540-8_8

But if manipulation is to be taken further, also a second challenge arises and that is *social* or *many-to-many*. Supposing that we know *how* to exert efficient influence, it is another issue *whom* to influence in a group of decision makers, so as to efficiently propagate an opinion in a society.

This chapter deals with efficient strategies for manipulation at both levels. This is not only relevant for aspiring master manipulators, but also for those who would like to brace themselves for a life in a manipulative environment. Our main conclusions are that successful manipulation requires the exploitation of weaknesses of those to be manipulated. So in order to avoid being manipulated against one's own interest, it is important to be aware of the possibility of malign manipulation and one's own weaknesses.

The chapter is divided into two parts. The first is addressed in Sect. 1 and deals with the pragmatic perspective. It first shows that standard models from decision and game theory predict that usually an ideally rational decision maker would see through any malign manipulative effort. But if this is so, there would not be much successful manipulation, and also not many malign persuasive attempts from other ideally rational agents. Since this verdict flies in the face of empirical evidence, we feel forced to extend our investigation to more psychologically adequate models of boundedly rational agency. Towards this end, we review models of (i) unawareness of the game/context model, (ii) depth-limited step-by-step reasoning, and (iii) descriptive decision theory. We suggest that it is cognitive shortcomings of this sort that manipulators have to exploit in order to be successful.

Whereas Sect. 1 has an overview character in that it summarizes key notions and insights from the relevant literature, Sect. 2 seeks to explore new territory. Following the gradient of recent interest in information dynamics in possibly structured groups of agents (cf. [4,50,71]), we investigate a model of social *opinion dynamics*, i.e., a model of how opinions spread and develop in a population of agents, which also allows agents to choose whom to influence and whom to neglect. Since the complexity of this social dimension of manipulation is immense, the need for simple yet efficient heuristics arises. We try to delineate in general terms what a good heuristic strategy is for social manipulation of opinions. For that reason, we report on a case study simulating the behavior of four concrete heuristics in different kinds of social interaction structures. Two interesting conclusions can be drawn from this case study. Firstly, strategies that aim at easily influenceable targets are efficient on a short time scale, while strategies that aim at influential targets are efficient on a longer time scale. Secondly, it helps to play a coalition strategy together with other likeminded manipulators, in particular so as not to get into one another's way. Taken together, these conclusions corroborate the general conclusion that effective social propaganda, like one-to-one strategic manipulation, requires making strategic use of particularly weak spots in the flow patterns of information within a society.

Another final contribution of this chapter is in what it is *not* about. To the best of our knowledge, there is little systematic work in the tradition of logic and game theory that addresses both the psychological and the social dimension of strategic manipulation at once. We therefore conclude the chapter with a brief outlook at the many vexing open issues that arise when this integrative perspective is taken seriously.

A Note on Terminology. Although the term "manipulation" usually has a negative connotation, we frequently use it here more broadly to include cases where the target of manipulation might benefit from being manipulated as well, or is at least indifferent. We consider any act of purpose-driven act of influencing another agent or group of agents as a manipulative act irrespective of any potential conflicts of interest. Still, the main challenge, especially from the pragmatic perspective, is how to be able to manipulate agents *against* their own self-interests.

When we speak of a "strategy" here, what we have in mind is mostly a very loose and general notion, much like the use of the word "strategy" in non-technical English, when employed by speakers merrily uninterested in any geeky meaning contrast between "strategy" and "tactic". When we talk about a "good strategy", we mean a communication strategy that influences other agents to act, or have an opinion, in accordance with the manipulator's preferences. This notion of communication strategy is different from the one used in other contributions to this volume.

Within game theory, the standard notion of a strategy is that of a *full contingency plan* that specifies at the beginning of a game which action an agent chooses whenever she might be called to act. When we discuss strategies of games in Sect. 1 as a formal specification of an agent's behavior, we do also use the term in this specific technical sense. In general, however, we talk about strategic manipulation from a more God's-eye point of view, referring to a good strategy as what is a good general principle which, if realized in a concrete situation, would give rise to a "strategy" in the formal, game-theoretic sense of the term.

1 Pragmatic Aspects of Persuasion and Manipulation

The pragmatic dimension of persuasion and manipulation chiefly concerns the use of language. Persuasive communication of this kind is studied in rhetoric, argumentation theory, politics, law, and marketing (cf. [80]). But more recently also pragmatics, the linguistic theory of language use, has turned its eye towards persuasive communication, especially in the form of *game-theoretic pragmatics*. This is a very welcome development, for two main reasons. Firstly, persuasive communication can learn from pragmatics: a widely used misleading device in advertisements—a paradigmatic example of persuasion—is *false implication* (e.g. [44]). A certain quality is claimed for the product without explicitly asserting its uniqueness, with the intention to make you assume that only that product has the relevant quality. Persuasion by false implication is reminiscent of *conversational implicature*, a central notion studied in linguistic pragmatics (e.g. [48]). Secondly, the study of persuasive communication *should* really be a natural part of linguistic pragmatics. The only reason why persuasion has been neglected for long is due to the fact that the prevalent theory of language use in linguistics is based on the Gricean assumption of *cooperativity* [34]. Though game theory can formalize Gricean pragmatics, its analysis of strategic persuasive communication is suitable for non-cooperative situations as well. Indeed, game theory is the natural framework for studying strategic manipulative communication.

To show this, the following Sects. 1.1 and 1.2 introduce the main setup of decision and game-theoretic models of one-to-one communication. Unfortunately, as we will see presently, standard game theory counterintuitively predicts that successful manipulation is rare if not impossible. This is because ideally rational agents would basically see through attempts of manipulation. Hence ideally rational manipulators would not even try to exert malign influence. In reaction to this counterintuitive predicament, Sect. 1.3 looks at a number of models in which some seemingly unrealistic assumptions of idealized rational agency are levelled. In particular, we briefly cover models of (i) language use among agents who are possibly unaware of relevant details of the decision-making context, (ii) language use among agents who are limited in their depth of strategic thinking, and (iii) the impact that certain surprising features and biases of our cognitive makeup, such as *framing effects* [45], have on decision making.

1.1 Decisions and Information Flow

On first thought it may seem that it is always helpful to provide truthful information and mischievous to lie. But this first impression is easily seen to be wrong. For one thing, it can sometimes be helpful to lie. For another, providing truthful but incomplete information can sometimes be harmful.

Here is a concrete example that shows this. Suppose that our decision maker is confronted with the decision problem whether to choose action a_1 or a_2, while uncertain which of the states $t_1, \ldots, t_6$ is actual:

$U(a_i, t_j)$	t_1	t_2	t_3	t_4	t_5	t_6
a_1	-1	1	3	7	-1	1
a_2	2	2	2	2	2	2

By definition, rational decision makers choose their actions so as to maximize their expected utility. So, if a rational agent considers each state equally probable, it is predicted that he will choose a_2 because that has a higher expected utility than a_1; namely, a_2 gives a sure outcome of 2, but a_1 only gives an expected utility of $5/3 = 1/6 \times \sum_i u(a_1, t_i)$. If t_1 is the actual state, the decision maker has made the right decision. This is not the case, however, if, for instance, t_3 were the actual state. It is now helpful for the decision maker to receive the false information that t_4 is the actual state: falsely believing that t_4 is actual, the decision maker would choose the action which is in fact best in the actual state t_3. And of course, we all make occasional use of *white lies*: communicating something that is false in the interest of tact or politeness.

Another possibility is providing truthful but misleading information. Suppose that the agent receives the information that states t_5 and t_6 are not the case. After updating her information state (i.e., probability function) by standard conditionalization, rationality now dictates our decision maker to choose a_1 because that now has the highest expected utility: $5/2$ versus 2. Although a_1 was perhaps the most rational action to choose given the decision maker's uncertainty, he still made the *wrong decision* if it turns out that t_1 is the actual state. One can conclude that receiving truthful information is not always helpful, and can sometimes even hurt.

Communication helps to disseminate information. In many cases, receiving truthful information is helpful: it allows one to make a better informed decision. But we have just seen that getting truthful information can be harmful as well, at least when it is partial information. As a consequence, there is room for malign manipulation even with the strategic dissemination of truthful information, unless the decision maker would realize the potentially intended deception. Suppose, for instance, that the manipulator prefers the decision maker to perform a_1 instead of a_2, independently of which state actually holds. If the decision maker and the manipulator are both ideally rational, the informer will realize that it doesn't make sense to provide, say, information $\{t_1, t_2, t_3, t_4\}$ with misleading intention, because the decision maker won't fall for this and will consider information to be *incredible*. A new question comes up: how much can an agent credibly communicate in a situation like that above? This type of question is studied by economists making use of signaling games.

1.2 Signaling Games and Credible Communication

Signaling games are the perhaps simplest non-trivial game-theoretic models of language use. They were invented by David Lewis to study the emergence of conventional semantic meaning [49]. For reasons of exposition, we first look at Lewisean signaling games where messages do not have a previously given conventional meaning, but then zoom in on the case where a commonly known conventional language exists.

A signaling game proceeds as follows. A sender S observes the actual state of the world $t \in T$ and chooses a message m from a set of alternatives M. In turn, R observes the sent message and chooses an action a from a given set A. The payoffs for both S and R depend in general on the state t, the sent message m and the action a chosen by the receiver. Formally, a *signaling game* is a tuple $\langle \{S, R\}, T, \Pr, M, A, U_S, U_R \rangle$ where $\Pr \in \Delta(T)$ is a probability distribution over T capturing the receiver's *prior beliefs* about which state is actual, and $U_{S,R} : M \times A \times T \to \mathbb{R}$ are utility functions for both sender and receiver. We speak of a *cheap-talk game*, if message use does not influence utilities.[1]

It is clear to see that a signaling game embeds a classical decision problem, such as discussed in the previous section. The receiver is the decision maker and the sender is the manipulator. It is these structures that help us to study manipulation strategies and assess their success probabilities.

---

[1] For simplicity we assume that T, M and A are finite non-empty sets, and that $\Pr(t) > 0$ for all $t \in T$.

To specify player behavior, we define the notion of a *strategy*. (This is now a technical use of the term, in line with the remarks above). A *sender strategy* $\sigma \in M^T$ is modelled as a function from states to messages. Likewise, a *receiver strategy* $\rho \in A^M$ is a function from messages to actions. The strategy pair $\langle \sigma^*, \rho^* \rangle$ is an equilibrium if neither player can do any better by unilateral deviation. More technically, $\langle \sigma^*, \rho^* \rangle$ is a *Nash equilibrium* iff for all $t \in T$:

(i) $U_S(t, \sigma^*(t), \rho^*(\sigma^*(t))) \geq U_S(t, \sigma(t), \rho^*(\sigma(t)))$ for all $\sigma \in M^T$, and
(ii) $U_R(t, \sigma^*(t), \rho^*(\sigma^*(t))) \geq U_R(t, \sigma^*(t), \rho(\sigma^*(t)))$ for all $\rho \in A^M$.

A signaling game typically has many equilibria. Suppose we limit ourselves to a cooperative signaling game with only two states $T = \{t_1, t_2\}$ that are equally probable $\Pr(t_1) = \Pr(t_2)$, two messages $M = \{m_1, m_2\}$, and two actions $A = \{a_1, a_2\}$, and where $U(t_i, m_j, a_k) = 1$ if $i = k$, and 0 otherwise, for both sender and receiver. In that case the following combination of strategies is obviously a Nash equilibrium:[2]

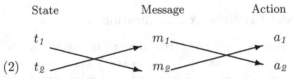

The following combination of strategies is an equally good equilibrium:

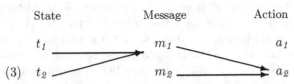

In both situations, the equilibria make real communication possible. Unfortunately, there are also Nash equilibria where nothing is communicated about the actual state of affairs. In case the sender's prior probability of t_2 exceeds that of t_1, for instance, the following combination is also a Nash equilibrium:

State   Message   Action

t_1 $\longrightarrow$ m_1 $\longrightarrow$ a_1
(3) t_2 $\longrightarrow$ m_2 $\longrightarrow$ a_2

Until now we assumed that messages don't have an *a priori* given conventional language is already in place that can be used or abused by speakers to influence their hearers for better or worse? Formally, we model this by a semantic denotation function $\llbracket \cdot \rrbracket : M \to \mathcal{P}(T)$ such that $t \in \llbracket m \rrbracket$ iff m is true in t.[3]

---

[2] Arrows from states to messages depict sender strategies; arrows from messages to actions depict receiver strategies.

[3] We assume for simplicity that for each state t there is at least one message m which is true in that state; and that no message is contradictory, i.e., there is no m for which $\llbracket m \rrbracket = \emptyset$.

Assuming that messages have a conventional meaning can help filter out unreasonable equilibria. In seminal early work, Farrell [22] (the paper goes back to at least 1984) proposed to refine the equilibrium set for cheap-talk signaling games by a notion of *message credibility*, requiring that R believe what S says if it is in S's interest to speak the truth (cf. [23]). Farrell's solution is rather technical and can be criticized for being unrealistic, but his general idea has been picked up and refined in many subsequent contributions, as we will also see below (cf. [28,52,58,67,76,81]). Essentially, Farrell assumed that the set of available messages is infinite and expressively rich: for any given reference equilibrium and every subset $X \subseteq T$ of states, there is always a message m_X with $[\![m_X]\!] = X$ that is not used in that equilibrium.[4] Such an unused message m is called a *credible neologism* if, roughly speaking, it can overturn a given reference equilibrium. Concretely, take an equilibrium $\langle \sigma^*, \rho^* \rangle$, and let $U_S^*(t)$ be the equilibrium payoff of type t for the sender. The types in $[\![m]\!]$ can send a *credible neologism* iff $[\![m]\!] = \{t \in T : U_S(t, BR([\![m]\!])) > U_S^*(t)\}$, where $BR([\![m]\!])$ is R's (assumed unique, for simplicity) optimal response to the prior distribution conditioned on $[\![m]\!]$. If R interprets a credible neologism literally, then some types would send the neologism and destroy the candidate equilibrium. A *neologism proof equilibrium* is an equilibrium for which no subset of T can send a credible neologism. For example, the previous two fully revealing equilibrias in (1) and (2) are neologism proof, but the pooling equilibrium in (3) is not: there is a message m^* with $[\![m^*]\!] = \{t_2\}$ which only t_2 would prefer to send over the given pooling equilibrium.

Farrell defined his notion of credibility in terms of a given reference equilibrium. Yet for accounts of online pragmatic reasoning about language use, it is not always clear where such an equilibrium should come from. In that case another reference point for pragmatic reasoning is ready-at-hand, namely a situation *without* communication entirely. So another way of thinking about $U_S^*(t)$ is just as the utility of S in t if R plays the action with the highest expected utility of R's decision problem. In this spirit, Van Rooij [69] determines the *relevance of information* against the background of the decision maker's decision problem. Roughly speaking, the idea is that message m is relevant with respect to a decision problem if the hearer will change his action upon hearing it.[5] A message is considered credible in case it is relevant, and cannot be used misleadingly. As an example, let's look at the following cooperative situation:

---

[4] This *rich language assumption* might be motivated by evolutionary considerations, but is unsuitable for applications to online pragmatic reasoning about natural language, which, arguably, is not at the same time cheap and fully expressive: some things are more cumbersome to express than others (cf. [28]).

[5] Benz [10] criticizes this and other decision-theoretic approaches, arguing for the need to take the speaker's perspective into account (cf. [9,11] for models where this is done). In particular, Benz [9,10] proved that any speaker strategy aiming at the maximization of relevance necessarily produces misleading utterances. This, according to Benz, entails that relevance maximization alone is not sufficient to guarantee credibility.

(4)

$U(t_i, a_j)$	a_1	a_2
t_1	1,1	0,0
t_2	0,0	1,1

If this was just a decision problem without possibility of communication and furthermore $Pr(t_2) > Pr(t_1)$, then R would play a_2. But that would mean that $U_{S^*}(t_1) = 0$, while $U_{S^*}(t_2) = 1$. In this scenario, message "I am of type t_1" is credible, under van Rooij's [69] notion, but "I am of type t_2" is not, because it is not relevant. Notice that if a speaker is of type t_2, he wouldn't say anything, but the fact that the speaker didn't say anything, if taken into account, must be interpreted as S being of type t_2 (because otherwise S would have said "I am t_1"). Assuming that saying nothing is saying the trivial proposition, R can conclude something more from some messages than is literally expressed. This is not unlike conversational implicatures [34].

So far we have seen that if preferences are aligned, a notion of credibility helps predict successful communication in a natural way. What about circumstances where this ideal condition is not satisfied? Look at the following table:

(5)

$U(t_i, a_j)$	a_1	a_2
t_1	1,1	0,0
t_2	1,0	0,1

In this case, both types of S want R to play a_1 and R would do so, in case he believed that S is of type t_1. However, R will not believe S's message "I am of type t_1", because if S is of type t_2 she still wants R to believe that she is of type t_1, and thus wants to mislead the receiver. Credible communication is not possible now. More in general, it can be shown that costless messages with a pre-existing meaning can be used to credibly transmit information only if it is known by the receiver that it is in the sender's interest to speak the truth.[6] If communicative manipulation is predicted to be possible at all, its successful use is predicted to be highly restricted.

We also must acknowledge that a proper notion of messages credibility is more complicated than indicated so far. Essentially, Farrell's notion and the slight amendment we introduced above use a *forward induction* argument to show that agents can talk themselves out of an equilibrium (cf. [18,75] for accessible discussions of forward induction). But it seems we didn't go far enough. To show this, consider the following game where states are again assumed equiprobable:

(6)

$U(t_i, a_j)$	a_1	a_2	a_3	a_4
t_1	10,5	0,0	1,4.1	-1,3
t_2	0,0	10,5	1,4.1	-1,3
t_3	0,0	0,0	1,4.1	-1,6

---

[6] The most relevant game-theoretic contributions are by Farrell [21,22], Rabin [67], Matthews [52], and Zapater [81]. More recently, this topic has been reconsidered from a more linguistic point of view, e.g., by Stalnaker [76], Franke [28] and Franke, de Jager and van Rooij [31].

Let's suppose again that we start with a situation with only the decision problem and no communication. In this case, R responds with a_3. According to Farrell, this gives rise to two credible announcements: "I am of type t_1" and "I am of type t_2", with the obvious best responses. This is because both types t_1 and t_2 can profit from having these true messages believed: a credulous receiver will answer with actions a_1 and a_2 respectively. A speaker of type t_3 cannot make a credible statement, because revealing her identity would only lead to a payoff strictly worse than what she obtains if R plays a_3. Consequently, R should respond to no message with the same action as he did before, i.e., a_3. But once R realizes that S could have made the other statements credibly, but didn't, she will realize that the speaker must have been of type t_3 and will respond with a_4, and not with a_3. What this shows is that to account for the credibility of a message, one needs to think of higher levels of strategic sophistication. This also suggests that if either R or S do not believe in common belief in rationality, then misleading communication might again be possible. This is indeed what we will come back to presently in Sect. 1.3.

But before turning to that, we should address one more general case. Suppose we assume that messages not only have a semantic meaning, but that speakers also obey Grice's Maxim of Quality and do not assert falsehoods [34].[7] Do we predict more communication now? Milgrom and Roberts [55] demonstrate that in such cases it is best for the decision maker to "assume the worst" about what S reports and that S has omitted information that would be useful. Milgrom and Roberts [55] show that the optimal equilibrium strategy will always be the *sceptical posture*. In this situation, S will know that, unless the decision maker is told everything, the decision maker will take a stance against both his own interests (had he had full information) and the interests of S. Given this, S could as well reveal all she knows.[8] This means that when speakers might try to manipulate the beliefs of the decision maker by being less precise than they could be, this won't help because an ideally rational decision maker will see through this attempt at manipulation. In conclusion, manipulation by communication is impossible in this situation; a result that is very much in conflict with what we perceive daily.[9]

---

[7] It is very frequently assumed in game-theoretic models of pragmatic reasoning that the sender is compelled to truthful signaling by the game model. This assumption is present, for instance, in the work of Parikh [63–65], but also assumed by many others. As long as interlocutors are cooperative in the Gricean sense, this assumption might be innocuous enough, but, as the present considerations make clear, are too crude a simplification when we allow conflicts of interest.

[8] The argument used to prove the result is normally called the *unraveling argument*. See [31] for a slightly different version.

[9] Shin [73] proves a generalization of Milgrom and Robert's result [55], claiming that there always exists a sequential equilibrium (a strengthened notion of Nash equilibrium by Kreps and Wilson [46] which we have not introduced here) of the persuasion game in which the sender's strategy is perfectly revealing in the sense that the sender will say exactly what he knows.

1.3   Manipulation and Bounded Rationality

Many popular and successful theories of meaning and communicative behaviour are based on theories of ideal reasoning and rational behavior. But there is a lot of theoretical and experimental evidence that human beings are not perfectly rational reasoners. Against the assumed idealism it is often held, for instance, that we sometimes hold inconsistent beliefs, and that our decision making exhibits systematic biases that are unexplained by the standard theory (e.g. [74,77]). From this point of view, standard game theory is arguably based on a number of unrealistic assumptions. We will address two of such assumptions below, and indicate what might result if we give these up. First we will discuss the assumption that the game being played is common knowledge. Then we will investigate the implications of giving up the hypothesis that everybody is ideally rational, and that this is common knowledge. Finally, we will discuss what happens if our choices are systematically biased. In all three cases, we will see more room for successful manipulation.

Unawareness of the game being played. In standard game theory it is usually assumed that players conceptualize the game in the same way, i.e., that it is common knowledge what game is played. But this seems like a highly idealized assumption. It is certainly the case that interlocutors occasionally operate under quite different conceptions of the context of conversation, i.e., the 'language game' they are playing. This is evidenced by misunderstandings, but also by the way we talk: cooperative speakers must not only provide information but also enough background to make clear how that information is relevant. To cater for these aspects of conversation, Franke [30] uses models for *games with unawareness* (cf. [25,36,39]) to give a general model for pragmatic reasoning in situations where interlocutors may have variously diverging conceptualizations of the context of utterance relevant to the interpretation of an utterance, different beliefs about these conceptualizations, different beliefs about these beliefs and so on. However, Franke [30] only discusses examples where interlocutors are well-behaved Gricean cooperators [34] with perfectly aligned interests. Looking at cases where this is not so, Feinberg [24,26] demonstrates that taking unawareness into account also provides a new rationale for communication in case of conflicting interests. Feinberg gives examples where communicating one's awareness of the set of actions which the decision maker can choose from might be beneficial for both parties involved. But many other examples exist (e.g. [61]). Here is a very simple one that nonetheless demonstrates the relevant conceptual points.

Reconsider the basic case in (5) that we looked at previously. We have two types of senders: t_1 wants his type to be revealed, and t_2 wishes to be mistaken for a type t_1. As we saw above, the message "I am of type t_1" is not credible in this case, because a sender of type t_2 would send it too. Hence, a rational decision maker should not believe that the actual type is t_1 when he hears that message. But if the decision maker is not aware that there could be a type t_2 that might want to mislead him, then, although incredible from the point of view of a perfectly aware spectator, from the decision maker's subjective point of view, the message "I'm of type t_1" is perfectly credible. The example is (almost) entirely trivial, but the essential point nonetheless significant. If we want to mislead, but also if we want to reliably and honestly communicate, it might be the very best thing to do to leave the decision maker completely in the dark as to any mischievous motivation we might pursue or, contrary to fact, might have been pursuing.

This simple example also shows the importance of choosing, not only *what* to say, but also *how* to say it. (We will come back to this issue in more depth below when we look at *framing effects*). In the context of only two possible states, the messages "I am of type t_1" and "I am not of type t_2" are equivalent. But, of course, from a persuasion perspective they are not equally good choices. The latter would make the decision maker aware of the type t_2, the former need not. So although contextually equivalent in terms of their extension, the requirements of efficient manipulation clearly favor the one over the other simply in terms of surface form, due to their variable effects on the awareness of the decision maker.

In a similar spirit, van Rooij and Franke [70] use differences in awareness-raising of otherwise equivalent conditionals and disjunctions to explain why there are conditional threats (7a) and promises (7b), and also disjunctive threats (7c), but, what is surprising from a logical point of view, no disjunctive promises (7d).

(7) a. If you don't give me your wallet, I'll punish you severely.   threat
     b. If you give me your wallet, I'll reward you splendidly.   promise
     c. You will give me your wallet or I'll punish you severely.   threat
     d. ? You will not give me your wallet or I'll reward you splendidly. threat

Sentence (7d) is most naturally read as a threat by accommodating the admittedly aberrant idea that the hearer has a strong aversion against a splendid reward. If that much accommodation is impossible, the sentence is simply pragmatically odd. The general absence of disjunctive threats like (7d) from natural language can be explained, van Rooij and Franke [70] argue, by noting that these are suboptimal manipulation strategies because, among other things, they raise the possibility that the speaker does *not* want the hearer to perform. Although conditional threats also might make the decision maker aware of the "wrong" option, these can still be efficient inducements because, according to van Rooij and Franke [70], the speaker can safely increase the stakes, by committing to more severe levels of punishment. If the speaker would do that for disjunctive promises, she would basically harm herself by expensive promises.

These are just a few basic examples that show how reasoning about the possibility of subjective misconceptions of the context/game model affects what counts as an optimal manipulative technique, but limited awareness of the context model is not the only cognitive limitation that real-life manipulators may wish to take into consideration. Limited reasoning capacity is another.

No common knowledge of rationality. A number of games can be solved by (iterated) elimination of dominated strategies. If we end up with exactly one (rationalizable) strategy for each player, this strategy combination must be a Nash equilibrium [60]. Even though this procedure seems very appealing, it crucially depends on a very strong epistemic assumption: *common knowledge of rationality*; not only must every agent be ideally rational, everybody must also know of each other that they are rational, and they must know that they know it, and so on *ad infinitum*.[10] However, there exists a large body of empirical evidence that the assumption of common knowledge of rationality is highly unrealistic (cf. [13, Chapter 5]). Is it possible to explain deception and manipulation if we give up this assumption?

Indeed, it can be argued that whenever we do see attempted deceit in real life we are sure to find at least a belief of the deceiver (whether justified or not) that the agent to be deceived has some sort of limited reasoning power that makes the deception at least conceivably successful. Some agents are more sophisticated than others, and think further ahead. To model this, one can distinguish different *strategic types* of players, often also referred to as *cognitive hierarchy models* within the economics literature (e.g. [14,68]) or as *iterated best response models* in game-theoretic pragmatics (e.g. [29,42,43]). A strategic type captures the level of strategic sophistication of a player and corresponds to the number of steps that the agent will compute in a sequence of iterated best responses. One can start with an unstrategic level-0 players. An unstrategic level-0 hearer (a credulous hearer), for example, takes the semantic content of the message he receives literally, and doesn't think about why a speaker used this message. Obviously, such a level-0 receiver can sometimes be manipulated by a level-1 sender. But such a sender can in turn be outsmarted by a level-2 receiver, etc. In general, a level-$(k+1)$ player is one who plays a best response to the behavior of a level-k player. (A *best response* is a rationally best reaction to a given belief about the behavior of all other players). A fully sophisticated agent is a level-ω player who behaves rationally given her belief in common belief in rationality.

Using such cognitive hierarchy models, Crawford [16], for instance, showed that in case sender and/or receiver believe that there is a possibility that the other player is less sophisticated than he is himself, deception is possible (cf. [17]). Moreover, even sophisticated level-ω players can be deceived if they are not sure that their opponents are level-ω players too. Crawford assumed that messages have a specific semantic content, but did not presuppose that speakers can only say something that is true.

Building on work of Rabin [67] and Stalnaker [76], Franke [28] offers a notion of *message credibility* in terms of an iterated best response model (see also [27, Chapter 2]). The general idea is that the conventional meaning of a message is a strategically non-binding *focal point* that defines the behavior of unstrategic level-0 players. For instance, for the simple game in (5), a level-0 receiver would be credulous and believe that message "I am of type t_2" is true and honest. But then a level-1 sender of type t_2 would exploit this naïve belief and also believe that her deceit is successful. Only if the receiver in fact is more sophisticated

---

[10] We are rather crudely glossing here over many interesting subtleties in the notion of rationality and (common) belief in it. See, for instance, the contributions by Bonanno [12], Pacuit [62] and Perea [66] to this volume.

than that, would he see through the deception. Roughly speaking, a message is then considered credible iff no strategic sender type would ever like to use it falsely. In effect, this model not only provably improves on the notion of message credibility, but also explains when deceit can be (believed to be) successful.

We can conclude that (i) it might be unnatural to assume common knowledge of rationality, and (ii) by giving up this assumption, we can explain much better why people communicate the way they do than standard game theory can: sometimes we communicate to manipulate others on the assumption that the others don't see it through, i.e., that we are smarter than them (whether this is justified or not).

Framing. As noted earlier, there exists a lot of experimental and theoretical evidence that we do not, and even cannot, always pick our choices in the way we should do according to the standard normative theory. In decision theory it is standardly assumed, for instance, that preference orders are transitive and complete. Still, already May [53] has shown that cyclic preferences were not extraordinary (violating transitivity of the preference relation), and Luce [51] noted that people sometimes seem to choose one alternative over another with a given consistent probability not equal to one (violating completeness of the preference relation). What is interesting for us is that due to the fact that people don't behave as rationally as the standard normative theory prescribes, it becomes possible for smart communicators to *manipulate* them: to convince them to do something that goes against their own interest. We mentioned already the use of *false implication.* Perhaps better known is the *money pump* argument: the fact that agents with intransitive preferences can be exploited because they are willing to participate in a series of bets where they will lose for sure. Similarly, manipulators make use of *false analogies.* According to psychologists, reasoning by analogy is used by boundedly rational agents like us to reduce the evaluation of new situations by comparing them with familiar ones (cf. [33]). Though normally a useful strategy, it can be exploited. There are many examples of this. Just to take one, in an advertisement for Chanel No. 5, a bottle of the perfume is pictured together with Nicole Kidman. The idea is that Kidman's glamour and beauty is transferred from her to the product. But perhaps the most common way to influence a decision maker making use of the fact that he or she does not choose in the prescribed way is by *framing.*

By necessity, a decision maker interprets her decision problem in a particular way. A different interpretation of the same problem may sometimes lead to a different decision. Indeed, there exists a lot of experimental evidence, that our decision making can depend a lot on how the problem is set. In standard decision theory it is assumed that decisions are made on the basis of information, and that it doesn't matter how this information is presented. It is predicted, for instance, that it doesn't matter whether you present this glass as being half full, or as half empty. The fact that it sometimes does matter is called the *framing effect.* This effect can be used by manipulators to present information such as to influence the decision maker in their own advantage. An agent's choice can be manipulated, for instance, by the addition or deletion of other 'irrelevant' alternative actions to choose between, or by presenting the action the manipulator wants to be chosen in the beginning of, or at multiple times in, the set of alternative actions.

Framing is possible, because we apparently do not always choose by maximizing utility. Choosing by maximizing expected utility, the decision maker integrates the expected utility of an action with what he already has. Thinking for simplicity of utility just in terms of monetary value, it is thus predicted that someone who starts with 100 Euros and gains 50, ends up being equally happy as one who started out with 200 Euros and lost 50. This prediction is obviously wrong, and the absurdity of the prediction was highlighted especially by Kahneman and Tversky. They pointed out that decision makers think in terms of *gains* and *losses* with respect to a *reference point*, rather than in terms of context-independent utilities as the standard theory assumes. This reference point typically represents what the decision maker currently has, but—and crucial for persuasion—it need not be. Another, in retrospect, obvious failure of the normative theory is that decision makers systematically overestimate low-probability events. How else can one explain why people buy lottery tickets and pay quite some money to insure themselves against very unlikely losses?

Kahneman and Tversky brought to light less obvious violations of the normative theory as well. Structured after the well-known Allais paradox, their famous Asian disease experiment [78], for instance, shows that in most people's eyes, a *sure* gain is worth more than a *probable* gain with an equal or greater expected value. Other experiments by the same authors show that the opposite is true for losses. People tend to be risk-averse in the domain of gains, and risk-taking in the domain of losses, where the displeasure associated with the loss is greater than the pleasure associated with the same amount of gains.

Notice that as a result, choices can depend on whether outcomes are seen as gains or losses. But whether something is seen as a gain or a loss depends on the chosen reference-point. What this reference-point is, however, can be influenced by the manipulator. If you want to persuade parents to vaccinate their children, for instance, one can set the outcomes either as losses, or as gains. Experimental results show that persuasion is more successful by loss-framed than by gain-framed appeals [59].

Framing effects are predicted by Kahneman and Tversky's *Prospect Theory*: a theory that implements the idea that our behavior is only boundedly rational. But if correct, it is this kind of theory that should be taken into account in any serious analysis of persuasive language use.

Summary. Under idealized assumptions about agents' rationality and knowledge of the communicative situation, manipulation by strategic communication is by and large impossible. Listeners see through attempts of deception and speakers therefore do not even attempt to mislead. But manipulation can prosper among boundedly rational agents. If the decision maker is unaware of some crucial parts of the communicative situation (most palpably: the mischievous intentions of the speaker) or if the decision maker does not apply strategic reasoning deeply enough, deception may be possible. Also if the manipulator, but not the decision maker, is aware of the cognitive biases that affect our decision making, these mechanism can be exploited as well.

2   Opinion Dynamics and Efficient Propaganda

While the previous section focused exclusively on the pragmatic dimension of persuasion, investigating *what* to say and *how* to say it, there is a wider social dimension to successful manipulation as well: determining *whom we should address*. In this section, we will assume that agents are all part of a social network, and we will discuss how to best propagate one's own ideas through a social network. We focus on this perspective, because it complements nicely recent investigations into the logic of information flow in structured societies (cf. [4,50,71] inter alia) and the exploration of evolutionary dynamics of language games on social networks (cf. [56,57,79,82] inter alia).

We present a novel variant of DeGroot's classical model of opinion dynamics [19] that allows us to address the question how an agent, given his position in a social web of influenceability, should try to strategically influence others, so as to maximally promote her opinion in the relevant population. More concretely, while DeGroot's model implicitly assumes that agents distribute their persuasion efforts equally among the neighbors in their social network, we consider a new variant of DeGroot's model where a small fraction of players is able to re-distribute their persuasion efforts strategically. Using numerical simulations, we try to chart the terrain of more or less efficient opinion-promoting strategies and conclude that in order to successfully promote your opinion in your social network you should: (i) spread your web of influence wide (i.e., not focussing all effort on a single or few individuals), (ii) choose "easy targets" for quick success and "influential targets" for long-term success, and (iii), if possible, coordinate your efforts with other influencers so as to get out of each other's way. Which strategy works best, however, depends on the interaction structure of the population in question. The upshot of this discussion is that, even if computing the theoretically optimal strategy is out of the question for a resource-limited agent, the more an agent can exploit rudimentary or even detailed knowledge of the social structure of a population, the better she will be able to propagate her opinion.

Starting Point: The DeGroot Model. DeGroot [19] introduced a simple model of opinion dynamics to study under which conditions a consensus can be reached among all members of a society (cf. [47]). DeGroot's classical model is a round-based, discrete and linear update model.[11] Opinions are considered at discrete time steps $t \in \mathbb{N}^{\geq 0}$. In the simplest case, an opinion is just a real number, representing, e.g., to what extent an agent endorses a position. For n agents in the society we consider the row vector of opinions $\mathbf{x}(t)$ with $\mathbf{x}(t)^T = \langle x_1(t), \ldots, x_n(t) \rangle \in \mathbb{R}^n$ where $x_i(t)$ is the opinion of agent i at time

---

[11] DeGroot's model can be considered as a simple case of Axelrod's [3] famous model of cultural dynamics (cf. [15] for overview).

t.[12] Each round all agents update their opinions to a weighted average of the opinions around them. Who influences whom how much is captured by *influence matrix* P, which is a (row) stochastic $n \times n$ matrix with P_{ij} the weight with which agent i takes agent j's opinion into account. DeGroot's model then considers the simple linear update in (1):[13]

$$\mathbf{x}(t+1) = P\,\mathbf{x}(t)\,. \tag{1}$$

For illustration, suppose that the society consists of just three agents and that influences among these are given by:

$$P = \begin{pmatrix} .7 & .3 & 0 \\ .2 & .5 & .3 \\ .4 & .5 & .1 \end{pmatrix}\,. \tag{2}$$

The rows in this influence matrix give the proportions with which each agent updates her opinions at each time step. For instance, agent 3's opinion at time $t+1$ is obtained by taking .4 parts of agent 1's opinion at time t, .5 parts of agent 2's and .1 parts of her own opinion at time t. For instance, if the vector of opinions at time $t = 0$ is a randomly chosen $\mathbf{x}(0)^T = \langle .6, .2, .9 \rangle$, then agent 3's opinion at the next time step will be $.4 \times .6 + .5 \times .2 + .1 \times .9 \approx .43$. By equation (1), we compute these updates in parallel for each agent, so we obtain $\mathbf{x}(1)^T \approx \langle .48, .49, .43 \rangle$, $\mathbf{x}(2)^T \approx \langle .48, .47, .48 \rangle$ and so on.[14]

DeGroot's model acknowledges the social structure of the society of agents in its specification of the influence matrix P. For instance, if $p_{ij} = 0$, then agent i does not take agent j's opinion into account at all; if $p_{ii} = 1$, then agent i does not take anyone else's opinion into account; if $p_{ij} < p_{ik}$, then agent k has more influence on the opinion of agent i than agent j.

It is convenient to think of P as the adjacency matrix of a fully-connected, weighted and directed graph, as shown in Fig. 1. As usual, rows specify the weights of outgoing connections, so that we need to think of a weighted edge in a graph like in Fig. 1 as a specification of how much an agent (represented by a node) "cares about" or "listens to" another agent's opinion. The agents who agent i listens to, in this sense, are the *influences* of i:

$$I(i) = \{j \mid p_{ij} > 0 \wedge i \neq j\}\,.$$

---

[12] We write out that transpose $\mathbf{x}(t)^T$ of the row vector $\mathbf{x}(t)$, so as not to have to write its elements vertically.

[13] Recall that if A and B are (n, m) and (m, p) matrices respectively, then $A\,B$ is the matrix product with $(A\,B)_{ij} = \sum_{k=1}^{m} A_{ik} B_{ki}$.

[14] In this particular case, opinions converge to a consensus where everybody holds the same opinion. In his original paper DeGroot showed that, no matter what $\mathbf{x}(0)$, if P has at least one column with only positive values, then, as t goes to infinity, $\mathbf{x}(t)$ converges to a unique vector of uniform opinions, i.e., the same value for all $\mathbf{x}_i(t)$. Much subsequent research has been dedicated to finding sufficient (and necessary) conditions for opinions to converge or even to converge to a consensus (cf. [1,41] for overview). Our emphasis, however, will be different, so that we sidestep these issues.

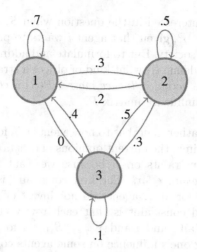

Fig. 1. Influence in a society represented as a (fully connected, weighted and directed) graph.

Inversely, let's call all those agents that listen to agent i as the *audience* of i:

$$A(i) = \{j \mid p_{ji} > 0 \wedge i \neq j\}.$$

One more notion that will be important later should be mentioned here already. Some agents might listen more to themselves than others do. Since how much agent i holds on to her own opinion at each time step is given by value p_{ii}, the diagonal $\mathtt{diag}(P)$ of P can be interpreted as the vector of the agents' *stubbornness*. For instance, in example (2) agent 1 is the most stubborn and agent 3 the least convinced of his own views, so to speak.

Strategic Promotion of Opinions. DeGroot's model is a very simple model of how opinions might spread in a society: each round each agent simply adopts the weighted average of the opinions of his influences, where the weights are given by the fixed influence matrix. More general update rules than (1) have been studied, e.g., ones that make the influence matrix dependent on time and/or the opinions held by other agents, so that we would define $\mathbf{x}(t+1) = P(t, \mathbf{x}(t))\, \mathbf{x}(t)$ (cf. [38]). We are interested here in an even more liberal variation of DeGroot's model in which (some of the) agents can *strategically* determine their influence, so as to best promote their own opinion. In other terms, we are interested in opinion dynamics of the form:

$$\mathbf{x}(t+1) = P(S)\,\mathbf{x}(t), \tag{3}$$

where P depends on an $n \times n$ *strategy matrix* S where each row S_i is a strategy of agent i and each entry S_{ij} specifies how much effort agent i invests in trying to impose her current opinion on each agent j.

Eventually we are interested in the question when S_i is a *good* strategy for a given influence matrix P, given that agent i wants to promote her opinion as much as possible in the society. But to formulate and address this question more precisely, we first must define (i) what kind of object a strategy is in this setting and (ii) how exactly the *actual influence matrix* $P(S)$ is computed from a given strategy S and a given influence matrix P.

Strategies. We will be rather liberal as to how agents can form their strategies: S could itself depend on time, the current opinions of others etc. We will, however, impose two general constraints on S because we want to think of *strategies as allocations of persuasion effort*. The first constraint is a mere technicality, requiring that $S_{ii} = 0$ for all i: agents do not invest effort into manipulating themselves. The second constraint is that each row vector S_i is a stochastic vector, i.e., $S_{ij} \geq 0$ for all i and j and $\sum_{j=1}^{n} S_{ij} = 1$ for all i. This is to make sure that strengthening one's influence on some agents comes at the expense of weakening one's influence on others. Otherwise there would be no interesting strategic considerations as to where best to exert influence. We say that S_i is a *neutral strategy* for P if it places equal weight on all j that i can influence, i.e., all $j \in A(i)$.[15] We call S neutral for some P, if S consists entirely of neutral strategies for P. We write S^* for the neutral strategy of an implicitly given matrix P.

Examples of strategy matrices for the influence matrix P in (2) are:

$$S = \begin{pmatrix} 0 & .9 & .1 \\ .4 & 0 & .6 \\ .5 & .5 & 0 \end{pmatrix} \qquad S' = \begin{pmatrix} 0 & .1 & .9 \\ .5 & 0 & .5 \\ 0 & 1 & 0 \end{pmatrix} \qquad S^* = \begin{pmatrix} 0 & .5 & .5 \\ .5 & 0 & .5 \\ 0 & 1 & 0 \end{pmatrix}.$$

According to strategy matrix S, agent 1 places .9 parts of her available persuasion effort on agent 2, and .1 on agent 3. Notice that since in our example in (2) we had $P_{13} = 0$, agent 3 cannot influence agent 1. Still, nothing prevents her from allocating persuasion effort to agent 1. (This would, in a sense, be irrational but technically possible). That also means that S_3 is *not* the neutral strategy for agent 3. The neutral strategy for agent 3 is S'_3 where all effort is allocated to the single member in agent 3's audience, namely agent 2. Matrix S' also includes the neutral strategy for agent 2, who has two members in her audience. However, since agent 1 does not play a neutral strategy in S', S' is not neutral for the matrix P in (2), but S^* is.

Actual Influence. Intuitively speaking, we want the actual influence matrix $P(S)$ to be derived by adjusting the influence weights in P by the allocations of effort given in S. There are many ways in which this could be achieved. Our present approach is motivated by the desire to maintain a tight connection with the original DeGroot model. We would like to think of (1) as the special case of (3) where every agent plays a neutral strategy. Concretely, we require that $P(S^*) = P$. (Remember that S^* is the neutral strategy for P.) This way, we can think

---

[15] We assume throughout that $A(i)$ is never empty.

of DeGroot's classical model as a description of opinion dynamics in which no agent is a strategic manipulator, in the sense that no agent deliberately tries to spread her opinion by exerting more influence on some agents than on others.

We will make one more assumption about the operation $P(S)$, which we feel is quite natural, and that is that $\mathtt{diag}(P(S)) = \mathtt{diag}(P)$, i.e., the agents' stubbornness should not depend on how much they or anyone else allocates persuasion effort. In other words, strategies should compete only for the resources of opinion change that are left after subtracting an agent's stubbornness.

To accommodate these two requirements in a natural way, we define $P(S)$ with respect to a reference point formed by the neutral strategy S^*. For any given strategy matrix S, let $\overline{S}$ be the column-normalized matrix derived from S. $\overline{S}_{ij}$ is i's *relative persuasion effort* affecting j, when taking into account how much everybody invests in influencing j. We compare $\overline{S}$ to the relative persuasion effort $\overline{S^*}$ under the neutral strategy: call $R = \overline{S}/\overline{S^*}$ the matrix of *relative net influences* given strategy S.[16] The actual influence matrix $P(S) = Q$ is then defined as a reweighing of P by the relative net influences R:

$$Q_{ij} = \begin{cases} P_{ij} & \text{if } i = j \\ \dfrac{P_{ij} R_{ji}}{\sum_k P_{ik} R_{ki}}(1 - P_{ii}) & \text{otherwise.} \end{cases} \tag{4}$$

Here is an example illustrating the computation of actual influences. For influence matrix P and strategy matrix S we get the actual influences $P(S)$ as follows:

$$P = \begin{pmatrix} 1 & 0 & 0 \\ .2 & .5 & .3 \\ .4 & .5 & .1 \end{pmatrix} \qquad S = \begin{pmatrix} 0 & .9 & .1 \\ 0 & 0 & 1 \\ 0 & 1 & 0 \end{pmatrix} \qquad P(S) \approx \begin{pmatrix} 1 & 0 & 0 \\ .27 & .5 & .23 \\ .12 & .78 & .1 \end{pmatrix}.$$

To get there we need to look at the matrix of relative persuasion effort $\overline{S}$ given by S, the neutral strategy S^* for this P and the relative persuasion effort $\overline{S^*}$ under the neutral strategy:

$$\overline{S} = \begin{pmatrix} 0 & 9/19 & 1/11 \\ 0 & 0 & 10/11 \\ 0 & 10/19 & 0 \end{pmatrix} \qquad S^* = \begin{pmatrix} 0 & .5 & .5 \\ 0 & 0 & 1 \\ 0 & 1 & 0 \end{pmatrix} \qquad \overline{S^*} = \begin{pmatrix} 0 & 1/3 & 1/3 \\ 0 & 0 & 2/3 \\ 0 & 2/3 & 0 \end{pmatrix}.$$

That $\overline{S^*}_{12} = 1/3$, for example, tells us that agent 1's influence on agent 2 $P_{21} = 1/5$ comes about in the neutral case where agent 1 invests half as much effort into influencing agent 2 as agent 3 does. To see what happens when agent 1 plays a non-neutral strategy, we need to look at the matrix of relative net influences $R = \overline{S}/\overline{S^*}$, which, intuitively speaking, captures how much the actual case $\overline{S}$ deviates from the neutral case $\overline{S^*}$:

$$R = \begin{pmatrix} 0 & 27/19 & 3/11 \\ 0 & 0 & 15/11 \\ 0 & 15/19 & 0 \end{pmatrix}.$$

---

[16] Here and in the following, we adopt the convention that $x/0 = 0$.

This derives $P(S) = Q$ by equation (4). We spell out only one of four non-trivial cases here:

$$Q_{21} = \frac{P_{21}R_{12}}{P_{11}R_{11} + P_{12}R_{21} + P_{13}R_{31}}(1 - P_{22})$$

$$= \frac{2/10 \times 27/19}{1/5 \times 27/19 + 1/2 \times 0 + 3/10 \times 15/19}(1 - 1/2)$$

$$\approx 0.27$$

In words, by investing 9 times as much into influencing agent 2 than into influencing agent 3, agent 1 gains effective influence of ca. $.27 - .2 = .07$ over agent 2, as compared to when she neutrally divides effort equally among her audience. At the same time, agent 1 loses effective influence of ca. $.4 - .12 = .28$ on agent 3. (This strategy might thus seem to only diminish agent 1's actual influence in the updating process. But, as we will see later on, this can still be (close to) the optimal choice in some situations).

It remains to check that the definition in (4) indeed yields a conservative extension of the classical DeGroot-process in (1):

Fact 1 $P(\overline{S}) = P$.

Proof. Let $Q = P(\overline{S})$. Look at arbitrary Q_{ij}. If $i = j$, then trivially $Q_{ij} = P_{ij}$. If $i \neq j$, then

$$Q_{ij} = \frac{P_{ij}R_{ji}}{\sum_k P_{ik}R_{ki}}(1 - P_{ii}),$$

with $R = \overline{S}^*/\overline{s}^*$. As $S_{ii} = 0$ by definition of a strategy, we also have $R_{ii} = 0$. So we get:

$$Q_{ij} = \frac{P_{ij}R_{ji}}{\sum_{k \neq i} P_{ik}R_{ki}}(1 - P_{ii}).$$

Moreover, for every $k \neq i$, $R_{kl} = 1$ whenever $P_{lk} > 0$, otherwise $R_{kl} = 0$. Therefore:

$$Q_{ij} = \frac{P_{ij}}{\sum_{k \neq i} P_{ik}}(1 - P_{ii}) = P_{ij}.$$

The Propaganda Problem. The main question we are interested in is a very general one:

(8) *Propaganda problem (full)*: Which individual strategies S_i are good or even optimal for promoting agent i's opinion in society?

This is a game problem because what is a good promotion strategy for agent i depends on what strategies all other agents play as well. As will become clear below, the complexity of the full propaganda problem is daunting. We therefore start first by asking a simpler question, namely:

(9) *Propaganda problem (restricted, preliminary)*: Supposing that most agents behave non-strategically like agents in DeGroot's original model (call them: *sheep*), which (uniform) strategy should a minority of strategic players (call them: *wolves*) adopt so as best to promote their minority opinion in the society?

In order to address this more specific question, we will assume that initially wolves and sheep have opposing opinions: if i is a wolf, then $x_i(0) = 1$; if i is a sheep, then $x_i(0) = -1$. We could think of this as being politically right wing or left wing; or of endorsing or rejecting a proposition, etc. Sheep play a neutral strategy and are susceptible to opinion change ($P_{ii} < 1$ for sheep i). Wolves are maximally stubborn ($P_{ii} = 1$ for wolves i) and can play various strategies. (For simplicity we will assume that all wolves in a population play the same strategy). We are then interested in ranking wolf strategies with respect to how strongly they pull the community's *average opinion* $\bar{x}(t) = 1/n \times \sum_{i=1}^{n} x_i(t)$ towards the wolf opinion.

This formulation of the propaganda problem is still too vague to be of any use for categorizing good and bad strategies. We need to be more explicit at least about the number of rounds after which strategies are evaluated. Since we allow wolf strategies to vary over time and/or to depend on other features which might themselves depend on time, it might be that some strategies are good at short intervals of time and others only after many more rounds of opinion updating. In other words, the version of the propaganda problem we are interested in here is dependent on the number of rounds k. For fixed P and $\mathbf{x}(0)$, say that $\mathbf{x}(k)$ results from a sequence of strategy matrices $\langle S^{(1)}, \ldots, S^{(k)} \rangle$ if for all $0 < i \leq k$: $\mathbf{x}(i) = P(S^{(i)}) \mathbf{x}(i-1)$.

(10) *Propaganda problem (restricted, fixed P)*: For a fixed P, a fixed $\mathbf{x}(0)$ as described and a number of rounds $k > 0$, find a sequence of k strategy matrices $\langle S^{(1)}, \ldots, S^{(k)} \rangle$, with wolf and sheep strategies as described above, such that $\bar{x}(k)$ is maximal for the $\mathbf{x}(k)$ that results from $\langle S^{(1)}, \ldots, S^{(k)} \rangle$.

What that means is that the notion of a *social influencing strategy* we are interested in here is that of an optimal *sequence* of k strategies, not necessarily a single strategy. Finding a good strategy in this sense can be computationally hard, as we would like to make clear in the following by a simple example. It is therefore that, after having established a feeling for how wolf strategies influence population dynamics over time, we will rethink our notion of a social influence strategy once more, arguing that the complexity of the problem calls for *heuristics* that are easy to apply yet yield good, if sub-optimal, results. But first things first.

Example: Lone-Wolf Propaganda. Although simpler than the full game problem, the problem formulated in (10) is still a very complex affair. To get acquainted with the complexity of the situation, let's look first at the simplest non-trivial case of a society of three agents with one wolf and two sheep: call it a *lone-wolf problem.* For concreteness, let's assume that the influence matrix is the one we considered previously, where agent 1 is the wolf:

$$P = \begin{pmatrix} 1 & 0 & 0 \\ .2 & .5 & .3 \\ .4 & .5 & .1 \end{pmatrix}. \tag{5}$$

Since sheep agents 2 and 3 are assumed to play a neutral strategy, the space of feasible strategies for this lone-wolf situation can be explored with a single parameter $a \in [0; 1]$:

$$S(a) = \begin{pmatrix} 0 & a & 1\text{-}a \\ 0 & 0 & 1 \\ 0 & 1 & 0 \end{pmatrix}.$$

We can therefore calculate:

$$\overline{S^*} = \begin{pmatrix} 0 & 1/3 & 1/3 \\ 0 & 0 & 2/3 \\ 0 & 2/3 & 0 \end{pmatrix} \qquad \overline{S(a)} = \begin{pmatrix} 0 & a/a+1 & 1-a/2-a \\ 0 & 0 & 1/2-a \\ 0 & 1/a+1 & 0 \end{pmatrix}$$

$$R = \begin{pmatrix} 0 & 3a/a+1 & 3-3a/2-a \\ 0 & 0 & 3/4-2a \\ 0 & 3/2a+2 & 0 \end{pmatrix} \qquad P(S(a)) = \begin{pmatrix} 1 & 0 & 0 \\ 4a/8a+6 & 1/2 & 3/8a+6 \\ 36-36a/65-40a & 9/26-16a & 1/10 \end{pmatrix}$$

Let's first look at the initial situation with $\mathbf{x}(0)^T = \langle 1, -1, -1 \rangle$, and ask what the best wolf strategy is for boosting the average population in just one time step $k = 1$. The relevant population opinion can be computed as a function of a, using basic algebra:

$$\overline{\mathbf{x}(1)}(a) = \frac{-224a^2 + 136a - 57}{-160a^2 + 140a + 195}. \tag{6}$$

This function is plotted in Fig. 2.

Another chunk of basic algebra reveals that this function has a local maximum at $a = .3175$ in the relevant interval $a \in [0; 1]$. In other words, the maximal shift towards wolf opinion in one step is obtained for the wolf strategy $\langle 0, .3175, .6825 \rangle$. This, then, is an exact solution to the special case of the propaganda problem state in (10) where P is given as above and $k = 1$.

How about values $k > 1$? Let's call any k-sequence of wolf strategies that maximizes the increase in average population opinion at each time step the **greedy** strategy. Notice that the **greedy** strategy does not necessarily select the same value of a in each round because each greedy choice of a depends on the actual sheep opinions x_2 and x_3. To illustrate this, Fig. 3 shows (a numerical approximation of) the **greedy** values of a for the current example as a function of all possible sheep opinions. As is quite intuitive, the plot shows that the more, say, agent 3 already bears the wolf opinion, the better it is, when greedy, to focus persuasion effort on agent 2, and vice versa.

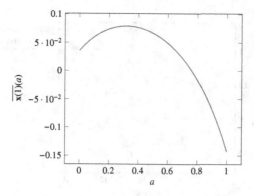

Fig. 2. Population opinion after one round of updating with a strategy matrix $S(a)$ for all possible values of a, as described by the function in Equation (6).

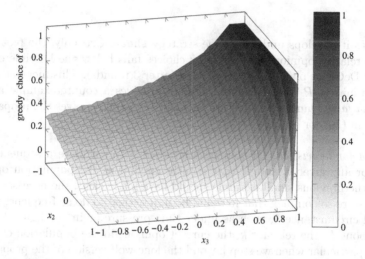

Fig. 3. Dependency of the **greedy** strategy on the current sheep opinion for the lone-wolf problem given in (5). The graph plots the best choice of effort a to be allocated to persuading agent 2 for maximal increase of population opinion in one update step, as a function of all possible pairs of sheep opinions x_2 and x_3.

It may be tempting to hypothesize that strategy **greedy** solves the lone-wolf version of (10) for arbitrary k. But that's not so. From the fourth round onwards even playing the neutral strategy **sheep** (a constant choice of $a = 1/2$ in each round) is better than strategy **greedy**. This is shown in Fig. 4, which plots the temporal development over 20 rounds of what we will call *relative opinion* for our current lone-wolf problem. Relative opinion of strategy X is the average population opinion as it develops under strategy X minus the average population

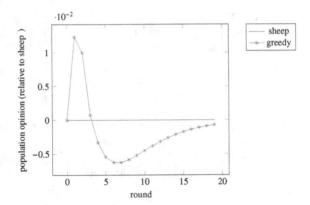

Fig. 4. Temporal development of relative opinion (i.e., average population opinion relative to average population opinion under baseline strategy **sheep**) for several wolf strategies for the influence matrix in (5).

opinion as it develops under baseline strategy **sheep**. Crucially, the plot shows that the relative opinion under **greedy** choices falls below the baseline of non-strategic DeGroot play already very soon (after 3 rounds). This means that the influence matrix P we are looking at here provides a counterexample against the *prima facie* plausible conjecture that playing **greedy** solves the propaganda problem in (10) for all k.

The need for heuristics. Of course, it is possible to calculate a sequence of a values for any given k and P that strictly maximizes the population opinion. But, as the previous small example should have made clear, the necessary computations are so complex that it would be impractical to do so frequently under "natural circumstances", such as under time pressure or in the light of uncertainty about P, the relevant k, the current opinions in the population etc. This holds in particular when we step beyond the lone-wolf version of the propaganda problem: with several wolves the optimization problem is to find the *set* of wolf strategies that are optimal *in unison*. Mathematically speaking, for each fixed P, this is a multi-variable, non-linear, constrained optimization problem. Oftentimes this will have a unique solution, but the computational complexity of the relevant optimization problem is immense. This suggests the usefulness, if not necessity, of simpler, but still efficient *heuristics*.[17] For these reasons we focus in the following on intuitive and simple ways of playing the social manipulation

---

[17] Against this it could be argued that processes of evolution, learning and gradual optimization might have brought frequent manipulators at least close to the analytical optimum over time. But even then, it is dubious that the agents actually have the precise enough knowledge (of influence matrix P, current population opinion, etc.) to learn to approximate the optimal strategy. Due to reasons of learnability and generalizability, what evolves or is acquired and fine-tuned by experience, too, is more likely a good heuristic.

game that make, for the most part, more innocuous assumptions about agents' computational capacities and knowledge of the social facts at hand. We try to demonstrate that these heuristics are not only simple, but also lead to quite good results on average, i.e., if uniformly applied to a larger class of games.

To investigate the average impact of various strategies, we resort to numerical simulation. By generating many random influence matrices P and recording the temporal development of the population opinion under different strategies, we can compare the average success of these strategies against each other.

Towards efficient heuristics. For reasons of space, we will only look at a small sample of reasonably successful and resource-efficient heuristics that also yield theoretical insights into the nature of the propaganda problem. But before going into details, a few general considerations about efficient manipulation of opinions are in order. We argue that in general for a manipulation strategy to be efficient it should: (i) not preach to the choir, (ii) target large groups, not small groups or individuals, (iii) take other manipulators into account, so as not to get into one another's way, and (iv) take advantage of the social structure of society (as given by P). Let's look at all of these points in turn.

Firstly, it is obvious that any effort spent on a sheep which is already convinced, i.e., holds the wolf opinion one, is wasted.[18] A minimum standard for a rational wolf strategy would therefore be to spend no effort on audience members with opinion one as long as there are audience members with opinion lower than one. All of the strategies we look at below are assumed to conform to this requirement.

Secondly, we could make a distinction between strategies that place all effort onto just one audience member and strategies that place effort on more than one audience member (in the most extreme case that would be *all* of the non-convinced audience members). Numerical simulations show that, on average, strategies of the former kind clearly prove inferior to strategies of the latter kind. An intuitive argument why that is so is the following. For concreteness, consider the lone-wolf greedy maximization problem plotted in Fig. 2. (The argument holds in general). Since the computation of $P(S)$ relies on the *relative* net influence R, playing extreme values ($a = 0$ or $a = 1$) is usually suboptimal because the influence gained on one agent is smaller than the influence lost on the other agent. This much concerns just one round of updating, but if we look at several rounds of updating, then influencing several agents to at least some extent is beneficial, because the increase in their opinion from previous rounds will lead to more steady increase in population opinion at later rounds too. All in all, it turns out that efficient manipulation of opinions, on a short, medium and long time scale, is achieved better if the web of influence is spread wide, i.e., if many or all suitable members of the wolves' audience are targeted with at

---

[18] Strictly speaking, this can only happen in the limit, but this is an issue worth addressing, given (i) floating number imprecision in numerical simulations, and (ii) the general possibility (which we do not explicitly consider) of small independent fluctuations in agents' opinions.

least *some* persuasion effort. For simplicity, the strategies we consider here will therefore target all non-convinced members of each wolf's audience, but variably distribute persuasion effort among these.

Thirdly, another relevant distinction of wolf strategies is between those that are sensitive to the presence and behavior of other wolves and those that are not. The former may be expected to be more efficient, if implemented properly, but they are also more sophisticated. This is because they pose stronger requirements on the agents that implement these strategies: wolves who want to hunt in a pack should be aware of the other wolves and adapt their behavior to form an efficient *coalition strategy*. We will look at just one coalition strategy here, but find that, indeed, this strategy is (one of) the best from the small sample that is under scrutiny here. Surprisingly, the key to coalition success is not to join forces, but rather to get out of each other's way. Intuitively, this is because if several manipulators invest in influencing the same sheep, they thereby decrease their *relative* net influence unduly. On the other hand, if a group of wolves decides who is the main manipulator, then by purposefully investing little effort the other wolves boost the main manipulator's relative net influence.

Fourthly and finally, efficient opinion manipulation depends heavily on the social structure of the population, as given by P. We surely expect that a strategy which uses (approximate) knowledge of P in a smart way will be more effective than one that does not. The question is, of course, what features of the social structure to look at. Below we investigate two kinds of socially-aware heuristics: one that aims for sheep that can be easily influenced, and one that aims for sheep that are influential themselves. We expected that the former do better in the short run, while the latter might catch up after a while and eventually do better in the long run. This expectation is borne out, but exactly how successful a given strategy (type) is also depends on the structure of the society.

The cast. Next to strategy `sheep`, the strategies we look at are called `influence`, `impact`, `eigenvector` and `communication`. We describe each in turn and then discuss their effectiveness, merits and weaknesses.

Strategy `influence` chooses a fixed value of a in every round, unlike the time-dependent `greedy`. Intuitively speaking, the strategy `influence` allocates effort among its audience proportional to how much influence the wolf has on each sheep: the more a member of an audience is susceptible to being influenced, the more effort is allocated to her. In effect, strategy `influence` says: "allocate effort relatively to how much you are being listened to". In our running example with P as in Equation (5) the lone wolf has an influence on (sheep) agent 2 of $P_{12} = 1/5$ and of $P_{13} = 2/5$ on agent 3. Strategy `influence` therefore chooses $a = 1/3$, because the wolf's influence over agent 2 is half as big as that over agent 3.

Intuitively speaking, strategy `impact` says: "allocate effort relatively to how much your audience is being listened to." The difference between `influence` and `impact` is thus that the former favors those the wolf has big influence over, while the latter favors those that have big influence themselves. To determine influence, strategy `impact` looks at the column vector P^T_j for each agent $j \in A(i)$ in wolf

i's audience. This column vector P^T_j captures how much *direct influence* agent j has. We say that sheep j has more direct influence than sheep j' if the sum of the j-th column is bigger than that of the j'-th. (Notice that the rows, but not the columns of P must sum to one, so that some agents may have more direct influence than others). If we look at the example matrix in equation (5), for instance, agent 2 has more direct influence than agent 3. The strategy `impact` then allocates persuasion effort proportional to relative direct influence among members of an audience. In the case at hand, this would lead to a choice of

$$a = \frac{\sum_k P_{k2}}{\sum_k P_{k2} + \sum_k P_{k3}} = 5/12 \, .$$

Strategy `eigenvector` is very much like `impact`, but smarter, because it looks beyond *direct* influence. Strategy `eigenvector` for wolf i also looks at how influential the audience of members of i's audience is, how influential their audience is and so on *ad infinitum*. This transitive closure of social influence of all sheep can be computed with the (right-hand) eigenvector of the matrix P^*, where P^* is obtained by removing from P all rows and columns belonging to wolves.[19],[20] For our present example, the right-hand unit eigenvector of matrix

$$P^* = \begin{pmatrix} .5 & .3 \\ .5 & .1 \end{pmatrix}$$

is approximately $\langle .679, .321 \rangle$. So the strategy `eigenvector` would choose a value of approximately $a = .679$ at each round.

Finally, we also looked at one coalition strategy, where wolves coordinate their behavior for better effect. Strategy `communication` is such a sophisticated coalition strategy that also integrates parts of the rationale behind strategy `influence`. Strategy `communication` works as follows. For a given target sheep i, we look at all wolves among the influences $I(i)$ of i. Each round a main manipulator is drawn from that group with a probability proportional to how much influence each potential manipulator has over i. Wolves then allocate 100 times more effort to each sheep in their audience for which they are the main manipulator in that round than to others. Since this much time-variable coordination seems only plausible, when wolves can negotiate their strategies each round, we refer to this strategy as `communication`.

We expect strategy `influence` and `communication` to outperform baseline strategy `sheep` in early rounds of play. `Communication` could be expected to be better than `influence` because it is the more sophisticated coalition strategy. On the other hand, strategies `impact` and `eigenvector` should be better at later rounds of updating because they invest in manipulating influential or "central"

---

[19] Removing wolves is necessary because wolves are the most influential players; in fact, since they are maximally stubborn, sheep would normally otherwise have zero influence under this measure.

[20] The DeGroot-process thereby gives a motivation for measures of eigenvector centrality, and related concepts such as the Google page-rank (cf. [41]). Unfortunately, the details of this fascinating issue are off-topic in this context.

agents of the society, which may be costly at first, but should pay off later on. We expect `eigenvector` to be better than `impact` because it is the more sophisticated social strategy that looks beyond *direct* influence at the *global* influence that agents have in the society.

Experimental set-up. We tested these predictions by numerical simulation in two experiments, each of which assumed a different *interaction structure* of the society of agents. The first experiment basically assumed that the society is *homogeneous*, in the sense that (almost) every wolf can influence (almost) every sheep and (almost) every sheep interacts with (almost) every sheep. The second experiment assumed that the pattern of interaction is *heterogeneous*, in the sense that who listens to whom is given by a scale-free small-world network. The latter may be a more realistic approximation of human society, albeit still a strong abstraction from actual social interaction patterns.

Both experiments were executed as follows. We first generated a random influence matrix P, conforming to either basic interaction structure. We then ran each of the four strategies we described above on each P and recorded the population opinion at each of 100 rounds of updating.

Interaction networks. In contrast to the influence matrix P, which we can think of as the adjacency matrix of a directed and weighted graph, we model the basic interaction structure of a population, i.e., the qualitative structure that underlies P, as an undirected graph $G = \langle N, E \rangle$ where $N = \{1, \ldots, n\}$, with $n \geq 2$, is the set of nodes, representing the agents, and $E \subseteq N \times N$ is a reflexive and symmetric relation on N.[21] If $\langle i, j \rangle \in E$, then, intuitively speaking, i and j know each other, and either agent could in principle influence the opinion of the other. For each agent i, we consider $N(i) = \{j \in N \mid \langle i, j \rangle \in E\}$ the set of i's *neighbors*. The number of i's neighbors is called agent i's *degree* $d_i = |N(i)|$. For convenience, we will restrict attention to *connected* networks, i.e., networks all of whose nodes are connected by some sequences of transitions along E. Notice that this also rules out agents without neighbors.

For a homogeneous society, as modelled in our first experiment, we assumed that the interaction structure is given by a totally connected graph. For heterogeneous societies, we considered so-called *scale-free small-world networks* [2,5]. These networks are characterized by three key properties which suggest them as somewhat realistic models of human societies (cf. [41]):

(1.) *scale-free*: at least some part of the distribution of degrees has a power law character (i.e., there are very few agents with many connections, and many with only a few);

(2.) *small-world*:

---

[21] Normally social network theory takes E to be an irreflexive relation, but here we want to include all self-connections so that it is possible for all agents to be influenced by their own opinion as well.

(a.) *short characteristic-path length*: it takes relatively few steps to connect any two nodes of the network (more precisely, the number of steps necessary increases no more than logarithmically as the size of the network increases);

(b.) *high clustering coefficient*: if j and k are neighbors of i, then it is likely that j and k also interact with one another.

We generated random scale-free small-world networks using the algorithm of Holme and Kim [40] with parameters randomly sampled from ranges suitable to produce networks with the above-mentioned properties. (We also added all self-edges to these graphs; see Footnote 21).

For both experiments, we generated graphs of the appropriate kind for population sizes randomly chosen between 100 and 1000. We then sampled a number of wolves averaging around 10 % of the total number of agents (with a minium of 5) and randomly placed the wolves on the network. Subsequently we sampled a suitable random influence matrix P that respected the basic interaction structure, in such a way that $P_{ij} > 0$ only if $\langle i, j \rangle \in E$. In particular, for each sheep i we independently sampled a random probability distribution (using the r-Simplex algorithm) of size d_i and assigned the sampled probability values as the influence that each $j \in N(i)$ has over i. As mentioned above, we assumed that wolves are unshakably stubborn ($P_{ii} = 1$).

Results. For the most part, our experiments vindicated our expectations about the four different strategies that we tested. But there were also some interesting surprises.

The temporal development of average relative opinions under the relevant strategies is plotted in Fig. 5 for homogeneous societies and in Fig. 6 for heterogeneous societies. Our general expectation that strategies `influence` and `communication` are good choices for fast success after just a few rounds of play is vindicated for both types of societies. On the other hand, our expectation that targeting influential players with strategies `impact` and `eigenvector` will be successful especially in the long run did turn out to be correct, but only for the heterogeneous society, not for the homogeneous one. As this is hard to see from Figs. 5 and 6, Fig. 7 zooms in on the distribution of relative opinion means at the 100th round of play.

At round 100 relative means are very close together because population opinion is close to wolf opinion already for all strategies. But even though the relative opinions at the 100th round are small, there are nonetheless significant differences. For homogeneous societies we find that *all* means of relative opinion at round 100 are significantly different ($p < .05$) under a paired Wilcoxon test. Crucially, the difference between `influence` and `impact` is highly significant ($V = 5050$, $p < .005$). For the heterogeneous society, the difference between `influence` and `impact` is also significant ($V = 3285$, $p < 0.01$). Only the means of `communication` and `influence` turn out not significantly different here.

Indeed, contrary to expectation, in homogeneous societies strategies preferentially targeting influenceable sheep were more successful on average for *every*

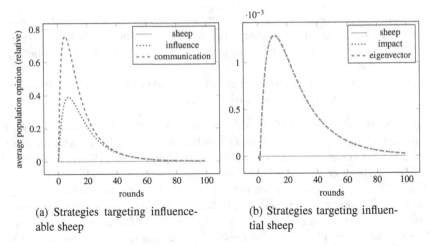

(a) Strategies targeting influence-able sheep

(b) Strategies targeting influential sheep

Fig. 5. Development of average population opinion in homogeneous societies (averaged over 100 trials). The graph in Fig. 5a shows the results for strategies targeting influenceable sheep, while one in Fig. 5b shows strategies targeting influential sheep. Although curves are similarly shaped, notice that the y-axes are scaled differently. Strategies `influence` and `communication` are *much* better than `impact` and `eigenvector` in the short run.

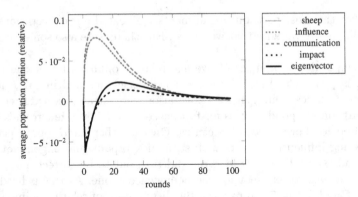

Fig. 6. Development of average relative opinion in heterogeneous societies (averaged over 100 trials).

$0 < k \leq 100$ than strategies preferentially targeting influential sheep. In other words, the type of basic interaction structure has a strong effect on the success of a given (type of) manipulation strategy. Although we had expected such an effect, we had not expected it to be that pronounced. Still, there is a plausible *post hoc* explanation for this observation. Since in homogeneous societies (almost) every wolf can influences (almost) every sheep, wolves playing strategies `impact` and `eigenvector` invest effort (almost) exactly alike. But that means

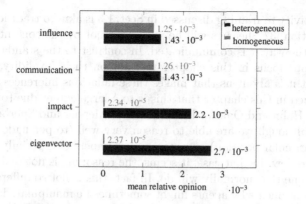

Fig. 7. Means of relative opinion at round 100 for heterogeneous and homogeneous societies. Strategies `impact` and `eigenvector` are efficient in the long run in heterogeneous societies with a pronounced contrast between more and less influential agents.

that most of the joint effort invested in influencing the same targets is averaged out, because everybody heavily invests in these targets. In other words, especially for homogeneous societies, playing a coalition strategy where manipulators do not get into each other's way is important for success. If this explanation is correct, then a very interesting practical advice for social influencing is ready at hand: given the ever more connected society that we live in, with steadily growing global connectedness through telecommunication and social media, it becomes more and more important for the sake of promoting one's opinion within the whole of society to team-up and join a coalition with like-minded players.

3 Conclusions, Related Work and Outlook

This chapter investigated strategies of manipulation, both from a pragmatic and from a social point of view. We surveyed key ideas from formal choice theory and psychology to highlight what is important when a single individual wants to manipulate the choice and opinion of a single decision maker. We also offered a novel model of strategically influencing social opinion dynamics. Important for both pragmatic and social aspects of manipulation were heuristics, albeit in a slightly different sense here and there: in order to be a successful one-to-one manipulator, it is important to know the heuristics and biases of the agents one wishes to influence; in order to be a successful one-to-many manipulator, it may be important to use heuristics oneself. In both cases, successful manipulation hinges on exploiting weaknesses in the cognitive make-up of the to-be-influenced individuals or, more abstractly, within the pattern of social information flow. To promote an opinion in a society on a short time scale, one would preferably focus on influenceable individuals; for long-term effects, the focus should be on influential targets.

The sensitivity to framing discussed in Sect. 1.3 is akin to traditional fallacies of argumentation [37]: hearers will be influenced not by the content of the message, but by the way it is communicated. In contrast to the standard literature on fallacies, our focus in this chapter was not on their invalidity, but on the question what it is about us that makes these fallacious inferences so common. We have argued in this chapter that this is to a large extent due to agents' limited abilities. Hahn and Oaksford [35] as well as Mercier and Sperber [54] argue instead that although we are able to reason very well (to persuade ourselves or others of a particular position), our reasoning is imperfect especially when stakes and targets are low. In that case, it seems, the reasoning is not really fallacious, but rather is one that normally will do. In fact, this is not so different from the reasons we mentioned why agents might sometimes be manipulated: they reason in a way that normally works well. Non-monotonic logics (including probabilistic logic) are natural tools to account for these types of inferences [32]. Indeed, non-monotonic reasoning seems a natural resource-compensation strategy, next to approximation and the division of the world into natural kinds. Although this reasoning is not always accurate, it makes perfect sense when balancing the cost of calculation versus the potential benefit of the result. In contrast to these reasons, however, we pointed out that even in argumentative situations, where hearers reason well, speakers can still manipulate by obfuscating states of the world that are to the speaker's disadvantage, and of which the hearer is unaware; or by making the hearer selectively aware of states of the world of which he was previously unaware, i.e., only of those which are to the sender's advantage.

Many important features of strategic manipulation have not been addressed and must be left for future work. Most strikingly, the model of social influencing given in the second part of the chapter is heavily simplistic in a number of ways. We have not at all addressed the case where several manipulators with different motives compete for influence over the population opinion. In that case, we would really consider a full game problem where what is a good manipulation strategy also depends on what competing manipulators do. We have also assumed that the pragmatic one-to-one aspect of opinion manipulation does not play a role when it comes to the social problem of opinion manipulation. Of course, there are obvious interactions: the social structure of the population will likely also affect which information to present to whom and how to present information to this or that guy. To the best of our knowledge, this is largely uncharted terrain for formal theories of strategic manipulation. Adding the broader social perspective to models of social influencing in formal choice models seems a very promising field for future research. A lot of work would need to be done here to tackle the immense complexity of this subject. The model presented in the second half of this chapter might be a first step in this direction.

Relation to other work presented in this volume. Gabriel Sandu's work that is presented in this volume [72] appears to be closely related to our own, but there are fundamental conceptual differences. Sandu works in the tradition of Hintikka's game semantics. Game semantics is an approach to formal semantics that seeks to ground the concepts of truth, meaning, and validity in terms of a dialogical view of communication and of winning strategies. While Sandu's approach is primarily about *semantics*, and the grounding of truth, we focus on (perhaps non-Gricean) *pragmatics*, on how agents can be influenced by means of communication. Whereas in Sandu's tradition the dialogues can be very long, but the meaning of the dialogue moves is always clear, the dialogues we studied were typically short, but vague, in that it might be hard to determine what was meant by a dialogue move. The roles of the participants of the dialogues are very different as well. In Sandu's semantic games, there are only two participants with fixed goals: either to verify or falsify a given formula. It is common knowledge between the participants that their goals are diametrically opposed. Although when we talk about one-to-one communication, we also limit ourselves to communication games with only two participants involved, the emphasis of the later part of our chapter is on influencing whole groups of agents. Equally important, the goals of our agents are not necessarily diametrically opposed but can show various degrees of alignment.

There are other interesting connections between this chapter and others presented in this volume. Eric Pacuit [62] explores a number of ways to reason strategically about a game situation. This links directly to the first part of this chapter, where we argued that knowing a decision maker's cognitive make-up opens possibilities of exploitation by a malignant communicator. Taking Pacuit's and our perspective together, a very interesting open question arises, namely which reasoning strategies (in the sense of Pacuit) are more or less vulnerable to malign influence by a strategic self-interested communicator.

Andrés Perea [66] acknowledges, like we do, the intuitive necessity to look for more cognitively realistic ways of solving games. But Perea's conceptual approach is a slightly different one from ours. While we are interested in integrating concrete psychological aspects of reasoning, Perea's contribution remains more conceptual in that it shows, roughly speaking, that a normatively compelling solution of a game problem can be reached at less cognitive effort than frequently assumed.

Indeed, both Perea's and Pacuit's contributions fit well with the work on reasoning in games and strategic interaction in Johan van Benthem's chapter in this book [7]. The logics discussed there feed into the general "Theory of Play" of [6], and so there is an interesting general question of how our approach to strategic reasoning relates to current dynamic-epistemic logics of games.

Finally, Jan van Eijck [20] discusses many different aspects of how the strategic reasoning of individuals can impact the well-fare of society as a whole. Our second model can well be seen as one special case of this more general perspective. Adding his approach to social strategizing to ours raises another interesting open issues that we have not explicitly addressed. The model of strategic influencing that we presented here did not actually specify whether the influence exerted by the strategic manipulators was beneficial or detrimental to society as a whole. Another related issue, brought up by Gabriel Sandu (p.c.), relates to the question of truth. What if the social opinion dynamics are not only affected by what others believe, but also by what is good and/or true?

In summary, unifying psychological and social aspects of manipulative strategizing in a unified framework is a giant's task that has close bearing on many central concerns raised in other chapters of this volume. We see a lot of potential for future research in this area, especially where it brings formal modelling and empirical research closer together.

Acknowledgements. This chapter profited from many insightful comments of the participants of the Workshop *Modeling Strategic Reasoning*. We are particularly thankful for the stimulating input from Rineke Verbrugge, Johan van Benthem, Anton Benz, Gabriel Sandu and Jakub Szymanik. Michael Franke gratefully acknowledges financial support by NWO-VENI grant 275-80-004.

References

1. Acemoglu, D., Ozdaglar, A.: Opinion dynamics and learning in social networks. Dyn. Games Appl. **1**(1), 3–49 (2011)
2. Albert, R., Barabási, A.-L.: Statistical mechanics of complex networks. Rev. Mod. Phys. **74**(1), 47–97 (2002)
3. Axelrod, R.: The dissemination of culture: a model with local convergence and global polarization. J. Conflict Resolut. **41**(2), 203–226 (1997)
4. Baltag, A., Christoff, Z., Hansen, J.U.: Logical models of information cascades. In: van Benthem, J., Liu, F. (eds.) Logic Across the Universities. Studies in Logic, pp. 405–432. College Publications, London (2013)
5. Barabási, A.-L., Albert, R.: Emergence of scaling in random networks. Science **286**(5439), 509–512 (1999)
6. van Benthem, J.: Logic in Games. MIT Press, Cambridge (2014)
7. van Benthem, J.: Logic of strategies: What and how? In: van Benthem et al. [8], pp. 321–332
8. van Benthem, J., Ghosh, S., Verbrugge, R. (eds.): Models of Strategic Reasoning. LNCS, vol. 8972. Springer, Heidelberg (2015)
9. Benz, A.: Utility and relevance of answers. In: Benz, A., Jäger, G., van Rooij, R. (eds.) Game Theory and Pragmatics, pp. 195–219. Palgrave, Hampshire (2006)
10. Benz, A.: On relevance scale approaches. In: Puig-Waldmüller, E. (ed.) Proceedings of Sinn und Bedeutung 11, pp. 91–105. Universitat Pompeu Fabra, Barcelona (2007)
11. Benz, A., van Rooij, R.: Optimal assertions and what they implicate. Topoi **26**, 63–78 (2007)
12. Bonanno, G.: Reasoning about strategies and rational play in dynamic games. In: van Benthem et al. [8], pp. 34–62
13. Camerer, C.F.: Behavioral Game Theory: Experiments in Strategic Interaction. Princeton University Press, Princeton (2003)
14. Camerer, C.F., Ho, T.-H., Chong, J.-K.: A cognitive hierarchy model of games. Q. J. Econ. **119**(3), 861–898 (2004)
15. Castellano, C., Fortunato, S., Loreto, V.: Statistical physics of social dynamics. Rev. Mod. Phys. **81**, 591–646 (2009)
16. Crawford, V.P.: Lying for strategic advantage: rational and boundedly rational misrepresentation of intentions. Am. Econ. Rev. **93**(1), 133–149 (2003)
17. Crawford, V.P.: Let's talk it over: Coordination via preplay communication with level-k thinking, Unpublished manuscript (2007)

18. van Damme, E.: Stable equilibria and forward induction. J. Econ. Theor. **48**, 476–496 (1989)
19. DeGroot, M.H.: Reaching a consensus. J. Am. Stat. Assoc. **69**(345), 118–121 (1974)
20. van Eijck, J.: Strategies in social software. In: van Benthem et al. [8], pp. 292–317
21. Farrell, J.: Communication, coordination and Nash equilibrium. Econ. Lett. **27**(3), 209–214 (1988)
22. Farrell, J.: Meaning and credibility in cheap-talk games. Games Econ. Behav. **5**, 514–531 (1993)
23. Farrell, J., Rabin, M.: Cheap talk. J. Econ. Perspect. **10**(3), 103–118 (1996)
24. Feinberg, Y.: Meaningful talk. In: Apt, K.R., van Rooij, R. (eds.) New Perspectives on Games and Interaction, pp. 105–119. Amsterdam University Press, Amsterdam (2008)
25. Y. Feinberg. Games with unawareness. Unpublished manuscript, Stanford University, April 2011
26. Feinberg, Y.: Strategic communication. In: Apt, K.R. (ed.) Proceedings of the 13th Conference on Theoretical Aspects of Rationality and Knowledge, pp. 1–11. ACM, New York (2011)
27. Franke, M.: Signal to Act: Game Theory in Pragmatics. Ph.D. thesis, Universiteit van Amsterdam (2009)
28. Franke, M., Franke, M.: Semantic meaning and pragmatic inference in non-cooperative conversation. In: Icard, T., Icard, T., Muskens, R., Muskens, R. (eds.) ESSLLI 2009. LNCS, vol. 6211, pp. 13–24. Springer, Heidelberg (2010)
29. Franke, M.: Quantity implicatures, exhaustive interpretation, and rational conversation. Semant. Pragmatics **4**(1), 1–82 (2011)
30. Franke, M.: Pragmatic reasoning about unawareness. Erkenntnis **79**(4), 729–767 (2014)
31. Franke, M., de Jager, T., van Rooij, R.: Relevance in cooperation and conflict. J. Logic Comput. **22**(1), 23–54 (2012)
32. Gabbay, D., Woods, J.: Resource-origins of nonmonotonicity. Stud. Logica. **88**, 85–112 (2008)
33. Gilboa, I., Schmeidler, D.: A Theory of Case-Based Decisions. Cambridge University Press, Cambridge (2001)
34. Grice, P.H.: Logic and conversation. In: Cole, P., Morgan, J.L. (eds.) Syntax and Semantics. Speech Acts, vol. 3, pp. 41–58. Academic Press, New York (1975)
35. Hahn, U., Oaksford, M.: The rationality of informal argumentation: a Bayesian approach to reasoning fallacies. Psychol. Rev. **114**(3), 704–732 (2007)
36. Halpern, J.Y., Rêgo, L.C.: Extensive games with possibly unaware players. In: Proceedings of the Fifth International Joint Conference on Autonomous Agents and Multiagent Systems, pp. 744–751 (2006)
37. Hamblin, C.L.: Fallacies. Methuen, London (1970)
38. Hegselmann, R., Krause, U.: Opinion dynamics and bounded confidence: models, analysis, and simulation. J. Artif. Soc. Soc. Simul. **5**(3), 1–33 (2002)
39. Heifetz, A., Meier, M., Schipper, B.C.: Dynamic unawareness and rationalizable behavior. Games Econ. Behav. **81**, 50–68 (2013)
40. Holme, P., Kim, B.J.: Growing scale-free networks with tunable clustering. Phys. Rev. E **65**(2), 026107-1–026107-4 (2002)
41. Jackson, M.O.: Social and Economic Networks. Princeton University Press, Princeton (2008)
42. Jäger, G.: Game-theoretical pragmatics. In: van Benthem, J., ter Meulen, A. (eds.) Handbook of Logic and Language, pp. 467–491. Elsevier, Amsterdam (2011)

43. Jäger, G., Ebert, C.: Pragmatic rationalizability. In: Riester, A., Solstad, T. (eds.) Proceedings of Sinn und Bedeutung, vol. 13, pp. 1–15. University of Stuttgart, Stuttgart (2009)
44. Kahane, H., Cavender, N.: Logic and Contemporary Rhetoric. Wadsworth Publishing, Belmont (1980)
45. Kahnemann, D., Tversky, A.: On the psychology of prediction. Psychol. Rev. **80**, 237–251 (1973)
46. Kreps, D.M., Wilson, R.: Sequential equilibria. Econometrica **50**(4), 863–894 (1982)
47. Lehrer, K.: Social consensus and rational agnoiology. Synthese **31**(1), 141–160 (1975)
48. Levinson, S.C.: Pragmatics. Cambridge University Press, Cambridge (1983)
49. Lewis, D.: Convention: A Philosophical Study. Harvard University Press, Cambridge (1969)
50. Liu, F., Seligman, J., Girard, P.: Logical dynamics of belief change in the community. Synthese **191**(11), 2403–2431 (2014)
51. Luce, D.R.: Individual Choice Behavior: A Theoretical Analysis. Wiley, New York (1959)
52. Matthews, S.A., Okuno-Fujiwara, M., Postlewaite, A.: Refining cheap talk equilibria. J. Econ. Theor. **55**, 247–273 (1991)
53. May, K.O.: Intransitivity, utility and the aggregation of preference patterns. Econometrica **22**(1), 1–13 (1945)
54. Mercier, H., Sperber, D.: Why do humans reason? Arguments from an argumentative theory. Behav. Brain Sci. **34**, 57–111 (2011)
55. Milgrom, P., Roberts, J.: Relying on the information of interested parties. RAND J. Econ. **17**(1), 18–32 (1986). Spring
56. Mühlenbernd, R.: Learning with neighbors: emergence of convention in a society of learning agents. Synthese **183**, 87–109 (2011)
57. Mühlenbernd, R., Franke, M.: Signaling conventions: Who learns what where and when in a social network. In: Scott-Phillips, T.C., Tamariz, M., Cartmill, E.A., Hurford, J.R. (eds.) The Evolution of Language: Proceedings of 9th International Conference (EvoLang 9), pp. 242–249. World Scientific, Singapore (2012)
58. Myerson, R.B.: Credible negotiation statements and coherent plans. J. Econ. Theor. **48**(1), 264–303 (1989)
59. O'Keefe, D.J., Jensen, J.D.: The relative persuasiveness of gain-framed and loss-framed messages for encouraging disease prevention behaviors. J. Health Commun. **12**, 623–644 (2007)
60. Osborne, M.J., Rubinstein, A.: A Course in Game Theory. MIT Press, Cambridge (1994)
61. Ozbay, E.Y.: Unawareness and strategic announcements in games with uncertainty. In: Samet, D. (ed.) Proceedings of TARK XI, pp. 231–238 (2007)
62. Pacuit, E.: Dynamic models of rational deliberation in games. In: Benthem et al. [8], pp. 3–33
63. Parikh, P.: Communication and strategic inference. Linguist. Philos. **473–514**(14), 3 (1991)
64. Parikh, P.: The Use of Language. CSLI Publications, Stanford University (2001)
65. Parikh, P.: Language and Equilibrium. MIT Press, Cambridge (2010)
66. Perea, A.: Finite reasoning procedures for dynamic games. In: van Benthem et al. [8], pp. 63–90
67. Rabin, M.: Communication between rational agents. J. Econ. Theor. **51**, 144–170 (1990)

68. Rogers, B.W., Palfrey, T.R., Camerer, C.: Heterogeneous quantal response equilibrium and cognitive hierarchies. J. Econ. Theor. **144**(4), 1440–1467 (2009)

69. van Rooij, R.: Quality and quantity of information exchange. J. Logic Lang. Inform. **12**, 423–451 (2003)

70. van Rooij, R., Franke, M.: Promises and threats with conditionals and disjunctions. In: Grewendorf, G., Zimmermann, T.E. (eds.) Discourse and Grammar: From Sentence Types to Lexical Categories, pp. 69–88. de Gruyter Mouton, Berlin (2012)

71. Ruan, J., Thielscher, M.: A logic for knowledge flow in social networks. In: Wang, D., Reynolds, M. (eds.) AI 2011. LNCS, vol. 7106, pp. 511–520. Springer, Heidelberg (2011)

72. Sandu, G.: Languages for imperfect information. In: van Benthem et al. [8], pp. 202–251

73. Shin, H.S.: The burden of proof in a game of persuasion. J. Econ. Theor. **64**(1), 253–264 (1994)

74. Simon, H.A.: Theories of decision-making in economics and behavioral science. Am. Econ. Rev. **49**, 253–283 (1959)

75. Stalnaker, R.: Belief revision in games: forward and backward induction. Math. Soc. Sci. **36**, 31–56 (1998)

76. Stalnaker, R.: Saying and meaning, cheap talk and credibility. In: Benz, A., Jäger, G., van Rooij, R. (eds.) Game Theory and Pragmatics, pp. 83–100. Palgrave MacMillan, Hampshire (2006)

77. Tversky, A., Kahnemann, D.: Judgement under uncertainty: heuristics and biases. Science **185**, 1124–1131 (1974)

78. Tversky, A., Kahnemann, D.: The framing of decisions and the psychology of choice. Science **211**(4481), 453–458 (1981)

79. Wagner, E.: Communication and structured correlation. Erkenntnis **71**(3), 377–393 (2009)

80. Walton, D.N., Krabbe, E.C.W.: Commitment in Dialogue: Basic Concepts of Interpersonal Reasoning. State University of New York, Albany (1995)

81. Zapater, I.: Credible proposals in communication games. J. Econ. Theor. **72**, 173–197 (1997)

82. Zollman, K.J.S.: Talking to neighbors: the evolution of regional meaning. Philos. Sci. **72**, 69–85 (2005)

Strategies in Social Software

Jan van Eijck[✉]

Center for Mathematics and Computer Science (CWI),
Amsterdam and Institute for Logic, Language and Computation (ILLC),
University of Amsterdam, Amsterdam, The Netherlands
jve@cwi.nl

Abstract. Viewing the way society has defined its rules and mechanisms as "social software", we want to understand how people behave given their understanding of the societal rules and given their wish to further their interest *as they conceive it*, and how social mechanisms should be designed to suit people furthering their interest *as they conceive it*. This chapter is written from the perspective of strategic game theory, and uses strategic game scenarios and game transformations to analyze societal mechanisms.

Keywords: Strategic game theory · Game transformation · Design of societal mechanism

> Know the enemy and know yourself; in a hundred battles you will never be in peril.
> When you are ignorant of the enemy but know yourself, your chances of winning and losing are equal.
> If ignorant both of your enemy and of yourself, you are certain in every battle to be in peril.

> Sun Tzu, The Art of War [37]

1 What Is Social Software?

Social software is a term coined by Parikh [42] for social procedures designed to regulate societal behaviour. Many of these mechanisms are connected to strategic reasoning. Parikh's paper is a plea to view social procedures as algorithms, and to study them with the methods of logic and theoretical computer science. See [14] for illuminating use of this methodology to explain rituals in societies. The discourses in Van Eijck and Verbrugge [18] give further informal introduction.

© Springer-Verlag Berlin Heidelberg 2015
J. van Benthem et al. (Eds.): Models of Strategic Reasoning, LNCS 8972, pp. 292–317, 2015.
DOI: 10.1007/978-3-662-48540-8_9

In fact, design and analysis of social software is at the intersection of various academic disciplines. It is related to what is called mechanism design in game theory and economics [26], to behavioral architecture in political theory [53], to rational decision making in decision theory [22,30], to multi-agent theory in artificial intelligence [47], and to auction theory in economics [32,38], to name but a few. If it is different from any of these, then the difference lies in the emphasis on the use of tools from logic and theoretical computer science, while bearing in mind that the objects of study are humans rather than microprocessors.

Indeed, the human participants in a social procedure are quite different from microprocessors interacting in a calculation. Unlike microprocessors, humans are, to some extent at least, aware of the social mechanisms they are involved in. This awareness may inspire them to act strategically: to use their knowledge of the mechanism to improve their welfare. Conversely, social mechanisms may be designed with this behaviour in mind. Ideally, the design of the mechanism should ensure that it cannot be exploited, or at least that the mechanism is resistant to exploitation attempts.

A central topic in economics, and in a branch of game theory called evolutionary game theory, is to explain how selfish behaviour can lead to beneficial outcomes on the societal level [48]. On the other hand, some economists have argued convincingly that modelling human beings as selfish misses a point: the scope of economics should be broadened to the study of interacting agents maximizing welfare *as they conceive it* [7].

Undoubtedly the most famous social mechanism that employs strategic behaviour is the mechanism of the free market, supposedly guided by Adam Smith's invisible hand, the hidden mechanism that fuses actions motivated by individual interests into a self-regulating social mechanism beneficent to all. In Smith's famous words:

> It is not from the benevolence of the butcher, the brewer or the baker that we expect our dinner, but from their regard to their own interest. We address ourselves not to their humanity but to their self-love, and never talk to them of our necessities but of their advantages. Nobody but a beggar chooses to depend chiefly upon the benevolence of their fellow-citizens. [49, Book 1,Chapter II]

The mechanism of the free market is designed, so to speak, to put individual self-interest at the service of society. But in other cases, social mechanism design has as one of its goals to discourage 'strategic behaviour', which now is taken to mean *misuse* of the mechanism to guarantee a better individual outcome. An example of this is auction design. Vickrey auctions, where bids are made simultaneously, bidders do not know the values of the other bids, and the highest bidder wins but pays the second-highest bid [55], are an example. The design of the procedure discourages the bidders from making bids that do not reflect their true valuation. Google and Yahoo use variations on this when auctioning advertisement space.

Many societal mechanisms are set up so as to ensure a desirable outcome for society. What is the social procedure that ensures that soldiers that are sent into battle actually fight? One force is the fact that the other soldiers are fighting — a chain-effect. An additional factor may be the public announcement to the effect that deserters will be shot. This reduces the choice that a soldier has to that between facing the risk of death while engaging in battle versus certain death when avoiding to fight. Surely, other factors are involved, having to do with how soldiers perceive their own behaviour and their relationship to each other and to the community they fight for: comradeship, the desire to return home as a hero rather than a coward. The point is that society has mechanisms in play to ensure that individuals behave in ways that, at first sight, are squarely against their self-interest.

Some societies stage public executions of criminals. Such stagings serve a strategic social goal: to inspire terror in aspiring criminals. Or maybe, to inspire terror in the population at large, in case the victims are convicted for political crimes. Some societies keep their citizens in check with the threat of corporal punishment — in Singapore you risk a blow with the stick for a relatively minor offence — while other societies consider such methods off-limits and barbarian. Someone interested in design and analysis of social software will want to understand such radical differences in attitude.

The mechanisms of performance-related pay and of investment bankers' bonuses are other examples of social procedures designed with the goal of influencing the strategies of workers, in order to increase productivity or profitability. While the current financial crisis is evidence of the dangers of this system, experimental economics also points out that very high rewards are in fact detrimental to performance [2].

On the other hand, in another setting such a mechanism may have considerable advantages. The bonus-malus system (BMS) used in the insurance industry adjusts the premium that a customer has to pay to insure a certain risk according to the individual claim history of the customer. This inspires caution in claiming damage on an insured vehicle, for instance, for a claim means that the customer loses her no-claim discount. Thus, the system is designed to induce strategic behaviour in the customers, for it now makes sense to not report minor damages to your car to the insurance company, as the loss of the no-claim discount outweighs the cost of the damage. This is in the interest of the insurance company, and indirectly in the interest of the public in need of car insurance, for it helps to keep premiums low. So why does the bonus system work well in this situation while creating disaster in other settings?

A general problem with social mechanism design is that technological fixes to societal problems have a tendency to misfire and create new problems, because the technological solution leads to paradoxical and unintended consequences. New roads lead to bigger traffic jams and uncontrolled growth of suburbia. Rent regulation, intended to protect tenants, may lead to poorer housing conditions for the less affluent. Worker protection laws may be a factor in causing unemployment because they make employers reluctant to hire new staff. Performance-related pay may induce bankers to take unreasonable risks. Tenner [52] gives many other examples, with insightful comments.

Still, insights from the design and analysis of algorithms can and should be applied to analysis and design in social interaction, all the time bearing in mind that agents involved in social interaction are *aware* of the societal mechanisms. This awareness often takes the form of strategic reasoning by people about how to further their best interest, *as they conceive it*, given the way society has defined its rules and mechanisms. The analysis and design of social software should take this awareness of participants into account.

The focus of this chapter is on strategic games rather than dynamic games. The structure of the chapter is as follows. In Sect. 2 we distinguish three levels at which strategizing might occur. In Sect. 3, we use the situation of the well-known prisoner's dilemma as a starting point for a discussion of what goes on in social software design and analysis. Section 4 discusses, in a game-theoretic setting, how strategies are affected by punishment, and Sect. 5 focusses on the influence of rewards on strategies. In Sect. 6, these same topics return in the tragedy of the commons scenario, closely related to the prisoner's dilemma. The theme of individual versus collective is brought out even more poignantly in renunciation games, presented in Sect. 7. Section 8 discusses the use of game scenarios in experiments about knowledge and trust in social protocols, and Sect. 9 concludes with a mention of logics for strategic games, together with some remarkable arguments for democracy.

2 Strategizing at Various Levels

The social problem of collective decision making involves strategizing at various levels. Consider as an example a scientific advisory board that has to rank a number of research proposals in order of quality. Participants in such a meeting strategize at various levels, and strategizing also takes place at the level of the scientific community at large.

Strategizing at the Micro-Level. How much should I, as a participant in such a meeting, reveal about my own true preferences (or: of my own knowledge and ignorance), in order to make me maximally effective in influencing the other participants?

Strategizing at Intermediate Level. How should the chair structure the decision making process, so as to ensure that consensus is reached and that the meeting terminates within a reasonable period of time? The chair could propose rules like "For any two proposals X and Y, once we have reached a decision on their relative merit, this order will remain fixed." Or: "A meeting participant who has close working relationships with the writer of a research proposal should leave the room when the merit of that proposal is discussed." Slightly more general, but still at the intermediate level: How should the general rules for ranking research proposals be designed? E.g., collect at least three independent reviews per proposal, and use the reviews to get at a preliminary ranking. Ask participants to declare conflicts of interest before the meeting starts. And so on.

Strategizing at the Macro-Level. How does the scientific community at large determine quality of research? How do the peer review system and the impact factor rankings of scientific journals influence the behaviour of researchers or research groups?

In other cases we can make similar distinctions. Take the case of voting as a decision making mechanism.

Micro-Level. At the micro level, individual voters decide what to do, given a particular voting rule, given their true preferences, and given what they know about the preferences of the other voters. The key question here is: "Should I vote according to my true preferences or not?" This is the question of *strategic voting*: deviating from one's true preference in the hope of a better outcome. In a school class, during an election for a football captain, excellent sportsmen may cast a strategic vote on a mediocre player to further their own interests.

Intermediate Level. At the intermediate level, organizers of meetings decide which voting procedures to adopt in particular situations. How to fix the available set of alternatives? Does the situation call for secret ballots or not? How to settle the order for reaching decisions about sub-issues?

Macro-Level. At the macro-level, there is the issue of the design and analysis of voting procedures, or the improvement of voting procedures that fail to serve their political goal of rational collective decision making in a changing society. Think of the discussion of the merits of "first past the post" election systems in single-member districts, which favour the development of a small number of large parties, versus proportional representation systems which make it possible for smaller parties to survive in the legislature, but also engender the need for coalitions of several parties to aggregate in a working majority.

Writers about strategizing in warfare make similar level distinctions. Carl von Clausewitz, who defines war as "an act of violence or force intended to compel our enemy to do our will," makes a famous distinction between tactics, the doctrine of the use of troops in battle, and strategy, the doctrine of the use of armed engagements to further the aims of the war [56]. In our terminology, these issues are at the micro- and at the intermediate level, while the political choices between war and peace are being made at the macro-level.

3   The Prisoner's Dilemma as an Exemplar

The game known as the "prisoner's dilemma" is an evergreen of game theory because it is a top-level description of the plight of two people, or countries, who can either act trustfully or not, with the worst outcome that of being a sucker whose trust gets exploited by the other player.

One particular choice for a player in such a situation is called a strategy. Further on, we will discuss how the choice of strategies in this sense is affected by redesign of the scenario, thus shifting attention to possible strategies for the social mechanism designer, so to speak.

But first, here is a brief recap. Agents I and II are imprisoned, in different cells, and are faced with a choice between cooperating with each other or defecting. If the two cooperate they both benefit, but, unfortunately, it pays to defect if the other cooperates. If they both defect they both lose. This situation can be described in the following payoff matrix.

	II cooperates	II defects
I cooperates	3, 3	0, 4
I defects	4, 0	1, 1

This table displays a two person non-zero-sum game. The first member of each payoff pair gives I's payoff, the second member II's payoff. The table outcome 4, 0 indicates that if I defects while II cooperates, the payoff for I is 4 and the payoff for II is 0. This indicates that for I it is profitable to cheat if II stays honest. In fact it is more profitable for I to cheat than to stay honest in this case, for honesty gives him a payoff of only 3.

For the prison setting, read the two options as 'keep silent' or 'betray (by talking to the prison authorities)'. For an armament race version, read the two options as 'disarm' or 'arm'.

What matters for the payoffs is the preference order that is implied by the numbers in the payoff matrix. Abbreviate the strategy pair where I cooperates and II defects as (c, d), and so on. Then the preference order for I can be given as $(d, c), (c, c), (d, d), (c, d)$, while the preference order for II swaps the elements of the pairs: $(c, d), (c, c), (d, d), (d, c)$. Replacing the payoffs by different numbers reflecting the same preference order does not change the nature of the game.

Suppose player I decides to follow a particular strategy. If player II has also made up her mind about what to do, this determines the outcome. Does player I get a better payoff if he changes his strategy, given that II sticks to hers? Player II can ask the same question. A situation where neither player can improve his outcome by deviating from his strategy while it is given that the other player sticks to hers is called a *Nash equilibrium*, after John Nash [33].

Observe that the strategy pair (d, d) is a Nash equilibrium, and no other strategy pair is. This is what makes the situation of the game a dilemma, for the outcome (c, c) would have been better for both.

Not only is (d, d) a Nash equilibrium of the game, but it holds that (d, d) is the *only* Nash equilibrium. What follows is that for each player, d is the optimal action, *no matter what the other player does*. Such a strategy is called a *dominant* strategy.

Using u_I for I's utility function, and u_{II} for II's utility function, we can say that what makes the game into a dilemma is the fact that $u_I(d, d) > u_I(c, d)$ and $u_I(d, c) > u_I(c, c)$, and similarly for II: $u_{II}(d, d) > u_{II}(d, c)$ and $u_{II}(c, d) > u_{II}(c, c)$.

The two-player prisoner's dilemma can be generalized to an n player prisoner's dilemma (NPD), which can be used to model situations where the invisible hand does *not* work to the benefit of all. See Sect. 6 below.

Here we remind the reader of some formal terminology for strategic n-person games. A strategic game G is a tuple

$$(\{1, \ldots, n\}, \{S_i\}_{i \in \{1, \ldots, n\}}, \{u_i\}_{i \in \{1, \ldots, n\}}),$$

where $\{1, \ldots, n\}$ with $n > 1$ is the set of players, each S_i is a set of strategies, and each u_i is a function from $S_1 \times \cdots \times S_n$ to $\mathbb{R}$ (the utility function for player i). I use N for $\{1, \ldots, n\}$, S for $S_1 \times \cdots \times S_n$ and u for $\{u_i\}_{i \in \{1, \ldots, n\}}$, so that I can use (N, S, u) to denote a game.

A member of $S_1 \times \cdots \times S_n$ is called a strategy profile: each player i picks a strategy $s_i \in S_i$. I use s to range over strategy profiles, and s_{-i} for the strategy profile that results by deleting strategy choice s_i of player i from s. Let (s'_i, s_{-i}) be the strategy profile that is like s for all players except i, but has s_i replaced by s'_i. Let S_{-i} be the set of all strategy profiles minus the strategy for player i (the product of all strategy sets minus S_i). Note that $s_{-i} \in S_{-i}$. A strategy s_i is a *best response* in s if

$$\forall s'_i \in S_i \ u_i(s) \geq u_i(s'_i, s_{-i}).$$

A strategy profile s is a (pure) Nash equilibrium if each s_i is a best response in s:

$$\forall i \in N \ \forall s'_i \in S_i \ u_i(s) \geq u_i(s'_i, s_{-i}).$$

Let $\mathrm{nash}(G) = \{s \in S \mid s \text{ is a Nash equilibrium of } G\}$.

A game G is *Nash* if G has a (pure) Nash equilibrium.

A strategy $s^* \in S_i$ weakly dominates another strategy $s' \in S_i$ if

$$\forall s_{-i} \in S_{-i} \ u_i(s^*, s_{-i}) \geq u_i(s', s_{-i}).$$

A strategy $s^* \in S_i$ strictly dominates another strategy $s' \in S_i$ if

$$\forall s_{-i} \in S_{-i} \ u_i(s^*, s_{-i}) > u_i(s', s_{-i}).$$

If a two-player game has a strictly dominant strategy for each player, both players will play that strategy no matter what the other player does, and the dominant strategy pair will form the only Nash equilibrium of the game. This is what happens in the prisoner's dilemma game.

Define a *social welfare function* $W : S_1 \times \cdots \times S_n \to \mathbb{R}$ by setting

$$W(s) = \sum_{i=1}^{n} u_i(s).$$

A strategy profile s of a game $G = (N, S, u)$ is a *social optimum* if

$$W(s) = \sup\{W(t) \mid t \in S\}.$$

For a finite game, s is a social optimum if $W(s)$ is the maximum of the welfare function for that game.

In the case of the prisoner's dilemma game, the social optimum is reached at (c, c), with outcome $W(c, c) = 3 + 3 = 6$.

We can turn the prisoner's dilemma setting into a playground for social software engineering, in several ways. In Sect. 4 we explore punishment mechanisms, while in Sect. 5 we look at welfare redistribution.

4   Appropriate Punishment

Suppose the social software engineer is confronted with a PD situation, and has to design a policy that makes defection less profitable. One way of doing that is to put a penalty P on defection. Notice that we now talk about engineering a strategy at a level different from the level where I and II choose their strategies in the game.

A penalty P on cheating does not have an immediate effect, for it can only be imposed if the one who cheats gets caught. Suppose the probability of getting caught is p. In case the cheater gets caught, she gets the penalty, otherwise she gets what she would have got in the original game.

Then adopting the policy amounts to a *change in the utility functions*. In other words, the policy change can be viewed as a *game transformation* that maps strategic game G to strategic game G^{pP}, where G^{pP} is like G except for the fact that the utility function is replaced by:

$$u_I^{pP}(c, c) = u_I(c, c),$$
$$u_I^{pP}(d, c) = pP + (1 - p)u_I(d, c),$$
$$u_I^{pP}(c, d) = u_I(c, d),$$
$$u_I^{pP}(d, d) = pP + (1 - p)u_I(d, d),$$

and similarly for u_{II}^{pP}. The utility for behaving honestly if the other player is also honest does not change. The new utility of cheating if the other is honest amounts to P in case you get caught, and to the old utility of cheating in case you can get away with it. The probability of getting caught is p, that of getting away unpunished is $1 - p$. Hence $u_I^{pP} = pP + (1 - p)u_I(d, c)$.

This allows us to compute the 'right' amount of punishment as a function of the utilities of being honest and of cheating without being caught, and the probability of being caught. Recall the assumption that the utility of staying honest while the other player cheats has not changed. Call this H. Let C be the reward for cheating without being caught. Let p is the probability of getting caught. Then a punishment of $\frac{H + pC - C}{p}$ is "just right" for making cheating lose its appeal. Technically, this is the least amount of punishment that turns the social optimum of the game into a Nash equilibrium.

For example, suppose the probability of getting caught cheating is $\frac{1}{9}$. Then the punishment that ensures that cheating loses its appeal in case the other player is honest, for the utilities shown above, equals $\frac{3+(1/9)4-4}{1/9} = -5$. This amounts to the following transformation of the prisoner's dilemma game:

$$
\begin{array}{c|cc}
 & c & d \\
\hline
c & 3,3 & 0,4 \\
d & 4,0 & 1,1
\end{array}
\Rightarrow (-5, \frac{1}{9}) \Rightarrow
\begin{array}{c|cc}
 & c & d \\
\hline
c & 3,3 & 0,3 \\
d & 3,0 & \frac{1}{3},\frac{1}{3}
\end{array}
$$

The new game has two Nash equilibria: (c,c) with payoff $(3,3)$, and (d,d), with payoff $(\frac{1}{3},\frac{1}{3})$. If the other player is honest, cheating loses its appeal, but if the other player cheats, cheating still pays off.

The punishment that ensures that cheating loses its appeal in case the other player is cheating (assuming the probability of getting caught is still the same) is higher. It equals $\frac{(1/9)-1}{1/9} = -8$. This corresponds to the following game transformation:

$$
\begin{array}{c|cc}
 & c & d \\
\hline
c & 3,3 & 0,4 \\
d & 4,0 & 1,1
\end{array}
\Rightarrow (-8, \frac{1}{9}) \Rightarrow
\begin{array}{c|cc}
 & c & d \\
\hline
c & 3,3 & 0,2\frac{2}{3} \\
d & 2\frac{2}{3},0 & 0,0
\end{array}
$$

In the result of this new transformation, the social optimum (c,c) is the only Nash equilibrium.

There are many possible variations on this. One reviewer suggested that in the case where cheating gets detected, there should also be an implication for the honest player. The cheating player should get the penalty indeed, but maybe the honest player should get what she would get in case both players are honest.

Another perspective on this is that punishment presupposes an agent who administers it, and that doling out punishment has a certain cost. Think of real-life examples such as confronting a queue jumper in a supermarket line. The act of confrontation takes courage, but if it succeeds all people in the queue benefit [19].

Game theory does not directly model what goes on in society, but game-theoretical scenarios can be used to *illuminate* what goes on in society. The transformation mechanism for the prisoner's dilemma scenario illustrates, for example, why societies with widespread crime need more severe criminal laws than societies with less crime. Also, the calculations suggest that if a society wants to avoid severe punishments, it has to invest in measures that ensure a higher probability of getting caught.

A game-theoretical perspective on crime and punishment is in line with rational thinking about what constitutes 'just punishment', which goes back (at least) to Beccaria [6]. What the analysis is still missing is the important principle that the punishment should somehow be in proportion to the severity of the crime. Such proportionality is important:

> If an equal punishment be ordained for two crimes that injure society
> in different degrees, there is nothing to deter men from committing the
> greater as often as it is attended with greater advantage. [6, Ch6]

Let us define a measure for social harm caused by the strategy of an individual player. Let a game $G = (N, S, u)$ be given. For any $i \in N$, define the individual harm function $H_i : S \to \mathbb{R}$, as follows:

$$H_i(s) = \sup_{s_i' \in S_i} W(s_i', s_{-i}) - W(s).$$

This gives the difference between the best outcome for society as i unilaterally deviates from her current strategy and the present outcome for society. Assuming that the set S_i is finite, we can replace this by:

$$H_i(s) = \max_{s_i' \in S_i} W(s_i', s_{-i}) - W(s).$$

That is, $H_i(s)$ gives a measure for how much player i harms society by playing s_i rather than the alternative s_i' that ensures the maximum social welfare. Clearly, in case s is a social optimum, $H_i(s) = 0$ for any i.

In the case of the prisoner's dilemma, if player II is honest, the cheating behaviour of player I causes 2 units of societal harm:

$$H_I(c,c) = 0, H_I(d,c) = W(c,c) - W(d,c) = 6 - 4 = 2.$$

Also in case II cheats, the cheating behaviour of I causes 2 units of societal harm:

$$H_I(d,d) = H(c,d) - H(d,d) = 4 - 2 = 2.$$

Finally, $H_I(c,d) = 0$, for playing honest if the other player is cheating is better for society than cheating when the other player is cheating.

Punishment can now be made proportional to social harm, as follows. If $G = (N, S, u)$ is a strategic game, $p \in [0,1]$, $\beta \in \mathbb{R}_{\geq 0}$, then $G^{p\beta}$ is the game $(N, S, u^{p\beta})$, where $u^{p\beta}$ is given by:

$$u_i^{p\beta}(s) := u_i(s) - p\beta H_i(s).$$

To see what this means, first consider cases of s and i with $H_i(s) = 0$. In these cases we get that $u_i^{p\beta}(s) = u_i(s)$. In cases where $H_i(s) > 0$ we get that the penalty for harming society is proportional to the harm. Observe that

$$u_i(s) - p\beta H_i(s) = (1 - p)u_i(s) + p(u_i(s) - \beta H_i(s)).$$

So, with probability $1 - p$ the crime gets undetected, and the player gets $u_i(s)$. With probability p, the crime gets detected, and the player gets $u_i(s) - \beta H_i(s)$, the original reward minus the penalty.

Now we have to find the least β that deters players from harming society. Games where no player has an incentive for harming society are the games that have a social optimum that is also a Nash equilibrium. For any game G it holds that $G^{0\beta} = G$, for all β, for if there is no possibility of detection, it does not matter what the penalty is. If the probability p of detection is non-zero, we can investigate the class of games $\{G^{p\beta} \mid \beta \in \mathbb{R}_{\geq 0}\}$.

Note that G and $G^{p\beta}$ have the same social optima, for in a social optimum s it holds for any player i that $H_i(s) = 0$. Moreover, if s is a social optimum of G, then $W(s) = W^{p\beta}(s)$.

As an example, consider the prisoner's dilemma again. We get:

$$u_I^{p\beta}(d,c) = u_I(d,c) - p\beta H_I(d,c) = 4 - 2p\beta.$$

To make (c,c) Nash, we need $4 - 2p\beta \leq 3$, whence $\beta \geq \frac{1}{2p}$ (recall that $p > 0$).

Nash equilibrium can be viewed as the outcome of the agents' strategic reasoning. It is the most commonly used notion of equilibrium in game theory, but that does not mean that this is the obviously right choice in any application. Here is one example of a modification. Call a strategy s_i a *social best response* in s if

$$\forall s_i' \in S_i \ (W(s) \leq W(s_i', s_{-i}) \to u_i(s) \geq u_i(s_i', s_{-i})).$$

What this means is that no other response for i *from among the responses that do not harm the social welfare payoff* is strictly better than the current response for i.

Call a strategy profile a *social equilibrium* if each s_i is a social best response in s:

$$\forall i \in \{1, \ldots, n\} \ \forall s_i' \in S_i \ (W(s) \leq W(s_i', s_{-i}) \to u_i(s) \geq u_i(s_i', s_{-i})).$$

The PD game has two social equilibria: (c,c) and (d,d). The strategy pair (c,c) is a social equilibrium because for each of the players, deviating from this profile harms the collective. The strategy pair (d,d) is a social equilibrium because it holds for each player that deviating from it harms that player.

A strategy profile is called Pareto optimal if it is impossible in that state to make a player better off without making at least one other player worse off. The profiles (c,c), (c,d) and (d,c) in the PD game are Pareto optimal, while (d,d) is Pareto-dominated by (c,c). This shows that Pareto optimality is different from being a social equilibrium.

If one would be allowed to assume that players are 'social' in the sense that they would always refrain from actions that harm society as a whole, then meting out punishment proportional to the social harm that is caused would make no sense anymore, for players would not cause any social harm in the first place. In a more realistic setting, one would assume a certain mix of socially responsible and socially irresponsible players, and study what happens in repeated game playing for populations of such player types [48]. If the distinction between socially responsible players and selfish players makes sense, the distinction between Nash equilibria and social equilibria may be useful for an analysis of social responsibility. I must leave this for future work.

5   Welfare Redistribution

For another variation on the prisoner's dilemma game, we can think of reward rather than punishment. The idea of using *welfare redistribution* to make a game more altruistic can be found in many places, and has made it to the textbooks. Consider the following exercise in Osborne [39], where the student is invited to analyze a variation on the prisoner's dilemma:

The players are not "selfish"; rather the preferences of each player i are represented by the payoff function $m_i(a) + \alpha m_j(a)$, where $m_i(a)$ is the amount of money received by player i when the action profile is a, j is the other player, and α is a given non-negative number.
[39, Exercise 27.1 on page 27]

This idea is worked out in Apt and Schaefer [1] for the general case of n player strategic games, where the *selfishness level* of a game is computed by transforming a game G to a different game $G(\alpha)$, with α a positive real number, and $G(\alpha)$ the result of modifying the payoff function of G by adding $\alpha W(s)$ to each utility ($W(s)$ is the social welfare outcome for the strategy profile s).

As an example, using $\alpha = 1$, we can transform the prisoner's dilemma game PD into $PD(1)$, as follows:

	c	d
c	3, 3	0, 4
d	4, 0	1, 1

$\Rightarrow (\alpha = 1) \Rightarrow$

	c	d
c	9, 9	4, 8
d	8, 4	3, 3

This gives a new game, and in this modified game, the only Nash equilibrium is (c, c). This means that the social optimum now is a Nash equilibrium. The selfishness level of a game G is defined as the least α for which the move from G to $G(\alpha)$ yields a game for which a social optimum is a Nash equilibrium. For the prisoner's dilemma game with the payoffs as given in the table on page 6, the selfishness level α can be computed by equating the payoff in the social optimum with the best payoff in the Nash equilibrium: $3 + 6\alpha = 4 + 4\alpha$, which gives $\alpha = \frac{1}{2}$.

There are also games G that have at least one social optimum, but that cannot be turned into a game $G(\alpha)$ with a socially optimal Nash equilibrium for any α. Apt and Schaefer [1] stipulate that such games have a selfishness level equal to ∞.

Instead of the selfishness level, I will use a reformulation of this idea which consists in computing what is the least amount of *welfare redistribution* that is necessary to convert a social optimum into a Nash equilibrium. In other words: *how far* do you have to move on the scale from pure capitalism to pure communism to ensure that a social optimum is a Nash equilibrium? (But whether this is more perspicuous remains a matter of taste, for I have tried in vain to convince the authors to adjust their definition).

The map for welfare redistribution is $G \mapsto G[\gamma]$, where $\gamma \in [0, 1]$ (our γ is a *proportion*), and the payoff u_i^γ in the new game $G[\gamma]$ is computed from the payoff u_i in G (assuming there are n players) by means of:

$$u_i^\gamma(s) = (1 - \gamma)u_i(s) + \gamma \frac{W(s)}{n}.$$

Here $W(s)$ gives the result of the welfare function on s in G.

Thus, player i is allowed to keep $1 - \gamma$ of her old revenue $u_i(s)$, and gets an equal share $\frac{1}{n}$ of $\gamma W(s)$, which is the part of the welfare that gets redistributed. This definition is mentioned (but not used) in Chen and Kempe [12].

Notice the similarity to the probability of punishment computation on page 8. Also notice that if $\gamma = 0$, no redistribution of wealth takes place (pure capitalism), and if $\gamma = 1$, all wealth gets distributed equally (pure communism).

The *civilization cost* of a game G is the least γ for which the move from G to $G[\gamma]$ turns a social optimum into a Nash equilibrium. In case G has no social optimum, the civilization cost is undefined.

Note the difference with the notion of the selfishness level of a game, computed by means of $u_i^\alpha(s) = u_i(s) + \alpha W(s)$. Summing over all the players this gives a new social welfare $W' = (1 + n\alpha)W$. If we rescale by dividing all new payoffs by $1 + n\alpha$, we see that this uses a different recipe: $q_i(s) = \frac{u_i(s) + \alpha W}{1 + n\alpha}$. Thus, the definitions of selfishness level and civilisation cost are *not* related by rescaling (linear transformation). Rather, they are related, for the case where $\gamma \in [0, 1)$, by the nonlinear transformation $\alpha = \frac{\gamma}{n(1-\gamma)}$. This transformation is undefined for $\gamma = 1$. Note that the map $G, \gamma \mapsto G[\gamma]$ is more general than the map $G, \alpha \mapsto G(\alpha)$, for the game $G[1]$ where all welfare gets distributed equally has no counterpart $G(\cdot)$. Setting α equal to ∞ would result in a 'game' with infinite payoffs.

An example of a game for which the selfishness level and the civilization cost are 0 is the stag hunting game (first mentioned in the context of the establishment of social convention, in Lewis [34], but the example goes back to Rousseau [46]), with s for hunting stag and h for hunting hare.

	s	h
s	2,2	0,1
h	1,0	1,1

These payoffs are meant to reflect the fact that stag hunting is more rewarding than hunting hare, but one cannot hunt stag on one's own.

Note the difference in payoffs with the prisoner's dilemma game: if your strategy is to hunt hare on your own, it makes no difference for your payoff whether the others also hunt hare or not. This game has two Nash equilibria, one of which is also a social optimum. This is the strategy tuple where everyone joins the stag hunt. So the selfishness level and the civilisation cost of this game are 0.

Here is how the result of redistribution of proportion γ of the social welfare is computed for the PD game, for the case of I (the computation for II is similar):

$$u_I^\gamma(c, c) = u_I(c, c),$$

$$u_I^\gamma(d, c) = (1 - \gamma)u_I(d, c) + \gamma \frac{W(d, c)}{2}$$

$$u_I^\gamma(c, d) = (1 - \gamma)u_I(c, d) + \gamma \frac{W(c, d)}{2}$$

$$u_I^\gamma(d, d) = u_I(d, d).$$

In the cases $u_I^\gamma(c, c)$ and $u_I^\gamma(d, d)$ nothing changes, for in these cases the payoffs for I and II were already equal.

The civilisation cost of the prisoner's dilemma, with the payoffs of the example, is computed by means of $3 = 4(1 - \gamma) + \frac{\gamma}{2}4$, which yields $\gamma = \frac{1}{2}$. This is the same value as that of the selfishness level, because substitution of $\frac{1}{2}$ for γ in the equation $\alpha = \frac{\gamma}{2-2\gamma}$ yields $\alpha = \frac{1}{2}$.

If we change the payoffs by setting $u_I(d, c) = u_{II}(c, d) = 5$, while leaving everything else unchanged, the cost of civilization is given by $3 = 5(1 - \alpha) + \frac{\alpha}{2}5$, which yields $\alpha = \frac{4}{5}$. The selfishness level in this case is given by $3 + 6\alpha = 5 + 5\alpha$, which yields $\alpha = 2$.

These were mere illustrations of how the effects of welfare redistribution can be studied in a game-theoretic setting. This analysis can help to understand social interaction in real life, provided of course that the game-theoretic model fits the situation. In the next section we will look at a more sophisticated model for the conflict between individual and societal interest than the prisoner's dilemma game model.

6   Tragedy-of-the-Commons Scenarios and Social Engineering

The tragedy of the commons game scenario that applies to games of competition for shares in a commonly owned resource was first analyzed in Gordon [23] and was made famous in an essay by Garrett Hardin:

> The tragedy of the commons develops in this way. Picture a pasture open to all. It is to be expected that each herdsman will try to keep as many cattle as possible on the commons. Such an arrangement may work reasonably satisfactorily for centuries because tribal wars, poaching, and disease keep the numbers of both man and beast well below the carrying capacity of the land. Finally, however, comes the day of reckoning, that is, the day when the long-desired goal of social stability becomes a reality. At this point, the inherent logic of the commons remorselessly generates tragedy. [25]

Bringing more and more goats to the pasture will in the end destroy the commodity for all. Still, from the perspective of an individual herdsman it is profitable until almost the very end to bring an extra goat.

The tragedy of the commons can be analyzed as a multi-agent version of the prisoner's dilemma. The players' optimal selfish strategies depend on what the other players do, and the outcome if all players pursue their individual interest is detrimental to the collective. One can also view this as a game of an individual herdsman I against the collective II. Then the matrix is:

	m	g
m	2, 2	0, 3
g	3, 0	−1, −1

Each player has a choice between g (adding goats) and m (being moderate). Assuming that the collective is well-behaved, it pays off to be a free rider. But if everyone acts like this, system breakdown will result.

In a more sophisticated multi-player version, assume there are n players. I use the modelling of Chap. 1 of Vazirani et al. [54]. The players each want to have part of a shared resource. Setting the value of the resource to 1, each player i has to decide on the part of the resource x_i to use, so we can assume that $x_i \in [0, 1]$. Note that in this model, each player can choose from an infinite number of possible strategies.

Let us stipulate the following payoff function. Let N be the set of agents. If $\sum_{j \in N} x_j < 1$ then the value for player i is $u_i = x_i(1 - \sum_{j \in N} x_j)$: the benefit for i decreases as the resource gets exhausted. If $\sum_{j \in N} x_j \geq 1$ (the demands on the resource exceed the supply), the payoff for the players becomes 0.

So what are equilibrium strategies? Take the perspective of player i. Let D be the total demand of the other players, i.e., $D = \sum_{j \in N, j \neq i} x_j < 1$. Then strategy x_i gives payoff $u_i = x_i(1 - (D + x_i))$, so the optimal solution for i is $x_i = (1 - D)/2$. Since the optimal solution for each player is the same, this gives $x = \frac{1-(n-1)x}{2}$, and thus $x = \frac{1}{n+1}$ as the optimal strategy for each player. This gives $D + x = \frac{n}{n+1}$, and payoff for x of $u = \frac{1}{n+1}(1 - \frac{n}{n+1}) = \frac{1}{(n+1)^2}$, and a total payoff of $\frac{n}{(n+1)^2}$, which is roughly $\frac{1}{n}$. This means that the social welfare in the Nash equilibrium for this game depends inversely on the number of players.

If the players had agreed to leave the resource to a single player, the total payoff would have been $u = x(1 - x)$, which is optimal for $x = \frac{1}{2}$, yielding payoff $u = \frac{1}{4}$. If the players had agreed to use only $\frac{1}{2}$ of the resource, they would have had a payoff of $\frac{1}{4n}$ each, which is much more than $\frac{1}{(n+1)^2}$ for large n. Tragedy indeed.

Can we remedy this by changing the payoff function, transforming the ToC into ToC$[\gamma]$ with a Nash equilibrium which also is a social optimum? It turns out we can, but only at the cost of complete redistribution of welfare. The civilization cost of the ToC is 1. Here is why. If all players decide to leave the resource to a single player i, the payoff for i is given by $u_i = x_i(1 - x_i)$. This is optimal for $x_i = \frac{1}{2}$, and the payoff for this strategy, in the profile where all other players play 0, is $\frac{1}{4}$. This is the social optimum.

Suppose we are in a social optimum s. Then $W(s) = \frac{1}{4}$. Player i deviates by moving from x_i to $x_i + y$. The new payoff is $(x_i + y)(\frac{1}{2} - y) = \frac{1}{2}(x_i + y) - y(x_i + y)$. The deviation is tempting if $(x_i + y)(\frac{1}{2} - y) > \frac{1}{2}x_i$. Solving for y gives: $y < \frac{1}{2}$.

Let s' be the profile where i plays $x_i + y$. Then $W(s') = (\frac{1}{2} + y)(\frac{1}{2} - y) = \frac{1}{4} - y^2$, so $W(s) - W(s') = y^2$.

$$u_i(s') - u_i(s) = \frac{1}{2}(x_i + y) - y(x_i + y) - \frac{1}{4} = y(\frac{1}{2} - x_i - y).$$

We can now calculate just how much welfare we have to distribute for a given alternative to social optimum s to lose its appeal for i. A tempting alternative s' for i in s loses its appeal for i in s when the following holds:

$$u_i^\gamma(s') \leq u_i^\gamma(s).$$

Write out the definition of u_i^γ:

$$(1-\gamma)u_i(s') + \gamma\frac{W(s')}{n} \le (1-\gamma)u_i(s) + \gamma\frac{W(s)}{n}.$$

Solve for γ:

$$\frac{n(u_i(s') - u_i(s))}{n(u_i(s') - u_i(s)) + W(s) - W(s')} \le \gamma.$$

In our particular case, this gives:

$$\frac{ny(\frac{1}{2} - x_i - y)}{ny(\frac{1}{2} - x_i - y) + y^2} = \frac{nx_i + ny - n}{nx_i + ny - n - y^2}.$$

We have that $0 \le x_i \le \frac{1}{2}$, $0 \le y < \frac{1}{2}$, Plugging these values in, we get:

$$\sup_{0 \le x_i \le \frac{1}{2}, 0 \le y < \frac{1}{2}} \frac{nx_i + ny - n}{nx_i + ny - n - y^2} = 1.$$

Since the social optimum s was arbitrary, it follows that the cost of civilization for the tragedy of the commons game is 1. (This corresponds to selfishness level ∞.)

Now for the key question: what does this all mean for policy making in ToC situations? One can ask what a responsible individual should do in a ToC situation to optimize social welfare. Let $D = \sum_{i \in N} x_i$, i.e., D is the total demand on the resource. Suppose j is a new player who wants to act responsibly. What should j do? If $D < \frac{1}{2}$, j should demand

$$x_j = \frac{1}{2} - D.$$

This will make the new demand equal to $\frac{1}{2}$, and the welfare equal to $D - D^2 = \frac{1}{4}$, which is the social optimum.

If $D = \frac{1}{2}$, any positive demand of j would harm the social welfare, so in this case j should put $x_j = 0$. An alternative would be to persuade the n other players to each drop their individual demands from $\frac{1}{2n}$ (on average) to $\frac{1}{2n+2}$. If this plea succeeds, j can also demand $\frac{1}{2n+2}$, and the new total demand becomes $\frac{n+1}{2n+2} = \frac{1}{2}$, so that again the social optimum of $\frac{1}{4}$ is reached.

If $D > \frac{1}{2}$, any positive demand of j would harm the social welfare, so again j should put $x_j = 0$. In this case, the prospect of persuading the other players to lower their demands may be brighter, provided the players agree that they all have equal rights. Once this is settled, it is clear what the individual demands should be for optimum welfare. The optimum individual demand is $\frac{1}{2n}$ if there are n players, and $\frac{1}{2n+2}$ if there are $n + 1$ players. Allowing in one extra player would cost each player $\frac{1}{4n} - \frac{1}{4n+4}$.

To change to the punishment perspective, suppose D is the demand in the old situation s. A new player comes in and demands x. Call the new situation

s'. Let D be the total demand in s. Then $W(s) = D - D^2$. If $D + x > 1$ then $W(s') = 0$. So in this case, the social damage equals the original welfare, and the appropriate punishment is $-W(s)$.

In the case where $x + D \leq 1$, the excess demand is anything in excess of $\frac{1}{2}$, so the appropriate punishment is the welfare deterioration caused by the excess demand y. Thus, the appropriate punishment is given by:

$$\frac{1}{4} - W(s') = \frac{1}{4} - (\frac{1}{2} + y)(\frac{1}{2} - y) = y^2.$$

If this is combined with the probability p of catching offenders, the penalty for excess demand y should be $\frac{y^2}{p}$.

Take an example case. Two players each demand $\frac{1}{5}$, so each gets $\frac{1}{5}(1 - \frac{2}{5}) = \frac{3}{25}$. We have $D = \frac{2}{5}$, and $W = D - D^2 = \frac{6}{25}$. A third player comes along and demands $\frac{1}{3}$. Then the new demand D' becomes $\frac{11}{15}$, which results in new welfare $W' = D' - D'^2 = \frac{44}{225}$. The welfare in the social optimum is $\frac{1}{4}$. The excess demand is $(\frac{2}{5} + \frac{1}{3}) - \frac{1}{2} = \frac{7}{30}$. The deterioration in welfare is $\frac{1}{4} - W' = \frac{1}{4} - \frac{44}{225} = \frac{49}{900}$. This is exactly equal to the square of the excess demand $\frac{7}{30}$.

A modern and pressing case of the tragedy of the commons is presented in the Fourth IPCC Assessment report:

> The climate system tends to be overused (excessive GHG concentrations) because of its natural availability as a resource whose access is open to all free of charge. In contrast, climate protection tends to be underprovided. In general, the benefits of avoided climate change are spatially indivisible, freely available to all (non-excludability), irrespective of whether one is contributing to the regime costs or not. As regime benefits by one individual (nation) do not diminish their availability to others (non-rivalry), it is difficult to enforce binding commitments on the use of the climate system [27, 28]. This may result in "free riding", a situation in which mitigation costs are borne by some individuals (nations) while others (the "free riders") succeed in evading them but still enjoy the benefits of the mitigation commitments of the former. [45, page 102]

The problem of collective rationality has been a key issue in practical philosophy for more than two millennia. Aristotle discusses it at length, in the *Politics*:

> For that which is common to the greatest number has the least care bestowed upon it. Every one thinks chiefly of his own, hardly at all of the common interest; and only when he is himself concerned as an individual. For besides other considerations, everybody is more inclined to neglect the duty which he expects another to fulfill; as in families many attendants are often less useful than a few. [3, paragraph 403, Book II]

What is important about the game-theoretical analysis is the insight that there are situations where lots of individual actions of enlightened self-interest may endanger the common good. There is not always an invisible hand to ensure a happy outcome.

The phenomenon that Aristotle alludes to is called the 'bystander effect' in Darley and Letane [16]: solitary people usually intervene in case of an emergency, whereas a large group of bystanders may fail to intervene — everyone thinks that someone else is bound to have called the emergency hotline already (pluralistic ignorance), or that someone else is bound to be more qualified to give medical help (diffused responsibility). See Osborne [39] for an account of this social phenomenon in terms of game theory, Pacuit, Parikh and Cogan [41] for a logical analysis, and Manning, Levine and Collins [36] for historical nuance about the often quoted and much discussed case of Kitty Genovese (who, according to the story, was stabbed to death in 1964 while 38 neighbours watched from their windows but did nothing).

Garrett Hardin, in his famous essay, also discusses how tragedy of the commons situations can be resolved. He makes a plea for the collective (or perhaps: enlightened individuals within the collective) to impose "mutual constraints, mutually agreed upon," and he quotes Sigmund Freud's *Civilisation and its Discontents* [20] to put the unavoidable tension between civilisation and the desires or inclinations of individuals in perspective.

On the other hand, Ostrom [40] warns against the temptation to get carried away by the game-theoretical analysis of ToC situations, and shows by careful study of real-world cases of institutions (fisheries, irrigation water allocation schemes) how — given appropriate circumstances — effective collective action can be organized for governing common pool resources without resorting to a central authority. See Baden and Noonan [5] for further discussion.

7   Renunciation Games

Let me depart now from the standard game theory textbook fare, and introduce three new games where an individual is pitted against a collective. The setup of the games is such that the social optimum of the game can only be reached at the expense of *one single* individual. I call such games renunciation games. When will an individual sacrifice his or her own interest to save society? It turns out that the nature of the renunciation game changes crucially depending on the temptation offered to the renouncer.

Pure Renunciation Game. The *pure renunciation game* has n players, who each choose a strategy in $[0, 1]$, which represents their demand. If at least one player renounces (demands 0), then all other players get as payoff what they demand. Otherwise, nobody gets anything. The payoff function for i is given by:

$$u_i(s) = \begin{cases} s_i & \text{if } \exists j \neq i : s_j = 0 \\ 0 & \text{otherwise.} \end{cases}$$

This game has n social optima $(0, 1, \ldots, 1), (1, 0, 1, \ldots, 1), \ldots, (1, \ldots, 1, 0)$, where the social welfare W equals $n - 1$. The social optima are also Nash equilibria.

No need for welfare redistribution, no need for punishment. The situation changes if there is a temptation for the renouncer in the game.

Renunciation Game with Mild Temptation. This *renunciation game* has n players, who each choose a strategy in $[0, 1]$, which represents their demand. If at least one player renounces (demands 0), then all other players get as payoff what they demand. Otherwise, if there is one player i who demands less than any other player, i gets what she demands, and the others get nothing. In all other cases nobody gets anything. The payoff function for i is given by:

$$u_i(s) = \begin{cases} s_i & \text{if } \exists j \neq i : s_j = 0 \\ & \text{or } \forall j \neq i : 0 < s_i < s_j \\ 0 & \text{otherwise.} \end{cases}$$

This game has n social optima. There are no Nash equilibria. The cost of civilization for the Renunciation Game is $\gamma = \frac{1}{2n-2}$. Indeed, this game has n social optima $(0, 1, \ldots, 1)$, $(1, 0, 1, \ldots, 1)$, $\ldots$, $(1, \ldots, 1, 0)$, where the social welfare W equals $n - 1$. In particular, the social optima are not Nash equilibria. For in a social optimum, the player who renounces (and receives nothing) can get any q with $0 < q < 1$ by playing q. That's the temptation.

Now focus on player 1 and compute the least γ for which the social optimum $(0, 1, \ldots, 1)$ turns into a Nash equilibrium in $G[\gamma]$. The payoff function for player 1 in $G[\gamma]$ satisfies:

$$u_1^\gamma(0, 1, \ldots, 1) = \gamma \frac{n-1}{n}.$$

For the social optimum to be Nash, this value has to majorize

$$u_1^\gamma(q, 1, \ldots, 1) = (1 - \gamma)q + \frac{\gamma}{n}q.$$

Since q can be arbitrarily close to 1, we get $u_1^\gamma(q, 1, \ldots, 1) < (1-\gamma) + \frac{\gamma}{n}$, Therefore $(0, 1, \ldots, 1)$ is a social optimum in $G[\gamma]$ iff $\gamma \frac{n-1}{n} \geq (1 - \gamma) + \frac{\gamma}{n}$. Solving this for γ gives $\gamma \geq \frac{1}{2n-2}$.

The situation changes drastically if there is heavy temptation.

Renunciation Game with Heavy Temptation. This renunciation game has n players, who each choose a strategy q in $[0, 1]$, which represents their demand. If at least one player renounces (demands 0), then all other players get as payoff what they demand. Otherwise, if there is one player i who demands less than any other player, i gets $n - 1$ times what she demands, and the others get nothing. In all other cases nobody gets anything. The payoff function for i is given by:

$$u_i(s) = \begin{cases} s_i & \text{if } \exists j \neq i : s_j = 0 \\ (n - 1)s_i & \text{if } \forall j \neq i : 0 < s_i < s_j \\ 0 & \text{otherwise.} \end{cases}$$

The civilization cost for Renunciation With Heavy Temptation is 1. Social optima are the same as before. We have to compute the least γ that turns social optimum $(0, 1, \ldots, 1)$ into a Nash equilibrium in $G[\gamma]$. The constraint on the payoff function for player 1 is:

$$u_1^\gamma(q, 1, \ldots, 1) = (1 - \gamma)(n - 1)q + \frac{\gamma}{n}(n - 1)q.$$

Since q can be arbitrarily close to 1, this gives

$$u_1^\gamma(q, 1, \ldots, 1) < (1 - \gamma)(n - 1) + \frac{\gamma}{n}(n - 1).$$

This puts the following constraint on γ:

$$\gamma\frac{n - 1}{n} \geq (1 - \gamma)(n - 1) + \frac{\gamma}{n}(n - 1).$$

Solving for γ gives $n\gamma \geq n$, and it follows that $\gamma = 1$.

These games are offered here as examples of new metaphors for social interaction, showing that the store-room of game-theoretic metaphors is far from exhausted. I hope to analyse renunciation games in future work.

8   Experiments with Knowledge and Trust

In many social protocols (scenarios for social interaction) the knowledge that the participants have about each other and about the protocol itself play a crucial role.

The prisoner's dilemma scenario, e.g., assumes that there is common knowledge among the players about the utilities. Also, it is assumed that there is common knowledge that the players cannot find out what the other player is going to do. If we change the scenario, by letting the players move one by one, or by communicating the move of the first player to the second player, this changes the nature of the game completely.

Suppose two players meet up with a host, who hands over a bill of ten euros to each of them, and then explains that they will each be asked whether they are willing to donate some or all of the money to the other player. The host adds the information that donated amounts of money will be doubled.

What will happen now depends on the set-up. If each player communicates in private to the host, we are back with the prisoner's dilemma situation. If the players are allowed to coordinate their strategies, and if they act under mutual trust, they will each donate all of their money to the other player, so that they each end up with 20 euros. If the first player is asked in public what she will do, it depends on what she believes the other player will do if it is his turn, and so on.

Experiments based on this kind of scenario have been staged by game theorists, to explain the emergence of trust in social situations. A relevant game is the so-called ultimatum game, first used in Güth, Schmittberger and Schwarze [24].

Player I is shown a substantial amount of money, say 100 euros. He is asked to propose a split of the money between himself and player II. If player II accepts the deal, they both keep their shares, otherwise they both receive nothing. If this game is played once, a split $(99, 1)$ should be acceptable for II. After all, receiving 1 euro is better than receiving nothing. But this is not what we observe when this game is played. What we see is that II rejects the deal, often with great indignation [11].

Evidence from experiments with playing the ultimatum game and repeated prisoner's dilemma games suggests that people are willing to punish those who misbehave, even if this involves personal cost.

Another game that was used in actual experiments, the investment game, suggests that people are also willing to reward appropriate behaviour, even if there is no personal benefit in giving the reward.

The investment game is played between a group of people in a room A and another group of people in a room B, and can be summarized as follows. Each person in room A and each person in room B has been given 10 euros as show up money. The people in room A will have the opportunity to send some or all of their money to an anonymous receiver in group B. The amount of money sent will be tripled, and this is common knowledge. E.g., an envelope sent with 9 euros will contain 27 euros when it reaches its recipient in room B. The recipient in group B, who knows that someone in group A parted with one third of the amount of money she just received, will then decide how much of the money to keep and how much to send back to the giver in room A. Consult Berg, Dickhaut and McCabe [9] for the results of the experiment.

Reputation systems such as those used in Ebay are examples of engineered social software. The design aim of these public ratings of past behaviour is to make sure that trust can emerge between players that exchange goods or services. Reputation can be computed: Kleinberg [29] gives a now-famous algorithm which ranks pages on the internet for authoritativeness in answering informative questions. One of the ways to strategically misuse reputation systems is by creating so-called "sybils": fake identities which falsely raise the reputation of an item by means of fake links. So a design aim can be to create reputation mechanisms that are *sybil proof*, see Cheng [13]. For further general information on reputation systems, consult Resnick [44].

These systems can also be studied empirically: how does the designed reputation system influence social behaviour? The same holds for the renunciation game scenarios from the previous section. Empirical studies using these scenarios might yield some revealing answers to the question "What do people actually do when being asked to renounce for the benefit of society?"

9   Conclusion

Several chapters in this book present relevant logics for strategic reasoning. Van Benthem [8] makes a plea for applying the general perspective of action logic to reasoning about strategies in games. In Van Eijck [17] it is demonstrated how propositional dynamic logic or PDL [31, 43] can be turned into a logic for reasoning about finite strategic games. Such logics can be used to study, e.g., voting rules or auction protocols from a logical point of view. In voting, think of casting an individual vote as a strategy. Now fix a voting rule and determine a payoff function, and you have an n player voting game. Next, represent and analyze this in PDL, or in any of the logic formalisms taken from this book.

Voting is a form of collective decision making. A key distinction in decision making is between cases where there is a correct outcome, and the challenge for the collective is to find that outcome, and cases where the notion of correctness does not apply, and the challenge for the collective is to arrive at a choice that everyone can live with.

A famous result from the early days of voting theory is Condorcet's jury theorem [15]. The case of a jury that has to reach a collective decision 'guilty or not', say in a murder trial, has a correct answer. For either the accused has committed the murder, or he has not. The trouble is that no member of the jury knows for sure what the answer is. Condorcet's jury theorem states the following:

> Suppose each voter has an independent probability p of arriving at the correct answer. If p is greater than $\frac{1}{2}$ then adding more voters increases the probability of a correct majority decision. If p is smaller than $\frac{1}{2}$ then it is the other way around, and an optimal jury consists of a single voter.

To see why this is true, assume there are n voters. For simplicity, we assume n is odd. Assume that m voters have made the correct decision. Consider what happens when we add two new voters. Then the majority vote outcome changes in only two cases.

1. m was one vote short to get a majority of the n votes, and both new voters voted correctly. In this case the vote outcome changes from incorrect to correct.
2. m was just equal to a majority of the n votes, but both new voters voted incorrectly. In this case the vote outcome changes from correct to incorrect.

In both of these cases we can assume that it is the last of the n voters who casts the deciding vote. In the first case, voter n voted correctly, in the second case voter n voted incorrectly. But we know that voter n has probability p of arriving at a correct decision, so we know that in case there is just a difference of a single vote between the correct and the incorrect decision among n voters, the probability of the n voters arriving at a correct decision is p. Now add the two new voters. The probability of case (1), from incorrect to correct, is $(1 - p)p^2$, and the probability of case (2), from correct to incorrect, is $p(1 - p)^2$. Observe that $(1 - p)p^2 > p(1 - p)^2$ iff $p > \frac{1}{2}$. The case where there is an even number of voters is similar, but in this case we have to assume that ties are broken by a fair coin flip, with probability equal to $\frac{1}{2}$ of arriving at the correct decision.

Condorcet's jury theorem is taken by some as an argument for democracy; whether the argument cuts wood depends of course on whether one believes in the notion of 'correct societal decisions'. See List and Goodin [35] for further discussion.

Let me finish, light-heartedly, with another famous argument for democracy, by Sir Francis Galton, in an amusing short paper 'Vox Populi' in *Nature*. Galton's narrative is one of the key story lines in Surowiecki [50]. Galton [21] starts as follows:

> In these democratic days, any investigation into the trustworthiness and peculiarities of popular judgments is of interest. The material about to be discussed refers to a small matter, but is much to the point.
>
> A weight-judging competition was carried on at the annual show of the West of England Fat Stock and Poultry Exhibition recently held at Plymouth (England). A fat ox having been selected, competitors bought stamped and numbered cards, for 6d. each, on which to inscribe their respective names, addresses, and estimates of what the ox would weigh after it had been slaughtered and "dressed." Those who guessed most successfully received prizes. About 800 tickets were issued, which were kindly lent me for examination after they had fulfilled their immediate purpose.

Galton then goes on to tell what he found. As it turned out, 13 tickets were defective or illegible, but the median of the 787 remaining ones contained the remarkably accurate guess of 1207 pounds, which was only 9 pounds above the actual weight of the slaughtered ox: 1198 pounds. The majority plus one rule gave the approximately correct answer.

What does this have to do with strategies and strategic reasoning, the reader might ask. The strategic reasoning is lifted to the meta-level now: Are we in a decision-making situation that is like weight-judging, or are we not? Is this a social situation where many know more than one, or isn't it? Does the optimal jury for this consist of a single person, or does it not? Which brings us to the key strategic question we all face when about to make the decisions in life that really matter: "Should I take this decision on my own, or is it better to consult others before making my move?"

Acknowledgement. Johan van Benthem, Robin Clark and Rainer Kessler sent their written comments on an early draft, in which Floor Sietsma was also involved. Later, I received helpful comments from Barteld Kooi.

The final version has benefitted from extensive reports by two anonymous reviewers. Since these reports were excellent, I have tried to implement almost all referee suggestions. Inspiring conversations with Mamoru Kaneko have led to further improvements.

Thanks are also due to book editors Rineke Verbrugge and Sujata Ghosh for detailed comments on the final version and for help with proof-reading, and to the other participants in the Lorentz workshop on Modeling Strategic Reasoning for inspiring feedback. Finally, I acknowledge communication with Krzysztof Apt and Guido Schaefer.

References

1. Apt, K.R., Schäfer, G.: Selfishness level of strategic games. In: Serna, M. (ed.) SAGT 2012. LNCS, vol. 7615, pp. 13–24. Springer, Heidelberg (2012)

2. Ariely, D., Gneezy, U., Loewenstein, G., Mazar, N.: Large stakes and big mistakes. Rev. Econ. Stud. **76**, 451–469 (2009)
3. Aristotle.: The Politics of Aristotle: Translated into English with Introduction, Marginal Analysis, Essays, Notes and Indices, vol. 1. Clarendon Press, Oxford (330 BC). Translated and annotated by B. Jowett (1885)
4. Aumann, R.J.: Agreeing to disagree. Ann. Stat. **4**, 1236–1239 (1976)
5. Baden, J.A., Noonan, D.S. (eds.): Managing the Commons, 2nd edn. Indiana University Press, Bloomington (1998)
6. Beccaria, C.: On Crimes and Punishment (Dei delitti e delle pene). Marco Coltellini, Livorno (1764)
7. Becker, G.S.: Nobel lecture: The economic way of looking at behavior. J. Polit. Econ. **101**(3), 385–409 (1993)
8. van Benthem, J.: In praise of strategies. In: van Eijck, J., Verbrugge, R. (eds.) Games, Actions and Social Software 2010. LNCS, vol. 7010, pp. 96–116. Springer, Heidelberg (2012)
9. Berg, J., Dickhaut, J., McCabe, K.: Trust, reciprocity, and social history. Games Econ. Behav. **10**(1), 122–142 (1995)
10. Brams, S.: Mathematics and Democracy: Designing Better Voting and Fair Division Procedures. Princeton University Press, Princeton (2008)
11. Camerer, C.F.: Behavioral Game Theory: Experiments in Strategic Interaction. Princeton University Press, Princeton (2003)
12. Chen, P.A., Kempe, D.: Altruism, selfishness, and spite in traffic routing. In: Proceedings 10th ACM Conference on Electronic Commerce, pp. 140–149 (2008)
13. Cheng, A., Friedman, E.: Sybilproof reputation mechanisms. In: Proceedings of the 2005 ACM SIGCOMM Workshop on Economics of Peer-to-Peer Systems, P2PECON 2005, pp. 128–132. ACM, New York (2005)
14. Chwe, M.S.Y.: Rational Ritual. Princeton University Press, Princeton and Oxford (2001)
15. Condorcet, M.: Essai sur l'Application de l'Analyse à la Probabilité des Décisions Rendues à la Pluralité des Voix. Imprimerie Royale, Paris (1785)
16. Darley, J.M., Letane, B.: Bystander intervention in emergencies: diffusion of responsibility. J. Pers. Soc. Psychol. **8**, 377–383 (1968)
17. van Eijck, J.: PDL as a multi-agent strategy logic. In: Schipper, B.C. (ed.) TARK 2013 - Theoretical Aspects of Reasoning About Knowledge, Proceedings of the 14th Conference - Chennai, India, pp. 206–215 (2013)
18. van Eijck, J., Verbrugge, R. (eds.): Discourses on Social Software. Texts in Logic and Games, vol. 5. Amsterdam University Press, Amsterdam (2009)
19. Fehr, E., Gächter, S.: Altruistic punishment in humans. Nature **415**, 137–140 (2002)
20. Freud, S.: Das Unbehagen in der Kultur (Civilization and Its Discontents). Internationaler Psychoanalytischer Verlag, Vienna (1930)
21. Galton, F.: Vox populi. Nature **75**, 450–451 (1907)
22. Gilboa, I.: Rational Choice. MIT Press, Cambridge (2010)
23. Gordon, H.S.: The economic theory of a common-property resource: the fishery. J. Polit. Econ. **62**, 124–142 (1954)
24. Güth, W., Schmittberger, R., Schwarze, B.: An experimental analysis of ultimatum bargaining. J. Econ. Behav. Organ. **3**(4), 367–388 (1982)
25. Hardin, G.: The tragedy of the commons. Science **162**, 1243–48 (1968)
26. Hurwicz, L., Reiter, S.: Designing Economic Mechanisms. Cambridge University Press, Cambridge (2006)

27. Kaul, I., Conceicao, P., Le Gouven, K., Mendoz, R.U.: Providing Global Public Goods. Oxford University Press, New York (2003)
28. Kaul, I., Grunberg, I., Stern, M.A.: Global Public Goods. Oxford University Press, New York (1999)
29. Kleinberg, J.M.: Authoritative sources in a hyperlinked environment. J. ACM **46**(5), 604–632 (1999)
30. Körner, T.W.: Naive Decision Making: Mathematics Applied to the Social World. Cambridge University Press, New York (2008)
31. Kozen, D., Parikh, R.: An elementary proof of the completeness of PDL. Theor. Comput. Sci. **14**, 113–118 (1981)
32. Krishna, V.: Auction Theory. Elsevier Science, USA (2009)
33. Kuhn, H.W., Nasar, S. (eds.): The Essential John Nash. Princeton University Press, Princeton (2002)
34. Lewis, D.K.: Convention: A Philosophical Study. Harvard University Press, Cambridge (1969)
35. List, C., Goodin, R.E.: Epistemic democracy: generalizing the Condorcet jury theorem. J. Polit. Philos. **9**(3), 277–306 (2001)
36. Manning, R., Levine, M., Collins, A.: The Kitty Genovese murder and the social psychology of helping: the parable of the 38 witnesses. Am. Psychol. **62**, 555–562 (2007)
37. Tzu, S.: The Art of War, translated and with an introduction by Samuel B. Griffith. Oxford University Press, 450 BC. Translation from 1963
38. Milgrom, P.: Putting Auction Theory to Work (Churchill Lectures in Economics). Cambridge University Press, Cambridge (2004)
39. Osborne, M.J.: An Introduction to Game Theory. Oxford University Press, New York (2004)
40. Ostrom, E.: Governing the Commons: The Evolution of Institutions for Collective Action. Cambridge University Press, Political Economy of Institutions and Decisions (1990)
41. Pacuit, E., Parikh, R., Cogan, E.: The logic of knowledge based obligation. Synthese **31**, 311–341 (2006)
42. Parikh, R.: Social software. Synthese **132**, 187–211 (2002)
43. Pratt, V.: Semantical considerations on Floyd-Hoare logic. In: Proceedings of 17th IEEE Symposium on Foundations of Computer Science, pp. 109–121 (1976)
44. Resnick, P., Kuwabara, K., Zeckhauser, R., Friedman, E.: Reputation systems. Commun. ACM **43**(12), 45–48 (2000)
45. Rogner, H.-H., Zhou, R., Bradley, R., Crabbé, P., Edenhofer, O., Hare, B., Kuijpers, L., Yamaguchi, M.: Introduction. In: Metz, B., et al. (eds.) Climate Change 2007: Mitigation. Contribution of Working Group III to the Fourth Assessment Report of the Intergovernmental Panel on Climate Change. Cambridge University Press, Cambridge (2007)
46. Rousseau, J.J.: Discours sur l'Origine et les Fondements de l'Inégalité Parmi les Hommes. Marc Michel Rey, Amsterdam (1755)
47. Shoham, Y., Leyton-Brown, K.: Multiagent Systems: Algorithmic, Game-Theoretic, and Logical Foundations. Cambridge University Press, New York (2008)
48. Sigmund, K.: The Calculus of Selfishness. Princeton Series in Theoretical and Computational Biology. Princeton University Press, Princeton (2010)
49. Smith, A.: An Inquiry into the Nature and Causes of the Wealth of Nations. Liberty Fund, Indianapolis (1776)

50. Surowiecki, J.: The Wisdom of Crowds: Why the Many Are Smarter Than the Few and How Collective Wisdom Shapes Business, Economies, Societies and Nation. Random House, New York (2004)
51. Taylor, A.D.: Social Choice and the Mathematics of Manipulation. Cambridge University Press, Cambridge (2005)
52. Tenner, E.: Why Things Bite Back - Technology and the Revenge Effect. Fourth Estate, London (1996)
53. Thaler, R.H., Sunstein, C.R.: Nudge: Improving Decisions About Health, Wealth, and Happiness. A Caravan book. Yale University Press, New Haven (2008)
54. Vazirani, V.V., Nisan, N., Roughgarden, T., Tardos, E.: Algorithmic Game Theory. Cambridge University Press, New York (2007)
55. Vickrey, W.: Counterspeculation, auctions, and competitive sealed tenders. J. Finance 16(1), 8–37 (1961)
56. von Clausewitz, M. (ed.): Vom Kriege, Hinterlassenes Werk des Generals Carl von Clausewitz. Ferdinand Dümmler, Berlin (1832–1834)

Future Perspective

Logic of Strategies: What and How?

Johan van Benthem[1,2]([⊠])

[1] Institute for Logic, Language and Computation (ILLC),
University of Amsterdam, Amsterdam, The Netherlands
[2] Department of Philosophy, Stanford University, Stanford, USA
johan.vanbenthem@uva.nl

Abstract. This piece is not a paper reporting on original research, but rather a slightly expanded write-up of some notes for a concluding discussion at the 2012 Workshop on 'Modeling Strategic Reasoning' at the Lorentz Center in Leiden, an interdisciplinary meeting on the importance of strategies in many fields, from game theory to linguistics, computer science, and cognitive science, that was the incubator for the present volume on the logic-based analysis of strategies and how we reason with, and about them. My modest purpose here is to highlight a few general, somewhat unresolved, decision points about this proposed program that seemed to resonate with the audience at the Workshop, but that may also present food for thought to a more general reader of this book. The emphasis in the presentation that follows is on logic, a view of strategies that figures prominently in my own work on logic and games, cf. [9]. Still, there are certainly other equally viable and illuminating formal viewpoints on the study of strategies, coming, for instance, from automata theory or dynamical systems, cf. [16,31].

Keywords: Strategy · Dynamic logic · Knowledge · Preference · Revision

1 What to Study in a Logic of Strategies?

If we take strategies seriously, what sort of logical analysis will make most sense? The workshop title mentioned in the Abstract looks harmless as titles go, but it hides some serious questions of what it is all about. Should the subject of the logical analysis be strategies themselves, or the way we reason about strategies (surely, not the same thing), or even just modeling reasoning about strategies, as done by real agents in games, thereby placing two layers of intellectual distance: 'reasoning' and 'modeling', on top of the original phenomenon itself?

In fact, several perspectives need to come together in logical analysis: the structure of strategies themselves and the agents using them, in what is sometimes called the internal 'first-person mode' of participants in a game or social activity, but also reasoning about strategies as an important external 'third-person' perspective on that same activity.[1] Though related, these levels are separate. The difference between the first- and third-person stance shows up, for

---

[1] I will leave the further 'modeling' layer in the title out of consideration altogether.

© Springer-Verlag Berlin Heidelberg 2015
J. van Benthem et al. (Eds.): Models of Strategic Reasoning, LNCS 8972, pp. 321–332, 2015.
DOI: 10.1007/978-3-662-48540-8_10

instance, in current discussions of computational complexity of logics for agency. One often sees claims that complexity results about logics of multi-agent activities tell us something about the complexity of these activities, cf. [14]. But such claims may involve a confusion of the above levels. For instance, solving extensive games with perfect recall may involve simple moves and strategies, even though the epistemic-temporal logic of agents with perfect recall is extremely complex, cf. [32]. More generally, the theory of a simple activity may well be difficult.[2]

Even when we decide to give strategies themselves their due, another issue arises. The core meaning of the very term 'strategy' is contentious, reflecting a broader issue of where to locate the essence of this notion. Some people think of what is strategic in behavior as typically involving some *structured plan* for the longer term, in line with the crucial role of programs in computer science, or plans in AI [3] and philosophy [20]. But others, for instance, cognitive scientists and social scientists [21,30] see the heart of strategic behavior in interest- or preference-driven action, often with ulterior goals beyond what is immediately observable.[3] In the latter case, standard computational logics, no matter how sophisticated (cf. the survey of modern fixed-point logics in [55]) may not suffice as a paradigm for studying strategies, as agents' preferences between runs of the system now become of the essence, something that has not been integrated systematically into computation (but see [51,53] for some attempts).

My own advocacy of the explicit logical study of strategies has mainly focused on the former structured plan aspect [7], and I will continue do so in this note – but the above two dimensions of strategic behavior are evidently not in conflict. They just need to be distinguished, and then brought into contact.

2   Locating Key Notions and Core Language

Logicians like to believe, and their methodology also tends to require, that their analysis starts with some stable practice of language use and reasoning patterns concerning the phenomenon at issue. But do strategies form such a natural practice that can bear the weight of the logical machinery that one would want to apply? At least, there is an issue of what would be natural boundaries for the theme. In serious logical analysis, one wants to find core families of notions that naturally belong together. For instance, to take another notion important to the agency in strategies, in epistemology, it makes little sense to study knowledge by itself without at the same time studying belief, and perhaps also the notion of evidence [28,34]. These notions form a natural trinity of what seem the basic epistemic notions tied up with the information that agents have about the world. Likewise, we may ask whether strategies should be an exclusive focus for the study envisioned here, or whether logical analysis only gets a proper perspective by taking on board further notions from the start.

---

[2] For this level distinction in dynamic-epistemic logics of agency, and what is 'easy' and 'hard' for acting agents versus for theorists, see also the discussion in [6].

[3] Sometimes this is seen as high rationality, but sometimes also as self-serving and not really nice, mirroring the pejorative meaning of 'strategizing' in common parlance.

It may be significant here that the linguistic terminology used around the notion of strategy shows a great variety, both in ordinary language and in academic research. People talk of strategies, tactics, plans, protocols, methods, agent types, and the like, which often amount to similar things. For instance, is a 'Liar' a type of person, a program producing a certain behavior, a method for dealing with other people, or a strategy? One can find instances of all these views in the literature, and in professional talk. Clearly, these terms are not all formally well-defined, though some cues for their use might be culled from natural language. In daily discourse, tactics means strategy writ small (a 'strategette'), while strategy is tactics writ large – and one feels that they are similar notions of modus operandi, but operating at different levels of describing activities. It might be worth aiming for further conceptual clarification here, and reserve terms for various uses in a natural family of descriptions for interactive behavior.[4]

In my own work on logic and games, [9], I have sometimes found a need for several related notions that all have their own place – though I do not claim they are standard. A *protocol* is a persistent style of behavior over a longer period of time, say, a linguistic practice such as cooperative answering. Such a practice is like an operating system, which then admits of running different *strategies* inside its compass for particular short-term purposes, such as conveying a message, or convincing your audience of a claim in argumentation. Moreover, these strategies are used by *agents*, viewed as embodied devices that can run different strategies, conforming to protocols that set up the space of possible behavior. But I admit that I often switch terms, much like other colleagues in my trade.[5]

Our common vocabulary around the notion of a strategy seems less stable than for, say, knowledge or belief. While I do not expect that plunging into linguistic semantics or philosophy is a magic key resolving these issues, a systematic look at natural language might be worth-while.[6] For now, however, we may just have to make do with fixing terms locally when communicating with colleagues. But I do think the variety of interactive notions mentioned above, operative at different levels of agency, is worth studying together under any name.

3 Starting from Best Practices

In addition to finding core notions as discussed above, what is the further raw material for a logical analysis of strategies? In addition to top-down worrying about conceptual structure and clean terminology, there is the more empirical

---

[4] In fact, this is exactly what happens when certain sub-communities of game theory, computer science, or AI do attach fixed meanings to some of these terms. Cf. [52].

[5] I freely use even further terms, such as 'plans' as being more open-ended than strategies, and also, as something one is aware of and commits to, more than strategies.

[6] Compare the not wholly unrelated case of epistemology and informational action, where natural language has a rich and telling repertoire of common expressions such as 'know', 'suspect', 'learn', 'note', 'discover', 'tell' that we use with a certain amount of stability and even sophistication when engaging in actions of our own, or reporting and reflecting on actions by others. For more on this theme, cf. [10].

approach of looking at best practice. Consider the somewhat related question of 'What is an algorithm?'. Perhaps the best way of approaching this issue is by giving a set of concrete examples, exemplars that we see as characteristic of the notion, and that help nurture our intuitions. Think of famous sorting algorithms, geometrical constructions, or algebraic procedures. Can we do something similar for our topic of strategies? Is there a core range of evergreens that attract our attention, and could serve as benchmarks for logical theorizing?

On various occasions, I have tried to collect concrete examples that colleagues around me find particularly motivating. But I never found a large set, and the items that recur are often abstract and logical in nature – perhaps due to a filter inherent to logicians' channels of thought. Elegant ubiquitous items giving strong effects for small effort are surprisingly simple *copying strategies*: Copy-Cat in linear game semantics [1], Tit-for-Tat in evolutionary games [5], or 'strategy stealing' in classical game theory [17,42]. These strategies are not quite the same, if you think them through, but what they have in common is a simple way of copying useful moves from somewhere else. At the above-mentioned Lorentz workshop, I became aware of new strategies of this kind. For instance, the most sophisticated examples of signaling strategies in 'IF logic' [35,50] are not concrete Skolem functions, the usual paradigm in that field, but generic identifying strategies like 'take the same object', 'take some other object'.

Perhaps surprisingly, much can be built from a modest copying repertoire for agents once we allow further game constructions. Game semantics for linear logic builds all its strategies in this way (cf. [2]), suggesting that copying plus compositionality might be a major part of understanding the working of complex strategies. Moreover, automata-based strategies in computational logic achieve significant mathematical proofs and results using 'shadow matches' and copying behavior from virtual games into one's actual play (cf. [31,55]).

And in the end, this may not just be logic-internal. Maybe the best practical game paradigm around is *Judo*, using one's opponent's moves to win it all.

4 Core Logic of Strategies

But here is yet another take on our program of studying strategies. In addition to designing formal languages, logicians have their own approach to zooming in on a notion, no matter what stable terminology or exemplars trail along with it. We think a notion is stable if there are some basic reasoning principles at its core, shedding light on a broad range of uses. I myself indeed like to believe that there is a core calculus of reasoning about strategic patterns in behavior, from first-person deliberation to third-person assessment of action in games.

One obvious candidate for such a calculus of reasoning about strategies has in fact long existed: namely, *propositional dynamic logic* PDL of programs with sequential operations [33]. The compositional structure of strategies often has a typical program-like IF ... THEN ... ELSE and WHILE ... DO ... character, and also, PDL's way of generalizing from strategies as unique-valued functions defined on turns of players to possibly many-valued binary *relations* makes a lot of sense when we generalize from strategies as unique-valued functions to plans offering choices.[7] What PDL delivers is a general way of reasoning about generic strategies (cf. [7,9,27,47,48] on various versions of this), though it can also handle specific functions or relations in single games. But is it enough?

One way of testing this might be quasi-empirical, cataloguing relevant basic results in game theory, computer science, and logic, toward a repertoire of ubiquitous proofs concerning strategies. What is a stable set of paradigmatic arguments that can be mined for recurring logical patterns, and serve as a benchmark for logics of strategies? My favorite sources are standard proofs of major results such as the Gale-Stewart theorem or the Von Neumann-Morgenstern-Nash fixed-point theorem (cf. [42]) – and one could add recent proofs from computer science, e.g., for the Positional Determinacy Theorem and related results in work on strategies in automata theory [29], or in the modal μ–calculus [31,55]. If you look at the details of what happens in such mathematical arguments, you will see a rich amount of logical finesse concerning strategies, including sophisticated simulation techniques that generalize far beyond these results themselves.

Of course, this still does not tell us what framework would be best for a base calculus of strategies. Propositional dynamic logic as above is one option favored by many authors, linear logic for game semantics is another major paradigm, more proof-theoretic or category-theoretic in nature [2], but one may also want to consider more recent paradigms such as the co-algebra of strategies in infinite games.[8] I will not pursue these various approaches here, but refer to [8] for more detailed case studies of calculi of strategies that fit basic proofs and counter-examples about games.[9] So far, however, none of these calculi have dealt with the preference-based sense of strategic action in terms of pursuing goals.[10]

5   Plans Across Changing Situations

So far, I have emphasized one key desideratum for a logical understanding of strategies, a grasp of fundamental valid patterns in reasoning about them. But there are further relevant intuitions that invite a logical angle. What seems particularly important to me is that a good strategy, or plan, should still work when circumstances change: its should be *robust* under, at least, small changes.

---

[7] As noted before, intuitively, a plan restricts my choices in helpful ways, but it need not fix my behavior uniquely: cf. [20] on the conceptual importance of this 'slack'.

[8] Coalgebraic strategies [54] are typically top-down objects that can be used by making an observation of their head after which an infinite tail of the strategy remains available. This never-ending feature is very different from the bottom-up behavior of terminating programs highlighted in PDL.

[9] [11] explores a follow-up to this concrete style of proof analysis for strategic reasoning in infinite games with simultaneous moves.

[10] Much further background, including game constructions associated with a strategy calculus in our sense, is found in [9]. That book also discusses how strategies can change our view of logic itself when we move from logic *of* games to logic *as* games, reading formulas as complex game expressions.

Of course, one can quibble about what is 'small' here, measured in what space, but the intuition seems clear, and it led to lively discussion at the Lorentz Workshop for this book, raising serious issues of implementation for these ideas.

Many strategies in the literature are very local. They fall apart under small changes in a game, and may not do anything useful any more. One sees this easily when computing the *Backward Induction* strategy, perhaps the most basic game-theoretic solution procedure. Its optimal path can shift wildly with addition or deletion of moves, but also with slight changes in preferences. For an analogy, consider computation or planning in AI: programs meeting certain specifications may quickly stop working under even slight changes in the model.[11]

Two options seem to arise for coping at this stage: 'recomputation' and 'repair'. Should we just create a new strategy in a new game, or gently revise a given strategy? Looking at practice, we often seem to start with the latter scenario, and only go the former route when forced by circumstances. But what would be a serious theory of strategy revision? For instance, along what comparison order should that take place? And can we say more precisely when gradual changes are sufficient, and when they have to be drastic? I think all this raises interesting issues of strategy structure, definability and model-theoretic preservation behavior that we logicians have not yet begun to address systematically.[12]

What I find intriguing is how, in modern epistemology, similar intuitions of robustness have led to powerful 'tracking theories' [37,41] viewing knowledge as true belief that stays correct under small counterfactual variations in the world. My hunch is that similar techniques may work for the notion of a strategy.

6   Plans, Knowledge and Understanding

My discussion so far fits a conception of strategies as pure algorithms composed out of atomic actions and factual tests. But in most topics of interest to agency, pure action is not enough. *Information* plays a crucial role in strategic behavior by the more interesting sorts of agents that logicians study. This topic has been studied for quite a while, and we know a lot about how to extend pure computational approaches. In particular, in the PDL format with epistemic logic added, one can get a long way with epistemic dynamic logics for planning [40] or 'knowledge programs' [28].[13] I cannot discuss these lines of work in this brief note, but they are highly relevant to any eventual logic of strategies.

---

[11] One might seek the robustness already in the standard game-theoretic notion of a strategy, that has to work under *every* eventuality. One can turn all relevant forms of change into moves in a 'supergame', asking for one strategy there. But the latter 'pre-encoding' seems far removed from our ordinary understanding of agency.

[12] Compare the nice example of repairing programs discussed in [38]. We know very little by way of relevant systematic results in logic. Thus, I am not even aware of model-theoretic preservation theorem under submodels or model extensions for such a simple logic as PDL with programs. However, re-planning in multi-agent systems has been investigated in computer science, cf. [25,26].

[13] Such natural extensions with explicit epistemic features do not seem to exist yet for other logical formats for strategies, such as linear game semantics.

Instead, I just want to point out that, despite this success, basic questions remain about the entanglement of information and action. In addition to plans having to refer to knowledge, there is also a further fundamental notion of *knowing a strategy*, or a plan that seems crucial to rational agency. This is not just a higher-order philosophical desideratum. Consider what we want a genuine process of *learning* to achieve for students: not just correct propositional knowledge that something is the case, but also the ability to engage in a certain practice based on the methods learned. In education, we teach *know-how* at least as much as 'know-that'. How can we add the latter notion to logics of strategies and information? There is no generally accepted current explication of what knowing a strategy means. One common line is to ask for a sufficient amount of propositional knowledge about what effects the plan, and remaining parts of it, will achieve.[14] But intuitively, much more seems involved.

The surplus might be highlighted intuitively in terms of *understanding a strategy* versus merely knowing it. What is the intuitive extra of understanding over knowledge? This issue has emerged in recent discussions in epistemology [46], and it also resonated with the audience at the Lorentz Workshop, where it triggered interesting discussion about what understanding involves. In addition to propositional knowledge of what a strategy, and parts of it, actually achieves as it unfolds, people mentioned more modal desirable features such as the earlier epistemic robustness: counterfactually knowing the effects of a strategy under changed circumstances, or the ability to modify a strategy on the fly as needed. Other desiderata included an ability to describe a strategy at different levels of detail, moving up or down as needed. There may be other key aspects, but my purpose here is just to raise the issue for the reader's consideration.[15]

7 Entanglement with Preferences and Goals

Having looked at combining action and information, let us briefly consider the other sense of strategic behavior mentioned in our introduction, that of being based on motives and goals. As a concrete instance, consider how action and *preference* are entangled in game theory and practical reasoning in general. Many of the issues discussed earlier return then in a much richer way.

A benchmark in the area that has kept generating surprising new angles is the Backward Induction algorithm [4,13,18]. Many current logics of strategies can define how this works, but there are intriguing issues in interpreting what the mixture of action and preference in these logics achieves, and what becomes of the notion of a strategy in this setting. Proposals range from generating strategies as advice for best behavior to viewing strategies as beliefs about the behavior of other agents. All this gets even more complex when we go to techniques such as

---

[14] This issue plays in the area of epistemic planning (cf. [3]), where different kinds of knowledge or beliefs become important: about where we are in following some current plan, but also beliefs about how we expect the process to develop over time.

[15] Similar issues arise in analyzing what it means to understand a formal *proof*, and useful intuitions might be drawn from our experience with mathematical practice.

Forward Induction that also take into account what history of play has gone on up until the present moment, and how to interpret observed moves.[16] For more on the state of the art in logical models of such reasoning styles, see [9].

8   Zooming in and Zooming Out

This may be a good place for a small digression clarifying what I am advocating for a logical study of strategies. Current work on game solution methods like Backward Induction may suggest that logics of strategies must get ever more expressively powerful, making everything explicit, *zooming in* on the tiniest details – turning simple intuitive arguments into elaborate arrays of logical formulas. But that would be only one half of the story. Often, logical analysis does just the opposite to achieve greater clarity in a given reasoning practice, *zooming out* to an abstraction level that hides details of a given type of strategy to see the laws of a bigger picture. In particular, it has been argued that practical reasoning needs coarse-grained modal top-level logics of 'best action' as a subset of all available moves in a game (cf. [43]), and similar ideas have occurred in recent logics that merge ideas from game theory and deontic logic toward a global theory of action (cf. [39,49]). Indeed, several logical abstraction levels can make sense for one and the same reasoning practice, and the case of strategies is no exception.[17]

9   Architecture of Diversity

I conclude with two points that return to my concern in this paper, the coherence of the area represented at our Workshop, and indeed the topic of this book.

The first is the striking diversity of the available logical paradigms clamoring for attention as candidates for a logic of strategies, and sometimes competing for our allegiance as if they were alternative religions. I myself am a firm believer in framework compatibility and convergence in the area of agency (and logic in general), though I will not argue for this here (cf. [12,15]). I believe that the study of strategies will benefit from a similar relaxed attitude.

The second point is the architecture of the phenomena we are after. A grand unification into one strategic format, may not be possible, or even desirable. But even without such a unification, there is the challenge of achieving beneficial coexistence. It has often been noted that the reality of many activities that humans engage in consists of a number of different games played at the same time, that allow for passing information, and indeed switches of scenarios. A telling example of such a setting is the array of different games that constitute (or at least, model) the different aspects of natural language use, from finite conversational scenarios to the infinite operating system of linguistic conventions.

---

[16] Some game-theoretic sources for Forward Induction are [19,44,45].

[17] In cognitive reality, zooming out and hiding procedural detail mirror processes of *automation* turning explicit skills into unconscious routines in the brain, cf. [21].

Accordingly, given that we tend to use strategies (pure, or entangled with information and preferences) in a complex array of differently structured tasks, what is the overall architecture that allows these plans to *mesh* and collaborate? We need a better understanding of ways of interfacing and connecting strategies for different tasks, making them work in parallel when on the same time-scale. But also, in line with what what was just said, we need to harmonize strategies for short-term terminating tasks (like the ones usually found in classical game theory) with those for long-term tasks (as in evolutionary game theory, cf. [36]). There may be hidden complexities in this connecting up of different strategies and their logics, as is known from long experience with combining logical systems.[18] And even beyond that, understanding the total architecture of strategies at these various levels may call for interfacing different mathematical paradigms, such as the PDL-style dynamic logic of programs that we have highlighted earlier with the probabilistic dynamical systems that underlie infinite games.

10 The Final Word for Reality

I have raised a number of theoretical issues that run through the logical study of strategies as an emerging area. Many of them may seem challenging common problems for the community in this book, rather than shared solutions. Let me add on a positive note all the same. Sometimes, when theoretical analysis seems to make things more, rather than less complex, there is a last resort: consulting the *empirical facts*. I feel that strategies reflect an undeniable human practice: social interaction has been claimed to be the human evolutionary feature par excellence [23,24,57]. It would be good then to also listen to cognitive studies of strategic behavior [56], since that is where our subject is anchored eventually. Now, making a significant connection with cognitive psychology may not be easy, since strategic structure with its delicate compositional, generic, and counterfactual aspects is not immediately visible and testable in actual psychological experiments. But that just means that, in addition to its logical, computational, and philosophical dimensions that have been mentioned here, the study of strategies also invites sophisticated empirical fact gathering.

Acknowledgments. I would like to thank my co-editors Sujata Ghosh and Rineke Verbrugge, as well as the very helpful anonymous reviewers of this volume. I also received valuable feedback from audiences for talks on the theme of designing an explicit logic of strategies.

References

1. Abramsky, S.: Concurrent interaction games. In: Davies, J., Roscoe, A.W., Woodcock, J. (eds.) Millennial Perspectives in Computer Science, pp. 1–12. Palgrave, UK (2000)

---

[18] For relevant issues, notions, and results, see the entry on combining logics in the *Stanford Encyclopedia of Philosophy* [22].

2. Abramsky, S., Jagadeesan, R.: Games and full completeness for multiplicative linear logic. J. Symbolic Logic **59**, 543–574 (1992)
3. Andersen, M.B., Bolander, T., Jensen, M.H.: Conditional epistemic planning. In: del Cerro, L.F., Herzig, A., Mengin, J. (eds.) JELIA 2012. LNCS, vol. 7519, pp. 94–106. Springer, Heidelberg (2012)
4. Aumann, R.: Backward induction and common knowledge of rationality. Games Econ. Behav. **8**, 6–19 (1995)
5. Axelrod, R.: The Evolution of Cooperation. Basic Books, New York (1984)
6. van Benthem, J.: Logical Dynamics of Information and Interaction. Cambridge University Press, Cambridge (2011)
7. van Benthem, J.: In praise of strategies. In: van Eijck, J., Verbrugge, R. (eds.) Games, Actions and Social Software 2010. LNCS, vol. 7010, pp. 96–116. Springer, Heidelberg (2012)
8. van Benthem, J.: Reasoning about strategies. In: Coecke, B., Ong, L., Panangaden, P. (eds.) Abramsky Festschrift. LNCS, vol. 7860, pp. 336–347. Springer, Heidelberg (2013)
9. van Benthem, J.: Logic in Games. The MIT Press, Cambridge (2014)
10. van Benthem, J.: Natural language and logic of agency. J. Logic Lang. Inform. **23**(3), 367–382 (2014)
11. van Benthem, J., Cui, J., Steinert-Threlkeld, S.: Logics for evolutionary games. Working paper, ILLC Amsterdam, Philosophy Stanford, and ILLC Guangzhou (2013)
12. van Benthem, J., Gerbrandy, J., Hoshi, T., Pacuit, E.: Merging frameworks for interaction. J. Philos. Logic **38**, 491–526 (2009)
13. van Benthem, J., Gheerbrant, A.: Game solution, epistemic dynamics and fixed-point logics. Fundamenta Informaticae **100**(1–4), 19–41 (2010)
14. van Benthem, J., Pacuit, E.: The tree of knowledge in action: towards a common perspective. In: Governatori, G., Hodkinson, I., Venema, Y. (eds.) Proceedings of Advances in Modal Logic (AiML IV), pp. 87–106. King's College Press, London (2006)
15. van Benthem, J., Pacuit, E.: Choices, actions, and games. In: Müller, T. (ed.) Nuel Belnap on Indeterminism and Free Action. Springer, Dordrecht (2013)
16. Bicchieri, C., Jeffrey, R., Skyrms, B. (eds.): The Logic of Strategy. Oxford University Press, Oxford (1999)
17. Binmore, K.: Game Theory: A Very Short Introduction. Oxford University Press, Oxford (2008)
18. Bonanno, G.: Branching time, perfect information games, and backward induction. Games Econ. Behav. **36**, 57–73 (2001)
19. Brandenburger, A.: Tutorial on game theory. First Amsterdam-Lausanne-London Graduate Workshop, London School of Economics (2007)
20. Bratman, M.: Shared cooperative activity. Philos. Rev. **101**(2), 327–341 (1992)
21. Calvo, P., Gomila, A. (eds.): Handbook of Cognitive Science. Elsevier, Amsterdam (2009)
22. Carnielli, W., Coniglio, M.E.: Combining logics. In: Zalta, E.N. (ed.) The Stanford Encyclopedia of Philosophy. Stanford University, spring 2014 edition (2014)
23. Damasio, A.: The Feeling of What Happens: Body Emotion and the Making of Consciousness. Heinemann, London (1999)
24. Dunbar, R.I.M., Shultz, S.: Evolution in the social brain. Science **317**(5843), 1344–1347 (2007)
25. Dunin-Kęplicz, B., Verbrugge, R.: A reconfiguration algorithm for distributed problem solving. Eng. Simul. **18**, 227–246 (2001)

26. Durfee, E.H.: Distributed problem solving and planning. In: Štěpánková, O., Luck, M., Mařík, V., Trappl, R. (eds.) ACAI 2001 and EASSS 2001. LNCS (LNAI), vol. 2086, pp. 118–149. Springer, Heidelberg (2001)

27. van Eijck, J.: PDL as a multi-agent strategy logic. In: Schipper, B.C. (ed.) TARK 2013: Proceedings of the 14th Conference on Theoretical Aspects of Rationality and Knowledge (2013)

28. Fagin, R., Halpern, J.Y., Moses, Y., Vardi, M.Y.: Reasoning About Knowledge. The MIT Press, Cambridge (1995)

29. Ghosh, S., Ramanujam, R.: Strategies in games: a logic-automata study. In: Bezhanishvili, N., Goranko, V. (eds.) ESSLLI 2010 and ESSLLI 2011. LNCS, vol. 7388, pp. 110–159. Springer, Heidelberg (2012)

30. Gintis, H.: The Bounds of Reason: Game Theory and the Unification of the Behavioral Sciences. Princeton University Press, Princeton (2008)

31. Grädel, E., Thomas, W., Wilke, T. (eds.): Automata, Logics, and Infinite Games. Springer, Heidelberg (2002)

32. Halpern, J., Vardi, M.: The complexity of reasoning about knowledge and time, I: Lower bounds. J. Comput. Syst. Sci. **38**, 195–237 (1989)

33. Harel, D., Kozen, D., Tiuryn, J.: Dynamic Logic. The MIT Press, Cambridge (2000)

34. Hintikka, J.: Knowledge and Belief. Cornell University Press, Ithaca (1962)

35. Hintikka, J., Sandu, G.: Game-theoretical semantics. In: van Benthem, J., ter Meulen, A. (eds.) Handbook of Logic and Language, pp. 361–410. Elsevier, Amsterdam (1997)

36. Hofbauer, J., Sigmund, K.: Evolutionary Games and Population Dynamics. Cambridge University Press, Cambridge (1998)

37. Holliday, W.: Knowing What Follows; Epistemic Closure and Epistemic Logic. Ph.D. thesis, Department of Philosophy, Stanford University (2012)

38. Huth, M., Ryan, M.: Logic in Computer Science. Cambridge University Press, Cambridge (2004)

39. Kooi, B., Tamminga, A.: Conditional obligations in strategic situations. In: Boella, G., Pigozzi, G., Singh, M., Verhagen, H. (eds.) Proceedings 3rd International Workshop on Normative Multi-agent Systems, pp. 188–200 (2008)

40. Moore, R.: A logic of knowledge and action (1985). Research report

41. Nozick, R.: Philosophical Explanations. Harvard University Press, Cambridge (1981)

42. Osborne, M.J., Rubinstein, A.: A Course in Game Theory. The MIT Press, Cambridge (1994)

43. van Otterloo, S.: A Security Analysis of Multi-Agent Protocols. Ph.D. thesis, ILLC, University of Amsterdam, and Department of Computing, University of Liverpool (2005). DS-2005-05

44. Pearce, D.G.: Rationalizable strategic behavior and the problem of perfection. Econometrica **52**(4), 1029–1050 (1984)

45. Perea, A.: Epistemic Game Theory: Reasoning and Choice. Cambridge University Press, Cambridge (2012)

46. Pritchard, D.: Knowledge, Understanding, and Epistemic Value. Cambridge University Press, Cambridge (2009)

47. Ramanujam, R., Simon, S.: Dynamic logic on games with structured strategies. In: Proceedings 11th International Conference on Principles of Knowledge Representation and Reasoning (KR-08), pp. 49–58. AAAI Press (2008)

48. Ramanujam, R., Simon, S.: A logical structure for strategies. In: Proceedings Logic and the Foundations of Game and Decision Theory (LOFT7). Texts in Logic and Games, vol. 3, pp. 183–208. Amsterdam University Press (2008)

49. Roy, O., Anglberger, A., Gratzl, N.: The logic of best actions from a deontic perspective. In: Baltag, A., Smets, S. (eds.) Johan van Benthem on Logic and Information Dynamics. Springer, Dordrecht (2014)

50. Sandu, G.: An alternative analysis of signaling games. In: Baltag, A., Smets, S. (eds.) Johan van Benthem on Logic and Information Dynamics. Springer, Dordrecht (2014)

51. Sergot, M.: Norms, action and agency in multi-agent systems. In: Sartor, G., Governatori, G. (eds.) DEON 2010. LNCS, vol. 6181, p. 2. Springer, Heidelberg (2010)

52. Shoham, Y., Leyton-Brown, K.: Multi-Agent Systems: Algorithmic Game-Theoretic and Logical Foundations. Cambridge University Press, Cambridge (2008)

53. van der Meyden, R.: The dynamic logic of permission. J. Logic Comput. **6**(3), 465–479 (1996)

54. Venema, Y.: Algebras and co-algebras. In: Blackburn, P., van Benthem, J., Wolter, F. (eds.) Handbook of Modal Logic, pp. 331–426. Elsevier, Amsterdam (2006)

55. Venema, Y.: Lectures on the modal mu-calculus (2007)

56. Verbrugge, R.: Logic and social cognition: The facts matter, and so do computational models. J. Philos. Logic **38**, 649–680 (2009)

57. de Weerd, H., Verbrugge, R., Verheij, B.: How much does it help to know what she knows you know? An agent-based simulation study. Artif. Intell. **199**, 67–92 (2013)

Author Index

Printed in the United States
By Bookmasters